Ada®
AN ADVANCED INTRODUCTION
including
REFERENCE MANUAL
FOR THE
ADA PROGRAMMING LANGUAGE

NARAIN GEHANI

Bell Laboratories
Murray Hill, New Jersey

PRENTICE-HALL, INC.
Englewood Cliffs, New Jersey 07632

Library of Congress Cataloging in Publication Data

Gehani, Narain (date)
  Ada, an advanced introduction.

  (Prentice-Hall software series)
  Bibliography: p.
  Includes index.
  1. Ada (Computer program language) I. Title.
II. Series.
QA76.73.A35G43 1984   001.64'24   83-11215
ISBN 0-13-003997-7

To
my wife,
our parents,
and
my grandparents

Previous edition published under the title *Ada: An Advanced Introduction.*

Ada is a registered trademark of the U.S. Government, Ada Joint Program Office. Any reference to the Ada Programming Language Reference Manual should be to the standard (ANSI/MIL-STD-1815A) which was published by the United States Department of Defense, Washington, D.C., 20301, 1983.

PRENTICE-HALL SOFTWARE SERIES
Brian W. Kernighan, advisor

Editorial/production supervision: Nancy Milnamow
Manufacturing buyer: Gordon Osbourne

Printed in the United States of America
10 9 8 7 6 5 4 3 2 1

ISBN 0-13-003997-7

Prentice-Hall International, Inc., *London*
Prentice-Hall of Australia Pty. Limited, *Sydney*
Editora Prentice-Hall do Brazil, Ltda., *Rio de Janeiro*
Prentice-Hall of Canada Inc., *Toronto*
Prentice-Hall of India Private Limited, *New Delhi*
Prentice-Hall of Japan, Inc., *Tokyo*
Prentice-Hall of Southeast Asia Pte. Ltd., *Singapore*
Whitehall Books Limited, Wellington, *New Zealand*

iii

Contents

Foreword

Ada Byron, Countess Lovelace, was the child of an unfortunate marriage. She cost her mother unexpected sums of money throughout her life and died at an early age. At the same time, she provided the needed connection between the machinery of computation and its potential application to the solution of human problems, stimulating and guiding the builder as well as the user.

Which, if any, of these attributes will apply to the life story of the Ada programming language, the subject of the present volume, is not as yet clear. This Ada has many supporters as well as some thoughtful critics. Its formidable list of advantages hardly needs reenumeration. Its restrictions are designed to enforce a programming discipline that facilitates the development of reliable and modular programs. Still, protective barriers can usually only delay and discourage self-injury by the desperate and the foolhardy. Ada's strong typing can be breached by *representation viewing*, appropriately renamed *unchecked conversion*; *goto*s are discouraged, but not altogether eliminated, because their use is necessary in rare cases; and so on. Ada's discipline is an aid to, but not a guarantee of, good programming practice. The familiar "Don't tell me your troubles, just get your job done" will still be a good recipe for bad programs, although the defects may now be buried a little deeper.

The long-term impact of the effort to create yet another programming language will ultimately depend upon the quality of programs written in it. Clearly, Ada does not have to become universal in order to be a useful aid in making large-scale programming a more productive enterprise. Truly modular programs appear to offer something for everyone. Write your module and deliver it early to avoid the last-minute rush at project deadline time. Test each module as it arrives, knowing that the system will work as long as each part checks out separately. Maintain the system by replacing bulky or obsolete parts. Too good to be true? We don't have all that long to wait to find out.

This book introduces problem solving in Ada by means of a set of well-chosen examples. The solutions to the problems are developed in the framework of stepwise refinement, thus providing the reader the added benefit of some practical instruction in top-down structured programming. At the same time, the reader ought to keep in mind that one of the big selling points of Ada is its modularity. Indeed, the extensive program libraries we can look forward to, and expect to make use of, might almost seem to argue for a *bottom-up* approach based on program components.

In practice, however, this dilemma is more apparent than real. The top-down approach of stepwise refinement is an iterative process. Each iteration aims at dividing the problem into tractable pieces, aiming toward pieces whose solutions are readily programmable or, better yet, fit an existing program module. At the same time, component-based programming involves purposeful browsing through the program library, looking for matches to pieces of the problem at hand; this implies that the problem must have somehow been decomposed into components at the beginning of this approach also.

In comparing the two approaches, the major issue is how well the decomposition will be carried out. Although we may not be able to rid ourselves of our bad habits entirely, we ought to recognize the value of the emphasis the author places on top-down programming. It offers us, among other things, the great advantage of understandability inherent in logically structured programs. Other programmers—and, after a short while, the original programmer—generally need to understand programs and need whatever help they can get in doing so.

Ideally, one would like to write programs which explain themselves. The examples in this book owe their clarity to the accessibility of their abstract solutions, hence their underlying structure. The refinements are gradual and understandable; they serve as examples of style as well as method. They illustrate the method's capabilities as a means of communication, from the programmer to the machine, as well as to readers of the program.

I think it is fair to say that this volume will itself help provide a "needed connection between the machinery of computation and its potential applications to the solution of human problems."

Murray Hill, N. J.   Arno A. Penzias

Preface

1. The Development of Ada

The high level programming language Ada is named in honor of Augusta Ada
Byron, the Countess of Lovelace and the daughter of the English poet Lord
Byron. She was the assistant, associate and supporter of Charles Babbage, the
mathematician and inventor of a calculating machine called the Analytical
Engine. With the help of Babbage she wrote a nearly complete program for
the Analytical Engine to compute the Bernoulli numbers circa 1830 [HUS80].
Because of this effort, the Countess may be said to have been the world's first
computer programmer.

To dispel exaggerated ideas about the powers of the Analytical Engine, e.g.,
that the Analytical Engine could think and feel, Ada wrote the following
assessment of its capabilities [MOO77]:

> The Analytical Engine has no pretensions whatever to *originate*
> anything. It can do whatever *we know how to order it to perform*. It
> can *follow* analyses; but it has no power of anticipating any analytical
> relations or truths. Its province is to assist us in making *available*
> what we are already acquainted with.

This assessment applies also to today's computers, even though they are far
more sophisticated than the Analytical Engine! Indeed the Countess' statement
is still quoted in modern debates on the nature and scope of artificial
intelligence [MCC79].

Ada, the language which bears the Countess' name, was designed at the
initiative and under the auspices of the United States Department of Defense
(DoD). DoD studies in the early and middle 1970s indicated that enormous
savings in software costs (about $24 billion between 1983 and 1999) might be
achieved if the DoD used one common programming language for all its
applications instead of the over 450 programming languages and incompatible
dialects used by its programmers.

As a result of these studies requirements were drawn up for a new
programming language that would replace most of the programming languages
being used by the DoD. Starting with Strawman (a jocular name), these
requirements were progressively refined by means of wide and public
consultation, both domestic and international. The United States armed
services, foreign military organizations, industrial organizations and universities

were involved in this process. The refined requirements were successively called Woodenman, Tinman, Ironman [FIS78] and finally Steelman [WAS80].

Although the motive for the new programming language was initially economic, it was propelled by the desire to have a good programming language that addressed important and recognized problems in software development. Requirements for the new language addressed technical issues such as language simplicity and completeness, program reliability, correctness, maintainability and portability, the development of large programs, real-time programming and error handling. In response to the trend toward multicomputers and away from large computers,[1] the requirements also demanded concurrent programming, i.e., the ability to write a program whose components could be executed in parallel on different computers or on the same computer via interleaved execution.

An international competition was held to design a language based on the above requirements. Seventeen companies submitted proposals out of which four were selected as semifinalists. Interestingly, all the semifinalists chose to base their languages on Pascal [JEN74]. The competition was won by a language designed by a team of computer scientists lead by Jean Ichbiah of CII Honeywell Bull. After some modifications, this language was named Ada [DOD80b]. In the process of getting Ada adopted as an ANSI standard, further revisions were made to Ada in an effort to simplify it and remove inconsistencies. Ada was adopted as an ANSI standard in February 1983 [DOD83].

Another step in DoD's efforts to standardize its software has been to initiate an Ada Compiler Validation project [GOO80]. The goal of this validation effort is to develop a set of standard tests that an Ada compiler must pass before it can be certified as implementing the standard Ada. In parallel with this effort, the process of developing requirements for the environment of Ada programs and the Ada user interface has been initiated [DOD80a].

Ada is a modern programming language with facilities found in Pascal-like languages such as the ability to define types, the common control structures and subprograms. Moreover, Ada incorporates many of the advances made in programming language design in the 1970s. It supports logical modularity by which data, types and subprograms can all be packaged. Physical modularity

---

1. A multicomputer is a computer architecture that consists of several different computers that do not share any memory. Processes on the different computers communicate with each other by sending messages. With the advent of one-chip computers and their rapidly decreasing price, multicomputers are fast becoming an attractive means of providing large amounts of computing power at low cost.

is made possible by separate compilation. Ada supports real-time programming by providing mechanisms for concurrency and exception handling. Systems programming is facilitated by providing access to system-dependent parameters and by precise control over representation of data.

Ada enforces a strict programming discipline with the intention of making programs more readable, reliable, portable, modular, maintainable, efficient and so on—all qualities of a good program. For example, the programmer must declare all objects, use objects in a manner consistent with their types, and access objects only according to Ada's visibility rules. At first, a programmer used to programming in a language that imposes little or no discipline may not like or appreciate Ada's strictness. After having written a few nontrivial programs, however, the programmer will readily appreciate this strictness, realizing that the intent of Ada's restrictions and strict checking is to detect more errors early and automatically, and to help the programmer to write good programs—not to inhibit creativeness and ingenuity.

2. About the Book

This book is written especially for readers who have a good knowledge of at least one procedural programming language such as Pascal, C, PL/I, Algol 60, Simula 67, Algol 68 or FORTRAN. The book focuses primarily on the novel aspects of Ada, which are illustrated by many fairly difficult and concrete examples written out in full. Interesting differences between Ada and other programming languages are commented upon.

The many example programs are developed using stepwise refinement [WIR71, GEH81] to assist the reader in understanding their design and development. Solution of a problem by stepwise refinement consists of solving the problem by decomposing or *refining* it into smaller subproblems and then solving the subproblems. This refinement is accomplished by giving an abstract version of the algorithm and the data structures that will be used in solving the problem. The abstract solution contains abstract instructions which are the subproblems. Such an approach is an important aid for mastering the complexity involved in the design of complex or large programs, since only a part of the problem is solved in any one refinement. Stepwise refinement also facilitates the understanding and explanation of programs and their design. The usefulness of this approach is clearly demonstrated by the design of large or complex programs such as the elevator algorithm given in the chapter on concurrency. The Appendix contains some remarks on the requirements for a good programming methodology and suggestions on how to develop programs via stepwise refinement.

The first chapter is an introduction to the features of Ada that are rather common—such as those found in programming languages like Pascal, C, PL/I or FORTRAN. Elaborate details about each feature are not provided. The remaining chapters focus on the novel aspects of Ada:

- Treatment of Types
- Packages—Encapsulation/Data Abstraction
- Concurrency or Tasking
- Exception Handling
- Generic Facilities
- Program Structure and Separate Compilation
- Representation Clauses and Implementation Dependent Features

A chapter is devoted to each topic. Throughout the book, the syntax is presented informally and by means of examples. The formal syntax of Ada can be found in the Ada Reference Manual [DOD83].

Each chapter begins with an introduction to the concepts that it will discuss. The facilities provided in Ada for implementing these concepts are introduced and illustrated with the aid of small examples. Finally, several complete examples are given to illustrate how these facilities are used in conjunction with the rest of Ada in solving problems. Care has been taken to ensure that the examples are realistic and nontrivial.

Because stepwise refinement is used to solve the problems, abstract versions of the problem solution appear prior to the final version of the solution in Ada. Reading these abstract versions of the problem solution should facilitate understanding the final solution in Ada. The final version can be skipped by the reader who is not interested in the details of the solution.

Throughout the book, pointers to the appropriate section of the Ada Reference Manual [DOD83] are provided (numbers in brackets, e.g. [5.2]) as an aid in looking up additional details. These pointers appear in chapter and section headings, and in the text.

An annotated bibliography of articles and books on Ada, influences on the design of Ada, stepwise refinement and other relevant topics is given at the end of the book. Following most of the items in the bibliography are brief comments that highlight their main and/or interesting points. The reader is urged to look through the bibliography, especially because it lists many interesting and classic articles and books, not all of which have been cited in the text.

3. Preparation of the Book

This book was written using the extensive document preparation tools available on the UNIX[TM] operating system. Some of the tools used were

- TROFF (formatter)
- MM (collection of TROFF macros for page layout)
- EQN (preprocessor for formatting equations)
- TBL (preprocessor for making tables)
- PIC (preprocessor for drawing figures)

The availability of these and other software tools, and the typesetting facilities available at Bell Laboratories, made writing the book less tedious.

4. Testing of the Example Programs

The program fragments and example programs given in the book have been tested using the Ada compiler being developed by New York University.[2] Since the programs are in machine readable form, it was fairly easy to extract them from the text, strip off the formatting commands and execute them.

The NYU Ada compiler is a prototype and is not yet complete. It implements a large subset of Ada, is written in SETL, requires an enormous amount of memory to run and at the same time is very slow. Consequently, some of the programs had to be modified slightly so that they used only the subset implemented by the NYU Ada compiler and they finished execution within a reasonable amount of time. Moreover, extensive program testing was not feasible because of the substantial resources required by the Ada compiler.

Murray Hill, N. J.   Narain Gehani

---

2. The NYU Ada compiler used for testing the example programs implemented the pre-ANSI version of Ada [DOD80b]. Modifications to Ada, resulting from the process of getting it adopted as an ANSI standard, had only a minimal impact on the examples in the book, e.g., call to parameterless functions had to be modified to eliminate the parentheses following the function name.

Acknowledgements

I am very grateful to the many friends and colleagues who have helped me in writing this book. The support and feedback I got from them was instrumental in shaping the form and content of the book.

First of all, my management at Bell Labs, J. O. Limb, H. G. Alles, R. W. Lucky and A. A. Penzias, enthusiastically supported and encouraged my writing the book. Without their support, this book would probably not have been written.

Perusing a manuscript for technical errors and poor explanations, and suggesting changes is a very time consuming task. I was fortunate, since several friends and colleagues took time out of their busy schedules, to give extensive comments, both technical and stylistic, on the manuscript. They are R. B. Allen, A. R. Feuer, D. Gay, D. Gries, B. W. Kernighan, J. P. Linderman, M. O'Donnell, and C. Wetherell. Brian Kernighan and Charlie Wetherell gave detailed comments on two versions of the manuscript. I am also indebted to Charlie for the discussions clarifying several fine points in Ada.

I am grateful to A. A. Penzias and David Gries for their exhaustive stylistic and editorial comments on the manuscript. Arno Penzias and Charlie Wetherell stressed the importance of an easy and informal writing style—a style which I have tried to follow.

I am also thankful for the helpful comments I got from H. G. Alles, C. D. Blewett, T. A. Cargill, J. DeTreville, R. A. Finkel, C. N. Fischer, D. D. Hill, J. O. Limb, R. A. Maddux, R. H. McCullough, J. Misra, M. E. Quinn, and J. E. Weythman.

G. Fisher and D. Shields gave me a copy of the New York University Ada Compiler, using which I was able to test the example programs. I would have been very uncomfortable had the programs in the book not been tested. I am particularly grateful to Gerry Fisher who was very helpful in providing me with revisions to Ada and answering questions about the compiler.

I appreciate the help of N. E. Bock, F. L. Dalrymple, R. L. Drechsler and Brian Kernighan in overcoming typesetting problems of one form or another.

Finally, I must thank J. Wait and J. Fegen of Prentice-Hall for their constant and encouraging support of this book.

Chapter 1: **Introduction** [1-6, 8]

As a modern programming language Ada incorporates many of the advances made in programming language research in the 1970s. This chapter focuses on the conventional part of Ada while the remaining chapters are devoted to the novel concepts in Ada not found in the commonly used high level programming languages. The unconventional part of Ada includes concepts such as data encapsulation, exception handling, concurrency and generic subprograms.[3] The conventional part of Ada includes concepts present in existing high level languages such as Pascal, C, PL/I and, to quite an extent, in FORTRAN. Like Pascal, but unlike C, PL/I and FORTRAN, Ada is strict in its treatment of types. It is even stricter than Pascal, from which its type philosophy has been derived.

The flavor of Ada programs is illustrated by a small program, CALCULATOR, which simulates a simple calculator that can add, subtract, multiply and divide. The data appears as a list of operations in the format

$$A \text{ operator } B$$

where *operator* is one of the symbols +, −, * or /, and the operands A and B are real values.

The reader familiar with high level languages ought to be able to understand the program CALCULATOR and most of the conventional part of Ada without much difficulty:

---

3. PL/I [IBM70] supports exception handling (albeit not very well) and provides limited facilities for supporting concurrency and generic subprograms.

```
--comments begin with two dashes and continue until the end of the line
with TEXT_IO; use TEXT_IO; --make input/output available
procedure CALCULATOR is
    type REAL is digits 10;
        --precision of real values is specified to be at least 10 digits
    package IO_REAL is new FLOAT_IO(REAL); use IO_REAL;
                    --input/output for REAL values is now available

    A, B: REAL;    --A and B are declared to be real variables
    OPR: CHARACTER;
    RESULT: REAL;
begin
    while not END_OF_FILE(STANDARD_INPUT) loop
            --function STANDARD_INPUT returns the default
            --input file
    GET(A); GET(OPR); GET(B);    --read the input
    case OPR is    --case statement
        when '+' => RESULT := A+B;
        when '-' => RESULT := A-B;
        when '*' => RESULT := A*B;
        when '/' => RESULT := A/B;
        when others => PUT("ERROR***BAD OPERATOR");
                    exit; --exit from the loop on bad input
    end case;
    PUT(RESULT); NEW_LINE;
    end loop;
end CALCULATOR;
```

CALCULATOR is an Ada main program. Any Ada subprogram can be executed as a main program provided all the *contextual information* needed by the subprogram has been specified. The contextual information

```
with TEXT_IO; use TEXT_IO;
```

makes CALCULATOR complete, i.e., CALCULATOR can be compiled and executed. The *with* clause specifies that CALCULATOR needs to use the predefined package TEXT_IO containing the text input and output facilities. The *use* clause allows subprograms in TEXT_IO to be referenced in CALCULATOR without explicitly stating that they belong to TEXT_IO. Package TEXT_IO provides subprograms to do input and output for some predefined types (e.g., CHARACTER), while for other types it provides templates of subprograms. Using the template FLOAT_IO for floating point input and output, given in TEXT_IO, the declaration

```
package IO_REAL is new FLOAT_IO(REAL);
```

creates a package containing input and output subprograms for values of floating point type REAL.

The rest of this chapter contains details and discussion of the facilities in the conventional part of Ada. The first section is a discussion of the basic elements of Ada. Then follow sections on types, expressions, statements, subprograms, visibility of entities, input and output, main programs and compilation units, pragmas and, finally, a set of complete examples.

1. Basics [2]

The *basic character set* of Ada consists of the upper case letters, the digits, the special characters

$$\texttt{"\# \& ' ( ) * + , - . / : ; < = > \_ |}$$

and the space character. The *expanded character set*, which may not be supported by all the Ada implementations, consists of the 95 character ASCII graphics character set. In addition to the basic character set, the expanded character set includes the lower case letters and the additional special characters

$$\texttt{! \$ \% ? @ [\textbackslash\ ] ^ ` \{ \} ~}$$

Any Ada program can be written using just the basic character set. Every Ada program can be converted to an equivalent Ada program that uses only the basic character set. Any lower case letter is equivalent to the corresponding upper case letter except within string and character literals.

Identifiers start with a letter and may be followed by any number of letters, digits and isolated underscore characters. Identifiers differing only in the upper and lower case letters, in corresponding positions, are considered identical.

Numeric literals are of two kinds—integers and reals. Some examples are

$$12 \qquad 12.0 \qquad 1.2E1 \text{ (or 1.2e1)}$$

Isolated underscores may be inserted between adjacent digits to facilitate ease of reading, as in

$$12\_000\_000$$

Literals can be written in a base other than decimal. For example 61.0 decimal can be written in base 8 as

$$8\#75.0\# \quad \text{ or } \quad 8\#7.5\#E1$$

where 1 is the exponent in the second example. Both the base and exponent are written in decimal notation. For bases above 10, the letters A through F are used for the extended digits.[4]

A *character literal* is formed by enclosing a character within single quotes. For example, the literals A, *, ´ and the space character are denoted as

´A´   ´*´   ´´´   ´ ´

Strings are formed by enclosing a sequence of zero or more printable characters within double quotes. The double quote character " must be written twice to be included once in a string. Catenation, denoted by &, is used to represent strings longer than one line and strings containing control characters. Examples of strings are

" "   ""   "A"   """"

"A normal string"

"This is a very very very very very very very very very very " & "long string"

"This string contains" & ASCII.CR & ASCII.LF & "control characters"

Note how the carriage return and line feed control characters (ASCII.CR and ASCII.LF) are specified. There is no direct denotation for them in Ada. They are *imported* from the ASCII *package* by qualification with the identifier that represents them, as will be explained later.

Comments start with two adjacent hyphens anywhere on a line and are terminated by the end of the line:

```
      ——all of Ada's statements must be terminated by a semicolon
   if MONTH = DECEMBER and DAY = 31 then
               ——end of the year
      YEAR := YEAR + 1;
   end if;
```

Ada has some identifiers, designated as *reserved words* [2.9], which have a special meaning in the language. Reserved words may not be used as names of program entities. Reserved words will be printed in boldface in the text to distinguish them from other identifiers.

A character not in the basic character set may be *transliterated* into the basic character set by using the identifier that represents it in the ASCII package (Appendix C of the Reference Manual [DOD83]). For example, ´$´ is represented by DOLLAR in the ASCII package and the alternative denotation

---

4. The maximum base is thus limited to 16.

using the basic character set is ASCII.DOLLAR. This alternative denotation must be used if an Ada implementation supports only the basic character set. In such a situation, for example, the string

"$AMOUNT"

would be written as

ASCII.DOLLAR & "AMOUNT"

The following *replacements* are allowed for unavailable characters:

| may be replaced by a !

\#   may be replaced by : throughout any based number

"   may be replaced by % as a string terminator,
provided the string does not contain "".
Any % character in the string must now be written
twice. A string containing " is represented by using
catenation and the alternative denotation from
the ASCII package, i.e., ASCII.QUOTATION

2. Types, Constants and Variables [3]

A *type* is a set of values plus a set of operations that can be performed upon these values [MOR73]. An *object* is an entity with which a type is associated; a value of this type can also be associated with the object.

An object is created and its type specified by means of a *declaration*. All objects must be explicitly declared in Ada.[5] An initial value may be given to an object in its declaration (which will override a default initial value associated with the object type). There are two kind of objects—*constants* and *variables*. The value given to a constant cannot be changed, while that given to a variable can be changed.

2.1 Object Declarations

Object declarations have the form[6]

---

5. Loop variables are an exception to this rule. They are implicitly declared by their presence in the loop heading.

6. Extended BNF notation, as used in the Ada Reference Manual, is used in defining the syntax:

- [a]   specifies the optional occurrence of item a
- {a}   specifies 0 or more occurrences of item a
- a | b   specifies either item a or item b

Bold and bigger characters will be used for the BNF meta symbols [ ]{ } and | to distinguish them from the Ada characters [ ]{} and |.

identifier_list: [constant] T [:= expression];
identifier_list: constant := N;

where T is a type or a *subtype* name with an optional *constraint*, or a constrained array type definition, *expression* is the initial value being given to the objects, and N is a *static* expression (i.e., an expression that can be evaluated at compile time). A constraint is a restriction on the set of possible values of the type it is associated with. (A *subtype* represents a type but with constraints on the associated set of values; every type is trivially a subtype of itself.)

2.1.1 Examples of Constant Declarations [3.2.1]:

PI: **constant** FLOAT := 3.1416;
        --a floating point real constant

NO_LINES, NO_WORDS: **constant** INTEGER := 1000;
        --integer constants

NO_BYTES: **constant** INTEGER := NO_WORDS * 4;
        --initialized to an expression; although this
        --expression is static, the initial expression
        --does not have to be static

GREET_1: **constant** STRING := "Welcome";
        --STRING is predefined type;
        --the string size is determined from the initial value.

GREET_2: **constant** STRING := GREET_1 & ASCII.CR & ASCII.LF
            & "This is the display editor";
        --note how the constant is defined on two lines and
        --that the two parts of the greeting will appear on
        --two lines, because of the carriage return and line
        --feed characters

WEEK: **constant array**(1..7) **of** DAY
        := (SUN, MON, TUE, WED, THU, FRI, SAT);
        --array of a user-defined type DAY whose elements are
        --initialized to appropriate days which are values of
        --type DAY. Positional notation has been used in the
        --initialization, i.e., WEEK(1) = SUN, etc.

A: **constant array**(1..10) **of** BOOLEAN := (1..10 => FALSE);
           --all the elements of this boolean array constant are
           --initialized to FALSE. Named notation has been
           --used for initialization, i.e., element indices have
           --been explicitly specified in the initial value

2.1.2 Number Declarations [3.2.2]: The type identifier may be left out in constants that are synonyms of numbers:

PI: **constant** := 3.1416;

2.1.3 Examples of Variable Declarations [3.2.1]:

PRESENT: BOOLEAN := FALSE;
HIGH, LOW: INTEGER;
           --HIGH and LOW are not initialized
HOUR: INTEGER **range** 0..24;
           --HOUR is an INTEGER variable whose values
           --have been restricted to lie between 0 and 24
           --by the range constraint *range 0..24*
COLOR_TABLE: **array**(1..N) **of** COLOR;
           --upper bound is a variable
X, Y: STRING(1..80);
GRID: **array**(1..100, 1..100) **of** FLOAT;
           --two-dimensional array
PAGE: **array**(1..60) **of** LINE;
           --an array of arrays where LINE
           --is some user-defined array type

All variables must be given a value before they are used in an expression; otherwise, an error occurs.

2.1.4 Type Definitions Allowed in Object Declarations: Only array type definitions, for example,

array(1..100) **of** INTEGER;

can be given directly in object declarations. In case of other type definitions, such as a record type definition, a type name representing the type definition must be declared and then used in the object declaration.[7]

---

7. Suppose that constant BOUNDS is to be declared having two values—a low limit and a high limit. BOUNDS can be declared as an array or a record constant. The following declaration of BOUNDS using an array definition is legal:

   BOUNDS: **constant** array(1..2) **of** INTEGER := (1, 100);

However, the alternative declaration of BOUNDS as a record constant

2.2 Type Declarations [3.3]

A *type declaration* associates a *name* with a *type definition*. Type declarations have the form

type name **is** type_definition;

where *name* is an identifier.

Type declarations are used to collect the common properties of objects, in one place in a program, and give them a name. This *type name* can then be used in subsequent declarations of these objects. Type declarations enhance program maintainability, since a change in the properties of the objects requires a change in only one place in the program [DOD79b].

Types that can be defined are enumeration, integer, real, array, record and access types. A type definition always defines a *distinct* (different from any other) type even if two type definitions are textually identical.

Except for array type definitions, a type identifier must always be used when declaring an object. For example, the declaration of S as an enumeration type variable with values ON and OFF

S: (ON, OFF);

is illegal, since the enumeration type definition

(ON, OFF)

cannot be used directly in an object declaration. However, using the enumeration type SWITCH declared as

type SWITCH **is** (ON, OFF);

variable S can be declared as

S: SWITCH;

BOUNDS: **constant record** LOW, HIGH: INTEGER; **end record** := (1, 100);

is illegal, since a record type definition has been used. Record type definitions are not allowed in the declaration of objects. An appropriate record type, say LIMITS, must be declared and then used to declare BOUNDS as a constant of a record type:

BOUNDS: **constant** LIMITS := (1, 100);

Allowing only array type definitions but not definitions of other types, e.g., record or access types, in object declarations is not uniform and therefore undesirable.

2.3 Scalar Types [3.5]

Scalar types, viz., the *discrete* and *real* types, are types with simple values (the values have no components). *Enumeration* types and *integers* are the discrete scalar types. Integer and real types are called the *numeric* types. Each scalar type T has the attributes T´FIRST and T´LAST.

> T´FIRST   Smallest value of type T
>
> T´LAST   Largest value of type T

2.3.1 Enumeration Types [3.5.1]: The set of values of an enumeration type is defined by explicitly listing the values. Enumeration type declarations have the form

> **type** ENUM **is** $(a_1, a_2, ..., a_n)$

where the enumeration literals a_i can be identifiers or character literals. The position of the values a_i determines their ordering, that is, $a_1 < a_2 < a_3$ and so on. Some examples of enumeration type definitions are

> **type** DAY **is** (MON, TUE, WED, THU, FRI, SAT, SUN);

> **type** COLOR **is** (YELLOW, BLUE, RED);

> **type** TRAFFIC_LIGHT **is** (RED, YELLOW, GREEN);
>
>   ——The literal value YELLOW belongs to two
>   ——enumeration types. YELLOW is said to be
>   ——overloaded. If the type of a literal cannot be
>   ——determined from the context then the type must be
>   ——explicitly supplied using a *qualified* expression,
>   ——for example, TRAFFIC_LIGHT´(YELLOW)

> **type** HEXADECIMAL **is**
>   ('0', '1', '2', '3', '4', '5', '6', '7', '8', '9',
>   'A', 'B', 'C', 'D', 'E', 'F');

> **type** MIXED **is** ('A','B','C','*','?','%', NONE);

type CHESS_PIECES **is**
       (WHITE_PAWN, WHITE_ROOK, WHITE_KNIGHT,
       WHITE_BISHOP, WHITE_QUEEN, WHITE_KING,
       BLACK_PAWN, BLACK_ROOK, BLACK_KNIGHT,
       BLACK_BISHOP, BLACK_QUEEN, BLACK_KING,
       BLANK);
      ――a chess board may be represented as squares
      ――associated with values of type CHESS_PIECE only;
      ――inclusion of piece BLANK allows indication of
      ――an empty square.

2.3.2 Character and Boolean Types [3.5.2, 3.5.3]: Ada provides two predefined enumeration types—CHARACTER and BOOLEAN. They are declared as

type CHARACTER **is** (*the ASCII character set*);
      ――see Appendix C of the Ada Reference Manual for
      ――a detailed listing of values of type CHARACTER

type BOOLEAN **is** (FALSE, TRUE);
      ――predefined boolean type

2.3.3 Integers [3.5.4]: Ada provides the predefined type INTEGER. An Ada implementation may also provide other predefined types such as SHORT_INTEGER and LONG_INTEGER. The smallest and largest integers supported by an implementation are given by the constants SYSTEM.MIN_INT and SYSTEM.MAX_INT. The predefined subtypes NATURAL and POSITIVE represent subsets of INTEGER values greater than or equal to zero (≥ 0) and greater than zero (> 0), respectively.

2.3.4 Attributes of Discrete (i.e., Enumeration and Integer) Types [3.5.5]: In addition to FIRST and LAST, some other attributes defined for every discrete type T are

T'POS(X)   The position number of X in its definition. For example

                 COLOR'POS(BLUE) = 2
                 POSITIVE'POS(3) = 3

T'SUCC(X)   The successor element of X in type T. For example

                 COLOR'SUCC(BLUE) = RED
                 NATURAL'SUCC(3) = 4

                T'SUCC(X) with X = T'LAST raises the error exception CONSTRAINT_ERROR.

T′PRED(X)   The predecessor element of X. The error exception CONSTRAINT_ERROR is raised if X = T′FIRST.

T′VAL(N)   The element of T with position number N. For example

$$COLOR′VAL(2) = BLUE$$
$$POSITIVE′VAL(2) = 2$$

The error exception CONSTRAINT_ERROR is raised if N < T′POS(T′FIRST) or N > T′POS(T′LAST).

2.3.5 Reals [3.5.6-3.5.10]: Ada provides elaborate facilities for reals [WIC81]. Values of type real are approximations to the mathematical reals. Reals come in two flavors—floating point and fixed point. Real values are represented differently in floating point and fixed point, and hence have different approximation errors.

Floating point reals are an approximation to the mathematical reals in which the error in representing a mathematical real is *relative* to its absolute value. On the other hand, the representation error in case of the fixed point reals is *independent* of its value. Consequently, small fixed point real values may have a correspondingly large relative error. The size of the error bounds for both types of reals depends upon the desired accuracy, called the *accuracy constraint*, which is specified by the user.

The error bound for floating point reals is specified by giving the minimum number of decimal digits that should be stored for the mantissa. The error bound for fixed point reals is specified as an absolute value called the *delta* of the fixed point real.

Associated with every real type definition is a set of numbers called the *model numbers*. The semantics of real arithmetic in Ada is defined in terms of these model numbers [BRO81]. Error bounds for the predefined real operations are also defined in terms of these numbers. Any implementation of a real type must include exact representations of these numbers. This requirement provides a basis for guaranteeing the consistency of real arithmetic computation across different implementations.

An implementation may provide a superset of the model numbers called the *safe numbers*. Safe numbers allow the programmer to exploit the extra precision provided by an implementation.

The characteristics of model and safe numbers, associated with a real type, can be determined using appropriate attributes which are provided for all real types.

2.3.5.1 Floating Point Reals [3.5.7]: Ada provides the user with the predefined floating point real type FLOAT. Additionally, an implementation may provide other predefined reals, such as SHORT_FLOAT and LONG_FLOAT.

2.3.5.2 Floating Point Attributes [3.5.8]: Some attributes defined for every floating point type F are

F'DIGITS	Precision in decimal digits
F'FIRST	The algebraically smallest value of type F
F'LAST	The algebraically largest value of type F
F'SMALL	Smallest positive model number associated with type F
F'LARGE	Largest positive model number associated with type F
F'EPSILON	Difference between model number 1.0 and the next greater model number

The values F'FIRST and F'LAST need not be model numbers.

2.3.5.3 Fixed Point Reals [3.5.9]: Fixed point real types are declared as

> **type** NEW_FIXED **is** *fixed_point_constraint*;

where *fixed_point_constraint*, the accuracy constraint for fixed point types, has the form

> **delta** DEL **range** L..R;

where DEL, L and R are static expressions of some real type. The delta value DEL, which must be positive, specifies the maximum absolute error that should occur in representing values of the fixed point type being specified. Elements of this fixed point type are consecutive multiples of DEL.

The range constraint *range L..R* must be specified in the definition of a fixed point type. A value satisfies a fixed point constraint if it satisfies any included range constraint.

Some examples of fixed point types are

> **type** CURRENCY **is delta** 0.01 **range** 0.0 .. 1_000_000_000_000.0;
> **type** HIGH_PRECISION **is delta** 0.0001 **range** 0.0 .. 500.0;

2.3.5.4 Fixed Point Attributes [3.5.10]: Some attributes defined for every fixed point type F are

F'DELTA	The delta value specified in the declaration of F

F'SMALL	The smallest positive model number associated with type F
F'LARGE	The largest positive model number associated with type F
F'FIRST	The smallest value of type F
F'LAST	The largest value of type F

2.4 Arrays [3.6, 4.3, 4.7]

An array is a composite object consisting of component objects (called elements) all of which have the same type (actually, the same subtype).[8] Array types come in two varieties—constrained and unconstrained. In case of a *constrained* array type, the bounds of the array are specified at the time the array type is defined or when an array object is declared. Constrained arrays are similar to Pascal arrays. In case of an *unconstrained* array type, the array bounds are not specified in its declaration. These bounds are supplied later, in type definitions using the unconstrained array type, in object declarations or during parameter passage. The unconstrained array type can be used only in type definitions and parameter declarations. It can be used for object declarations only if the constraints are supplied. It is the unconstrained array type that allows procedures and functions to accept actual parameter arrays of different sizes.[9]

2.4.1 Constrained Arrays: The constrained array type has the form

    array index_constraint **of** C

where subtype C is the type of the array components. C can be any type including an array (or a task) type. The *index_constraint* specifies the type of the array indices and is of the form

---

8. Requiring all elements of an array to be of the same subtype, instead of the same type, eliminates the possibility of *ragged* arrays. An array is ragged if its components have different sizes, e.g., a one-dimensional array whose components are one-dimensional arrays of different sizes. Arrays with different number of elements can be of the same *unconstrained* array type, i.e., an array type in which the array size is not specified. On the other hand, all arrays of the same array subtype have the same number of elements, since the size of the array is specified in the subtype.

9. The lack of unconstrained arrays (or a facility similar to it) is one of Pascal's major drawbacks, since a subprogram cannot be called with actual parameter arrays of different sizes (corresponding to the same formal parameter). It is possible to pass arrays of different sizes as parameters in many programming languages, e.g., PL/I, Algol 68, and C. The ISO Pascal Standard [ISO81] eliminates this drawback by providing *conformant arrays*.

(discrete_range {, discrete_range})

where *discrete_range* is a range of the form *L..U*, or is a type or subtype name followed, possibly, by a range constraint of the form *range L..U*. The expressions L and U defining the bounds of the discrete ranges can be dynamic, that is, they can depend upon computed results. An array whose bounds are not static is called a *dynamic array*. Some examples illustrating constrained array types are

       type SALES **is array**(MONTHS) **of** FLOAT;
               --MONTHS is a user-defined enumeration type
       type CHESS_BOARD **is array**(1..8, 1..8) **of** CHESS_PIECES;
       type CARD **is array**(INTEGER **range** 1..80) **of** CHARACTER;
               --objects of type CARD must be indexed by objects of
               --type INTEGER or subtypes of INTEGER, with values
               --between 1 and 80

Some examples of array object declarations are

       SET: **array**(1..SET_SIZE) **of** BOOLEAN;   --dynamic array
       WEEKLY_SALES: **array**(DAY **range** MON..SAT) **of** FLOAT;

An array is a *null array* if at least one of its indices defines a *null range*. A range L..U is null if L > U. A null array has no components.

2.4.2 Unconstrained Arrays: Unconstrained array types definitions have the form

       array(index {, index}) **of** C

where subtype C is the array component type and *index* is of the form

       T **range** <>

T is a type or subtype name. <> is called the *box* and stands for an undefined range whose bounds are to be supplied later.

When declaring unconstrained array type objects, the *index_constraint* must be supplied. Different objects of the same unconstrained array type can have different bounds. For example, consider the unconstrained array type declarations

       type VECTOR **is array**(INTEGER **range** <>) **of** FLOAT;
       type MATRIX **is array**
              (INTEGER **range** <>, INTEGER **range** <>) **of** FLOAT;

Some examples of arrays objects declared using these types and appropriate index constraints are

X: VECTOR(1..10);   ——1..10 is the index constraint
Y: VECTOR(−200..0);
            ——X and Y are of the same type VECTOR but they
            ——have different bounds

M: MATRIX(1..25, 1..40);

The use of an unconstrained type in parameter declarations is illustrated by the definition of procedure SORT:

procedure SORT(V: **in out** VECTOR);

Procedure SORT can be called with any array of type VECTOR, such as X, regardless of the size of the array. The bounds of the formal parameter array V are obtained from the corresponding actual parameter and are given by the attributes V′FIRST and V′LAST.

2.4.3 Strings [3.6.3]: Ada provides the predefined string type

type STRING **is array**(POSITIVE **range** < >) **of** CHARACTER;

Strings are one-dimensional arrays of characters. Some examples of the use of the STRING type are

type LINE **is new** STRING(1..80);
            ——defines a new type LINE whose values are strings
            ——of length 80. Type LINE is different from
            ——STRING(1..80); see derived types in Chapter 2 on
            ——More About Types
NAME: STRING(1..20);
L: LINE;

The relational operators =, /=, <, <=, >= and >, and the catenation operator & are predefined for strings.

As an example illustrating the use of strings, consider the subprogram REVERSE_STRING, which reverses strings of type STRING regardless of their length:

procedure REVERSE_STRING(S: **in out** STRING) **is**
      ––reverse string S; the bounds of S will be those
      ––of the corresponding actual parameter

  L: **constant** INTEGER := S'FIRST;
  U: **constant** INTEGER := S'LAST;
      ––the bounds of S are determined using the array attributes
      ––FIRST and LAST
  C: CHARACTER;

begin
  for I **in** L..(L+U)/2 **loop**
    C := S(I);
    S(I) := S(U−I+1);
    S(U−I+1) := C;
  end loop;
end REVERSE_STRING;

2.4.4 Array Elements, Slices and Aggregates [4.1.1, 4.1.2, 4.3, 4.3.2]: The element of an n-dimensional array A with subscripts $i_1, i_2, ..., i_n$ is referenced using the notation

$A(i_1, i_2, ..., i_n)$

Portions of one-dimensional arrays, called *slices*, can be referenced by using the notation

A(discrete_range)

For example, the slice $X(1..5)$ refers to the first 5 elements of X. Slicing does not produce copies of the elements of the array being sliced; changing an element of a slice is equivalent to changing the corresponding element of the array being sliced and vice versa. For example, the assignment

$X(1..5)(2) := X(1..5)(2) + 1.0;$

is equivalent to the assignment

$X(2) := X(2) + 1.0;$

Array values, called *array aggregates*, can be constructed directly from component values. Array aggregates can be used for assignment to array objects or in expressions. Array aggregates can be formed using a *positional* notation, a *named* notation or a combination of these two notations. An aggregate must be *complete*; that is, a value must be given for every component of the composite value.

The type of an array aggregate is determined from the context unless its type is explicitly stated. The type of an array aggregate may be explicitly stated by qualifying it with a type or subtype name:

    T′aggregate

where T is a type or a subtype. This qualification is required when the type of the aggregate cannot be unambiguously determined from the context. The aggregate type must be the same as the base type of the explicitly specified type or subtype.

Some examples of array aggregates and slices are given below:

(1, 2, 3, 4, 5)	is a one-dimensional array value with 5 elements specified using positional notation; the ith element has value i.
(1..10 => 5.5)	is a one-dimensional array value with 10 elements, each having the value 5.5; named notation has been used to construct the aggregate.
CARD′(1 | 45 => ′*′, **others** => ′_′)	is an array value of type CARD (type of the aggregate is explicitly stated) with components 1 and 45 having the value ′*′. All other elements have the value ′_′. The index range is determined from type CARD. The choice **others** must be the last choice.
(′T′, ′e′, ′s′, ′t′)	is a one-dimensional array of characters.
"Test"	same as above; "..." is an alternative notation for writing one-dimensional CHARACTER array aggregates.
M := (1..25 => (1..25 => 0.0));	the right hand side specifies a two-dimensional array aggregate value. It is depicted as an array of 25 one-dimensional arrays, each of whose elements has the value 0.0. Named notation has been used to specify the elements.
X(1..5) : = (2 => 5.0, 1 | 3..5 => 0.0);	assigns to the slice of the array X an aggregate with 5 elements; the second element of the aggregate has the value 5.0 while elements 1, 3, 4 and 5 have the value 0.0.

The bounds of a positional aggregate or any aggregate containing the choice **others** are determined from the context [4.3.2]. An N-dimensional array aggregate is written as a one-dimensional array aggregate consisting of $(N-1)$-dimensional array values.

2.4.5 Array Attributes [3.6.2]: The following attributes are defined for each array object or constrained array subtype A:

A'FIRST	Lower bound of the first index; same as A'FIRST(1)
A'FIRST(N)	Lower bound of the Nth index
A'LAST	Upper bound of the first index; same as A'LAST(1)
A'LAST(N)	Upper bound of the Nth index
A'LENGTH	Size of the first index (if the indices are integers, then A'LENGTH = A'LAST − A' FIRST + 1); same as A'LENGTH(1)
A'LENGTH(N)	Size of the Nth index (if the indices are integers, then A'LENGTH(N) = A'LAST(N) − A' FIRST(N) + 1)
A'RANGE[10]	The subtype A'FIRST..A'LAST corresponding to the legal values for the first index; same as A'RANGE(1)
A'RANGE(N)	The subtype A'FIRST(N)..A'LAST(N) corresponding to the legal values for the Nth index.

2.5 Records [3.7]

A record is a composite object consisting of named components that may be of different types (components of a record are *heterogeneous* whereas the components of an array are *homogeneous*). Record types are defined as

---

10. RANGE is a misnomer! DOMAIN would have been more appropriate. The domain of an array is the set of legal subscripts for it, while the range of an array is the set of values of its elements.

record
    component_declarations | **null**
end record

A component declaration declares one or more components to be of a specified type using a type or subtype name followed, optionally, by a constraint. If there are no components in a record, then the record type definition must contain the reserved word **null**; such a record is called a *null record*.

A component C of a record object R is referenced using the *selected component* notation:

    R.C

Some examples of record types are

```
type POSITION is
   record
      X, Y: FLOAT;
   end record;

type SEQUENCE is
   record
      SEQ: STRING(1..MAX_SIZE);
      L: POSITIVE range 1..MAX_SIZE;
   end record;

type DATE is
   record
      YEAR: INTEGER range 1901..2099;
      MONTH: INTEGER range 1..12;
      DAY: INTEGER range 1..31;
   end record;
```

Objects of a record type can be given default initial values by specifying the values for the record components in the record type definition.[11] A default initial value can be overridden by an explicitly supplied initial value. For example, all objects of type POSITION can be given the default initial value of (0.0, 0.0) by declaring POSITION alternatively as

---

11. Default values for objects of a type T can be specified only if T is a record type!

```
type POSITION is
  record
    X, Y: FLOAT := 0.0;
  end record;
```

As a result of the declarations

```
P1: POSITION;                    --default initialization
P2: POSITION := (1.0, 1.0);      --explicit initialization
```

P1.X and P1.Y have the value 0.0 while P2.X and P2.Y have the value 1.0.

The use of records is illustrated by the function subprogram DISTANCE that computes the distance between two positions, (x_1, y_1) and (x_2, y_2), which is given by the expression

$$\sqrt{(x_1-x_2)^2+(y_1-y_2)^2}$$

Function DISTANCE is declared as

```
function DISTANCE(P1, P2: POSITION) return FLOAT is
begin
  return SQRT((P1.X - P2.X) ** 2 + (P1.Y - P2.Y) ** 2);
end;
```

where SQRT is a user-defined function that computes the square root.

2.5.1 Record Aggregates [4.3.1]: Record values, called *record aggregates*, can be constructed directly from component values. Record aggregates can be used in assignments to record objects. A value must be provided for each component regardless of whether or not a default initial value exists for the component. Like array aggregates, record aggregates can be specified using either the positional or the named notation.

The following record aggregate examples use the type POSITION, declared earlier, and the type COMPLEX declared as

```
type COMPLEX is
  record
    R, I: FLOAT;
  end record;
```

Some record aggregate examples are

(5.0, 6.0)   The positional notation is fine as long as the type can be determined from the context; otherwise the aggregate must be qualified with the type as shown in the following examples.

POSITION´(5.0, 6.0)   The aggregate type is specified explicitly.

COMPLEX´(5.0, 6.0)

2.6 Access Types [3.8, 4.1.3]

Static objects are created by specifying them in a declaration. *Dynamic* objects, on the other hand, are created dynamically and explicitly during program execution. The storage *allocator*, which is called *new*, is used to create dynamic objects. The number of dynamic objects, unlike the number of static objects, is not fixed by the program text—they can be created or destroyed as desired during program execution. Dynamic objects, unlike static objects, do not have explicit names and must be referred to using *access type* objects that point to them.[12]

The allocator *new* returns a value of an access type when a dynamic object is created. It is this value that is used to refer to the dynamic object. This access type value may be assigned to more than one object of the same access type. Thus, a dynamic object may be referred to using one or more objects of an access type; an object that can be referred to via two or more access type objects is said to have *aliases*.

Access types are defined by

access T [constraint]

where T is a type or subtype name and the *constraint* is a discriminant or index constraint. Objects of this access type are used to refer to objects of type T.

The access value **null** is associated with all access types. All objects of an access type are given the **null** value as the default initial value. The value **null** indicates that no object is being referred to by the access type object. Using this value to refer to a dynamic object is an error and raises an exception.

Some examples of access type declarations are

---

12. Access types are really pointers! Ada uses a different terminology to avoid the connotation of unsafeness usually associated with pointers. Also Ada's access types have more restrictions than those, if any, on pointers in most programming languages.

The lack of restrictions on pointers, as in PL/I, allows a pointer to refer to any type of object. This freedom defeats type checking, because the compiler cannot determine the type of the object being accessed. Pointers can be used to access portions of memory, which were used by the objects pointed to by them but which have since been deallocated. Pointer arithmetic is allowed in some languages, and if proper checking is not done, illegal access to other parts of storage is possible.

  type TITLE **is access** STRING(1..40);
          ——refers to strings of length 40
  type LOCATION **is access** POSITION;
  type FIGURE **is access** GEOMETRIC_FIGURE;

Dynamic objects are created during program execution by a call to the allocator, which is of the form

  new T ⟦′(expression) | ′aggregate | discriminant or index constraint⟧

where T is a type or subtype name. An initial value for the dynamic object may be explicitly supplied at creation time. If T is an unconstrained type, then a constraint or an initial value must be supplied when creating dynamic objects of type T.

Using access type objects declared as

  T1, T2: TITLE;
  A, B: LOCATION;
  F: FIGURE;

some examples of dynamic objects created using the allocator are

  T1 := **new** STRING(1..40);   ——index constraint supplied
  T2 := **new** STRING′(1..40 => ′ ′); ——initial value supplied
  A := **new** POSITION′(Y => 5.0, X => 10.0);
  B := **new** POSITION;
  F := **new** GEOMETRIC_FIGURE(CIRCLE); ——constraint supplied

The access value represented by an access type object P is referred to simply as P. The notation for referring to dynamic objects is P.**all**, where P is an access type object or a function call returning a value of an access type. If P refers to an object of a record type, then component C of that record object is referred to as P.C. For example, using variables A and B as declared above, the assignment

  B.**all** := A.**all**;

copies the value of the object referred to by A into the object referred to by B. This assignment is equivalent to the assignments of the components of A to the components of B

  B.X := A.X;
  B.Y := A.Y;

On the other hand, the assignment

  B := A;

just copies the value of A into B, with the result that B also refers to the object pointed to by A. The object, if any, referred to by B prior to the assignment becomes inaccessible unless another access type object refers to it.

2.6.1 Lifetime of a Dynamic Object: A dynamic object remains in existence as long as the object can be accessed. Conceptually, dynamic objects can be accessed only as long as the declaration of the corresponding access type is available. The storage allocated for the dynamic objects may be reclaimed when they are no longer accessible or have been deallocated. Inaccessible objects will be automatically deallocated if the implementation provides a *garbage collector.* Otherwise, these objects must be deallocated explicitly if the space occupied by them has to be used for other purposes. Explicit deallocation is done using *instantiations* of the generic procedure UNCHECKED_DEALLOCATION. Care must be taken to avoid errors resulting from the *dangling pointer* problem [PRA75], i.e., referencing objects that have been explicitly deallocated.

The total amount of storage set aside for objects of a particular access type can be specified by means of a length specification (see Chapter 8 on Representation Clauses and Implementation Dependent Features).

3. Expressions [4.4]

Expressions are formed using operators and operands. In evaluating an expression, operators with a higher precedence are applied first. Operators having the same precedence are applied in textual order from left to right. Parentheses may be used to change the order of evaluation imposed by the precedence of the operators.

A *static expression* [4.9] is an expression whose operands have values that can be determined without program execution. Static expressions can therefore be evaluated at compile time (without executing the program).

Static expressions consist of literals, literal expressions, constants initialized to static expressions, aggregates composed of static expressions, predefined operators, static attributes, function attributes with static expressions as actual parameters and so on.

Operator precedence and semantics are given in the following sections and tables:

3.1 Operator Precedence [4.5]

The operators are listed in order of increasing precedence:

logical	**and | or | xor | and then | or else**
relational/membership	**= | /= | < | <= | > | >= | in | not in**
adding (binary)	**+ | − | &**
adding (unary)	**+ | −**
multiplying	*** | / | mod | rem**
highest precedence	**** | abs | not**

3.2 Operator Semantics

3.2.1 Logical Operators [4.5.1]:

Operator	Operation	Operand Types	Result Type
and	conjunction	boolean	same boolean
		boolean array	same boolean array
or	inclusive disjunction	boolean	same boolean
		boolean array	same boolean array
xor	exclusive disjunction	boolean	same boolean
		boolean array	same boolean array
and then	short circuit *and*	boolean	same boolean
or else	short circuit *or*	boolean	same boolean

A *boolean* type refers to either the predefined type BOOLEAN or any type derived from a boolean type (derived types are discussed in Chapter 2 on More About Types).

The result of an expression formed using the logical operators **and, or** or **xor** is determined by evaluating both operands. In case of the short circuit logical operators (**and then** and **or else**), the second operand is evaluated only if the result of the expression cannot be determined from evaluating the first operand. The phrase *optimization of boolean expressions*[13] has been used to mean that when generating code for boolean expressions, the normal logical operators (**and, or**) will be treated as if they were really short circuit logical operators [GRI71]. As long as the boolean expressions do not contain side effects this

---

13. Optimization is a misnomer! The phrase *code improvement* should be used instead, since the code produced after the so called optimization is usually not the most efficient code.

optimization poses no problems.

Programs relying on the knowledge that the boolean expressions are optimized in a particular implementation may become implementation dependent, because they may not produce correct results on an implementation that does not optimize boolean expressions. For example, evaluating the expression

$$I \mathrel{/}= 0 \text{ and } A(I)$$

in which the lower bound of array A is 1 will cause no problems when I is equal to 0, if optimized code is produced, but will result in a *subscript out of range* error otherwise.

By separating the logical operators into the regular and short circuit forms, Ada provides the programmer with the option to specify exactly what is wanted. The use of short circuit operators can lead to elegant code [DIJ76]. For example, without the short circuit operator **and then**, the Ada program segment

```
I := 1;
while I <= N and then X(I) /= KEY loop
    I := I + 1;
end loop;
--if I <= N then I is the subscript of KEY in X
```

that searches the array slice X(1..N) for a value KEY may be written (inelegantly) using an additional BOOLEAN variable PRESENT as

```
I :=  0;
PRESENT := FALSE;
while I < N and not PRESENT loop
    I := I + 1;
    PRESENT := X(I) = KEY;
end loop;
--if PRESENT is TRUE then I is the subscript of KEY in X
```

The additional variable must be used to avoid a subscript error in case KEY is not present in the array.[14] The **and then** operator allows evaluation of its second operand

---

14. Just writing the first program segment using simply **and** instead of **and then** as in

```
while I <= N and X(I) /= KEY loop I := I + 1; end loop;
```

causes a subscript error when I > N.

$$X(I) \mathrel{/=} KEY$$

only if its first operand

$$I \mathrel{<=} N$$

is true, so that $X(I)$ is a valid element of X.

3.2.2 Relational and Membership Operators [4.5.2]:

Operator	Operation	Operand Types	Result Type
= /=	equality inequality	any type	BOOLEAN
< <= > >=	test for ordering	any scalar type discrete array type	BOOLEAN BOOLEAN

Operator	Operation	Left Operand Type	Right Operand Type	Result Type
in **not in**	membership test to determine if a value belongs to a range, type or subtype	value of the right operand type	range, type or subtype name	BOOLEAN

3.2.3 Binary Adding Operators [4.5.3]:

Operator	Operation	Left Operand Type	Right Operand Type	Result Type
+	addition	numeric	same numeric	same numeric
−	minus	numeric	same numeric	same numeric
&	catenation	array type element type array type element type	same as left array type array type element type element type	same as left same array type same array type any array type

The catenation operator & can be used to catenate two arrays, extend an array at either end by one element and to form an array of two elements.

3.2.4 Unary Adding Operators [4.5.4]:

Operator	Operation	Operand Type	Result Type
+	identity	numeric	same numeric type
−	negation	numeric	same numeric type

3.2.5 Multiplying Operators [4.5.5]:

The first table in this section shows the multiplying operators for integer and floating point real values; the second table shows the multiplying operators for fixed point reals:

Operator	Operation	Operand Types	Result Type
*	multiplication	integer floating	same integer type same floating type
/	integer division floating division	integer floating	same integer type same floating type
mod	modulus	integer	same integer type
rem	remainder	integer	same integer type

The remainder operator **rem** and the modulus operator **mod** applied to operands with the same absolute value produce the same result only when both operands are of the same sign. Operation (A **rem** B) is defined by the relation

$$A = (A/B)*B + (A \text{ rem } B)$$

where A and B are integers, / represents integer division, and (A **rem** B) has the sign of A and an absolute value less than the absolute value of B. On the other hand, (A **mod** B) has the sign of B and an absolute value less than the absolute value of B. Subject to these restrictions, (A **mod** B) is defined by the relationship

$$A = B*N + (A \text{ mod } B)$$

where N is some integer.

Operator	Operation	Left Operand Type	Right Operand Type	Result Type
*	multiplication	fixed integer fixed	integer fixed fixed	same as left operand same as right operand *universal fixed*
/	division	fixed fixed	integer fixed	same as left operand *universal fixed*

The *universal fixed* point type, a type with arbitrarily fine precision, is not available to the user. Values of this type must be explicitly converted to some fixed point type before they can be used.

3.2.6 Highest Precedence Operators [4.5.6]:

Operator	Operation	Operand Type	Result Type
abs	absolute value	numeric	same numeric
not	logical negation	boolean boolean array	same boolean same array type

Operator	Operation	Left Operand Type	Right Operand Type	Result Type
**	exponentiation	integer floating	positive integer integer	left operand type left operand type

4. Statements [5]

In this section, Ada statements that are conventional in nature (such as those found in Pascal) are discussed. Statements such as those pertaining to concurrency, raising exceptions and the insertion of machine code are left for later chapters.

4.1 Null Statement [5.1]

Ada has a statement that does nothing. This statement is

   null;

The *null* statement is used in situations where no action is to be performed, but where the Ada syntax requires the presence of at least one statement.

4.2 Assignment [5.2]

Assignment statements have the form

   V := E;

where V is a variable name and E is an expression. Executing the assignment statement causes the value of E to be assigned to the variable represented by V. The type of both V and E must be the same. Additionally, the value of E must satisfy constraints imposed by the type of V. Assignment is defined for all types. For example, whole arrays, slices or records can be assigned values directly.

4.3 If Statement [5.3]

The *if* statement has the form

> **if** boolean_expression **then**
>   sequence_of_statements
> {**elsif** boolean_expression **then**
>   sequence_of_statements}
> [**else**
>   sequence_of_statements]
> **end if;**

The sequence of statements corresponding to the first boolean expression that is true is executed. Otherwise, the sequence of statements corresponding to the *else* part, if any, is executed. The following program segment, illustrating the use of the *if* statement, is taken from the abstract version of the program to sort an array, using the quicksort technique, given at the end of the chapter:

> **if** One element **then**
>   **null;**
> **elsif** Two elements **then**
>   Order them
> **elsif** More than two elements **then**
>   Partition the array into two parts and sort each part
> **end if;**

4.4 Case Statement [5.4]

The *case* statement is used to select one alternative sequence of statements out of many. It has the form

> **case** expression **is**
>   **when** choice {| choice} => sequence_of_statements
>   {**when** choice {| choice} => sequence_of_statements}
> **end case;**

The expression in the *case* statement must be of a discrete type. The sequence of statements corresponding to a choice matching the value of the expression is executed. The choices must be static expressions of a discrete type or discrete ranges. A choice that is a discrete range is an abbreviation for a list of choices representing the values in the range. The choices must cover all possible values the expression in the *case* statement might have and must be mutually exclusive. The choice **others** may be given for the last alternative as a shorthand for the remaining possible values of the expression.

An example of a *case* statement is a program segment from a simple Polish notation interpreter.

```
case C is
   when '+' => ADD;
   when '-' => SUBTRACT;
   when '*' => MULTIPLY;
   when '/' => DIVIDE;
   when others => PUT_ON_STACK;
end case;
```

The *case* statement is clearer and more efficient to implement than the multiway branch using the *if* statement:

```
if C = '+' then ADD;
elsif C = '-' then SUBTRACT;
elsif C = '*' then MULTIPLY;
elsif C = '/' then DIVIDE;
else PUT_ON_STACK;
end if;
```

The *case* statement, unlike the *if* statement, can be used only when the choice depends upon the value of a discrete expression.

4.5 Loops [5.5]

The *loop* statement has three forms:

```
while boolean_expression loop
   sequence_of_statements
end loop;

for loop_parameter in [reverse] discrete_range loop
   sequence_of_statements
end loop;

loop
   sequence_of_statements
end loop;
```

The first loop, called the *while* loop, is executed repeatedly as long as the boolean_expression is TRUE. For example, the following loop is executed until the end of file P is reached. The statements inside the loop copy a value from file P to file R:

```
while not END_OF_FILE(P) loop
   READ(P, X);
   WRITE(R, X);
end loop;
```

In the second form, called the *for* loop, the loop is executed once for each value in the discrete range with the loop parameter being equal to that value. The values are assigned to the loop parameter in increasing order when the keyword **reverse** is absent and in decreasing order when **reverse** is present. The loop parameter is not declared explicitly. It is implicitly declared by its presence in the loop and has the type of the specified discrete range. The loop parameter is local to the loop and its value cannot be changed in the loop body. No value can be assigned to it, nor can it be passed to a procedure in a manner that could allow its value to be modified. The loop parameter acts like a constant within the loop body. In the following example, the loop is executed once for each subscript of A, except the last one, with the loop parameter I being assigned the subscripts in decreasing order:

```
--from the program to evaluate a polynomial using Horner's
--rule given at the end of the chapter

for I in reverse A'FIRST..A'LAST-1 loop
    --loop variable I is implicitly declared by its presence
    --in the loop  header

    SUM := SUM * V + A(I);
end loop;
```

A *for* loop is not executed if a *null range* is specified. For example, this loop is not executed at all if LAST is equal to 0:

```
for J in 1..LAST loop
        --search table ST for the record with
        --value X in its ID field
    if ST(J).ID = X then
        return TRUE;
    end if;
end loop;
```

The third form of the loop is used when neither the *for* loop nor the *while* loop can be conveniently used. In this form, the loop iterates until it is exited explicitly, e.g., by executing an *exit*, a *return* or a *goto* statement, or implicitly when an exception is raised. The third loop form is also used to express infinite cycles that occur in *tasks* (concurrent programs) that are designed never to stop. Examples of such programs are a clock that runs forever and an infinite process that reads characters from a buffer and outputs their upper case form. The second of these examples is illustrated by the following program segment:

```
loop
    BUFFER.READ(X);
    PUT(UPPER(X));
end loop;
```

Execution of the statement BUFFER.READ is suspended when the buffer is empty and is resumed after at least one character has been put into the buffer.

4.5.1 Naming Loops: A loop may be named by prefixing it with an identifier, for example,

> L:

A named loop must be terminated by its name, for example,

> **end loop** L;

Loop names are used in *exit* statements. Also, naming loops is helpful when loops are nested several levels deep and when the first and last lines of the loop are textually far apart.

4.6 Blocks [5.6]

A *block* statement is a sequence of statements preceded optionally by a set of local declarations and followed optionally by a sequence of exception handlers (exception handling is discussed in Chapter 5 on Exceptions). A block can be named just as a loop can be named.

```
[ declare
     declarative_part ]
  begin
     sequence_of_statements
[ exception
     exception handlers ]
  end;
```

Blocks are used to confine the scope of declarations and exception handlers to the statements with which they are logically associated. Without blocks, these declarations would be visible to all other statements and it would not be possible to locally handle exceptions raised in these statements. Storage for objects declared in the block is allocated upon entering the block and is reclaimed on exit.

As an example, suppose that a program segment to exchange the values of two strings A and B of type STRING(1..80) is to be written. Using blocks, the program segment can be written as

```
declare
   TEMP: STRING(1..80);
begin
   TEMP := A;
   A := B;
   B := TEMP;
end;
```

TEMP is local to the statements that need to use it and is not visible to any other statements in the rest of the program. Storage for TEMP is allocated on block entry and released on block exit.

4.7 Exit Statement [5.7]

An *exit* statement is used to exit from a loop, either unconditionally (when no boolean expression has been specified) or conditionally (when a boolean expression is present).

exit [loop_name] [**when** boolean_expression];

Unless a loop name is specified, the innermost loop surrounding the *exit* statement is the one exited.

4.8 Return [5.8]

A *return* statement is used to return from a function, a procedure or an *accept* statement. In case of a function, the *return* statement is also used to return the value computed by the function. A *return* statement of the form

return expression;

must be used to return from a function. The value returned by the function is the value of *expression*. To return from a procedure, the form

return;

is used.

4.9 Goto [5.9]

Each statement can be prefixed by a label of the form

<< identifier >>

Labels identify the statements they are associated with and are used in *goto* statements. The *goto* statement is used for explicitly transferring control to a statement whose label has been specified. The *goto* statement has the form

goto label;

The unrestricted use of the *goto* statement is considered to be harmful, because it hampers program understandability [DIJ68b, KNU74]. Consequently a very restricted version of the *goto* statement is provided in Ada. The *goto* statement cannot be used to transfer control out of a subprogram, package or task body, or an *accept* statement. It cannot be used to transfer control from outside into a compound statement, an *if* statement, a *case* statement or any other control structure.

5. Subprograms [6]

There are four forms of *program units* from which programs can be composed—subprograms, packages, tasks and generic units. Subprograms can be compiled *separately* and are called *compilation units.*[15] Subprograms in Ada come in two varieties—procedures and functions. A procedure is executed for its effect (e.g., changing the values of the **in out** parameters, supplying values to **out** parameters or updating global variables) and functions are used to return values.

Subprograms are invoked (executed) by means of subprogram calls. A procedure call is a statement, while a function call is an operand in an expression. Execution of a procedure terminates upon reaching the end of the procedure or by executing a *return* statement. Execution of a function must terminate by executing a *return* statement that returns the function result. Subprograms in Ada are recursive and reentrant.

A subprogram consists of two parts:

- a subprogram specification and

- a subprogram body.

A subprogram specification consists of the name of the subprogram, the names and types of its parameters, and, in case of a function, the type of the result. Subprogram specifications are of the form

      procedure name [(formal parameters)] ;

      function name [(formal parameters)] **return** T;

where *name* is an identifier (or alternatively, in case of a function, an operator symbol surrounded by double quotes) and T is a type or subtype name. Some examples of subprogram specifications are

---

15. A program is a collection of one or more compilation units submitted to the compiler together or separately. Subprogram and package declarations and bodies, generic declarations and instantiations, and subunits (bodies of subprograms, packages and tasks declared in other compilation units) are the compilation units of Ada.

procedure EXTEND(S: **in out** SEQUENCE);

function SQRT(X: **in** NON_NEGATIVE_REAL;
                  EPS: **in** POS_REAL := 0.001) **return** FLOAT;

function NULL_SEQ **return** SEQUENCE;

Subprogram bodies have the form[16]

procedure name [(formal parameters)] **is**
    declarations
begin
    sequence_of_statements
[**exception**
    exception handlers]
end name;

function name [(formal parameters)] **return** T **is**
    declarations
begin
    sequence_of_statements
[**exception**
    exception handlers]
end name;

As stated above, T is the type of the function result.

In the *declarations* part of a subprogram body, declarations of all objects, types, subtypes, representation specifications and exceptions must come before the bodies of subprograms, packages and tasks.

A subprogram specification can be omitted only if the subprogram will be called after its body has been given (assuming it has not been declared in the visible part of a package). In this case the body of the subprogram acts as its own specification.

---

16. Supplying the subprogram name at the end of its body, i.e., after the reserved word **end**, is optional in Ada. However, it is good programming style to end a subprogram body with its name, since it aids program readability. For this reason, the forms shown for subprogram bodies do not indicate that the subprogram name at the end of its body is optional. This style will also be used for package specification and body, task specification and body, etc.

5.1 Formal Parameters

Formal parameters of a subprogram are local to the subprogram. They can have one of three modes—**in**, **out** and **in out**:[17]

formal parameter mode	formal parameter behavior
in	The formal parameter acts like a constant in the subprogram with its value being supplied by the corresponding actual parameter. **in** is the default mode if no mode is explicitly specified. This mode should be used when a value is supplied by the actual parameter to the corresponding formal parameter and no value is expected back from the subprogram.
out	The formal parameter acts like a local variable. Its value is assigned to the corresponding actual parameter on normal termination of the subprogram. This mode should be used when the actual parameter is to be supplied a value from the corresponding formal parameter.
in out	The formal parameter behaves like an initialized local variable. Its initial value is that of the corresponding actual parameter. On normal termination of a subprogram, the value of a formal parameter is assigned to the corresponding actual parameter. This mode is used when the actual parameter supplies a value to the corresponding formal parameter and it in turn is supplied a value by the formal parameter on normal termination of the subprogram.

The formal parameters of a function must all have the mode **in**. (The intent of this restriction is to discourage the definition of functions with side effects; however, global variables can still be changed to produce side effects.)

---

17. These modes are known in the computer science literature [GRI71, PRA75] as *value, result* and *value result* respectively.

5.2 Examples of Subprograms

5.2.1 Swap: The following procedure subprogram swaps or interchanges the values of two floating point variables:

```
procedure SWAP(X, Y: in out FLOAT) is
    T: FLOAT;   ――temporary variable
begin
    T := X;
    X := Y;
    Y := T;
end SWAP;
```

5.2.2 Square Root by Newton's Method: Function SQRT calculates the positive square root of a floating point real using Newton's method. The $k+1^{th}$ approximation a_{k+1} to the square root of a value X is given by the iterative formula

$$a_{k+1} = 0.5\ (a_k + \frac{X}{a_k})$$

The iteration is stopped when the absolute difference between two successive approximations of the square root is less than EPS, which is a very small positive number. SQRT uses subtypes NON_NEGATIVE_REAL and POS_REAL declared as

```
    subtype NON_NEGATIVE_REAL
                is FLOAT range 0.0 .. FLOAT'LAST;
    subtype POS_REAL
                is FLOAT range FLOAT'SMALL .. FLOAT'LAST;
```

NON_NEGATIVE_REAL values are values of type FLOAT $\geqslant 0.0$ while POS_REAL values are $\geqslant$ the smallest positive (non-zero) model number associated with FLOAT.

```
function SQRT(X: in NON_NEGATIVE_REAL;
              EPS: in POS_REAL := 0.001) return FLOAT is

    --only floating point numbers ≥ 0.0 are accepted,
    --the positive square root is returned with the specified
    --accuracy EPS, which has a default value of 0.001

OLD_VALUE: FLOAT;
    --the kth approximation of the square root
NEW_VALUE: FLOAT;
    --the k+1th approximation of the square root
begin
    OLD_VALUE := 0.0;     --just some value to go through the loop;
    NEW_VALUE := X/2.0; --the initial guess

    while abs (NEW_VALUE-OLD_VALUE) > EPS loop
        OLD_VALUE := NEW_VALUE;
        NEW_VALUE := 0.5 * (OLD_VALUE + X/OLD_VALUE);
    end loop;

    return NEW_VALUE;
end SQRT;
```

5.2.3 Matrix Addition: The operator +, which denotes integer and real addition, will now be extended so that it also represents matrix addition. This example illustrates the use of an unconstrained array type as the type of a formal parameter and *operator overloading.* The unconstrained array type allows arrays of different sizes to be passed as actual parameters to a subprogram. Operator overloading is the declaration of an operator with operand types other than the built-in ones.

Matrix addition will be declared for matrices of the unconstrained array type MATRIX, which was defined earlier as

```
type MATRIX is array
            (INTEGER range <>, INTEGER range <>) of FLOAT;
```

The overloaded + is declared as

function "+"(X, Y: MATRIX) **return** MATRIX **is**

      ——Matrices X and Y can have any bounds but they must
      ——be the same for matrix addition. This requirement could be
      ——checked explicitly in the subprogram.
      ——The mode of the formal parameters has not been specified and
      ——is assumed to be **in** by default. This mode is the only
      ——one allowed for formal parameters of a function.

      SUM: MATRIX(X´FIRST..X´LAST, X´FIRST(2)..X´LAST(2));
        ——note how the bounds of SUM are supplied
begin
    for I **in** X´RANGE(1) **loop**
      for J **in** X´RANGE(2) **loop**
          ——**for** loop variables are implicitly declared
        SUM(I, J) := X(I, J) + Y(I, J);
               ——the + used here is that for FLOAT
      end loop;
    end loop;
    return SUM;
  end "+";

In overloading + for matrix addition, the type of the elements of MATRIX does not matter as long as the operator + used inside the body of the overloaded + is defined for the element type. For example, suppose that the declaration of MATRIX is modified so that the matrix elements are now of type INTEGER instead of type FLOAT. The overloaded declaration of + remains legal for the modified type MATRIX, since + is also defined for type INTEGER.

All operators, except the membership and the short circuit operators, can be overloaded.

The declaration of the formal parameters X and Y

    X, Y: MATRIX;

could alternatively have been written as

    X: MATRIX; Y: MATRIX;

It would have been nice had Ada differentiated between these two forms of declaring unconstrained type objects—the first form, unlike the second form, could require that the bounds of the corresponding actual parameters be identical. Explicit checks to ensure that the bounds of X and Y in the declaration of + would then not be needed.

5.3 Subprogram Calls, Actual Parameters and Parameter Matching [6.4]

Subprogram calls have the form

procedure_name [(actual parameter list)];

function_name (actual parameter list) | function_name

Actual parameters may be specified in positional or named notation. Actual parameters may be given default initial values by associating the default initial values with the corresponding formal parameters. Such actual parameters may be omitted, but the named notation must then be used for the rest of the actual parameters in the subprogram call.

A procedure call is a statement by itself, e.g.,

SWAP(P, Q);
PUT(UPPER(CHAR));

A function call, on the other hand, can be used only as part of an expression, since functions return values.

SQRT(5.0)
        −−default value is used for the second actual
        −−parameter, i.e., 0.001; see the declaration
        −−of SQRT in section 5.2.2

SQRT(Y, 0.05) > 3.0

SQRT(EPS => 0.05, X => Y)
        −−alternative version of the above using
        −−named notation for parameters

A := B + C + D;
        −−A, B, C and D are arrays of type MATRIX
        −−with the same bounds. The + operator used here
        −−is the one overloaded for arrays of type MATRIX

The types of the formal and actual parameters must match exactly. In the case of parameters of a scalar type the range constraints must be satisfied. Index and discriminant constraints must be satisfied for access types. For parameters of an array type, a record or a private type with discriminants, the constraints specified for the formal parameter type must be satisfied. The bounds of an unconstrained array type formal parameter are obtained from the corresponding actual parameter.

5.4 Subprogram Overloading [6.6]

Subprogram overloading is the use of the same subprogram name for *different* subprograms. For example, in most programming languages the same name + designates the various functions used for adding different types of integers and reals. Overloading is convenient, since the user has to remember only one name for the addition functions and since it corresponds to common mathematical notation. A programming language should also allow users to overload subprograms, particularly if a user is allowed to define new types. For example, it would be nice if the operator + could be overloaded to represent addition of user-defined types such as complex, rational and polynomial.

Ideally the same name should be used for subprograms that are similar in some important ways, e.g., they use the same abstract algorithm but differ in details such as the type and number of their parameters. It would be bad practice to use the same name for subprograms that implement significantly different ideas. For example, it would not be good style to use the name MAX both for a function that computes the maximum value of a real array and a function that determines a value occurring the maximum number of times in an array of strings. However, it makes sense to use the name MAX for functions that compute the maximum values of real, integer and character arrays, and so on.

Ada allows the user to overload subprogram names. Overloading a subprogram hides the subprogram being overloaded if it and the new subprogram have *identical* specifications. Two subprograms have identical specifications if both subprograms have the same

- name,
- number of parameters,
- types (actually *base* types) for the corresponding parameters and
- result type (in case of function subprograms only).

A call to an overloaded subprogram name is illegal if it is ambiguous, i.e., if it cannot be decided exactly to which one of the overloaded subprograms it refers. Such ambiguities can be resolved in several ways, such as prefixing the name of the subprogram by the name of the *package* it is contained in or by *renaming* it.

6. Visibility Rules [8]

The discussion of the visibility of entities in this section refers mainly to identifiers (variable names, subprogram names and so on) but also to literals, enumeration values and other entities.

A *declaration* associates an identifier with a program entity such as a variable, type definition, subprogram or formal parameter. An entity can be declared in several ways, such as in

- the declarative part of a subprogram, block or a package,
- a package specification,
- a record as one of its components,
- a subprogram formal parameter,
- in a loop implicitly as a loop parameter (simply by the occurrence of an identifier in the loop heading).

6.1 Scope of Entities [8.2]

The *scope* of an entity is the region of the program text where its declaration is in effect. The scope of

1. an entity declared in a block, subprogram or task extends from the declaration to the end of the block, subprogram or task.

2. an entity declared in the visible part of a package declaration extends to the scope of the package declaration, which includes the rest of the package specification and the package body. On the other hand, the scope of an entity declared in the *private part* of a package extends to the end of the package specification and the package body.

3. an entry in a task declaration extends from its declaration to the end of the scope of the task declaration. It includes the task body.

4. a record component extends from its declaration to the end of the scope of the record definition.

5. a loop parameter extends from its first occurrence to the end of the associated loop.

6. the scope of a parameter (including a generic parameter) extends from its declaration to the end of the scope it is declared in.

(Only the first item of this list is directly relevant to this chapter; the remaining items are included to make the discussion complete.)

6.2 Visibility of Entities

The scope of entities with the same identifier can overlap as a result of overloading of subprograms and enumeration literals, nesting and so on. Ada *program units* such as subprogram, tasks and packages along with statements and blocks can be nested. Ada's visibility rules for entities are similar to those of Algol 60. In addition, Ada provides the user with a mechanism to control visibility to some degree.

An entity is said to be *directly visible* if the entity can be referred to directly by using the identifier associated with it. If the entity is not directly visible, then context can sometimes be added to make it directly visible. For example, a component C of a package P can be made visible in the context in which the package P is visible by using the *selected component notation* P.C for it.

An identifier associated with an entity for which overloading is not possible (e.g., variables, constants, loop parameters and labels) is *hidden* in an inner construct if the inner construct contains an entity with the same identifier. Within the inner construct, the hidden outer entity is not directly visible. An entity that can be overloaded is said to be *hidden* in an inner construct when the inner construct contains a declaration for another entity with the same identifier and with identical specifications. For example, a subprogram, which can be overloaded, is hidden in an inner construct only when a subprogram with an identical specification is declared in the inner constructs.

Enumeration literals are treated like parameterless functions in determining the visibility of entities. Consequently, an enumeration literal may hide a parameterless function and vice versa.

The following program segment illustrates the difference between the visibility rules for entities that can be overloaded and those that cannot:

```
procedure P is
    A, B: FLOAT;
    procedure Y is  ...  end Y;
    procedure Q is
        A: INTEGER;
        function B return INTEGER is  ...  end B;
        procedure Y(X: FLOAT) is  ...  end Y;
    begin
            ——variables A and B of the outer procedure P are
            ——not directly visible here, because Q contains entities
            ——with the same identifier; however, they can be referred to
            ——using the selected component notation P.A and P.B;
            ——procedure Y, declared outside Q, is visible, because the
            ——procedure Y inside Q has a different specification
        :
    end Q;
    :
begin
    :
end P;
```

6.3 Making Package Components Directly Visible

If a package is visible at a given point in a program, then its components are also visible at that point, using the selected component notation. The *use* clause can be used to make the components of such a package directly visible.

Use clauses do not result in an identifier being hidden, although they may cause overloading of an identifier. If an entity cannot be made visible by means of a *use* clause (because a similar entity is already directly visible), then the selected component notation must be used. In case of overloading, identifiers made visible are considered only if a valid interpretation of the program cannot be found without them.

6.4 Renaming Entities [8.5]

Ada provides a facility, the *renaming declaration*, for giving an alternative name to an entity. Both the original name and the new name can be used to refer to the renamed entity. Renaming can be used to resolve name conflicts (e.g., those caused by overloading) and for convenient abbreviations.

For example, a procedure or function can be given another name. The procedure TEXT_IO.PUT for writing character values to the standard output is renamed PUT for convenience in using the declaration

> **procedure** PUT(A: CHARACTER) **renames** TEXT_IO.PUT;
> −−shorthand notation for PUT

The operator +, overloaded for matrix addition, can be renamed MATRIX_SUM by the declaration

> **function** MATRIX_SUM(X, Y: **in** MATRIX) **return** MATRIX
> **renames** "+";

The statement

>   A := B + C + D;

where A, B, C and D are all arrays of type MATRIX having the same bounds can now also be written as

>   A := MATRIX_SUM(D, MATRIX_SUM(B, C));

Operators can be renamed as functions and vice versa. A function corresponding to a unary operator must have exactly one formal parameter while a function corresponding to a binary operator must have exactly two formal parameters.

7. Input/Output [14]

General high level input and output facilities are provided by the predefined packages SEQUENTIAL_IO, DIRECT_IO and TEXT_IO. They define the file types, file *modes* and file operations. SEQUENTIAL_IO and DIRECT_IO, which are generic, are used to interface with files in binary format. TEXT_IO is used to read from or write to a text file, i.e., a file represented as a sequences of characters. (Text files, unlike binary files, are human readable.) A package, named LOW_LEVEL_IO, is also provided for controlling peripheral devices directly.

An *external* [14.1] file is anything external to a program that can produce or receive a value. It is identified by a *name*, which is a string. System dependent characteristics of a file, such as its *access rights* and its physical organization, are given by a second string, called the *form*. An external file cannot be operated upon directly. An *internal* file object (called simply a file unless there is an ambiguity) must first be created and then associated with an external file. It is this internal file which is used in performing file operations, such as reading from or writing to the associated external file. Files, both internal and external, are homogeneous objects, i.e., they contain only elements of the same type.

7.1 Direct and Sequential Files [14.2]

Two kinds of access to external files are supported—direct and sequential. A file that is used for direct access is called a *direct* file. (Of course, the associated external file must reside on a medium that supports direct access, e.g, a disk.) Such a file is viewed as a set of elements occupying consecutive positions in a linear order. Elements at arbitrary positions can be accessed and updated. The position of an element is given by its index. The index of the first element, if any, is one. The number of elements in a file is called is its *current size*. A direct access file can have one of three modes—read only (IN_FILE), write only (OUT_FILE) and read/write (INOUT_FILE).

An internal file object used for sequential access is called a *sequential* file. Elements in a sequential file cannot be accessed by position; they must be accessed sequentially. Unlike direct access files, sequential files can have only two modes—read only (IN_FILE) and write only (OUT_FILE).

7.1.1 Using Direct and Sequential Files: Files with elements of type T are declared and used in a subprogram (or a package) in the following manner:

1. Specify the appropriate generic input/output package that the subprogram (or package) is to be compiled with, by using a *with* statement, e.g.,

     with SEQUENTIAL_IO;

2. Instantiate the generic input/output package for elements of type T, e.g.,

package T_IO **is**
    new SEQUENTIAL_IO(ELEMENT_TYPE => T);

Package T_IO contains the declaration of type FILE_TYPE (which is used for declaring files with elements of type T), modes applicable to sequential files, (i.e., IN_FILE and OUT_FILE) and operations for sequential files with elements of type T.

3. Create internal files of type T_IO.FILE_TYPE. For example,

    A, B: T_IO.FILE_TYPE;

declares A and B to be internal files with elements of type T.

4. Establish the connection between the internal and external files by opening an existing external file or creating a new one; the mode of the internal file is specified at the same time, e.g.,

    T_IO.OPEN(A, IN_FILE, "student.grades");
    ——associates file A with an existing external file
    ——"student.grades" from which values can be read
    ——but not written to

    T_IO.CREATE(B, OUT_FILE, "student.statistics");
    ——associates file B with a newly created external file
    ——"student.statistics" and leaves it in an open state
    ——for writing; B is a write only file

5. Process the files, e.g., read values from A and write these or other values to B, using procedures T_IO.READ and T_IO.WRITE, e.g.,

    T_IO.READ(A, X);
     :
    T_IO.WRITE(B, Y);

where X is a variable and Y is an expression, both of type T.

6. When processing of the files is complete, connection between external and internal files is severed by closing the internal files using the operation T_IO.CLOSE, e.g.,

    T_IO.CLOSE(A);
    T_IO.CLOSE(B);

7. The need for explicitly prefixing entities provided by package T_IO can be avoided (except in case of ambiguity) by giving a *use* clause of the form

    use T_IO;

For example, operation

    T_IO.CLOSE(A);

can now be written simply as

    CLOSE(A);

7.2 Direct and Sequential File Operations

An instantiation of DIRECT_IO and SEQUENTIAL_IO makes the following file management operations available for the file type provided by the instantiation:

procedures	functions
CREATE	MODE
OPEN	NAME
CLOSE	FORM
DELETE	IS_OPEN
RESET	

7.2.1 Additional Sequential File Operations [14.2.2]: In addition to file management operations, an instantiation of SEQUENTIAL_IO also makes the following operations available:

procedures	functions
READ	END_OF_FILE
WRITE	

7.2.2 Additional Direct File Operations [14.2.4]: In addition to the file management operations, an instantiation of DIRECT_IO also makes the following operations available:

procedures	functions
READ	INDEX
WRITE	SIZE
SET_INDEX	END_OF_FILE

7.3 Text Files [14.3]

Package TEXT_IO provides file management operations (similar to those provided by DIRECT_IO and SEQUENTIAL_IO), operations for default input and output file manipulation, input and output operations, and layout control operations.

TEXT_IO provides procedures GET and PUT for reading and writing, instead of READ and WRITE as provided by DIRECT_IO and SEQUENTIAL_IO. GET and PUT do the necessary conversions between the internal representation of a value and its character representation on the text file. Only one item at a time, can be input or output by means of GET and PUT (READ and WRITE also operate on one item at a time). GET and PUT must be called an appropriate number of times, if more than one item is to be input or output.

Procedures GET and PUT are overloaded for types CHARACTER and STRING. To get versions of GET and PUT, for enumeration types, integers and reals, appropriate generic packages, provided in TEXT_IO, must be instantiated. GET and PUT are also overloaded, for numeric and enumeration types, so that an item can also be read from or written to a string (instead of a file). If a file name is not specified, when using GET or PUT, then by default, *standard input* and *standard output* files are used. These files are associated with the appropriate external files by an Ada implementation.

Logically, a text file may be viewed as a sequence of pages, a page as a sequence of lines, and a line as a sequence of characters. The ends of a file, page and line are marked by a *file terminator*, a *page terminator* and a *line terminator*, respectively. Terminators can be generated and recognized by appropriate subprograms, e.g., NEW_LINE and END_OF_FILE. Terminators are implementation dependent and their exact nature need concern only users interested in the input and output of control characters.

Facilities provided by TEXT_IO are now summarized:

1. File management operations

2. Function END_OF_FILE

3. Character input and output operations

4. String input and output operations (a string read using GET or written using PUT can span several lines; procedures GET_LINE and PUT_LINE read and write whole lines)

5. Generic package INTEGER_IO

6. Generic package FLOAT_IO

7. Generic package FIXED_IO

8. Generic package ENUMERATION_IO

9. Default input and output file manipulation operations

10. Layout control operations

11. Exceptions

Operations provided for default input and output file manipulation are

procedures	functions
SET_INPUT	STANDARD_INPUT
SET_OUTPUT	STANDARD_OUTPUT
	CURRENT_INPUT
	CURRENT_OUTPUT

Operations provided for layout control are

procedures	functions
SET_LINE_LENGTH	LINE_LENGTH
SET_PAGE_LENGTH	PAGE_LENGTH
NEW_LINE	END_OF_LINE
SKIP_LINE	END_OF_PAGE
NEW_PAGE	COL
SKIP_PAGE	LINE
SET_COL	PAGE
SET_LINE	

7.3.1 Using Text Files: The use and manipulation of text files is now summarized. TEXT_IO is made available to subprograms and packages compiled separately by prefixing them with

with TEXT_IO;

Text file operations and objects need not be qualified by TEXT_IO provided the following *use* clause has been given (assuming there is no ambiguity):

use TEXT_IO;

Text files are used in a manner similar to direct and sequential files. Package TEXT_IO, unlike DIRECT_IO and SEQUENTIAL_IO, is not generic and is therefore not instantiated. After declaring internal files, they are associated with external files by creating a new external file or opening an existing one. Text files are sequential files; consequently, only two modes are applicable to them—read only (IN_FILE) and write only (OUT_FILE).

TEXT_IO provides operations GET and PUT, instead of READ and WRITE. GET and PUT for character and string values are directly available, while for integers, reals and enumeration (including boolean) types, they are obtained by appropriately instantiating the generic packages INTEGER_IO, FLOAT_IO, FIXED_IO and ENUMERATION_IO.

Assuming the above *use* clause has been given, GET and PUT for INTEGER and COLOR types are made available by the declarations

package IO_INTEGER **is new** INTEGER_IO(INTEGER);
package IO_COLOR **is new** ENUMERATION_IO(COLOR);

The *use* clause

use IO_INTEGER, IO_COLOR;

obviates the need to prefix GET and PUT for types INTEGER and COLOR by IO_INTEGER and IO_COLOR.

7.4 Interactive Input

One problem area is interactive input in which Ada suffers from a problem similar to that in Pascal [FEU82]. For example, use of the paradigm

while not END_OF_FILE(STANDARD_INPUT) **loop**
    Request data from user
    Read data
    :
end loop;

to read input interactively from a terminal causes trouble. Function END_OF_FILE cannot be evaluated when there is no data, since it cannot be determined whether the data has been exhausted or that the data has not been supplied as yet. Consequently, evaluation of END_OF_FILE will be delayed until the user supplies the data—but the user has no way of knowing that the program is waiting for the data because the prompt will not be printed.

This problem can be avoided by using the following paradigm [GEHA83a] that uses the exception END_ERROR which is raised when an attempt is made to read past the end of file:

```
begin
        --begin a block so that the end of file exception
        --END_ERROR can be handled locally
    loop
        Request data from user
        Read data
                --this requires that either the data or an
                --indication of end of the file be supplied; in case
                --of an end of file, the END_ERROR exception is
                --raised by the read operation and control transfers
                --to the exception handler following the loop
            .
            .
    end loop;
    exception
        when END_ERROR => null;
                --the exception handler does nothing.  Execution
                --of the block terminates.
                --Note the use of a null statement--at least
                --one statement is required in an exception handler
                --by the Ada syntax.
    end;
```

This solution is inelegant since it requires the use of an exception and enclosure of the program segment reading the data in a *begin* block (so that the exception can be handled locally) and the use of a null exception handler.

A better solution [WET83] that avoids the above problems is

```
loop
    Request data from user
    exit when END_OF_FILE(STANDARD_INPUT);
    Read data
        .
        .
end loop;
```

8. Main Programs and Compilation Units

Any complete subprogram can be a *main program* in Ada. This philosophy is different from that adopted by most languages, such as FORTRAN, Pascal or PL/I, but is similar to that adopted by LISP. The main program will be executed from the command line in the environment, provided by an operating system, to support the development and execution of Ada programs. The main program must of course be prefixed by all the contextual information, such as the names of *compilation units*, necessary for its execution.

A main program can be a procedure or a function subprogram. If it is a procedure, then the result of executing the main program will be the side effects of the procedure, such as the creation of output on external files. If the main program is a function then the result of executing the main program will be the function result. A main program can have formal parameters. The corresponding actual parameters must be supplied on the command line using the notation specified by the environment in which the Ada program is being executed.

A program in Ada is a collection of one or more compilation units. A compilation unit is a declaration or a body of a subprogram or a package prefixed by any necessary *contextual information*. The contextual information consists of *with* and *use* clauses. The *with* clauses specify the compilation units required for the successful compilation of the declaration or body of the subprogram or the package. These compilation units must have been compiled before (or be predefined) since the *with* clauses specify dependencies between compilation units. The *use* clauses make the entities inside the specified compilation units directly visible inside the declaration or body that is being compiled.

9. Pragmas [2.8]

Pragmas are instructions (suggestions in some cases) to the compiler. For example, an Ada compiler can be instructed to pack arrays or records as densely as possible. Pragmas may be used to tune the behavior of the compiler so that it best meets the needs of the programmer. Suppose subprogram SWAP is being called repeatedly from a program segment whose execution speed is critical:

```
loop
   ⋮
   SWAP(A, B);
   ⋮
end loop;
```

The overhead associated with calling and returning from SWAP can be eliminated if the programmer replaces the call to SWAP by its body. Obliterating logical modularity, as represented by subprogram SWAP, in favor of execution speed is not desirable, since it makes a program less readable, less understandable and less modifiable. Logical modularity can be retained without sacrificing execution speed by having the compiler, instead of the programmer, make the replacement. Pragma INLINE instructs the compiler to replace all calls of the specified subprogram by its body:

  pragma INLINE(SWAP); --replace calls to the subprogram
            --SWAP by a copy of its body

A pragma can appear after a semicolon and wherever a statement, a declaration, a clause such as *use* and *with* clause, an *alternative*, a *variant* or an *exception handler* is allowed. There are some minor restrictions on this rule that apply to all pragmas. Further restrictions are associated with specific pragmas to ensure that they appear in places where they are meaningful. Pragmas may be language-defined (Appendix B of the Ada Reference Manual) or implementation-defined (Appendix F of the Ada Reference Manual). Some more examples of pragmas are

  pragma OPTIMIZE(SPACE);
     --try to optimize for space
  pragma LIST(OFF);
     --suspend printing of the program listing

10. Complete Examples

Several complete examples are given to illustrate the Ada concepts presented so far. The first example, taken from mechanical engineering, illustrates a numerical iteration method. The rest of the examples, from computer science, are on topics such as sorting, matrix multiplication and polynomial evaluation.

Stepwise refinement is used to illustrate the development of examples whenever necessary. Some desirable features of a good programming methodology and suggestions for stepwise refinement are given in the Appendix. The notation P_i is used to indicate the ith refinement of the program with P_0 being the initial refinement.

10.1 Steady State Temperature Distribution

This example is a heat transfer problem taken from mechanical engineering. The problem is to find the steady state temperature distribution across the walls of the air duct (or chimney) shown in the figure given below, the inside and outside temperatures being T_IN and T_OUT.

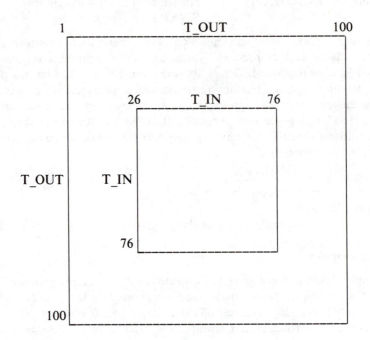

Cross Section of Duct

A heat transfer analysis of this problem reduces it to the simpler problem of solving the Laplace equation $\nabla^2 t = 0$ (t is the temperature) over the same cross section. The method used to solve the Laplace equation is Jacobi iteration (more on Jacobi method at the end of the example). It is defined as follows:

P_0:

Guess a temperature distribution for the cross section

loop

Let the temperature distribution computed in the
last iteration be the old temperature distribution
for this iteration;

Calculate the new temperature distribution from the
old one by letting the new temperature at each point
be the average of the old temperatures at the four
surrounding points

exit when the maximum absolute change in the
temperature at all the points is < EPS

end loop;

where $0.0 < EPS \ll 1.0$ is the desired accuracy of the result.

In the Ada program, arrays of size 100×100 are used (i.e., indices will have
values between 1 and 100) to represent the duct; the array REGION is defined
as

REGION(I, J) has the value TRUE if the point I, J
is inside the duct boundaries and FALSE otherwise

Array REGION simplifies testing to determine whether or not a point is within
the duct boundaries. The boundary temperatures are constant and it is not
necessary to visit points on the boundaries. Exclusion of the outside boundary
points is achieved easily by simply looping between 2 and 99 inclusive.
Consequently, REGION will be defined only for points I and J between the
limits 2 and 99.

Instead of comparing the complete old and new temperature distributions to
compute the maximum absolute temperature change at any point, this change
will be computed on a continuing basis every time a new temperature at a point
is computed. The abstract instruction *Calculate the new temperature
distribution from the old* ... in the above algorithm is therefore refined as

```
MAX_CHANGE := 0.0;
for all points I, J in REGION loop
    New temperature at point I, J is the average of the
    old temperatures at the four surrounding points;

    Let the new value of MAX_CHANGE be the  maximum of the
    old value of MAX_CHANGE and the absolute difference
    between the old and new temperatures at the point I, J
end loop;
```

The instruction **exit when** *the maximum* ... can now be refined as

```
exit when MAX_CHANGE < EPS;
```

The Ada main program based on the above algorithm and refinements is

```
with TEXT_IO;
        --the string I/O routines, the generic FLOAT, INTEGER
        --packages and other I/O routines become available

use TEXT_IO;     --the above routines no longer need to be
                 --qualified by TEXT_IO

procedure DUCT_TEMPERATURE is

    package IO_FLOAT is new FLOAT_IO(FLOAT);
            --instantiation of the generic FLOAT package
    package IO_INTEGER is new INTEGER_IO(INTEGER);
            --instantiation of the generic INTEGER package
    use IO_FLOAT, IO_INTEGER;
            --GET and PUT for FLOAT and INTEGER are now
            --directly visible



    subtype OUTSIDE is INTEGER range 1..100;
            --outside dimension of the duct
    type DUCT is array(OUTSIDE, OUTSIDE) of FLOAT;

    IN_TEMP, OUT_TEMP, EPS, MAX_CHANGE: FLOAT;
    OLD_TEMP, NEW_TEMP: DUCT;
                --contain the old and the new temperature
                --distributions in the duct
    REGION: constant array(2..99, 2..99) of BOOLEAN :=
            (2..25  => (2..99 => TRUE),
             26..75 => (26..75 => FALSE, 2..25 | 76..99 => TRUE),
             76..99 => (2..99 => TRUE));
```

```
                    ——note the elegant use of an array aggregate

                    ——the aggregate could not have been written as
                    ——(26..75 => (26..75 => FALSE), others => TRUE),
                    ——since (1) a two-dimensional array aggregate must be
                    ——written as a list of one-dimensional array values and
                    ——(2) the choice others can be used only in an
                    ——aggregate if its type has been explicitly supplied.

function MAX(A, B: in FLOAT) return FLOAT is
begin
    if A < B then return B; else return A; end if;

        ——The above style has been used for the if statement
        ——instead of the style usually used, as shown below, because
        ——of its small size. Style should not be rigid; it should
        ——be flexible to suit needs
        ——
        ——        if A < B then
        ——            return B;
        ——        else
        ——            return A;
        ——        end if;


end MAX;


begin

        ——Read in the boundary temperatures and the result accuracy

        PUT("What is the inside temperature?"); NEW_LINE;
        GET(IN_TEMP);

        PUT("What is the outside temperature?"); NEW_LINE;
        GET(OUT_TEMP);

        PUT("What is the desired accuracy?"); NEW_LINE;
        GET(EPS);

    ——initialize NEW_TEMP to the guessed temperature
    ——the boundaries are initialized to the specified temperatures
    ——and the inside region to the average of the two boundary
    ——temperatures
```

```
for I in OUTSIDE loop
    for J in OUTSIDE loop
        if I = OUTSIDE'FIRST
            or I = OUTSIDE'LAST
            or J = OUTSIDE'FIRST
            or J = OUTSIDE'LAST then
            NEW_TEMP(I, J) := OUT_TEMP;
                --outside boundary points
        elsif REGION(I, J) then
            NEW_TEMP(I, J) := (IN_TEMP + OUT_TEMP) / 2.0;
                                --inside region
        else
            NEW_TEMP(I, J) := IN_TEMP;
                --points on inside boundary and within it;
                --the array points enclosed by the inside boundary
                --will never be used
        end if;
    end loop;
end loop;

--compute the steady state temperature distribution

loop
    OLD_TEMP := NEW_TEMP;
                --ready for next iteration
                --note use of array assignment
    MAX_CHANGE := 0.0;
                --maximum change for any of the points
                --examined up to now
    for I in OUTSIDE'FIRST+1 .. OUTSIDE'LAST-1 loop
        for J in OUTSIDE'FIRST+1 .. OUTSIDE'LAST-1 loop
            if REGION(I, J) then
                NEW_TEMP(I, J) := (OLD_TEMP(I-1, J) +
                        OLD_TEMP(I+1, J) +
                        OLD_TEMP(I, J-1) +
                        OLD_TEMP(I, J+1)) /4.0;
                MAX_CHANGE := MAX(MAX_CHANGE,
                    abs (NEW_TEMP(I, J)-OLD_TEMP(I, J)));
            end if;
        end loop;
    end loop;

    exit when MAX_CHANGE < EPS;
end loop;
```

--Print the final version of the temperature distribution
--Identify each new row

```
    for I in OUTSIDE loop
        PUT("ROW"); PUT(I);
        NEW_LINE;
                    --default value of 1 is used for the actual
                    --parameter in the call to NEW_LINE

        for J in OUTSIDE loop
            PUT(NEW_TEMP(I, J));
        end loop;

        NEW_LINE(2);
    end loop;
end DUCT_TEMPERATURE;
```

The initialization of the array NEW_TEMP to the guessed temperature could alternatively have been written using an aggregate:

```
NEW_TEMP :=
    (1 | 100 => (1..100 => OUT_TEMP),
                    --top and bottom boundaries
     26..75 => (26..75 => IN_TEMP, 1 | 100 => OUT_TEMP,
                    2..25 | 76..99 => (OUT_TEMP + IN_TEMP)/2.0),
                --rows that include the inside boundary and
                --points within it

     2..25 | 76..99 => (1 | 100 => OUT_TEMP,
                        2..99 => (OUT_TEMP + IN_TEMP)/2.0));
                --the rest of the points
```

This initialization will probably be implemented more efficiently than the previous one, because the control flow is not explicitly specified and this gives more freedom to the compiler in generating code. Moreover, this initialization does not contain any explicit tests. Deciding which initialization is more readable is left to the reader.

The Jacobi iteration method always converges. New values (temperatures in this example) at the points are not used until the next iteration. In a variation of this method, called the Gauss-Seidel method, new values are used as soon as they are computed. The Gauss-Seidel method converges twice as fast as the Jacobi method, but there are situations in which the Gauss-Seidel method will not converge [DAH74]. The Gauss-Seidel method requires less storage, since only one array of values is needed.

10.2 The Mode of a Sorted Array

The problem is to write a subprogram that determines the most frequently occurring value, called the *mode*, of a sorted integer array. The frequency of the mode is also to be computed. The elegant algorithm used to compute the mode is based on the following observation made by Griffiths (in [GRI75]).

Let A be a sorted one dimensional array with a lower bound L and an upper bound U. The frequency of the mode, MF, of the slice $A(L..I-1)$ will be different from the frequency of the mode of the slice $A(L..I)$, only if $A(I)=A(I-1)$ and all the elements of the slice $A(I-MF..I-1)$ are equal. These conditions imply that

$$A(I) = A(I-1) = ... = A(I-MF)$$

and this relationship is true if and only if $A(I)=A(I-MF)$, since A is sorted. Therefore the frequency of the mode of $A(L..I)$ is $MF+1$, since there are now $MF+1$ equal elements of A.

The mode of a sorted array is computed by the procedure MODE, which is declared as

```
procedure MODE(A: in INT_VECTOR; MF, MV: out INTEGER) is
                --Assuming that A has at least one element,
                --MV will contain the mode of A on return and
                --MF will contain the frequency of MV on return

    L: constant INTEGER := A'FIRST;
    U: constant INTEGER := A'LAST;
        --array bounds do not have to be passed, since
        --they can be determined using attributes
    I: INTEGER;
begin
    MV := A(L);
    MF := 1;
    I := L+1;
    while I <= U loop
        if A(I) = A(I-MF) then
            MF := MF + 1;
            MV := A(I);
        end if;
        I := I+1;
    end loop;
end MODE;
```

The type INT_VECTOR used in procedure MODE is an unconstrained array type:

       type INT_VECTOR is array (INTEGER **range** <>) **of** INTEGER;

This algorithm is linear, i.e., every element of the sorted array is examined exactly once in computing the mode.[18]

10.3 The Towers of Hanoi

There are three rods X, Y and Z and there are N disks, all of different sizes. These disks are stacked up in decreasing order of size, like a tower, on rod X.

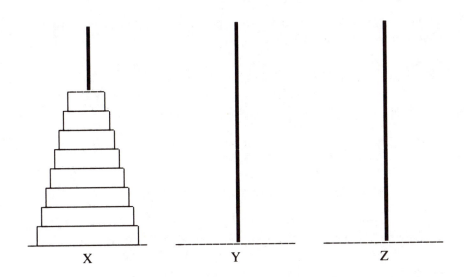

The Towers of Hanoi

The problem is to move these disks from rod X to rod Y so that they also end

---

18. The algorithm to compute the mode can be made sublinear on the average, i.e., not all elements of the array need be examined to compute the mode. The variable I is incremented by MF when $A(I) \neq A(I-MF)$ and then the array A is scanned backward from the element $A(I)$ to find the beginning of the sequence of elements equal to $A(I-MF)$. Computation of the new mode is resumed from this point. This improvement was suggested by John P. Linderman, a colleague at Bell Labs, and several others. Modifications, leading to improvements faster than the linear backward scan improvement, have also been suggested.

up in a decreasing size order on Y. Rod Z can be used as a temporary holding place. Only one disk can be moved at a time. Any disk may be placed on an empty rod but only a smaller disk can be placed on top of another disk. (The disks must never be placed on the ground.) The program is to read in the number of disks and print a series of move instructions.

The basic algorithm that generates the moves is

P_0

      move N−1 disks from X to Z using Y as temporary storage
      move the Nth disk from X to Y directly
      move N−1 disks from Z to Y using X as temporary storage

This algorithm is recursive and is further refined to include the termination condition and some more details.

P_1:

```
procedure Hanoi(N, X, Y, Z) is
        --move N disks from X to Y using Z as temporary storage
    begin
      if N /= 0 then
            --move N−1 disks from X to Z using Y
          Hanoi(N−1, X, Z, Y)

      Move disk N from X to Y

            --move N−1 disks from Z to Y using X
          Hanoi(N−1, Z, Y, X)
        end if;
    end
```

The *Principle of Induction* is used to show that this algorithm works. To show that a proposition P is true for all values of n ⩾ 0, the The Principle of Induction states that it must be shown that

1. P is true for n = 0.

2. P is true for n = k by assuming P is true for n = k−1.

Using the Principle of Induction it is fairly easy to show that procedure Hanoi works for all positive values of N. Clearly it works for N = 0, because it does nothing. Assume that it moves k−1 disks correctly. To move k disks from X to Y Hanoi first moves k−1 disks from X to Z. Then it moves the kth disk from X to Y. Finally, Hanoi moves the k−1 disks on Z to X. Thus the k disks are correctly moved from X to Y and by the Principle of Induction we conclude that Hanoi works correctly for all values of N that are positive.

The complete program (including a main program) is

```
with TEXT_IO; use TEXT_IO;
procedure TOWERS_OF_HANOI is

    package IO_INTEGER is new INTEGER_IO(INTEGER);
    use IO_INTEGER;

    NUMBER_OF_DISKS: NATURAL;
        --NATURAL is a subtype of INTEGER representing integer
        --values ≥0

    procedure HANOI(N: NATURAL; X, Y, Z: CHARACTER) is
        --move N disks from X to Y using Z as temporary storage
    begin
      if N /= 0 then

        --move the top N-1 disks to Z using Y
        --as a temporary holder
           HANOI(N-1, X, Z, Y);

        --output the move instruction
           PUT("Move disk "); PUT(N);
           PUT(" from "); PUT(X); PUT(" to "); PUT(Y);
           NEW_LINE;

        --move the N-1 disks on Z to Y using X
        --as the temporary holder this time
           HANOI(N-1, Z, Y, X);
      end if;
    end HANOI;

  begin

    PUT("How many disks have to be moved?"); NEW_LINE;
    GET(NUMBER_OF_DISKS);
    HANOI(NUMBER_OF_DISKS, 'X', 'Y', 'Z');

  end TOWERS_OF_HANOI;
```

10.4 Insertion Sort

Using insertion sort,[19] write a procedure to sort nonnull arrays of type *vector* in nondecreasing order. Sorting an array A, with L and U being its lower and upper bounds (L $\leqslant$ U), results in $A_L \leqslant A_{L+1} \leqslant \cdots \leqslant A_{U-1} \leqslant A_U$ with the new values of the array A being a permutation of its old values.[20]

Type VECTOR is declared as the unconstrained array type

> **type** VECTOR **is array**(INTEGER **range** <>) **of** FLOAT;

The program is developed as follows:

P_0:   Sort array A

Pictorially, the state of array A at different stages of the insertion sorting process can be depicted as shown below:

Initially,

L   U

```
┌──┬──────────────────────────────────────────────────┐
│  │                                                  │
└──┴──────────────────────────────────────────────────┘
```

  sorted   unsorted
   part   part

finally,

L   U

```
┌──────────────────────────────────────────────────┬──┐
│                                                  │  │
└──────────────────────────────────────────────────┴──┘
```

                          sorted   unsorted
                           part   part

and at some intermediate stage

---

19. The third volume of D. E. Knuth's encyclopedic series titled *The Art of Computer Programming* [KNU73] contains an exhaustive discussion of various sorting algorithms and their performance.

20. Without the permutation requirement, changing the value of the array A such as assigning 0.0 to every element suffices, since the ordering condition $A_L \leqslant A_{L+1}...$ is then satisfied.

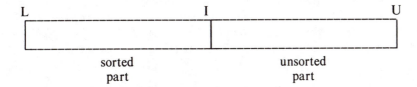

sorted   unsorted
part   part

The insertion sort algorithm can be stated abstractly as

P_1:

```
I := L; --A(L..I) is (trivially) sorted so far
while I /= U loop
    Extend sorted portion to include A(I+1)
    I := I+1;
end loop;
```

$A(L..I)$ is sorted represents the loop invariant.[21] It is true initially, since I is equal to L and the one element slice A(L..L) is trivially sorted. Upon termination of the loop I = U implying that A(L..U), i.e., the whole array, is sorted. It must be shown that the loop body leaves the loop invariant unchanged and for this the reader is referred to [DIJ76] and [CON73].

The abstract instruction *Extend sorted portion to include $A(I+1)$* of the refinement P_1 is refined as

```
T := A(I+1);
Shift all elements of A(L..I) > T one place to the right so that
    A(L..J-1) <= T and A(J+1..I+1) > T
A(J) := T;
```

The second statement of the above refinement *Shift all elements ...* is refined as

```
J := I+1;       --A(J+1..I+1) > T
while A(J-1) > T loop
    Shift A(J-1) to the right
    J := J-1;
end loop;
```

---

21. A loop invariant is a property that can be shown to be true before a loop is entered, true just before and after each time the loop body is executed, and true after the loop has terminated. Properly selected loop invariants can be used to demonstrate the correctness of programs containing loops. They also enhance program readability and understandability.

The condition A(J+1..I+1) > T is vacuously true prior to execution of the loop, since J = I+1 implies that the set of elements represented by A(J+1..I+1) is empty. On termination of the loop A(J+1..I+1) > T and A(J−1) <= T. This, along with the fact that at the start of the loop A(L..I) was sorted, leads to A(L..J−1) <= T.

The boolean expression in the above loop will lead to a *subscript out of range* error when J = L. When J = L we will have shifted all the elements one place to the right and the loop should terminate. So the boolean expression in the above loop is modified to use the short circuit operator **and then**, leading to

J /= L **and then** A(J−1) > T

The statement *Shift A (J−1) to the right* is refined as

A(J) := A(J−1);

Collecting all the refinements together and adding the appropriate procedure heading, and variable and constant declarations, we get the final version of INSERTION_SORT:

procedure INSERTION_SORT(A: **in out** VECTOR) **is**

```
    I, J: A'RANGE;
    T: FLOAT;
    L: constant INTEGER := A'FIRST;
    U: constant INTEGER := A'LAST;

begin
    I := L;
    while I /= U loop
      T := A(I+1);
      J := I+1;
      while J /= L and then A(J−1) > T loop
         A(J) := A(J−1);
         J := J−1;
      end loop;
      A(J) := T;
      I := I+1;
    end loop;
end INSERTION_SORT;
```

10.5 Quicksort

The problem is to sort an array as described in the example on insertion sort, but this time using the quicksort technique [HOA62]. Quicksort is on the verage more efficient than insertion sort [KNU73].[22]

$_0$:   Quicksort(A, L, U)

$_1$:

>   **if** One element **then**
>   >   **null;**
>   **elsif** Two elements **then**
>   >   Order them
>   **elsif** More than two elements **then**
>   >   Partition A such that

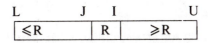

(one element in the middle)

or

(at least one element per partition in this case)[23]

where R is an arbitrary value
from the array A

---

22. The average running time of quicksort is of the order N log N, while that of insertion sort is N^2. In the worst case situations, both algorithms are of order N^2.

23. It is necessary for each partition to have at least one element to ensure that the recursion terminates.

——I represents the scan from left to right
——J represents the scan from right to left

Quicksort(A, L, J);
                ——the left partition which has elements <= R
Quicksort(A, I, U);
                ——the right partition which has elements >= R

——the values of elements, if any, with subscripts greater
——than J but less than I are all equal to R and these
——do not need to be sorted, since they are already in
——the right positions

end if;

Partitioning an array A into a left part that contains elements less than or equal to R (an arbitrary value from the array A) and a right part that contains elements greater than or equal to R is based on the following algorithm. Scan A from the left (to determine the left partition) until an element A(I) that is greater than or equal to R is found. Next scan A from the right (to determine the right partition) until an element A(J) that is less than or equal to R is found. Exchange A(I) and A(J) so that they belong to the correct partitions. The scans are then moved one step forward, i.e., I is increased by 1 and J decreased by 1. If the scans have not crossed, then the scanning is resumed.

Neither scan can go past the other, because the values contained in the partition represented by the first scan stop the second scan. Initially the right scan has no elements, but the left scan will still stop provided the value R is picked from the elements of the array A. Picking R from A and using weak inequalities (i.e. $\leq$ and $\geq$ instead of < and >, respectively) guarantees that *both* scans will halt, at R if not before.

At the end of the scan, if I is equal to J, then after the exchanging of the elements[24] and the updating of I and J, the state of the array A is represented by the first of the two partitions shown above. On the other hand, had I been equal to J−1 then we would arrive at the second partition (with each partition containing one element, since at least one exchange of elements would have been performed).

---

24. No real exchange takes place when I is equal to J, since A(I) and A(J) are aliases for the same array element.

The array partitioning algorithm was described *operationally*, i.e., by giving steps implementing it. An alternative way of describing an algorithm with a loop is to give an invariant for the loop and describe how the components of the invariant are changed by the loop to achieve the desired goal. An appropriate loop invariant for the partitioning algorithm is

$$A(L..I-1) \leqslant R \text{ and } A(J+1..U) \geqslant R$$

The invariant can be represented pictorially as

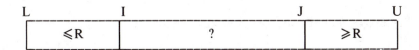

The purpose of the loop will be to increase I and decrease J while keeping the invariant true. This description of partitioning is easier to understand than the operational description which is clouded by details describing the implementation of the algorithm. Moreover, a description using a loop invariant is more flexible than operational description, since the programmer is free to implement the algorithm in any way provided it conforms to the loop invariant.[25]

The algorithm given in refinement P_1 is refined further as follows:

P_2:   The boolean expressions *One element* and *Two elements* are refined as

$$U - L = 0$$

and

$$U - L = 1$$

---

25. For more discussion on the use of invariants in program development and reasoning about loops see *The Science of Programming* by David Gries [GRI81].

The statement *Order them* is refined as

```
if A(U) <= A(L) then
     SWAP(A(L), A(U));
end if;
```

The boolean expression *More than two elements* is refined as

$$U - L > 1$$

The statement *Partition A such that* ... is refined as

```
R := A((U+L)/2);        --R is the middle element
I := L; J := U;
               --A(L..I-1) ≤ R and A(J+1..U) ≥ R
               --this is the loop invariant
while I <= J loop
     Extend left partition by increasing I
     Extend right partition by decreasing J
     Rearrange the elements so that the loop
     invariant is restored
end loop;
```

P_3:   The statement *Extend left partition* ... is refined as

```
while A(I) < R loop
     I := I+1;
end loop;        --A(I) ≥ R
```

The statement *Extend right partition* ... is refined as

```
while A(J) > R loop
     J := J-1;
end loop;        --A(J) ≤ R
```

The statement *Rearrange the elements* ... is refined as

```
if I <= J then
     SWAP(A(I), A(J));
     I := I+1;
     J := J-1;
end if;
```

Procedure SWAP used here was defined earlier. Collecting all the refinements
together, we get the final version of the quicksort program:

```
procedure QUICKSORT(A: in out VECTOR) is

    L: constant A'RANGE := A'FIRST;
    U: constant A'RANGE := A'LAST;
    I, J: A'RANGE;    --I and J can contain only values
                      --that are legal subscripts of A
    R : FLOAT;

begin

    if U−L = 0 then
       null;
    elsif U−L = 1 then
       if A(U) < A(L) then
          SWAP(A(L), A(U));
       end if;
    elsif U−L > 1 then
       R := A((U+L)/2);
       I := L;
       J := U;

       --Partition array with R as the dividing element
       while I <= J loop

          while A(I) < R loop
             I := I+1;
          end loop;

          while A(J) > R loop
             J := J−1;
          end loop;

          if I <= J then
             SWAP(A(I), A(J));
             I := I+1;
             J := J−1;
          end if;

       end loop;

       QUICKSORT(A(L..J));
```

```
                    −−note use of slices. A new copy of the
                    −−elements is not generated for the slice
            QUICKSORT(A(I..U));

        end if;
    end QUICKSORT;
```

The first two cases of the main *if* statement in procedure QUICKSORT can be coalesced into one case:

```
    if U−L <= 1 then
        if A(U) < A(L) then
            SWAP(A(L), A(U));
        end if;
    elsif ...
```

The amount of storage used by quicksort during recursion can be reduced by sorting first the smaller of the two slices, A(L..J) and A(I..U), and then the bigger slice.

10.6 Matrix Multiplication

Write a procedure MAT_MULT that multiplies two matrices A and B and puts the result in a third matrix C. Each matrix is of the unconstrained type

```
    type MATRIX is array
            (INTEGER range <>, INTEGER range <>) of FLOAT;
```

When multiplying two matrices, say A and B, the number of columns of A must be equal to the number of rows of B. The number of rows in the matrix that will be assigned the product should equal the number of rows of A and the number of columns in it should equal the number of columns in B. For programming simplicity, it is assumed that the corresponding index subtypes of the matrices of A and B, and the result matrix match.

The initial refinement for matrix multiplication is

P_0:

```
    Check that the bounds are correct for matrix multiplication
    for I in A'RANGE(1) loop
        for J in B'RANGE(2) loop
```

$$\text{Compute } C(I, J) = \sum_{K \in A'RANGE(2)} A(I, K) \times B(K, J);$$

```
        end loop;
    end loop;
```

P_0 is refined to give the following Ada procedure:

```
procedure MAT_MULT(A, B: in MATRIX; C: out MATRIX) is
begin

    if A'FIRST(1) /= C'FIRST(1)
            or A'LAST(1) /= C'LAST(1)
            or A'FIRST(2) /= B'FIRST(1)
            or A'LAST(2) /= B'LAST(1)
            or B'FIRST(2) /= C'FIRST(2)
            or B'LAST(2) /= C'LAST(2) then
        raise ERROR;        --raising exceptions will be discussed
                            --later in the chapter on exceptions
    end if;

    for I in A'RANGE(1) loop
        for J in B'RANGE(2) loop
            C(I, J) := 0.0;
            for K in A'RANGE(2) loop
                C(I, J) := C(I, J) + A(I, K) * B(K, J);
            end loop;
        end loop;
    end loop;

end MAT_MULT;
```

When there is an error in the bounds of the matrices, the subprogram MAT_MULT raises the exception ERROR and terminates. This error condition must be handled by the caller of MAT_MULT.

Using MAT_MULT, the multiplication operator * can be easily overloaded for matrix multiplication:

```
function "*"(A, B: in MATRIX) return MATRIX is
    C: MATRIX(A'FIRST(1)..A'LAST(1), B'FIRST(2)..B'LAST(2));
begin
    MAT_MULT(A, B, C);
    return C;
end "*";
```

10.7 Horner's Rule

The straightforward evaluation of the polynomial

$$A(x) = a_n x^n + a_{n-1} x^{n-1} + \cdots + a_1 x + a_0$$

requires at least 2n multiplications whereas evaluation by Horner's rule requires only n multiplications [AHO75]. Horner's rule is given by the following evaluation scheme:

$$A(x) = (...((a_n x + a_{n-1})x + a_{n-2})x + \cdots + a_1)x + a_0$$

Evaluation of a polynomial by Horner's scheme is implemented by the function EVAL_POLY, where the type COEFF is declared as

type COEFF **is array**(INTEGER **range** < >) **of** FLOAT;

The formal parameter array A expects the coefficients of the polynomial $a_n, a_{n-1}, ..., a_1$ to be in the elements $A(n), A(n-1), ..., A(0)$. V is the value at which the polynomial is to be evaluated:

```
function EVAL_POLY(A: in COEFF; V: in FLOAT) return FLOAT is
    SUM: FLOAT;
begin
    SUM := A(A'LAST);
    for I in reverse A'FIRST..A'LAST-1 loop    --note use of reverse
        SUM := SUM * V + A(I);
    end loop;
    return SUM;
end EVAL_POLY;
```

Chapter 2: **More About Types** [3]

Ada requires that object types be explicitly specified in the interest of better program readability, error detection and code generation. Ada is also very strict in its treatment of types to enhance program reliability. Every object must be used consistently with respect to its type. Ada provides a wide variety of types and type definition mechanisms that allow a programmer to define types appropriate to the application. For example

- floating point types of any desired accuracy, subject to implementation restrictions, can be declared.

- records can be parameterized.

- the set of values associated with an existing type can be restricted so that erroneous use of values outside the restricted set can be detected automatically.

- a new type, with values and operations similar to an existing type, can be declared. This new type, however, is different from the existing type from which it was derived. Thus, a variable representing the age of a person cannot be inadvertently assigned to a variable representing the person's social security number.

1. Strong Typing

Ada is *strongly typed*. The concept of strong typing was first popularized by the programming language Pascal. Since the design of Pascal the trend has been toward strong typing in programming languages, e.g., Euclid, Modula, Clu, Mesa and now, Ada. Although the phrase *strongly typed programming language* has been used for about a decade, it has been used loosely and it is hard to find a definition for it. In the context of the discussion in this book the following definition will be used:

Definition: A language is *strongly typed* [Gehani and Wetherell in FEU82] if

1. every object in the language belongs to exactly one type,

2. type is a *syntactic property*, i.e., the type of an expression can be determined from the program syntax,[26] and

3. type conversion occurs by converting a *value* from one type to another; conversion *does not* occur by viewing the representation of a value as a different type. In FORTRAN, for example, viewing the representation of a value as a different type is possible by means of the *equivalence* statement.

Specification of the type of an object provides the compiler with information about the intended usage of the object. A strongly typed language requires that objects be used in a fashion that is consistent with their types. For example, the bit pattern representing an integer value cannot be interpreted as a real, a character cannot be interpreted as an integer or an array name cannot be interpreted as a pointer to the beginning of the storage allocated for the array. Consequently, program errors resulting from usage of an object that is inconsistent with its type can be detected at compile time.

Limited experiments have suggested that strongly typed languages lead to increased program clarity and reliability [GAN77]. Violation of strong typing by means of *representation viewing* also hampers program portability, since the representation of an object may be different on different implementations.

Ada is a strongly typed language. However, its typing mechanism can be breached (i.e., bypassed) by means of specific mechanisms provided in the language. Programs that use these mechanisms are designated as *unchecked programs*, since potential errors resulting from the breach can no longer be detected. Breaching of strong typing may be necessary in rare cases (usually in machine dependent system programming) and must be used with great caution.

2. Subtypes [3.3]

Suppose variable CUR_FLOOR is to be used to indicate the current floor number in a program to control the elevator in an eight-floor building. CUR_FLOOR can be declared to be of type INTEGER, but in this case erroneous assignments to CUR_FLOOR outside the range 1 to 8 will not be automatically detected. It would be desirable to restrict the values of CUR_FLOOR to lie between 1 and 8 so that attempts to assign values outside this range to CUR_FLOOR are automatically flagged as errors. The *subtype* mechanism is used to specify such a restriction.

The set of values of a type T can be restricted by associating a constraint with it. The set of operations, except for assignment, is not affected. The new set of values plus the old set of operations is said to constitute a *subtype*; T is its *base*

---

26. This property of a strongly typed language was pointed out by Professor David Gries.

ype. Subtype declarations do not introduce a new type. Every type T is a
ubtype of itself. Subtypes are declared as

> subtype identifier **is** subtype_indication;

vhere *subtype_indication* is a type or subtype name followed by an optional
:onstraint. Constraints can be of four kinds—*range*, *index*, *accuracy*, and
liscriminant. For example, the range constraint *range 1..8* is used in the
leclaration of subtype STORIES

> subtype STORIES **is** INTEGER **range** 1..8;

o restrict the legal values of all objects of the subtype STORIES to be the
ntegers between 1 and 8.

Certain characteristics of types and subtypes, such as specific values and
operations, are available to the user and are called *attributes* of the types and
:he subtypes. The base type of any subtype (or type) T is given by the
attribute T′BASE. This attribute can be used only to form other attributes,
e.g., T′BASE′FIRST, which denotes the smallest element of the base type of T.
(A list of all the predefined attributes is given in Appendix A of the Ada
Reference Manual.)

By declaring a subtype, a user provides additional information that enhances
program readability and allows a compiler to ensure that all values assigned to
variables of the subtype satisfy the constraints associated with it. An
optimizing compiler can use the restrictions on the set of values specified by a
subtype to optimize the amount of storage required for objects of the subtype
(compared to the storage required for objects of the base type of the subtype).

2.1 Examples of Subtypes

> subtype WEEKDAY **is** DAY **range** MON..FRI;
> > ——type DAY is defined above
> > ——note the range constraint

> subtype WEEKEND **is** DAY **range** SAT..SUN;

> subtype BUFFER_SIZE **is** INTEGER **range** 0..MAX;

> subtype GRADES **is** VECTOR(1..50);
> > ——VECTOR is an unconstrained array type; the index
> > ——constraint 1..50 is supplied in the subtype declaration

> **subtype** MALE **is** PERSON(SEX => M);
> −−PERSON is a record type with a discriminant;
> −−the discriminant SEX is constrained to
> −−have the value M (record types with discriminants
> −−will be discussed later in this chapter)

3. Derived Types [3.4]

Suppose two variables P and S represent the price of fuel and the speed of a train. Both P and S can be declared to be of some real type, say FLOAT, but then inadvertent mistakes such as assigning P to S or vice versa cannot be detected automatically. It would be desirable to specify that P and S are of types CURRENCY and SPEED that have the same set of values and the same set of operations as FLOAT, but that are different from each other and from FLOAT. Mistaken use of variables of type CURRENCY for those of type SPEED or FLOAT, and so on, should be detected automatically. Such a facility is provided by the *derived types* in Ada.[27]

A derived type is a new and distinct type derived from an existing type, called the *parent* type. The values and operations of the derived type are copies of the values and operations of its parent type. Derived types are declared as

> **type** NEW_TYPE **is new** OLD_TYPE [constraint];

The constraint specified in the declaration of the derived type NEW_TYPE must be compatible with any constraints imposed by the parent type OLD_TYPE. As with subtypes, constraints can be of four kinds—*range, index, accuracy*, and *discriminant*.

Conversion is possible between a derived type and its parent type. The derived type uses the same notation for the literals and aggregates as the parent type. Such literals and aggregates are termed *overloaded*, since they designate values for more than one type. The type of the literal or the aggregate must be determinable from the context; otherwise it must be supplied explicitly by the programmer.

---

27. This strategy does not provide for a general treatment of values with different *units of measure* or for automatic conversion between values having equivalent units of measure [GEH77, GEH82b, GEH82c].

3.1 Examples of Derived Types

> **type** PRIMARY_COLOR **is new** COLOR;
> >   ——no new constraint is imposed
>
> **type** AGE **is new** INTEGER **range** 0..150;
> >   ——range constraint imposed
>
> **type** CARD **is new** LINE(1..80);
> >   ——index constraint imposed

4. Type Equivalence

Type equivalence has been classified into two broad classes—*name* and *structural* [WEL77]. When are two types equivalent in Ada? Ada uses the concept of name equivalence[28] to decide when two types are equivalent. Two objects have *equivalent types* if and only if they are declared using the same type identifier.

Each instance (or elaboration) of a type definition such as

> **array**(1..10) **of** INTEGER

creates a new type, called an *anonymous* type, which is different from all other types. For example, A and B declared separately in *single object declarations*

> A: **array**(1..10) **of** INTEGER;
> B: **array**(1..10) **of** INTEGER;

are not of the same type, because each declaration creates a new anonymous array type definition. Even if A and B had been declared together in one *multiple object declaration*

> A, B: **array**(1..10) **of** INTEGER;

they would be of different types, since a multiple object declaration is equivalent to a series of single object declarations [3.3.1].

As another example, consider the type identifier ARRAY10 declared as

> **type** ARRAY10 **is array**(1..10) **of** INTEGER;

As a result of the declarations

---

28. Name equivalence is conceptually simpler and much easier to implement than structural equivalence. Under structural type equivalence, two types are equivalent if and only if their components are of the same type regardless of the names of the components. There are several variations of this scheme.

        E, F: ARRAY10;
        G: ARRAY10;

E, F and G all have the same type, since they are all declared with the same
type identifier.

5. Type Conversions [4.6]

An expression E may be converted to another type or subtype by qualifying it
with the type or subtype name T; this is written as

        T(E)

Type conversions are allowed only among

Numeric Types	E can be an expression of any numeric type. Conversion of reals to integers is by rounding to the nearest integer.
Derived Types	T and the type of E must be derivable from each other, directly or indirectly, or there must exist a third type from which they are derived directly or indirectly. This conversion may result in a change of representation [13.6].
Array Types	Both T and E must have the same dimensionality, the same index and component types. In case the index types are different they should be convertible to each other. If the component types are access or record types then they must both either be constrained or unconstrained. If T denotes a constrained type and E has exactly the number of elements required by T then the bounds of the result are those imposed by T. If T denotes an unconstrained type, then the bounds of the result are the same as those of E.

Whenever a type conversion is allowed, the reverse conversion is also allowed.

5.1 Implicit Conversions

Ada does not allow implicit conversions.[29] Some computer scientists believe that implicit conversions should rarely be permitted even if they make sense mathematically, because conversions make programs more difficult to understand [LIS76].

Going from a subtype to its base type or vice versa (provided the value is a legal value for the subtype) is not considered a type conversion, because a subtype declaration does not really introduce a new type. An object of a subtype S effectively has type T, the base type of S, but the values that can be assigned to the object have been restricted as specified in the declaration of S.

6. Qualifying Expressions with their Types

The type of an expression is determined from its operand types and the types of values returned by the operators. A *qualified expression* is used to state explicitly the type of an expression or an aggregate. Qualification of an expression or an aggregate with the type is necessary in situations where the type cannot be determined from the context. As an example, consider two literals A and B, which both belong to two different enumeration types E and F. Then the expression

$$A < B$$

is ambiguous, because it cannot be determined from the context whether A and B belong to E or F. The value of such an expression may be different depending upon the type of A and B. For example, A may precede B in E so that A < B is TRUE (for type E) while A may follow B in F so that A < B is FALSE (for type F). This ambiguity can be resolved by *qualifying* A and B with their types. If both A and B are to be of type E, then the above expression can be unambiguously written as

$$E'(A) < E'(B)$$

or even

$$E'(A) < B$$

A *qualified expression* has the form

$$T'(\text{expression}) \mid T'\text{aggregate}$$

where T is a type or subtype name. The expression or the aggregate must have the same type as the base type of T.

---

29. PL/I and Algol 68 take the opposite approach. In PL/I just about any type can be implicitly converted to any other type.

7. More Types

This section contains more details about scalar types (particularly integers and reals), record types and access types. The use of constraints in defining new integer and real types is illustrated along with facilities for parameterizing record types and defining recursive types.

7.1 Scalar Types

A range constraint specifies that only a subset of the values of a type will be used. A range constraint is said to be *compatible* with an earlier range constraint if the set of values specified by the later range constraint is a subset of the values specified by the earlier constraint. A new range constraint must be compatible with earlier ones. A value is said to *satisfy* a range constraint if it is in the set of values specified by the range constraint.

7.1.1 Boolean: A boolean type is either the predefined type BOOLEAN or a type derived from a boolean type. The predefined comparison and membership operators produce a value of type BOOLEAN.

7.1.2 Integers: Additional integer types can be declared as

> **type** NEW_INTEGER **is range** L..R;

where NEW_INTEGER is the name of the type being declared, and L and R specify the smallest and largest value of type NEW_INTEGER. This type declaration is equivalent to

> **type** *integer_type* **is new** *predefined_integer_type*;
> **subtype** NEW_INTEGER **is** *integer_type*
> > **range** *integer_type*(L) .. *integer_type*(R);

where *predefined_integer_type* is selected by the Ada implementation to be one of the predefined integer types that includes the values in the range L to R. Some examples are

> **type** RANK **is range** 1..10;
> **type** ID **is range** 1..INTEGER'LAST;
> **type** PRIORITY **is new** INTEGER **range** 1..10;

    subtype NATURAL **is** INTEGER **range** 0..INTEGER'LAST;
            --predefined subtype in Ada

    subtype POSITIVE **is** INTEGER **range** 1..INTEGER'LAST;
            --predefined subtype in Ada

    subtype HIGH_PRIORITY **is** PRIORITY **range** H..10;
            --the bounds on the values of types and subtypes
            --can be static or dynamic expressions. H must
            --be ≤ 10 at run time, otherwise a constraint error
            --will occur (the exception CONSTRAINT_ERROR
            --will be raised)

    type FILE_ID **is new** ID;   --derived type

The types ID, FILE_ID and the subtype POSITIVE have the same set of values; however, they are all different.

7.2 Reals

Real types with any desired accuracy (subject to the limitations of the implementation) can be defined by specifying the *accuracy constraint*.

7.2.1 Floating Point Types: The accuracy constraint for floating points, called the *floating point constraint*, is of the form

    digits D [**range** L..R]

where D is a positive static expression of type integer, and L and R are static expressions of some real type. D is the precision of the real type being defined and indicates the minimum number of digits that should be stored for the mantissa. The optional range constraint specifies that the values will range between L and R.

A new floating point type NEW_FLOAT is declared as

    type NEW_FLOAT **is digits** D [**range** L..R];

This declaration is equivalent to

    type *float_type* **is new** *predefined_float_type*;
    subtype NEW_FLOAT **is** *float_type* **digits** D
                    [**range** *float_type*(L) .. *float_type*(R)];

where *predefined_float_type* is chosen appropriately by the Ada implementation so that the specified floating point constraint is satisfied. A value satisfies a floating point constraint if it satisfies any included range constraint.

Some examples of floating point types are

type WT_KG **is digits** 6;
type TEMPERATURE **is digits** 8 **range** 0.00 .. 1000.00;

subtype APPROX_TEMPERATURE **is** TEMPERATURE **digits** 6;

type WT_LB **is new** WT_KG;
                          −−weights in the two different units of measure
                          −−will not be mixed inadvertently now
type MASS **is new** REAL **digits** 7 **range** 0.0 .. 1.0E10;

For a subtype, a derived type or an object declaration, one can specify either the floating point constraint or just the range constraint. In defining a new floating point type or a floating point subtype F, the floating point constraint must be compatible with any earlier floating point constraints on the base or the parent type, i.e., the number of digits must not exceed those specified in the earlier constraint. Also if both F and the base or the parent type have range constraints, then the new range constraint must be compatible with the earlier ones.

7.2.2 Portability of Programs with Floating Point Objects: Different Ada implementations may implement predefined floating point types such as FLOAT with different precisions. Portability of programs with floating point objects can be achieved by using floating point types declared to have the desired precision. For example, a user may declare a new floating point type REAL as

         type REAL **is digits** 10;

and use it instead of FLOAT. When a program with such a type is moved from one Ada implementation to another, it is the responsibility of the Ada implementation to implement REAL with at least the precision specified (10 digits in this example).

This strategy is much better than that provided in other languages, say FORTRAN. FORTRAN does not define the accuracy of its single precision floating point; the accuracy varies on common systems from 24 to 48 bits. Consequently, the user has to select between single precision and double precision according to the implementation [DOD79b]. For example, in moving FORTRAN programs from the 60 bit CDC 6600 to the 32 bit IBM 370, users must change single precision variables to double precision to get approximately the same degree of accuracy. This can be extremely inconvenient.

7.3 Fixed Point Types

As stated in Chapter 1, the accuracy constraint for fixed point types, *fixed_point_constraint*, has the form

       delta DEL **range** L..R;

where DEL is the maximum error permitted in implementing the fixed point type and, L and R are expressions specifying the range of values. When declaring fixed point subtypes or derived types, specification of the range constraint is optional.

A new fixed point type NEW_FIXED is declared as

       type NEW_FIXED **is delta** DEL **range** L..R;

This declaration is equivalent to

       type *fixed_type* **is new** *predefined_fixed_type*;
       subtype NEW_FIXED **is** *fixed_type* **delta** DEL
                   range *fixed_type*(L) .. *fixed_type*(R);

where *predefined_fixed_type* is chosen appropriately by the Ada implementation so that the specified fixed point constraint is satisfied.

Some examples of fixed point subtypes and derived types are

       subtype LOW_PRECISION **is** HIGH_PRECISION **delta** 0.1;
             --HIGH_PRECISION was declared in Chapter 1 as
             --a fixed point type with a delta of 0.00001
       type DOLLARS **is new** CURRENCY;
             --CURRENCY is a floating point type
       type RUPEES **is new** CURRENCY;

A fixed point constraint must be compatible with any previous fixed point constraint. The delta of the later constraint must not be less than the earlier delta. If both have range constraints, then the later constraint must be compatible with the earlier ones.

7.4 Record Types

Objects of a record type need not have the same number and type of components. Record types can be parameterized to implement objects that are basically similar but that differ in some details, such as the size and the number of components.

7.4.1 Record Types with Discriminants [3.7.1]: Discriminants are used to parameterize record type definitions. They allows values of a record type to have alternative forms. Discriminants must be of a discrete type and are specified in the declaration of a record type. A discriminant is a named component of any object of such a record type. Within a record type definition a discriminant may be used only

1. as part of the default expression specifying the initial value of a record component,

2. as the discriminant of a variant part and

3. in a component subtype definition, either as an index bound or a discriminant value.

In the last case, the discriminant must be used by itself and not as the component of a larger expression. A discriminant does not have to be used within the record type definition.

Discriminants may be given default initial values. The default initial values can be overridden by explicitly giving initial values at object declaration time or while defining a subtype. When an object is being declared, an explicit initial value *must* be given for the discriminant if a default initial value has not been specified. The value of a discriminant in an object can be changed only by assigning the entire object a new value and not by assigning a value to just the discriminant.[30]

Examples of record types with discriminants are

```
type RECTANGLE(L, B: INTEGER := 10) is
        --the record type RECTANGLE is parameterized by the
        --discriminants L and B that represent the sides of the
        --rectangle. L and B are given a default initial value of 10,
        --which can be overridden by explicitly supplied initial values
    record
        R: MATRIX(1..L, 1..B);
            --MATRIX was declared in Chapter 1 as a
            --two-dimensional array with FLOAT elements
    end record;

type SQUARE(SIDE: POSITIVE) is
        --SIDE is the discriminant. It does not have a default
        --initial value; SIDE must be given a value when
        --an object of type SQUARE is declared
    record
        SQ: RECTANGLE(SIDE, SIDE);
    end record;
```

---

30. This restriction prevents a discriminant value from being changed without a corresponding change in the component values. In case of *variant records* (discussed in the next section), a change in the value of the discriminant may result in change in the type and number of record components. Without this restriction it would be possible to breach strong typing. The lack of this restriction is a major loophole in Pascal's typing mechanism.

type BUFFER(SIZE: BUFFER_SIZE := 128) **is**
           --BUFFER_SIZE was declared earlier as an integer
           --subtype with values in the range 0..MAX
  record
    POS: BUFFER_SIZE;
    VALUE: STRING(1..SIZE);
  end record;

type ITEM(NUMBER: POSITIVE) **is**
    --discriminant is not used inside the record definition
  record
    CONTENT: INTEGER;
  end record;

Objects of record types with discriminants are declared as

  R1: RECTANGLE;   --has the default size of 10 by 10
  R2: RECTANGLE(5, 50);
      --default initial values overridden. Initial
      --values supplied in positional notation
  R3: RECTANGLE(L => 10, B => 50);
      -- named notation used to supply initial values
  S: SQUARE(SIDE => 10);
      --discriminant must be given an explicit initial value
      --if a default initial value has not been specified
  B1: BUFFER(SIZE => 64, POS => 0, VALUE => (1..64 => ' '));
      --initial values supplied for all the components
      --of the record including the discriminant
  B2: BUFFER(64, 0, (1..64 => ' '));
      --this declaration, uses positional notation. It is
      --equivalent to the one for B1.
      --The discriminant comes before the other components.

Discriminants are like the other components of a record except that they cannot be directly assigned a value. Discriminants L and B, of variable R1, are modified by the assignment

    R1 := (L => 15, B => 20, R => (1..15 => (1..20 => 75.0)));

However, the following set of assignments, apparently equivalent to the above assignment, causes an error, because direct assignment to discriminants is not allowed:

    R1.L := 15;
    R1.B := 20;
    R1.R := (1..15 => (1..20 => 75.0));

7.4.2 Variant Records [3.7.3]: Programs often contain objects that are conceptually very similar to each other, differing only in some minor details. It would be nice to be able to specify them as being of the same type. For example, all values representing information about motorized vehicles may be specified to be of type VEHICLE. Different vehicles such as cars, buses and trucks have common information such as the names of the owner and the manufacturer, the model and the year of make of the vehicle. However, some information is not applicable to all vehicles. For example, tonnage (capacity in weight) is applicable only to trucks while the maximum seating capacity is relevant for buses only. Another example is the representation of geometric figures. Common information might include items such as area and perimeter. However, applicable information about their dimensions is different and depends upon their shape.

Variant records[31] are used to implement record types, such as VEHICLE, that have basically similar values but which differ in some small details. Variant records are a special case of records with discriminants. A record may have a variant part that specifies alternative lists of components. A component list can be empty in which case it must be specified as **null**. Each list is prefixed by a set of *choices*. The component list selected is one that has a choice that is equal to the value of the discriminant. Only components of the selected list can be referenced; referencing components of the other lists in the variant will result in an error.

The general form of a record definition is

    record
        component_declarations [variant_part] | **null**
    end record

The variant part of a record has the form

    case discriminant_name **is**
        when choice {| choice} => component_list
        {**when** choice {| choice} => component_list}
    end case;

where a choice can be a static expression, a static discrete range or the keyword **others**. The particular list of components selected corresponds to a choice that has a value equal to the discriminant value. A choice that is a discrete range is an abbreviation for a list of choices representing all values of the range. The keyword **others** can appear only as the choice for the last

---

31. The concept of variant records was first introduced in Pascal.

alternative. It appears by itself and stands for all possible values the discriminant can assume that have not been covered by the choices prefixing the preceding alternatives.

The following two examples illustrate the use of variant records. The first record type, GEOMETRIC_FIGURE, uses type SHAPE, which is declared as

```
type SHAPE is (RECT, CIRCLE, POINT);
```

GEOMETRIC_FIGURE has three or four components depending upon the value of the discriminant S:

```
type GEOMETRIC_FIGURE(S: SHAPE) is
   record
      PERIMETER: FLOAT;     ——perimeter of a point is 0.0
      case S is
         when RECT => L, B: INTEGER range 0..INTEGER'LAST;
         when CIRCLE => RADIUS: FLOAT := 1.0;
         when POINT => P: POSITION;
      end case;
   end record;
```

The first component, the discriminant S, is used to indicate the type of the geometric figure, that is, whether it is a rectangle, a circle or a point. The second component is PERIMETER. If S is RECT then an object of type GEOMETRIC_FIGURE will have two more components L and B. Otherwise it has only one more component, RADIUS or P.

Examples of declarations of variables of type GEOMETRIC_FIGURE are

```
C: GEOMETRIC_FIGURE(CIRCLE);
            ——C has components S, PERIMETER and RADIUS
R: GEOMETRIC_FIGURE(RECT);
            ——R has components S, PERIMETER, L and B
```

The radius of circle C has the default initial value 1.0, whereas the dimensions of rectangle R have no default initial values.

The second example [DOD83] shows how record type PERIPHERAL is used to represent different types of peripheral devices. Two enumeration types DEVICE and STATE used in this example are declared as

```
type DEVICE is (PRINTER, DISK, DRUM);
type STATE is (OPEN, CLOSED);
```

Each peripheral device has a component STATUS indicating the availability of the device.

```
type PERIPHERAL(UNIT: DEVICE := DISK) is
                --UNIT has the default initial value DISK
   record
      STATUS: STATE;
      case UNIT is
        when PRINTER =>
           LINE_COUNT: INTEGER range 1..PAGE_SIZE;
        when others =>
           CYLINDER: CYLINDER_INDEX;
           TRACK: TRACK_NUMBER;
      end case;
   end record;
```

In this example the drum is treated as logically similar to a disk, except that it has one cylinder while a disk has many. Examples of subtypes of PERIPHERAL are

```
subtype DRUM_UNIT is PERIPHERAL(DRUM);
subtype DISK_UNIT is PERIPHERAL(DISK);
```

Examples of peripherals, which are constrained record objects of type PERIPHERAL, are

```
BACKUP_DISK: PERIPHERAL;
WRITER: PERIPHERAL(UNIT => PRINTER);
             --default initial value of UNIT overridden
ARCHIVE: DISK_UNIT;
```

The discriminant should be treated like any other component; it precedes all other components of a record, as illustrated by the aggregate assignment

```
ARCHIVE := (DISK, CLOSED, 9, 1);
```

7.5 Access Types—Recursive and Mutually Dependent

Direct recursion in record type definitions is not allowed. Indirect recursion is allowed and is accomplished by means of access types. *Incomplete type declarations* must be used to define *recursive* and *mutually dependent* access types.

Consider the declaration of record type EMPLOYEE which contains three components representing the name, the identification number and the manager of an employee—NAME, ID and MANAGER. Since the manager is also an employee, component MANAGER must also be declared to be of type EMPLOYEE, thus making the definition of EMPLOYEE recursive. Since direct recursion is not allowed in Ada, an intermediate access type, say MGR, is used.

Type EMPLOYEE is declared by first giving an incomplete declaration for it:

    type EMPLOYEE;   ——incomplete type declaration

Type MGR is then declared as

    type MGR **is access** EMPLOYEE;

Finally, type EMPLOYEE is declared completely.

```
type EMPLOYEE is
  record
      NAME: STRING(1..30);
      ID: INTEGER;
      MANAGER: MGR;
  end record;
```

The incomplete type declaration is required, because in Ada every object and type must be declared (an incomplete declaration suffices) before use. Of course, the complete declaration must be supplied later.

Type EMPLOYEE could not have been declared as

```
type EMPLOYEE is
  record
      NAME: STRING(1..30);
      ID: INTEGER;
      MANAGER: access EMPLOYEE;   ——**ILLEGAL**
  end record;
```

since Ada does not allow an access type definition to be used in an object declaration, as illustrated by the above declaration of component MANAGER in the record type EMPLOYEE.

8. Examples

The examples in this section focus on the additional capabilities of records and access types. In the first example, the area of a geometric figure represented by a variant record is computed. This example illustrates the suitability of using *case* statements for dealing with variant records. The second and third examples concern printing and searching a binary tree, each node of which is represented by a recursive record type. Recursive programming blends very well with accessing recursive types.

8.1 Using Variant Records

Function AREA computes the area of an object of type GEOMETRIC_FIGURE (declared earlier in the section on variant records):

```
function AREA(F: GEOMETRIC_FIGURE) return FLOAT is
    PI: constant := 3.1416;
begin
    case F.S is
        --The choice is based on the discriminant of F
        when RECT => return FLOAT(F.L * F.B);
                            --note explicit conversion to real
        when CIRCLE => return PI * F.RADIUS * F.RADIUS;
        when POINT => return 0.0;
    end case;
end AREA;
```

8.2 Printing a tree

The problem is to print the values at the nodes of a binary tree with root R. Each node is of the form

VALUE	
LEFT	RIGHT

where the component VALUE is the value (of type INTEGER), and the components LEFT and RIGHT designate the left and right subtrees. The presence of a **null** value in components LEFT or RIGHT indicates an empty subtree. The node type is given by the following declarations, which are part of package TREE:

```
type NODE;    --incomplete type declaration

type BRANCH is access NODE;

type NODE is
                --type declaration being completed
    record
        VALUE: INTEGER;
        LEFT, RIGHT: BRANCH;
    end record;
```

Note how recursive types are defined in Ada. As mentioned earlier, instead of specifying the recursion directly, an access type must be used. First an incomplete type declaration is given. Using this incomplete type declaration, an access type is declared. Finally, the incomplete type declaration is completed.

The name of an incomplete type can be used only in the declaration of an access type.[32] Consequently, the following alternative formulation is illegal:

```
type BRANCH;     --incomplete type declaration

type NODE is
  record
    VALUE: INTEGER;
    LEFT, RIGHT: BRANCH;
           --illegal use of the incomplete type BRANCH
  end record;

type BRANCH is access NODE;
```

The procedure to print the binary tree, PRINT, is based on the abstract algorithm

```
if the tree is not empty then
    print the left sub-tree
    print the root of the tree
    print the right sub-tree
end if;
```

that prints the nodes in *inorder*. Any printing order may be used, since no specific order was specified in the problem statement. Procedure PRINT is

---

32. Otherwise, it becomes harder to compile definitions that use the incomplete type.

```
with TEXT_IO, TREE;
      --include these packages in the compilation unit
use TEXT_IO, TREE;
      --make their components directly visible
procedure PRINT(R: in BRANCH) is

    package IO_INT is new INTEGER_IO(INTEGER);
    use IO_INT;

begin
    if R /= null then
            PRINT(R.LEFT);

            PUT(R.VALUE);
                    --integer PUT from IO_INT
            NEW_LINE;

            PRINT(R.RIGHT);
    end if;
end PRINT;
```

8.3 Binary Tree Search

The problem is to write two equivalent functions, one recursive and the other iterative, that search an *ordered binary tree* with a root R (of type BRANCH that was defined earlier) for a value X. The two functions return TRUE if X is in the tree and FALSE otherwise.

Ordered binary trees are binary trees that are ordered according to some rule. One definition of an ordered binary tree is that it is a binary tree in which the left child of a node always has a value that is less than that of its parent and the right child always has a value greater than that of its parent.

```
      --recursive version of binary tree search
    function BIN_SRCH_REC(R: in BRANCH; X: in INTEGER)
                                return BOOLEAN is
    begin
        if R = null then return FALSE;
        elsif X = R.VALUE then return TRUE;
        elsif X < R.VALUE then return BIN_SRCH_REC(R.LEFT, X);
        else return BIN_SRCH_REC(R.RIGHT, X);
        end if;
    end BIN_SRCH_REC;
```

```
--iterative version of binary tree search
function BIN_SRCH_ITER(R: in BRANCH; X: in INTEGER)
                                    return BOOLEAN is
   T: BRANCH;  --temporary variable for tree traversal
begin
   T := R;
   loop
      if T = null then return FALSE;
      elsif X = T.VALUE then return TRUE;
      elsif X < T.VALUE then T := T.LEFT;
      else T := T.RIGHT;
      end if;
   end loop;
end BIN_SRCH_ITER;
```

In this example, both the recursive and iterative versions are simple and easy to understand. However, some problems are best expressed recursively, e.g., the Towers of Hanoi problem and the quicksort algorithm given Chapter 1. Many programmers avoid recursion and treat it as a novelty [GRI75]. Languages such as FORTRAN and COBOL do not allow recursion, and this limitation has inhibited many programmers from thinking recursively. Also the examples of recursion, commonly given in the introductory texts, such as factorial and Fibonacci numbers, are often best expressed iteratively and are therefore not convincing examples of the appropriateness of recursion.

Chapter 3: **Packages** [7]

1. Introduction

Packages, subprograms, tasks and generic units constitute the four forms of program units from which Ada programs are composed. Packages, like subprograms, can be compiled separately, thus allowing partitioning of large programs into smaller and more manageable parts. Partitioning programs into smaller pieces helps in building, understanding and maintaining large systems [HOR79]. Packages are generally defined in two parts—the package specification and the package body. The specification specifies the facilities provided by the package. The body implements the facilities. Package specifications and package bodies can be compiled separately. However, the compilation of a package specification must precede the compilation of the corresponding package body.

Packages are an information hiding and data encapsulation mechanism. They can be used to group logically related entities such as constants, variables, types and subprograms. The user of a package can see only the package specification and not the implementation details supplied in the package body. Moreover, only the entities specified in the *visible* part of a package specification can be referred to by the package user.

As the implementation details of a package are hidden from the package user, the user cannot exploit this knowledge in a program; thus a program cannot be made dependent on the package implementation. Consequently, once the package specification has been agreed upon, the package implementor is free to implement the package in any way consistent with the package specification. The implementation of a package can be changed in any way provided it remains consistent with the package specifications.

2. Package Specifications [7.2]

The specification of a package has the form

```
package identifier is
    basic declarative items
[ private
    basic declarative items]
end identifier;
```

97

A *basic declarative item* is either a *basic declaration*, a *use* clause or a *representation* clause. A *basic declaration* is any declaration except the body of a subprogram, package or a task, or a *body stub* (body stubs are discussed in Chapter 7 on Program Structure and Separate Compilation).

The body of a subprogram, package (if there is one), task or a generic unit declared in a package specification must be given in the package body. Alternatively, a body stub or an INTERFACE pragma may be given.

Two sets of declarations can appear in a package specification. The first set constitutes the *visible* part of the package. Objects declared here can be accessed using the selected component notation (i.e., by prefixing the object with the name of the package and a period) or directly by means of the *use* clause.

The second set of declarations follows the keyword **private**; it is not visible outside the package. These declarations contain structural or implementation details of private types that were declared in the visible part of the package. These details, which do not concern the user of the package, are provided in the package specification only to help the compiler in implementing the visible part of the package (e.g., the representation of a private type declared in the visible part of the package must be given in the private part so that the compiler can determine how much storage is to be allocated for objects of this type).

Nothing declared in the body of the package is visible outside the body. This restriction on visibility along with the restriction provided by the private part of a package specification supports the information hiding provided by packages.

Some examples of package specifications are now given. The first example is the package PLOTTING_DATA, which consists only of a group of common variables and has no corresponding package body [DOD83].

```
package PLOTTING_DATA is
    PEN_UP: BOOLEAN;
    CONVERSION_FACTOR,
    X_OFFSET, Y_OFFSET,
    X_MIN, X_MAX,
    Y_MIN, Y_MAX: FLOAT;
    X_VALUE: array(1..500) of FLOAT;
    Y_VALUE: array(1..500) of FLOAT;
end PLOTTING_DATA;
```

These declarations can be used by more than one subprogram.[33]

The second example is a package ORDERED_SET that implements a set whose elements are ordered by the time value associated with them. The elements are of a discrete type ID and the time values of the predefined type DURATION. The elements represent job identification numbers and the time value represents job execution time in seconds. Type ID is declared as

> **type ID is range** 1..100;

and this declaration is directly visible in the context in which ORDERED_SET is being declared. The specification of ORDERED_SET is

```
package ORDERED_SET is
    procedure INSERT(JOB: in ID; T: in DURATION);
            --add JOB to the set; JOB is a job that requires
            --T seconds of execution time
    procedure SMALLEST(JOB: out ID);
            --Store in JOB, a job from the ordered set with the
            --smallest execution time; this job is deleted from the
            --set; SMALLEST should be called after ensuring
            --that the set is not empty.

            --SMALLEST is not implemented as a function, since it
            --has the side effect of deleting an element.
            --Functions should not have any side effects.
            --A function should always return the same value if it
            --is called with the same actual parameters.
            --This convention corresponds to the mathematical
            --notion of a function

    function EMPTY return BOOLEAN;
end ORDERED_SET;
```

Declarations given in a package specification are visible outside the package at points in a program only if the package name is visible at these points. Identifiers in the visible part of the package specification can be referred to using selected component notation—the name of the item prefixed with the name of the package and a period. For example,

> ORDERED_SET.EMPTY

---

33. The use of these data declarations by parallel processes, called *tasks*, will cause the *concurrent update* problem [BR173] unless great care is taken.

The items can be made directly visible by means of the *use* clause. If the *use* clause

    use ORDERED_SET;

has appeared, then the function EMPTY can be referred to directly as

    EMPTY

provided no parameterless BOOLEAN function with the same name already exists, in which case EMPTY will refer to the existing function. Also, if two identical identifiers are made visible with the aid of *use* clauses then an ambiguity may result. To avoid the ambiguity, these identifiers must be qualified.

3. Package Bodies [7.3]

A package body has the form

    package body identifier **is**
       declarations
    [**begin**
       sequence_of_statements
    [**exception**
       exception handlers]]
    end identifier;

The body of a package constitutes the implementation of a package. It contains local declarations and the bodies of the subprograms, packages and tasks whose specifications were given in the package specification. All items declared in a package specification are visible in the corresponding package body. However, the implementations of these items, given in the package body, are not visible outside. Items declared locally in a package body are likewise not visible outside the package body.

A package body can also contain a sequence of statements that are executed when the package body is processed. These statements can be used to initialize the objects declared in the specification and body of the package. Exceptions raised by the execution of the statements are handled by the exception handlers given in the package body. If no handler is provided for an exception then, when this exception occurs, it is *propagated* to the part of the program containing the package body (this will be discussed in Chapter 5 on Exceptions).

As an example, the body of package ORDERED_SET, which implements the ordered set specified earlier, is declared. It uses a BOOLEAN array IN_SET to indicate the jobs that are present in the set along with an array RANK that contains their execution times. IN_SET(I) is TRUE if job I is present in the set and FALSE otherwise. RANK(I) contains the execution time associated with job I (when it is present in the set). The set is empty when all elements of IN_SET are FALSE.

When the set is not empty, then the job SMALL with the smallest execution time is determined and deleted from the set by means of the following algorithm:

> T := maximum possible execution time
> **for** all jobs I in the set **loop**
> > Let SMALL be the job I if its execution time RANK(I) is $\leqslant$ T;
> > in this case let T be equal to RANK(I).
> **end loop**
> Delete SMALL from the set

The elements present in the set cannot be directly generated as specified in the above loop heading. All elements that can possibly be in the set must be generated and those not actually present in the set screened out by means of an explicit test in the loop body. Consequently, the algorithm to find the smallest job is refined as

> **for** all jobs I that can be in the set **loop**
> > Let SMALL be the job I if it is in the set and if its execution time
> > RANK(I) is $\leqslant$ T; in this case let T be equal to RANK(I).
> **end loop**

The package ORDERED_SET is implemented as

```ada
--ID is available in this environment
package body ORDERED_SET is

    IN_SET: array(ID) of BOOLEAN := (ID => FALSE);
                    --initially the set is empty
    RANK: array(ID) of DURATION;

    procedure INSERT(JOB: in ID; T: in DURATION) is
            --if an element is present in the set, then inserting it
            --has no effect as is the case with mathematical sets
    begin
       IN_SET(JOB) := TRUE;
       RANK(JOB) := T;
    end INSERT;

    procedure SMALLEST(JOB: out ID) is
                    --SMALLEST should be called only if the
                    --set is not empty
       T: DURATION := DURATION'LAST;
       SMALL: ID;
    begin
       for I in ID loop     --searching for the smallest rank job
          if IN_SET(I) and then RANK(I) <= T then
             SMALL := I;
             T := RANK(I);
          end if;
       end loop;
       IN_SET(SMALL) := FALSE;     --delete the job from the set
       JOB := SMALL;
    end SMALLEST;

    function EMPTY return BOOLEAN is
    begin
       for I in ID loop
          if IN_SET(I) then
             return FALSE;
          end if;
       end loop;
       return TRUE;
    end EMPTY;

end ORDERED_SET;
```

As an exercise for the reader, the package body should be reimplemented using ordered lists to store the elements of the set.[34]

4. Private Types [7.4]

The implementation details of types declared in a package specification may be hidden from the user of the package by designating the types to be *private*. A type is designated as private by associating with it either the attribute **private** or the attribute **limited private**. A *limited private* type is also called a *limited* type. A private type is declared using a *private type declaration* given in the visible part of a package specification. For example,

> **type** SET **is private**;
> **type** ORD_SET **is limited private**;
> **type** QUEUE **is limited private**;

The full type declaration is given later in the private part of a package specification instead of the package body. The full type declaration is given in the package specification itself to ensure that the specification contains sufficient information to allow the compilation of a unit using the package.

Objects of private types can be declared, passed as parameters, compared for equality and inequality and assigned values of other objects of the same type. Limited private type objects, however, can be declared and passed only as parameters.

The private type declaration and the corresponding full type declarations offer two different views of a private type—one each for the outside and the inside worlds. Outside the package in which a private type is declared, objects of this private type can be manipulated and operated upon only in a restricted manner;

---

34. When the maximum cardinality of a set is much larger than its cardinality at any given time, it is more storage efficient to use a list representation for the set than a BOOLEAN array representation. The storage used in a list representation is proportional to the number of elements in the set and is allocated or deallocated when an element is added to or deleted from the set. In the BOOLEAN array representation, storage for all possible elements must be allocated regardless of whether or not the elements are present in the set.

Operations on the set such as addition, deletion and membership tests are faster when a BOOLEAN array representation is used and their speed is independent of the set cardinality. In a list representation the addition operation is fast and its speed is independent of the set cardinality, but the speeds of the deletion operation and the membership test are proportional to the set cardinality. The membership test can be speeded up by using an ordered list, but this slows the addition operation, making its speed proportional to the set cardinality. Speedup of the membership test is advantageous when the frequency of the membership tests is much greater than the frequency of adding elements to the set. More discussion on set representations can be found in *The Design and Analysis of Computer Algorithms* [AHO75].

inside this package, on the other hand, private type objects are like objects of any ordinary (i.e., non-private) types.

Constants of a private type can be declared in the visible part of a package, but their values must be given only in the private part using a complete redeclaration. Private types implemented as records can have discriminants.

The implementation of a private type is visible inside the corresponding package body, so that the implementor of a private type can define operations on objects of the private type. This implementation is hidden from the users of a private type; this forces them to manipulate private type objects using only the operations automatically provided with the private type and those provided by the implementor of the private type.

The use of private types is illustrated in the examples discussed below.

4.1 More on Ordered Sets

The implementation of an ordered set by the package ORDERED_SET, given earlier, is inflexible, because only one instance of a set is made available to the user. This can be remedied by defining, in the package specification, a type ORD_SET which is a record consisting of two components—the BOOLEAN array IN_SET and the array RANK of type DURATION (these were defined in the body of ORDERED_SET). These arrays will be used as before to represent the set. The operations will now be redefined to include a parameter of type ORD_SET. Users will declare ordered sets by declaring objects of type ORD_SET. A user can now have as many ordered sets as desired by declaring an appropriate number of objects of type ORD_SET. Operations on a specific ordered set are performed by passing that ordered set as a parameter to the operation in question.

The specification of ORDERED_SET2 (ORDERED_SET modified as discussed) is

```
package ORDERED_SET2 is

    type SET_ARRAY is array(ID) of BOOLEAN;
    type RANK_ARRAY is array(ID) of DURATION;
    type ORD_SET is
      record
        IN_SET: SET_ARRAY := (ID => FALSE);
        RANK: RANK_ARRAY;
      end record;

    procedure INSERT(S: in out ORD_SET;
                             JOB: in ID; T: in DURATION);
    procedure SMALLEST(S: in out ORD_SET; JOB: out ID);
    function EMPTY(S: in ORD_SET) return BOOLEAN;

  end ORDERED_SET2;
```

Assuming that the proper *use* clause has been given, ordered sets are declared as

```
A, B, C: ORD_SET;    --three ordered sets
```

Although this modification has solved the problem of being able to provide more than one ordered set, another problem arises now. The user of the package can directly manipulate the implementation of the ordered sets. This manipulation is possible, because the implementation of type ORD_SET, i.e., a record consisting of two arrays IN_SET and RANK, is visible outside the package specification. Moreover, the types SET_ARRAY and RANK_ARRAY are unnecessarily visible to the user. Information hiding, as provided by the package ORDERED_SET, no longer exists.

In situations like this, private types are useful in hiding the implementation details. The implementation of ORD_SET can be hidden from the user by declaring it as a limited private type. The user cannot even make copies of ORD_SET objects or compare them, since ORD_SET is declared to be a *limited* private type. The specification of the modified ORDERED_SET2, modified to declare ORD_SET as a limited private type, is

```
package ORDERED_SET2 is

    type ORD_SET is limited private;

    procedure INSERT(S: in out ORD_SET;
                              JOB: in ID; T: in DURATION);
    procedure SMALLEST(S: in out ORD_SET; JOB: out ID);
    function EMPTY(S: in ORD_SET) return BOOLEAN;

private
    type SET_ARRAY is array(ID) of BOOLEAN;
    type RANK_ARRAY is array(ID) of DURATION;
    type ORD_SET is
        record
            IN_SET: SET_ARRAY := (ID => FALSE);
            RANK: RANK_ARRAY;
        end record;

end ORDERED_SET2;
```

The body of ORDERED_SET2 will look like

```
package body ORDERED_SET2 is

    procedure INSERT(S: in out ORD_SET;
                              JOB: in ID; T: in DURATION) is
                --the ordered set being manipulated is
                --supplied as a parameter
    begin
        S.IN_SET(JOB) := TRUE;
        S.RANK(JOB) := T;
    end INSERT;

    --body of procedure SMALLEST
            --similar to that given in ORDERED_SET except
            --that the ordered set being manipulated is
            --supplied as a parameter
    --body of function EMPTY
            --same comment as for SMALLEST
end ORDERED_SET2;
```

Note that it was possible to provide a default initial value for objects of type
ORD_SET only, because ORD_SET is a record type. It is not possible to
associate default values with types that are not records. One could, of course,
embed every type in a record type to get this initialization facility.

4.2 A Key Manager

Another example that illustrates the use of private types is a key manager [DOD83]. A different key is supplied every time a key is requested by the package user. All that a user can do with the keys is to assign them, compare them for equality and determine which key is smaller. The user cannot forge objects of type KEY:

```
package KEY_MANAGER is

    type KEY is private;
    NULL_KEY: constant KEY;
            --deferred constant because it is of a private type;
            --value has to be supplied in the private part

    procedure GET_KEY(K: out KEY);
            --GET_KEY is not defined as a function, because every
            --time it is called it returns a different value.

    function "<"(X, Y: in KEY) return BOOLEAN;

private
    type KEY is new NATURAL;
    NULL_KEY: constant KEY := 0;
            --a complete redeclaration of the deferred constant
            --is given to assign it a value

end KEY_MANAGER;
```

The only operations that can be performed on objects of type KEY outside the package KEY_MANAGER are assignment, comparison for equality and inequality, and the less than operation, <, defined in the package. The body of KEY_MANAGER is

```
package body KEY_MANAGER is

    LAST_KEY: KEY := 0;
            --LAST_KEY is global to the subprograms in the
            --package; this is how one gets the effect of
            --own or static variables in Ada

    procedure GET_KEY(K: out KEY) is
    begin
        LAST_KEY := LAST_KEY + 1;
        K := LAST_KEY;
    end GET_KEY;

    function "<"(X, Y: in KEY) return BOOLEAN is
    begin
        return INTEGER(X) < INTEGER(Y);
                --if the key values X and Y are not converted back
                --to the parent type INTEGER of KEY, then X < Y
                --would recursively invoke < defined for KEY.
                --KEY can be converted to INTEGER, because it is a
                --type derived from INTEGER
    end "<";

end KEY_MANAGER;
```

5. Abstract Data Types

Packages can be used to implement *abstract data types*. Abstract data types
are user-defined types for which the user supplies not only the set of values but
also the operations on the values. Abstract data types provide data abstraction
in much the same way that subprograms provide control abstraction. Details of
how an abstract data type is implemented are hidden from the user. Hiding
the details prevents the user from

1. making programs dependent on the representation. The representation of
    an abstract data type can be changed without affecting the rest of the
    program. For example, the abstract data type *set* may be implemented
    as a boolean array initially, but this representation may be changed to an
    ordered list later on for reasons of storage efficiency.

2. accidentally or maliciously violating the integrity of an abstract data type
    object. Integrity of abstract data type objects is preserved by forcing the
    user to manipulate these objects using only the operations provided by the
    designer of the abstract data type.

Abstract data types objects are declared and manipulated in exactly the same way as the predefined data types in the language. A package is not a true abstract data type facility, since it only partially supports the definition of abstract data types [SCH80]. For example, it is not possible to declare an array of packages.

A package is basically an information hiding mechanism. One cannot directly define an abstract data type T and declare objects of type T. In Ada one defines an information hiding package, say FENCE_FOR_T, and inside it specifies a private type definition T and the operations for T:

 package FENCE_FOR_T **is**

  type T **is private;** -- or limited private

  --operations for objects of type T

 private

  type T **is** ... ;

 end FENCE_FOR_T;

 package body FENCE_FOR_T **is**

 end FENCE_FOR_T;

Objects are then declared as being of type T from the package FENCE_FOR_T.

  X, Y, Z: FENCE_FOR_T.T;

The operations are semantically associated with the package FENCE_FOR_T instead of directly with the type T. They must be qualified by the package name. Of course, the need for the qualification may be eliminated by the *use* clause

  use FENCE_FOR_T;

However, the operations are still associated with package FENCE_FOR_T and not type T.

Type ORD_SET, declared in the previous section, is an example of an abstract data type declaration using the facilities provided by Ada. Its *fence* is represented by the package ORDERED_SET2.

6. Examples of Packages and Programming with Packages

Several examples are now given to illustrate further the use of packages. The first example, a symbol table manager, is an essential part of every compiler. The symbol table is implemented first using an array and then using an ordered binary tree. The specifications of the symbol table package do not change with the implementation. The second example is a package that implements a set of priority queues that may be used to schedule jobs with different priorities in an operating system. The last two examples, the *no equal subsequence* problem and the *eight queens* problem, illustrate the *trial and error* method of finding a solution to a problem. The trouble with this approach is that the number of possible candidates for a solution can be very large. Consequently, all candidates should not be generated and checked to see if they represent a solution [WIR71]. The set of possible candidates must be reduced considerably without eliminating a candidate that may represent a desired solution.

The reader is urged to try solving the problems before looking at the solutions given.

6.1 A Symbol Table Manager

The problem is to write a symbol table manager. Operations to perform the following actions are to be provided:

1. Insert an item and the information associated with it into the symbol table.

2. Retrieve the information associated with an item in the symbol table.

3. Determine whether or not the symbol table is full.

4. Check to see if an item is in the symbol table.

5. Reinitialize (reset) the symbol table.

Only unique items will be inserted into the symbol table. An insertion may not be made if the symbol table is full.

The items are strings of length 20 (padded with blanks if necessary) and the symbol table should be able to hold at least 200 items. The only information that is to be associated with an item is whether the item is a variable identifier, a function or procedure name, a keyword, or a label name. The example is a simplified version of a real symbol table, because block structure is not handled and the information associated with the items is straightforward.

The specification of the SYMBOL_TABLE_MANAGER package is

```
package SYMBOL_TABLE_MANAGER is

    N: constant := 200;   --size of the symbol table
    ITEM_SIZE: constant := 20;
        --it is good programming style to give constants
        --symbolic names. This enhances program readability
        --and makes it easy to change values of the constants.

    type ITEM is new STRING(1..ITEM_SIZE);
    type ITEM_TYPE is (VAR, FUN, PROC, KEYWD, LABEL);

    procedure ADD(X: in ITEM; I: in ITEM_TYPE);
    function IN_TABLE(X: in ITEM) return BOOLEAN;
    function GET(X: in ITEM) return ITEM_TYPE;
    function FULL return BOOLEAN;
    procedure CLEAR;   --empty table

end SYMBOL_TABLE_MANAGER;
```

The symbol table will be implemented as an array. Searches for the items will be done by searching the array sequentially.

```
package body SYMBOL_TABLE_MANAGER is

    type ITEM_INFO is
        record
            ID: ITEM;
            T: ITEM_TYPE;
        end record;

    ST: array(1..N) of ITEM_INFO;
                    --the symbol table representation
    LAST: INTEGER range 0..N := 0;
                    --symbol table entries are in ST(1..LAST)

    procedure ADD(X: in ITEM; I: in ITEM_TYPE) is
    begin
        LAST := LAST + 1;
                    --assuming that an item is inserted only
                    --when the symbol table is not full
                    --and the item is not in the table
        ST(LAST).ID := X;
        ST(LAST).T := I;
    end ADD;
```

```
function IN_TABLE(X: in ITEM) return BOOLEAN is
begin
    for J in 1..LAST loop      --search the table; the loop
                               --is not executed if LAST is 0
        if ST(J).ID = X then
            return TRUE;
        end if;
    end loop;
    return FALSE;
end IN_TABLE;

function GET(X: in ITEM) return ITEM_TYPE is
                --GET should be called only after ensuring
                --that item X is in the symbol table
begin
    for J in 1..LAST loop
        if ST(J).ID = X then
            return ST(J).T;
        end if;
    end loop;
end GET;

function FULL return BOOLEAN is
begin
    return LAST = N;
end FULL;

procedure CLEAR is
begin
    LAST := 0;
end CLEAR;

end SYMBOL_TABLE_MANAGER;
```

This simple representation of the symbol table will not be efficient if the number of searches to be performed is large. A hashed table or an ordered binary tree representation will be better, because the average search time will be much less.

6.1.1 An Alternative Representation of the Symbol Table: The SYMBOL_TABLE_MANAGER will now be reimplemented using an ordered binary tree representation for the symbol table. As long as no changes are made to the specifications of the SYMBOL_TABLE_MANAGER or the semantics of the subprograms defined in it, the program units using the package SYMBOL_TABLE_MANAGER *will not have to be modified.* The binary tree representation of the symbol table also illustrates the use of access types and how dynamic objects are allocated and created via the allocator *new*.

The procedure INSERT for adding an element X and the information associated with it to a binary tree with root R is declared as

```
procedure INSERT(X: in ITEM; I : in ITEM_TYPE;
                             R: in out NEXT_ELEMENT);
```

which is described abstractly as

```
if R = null then
    add the element X with the associated information I at R
elsif X < R.ID then
    INSERT(X, I, R.LEFT);
else
    INSERT(X, I, R.RIGHT);
end if;
```

The other procedures are straightforward. For variety, iteration is used instead of recursion in functions IN_TABLE and GET:

```
package body SYMBOL_TABLE_MANAGER is

    type ITEM_INFO;        ——an incomplete type declaration.
    type NEXT_ELEMENT is access ITEM_INFO;
    type ITEM_INFO is    ——the complete type declaration
        record
            ID: ITEM;
            T: ITEM_TYPE;
            LEFT, RIGHT: NEXT_ELEMENT;
        end record;

    ROOT: NEXT_ELEMENT;
                ——points to the root of the binary tree implementation
                ——of the symbol table; it is used as a global variable.
                ——R is initially null, which is the default
                ——initial value
    NUM_ELEMENTS: INTEGER range 0..N := 0;
```

```
procedure ADD(X: in ITEM; I: in ITEM_TYPE) is
        --ADD uses INSERT to implement the recursive
        --algorithm described above. Duplicate items must
        --not be inserted. Items should be inserted only
        --after ensuring that the table is not full

    procedure INSERT(X: in ITEM; I : in ITEM_TYPE;
                            R: in out NEXT_ELEMENT) is
    begin
        if R = null then
            R := new ITEM_INFO(X, I, null, null);
                    --dynamic object explicitly initialized
                    --at allocation time
        elsif X < R.ID then
            INSERT(X, I, R.LEFT);
        else
            INSERT(X, I, R.RIGHT);
        end if;
    end INSERT;

begin
    INSERT(X, I, ROOT);
    NUM_ELEMENTS := NUM_ELEMENTS + 1;
end ADD;

function IN_TABLE(X: in ITEM) return BOOLEAN is
    R: NEXT_ELEMENT := ROOT;
                --temporary variable used for tree traversal
begin
    while R /= null loop
        if X = R.ID then
            return TRUE;
        elsif X < R.ID then
            R := R.LEFT;
        else
            R := R.RIGHT;
        end if;
    end loop;
    return FALSE;
end IN_TABLE;
```

```
function GET(X: in ITEM) return ITEM_TYPE is
   R: NEXT_ELEMENT := ROOT;
                  --temporary variable used for tree traversal
begin
   while R /= null loop
      if X = R.ID then
         return R.T;
      elsif X < R.ID then
         R := R.LEFT;
      else
         R := R.RIGHT;
      end if;
   end loop;
end GET;

function FULL return BOOLEAN is
begin
   return NUM_ELEMENTS = N;
end FULL;

procedure CLEAR is
begin
   ROOT := null;
   NUM_ELEMENTS := 0;
end CLEAR;

end SYMBOL_TABLE_MANAGER;
```

The number of items that can be inserted into the symbol table has been restricted to 200 in the ordered binary tree implementation to conform to the specifications of the symbol table package. This restriction is not really necessary in the binary tree implementation, because storage for the items is allocated dynamically, as needed. Items can be inserted into the symbol table as long as storage is available.

The storage area for the binary tree is lost whenever operation CLEAR is executed. This storage will be reclaimed by a garbage collector if the Ada implementation provides one. If reclamation of the storage is important and the implementation does not provide a garbage collector then the user can use an instantiation of the generic procedure UNCHECKED_DEALLOCATION provided by Ada[35] to deallocate unused storage explicitly. As mentioned before, the user must be very careful when deallocating storage explicitly, since the effect of referring to an access value that points to a deallocated object is unpredictable.

6.2 Set of Priority Queues

This example illustrates the use of data refinement, i.e., the use of a simpler package to construct a more complicated one.

Consider an operating system in which jobs are to be scheduled according to their priority (10 being the highest priority and 1 the lowest). The next job that is to be executed is the one with the highest priority. If there is more than one job with the highest priority, then the one that has waited the longest is executed. Each queue associated with a priority should be able to hold 50 jobs. Jobs will be added to a queue only after checking to make sure that the queue is not full. A request for the next job to be executed will be made only after ensuring that there is at least one queue that is not empty.

The set of priority queues will be implemented as the package PRIORITY_QUEUES whose specifications are given below. Type JOB_ID is assumed to be available in the environment where the package PRIORITY_QUEUES is being declared:

> **package** PRIORITY_QUEUES **is**
>
> **type** PRIORITY **is new** INTEGER **range** 1..10;
>
> **procedure** ADD(P: **in** PRIORITY; J: **in** JOB_ID);
> **procedure** NEXT(J: **out** JOB_ID);
> **function** FULL(P: **in** PRIORITY) **return** BOOLEAN;
> **function** ANY_JOB **return** BOOLEAN;
>   −−returns TRUE if there is at least one job and
>   −−FALSE otherwise
>
> **end** PRIORITY_QUEUES;

Package PRIORITY_QUEUES will be implemented using a package FIFO (first-in first-out) which defines the type QUEUE. The different priority queues can then be implemented as an array of QUEUEs. The operations on objects of type QUEUE are supplied by package FIFO. The specification of

---

35. A list of free elements can be kept in the package body. Freed elements will be added to this list. Storage from this list will be used as and when needed. The storage allocator *new* will be called only when the list is empty. This list will be initially empty.

FIFO is

```
package FIFO is

    MAX_SIZE: constant := 50;
    type QUEUE is limited private;

    procedure ADD(Q: in out QUEUE; J: in JOB_ID);
    procedure FIRST(Q: in out QUEUE; J: out JOB_ID);
                    --return and delete the first job in the queue
    function FULL(Q: in QUEUE) return BOOLEAN;
    function EMPTY(Q: in QUEUE) return BOOLEAN;

private
    type JOBS is array(1..MAX_SIZE) of JOB_ID;
    type QUEUE is
        record
            X: JOBS;
            FIRST, LAST: INTEGER range 1..MAX_SIZE := 1;
            CUR_SIZE: INTEGER range 0..MAX_SIZE := 0;
        end record;
end FIFO;
```

The CUR_SIZE values in the queue will be, in the order inserted, in

X(FIRST), X(FIRST mod MAX_SIZE + 1), ...

The body of package FIFO is

```
package body FIFO is
    procedure ADD(Q: in out QUEUE; J: in JOB_ID) is
    begin
        if FULL(Q) then
            PUT("ERROR: Queue Full"); NEW_LINE; return;
                --a better alternative would be to raise an exception
                --indicating to the caller of ADD that the queue is
                --full and that corrective action should be taken;
                --robust programs, check error conditions even if their
                --specifications do not explicitly require the checking
        end if;
        Q.X(Q.LAST) := J;
        Q.LAST := Q.LAST mod MAX_SIZE + 1;
                    --mod has a higher precedence than +
        Q.CUR_SIZE := Q.CUR_SIZE + 1;
    end ADD;
```

```
procedure FIRST(Q: in out QUEUE; J: out JOB_ID) is
begin
   if EMPTY(Q) then
      PUT("ERROR: Queue Empty");
                  --see the comment given in subprogram ADD
      NEW_LINE;
      return;
   end if;

   J := Q.X(Q.FIRST);
   Q.FIRST := Q.FIRST mod MAX_SIZE + 1;
   Q.CUR_SIZE := Q.CUR_SIZE - 1;
end FIRST;

function FULL(Q: in QUEUE) return BOOLEAN is
begin
   return Q.CUR_SIZE = MAX_SIZE;
end FULL;

function EMPTY(Q: in QUEUE) return BOOLEAN is
begin
   return Q.CUR_SIZE = 0;
end EMPTY;
end FIFO;
```

Use of variable CUR_SIZE is not necessary, since its value can be easily computed from variables FIRST and LAST. However, CUR_SIZE enhances program understandability.

Using the specifications of the package FIFO (i.e., the items declared in it), the package body of PRIORITY_QUEUES is now declared:

```
package body PRIORITY_QUEUES is

    P_Q: array(PRIORITY) of FIFO.QUEUE;
                    --the 10 priority queues; one for each priority

    procedure ADD(P: in PRIORITY; J: in JOB_ID) is
    begin
        FIFO.ADD(P_Q(P), J);
    end ADD;

    procedure NEXT(J: out JOB_ID) is
    begin
        for I in reverse PRIORITY loop
                        --search higher priority queues first
            if not FIFO.EMPTY(P_Q(I)) then
                FIFO.FIRST(P_Q(I), J);
                return;
            end if;
        end loop;
        PUT("ERROR: No Jobs");
        NEW_LINE;
    end NEXT;

    function FULL(P: in PRIORITY) return BOOLEAN is
    begin
        return FIFO.FULL(P_Q(P));
    end FULL;

    function ANY_JOB return BOOLEAN is
            --returns TRUE if there is a job of any priority
            --and FALSE otherwise
    begin
        for I in PRIORITY loop
            if not FIFO.EMPTY(P_Q(I)) then
                return TRUE;
            end if;
        end loop;
        return FALSE;
    end ANY_JOB;

end PRIORITY_QUEUES;
```

The subprogram using these packages may look something like

```
with TEXT_IO; use TEXT_IO;
procedure OPERATING_SYSTEM is
    --declaration of type JOB_ID
    --specification and body of package FIFO
    --specification and body of package PRIORITY_QUEUES
    .
    .
    .
    .

begin
    .
    .
    .

    end OPERATING_SYSTEM;
```

6.3 No Equal Subsequence Problem [WIR73, DEN75]

Construct a sequence of length N consisting of the character elements 1, 2 and 3 such that it contains no adjacent equal subsequences. Examples of such sequences are the null sequence, 1, 12, 121 and so on. Some sequences that are invalid or not acceptable are 11, 1211, 1212 and 122.

The solution used generates a series of sequences such that

1. every valid sequence (containing no adjacent equal subsequences) is generated.

2. it is easy (efficient) to check if a sequence is valid or not.

We will start with the null sequence and extend it until we get a valid sequence of length N. The intermediate sequences will be extended only after ensuring that they are valid since all subsequences of a valid sequence are valid. If an intermediate sequence is not valid then it will be transformed until another valid sequence is found. By using this strategy the generation (and therefore validation) of many invalid sequences is ruled out, thus speeding up the finding of a valid sequence of length N.

Two operations will be used to extend and transform the intermediate sequences:

1. EXTEND(S): Extend the sequence S by appending a 1 to it.

2. NEXT(S): Change S to the next sequence in lexicographic order. (If the last element of S is a 1 or 2, increment it to 2 or 3, respectively; if the last element is a 3, delete it and apply NEXT to the truncated sequence.)

The algorithm GENERATE that generates the desired sequence is abstractly defined as

Start with a null sequence
while Length of sequence is not N or it is not a valid sequence **loop**
    if The sequence is valid **then**
        EXTEND the sequence
    else
        Find the NEXT sequence. If there is none then set the
        sequence to null and quit
end loop

The obvious strategy of checking all subsequences for determining the validity of a sequence is very inefficient. An examination of the algorithm GENERATE shows that a new sequence is obtained in one of two ways:

1. by extending a valid sequence S with the character 1, that is, by operation EXTEND(S), or

2. by taking a sequence S, which without its last element is a valid sequence, and changing its last element, that is, by operation NEXT(S).

Consequently, to determine the validity of a new sequence, it suffices to check only those adjacent subsequences that include the new (i.e., the last) element for equality. Using this fact makes validity checking efficient.

The largest subsequence containing the last element that must be considered in the above validity test will have half the length of the sequence. This observation is based on the fact that, for larger subsequences, there does not exist an adjacent subsequence of equal length.

Function VALID that checks the validity of a string is abstractly defined by the algorithm

Let S be the sequence to be tested for validity
Let I be 0 (length of subsequence of S containing its last element)
while I < half the length of S **loop**
    Increase I by 1
    if the subsequence of length I that contains the last element
        of S is equal to its adjacent subsequence **then**
            return FALSE
    end if
end loop
return TRUE

The following package, VALID_SEQUENCE_PACKAGE, will be used in procedure GENERATE:

```
package VALID_SEQUENCE_PACKAGE is

   MAX_SIZE: constant := 100;
   type SEQUENCE is private;

   function LENGTH(S: in SEQUENCE) return INTEGER;
   function VALID(S: in SEQUENCE) return BOOLEAN;
   function NULL_SEQ return SEQUENCE;
   function IS_NULL(S: in SEQUENCE) return BOOLEAN;
   procedure EXTEND(S: in out SEQUENCE);
   procedure NEXT(S: in out SEQUENCE);
   procedure PRINT(S: in SEQUENCE);
               --PRINT uses the package TEXT_IO; the body of
               --this package must be compiled with TEXT_IO

private
   type SEQUENCE is
      record
         SEQ: STRING(1..MAX_SIZE);
         L: INTEGER range 0..MAX_SIZE;
      end record;

end VALID_SEQUENCE_PACKAGE;
```

Procedure GENERATE is defined as

```
use VALID_SEQUENCE_PACKAGE;
procedure GENERATE(N: in POSITIVE; S: out SEQUENCE) is
begin
   S := NULL_SEQ;
   while LENGTH(S) /= N or not VALID(S) loop
      if VALID(S) then
         EXTEND(S);
      else
         NEXT(S);
         if IS_NULL(S) then
            return;   --no valid sequence of the desired length
         end if;
      end if;
   end loop;
end GENERATE;
```

GENERATE returns a null sequence if a valid sequence of the desired length
does not exist. The body of the package is now defined:

```
package body VALID_SEQUENCE_PACKAGE is

   function LENGTH(S: in SEQUENCE) return INTEGER is
   begin
      return S.L;
   end LENGTH;

   function VALID(S: in SEQUENCE) return BOOLEAN is
      I: INTEGER := 0;
                        --I represents the length of the adjacent
                        --subsequences being compared. The right
                        --subsequence includes the last element of S;
                        --it is the element by which S was extended
   begin
      while I < S.L/2 loop
                        --max subsequence length for comparison
                        --is half the sequence length
         I := I + 1;
         if S.SEQ(S.L−2*I+1 .. S.L−I)
                           = S.SEQ(S.L−I+1 .. S.L) then
                        --equality and inequality are defined for strings
            return FALSE;
         end if;
      end loop;
      return TRUE;
   end VALID;

   function NULL_SEQ return SEQUENCE is
      S: SEQUENCE;
   begin
      S.SEQ := (1..MAX_SIZE => ' ');   --string of blanks
      S.L := 0;
      return S;
   end NULL_SEQ;

   function IS_NULL(S: in SEQUENCE) return BOOLEAN is
   begin
      return S.L = 0;
   end IS_NULL;

   procedure EXTEND(S: in out SEQUENCE) is
   begin
      S.L := S.L + 1;
      S.SEQ(S.L) := '1';
```

```
    end EXTEND;

    procedure NEXT(S: in out SEQUENCE) is
    begin
       while S.SEQ(S.L) = '3' loop
          S.L := S.L - 1;   --delete the character 3
          if S.L = 0 then
             return;   --a sequence of length N cannot be found
          end if;
       end loop;
       S.SEQ(S.L) := CHARACTER'SUCC(S.SEQ(S.L));
                                   --successor of 1 or 2
    end NEXT;

    procedure PRINT(S: in SEQUENCE) is
    begin
       TEXT_IO.PUT(S.SEQ);
       TEXT_IO.NEW_LINE;
    end PRINT;

  end VALID_SEQUENCE_PACKAGE;
```

package VALID_SEQUENCE_PACKAGE implements sequences as strings of 100 characters. This implementation is wasteful, since storage for strings of length 100 must be allocated even if the valid sequence desired is much shorter. It is also restrictive, since the package cannot be used to generate a valid string of length greater than 100.

These problems are eliminated by making the sequence size a discriminant, that is a parameter, of the private type SEQUENCE and letting the user supply the length when declaring sequences. Specification of package VALID_SEQUENCE_PACKAGE is modified to allow for sequences of any length:

package VALID_SEQUENCE_PACKAGE **is**

   type SEQUENCE(SIZE: POSITIVE) **is private**;
           --example of a private type with a discriminant

   --specifications of the operations as before

private
   type SEQUENCE(SIZE: POSITIVE) **is**
     record
       SEQ: STRING(1..SIZE);
       L: INTEGER **range** 0..SIZE;
     end record;

   end VALID_SEQUENCE_PACKAGE;

The body of the VALID_SEQUENCE_PACKAGE remains the same. Sequences of the desired length can now be declared as

   S1: SEQUENCE(10);
   S2: SEQUENCE(50);

6.4 The Eight Queens Problem

The problem is to place eight queens on a chess board so that they do not attack each other, i.e., every row, column and diagonal of the chess board has at most one queen (in this case, exactly one queen will be on each row and each column, since there are exactly eight rows and eight columns on a chess board).

A placement of the eight queens on the board is called a *configuration*. A configuration is partial if all the eight queens have not been placed. A configuration is *safe* if none of the queens attack each other.

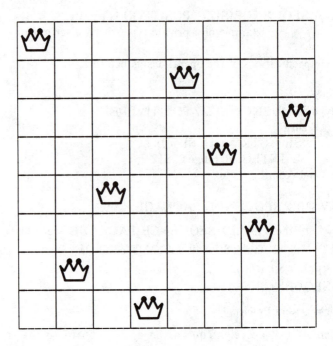

The Eight Queens
(safely placed)

This problem has been studied extensively in the computer science literature [WIR71, Dijkstra in DAH72, WIR76]. It is interesting, because of the trial and error nature of its solution and the choice of the data structure used to represent the chess board.

There are about 2^{32} ways ($\frac{64!}{56! \times 8!}$ combinations) in which the eight queens can be placed. Consequently, only a very poor strategy will attempt to generate all possible configurations in attempting to find a safe configuration. One good strategy is to start with an empty chess board and follow the rule that another queen will be placed only if the queens already on the board constitute a safe partial configuration. This strategy eliminates the consideration of a very large number of unsafe configurations [WIR71].

The solution is given by a recursive backtracking algorithm [WIR71, WIR76]. The procedure call

PLACE_QUEENS(I, SUCCESSFUL);

vill place the queens numbered I to 8 on the chess board if it is possible to do
t safely. It first places queen number I safely on some row in column I and
hen calls itself recursively to place the queens numbered I+1 to 8. If the
ecursive call fails then it tries another row and repeats the recursive call. If
ll rows have been tried without success then it returns with failure.

'rocedure PLACE_QUEENS(I, SUCCESSFUL) returns with success (i.e.,
vith the value TRUE for the variable SUCCESSFUL) when queens numbered
to 8 have been successfully placed. It is defined abstractly as

```
J := 0; --J+1 will be the next row in column I
         --on which queen I will be placed
SUCCESSFUL := FALSE;   --no success as yet
while not SUCCESSFUL and More rows to try loop
    J := J+1;   --try next row J in column I
    if Square with column I and row J is safe then
        Put queen I on column I and row J
        if All eight queens have not been placed then
            --try to place the remaining queens
                PLACE_QUEENS(I+1, SUCCESSFUL);
            if Not successful then
                Remove queen I from column I and row J
            end if;
        else SUCCESSFUL := TRUE;
        end if;
    end if;
end loop;
```

A package CHESS_BOARD with operations to

1. put a queen on the chess board,

2. remove a queen from the chess board,

3. determine if a square is safe or not and

4. print a configuration

s specified now:

package CHESS_BOARD **is**

    procedure PUT_QUEEN(ROW, COL: **in** INTEGER);
    procedure REMOVE_QUEEN(ROW, COL: **in** INTEGER);
    function SAFE(ROW, COL: **in** INTEGER) **return** BOOLEAN;
    procedure PRINT_POSITIONS;

    end CHESS_BOARD;

The chess board can be implemented directly as an 8 by 8 matrix of BOOLEAN elements. However, checking to see if a square is safe is not very efficient in this representation, because all the squares from which this square may be under attack may have to be examined. This operation will be executed very frequently and therefore it is important that the operation be implemented efficiently.

In the algorithm for placing the queens, only one queen is placed in each column—queen I is placed in column I. Consequently, a square for placing queen I in column I is safe if there is no queen on the row or the diagonals passing through it. With this in view, Wirth [WIR71] points out that a much better implementation of the chess board would be to use the following arrays:

ROW_POS(I)	is the row position of queen I (queen I is placed in column I) $1 \leqslant I \leqslant 8$
R(J)	is TRUE if there is no queen on row J, $1 \leqslant J \leqslant 8$ and FALSE otherwise
LD(K)	is TRUE if there is no queen on K^{th} diagonal pointing *left* and *down* (/), $2 \leqslant K \leqslant 16$; this kind of diagonal at the square ROW, COL is represented by the element COL+ROW of the array LD (the expression COL+ROW has the same value on all the squares of such diagonals).
RD(K)	is TRUE if there is no queen on K^{th} diagonal pointing *right* and *down* (\ ), $-7 \leqslant K \leqslant 7$; this kind of diagonal at the square ROW, COL is given by the element COL−ROW of the array RD (the expression COL−ROW has the same value on all the squares of such diagonals).

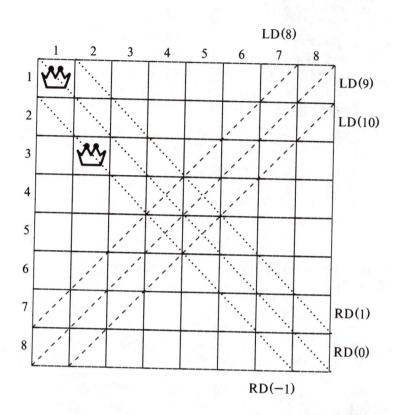

State of Board with 2 Queens

ROW_POS(1) = 1, ROW_POS(2) = 3
R(1) = FALSE, R(3) = FALSE, other elements of R are TRUE
LD(2) = FALSE, LD(5) = FALSE, other elements of LD are TRUE
RD(0) = FALSE, RD(−1) = FALSE, other elements of RD are TRUE

A square with row ROW and column COL can be determined to be safe simply by evaluating the BOOLEAN expression

R(ROW) **and** LD(COL+ROW) **and** RD(COL−ROW)

Assuming that there is no queen in the column COL, the square on row ROW is safe if this expression is TRUE, i.e., there is no queen attacking this square from the diagonals and the row going through it.

The body of the package CHESS_BOARD is

```
package body CHESS_BOARD is
    ROW_POS: array(1..8) of INTEGER;
    R: array(1..8) of BOOLEAN := (1..8 => TRUE);
    LD: array(2..16) of BOOLEAN := (2..16 => TRUE);
    RD: array(-7..7) of BOOLEAN := (-7..7 => TRUE);

    procedure PUT_QUEEN(ROW, COL: in INTEGER) is
    begin
        ROW_POS(COL) := ROW;
        R(ROW) := FALSE;
        LD(COL+ROW) := FALSE;
        RD(COL-ROW) := FALSE;
    end PUT_QUEEN;

    procedure REMOVE_QUEEN(ROW, COL: in INTEGER) is
    begin
        R(ROW) := TRUE;
        LD(COL+ROW) := TRUE;
        RD(COL-ROW) := TRUE;
        --ROW_POS(COL) could also be set to a value indicating
        --that there is no queen in the column COL, but this is not
        --necessary, since this element will be reset when another
        --queen is placed in column COL
    end REMOVE_QUEEN;

    function SAFE(ROW, COL: in INTEGER) return BOOLEAN is
    begin
        return R(ROW) and LD(COL+ROW) and RD(COL-ROW);
    end SAFE;

    procedure PRINT_POSITIONS is
    begin
        for I in 1..8 loop
            PUT("Queen number "); PUT(I);
            PUT(" is in column "); PUT(I);
            PUT(" and row "); PUT(ROW_POS(I));
            NEW_LINE;
        end loop;
    end PRINT_POSITIONS;
end CHESS_BOARD;
```

The procedure EIGHT_QUEENS that prints a safe configuration is

```
with TEXT_IO; use TEXT_IO;
procedure EIGHT_QUEENS is
    package IO_INTEGER is new INTEGER_IO(INTEGER);
    use IO_INTEGER;
    --insert specification and body of CHESS_BOARD here
    use CHESS_BOARD;

    procedure PLACE_QUEENS(I: in INTEGER;
                           SUCCESSFUL: out BOOLEAN) is
        J: INTEGER := 0;
                --J is the row number and I is the column number
    begin
        SUCCESSFUL := FALSE;
        while not SUCCESSFUL and J /= 8 loop
            J := J+1;
            if SAFE(J, I) then
                PUT_QUEEN(J, I);
                if I < 8 then
                    PLACE_QUEENS(I+1, SUCCESSFUL);
                    if not SUCCESSFUL then
                        REMOVE_QUEEN(J, I);
                    end if;
                else
                    SUCCESSFUL := TRUE;
                end if;
            end if;
        end loop;
    end PLACE_QUEENS;

    SUCCESSFUL: BOOLEAN;
begin     --body of main procedure EIGHT_QUEENS
    PLACE_QUEENS(1, SUCCESSFUL);    --place all 8 queens
    if SUCCESSFUL then
        PRINT_POSITIONS;
                --we do not really need to test for the
                --success of procedure PLACE_QUEENS as
                --safe configurations are known to exist.
    end if;
end EIGHT_QUEENS;
```

A variation of the eight queens problem, as an exercise for the reader, would be to print out all possible safe board positions the queens could be placed in. *Hint*: When all the queens have been placed safely, the board position is printed out and SUCCESSFUL set to FALSE to force PLACE_QUEENS to look for additional safe board positions. Another variation would be to generalize the problem to N queens and an N by N chess board.

Chapter 4: **Concurrency** [9]

1. Introduction

Ada provides high level facilities for expressing concurrent algorithms. An Ada implementation may provide true concurrency if the underlying computer is a multicomputer or a multiprocessor, or it may simulate concurrency by multiprogramming (i.e., interleaved execution). The ability to express concurrency in a programming language is desirable for two reasons. First, many algorithms are described naturally using concurrency. Second, programs with concurrency explicitly specified may be implemented more efficiently on multicomputers and multiprocessors than can sequential programs.

The model of concurrency in Ada is based on Hoare's Communicating Sequential Processes [HOA78] in which parallel processes synchronize and communicate by means of input and output statements. This model was strongly influenced by Brinch Hansen's Distributed Processes [BRI78]. The designers of Ada rejected control of concurrency by mechanisms such as semaphores, events and signals because of the low level nature of these mechanisms. Monitors were rejected, because they are not always easy to understand, and because their associated signals are low level in nature [DOD79b].

2. Tasks and Rendezvous [9.5]

Parallel processes in Ada are called *tasks*. Tasks, along with subprograms, packages and generic units, constitute the four kinds of program units from which programs are composed. Tasks may have *entries* in them, which may be called by other tasks. Synchronization between two tasks occurs when the task *issuing* an entry call and the task *accepting* an entry call establishes a *rendezvous*. The two tasks communicate with each other during the rendezvous. Entries are also the primary means of communication between tasks.[36] Communication in both directions takes place via actual parameters in the entry call and the corresponding formal parameters in the *accept* statement accepting the entry call.

---

36. Tasks can also communicate via global variables.

133

The rendezvous concept is explained pictorially in Figure 4.1.

Rendezvous

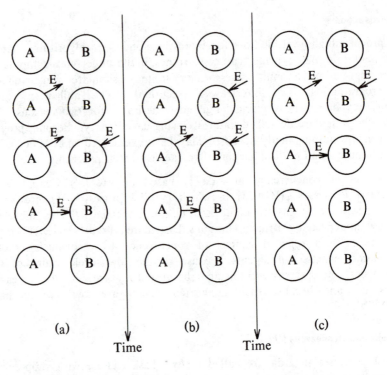

(a)   (b)   (c)

Time   Time

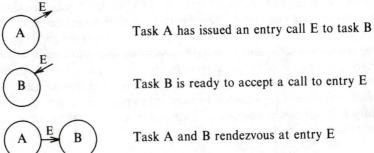

Task A has issued an entry call E to task B

Task B is ready to accept a call to entry E

Task A and B rendezvous at entry E

Figure 4.1

Three situations are illustrated. In the first case (a), task A issues the entry call E before task B is ready to accept it. Task A waits (its execution is suspended) until task B is ready to rendezvous. Having established the rendezvous, the two tasks interact (i.e., communicate). They both resume execution in parallel after completing the rendezvous.

In the second case (b), task B is ready to accept the entry call before A is ready to issue one. This time task B waits for task A to get ready for the rendezvous.

Finally (c), it is also possible for task A to issue the entry call at exactly the same moment that B gets ready to accept it.

The naming scheme used for the rendezvous is asymmetric; the caller (entry call issuer) is required to specify the name of the called task (entry call acceptor), while the called task does not specify the name of the caller. This asymmetry is present to allow the development of libraries containing *server* tasks.

Several tasks can rendezvous with each other, in groups of two or more, at any given instant. Generally, a task will complete a rendezvous with another task before engaging in a rendezvous with a third task.

However, there are situations where two tasks rendezvousing with each other need to interact with a third task before completing their rendezvous. Suppose task A calls task B for some information; task B can supply this information but only after interacting with task C. It is possible to write such interactions between tasks. The task accepting an entry call can, in the middle of a rendezvous, interact with other tasks. For example, suppose task A calls task B; task B can call task C in the middle of the rendezvous:

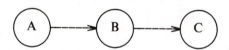

Task B in rendezvous with tasks A and C

In this situation task B must complete its rendezvous with task C before ending its rendezvous with task A. Alternatively, task B can accept an entry call from task T_1 in the middle of its rendezvous with task A. While communicating with T_1 it can accept another entry call from task T_2, and so on in a similar fashion with the additional tasks $T_3, ..., T_{n-1}, T_n$.

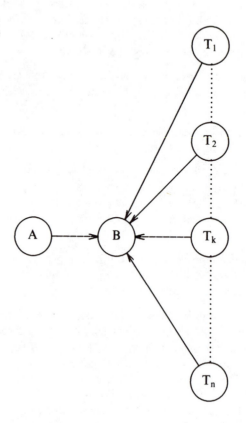

Task B in rendezvous with tasks
$A, T_1, T_2,..., T_n.$

Task B must complete its rendezvous with the tasks in the reverse of the order
in which they were established, i.e., $T_n, ..., T_1, A$.

3. Task Specification and Body [9.1]

Tasks, subprograms, packages and generic units are the four program units in
Ada from which programs are composed. Like a subprogram or a package, a
task consists of two parts—a specification and a body.

A task specification has either the form

      task identifier;

or the form

      task identifier **is**
          entry declarations
          representation clauses
      end identifier;

The first form is a task without entries, so it cannot be called by other tasks for a rendezvous. (The *representation clauses* in a task specification will be illustrated in the examples. Additional discussion can be found in Chapter 8 on Representation Clauses and Implementation Dependent Features.)

A task body has the form

      task body identifier **is**
          declarations
      begin
          sequence_of_statements
      [**exception**
          exception handlers]
      end identifier;

(*Exception handlers* will be discussed in Chapter 5 on Exceptions.)

As an example, consider a task PRODUCER that reads text from the standard input file and sends it to another task, CONSUMER (Figure. 4.2). CONSUMER converts all lower case characters to upper case and writes them on the standard output file.

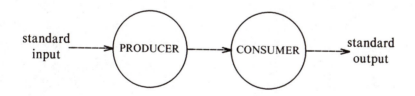

Figure 4.2

The specifications of the two tasks are

```
task PRODUCER;

task CONSUMER is
    entry RECEIVE(C: in CHARACTER);
            --C is a formal parameter, just as in a subprogram
end CONSUMER;
```

PRODUCER reads characters, one at a time, from the standard input and sends them to CONSUMER:

```
task body PRODUCER is
    C: CHARACTER;
begin
    while not END_OF_FILE(STANDARD_INPUT) loop
        GET(C);
        CONSUMER.RECEIVE(C);
    end loop;
end PRODUCER;
```

Entry calls are similar to procedure calls but, they must include the name of the task that contains the entries, e.g., CONSUMER.RECEIVE(C). (For the moment, entry calls may be thought of as being procedure calls that take effect when the two tasks rendezvous.) PRODUCER will terminate upon exhausting the data on the standard input.

CONSUMER accepts characters from PRODUCER and prints them on the standard output file:

```
task body CONSUMER is
   X: CHARACTER;
begin
   loop
      accept RECEIVE(C: in CHARACTER) do
            --the names of the calling tasks are not specified
         X := C;
            --X is needed to record the value of C for use
            --outside the accept statement, since C is local
            --to the accept statement
      end RECEIVE;
      PUT(UPPER(X));
            --output the upper case form. The PUT statement
            --has been placed outside the accept statement
            --so that the caller is not delayed while the
            --PUT statement is being executed.
   end loop;
end CONSUMER;
```

The two tasks rendezvous when PRODUCER has issued the entry call RECEIVE and CONSUMER is ready to accept it. They synchronize at the entry RECEIVE. PRODUCER is suspended until CONSUMER records the character sent to it (i.e., until CONSUMER reaches the end of the *accept* statement associated with entry RECEIVE).

As mentioned before, PRODUCER will terminate upon reaching the end of its body. However, CONSUMER will not terminate, because it never reaches the end of its body. It has an endless loop and will keep waiting at the *accept* statement, indicating its willingness to accept another call and rendezvous.

Only subprograms and packages are compilation units; only they can be compiled by themselves. Consequently, tasks must occur textually within a subprogram or a package. PRODUCER and CONSUMER, along with function UPPER, are put into procedure CONVERT_TO_UPPER_CASE to form a main program:

```
with TEXT_IO; use TEXT_IO;
    --package TEXT_IO contains the input and output
    --procedures GET and PUT and functions
    --END_OF_FILE and STANDARD_INPUT

procedure CONVERT_TO_UPPER_CASE is

  task PRODUCER;

  task CONSUMER is
    entry RECEIVE(C: in CHARACTER);
  end CONSUMER;


  --the characters a-z and A-Z appear sequentially in the Ada
  --character set (ASCII). The relative positions of the
  --corresponding upper and lower case letters are the same.
  --Translation from lower case to upper case is based on this
  --observation.
  function UPPER(C: in CHARACTER) return CHARACTER is
  begin
    if C >= 'a' and C <= 'z' then
      return CHARACTER'VAL(CHARACTER'POS(C)
             - CHARACTER'POS('a') + CHARACTER'POS('A'));

        --CHARACTER'POS(C) is the position of
        --character C in enumeration type CHARACTER.
        --CHARACTER'VAL(I) returns the character in
        --position I.

        --The test C in 'a'..'z' could
        --have alternatively been used in the if statement
    else
      return C;
    end if;
  end UPPER;

  task body PRODUCER is
    C: CHARACTER;
  begin
    while not END_OF_FILE(STANDARD_INPUT) loop
      GET(C);
      CONSUMER.RECEIVE(C);
    end loop;
  end PRODUCER;
```

```
task body CONSUMER is
    X: CHARACTER;
begin
    loop
        accept RECEIVE(C: in CHARACTER) do
            X := C;
        end RECEIVE;
        PUT(UPPER(X));
    end loop;
end CONSUMER;


begin      --PRODUCER and CONSUMER become active
    null;
        --according to the syntax, a subprogram body must
        --have at least one statement even if it is the
        --null statement
end CONVERT_TO_UPPER_CASE;
```

The two tasks become active immediately before the executable part of the procedure CONVERT_TO_UPPER_CASE is entered (which is just the **null** statement).[37]

3.1 Queuing of Entry Calls [9.5]

Several tasks can issue calls to the same entry of another task. These entry calls are put in a queue associated with the entry and accepted in first-in first-out (FIFO) order. In Figure 4.3, tasks A and B are both interested in rendezvousing with task C at entry E. Tasks A and B issue entry calls before task C has indicated its readiness to accept an entry call. Task C rendezvous first with task B, because it issued the entry call before task A:

---

37. The loop in the body of PRODUCER could have been written simply as
```
loop
    GET(C);
    CONSUMER.RECEIVE;
end loop;
```
On reaching the end of the file, an execution of GET will raise an exception, which will cause termination of the task since no exception handler has been provided (see Chapter 5 on Exceptions).

Queuing of Entry Calls

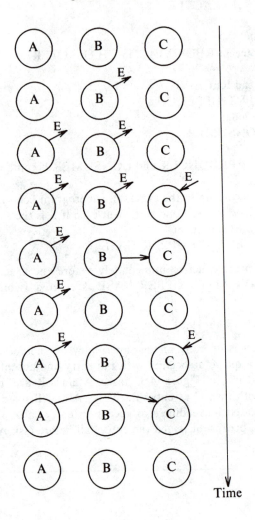

First B calls C and then A calls C
C services B first and then A

Figure 4.3

4. Entries and Accept Statements [9.5]

Entry declarations and calls are syntactically similar to procedure declarations and calls. An entry declaration can occur only in the specification of a task. The corresponding *accept* statements are given in the body of the task. More than one *accept* statement can be given for an entry declaration. Communication between two tasks takes place, when they rendezvous, through the actual parameters in the entry call and the formal parameters in the corresponding *accept* statement.

When a task issues an entry call and the task with the entry is not ready to accept the call (i.e., it is not ready to rendezvous) then the calling task is suspended and put on a queue associated with the entry. Tasks in an entry queue are removed from the queue, one by one, as their entry calls are accepted. The number of tasks waiting at an entry E of a task T is given by the attribute E'COUNT. At any given time a task can be in at most one entry queue.

The task accepting the entry call suspends execution of the calling task as long as necessary to exchange information. The duration of the suspension is equal to the time it takes to execute the statements associated with the *accept* statement. Unlike the called task, the calling task cannot suspend execution of the called task. This one-sided suspension of execution is another asymmetry in Ada's tasking mechanism. Tasks can also wait to accept entry calls from more than one task and issue calls for an immediate rendezvous or one within some specified time period.

If a task calls its own entry *deadlock* occurs, i.e., although the task has not completed or terminated, it will not be able to continue execution. Deadlock occurs because execution of the calling task, which is the same as the called task in this case, is suspended. Such calls are not prohibited in Ada although an implementation may not allow these calls or it may warn the user of their consequences.

As an example of the ability of the called task to suspend the calling task, consider a task A interacting with a task DATABASE that manages a database. When A establishes rendezvous with DATABASE to add information to the database, DATABASE delays A only as long as is necessary to get the information from A. Task A is then allowed to proceed while DATABASE does the conversion of information into the proper format and the actual insertion of the information into the database. On the other hand, when A establishes a rendezvous with DATABASE to retrieve information from the database, A is delayed until the computation and lookups necessary to find the requested information have been done and the information has been given to A.

An attempt to call an entry of a task that has completed, terminated or become *abnormal* results in an error (the exception TASKING_ERROR is raised).

Attribute T′CALLABLE (of type BOOLEAN) of a task T can be used t
determine whether a task T has completed, terminated or become abnormal.

4.1 Syntax

The syntax of entry declarations, entry calls and *accept* statements is illustrate
by means of examples. The following are some examples of entry declarations:

```
entry SIGNAL;                    ——no parameters
entry SET(T: in DURATION);
entry READ(C: out CHARACTER);
entry WRITE(C: in CHARACTER);
```

A family of entries (i.e., an array of entries) can also be declared:

```
entry REGISTER_REQUEST(ID)(D: in out DATA);
                    ——sign in for service
entry D_WRITE(1..5)(B: in BLOCK);   ——for 5 disks
```

Some examples of entry calls are

```
ALARM.SET(NEXT_MOVE_TIME);
BUFFER.READ(C);
DISKS.D_WRITE(J)(B);    ——write block B on disk J
```

Examples of *accept* statements are

```
accept  SIGNAL;
```

```
accept SET(T : in DURATION) do
   PERIOD := T;
       ——calling task suspended while this assignment is executed
end SET;
```

```
accept READ(C: out CHARACTER) do
  C := Q(INB mod N + 1);
end READ;
```

```
——accept statement corresponding to the Ith member
——of the entry family D_WRITE
accept D_WRITE(I)(B: in BLOCK) do
   ——sequence of statements
end D_WRITE;
```

As mentioned before, the calling task is blocked while information exchang
takes place. The duration of blocking is the amount of time it takes the calle
task to execute the statements contained within the **do** ... **end** part (if any)
following the *accept* statement.

5. Delay Statement [9.6]

A task can temporarily suspend its execution by executing a *delay* statement. The statement

delay T;

causes suspension of the task executing the statement for at least T seconds. T is an arithmetic expression of the predefined fixed point type DURATION. If T is zero or negative, execution of the *delay* statement has no effect.

6. Activation, Completion, Dependence and Termination of Tasks [9.3. 9.4]

Tasks declared immediately within a declarative part (that is tasks that are not nested within a declaration) become active just prior to the execution of the first statement following the declarative part. (In case a package body does not have any statements then a *null* statement is assumed.) The tasks are activated in an arbitrary order; this prevents the user from relying upon the order of task activation and allows the implementation to activate the tasks in any order, such as the most efficient one.

A task, block or a subprogram is said to have *completed* execution when the statements associated with it have been executed, i.e., the end of its body has been reached.

Each task depends upon a *master*—a task, a currently executing block or subprogram, or a library package. A task created using the storage allocator (see section on *task types*) depends upon the master containing the associated access type definition. Other tasks depend upon the master whose execution created them.

A task terminates if it

1. has completed and it has no dependent tasks.

2. has completed and all dependent tasks have terminated.

3. is waiting at a *terminate* alternative and

   • it depends upon a master which has completed execution, and

   • all dependent tasks of this master have either already terminated or are waiting at a *terminate* alternative.

A block or a subprogram is left only if all dependent tasks have terminated.

7. Select Statement [9.7]

There are three kinds of *select* statements—the *selective wait*, the *conditional entry* call and the *timed entry* call. The *selective wait* statement allows a task to accept entry calls from more than one task in a non-deterministic fashion.

The conditional entry call, unlike the normal entry call, is a non-blocking entry call. The calling task does not wait if the called task is not ready but goes on to do other things. The timed entry call is similar to the conditional entry call except that the calling task waits a specified period for the called task to get ready to accept the entry call before giving up and going on to other work.

7.1 Selective Wait [9.7.1]

The *selective wait* statement has the form

```
select
    select_alternative
{ or
    select_alternative}
[ else
    sequence_of_statements]
end select;
```

where a *select_alternative* is of the form

```
[ when condition => ]
              selective_wait_alternative
```

An alternative of the *select* statement is said to be *open* if there is no *when* clause before it or if the condition in the *when* clause is true. Otherwise it is said to be *closed*.

A *selective_wait_alternative* can be one of

```
    accept_statement [sequence_of_statements]
  | delay_statement [sequence_of_statements]
  | terminate;
```

A *selective wait* statement can have at most one *terminate* alternative. If a terminate alternative is present then the *selective wait* statement cannot contain the delay statement as an alternative. An *else* part is not allowed in a *selective wait* statement containing a terminate or a delay alternative.

The execution of a *selective wait* statement is defined as follows:

1. Determine all the open alternatives and start counting time for the *delay* statements (if any).

2. If there are open alternatives or there is an *else* part in the *selective wait* statement then the steps given below are followed in determining the next course of action:

    a. Select any one of the open alternatives that is an *accept* statement and for which a rendezvous can be established. Perform the rendezvous and execute the sequence of statments inside the *accept* statement and those following it.

b. Select an open alternative containing a *delay* statement with the shortest delay period, if no alternative has been selected yet. Execute the sequence of statements following the *delay* statement.

c. A *terminate* alternative may be selected if all dependent tasks of the master associated with the task containing the *terminate* alternative have terminated or are waiting at a *terminate* alternative. The selection of the *terminate* alternative is subject to the condition that there are no calls pending to any entry of the task containing the *terminate* alternative.

d. If no open alternative can be selected immediately or all the alternatives are closed then the *else* part is selected; if there is no *else* part then execution is suspended until an open alternative can be selected.

3. If all the alternatives are closed and there is no *else* part in the *selective wait* statement then raise the exception PROGRAM_ERROR.

The body of task CONSUMER, given earlier, is now modified so that it terminates instead of executing forever. The *accept* statement in CONSUMER is made part of a *select* statement that also has a terminate alternative. CONSUMER will now terminate by the selection of the terminate alternative after it determines that PRODUCER has terminated.

```
task body CONSUMER is
    X: CHARACTER;
begin
    loop
        select
            accept RECEIVE(C: in CHARACTER) do
                X := C;
            end RECEIVE;
            PUT(UPPER(X));
        or
            terminate;
        end select;
    end loop;
end CONSUMER;
```

The *terminate* alternative is selected in a task only after it is determined that all other tasks interacting with it have terminated.

7.2 Conditional Entry Call [9.7.2]

A conditional entry call is used to attempt an immediate rendezvous. If an immediate rendezvous is possible then the rendezvous takes place and the sequence of statements following the entry call is executed; otherwise the alternative sequence of statements specified in the *else* alternative is executed. A conditional entry call has the form

```
select
     entry_call [sequence_of_statements]
else
     sequence_of_statements
end select;
```

A conditional entry call can be used by a task to poll another task repeatedly to determine if it is ready to rendezvous. For example, a task X containing the following loop tries to read a card by calling entry READ of the card reader driver CARD. If CARD is not ready to rendezvous, task X does some local computations instead of wasting time waiting for CARD to be ready. This process is repeated indefinitely until a card can be read. Of course, it might be wiser to restrict the number of rendezvous attempts to a finite number:

```
loop
    select
        CARD.READ(C);
        process the card C
        exit;
    else
        do local computation
    end select;
end loop;
```

7.3 Timed Entry Call [9.7.3]

A timed entry call is an attempt to establish a rendezvous within some specified time period. If a rendezvous can be established within the specified period, then rendezvous takes place and the statements following the entry call are executed. Otherwise the statements following the specified delay period are executed. The timed entry call has the form

```
select
     entry_call [sequence_of_statements]
or
     delay_statement [sequence_of_statements]
end select;
```

The timed entry call can be used to monitor a critical device that must respond within a specified time period. If such a device does not respond within this period, then immediate corrective action must be taken. For example, in a nuclear reactor the task measuring the temperature of the walls of the vessel containing the fuel rods must supply a new temperature reading regularly within every 0.1 seconds. Otherwise an alarm, exception NO_TEMP_READING, is raised so that corrective action can be taken. This monitoring is implemented as

```
loop
    select
        accept NEW_TEMP(A: in TEMPERATURE) do
            T := A;
        end NEW_TEMP;
        :
        :
        process latest temperature T
        :
    or
        delay 0.1;
            --wait one tenth of a second before raising an alarm
        raise NO_TEMP_READING;
            --alarm is raised; exceptions are discussed in
            --Chapter 5 on Exceptions
    end select;
end loop;
```

8. Mutual Exclusion

The rendezvous mechanism can be used to implement *mutual exclusion* of operations in time. Mutual exclusion is needed when several tasks update common data to ensure consistency of the data [BRI73]. Mutual exclusion is easily achieved in Ada by ensuring that only two tasks are involved in a particular rendezvous. One task can be assigned to monitor the region of shared data where mutual exclusion is desired. For example, task SHARED_DATA monitors shared data that is updated and read by several tasks:

```
task SHARED_DATA is
    entry UPDATE(formal parameters);
    entry READ(formal parameters);
end SHARED_DATA;

task body SHARED_DATA is
    .
    .
    declarations for the shared data
    .
    .
begin
    loop
        --accept, one at a time, calls to update or read the shared data
        select
            accept UPDATE(formal parameters) do
                Record the parameters
            end UPDATE;
            --let the task supplying the update resume execution
            --while the actual update is done
            Perform the update
        or
            accept READ(formal parameters) do
                Set the parameters to the appropriate values
            end READ;
        or
            --quit if all tasks interested in the shared data
            --have quit or are ready to quit
                terminate;
        end select;
    end loop;
end SHARED_DATA;
```

The common data is accessed by the entry calls

```
SHARED_DATA.UPDATE(actual parameters);
```

and

```
SHARED_DATA.READ(actual parameters);
```

This example shows that is very easy to achieve mutual exclusion in Ada.

It is often desirable to allow more than one task to read the shared data at the same time, since this results in a smaller average waiting time for the tasks. To allow this, a task must be designed that grants permissions to update or read the shared data but does not monitor the shared data itself, as is done by the task SHARED_DATA. The user tasks inform the permissions task when they are finished with the data so that the permissions task can keep track of the tasks accessing the shared data.

9. Task Types [9.1, 9.2]

Task types facilitate the declaration of similar tasks, since several tasks can be declared collectively in an array or individually. The declaration of a task type is syntactically similar to the declaration of a task, with the only difference being the presence of the keyword *type* in the task specification. For example a task type FORK is declared as

```
task type FORK is
    entry PICK_UP;
    entry PUT_DOWN;
end FORK;
```

The declaration

```
F1, F2: FORK;
```

declares two tasks F1 and F2. These tasks become active, as before, just prior to execution of the first statement of the subprogram or package in which they are declared. Arrays whose elements are tasks are declared just like arrays with other types of elements. For example, each element of array F declared as

```
F: array(ID) of FORK;
```

is a task.

Task types are like limited private types. Objects of task types are constants and cannot be assigned to or compared for equality. Tasks can be passed as parameters; the actual parameter and the corresponding formal parameter designate the same task for all parameter modes. If an application needs to create tasks dynamically or to store and exchange the identities of the tasks, then access types must be used. For example, consider access type ANOTHER_FORK declared as

```
type ANOTHER_FORK is access FORK;
```

and variable EXTRA_FORK declared as

```
EXTRA_FORK: ANOTHER_FORK;
```

A task can be created dynamically by calling the allocator as illustrated by the statement

```
EXTRA_FORK := new FORK;
```

Allocated tasks become active when allocated. All allocated tasks must have terminated or be ready to terminate when the scope of the block, subprogram or task in which the access type is declared is about to be left; otherwise, Ada prevents the scope from being left.

10. Abort Statement [9.10]

A task can be explicitly terminated by means of an *abort* statement. The statement

    abort T_1, T_2, ..., T_n;

causes all of the tasks T_1, T_2, ..., T_n, that have not already terminated, to become *abnormal* thus preventing any further rendezvous with these tasks. A task that depends upon an abnormal task also becomes abnormal.

A task that becomes abnormal terminates immediately if it is waiting at an entry call, an *accept* statement, a *select* statement, or a *delay* statement; otherwise, termination occurs as soon as the task reaches a synchronization point such as the start or the end of a *accept* statement, an exception handler and so on.

If the calling task becomes abnormal in the middle of a rendezvous, it is allowed to complete the rendezvous before being terminated; the called task is unaffected. If the task containing the *accept* statement becomes abnormal in the middle of a rendezvous, then the exception TASKING_ERROR is raised in the calling task at the point of entry call.

The exception TASKING_ERROR is raised, at the point of entry call, in all tasks waiting or attempting to rendezvous with an aborted task. The task attribute CALLABLE has the value FALSE if the task has become abnormal (or has completed or terminated).

A task in Ada can abort any task including itself. However, the tasks specified must be visible at the place in the program where they are aborted. Although this blanket ability to abort tasks can be misused, it may be required in applications, such as the control of nuclear reactors and missiles, where misbehaving tasks may have to be terminated in an effort to avoid a catastrophe. The *abort* statement should be used only in well understood situations.

11. Interrupts [13.5.1]

Hardware interrupts are handled elegantly in Ada. Queued interrupts are treated like ordinary entry calls, while interrupts that are lost if not processed immediately are treated like conditional entry calls. A task entry can be associated with a hardware interrupt by specifying that the entry should be located at the interrupt address. This specification is implementation dependent. An *accept* statement executed in response to an interrupt is accorded the highest priority (higher than any user task) so that efficient use can be made of devices and good response achieved in real-time control situations. (Further discussion on the association of entries with hardware interrupt addresses is given in Chapter 8 on Representation Clauses and Implementation Dependent Features.)

12. Task Priorities [9.8]

Each task may be assigned a priority that overrides the default priority assigned to a task by the implementation. Tasks can be assigned a priority by using the PRIORITY pragma which is of the form

   pragma PRIORITY(P);

which is included in the specification of the task. P is a static expression of the implementation defined integer subtype PRIORITY. The higher the value of P, the higher the priority of the task.

The priority of a task is static and cannot be changed dynamically. A task with a higher priority is always given preference in the selection of a task for a rendezvous. For example, suppose that two tasks A and B, A having a higher priority than B, are ready to rendezvous with a third task C. If A and B have called different entries of C, then A will be selected, because of its higher priority. If A and B have called the same entry of C then the task selected will be the one that called C first; in this case the priorities do not make any difference. The order of scheduling tasks of equal priority is not specified and is left to the implementation. Priorities should be used to indicate the importance or the urgency of a task. They should not be used to control synchronization.

13. Task and Entry Attributes [9.9]

The following attributes are defined for tasks and task types:

T'CALLABLE	FALSE if task T has completed, terminated or become abnormal, and TRUE otherwise.
T'TERMINATED	TRUE if task T has terminated and FALSE otherwise.
E'COUNT	the number of tasks waiting to rendezvous at entry E

14. Examples

The power of Ada's tasking facilities is now demonstrated by several complete examples including one large example. The examples show how low level synchronization facilities such as signals and semaphores can be implemented, how tasks can communicate via a buffer and how tasks can be scheduled using a desired scheduling algorithm instead of the FIFO scheduling discipline provided by Ada. The *dining philosophers* problem was chosen, because it illustrates many of the problems encountered in concurrent programming. Real-time programming is illustrated by programs to control a traffic light and an elevator car. These examples also show how hardware interrupts are treated like entry calls. The program that controls the movement of an elevator car is quite large and illustrates most of the aspects of Ada discussed so far.

14.1 Implementing Signals via Ada Tasks

Signals are a low level facility used for synchronizing parallel processes (tasks in Ada terminology) in several programming languages (for example, PL/I [IBM70] and Modula-2 [WIR80]). When a signal is sent, one of the processes, if any, waiting for this signal is allowed to proceed further. If no process is waiting, then the signal is lost.

Signals can be implemented as tasks in Ada. For example, the signal SIGNAL is implemented as a task SIGNAL with entries WAIT and WAKEUP:

```
task SIGNAL is
   entry WAIT;
   entry WAKEUP;
end SIGNAL;
```

A call to the entry WAIT of the task SIGNAL makes the calling task wait until after SIGNAL accepts a WAKEUP entry call. Only one waiting task is released per rendezvous at the WAKEUP entry. Accepting a WAKEUP entry call has no effect if no tasks are waiting—this is the equivalent of a signal being lost. The task SIGNAL is implemented as

```
task body SIGNAL is
begin
   loop
      accept WAKEUP;
      --release one waiting task (if any)
         if WAIT'COUNT > 0 then
            accept WAIT;
         end if;
   end loop;
end SIGNAL;
```

The COUNT attribute of an entry should be used carefully to avoid subtle errors. For example, the above implementation of the task SIGNAL would be erroneous if tasks calling the entry WAIT withdraw the calls after some time period, i.e., timed entry calls. The error occurs when all the calls to WAIT are withdrawn after the task SIGNAL has determined that WAIT'COUNT is greater than 0 but before it has had a chance to accept an entry call.[38]

A separate task must be declared for every signal to be provided. If several signals have to be implemented then it will be more convenient to declare a task type to implement the signals. For example, instead of declaring SIGNAL a task type SIGNAL_TYPE is declared (SIGNAL_TYPE is identical to SIGNAL except for the keyword **type** in its specification). Several signals S1, S2, S3, S4 and S5 can now be easily declared as

S1, S2, S3, S4, S5: SIGNAL_TYPE;

A task cannot exist by itself: it must be part of a subprogram or a package. A task that is to be made available to the users must be enclosed in a package. For example, the task SIGNAL might be enclosed in a package SIGNAL_PACKAGE, which is declared as

---

38. Suppose that timed entry calls were being used to call the entry WAIT in this example. Then the problem resulting from their use could be avoided by using the *selective wait* statement

```
select
    accept WAIT;
else
    null;
end select;
```

is used instead of the *if* statement using the COUNT attribute of WAIT

```
if WAIT'COUNT > 0 then
    accept WAIT;
end if;
```

```
package SIGNAL_PACKAGE is
  procedure WAIT_SIGNAL;
  procedure WAKEUP_SIGNAL;
end SIGNAL_PACKAGE;

package body SIGNAL_PACKAGE is

    --specification of task SIGNAL

    --the specification of SIGNAL must be given before the following
    --subprograms, since they call entries of SIGNAL

  procedure WAIT_SIGNAL is
  begin
      SIGNAL.WAIT;
  end WAIT_SIGNAL;

  procedure WAKEUP_SIGNAL is
  begin
      SIGNAL.WAKEUP;
  end WAKEUP_SIGNAL;

    --body of task SIGNAL

end SIGNAL_PACKAGE;
```

Entries of task SIGNAL are called by using the appropriate procedure provided by SIGNAL_PACKAGE. In this example, the task specification and body are both declared in the body of the encapsulating package. Alternatively, specification of task SIGNAL could have been given in the specification of SIGNAL_PACKAGE and entries of task SIGNAL called directly, e.g.,

```
SIGNAL_PACKAGE.SIGNAL.WAIT;
```

Suppose that a user wants a different kind of signal—when a signal is received, all waiting processes, instead of one, are allowed to proceed. The above implementation of signals can be easily modified to allow this. Task SIGNAL_ALL is similar to task SIGNAL except that, after accepting a WAKEUP entry call, SIGNAL_ALL releases all waiting tasks:

```
task SIGNAL_ALL is
  entry WAIT;
  entry WAKEUP;
end SIGNAL_ALL;
```

```
task body SIGNAL_ALL is
begin
   loop
      accept WAKEUP;

      ——all processes waiting at the time of evaluation
      ——of the loop expression WAIT'COUNT (the number of
      ——processes waiting at the entry WAIT) will be released
      ——in FIFO order

      for I in 1 .. WAIT'COUNT loop
         accept WAIT;
      end loop;

   end loop;
end SIGNAL_ALL;
```

4.2 Semaphores

A *semaphore* is synchronization tool invented by E. W. Dijkstra [DIJ68]. A semaphore is a variable that is used to exchange timing signals between concurrent processes (tasks in Ada) by means of the operations P (wait) and V (signal)[39] [BRI73].

One use of semaphores is to implement mutual exclusion. A process executes the P operation before accessing the shared data and the V operation after its access is complete. The process executing the P operation is delayed if any other process is in the midst of accessing the shared data. It will be allowed to continue only after the process accessing the shared data has finished and executed its own V operation. In one version of the semaphore, processes executing the P operation are queued and released in FIFO order as a result of the V operations.

The following task type SEMAPHORE is used to implement semaphores:

```
task type SEMAPHORE is
   entry P;
   entry V;
end SEMAPHORE;
```

---

39. P and V are abbreviations for Dutch words.

```
task body SEMAPHORE is
begin
   loop
        accept P;
        accept V;
   end loop;
end SEMAPHORE;
```

Semaphores are declared by declaring tasks of type SEMAPHORE.

```
S1: SEMAPHORE;
```

To have exclusive access to the shared data, all the concurrent processes accessing the shared data must have code segments of the form

```
S1.P;
access the shared data
S1.V;
```

The semaphore is a low level synchronization tool and its usage is error prone [BRI73, DOD79b]. For example, synchronization calls can be inadvertently left out or the P operations mistakenly bypassed. It is to avoid such errors that Ada has selected the high level rendezvous for synchronization and mutual exclusion.

14.3 Task Communication via a Buffer Task

Communication between tasks in Ada is not automatically buffered. If buffering is needed then it must be explicitly provided by an intervening task.

The tasks PRODUCER and CONSUMER, in the procedure CONVERT_TO_UPPER_CASE given earlier, have to rendezvous once for each character transmitted. Variations in speed of the tasks PRODUCER and the CONSUMER are not possible, since there is no buffering of communication between them.

A modified version of the procedure described above, called CONVERT_TO_UPPER_CASE2, is now presented in which communication between PRODUCER and CONSUMER is buffered to allow variations in speed. Buffering is accomplished by introducing an intervening task called BUFFER with a maximum buffering capacity of 50 characters. Both the tasks PRODUCER and CONSUMER now call BUFFER to send and receive characters instead of interacting directly with each other. PRODUCER is forced to wait if it is producing characters much faster than CONSUMER can digest (i.e., when BUFFER contains 50 characters). On the other hand, CONSUMER is forced to wait if it consumes much faster than PRODUCER produces (i.e., when BUFFER is empty).

```ada
with TEXT_IO; use TEXT_IO;
procedure CONVERT_TO_UPPER_CASE2 is

   task PRODUCER;        --sends characters to the buffer
   task CONSUMER;        --reads characters from the buffer
   task BUFFER is        --buffers up to 50 characters
      entry WRITE(C: in CHARACTER);
      entry READ(C: out CHARACTER);
   end BUFFER;

   function UPPER(C: in CHARACTER) return CHARACTER is

      --as declared previously in
      --procedure CONVERT_TO_UPPER_CASE

   end UPPER;

   task body PRODUCER is
      C: CHARACTER;
   begin
      while not END_OF_FILE(STANDARD_INPUT) loop
         GET(C);
         BUFFER.WRITE(C);
      end loop;
   end PRODUCER;

   task body CONSUMER is
      X: CHARACTER;
   begin
      loop
         BUFFER.READ(X);
         PUT(UPPER(X));
      end loop;
   end CONSUMER;
```

```
task body BUFFER is
   N: constant INTEGER := 51;
   Q: array(1..N) of CHARACTER;
         --max number of elements in the buffer will be N-1,
   INB, OUTB: INTEGER range 1..N := 1;
         --INB mod  N + 1: next free space in Q
         --OUTB mod N + 1: first element in Q, if any
         --INB = OUTB: Q is empty; initially true
         --INB mod N + 1 = OUTB: Q is full; as a
         --consequence the buffer always has one unused
         --element in this implementation scheme
begin
   loop
      select
         when INB mod N + 1 /= OUTB =>      --Q not full
               --a character can be accepted
               accept WRITE(C: in CHARACTER) do
                  Q(INB mod N + 1) := C;
               end WRITE;
                     --PRODUCER can resume execution
            INB := INB mod N + 1;
         or when INB /= OUTB =>          --Q not empty
               --a character can be read
               accept READ(C: out CHARACTER) do
                  C := Q(OUTB mod N + 1);
               end READ;
                     --CONSUMER can resume execution
            OUTB := OUTB mod N + 1;
      or
            terminate;
      end select;
   end loop;
end BUFFER;


begin
      --PRODUCER, CONSUMER and BUFFER become active
   null;
end CONVERT_TO_UPPER_CASE2;
```

On reaching the end of standard input, task PRODUCER terminates. However, CONSUMER does not terminate after all the characters supplied by PRODUCER have been processed. BUFFER cannot terminate until both PRODUCER and CONSUMER have terminated or are willing to terminate.

CONSUMER cannot be modified easily as was possible in case of procedure CONVERT_TO_UPPER_CASE given earlier. Modification is not simple now, because a terminate alternative cannot be used in the task in CONSUMER as it does not accept entry calls (the terminate alternative can be used only in *selective wait* statements). However, this problem can be rectified in one of several ways. For example

1. modify PRODUCER to send an *end of transmission* character when it is done; modify CONSUMER to terminate when it gets this character from BUFFER. With this approach one character must be reserved to indicate termination.

2. add additional entries to BUFFER by which PRODUCER informs BUFFER that it will not be sending any more data and CONSUMER determines that no more data will be available. CONSUMER aborts when it determines that no more data is available.

3. Add an entry to BUFFER by which a task can determine if BUFFER has any characters. CONSUMER completes execution by exiting the loop when it determines that PRODUCER has completed or terminated (using the attribute CALLABLE), and BUFFER has no characters.

4. Restructure the program.

None of these alternatives is very satisfactory. The first one seems to be the best.

Tasks PRODUCER and CONSUMER are suspended by BUFFER as long as it is necessary for BUFFER to communicate with them, i.e, until the end of the *accept* statement corresponding to the entry called by them. It would be inefficient to hold up these tasks longer than necessary. For example, the *accept WRITE* statement in BUFFER could alternatively have been written as

```
accept WRITE(C: in CHARACTER) do
   Q(INB mod N + 1) := C;
   INB := INB mod N + 1;
end WRITE;
```

This would be inefficient, since PRODUCER will be unnecessarily suspended while BUFFER is doing its internal bookkeeping (incrementing INB). Statements inside the **do** ... **end** of an *accept* statement should be kept to a minimum to avoid delaying the calling task unnecessarily.

14.4 Controlling Task Scheduling

Entry calls are accepted in first-in first-out order. In some situations, a different scheduling discipline is desired. For example, disk access requests may be accepted in an order that minimizes head movement and an operating system may schedule jobs with the smallest execution times first to minimize the average waiting time.

One strategy that can be used to implement a different scheduling scheme is to use a family of entries. Suppose requests for service are classified into three categories declared as

      type REQUEST_LEVEL **is** (URGENT, NORMAL, LOW);

Urgent requests are accepted before any other kind of requests. Normal requests are accepted only if there are no urgent requests pending. Finally, requests in the low category are accepted only if there are no urgent or normal priority requests pending. Within each category requests are accepted in FIFO order.

This scheme is implemented by a task SERVICE that contains the declaration of an entry family REQUEST:

      task SERVICE **is**
        entry REQUEST(REQUEST_LEVEL) (D: **in out** DATA);
      end SERVICE;

Each member of REQUEST handles one request category. For example, the entry call

      SERVICE.REQUEST(URGENT)(D);   ——D is the data

is a request for urgent service.

The body of task SERVICE is

```
task body SERVICE is
  --local declarations
begin
  loop
    select
        accept REQUEST(URGENT)(D: in out DATA) do
          :
          process the request
          :
        end REQUEST;
          :
    or when REQUEST(URGENT)'COUNT = 0 =>
              --the number of tasks waiting at an entry is
              --given by the COUNT attribute
        accept REQUEST(NORMAL)(D: in out DATA) do
          :
          process the request
          :
        end REQUEST;
          :
    or when REQUEST(URGENT)'COUNT = 0
              and REQUEST(NORMAL)'COUNT = 0 =>
        accept REQUEST(LOW)(D: in out DATA) do
          :
          process the request
          :
        end REQUEST;
          :
    end select;
  end loop;

end SERVICE;
```

Scheduling algorithms such as those for minimizing disk head movement or average process waiting time cannot be implemented with this scheme. To implement a general scheduling scheme, use a two stage process involving two entry calls. First, the task requesting service gets an identification number and issues an entry call indicating that it wants service. This call is accepted immediately and the identification of the calling task is noted by SERVICE—this is the signing-in stage. Next, the caller issues another entry call that is accepted by SERVICE only when it can perform the service—this is the waiting-for-service stage.

The reason for making two entry calls is that SERVICE cannot schedule the calling task, say A, until it rendezvous with A to get information about the request and the resources required. Task A is then given a unique identification number, which it must use to get service. This registering of the request takes place during the first call to SERVICE, at its entry REGISTER_REQUEST. After this, A calls SERVICE again, this time calling a member of the entry family GET_SERVICE corresponding to its identification number. A is then delayed until it gets the requested service. The next task to be served, the task whose call to the entry GET_SERVICE is accepted, is determined by SERVICE using some specified scheduling algorithm.

Task SERVICE is an implementation of the abstract algorithm

loop
     Accept all jobs waiting to sign in for service
     Provide service to one job (if any)
end loop

It is inconvenient and error prone to let the calling task actually make the two entry calls. Instead, they are encapsulated in a procedure body and the task requesting service issues only one procedure call (which is syntactically similar to an entry call). However, a subprogram specification cannot be in a task specification. Consequently, task SERVICE is enclosed in a package SERVICE_PACKAGE:

```
package SERVICE_PACKAGE is
  --definition of type DATA
  procedure GET_SERVICE(D: in out DATA);
end SERVICE_PACKAGE;

package body SERVICE_PACKAGE is

  subtype ID is INTEGER range 1..100;
  --procedure NEXT_ID, FREE_ID and data to allocate/deallocate
  --identification for tasks requesting service. These are used
  --in procedure GET_SERVICE.

  --other local declarations of SERVICE_PACKAGE

  task SERVICE is
    entry REGISTER_REQUEST(ID)(D: in out DATA);  --sign in
          --Family of entries with index type ID
          --A job that is assigned the unique identification
          --number J of type ID calls entry J for service
    entry SERVE_REQUEST(ID)(D: in out DATA);
  end SERVICE;

  procedure GET_SERVICE(D: in out DATA) is
  begin
    Get a unique identifier I
    --register service request; member I of the entry
    --family REGISTER_REQUEST is called with data D
      SERVICE.REGISTER_REQUEST(I)(D);
    --wait for service
      SERVICE.SERVE_REQUEST(I)(D);
    Free identifier I
  end GET_SERVICE;

  task body SERVICE is
  begin
    loop

      for I in ID loop
              --a loop is used to accept calls of an
              --entry family
          select
                  --poll each member of the entry family;
                  --there can be only one call per member, since
                  --jobs requesting service are assigned unique
```

```
        --identification numbers
      accept REGISTER_REQUEST(I)(D: in out DATA) do
        .
        .
        --add job I to waiting list
      end REGISTER_REQUEST;
    else
      null;
    end select;
  end loop;

  if there is any task waiting for service then
      --Let K be the next job to be provided service
      --determined using the specified scheduling algorithm
      accept SERVE_REQUEST(K)(D:in out DATA) do
        .
        .
      end SERVE_REQUEST;
  end if;

  end loop;

  end SERVICE;

end SERVICE_PACKAGE;
```

14.5 The Ranked Signals of Modula [WIR77a, WIR77b, WIR77c]

The problem is to implement Modula's primitives for synchronizing concurrent processes. Processes synchronize using signals in Modula. The synchronization primitives allow the specification of a process *delay rank* (the process with the least delay rank has the highest priority). Package SIGNAL_PACKAGE, given earlier, did not allow specification of a delay rank; moreover, it provided only one signal. Using the new package implementing signals, a user will be able to specify the delay rank of a process and declare more than one signal.

The Modula synchronization primitives are

wait(S, R)	Delay the calling process until it gets signal S and give the process delay rank R (a positive integer expression).
wait(S)	Same as *wait (S, 1)*.
send(S)	Send a signal to the process waiting for signal S that has the least delay rank. If several processes have the same delay rank then the process waiting the longest gets the signal. The

process getting the signal resumes execution.

awaited(S)   Function that returns the value TRUE if there is a process waiting for the S signal. Otherwise it returns the value FALSE.

These primitives will be implemented as subprograms in a package SIGNALS_PACKAGE which also provides the limited private type SIGNAL for declaring signals. Type SIGNAL is implemented as a task type whose entries are called by the subprograms of SIGNALS_PACKAGE implementing the Modula primitives. For simplicity, the delay rank will be implemented as an integer value between 1 and 10 of type RANK (instead of an arbitrary integer value).

New signals can be declared as

S: SIGNALS_PACKAGE.SIGNAL;

(assuming of course that the package is visible at the point of declaration). If the *use* clause

use SIGNALS_PACKAGE;

has been given then the above declaration for the signal S can be written simply as

S: SIGNAL;

The specification of SIGNALS_PACKAGE is

```
package SIGNALS_PACKAGE is

    type RANK is range 1..10;
    type SIGNAL is limited private;

    procedure WAIT(S: in SIGNAL; R: in RANK := 1);
            --call WAIT(S) is equivalent to call WAIT(S, 1),
            --because of the default value of formal parameter R
    procedure SEND(S: in SIGNAL);
    function AWAITED(S: in SIGNAL) return BOOLEAN;

private

    task type SIGNAL is
        entry WAIT_SIGNAL(RANK);   --family of entries
        entry SEND_SIGNAL;
        entry AWAITED_SIGNAL(B: out BOOLEAN);
    end SIGNAL;

end SIGNALS_PACKAGE;
```

Each subprogram contains a call to the corresponding entry of the task implementing the specified signal. The implementation of task type SIGNAL is straightforward. Having accepted a SEND_SIGNAL entry call, SIGNAL then accepts the first call to an element of the WAIT_SIGNAL entry family with the lowest index (i.e., lowest delay rank) that has entry calls pending. This allows the task whose entry call was accepted to resume execution. The call AWAITED_SIGNAL is used to query SIGNAL to find out if there are any tasks waiting for a signal. Determining whether or not any task is waiting for a signal is done by examining the COUNT attribute of each member of the WAIT_SIGNAL entry family.

The body of task type SIGNAL is

```
task body SIGNAL is
begin
  loop
    select
      accept SEND_SIGNAL;
                --accept a send signal and give it to the
                --process with least delay rank (if any)

      for I in RANK loop
        select
          accept WAIT_SIGNAL(I);
          exit;
        else
          null;
        end select;
      end loop;

  or

      accept AWAITED_SIGNAL(B: out BOOLEAN) do
        B := FALSE;
        for I in RANK loop
          if WAIT_SIGNAL(I)'COUNT /= 0 then
            B := TRUE;
            exit;
          end if;
        end loop;
      end AWAITED_SIGNAL;

  or

      terminate;

    end select;

  end loop;
end SIGNAL;
```

The body of SIGNALS_PACKAGE is

```
package body SIGNALS_PACKAGE is

    procedure WAIT(S: in SIGNAL; R: in RANK := 1) is
    begin
        S.WAIT_SIGNAL(R);
    end WAIT;

    procedure SEND(S: in SIGNAL) is
    begin
        S.SEND_SIGNAL;
    end SEND;

    function AWAITED(S: in SIGNAL) return BOOLEAN is
        B: BOOLEAN;
    begin
        S.AWAITED_SIGNAL(B);
        return B;
    end AWAITED;

    ——The body of task type SIGNAL, given earlier,
    ——is inserted here

end SIGNALS_PACKAGE;
```

14.6 Shortest Job Next Scheduler

The problem is to implement a task that schedules jobs in the order of increasing execution time, i.e., shortest-job-next order. The scheduler is given jobs (job identification number, of type ID and expected execution time of the job) by several input processes. Several job dispatching processes ask for the next job to be executed from the scheduler. The scheduler selects a job with the shortest-execution-time to give to the next dispatching process requesting a job.

The scheduler uses the package ORDERED_SET declared in Chapter 3 on Packages. The specification of ORDERED_SET is reproduced:

```
package ORDERED_SET is
    procedure INSERT(JOB: in ID; T: in DURATION);
    procedure SMALLEST(JOB: out ID);
    function EMPTY return BOOLEAN;
end ORDERED_SET;
```

The specification of task SCHEDULER is

```
task SCHEDULER is
    entry ADD(JOB: in ID; T: in DURATION);
    entry NEXT(JOB: out ID);
            --return the next job to be executed and delete
            --it from the list of jobs to be scheduled
end SCHEDULER;
```

SCHEDULER accepts jobs from the input processes and inserts them into the ordered set. When there are jobs in the ordered set, SCHEDULER accepts requests from the dispatching processes to which it hands out jobs in increasing execution time order. Assuming that the *use* clause

```
use ORDERED_SET;
```

has been given, the body of SCHEDULER is declared as

```
task body SCHEDULER is
    I: ID;
    PERIOD: DURATION;
begin
    loop
        select
                accept ADD(JOB: in ID; T: in DURATION) do
                    I := JOB;
                    PERIOD := T;
                end ADD;
                INSERT(I, PERIOD);
        or when not EMPTY =>
                accept NEXT(JOB: out ID) do
                    SMALLEST(JOB);
                end NEXT;
        end select;
    end loop;
end SCHEDULER;
```

14.7 The Traffic Light

The problem is to write a task that controls the traffic light at the intersection of a main road and a lightly used side road. Few pedestrians cross the main road. Vehicles must stop when the light is red. Normally the traffic light is green for the main road and red for the side road. The light changes to red for the main road and green for the side road when

1. a sensor detects that a car has arrived at the intersection from the side road.

2. a pedestrian, who wants to cross the main road, presses a button provided for the purpose.

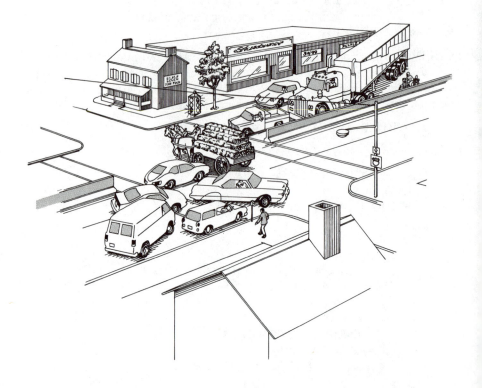

Traffic Light at a Lightly Used Side Road

Both the sensor and the pedestrian button cause an interrupt at location 8#2000# (octal 2000).

The following specifications for the traffic light must be observed.

1. The traffic flow on the main road is to be stopped only if the main road has had the green light for at least 3 minutes.

2. The traffic flow on the main road should be stopped for only 30 seconds at a time.

3. Multiple requests for stopping the flow of traffic on the main road have the same effect as one request. This rule circumvents the unnecessary changes in the traffic light that would otherwise be caused by the repeated pressing of the button by an impatient pedestrian.

A package TRAFFIC_LIGHT with the following specifications is available:

package TRAFFIC_LIGHT **is**

    procedure START_LIGHT;
          --start the traffic light with green for the main road
    procedure CHANGE_LIGHT;
          --change the traffic light from green to red in one
          --direction and red to green in the other

    end TRAFFIC_LIGHT;

Package TRAFFIC_LIGHT encapsulates the physical control of switches so that we need not worry about them.

The implementation of CONTROL_TRAFFIC_LIGHT uses the following abstract algorithm

    Start the traffic light
    loop
      Wait 3.0 minutes
      Accept request to stop main road traffic and change light
      Wait 30.0 seconds
      Clear additional requests to stop main road traffic
      Change light
    end loop

Procedure CONTROL_TRAFFIC_LIGHT is declared as

```
with TRAFFIC_LIGHT; use TRAFFIC_LIGHT;

procedure CONTROL_TRAFFIC_LIGHT is

  task LIGHT is
    entry STOP_MAIN;     --pedestrian button and sensor
    for STOP_MAIN use at 8#2000#;
          --an interrupt is an entry call in Ada. The interrupt
          --location is associated with the entry call. This
          --representation specification is implementation dependent
  end LIGHT;

  task body LIGHT is
    CUT_OFF: constant DURATION := 180.0;
       --main road traffic must flow at least 3 minutes
    SIDE_ROAD_OPEN: constant DURATION := 30.0;

  begin
    START_LIGHT;
    loop
       delay CUT_OFF;
       accept STOP_MAIN; CHANGE_LIGHT;
       delay SIDE_ROAD_OPEN;
       --clear out multiple requests to stop main road traffic
          for I in 1..STOP_MAIN'COUNT loop
             accept STOP_MAIN;
          end loop;
       CHANGE_LIGHT;
    end loop;

  end LIGHT;
begin
  null;
end CONTROL_TRAFFIC_LIGHT;
```

The actual times corresponding to the minimum time for which the main road
has the green light and the time for which the side road has the green light will
be slightly greater than CUT_OFF and SIDE_ROAD_OPEN. This difference
occurs, because of the time spent in executing the other statements in the loop;
consequently a cumulative time drift occurs in the loop. When performing
actions where it is undesirable to have such a cumulative drift, a program
segment of the form given below should be used [BAR80]:

```
INTERVAL: DURATION := ...;
NEXT_TIME: TIME := ...;
              --next time the action is to be performed
    :
loop
    delay NEXT_TIME - CLOCK;
    Action
    NEXT_TIME := NEXT_TIME + INTERVAL;
end loop;
```

Function CLOCK is from the predefined package CALENDAR [9.6], whose specification is

```
package CALENDAR is
   type TIME is private;

   subtype YEAR_NUMBER is INTEGER range 1901..2099;
   subtype MONTH_NUMBER is INTEGER range 1..12;
   subtype DAY_NUMBER is INTEGER range 1..31;
   subtype DAY_DURATION is DURATION range 0.0 .. 86_400.0;

   function CLOCK return TIME;

   function YEAR(DATE: TIME) return YEAR_NUMBER;
   function MONTH(DATE: TIME) return MONTH_NUMBER;
   function DAY(DATE: TIME) return DAY_NUMBER;
   function SECONDS(DATE: TIME) return DAY_DURATION;

   procedure SPLIT(DATE: in TIME;
                   YEAR: out YEAR_NUMBER;
                   MONTH: out MONTH_NUMBER;
                   DAY: out DAY_NUMBER;
                   SECONDS: out DAY_DURATION);

   function TIME_OF(YEAR: YEAR_NUMBER;
                    MONTH: MONTH_NUMBER;
                    DAY: DAY_NUMBER;
                    SECONDS: DAY_DURATION := 0.0) return TI

   function "+"(LEFT: TIME; RIGHT: DURATION) return TIME;
   function "+"(LEFT: DURATION; RIGHT: TIME) return TIME;
   function "-"(LEFT: TIME; RIGHT: DURATION) return TIME;
   function "-"(LEFT: TIME; RIGHT: TIME) return DURATION;

   function "<"(LEFT, RIGHT: TIME) return BOOLEAN;
   function "<="(LEFT, RIGHT: TIME) return BOOLEAN;
   function ">"(LEFT, RIGHT: TIME) return BOOLEAN;
   function ">="(LEFT, RIGHT: TIME) return BOOLEAN;

   TIME_ERROR: exception; --can be raised by TIME_OF, "+" and "

private
   --implementation-dependent
end CALENDAR;
```

14.8 The Mortal Dining Philosophers

This problem is an adaptation of the one posed by E. W. Dijkstra. Five philosophers spend their lives eating spaghetti and thinking. They eat at a circular table in a dining room. The table has five chairs around it and chair number I has been assigned to philosopher number I $(1 \leqslant I \leqslant 5)$. Five forks have also been laid out on the table so that there is one fork between every two chairs. Consequently there is one fork to the left of each chair and one to its right. Fork number I is to the left of chair number I.

The Five Philosophers

In order to be able to eat, a philosopher must enter the dining room and sit in the chair assigned to him. A philosopher must have two forks to eat (the forks are placed to the left and right of every chair). If he cannot get two forks

immediately then the philosopher must wait until he gets them before he ca
eat. The forks are picked up one at a time with the left fork being picked u
first. When a philosopher is finished eating (after a finite amount of time), h
puts the forks down and leaves the room.

The dining philosophers problem has been studied extensively in the compute
science literature. It is used as a benchmark to check the appropriateness o
the facilities for concurrent programming and proof techniques for concurren
programs. It is interesting, because, despite its apparent simplicity, i
illustrates many of the problems encountered in concurrent programming sucl
as shared resources and *deadlock*. The forks are the resources shared by th
philosophers who represent the concurrent processes.

The five philosophers and the five forks will be implemented as tasks using tw
arrays of tasks in the procedure DINING. On activation, each philosophe
first gets an identification number (equal to the array index he is associate
with). Using this number, a philosopher can determine the identificatio
numbers of the forks on either side of him. Each philosopher is mortal an
passes on to the next world soon after having eaten 100,000 times.

```
procedure DINING is
    subtype ID is INTEGER range 1..5;

    task type PHILOSOPHER is
        entry GET_ID(J: in ID);
                --get an identification number
    end PHILOSOPHER;

    task type FORK is
        entry PICK_UP;
        entry PUT_DOWN;
    end FORK;

    F: array(ID) of FORK;               --the 5 forks
    P: array(ID) of PHILOSOPHER;     --the 5 philosophers

    task body FORK is
                --A fork can be picked up by one philosopher at a time.
                --It must be put down before it can be picked up again.
                --The forks terminate when the philosophers terminate.
    begin
        loop
            select
                    accept PICK_UP;
                    accept PUT_DOWN;
```

```
              or
                    terminate;
              end select;
           end loop;
        end FORK;


        task body PHILOSOPHER is
           I: ID;   --index or number of this philosopher
           LIFE_LIMIT: constant := 100_000;
           TIMES_EATEN: INTEGER := 0;
           LEFT, RIGHT: ID;        --fork numbers
        begin
           accept GET_ID(J: in ID) do
                            --get the identification number
              I := J;
           end GET_ID;


           LEFT := I;      --number of the left fork
           RIGHT := I mod 5 + 1;   --number of the right fork

           while TIMES_EATEN /= LIFE_LIMIT loop
              --think for a while; then enter dining room and sit down
              --pick up forks
                 F(RIGHT).PICK_UP;
                 F(LEFT).PICK_UP;
              --eat
              --put down forks
                 F(LEFT).PUT_DOWN;
                 F(RIGHT).PUT_DOWN;

              TIMES_EATEN := TIMES_EATEN + 1;
              --get up and leave dining room
           end loop;
        end PHILOSOPHER;


     begin
        for K in ID loop
              --give identification numbers to the philosophers
           P(K).GET_ID(K);
        end loop;
     end DINING;
```

Philosophers and forks were both implemented as arrays of tasks. It would have been convenient if Ada had allowed a task that is an element of an array to determine its index in the array so that it could distinguish itself from the other elements of the array. The above program would then become simpler since there would be no need to supply the identification numbers explicitly to the philosophers.

A variation of the above problem for the reader to try is to allow a philosopher to sit on any chair. This variation will result in a smaller average waiting time for eating for the philosophers. *Hint*: this scheme can be implemented by declaring a new task that is called by every philosopher to request a chair (preferably one with free forks). On leaving the dining room a philosopher informs this task that the chair is vacant.

Who Eats Next?

In the solution given, no individual philosopher will be blocked indefinitely from eating, i.e., *starve*, because the philosophers pick up the forks in first-in first-out order (the discipline associated with all entry queues). However, there is a possibility of deadlock in the solution given above, e.g., each philosopher picks up one fork and waits to get another fork so that he can start to eat. Assuming that all the philosophers are obstinate and that none of them will give up his fork until he gets another fork and has eaten, everything will be in a state of suspension.

Deadlock can be avoided in several ways, for example, a philosopher may pick up the two forks needed by him only when both the forks are available (*Hint*: by using *when* conditions in the *select* statement). Alternatively, one could add another task called the HOST that makes sure that there are at most four philosophers in the dining room at any given time. Each philosopher must request permission to enter the room from the HOST and must inform it on leaving.

Task HOST is declared as

```
task HOST is
    entry ENTER;
    entry LEAVE;
end HOST;


task body HOST is
    I: INTEGER := 0;     --number of philosophers in the room
    begin
      loop
        select
          when I < 4 =>
                --a philosopher can enter if there are less
                --than 4 philosophers in the dining room
            accept ENTER;
            I := I + 1;
        or
            accept LEAVE;    --philosopher is leaving
            I := I - 1;
        or
            terminate;
        end select;
      end loop;
end HOST;
```

Clearly there is no possibility of a deadlock with this change, since there will be at least one philosopher in the room who will be able to eat. Since they all eat for a finite time, he will leave and some other philosopher will be able to eat.

14.9 Elevator Control

This example of a real-time application illustrates just about all the facilities in Ada discussed so far—packages, tasks, *delay* statements and representation specifications. The problem is to design a procedure RUN_ELEVATOR that controls an elevator serving 8 floors of a building, numbered from 1 to 8 (no basement).

At each floor in the building are two elevator call buttons—UP and DOWN (except for the first floor which does not have a DOWN button and the top floor which does not have an UP button). Inside the elevator there are 8 FLOOR buttons, one for each of the 8 floors and an OPEN button. FLOOR button marked I is depressed by a passenger to get off at floor I and the OPEN button is depressed to prolong the period the elevator door is open.

The Elevator Entrance

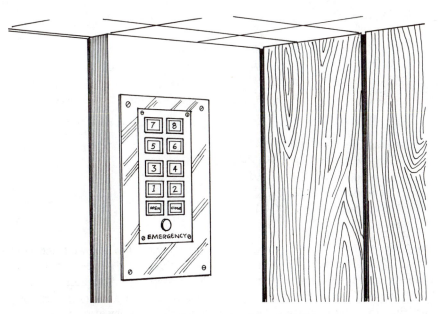

The Request Buttons Inside the Elevator

14.9.1 Elevator Specification: The elevator car behaves as follows:

1. It services the 8 floors carrying, passengers up and down. Its *home* floor
    is the first floor (the building lobby). Whenever there are no requests for
    use, it stations itself at the home floor.

2. When going up, the elevator services all requests for stops on floors above
    its current position; similarly when it is going down. The elevator tries to
    minimize the number of changes in direction. (No person waits forever.)

3. The elevator opens its door for 5 seconds. Every time the OPEN button
    is pressed, the door is kept open for one extra second. However, pressing
    the OPEN button when the door is closed has no effect.

14.9.2 Physical Details of the Elevator: Depressing an elevator button causes
a hardware interrupt (with a possible parameter) on the computer associated
with the elevator. These interrupts are queued automatically. Hardware
addresses corresponding to these interrupts are

Button	Address	Function
DOWN(I)	8#1000#	Request to go down from floor I
UP(I)	8#1010#	Request to go up from floor I
FLOOR(I)	8#1020#	Stop at floor I
OPEN	8#1030#	Delay closing door by one second

A package ELEVATOR with the following specification is available.

```
package ELEVATOR is
    procedure MOVE_UP_ONE_FLOOR;
    procedure MOVE_DOWN_ONE_FLOOR;
    procedure CLOSE_DOOR;
    procedure OPEN_DOOR;
end ELEVATOR;
```

14.9.3 Elevator Movement Timing Characteristics: The elevator movement consists of three phases—the car first accelerates to steady speed, then travels at steady speed and, finally, decelerates to a stop. The elevator takes 1.80 seconds to go from a stationary position at floor I to a stationary position at floor I+1 (the characteristics are the same whether the elevator is going up or down)—0.40 seconds to accelerate to steady speed while covering the distance A_IB_I, 1.00 seconds traveling at steady speed to cover the distance B_IC_I, and 0.40 seconds decelerating to a stop while covering the distance C_ID_I. A_IB_I is equal to C_ID_I, A_I coincides with D_{I-1} and D_I coincides with A_{I+1}.

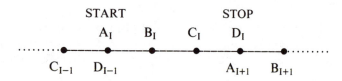

The distance between floor I and I+1 is represented by A_ID_I. The elevator will start decelerating at point C_I unless a signal to skip floor I+1 is given.

If there is no need for the elevator to stop at the next floor then it must be given another move command before it starts decelerating, i.e., at or before position C_I. There are two cases:

1. Suppose the elevator is in a stationary position at the time the first move command is given. Then the elevator should be given the next move command at most 1.40 seconds after the previous move command.

2. Suppose the elevator starts from floor I−1 or earlier. It does not stop at floor I and is not to stop at floor I+1 either. It was last instructed to keep moving at position C_{I-1}. It must now be instructed to keep moving at C_I. Traveling at steady speed the elevator covers the distance $A_I B_I$ or $C_I D_I$ in half the time it takes when accelerating or decelerating. Consequently, it covers the distance $C_{I-1} C_I$ in 1.40 seconds. The next move command, as in the first case, must be given at most 1.40 seconds after the previous move command.

The timing characteristics of a real elevator will be considerably different. For example, a real elevator might take less time to go down a floor and the time it takes to traverse a floor might depend on the load it is carrying. The timing characteristics given here have been simplified considerably so as to focus on those aspects that illustrate interesting facets of Ada.

14.9.4 Solution: In reading the solution, the reader is urged to keep in mind how reasonable elevators operate. Requests for elevator service, to go up or down, or to get off, are accepted by a task REQUEST_DB (requests data base), which also keeps track of these requests. Task ELEVATOR_CONTROL controls the elevator using commands provided in the package ELEVATOR. It also accepts requests from passengers, made by depressing the OPEN button, to keep the elevator door open longer than the normal period. Task ELEVATOR_CONTROL interacts with the task REQUEST_DB to

1. determine the next elevator destination based on pending requests for elevator service, and

2. supply information specifying the floors that have been serviced.

The interaction between tasks ELEVATOR_CONTROL, REQUEST_DB, package ELEVATOR and the elevator itself is illustrated in Figure 4.4:

At any time, the elevator will be in one of three states—UP, DOWN or NEUTRAL. States UP and DOWN indicate that the elevator is going in the direction implied by its state in response to passenger requests. The NEUTRAL state indicates that the elevator is not responding to a request but that it might be headed toward its home floor if it is not already there.

The Elevator System

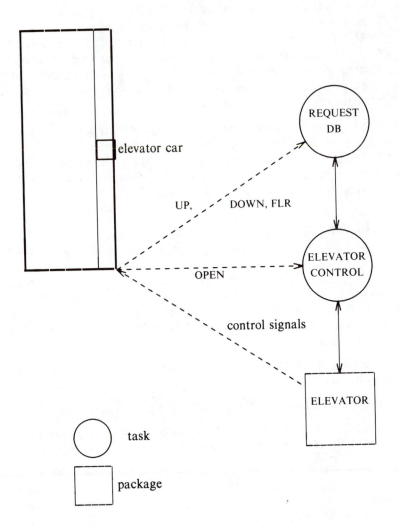

Figure 4.4

Some constant and type declarations used in the implementation are

```
HOME: constant := 1;
N: constant := 8;    --number of floors

subtype STORIES is INTEGER range 1..N;
type STATE is (UP, DOWN, NEUTRAL);

NORMAL_OPEN_TIME: constant DURATION := 5.0;
EXTRA_OPEN_TIME: constant DURATION := 1.0;
NEXT_MOVE_TIME: constant DURATION := 1.39
       --the next move command must be given at most
       --1.40 seconds after the previous move command;
       --selection of 1.39 is arbitrary except for the
       --above constraint
```

The specification of task ELEVATOR_CONTROL is

```
task ELEVATOR_CONTROL is
  entry OPEN;    --keep the door open one second longer
  --associate hardware interrupt location with entry OPEN
     for OPEN use at 8#1030#;
end ELEVATOR_CONTROL;
```

The specification of task REQUEST_DB is

```
task REQUEST_DB is
  entry DEST(CUR_STATE: in STATE; CUR_FLOOR: in STORIES;
                    NEW_STATE: out STATE;
                    NEW_FLOOR: out STORIES);
        --computes the new destination and direction
        --based on the current location, current
        --direction and pending requests
  entry REQUESTS(B: out BOOLEAN);
        --TRUE returned in B if there is any pending request
        --for elevator service and FALSE otherwise
  entry CLEAR_GO(DIR: in STATE; I: in STORIES);
        --picked up passenger(s) going up or down from floor I
  entry CLEAR_OFF(I: in STORIES);
        --passenger(s) let off at floor I

  --the following entries correspond to passenger
  --requests for elevator service
      entry DOWN(I: in STORIES);
      entry UP(I: in STORIES);
      entry FLOOR(I: in STORIES);

  --associate hardware interrupt locations with entries
      for DOWN use at 8#1000#;
      for UP use at 8#1010#;
      for FLOOR use at 8#1020#;
  end REQUEST_DB;
```

The procedure used by task ELEVATOR_CONTROL to control the elevator is described abstractly as

P_0:

```
loop
    Respond to requests, if any; otherwise position
    car at the home floor
end loop
```

The statement *Respond to requests, ...* is refined as

P₁:

> **if** There are no requests pending **then**
> > If at home floor then sleep for 1 second (to avoid *busy waiting*); otherwise, move elevator toward home floor and wait till it is time to give the next move instruction
>
> **else**
> > Compute destination (it might have changed)
> > **if** Elevator is not responding to a request or
> > > is not about to reach its destination **then**
> > > Give a move instruction to the elevator and wait until it is time to give the next move instruction
> >
> > **else**
> > > Let passengers get off and on; respond to requests to keep door open longer and clear requests to get off
> > > **if** There are requests pending **then**
> > > > Compute destination
> > > > Give a move instruction to the elevator and wait until it is time to give the next move instruction
> > >
> > > **end if**
> >
> > **end if**
>
> **end if**

When at the home floor, the program controlling the elevator delays itself by one second every time to minimize needless execution (busy waiting). This delay will allow additional execution time to be allocated to REQUEST_DB and other programs or tasks on the computer.

The following variables will be used in further refinements of the task ELEVATOR_CONTROL and in the final program:

CUR_FLOOR	The floor the elevator is at or about to reach.
CUR_STATE	The current state of the elevator.
NEW_STATE	The new state of the elevator.
NEW_FLOOR	The elevator destination.

Continuing the refinement, the boolean expression *There are no requests pending* is refined to be the expression

not REQUESTS

where REQUESTS is declared as

```
function REQUESTS return BOOLEAN is
   B: BOOLEAN;
begin
   REQUEST_DB.REQUESTS(B);    --entry call
   return B;
end REQUESTS;
```

The statement *If at home floor then sleep for 1 second ...* of P_1 is refined as

```
CUR_STATE := NEUTRAL;    --not responding to any requests
if CUR_FLOOR = HOME then
   delay 1.0;    --sleep for one second
else
   MOVE(CUR_STATE);
   delay NEXT_MOVE_TIME;
end if;
```

Procedure MOVE is declared as

```
procedure MOVE(DIR: in STATE) is
begin
   case DIR is
      when UP =>
            MOVE_UP_ONE_FLOOR;
            CUR_FLOOR := CUR_FLOOR + 1;
      when DOWN | NEUTRAL =>
            MOVE_DOWN_ONE_FLOOR;
            CUR_FLOOR := CUR_FLOOR - 1;
   end case;
end MOVE;
```

The statement *Compute destination* is replaced by the entry call

```
REQUEST_DB.DEST(CUR_STATE, CUR_FLOOR,
                  NEW_STATE, NEW_FLOOR);
```

The boolean expression *Elevator is not responding to a request or is not about to reach its destination* is refined as

```
CUR_STATE = NEUTRAL or else CUR_FLOOR /= NEW_FLOOR
```

The statement *Give a move instruction to the elevator and wait...* of the abstract algorithm P_1 is refined as

```
CUR_STATE := NEW_STATE;
    --new floor and direction were computed just before reaching
    --the current floor; no new calls have been accepted since
MOVE(CUR_STATE);
delay NEXT_MOVE_TIME;
```

Requests to keep the elevator door open are honored only when the elevator door is open; when the door is closed they are ignored.

The statement *Let the passengers get off and ...* is refined as

Clear any previous requests to open the door for extra time and
open the door for the normal time.
Close the door but delay closing if the open button has been pressed
Clear requests to get off and on

These three statements are refined as

(1) *Clear any previous requests to open the door for ...*

```
for I in 1..OPEN'COUNT loop
    accept OPEN;
end loop;
OPEN_DOOR;
delay NORMAL_OPEN_TIME;
```

(2) *Close the door but delay closing if the open button ...*

```
while OPEN'COUNT /= 0 loop
    accept OPEN;
    delay EXTRA_OPEN_TIME;
end loop;
CLOSE_DOOR;
```

(3) *Clear requests to get off and on*

```
CLEAR_OFF(CUR_FLOOR);
if There are requests pending then
    Compute destination
    CLEAR_GO(NEW_STATE, CUR_FLOOR);
end if;
```

Just before reaching a floor, the elevator indicates to the would be passengers the direction in which it will be going next[40] so that the passengers going in that direction may get on.

The boolean expression *There are requests pending* is refined to be just the function call

REQUESTS

These refinements when collected together make up the executable part of the task ELEVATOR_CONTROL body. The job of collecting the refinements is left to the reader. Procedure RUN_ELEVATOR, which contains the tasks ELEVATOR_CONTROL and REQUEST_DB, is now declared:

---

40. The direction may be indicated by means of colored lights. Direction indicators are not implemented in this algorithm.

```
with ELEVATOR; use ELEVATOR;
        --ELEVATOR is compiled separately (see Chapter 7
        --on Program Structure and Separate Compilation)
procedure RUN_ELEVATOR is

    N: constant := 8;    --number of floors
    subtype STORIES is INTEGER range 1..N;
    type STATE is (UP, DOWN, NEUTRAL);
    HOME: constant := 1;

    NORMAL_OPEN_TIME: constant DURATION := 5.0;
    EXTRA_OPEN_TIME: constant DURATION := 1.0;
    NEXT_MOVE_TIME: constant DURATION := 1.39;

    --specification and body of the task REQUEST_DB
    --specification of task ELEVATOR_CONTROL

    task body ELEVATOR_CONTROL is
        CUR_FLOOR: STORIES := HOME;
            --the elevator starts out positioned at its home floor
        NEW_FLOOR: STORIES;
        CUR_STATE: STATE := NEUTRAL;
        NEW_STATE: STATE;

        --the body of the procedure MOVE
        --the body of the function REQUESTS

    begin
        --The body of this task which was developed by stepwise
        --refinement is inserted here.
    end ELEVATOR_CONTROL;

begin
    null;
end RUN_ELEVATOR;
```

14.9.5 REQUEST_DB: Task REQUEST_DB accords entry calls made by task ELEVATOR_CONTROL a higher priority than requests from passengers for elevator service. It is important that task ELEVATOR_CONTROL be serviced as promptly as possible so that it can control the movement of the elevator within the constraints of the elevator's timing characteristics.

The infinite loop executed by REQUEST_DB can be abstractly described as

```
loop
  select
      Accept request to compute new destination
  or
      Accept information regarding the passengers
        picked up at floor I
  or
      Accept information specifying that passengers
        were let off at floor I
  or
      Accept an inquiry to find out if any elevator
        service requests are pending
  else
      Accept passenger requests for elevator service
  end select
end loop
```

Task REQUEST_DB will use BOOLEAN arrays F, U and D to record requests from passengers to get off at floors, and to go up or down.

F(I)	a TRUE value indicates that a passenger wants to get off at floor I
U(I)	a TRUE value indicates that a passenger wants to go up from floor I
D(I)	a TRUE value indicates that a passenger wants to go down from floor I

The statement *Accept request to compute new destination* is refined as

```
accept DEST(CUR_STATE: in STATE; CUR_FLOOR: in STORIES;
           NEW_STATE: out STATE;
           NEW_FLOOR: out STORIES) do
      DESTINATION(CUR_STATE, CUR_FLOOR,
                  NEW_STATE, NEW_FLOOR);
end DEST;
```

The statement *Accept information regarding the passengers picked up at floor I* is refined to be

```
accept CLEAR_GO(DIR: in STATE; I: in STORIES) do
    case DIR is
        when UP => U(I) := FALSE;
        when DOWN => D(I) := FALSE;
        when NEUTRAL => raise PROGRAM_ERROR;
                --raise the predefined exception PROGRAM_ERROR;
                --raising this exception will result in the
                --execution of the program being abandoned.
                --Exceptions are discussed in Chapter 5
    end case;
end CLEAR_GO;
```

The statement *Accept information specifying that passengers were let off at floor I* is refined as

```
accept CLEAR_OFF(I: in STORIES) do
    F(I) := FALSE;
end CLEAR_OFF;
```

The statement *Accept an inquiry to find out if any elevator service requests are pending* is refined as

```
accept REQUESTS(B: out BOOLEAN) do
    B := ANY(F) or ANY(U) or ANY(D);
end REQUESTS;
```

where ANY is a user-defined function that returns TRUE if any one of the elements of its array actual parameter has the value TRUE.

Finally, the statement *Accept passenger requests for elevator service* is refined as

```
select
    accept UP(I: in STORIES) do
        U(I) := TRUE;
    end UP;
or
    accept DOWN(I: in STORIES) do
        D(I) := TRUE;
    end DOWN;
or
    accept FLOOR(I: in STORIES) do
        F(I) := TRUE;
    end FLOOR;
else
    null;
end select
```

The body of the task REQUEST_DB is now given:

```
task body REQUEST_DB is

    type STATUS is array(INTEGER range <>) of BOOLEAN;
    F, U, D: STATUS(1..N) := (STORIES => FALSE);
        --F, U, & D contain requests to get off, go up
        --and down, respectively

    function ANY(A: in STATUS) return BOOLEAN is
        --returns TRUE if any element of A is true and false otherwise
    begin
        for I in A'RANGE loop
            if A(I) then
                return TRUE;
            end if;
        end loop;
        return FALSE;
    end ANY;

    function LOWEST(A, B : in STATUS) return STORIES is
        --call only when at least 1 element of A or B is TRUE; returns
        --lowest index in the 2 arrays such that element is TRUE
    begin
        for I in A'RANGE loop
            if A(I) or B(I) then return I; end if;
        end loop;
    end LOWEST;
```

```
function HIGHEST(A, B : in STATUS) return STORIES is
    --call only when at least 1 element of A or B is TRUE; returns
    --highest index in the 2 arrays such that element is TRUE
begin
    for I in reverse A'RANGE loop
        if A(I) or B(I) then
            return I;
        end if;
    end loop;
end HIGHEST;
```

```
    --the body of procedure DESTINATION (developed
    --following this task)
```

```
begin
```

```
    --the infinite loop whose refinements were given above
```

```
end REQUEST_DB;
```

Task REQUEST_DB is executed continuously without ever delaying itself. If REQUEST_DB is modified to eliminate busy waiting, care must be taken to ensure that ELEVATOR_CONTROL is always serviced in time for it to control the elevator properly.

Procedure DESTINATION computes the new destination depending upon the current direction of the elevator. While doing so it tries to minimize changes in elevator direction. It will not suggest a change in the elevator direction if there exists a request for elevator service that does not require changing direction. This means that when the elevator is going up, it will not stop on intermediate floors for requests to go down; it will stop for them on its way down. The elevator behaves in a similar fashion when it is going down.

Procedure DESTINATION should be called only after ensuring that there is at least one request for elevator service. It is specified as

```
procedure DESTINATION(CUR_STATE: in STATE;
                      CUR_FLOOR: in STORIES;
                      NEW_STATE: out STATE; NEW_FLOOR: out STORIES);
```

and implements the following abstract algorithm:

if If the elevator is not responding to requests or is going up **then**
  Process requests from the current floor or above to compute the new
  destination such that a change of the elevator direction is not
  required; if there are no such requests then change the direction
  to down and compute the new destination
else
  Process requests from the current floor or below to compute the new
  destination such that a change of direction is not required;
  if there are no such requests then change the direction to up and
  compute the new destination
end if

This algorithm is further refined as

if Current direction is NEUTRAL or UP **then**
  if There are requests from current floor or above to go up
                 or from passengers to get off above **then**
    NEW_FLOOR is the lowest floor up (current floor or above)
    requiring service
    NEW_STATE is UP
  elsif There are requests to come down from above **then**
    NEW_FLOOR is the highest floor up requiring service
    NEW_STATE is UP
  else −−change directions and compute recursively
    DESTINATION(DOWN, CUR_FLOOR,
                 NEW_STATE, NEW_FLOOR)
  end if
else
  if There are requests from current floor or below to go down
                 from passengers to get off below **then**
    NEW_FLOOR is the highest floor down (current floor or below)
    requiring service
    NEW_STATE is DOWN
  elsif There are requests to come up from below **then**
    NEW_FLOOR is the lowest floor down requiring service
    NEW_STATE is DOWN
  else −−change directions and compute recursively
    DESTINATION(UP, CUR_FLOOR, NEW_STATE, NEW_FLOOR
  end if
end if

As mentioned before, DESTINATION should be called only when there is at
least one request for elevator service. Termination of recursion can be shown
easily if there is at least one request. There will be at most one recursive call.

This procedure, as designed, gives preference to requests in the upward direction (because when direction is NEUTRAL it looks for requests on the floors above the current floor).

The Ada version of procedure DESTINATION is

```
procedure DESTINATION(CUR_STATE: in STATE;
                      CUR_FLOOR: in STORIES;
                      NEW_STATE: out STATE;
                      NEW_FLOOR: out STORIES) is
   --uses global variables U, F, D but does not change them.
begin
   if CUR_STATE = NEUTRAL or CUR_STATE = UP then
      if ANY(U(CUR_FLOOR..U'LAST)) or
                  ANY(F(CUR_FLOOR..F'LAST)) then
      NEW_FLOOR := LOWEST(U(CUR_FLOOR..U'LAST),
                  F(CUR_FLOOR..F'LAST));
      NEW_STATE := UP;
      elsif ANY(D(CUR_FLOOR..D'LAST)) then
         NEW_FLOOR := HIGHEST(D(CUR_FLOOR..D'LAST),
                  (CUR_FLOOR..D'LAST => FALSE));
            NEW_STATE := UP;
      else
         DESTINATION(DOWN, CUR_FLOOR,
                  NEW_STATE, NEW_FLOOR);
      end if;

   else
      if ANY(D(D'FIRST..CUR_FLOOR)) or
                  ANY(F(F'FIRST..CUR_FLOOR)) then
         NEW_FLOOR := HIGHEST(D(D'FIRST..CUR_FLOOR),
                  F(F'FIRST..CUR_FLOOR));
            NEW_STATE := DOWN;
      elsif ANY(U(U'FIRST..CUR_FLOOR)) then
         NEW_FLOOR := LOWEST(U(U'FIRST..CUR_FLOOR),
                  (U'FIRST..CUR_FLOOR => FALSE));
         NEW_STATE := DOWN;
      else
         DESTINATION(UP, CUR_FLOOR,
                  NEW_STATE, NEW_FLOOR);
      end if;
   end if;
end DESTINATION;
```

14.9.6 Extensions to the Elevator Problem: When moving to the home floor, the elevator stops at every floor although it does not open the door. These unnecessary stops causes additional wear and tear on the machinery. Modification of task ELEVATOR_CONTROL to eliminate this characteristic is left for the reader.

From the user's viewpoint, the elevator can be made more sophisticated by adding buttons for *emergency stop*, quick closing of the door and indicator lights at each floor. The home floor for the elevator is the first floor. The algorithm given exploits this information, since the elevator is always instructed to go down if it is not at the home floor and there are no requests. Selecting a floor different from the top or the bottom floors as the home floor will make the algorithm slightly more complicated, since the elevator may have to go up or down to reach its home floor instead of just going down.

Another dimension of complexity can be added to this problem by extending it to handle a bank of elevators. The elevators do not work independently and must be scheduled appropriately by a central scheduler. A possible approach is to define an array of tasks, one for each elevator, and a scheduler task. Each elevator task controls the physical movement of one elevator and communicates with the scheduler to find out where the elevator is to go next.

14.10 Disk Scheduler

The disk scheduler algorithm [HOA74] is similar to the above elevator algorithm, but simpler. Unlike the elevator, requests are only of one kind (to access some part of the disk), and there is more flexibility in handling them. For example, short requests may be given priority over large ones or requests may be accepted in FIFO order.

Prior to doing a disk read/write, a task asks the disk scheduler for permission to access a specific cylinder of the disk. When the request is granted, the task is free to access the disk. On completion, it informs the scheduler that it is done. The scheduler task has the specifications

```
task DISK_SCHEDULER is
    entry REQUEST(CYLINDER);      ——one entry for each cylinder
    entry DONE;
end DISK_SCHEDULER;
```

where the subtype CYLINDER is declared as

```
subtype CYLINDER is INTEGER range 1..MAX_CYLINDER;
```

It is left to the reader to implement the body of the task DISK_SCHEDULER.

Chapter 5: **Exceptions** [11]

1. Introduction

An *exception* is an event that occurs unexpectedly or infrequently, for example, an error or exhaustion of data. Specific examples of exceptions are

1. symbol table overflow,

2. division by zero,

3. bad input caused by a non-numeric character in data that is supposed to be numeric and

4. overheating of a car caused by lack of sufficient coolant.

The ability to respond to exceptions is particularly essential for the reliability of real-time systems. In many cases systems are designed to run forever. Design of such programs requires an ability to handle, without program termination, the exceptions that will occur sooner or later.

Exception handling has been classified into two categories:

1. A normal programming technique used for infrequent events that are not necessarily errors or boundary conditions [GOO75]. The passing of control to an exception handler is like a subprogram call, as is the case with PL/I's ON conditions [IBM70].

2. A programming technique used for handling errors and limiting conditions [BRO76]. Normal program execution is terminated when an exception occurs and execution of an exception handler is initiated. After the exception has been handled, execution is not resumed at or near the point in the program where the exception occurred.

Exception handling in Ada falls into the second category. The occurrence of an exception results in suspension[41] of execution of the *normal* part of a program. Bringing the exception to the attention of the appropriate program statements that must respond to this unusual situation is called *raising* the

---

41. Charles Wetherell, a colleague at Bell Labs, prefers the term *interruption* to *suspension*, the term used by the Ada designers, since it does not suggest any return to the point of error.

exception. These statements, which are specified in an *exception handler*, are then executed to *handle* the exception. Exception handlers are specified at the end of a block, a subprogram, a package or a task. Execution of an exception handler completes execution of the block, subprogram, package and task. After the exception has been handled, execution is not resumed at or near the point where the exception was raised.

If no exception handlers are provided, then execution of the program segment (which may be a block, subprogram, package, or task) in which the exception was raised is abandoned and the responsibility of responding to the exception is transferred to another part of the program. This transferring of responsibility is called *propagating* the exception.

A language does not need to provide a special mechanism for handling exceptions (most programming languages do not), since explicit tests can be used to detect the occurrence of an exception.[42] These tests must be placed at all places in the program where the exception might occur. However, the lack of an exception handling facility in a programming language results in [LEV77, BLA80]

1. *reduced program clarity*: Program clarity suffers, because the processing of all events, both normal computation and exceptions, is intermingled and not identified as different. Consequently, the reader of a program may experience difficulty in distinguishing the normal part of the program from the exception handler.

2. *impracticality*: For some classes of exceptions (e.g., numeric errors and I/O completions) the exception may occur anywhere in the program—in the middle of a statement, for example. For such exceptions it is clearly impractical to test explicitly for their occurrence at all possible points in a program.

3. *inefficient implementation*: Consider a function SEARCH that searches a one-dimensional array A with positive integer subscripts for a value X. SEARCH returns as its result an integer that is the index of X in A if X is present and −1 otherwise. This specification of a search function is reasonable for a language like FORTRAN or C. The result can be used to index A but only after explicitly checking to ensure that it does not have the value −1.

---

42. Even these tests are usually not provided in most programming languages!

Such a search function can be better designed in Ada by using an exception. For example, the range of SEARCH can be specified more precisely to be the domain of the subscripts of A. If X is present in the array, then SEARCH returns the index of X in A; if X is not present, then this is indicated to the calling subprogram by raising an exception. The compiler can now use a more compact representation for the result type of SEARCH, since it does not include the failure value. Explicit subscript checks, when the result of SEARCH is used to index into A, are no longer required, since SEARCH always returns a valid subscript when X is present. When X is not present control transfers to the exception handler. Thus the lack of an exception facility could result in inefficiency.

2. Declaring Exceptions [11.1]

Exceptions are declared using declarations of the form

list of exception names: **exception**;

Some examples of exception declarations are

TEMP_OUTSIDE_LIMITS: **exception**;
FIRE, BREAK_IN: **exception**;
STACK_OVERFLOW, STACK_UNDERFLOW: **exception**;

The identity of the exceptions is established at compile time (instead of run time). This treatment of exception identity is similar to the treatment of procedure and package declarations but different from the treatment of variable declarations in procedures—new new local variables are allocated every time a procedure is called. Consequently, different calls to a subprogram or different instances of a recursive subprogram do not result in new exceptions being declared. Different *instantiations* of generic subprograms and packages, however, do result in different exceptions being defined.

All user-defined exceptions must be raised explicitly when conditions warrant. Ada provides some *predefined exceptions* defined in the package STANDARD (Appendix C of the Ada Reference Manual). These are generally raised automatically by Ada when the conditions stated below are satisfied, but they may also be raised explicitly by the user. The predefined exceptions are

exception	when raised
CONSTRAINT_ERROR	This exception is raised when a range, index, or discriminant constraint is violated. It is also raised when an attempt is made to reference a nonexistent component of an array or a record, or when an access object with the value **null**

	is used to refer to an object.
NUMERIC_ERROR	This exception is raised when the result of a predefined numeric type does not lie within the implemented range of the numeric type, e.g., division by 0, multiplication of two large numbers. (Raising this exception is implementation dependent.)
PROGRAM_ERROR	This exception is raised to indicate a variety of errors not covered by the other predefined exceptions, e.g., when a *select* statement without an *else* part has no open alternatives, the exception PROGRAM_ERROR is raised.
STORAGE_ERROR	This exception is raised during the execution of the storage allocator when all available space for the specified access type has been exhausted.
TASKING_ERROR	Problems during task communication cause this exception to be raised.

3. Raising Exceptions [11.3]

Exceptions are raised explicitly by means of the *raise* statement, which has the form

    raise [exception_name];

Some examples are

    raise TEMP_OUTSIDE_LIMITS;
    raise NUMERIC_ERROR;   −−predefined exception is raised
    raise STACK_OVERFLOW;
    raise;   −−reraise the exception in question

A *raise* statement without an exception name can appear only in an exception handler (if the exception handler is not in a nested subprogram, package or a task). It causes reraising of the exception that caused the exception handler containing the *raise* statement to be activated.

4. Specifying Exception Handlers [11.2]

Exception handlers are specified at the end of a block, a subprogram, package and a task body following the key word **exception**. Each exception handler contains a sequence of one or more statements to handle the associated exceptions. Exception handlers have the form

when exception_choice {| exception_choice} =>
sequence_of_statements

where *exception_choice* is the name of an exception or the keyword **others**.

If the exception choice **others** appears, it must appear by itself in an exception handler and this handler must be the last one specified in the block, subprogram, package or task. The choice **others** stands for all exceptions that may be raised in the block, subprogram, package or task but for which an exception handler has not been explicitly specified. It also represents exceptions that are not visible, that is, those defined, raised and propagated from other parts of a program but for which no handlers were provided.

If an exception is to be reraised in an exception handler associated with the choice **others**, so that the exception is propagated to some other part of the program and the execution of the handler terminated, then the abbreviated *raise* statement

raise;

must be used. Using this form of the *raise* statement is necessary, because the name of the exception activating the handler is not known in the handler—it is anonymous.

When an exception is raised, the remainder of the statements in the block, subprogram, package or task are not executed. Instead execution of the appropriate exception handler, if any, is initiated. If no exception handler is provided for an exception (explicitly or implicitly using the choice **others**), execution of the block, subprogram, package or task is abandoned and the exception is propagated. If an exception cannot be handled in the main program, then the program is terminated.

The exception handler has the same rights and capabilities as the block, subprogram, package or task in which the exception is raised. For example, an exception handler associated with a subprogram has access to the local variables and parameters of the subprogram, and can contain the *return* statement.

Some examples of exception handlers are

```
when NUMERIC_ERROR => return INTEGER'LAST;

when TEMP_OUTSIDE_LIMITS =>
    ——call the appropriate procedures to initiate
    ——IMMEDIATE SHUT DOWN of the reactor
    ——give reason for shut down
      if T < T_MIN then
          PUT("SHUT DOWN => Vessel OVERCOOLING");
      else
          PUT("SHUT DOWN => Vessel OVERHEATING");
      end if;
```

5. Activation of Exception Handlers [11.4]

The specific exception handler activated to take care of an exception depends upon the execution path of the program and not the textual layout of the program—the association of a handler with an exception is dynamic and not static. Suppose no exception handler is provided in a subprogram S for an exception E. Exception E, when raised, will be propagated to the caller of S and handled there instead of being handled in the part of the program containing the declaration of S.

The selection of a handler for an exception also depends upon whether the exception was raised during execution of a statement or during elaboration (processing) of a declaration.

5.1 Exceptions Raised During Statement Execution

If an exception is raised during execution of a statement, then execution of local exception handler, if any, replaces execution of the remainder of the block, subprogram, package or task in which the exception occurs. Otherwise, if no local exception handler has been specified, the exception is propagated to other parts of the program as explained below.

If the exception is raised in

1. a *subprogram*, then execution of the subprogram is abandoned and the exception raised at the point at which the subprogram was called. If the subprogram is a main program then execution of the program is terminated.

2. a *block*, then execution of the block is abandoned and the exception raised immediately following the block in the surrounding program.

3. a *package body*, then elaboration of the package body is abandoned. If the package is a library unit, then execution of the main program is abandoned. Otherwise, the exception is raised in the part of the program containing the package body or its *stub* (stubs are discussed in Chapter 7

on Program Structure and Separate Compilation).

4. a *task*, then the execution of task is completed.

5. the sequence of statements of an *exception handler* (but not in a block nested in the exception handler), then execution of the exception handler is terminated and the new exception propagated, depending upon whether the exception handler was in a block, subprogram, package or task (following these rules).

5.2 An Example

Consider a procedure ROOTS that computes the roots r_1 and r_2 of a quadratic equation; the roots are given by the equations

$$r_1 = \frac{-b+\sqrt{b^2-4ac}}{2a}$$

and

$$r_2 = \frac{-b-\sqrt{b^2-4ac}}{2a}$$

where $a \neq 0$ and $b^2-4ac > 0$.

ROOTS uses function SQRT (defined in Chapter 1) to compute the roots. The exception CONSTRAINT_ERROR is propagated to ROOTS from the function SQRT. CONSTRAINT_ERROR is raised in SQRT when SQRT is called with a negative actual parameter. It is propagated because SQRT does not contain any exception handlers. The exception NUMERIC_ERROR is raised in ROOTS when an attempt is made to divide by zero (this happens when the coefficient *a* is zero) or when multiplication results in a very large number. ROOTS propagates an indication of an abnormal condition by raising the exception ERROR in the caller after having handled any exception raised in it:

```
with TEXT_IO; use TEXT_IO;
        --makes string I/O available and directly visible in ROOTS
with SQRT;
        --make the separately compiled SQRT available inside ROOTS
procedure ROOTS (A, B, C: FLOAT; R1, R2: out FLOAT) is
    TEMP: FLOAT;
    ERROR: exception;
            --to be propagated to the caller of ROOTS if an
            --exception is raised in ROOTS or propagated to ROOTS
begin
    TEMP := SQRT(B * B - 4.0 * A * C);
    R1 := (-B + TEMP ) / (2.0 * A);
    R2 := (-B - TEMP ) / (2.0 * A);
exception
    when NUMERIC_ERROR =>
        PUT("ERROR******* OVERFLOW or DIVIDE BY ZERO");
        raise ERROR;
    when CONSTRAINT_ERROR =>
        PUT("ERROR******* B*B-4*A*C is negative");
        raise ERROR;
end ROOTS;
```

Exception ERROR must be handled by the caller of the subprogram ROOTS by means of an exception handler with the keyword **others**, because the name ERROR is not visible outside ROOTS.

The caller of ROOTS will not be able to determine the cause of the exception, i.e., whether the exception was raised due to a constraint error or a numeric error, since the same exception ERROR is raised at the point of call. This information can be provided to the caller of ROOTS by having ROOTS reraise the exceptions NUMERIC_ERROR or CONSTRAINT_ERROR (instead of raising ERROR) by using the statement

> **raise**;

These exceptions, being predefined, would be visible to the caller of ROOTS.

5.3 Exceptions Raised During Declaration Processing

The occurrence of an exception in the processing of a declarative part, or in the declaration of a subprogram, package or a task, causes the processing to be abandoned. Propagation of the exception depends upon where it was raised. If the exception is raised in a

1. declaration in a *subprogram body*, then the exception is propagated to the part of the program calling the subprogram. If the subprogram is a main program, then execution of the program is terminated.

2. declaration in a *block*, then the exception is propagated to the surrounding program.

3. declaration in a *package body*, then the exception is propagated to the part of the program containing the package. If the package is a library unit then execution of the main program is terminated.

4. declaration in a *task body*, then the exception TASKING_ERROR is propagated to the part of the program that caused activation of the task; the task becomes completed.

5. *subprogram, package or task declaration (i.e., specification)*, then the exception is propagated to the part of the program containing the declaration. If the declaration is that of a library unit, then execution of the main program is terminated.

6. Exceptions and Tasks [11.5]

During a rendezvous or a rendezvous attempt, the following situations cause exceptions to be raised or propagated:

1. *The called task completes before accepting an entry call or is already completed at the time of the call.* Exception TASKING_ERROR is raised in the calling task at the point of the entry call.

2. *The called task becomes abnormal during rendezvous.* Exception TASKING_ERROR is raised in the calling task at the point of the entry call.

3. *An exception raised in the accept statement is not handled locally.* The exception is propagated to the calling task at the point of the entry call and to the part of the program containing the *accept* statement.

Abnormal termination of the calling task does not affect the called task. If the rendezvous has not started then the rendezvous is canceled. Otherwise, the rendezvous is allowed to complete normally.

7. Retrying an Operation Raising an Exception

When an exception occurs, execution cannot be resumed just before, at or just after the point at which the exception is raised. Execution of an appropriate handler replaces the execution of the remainder of the block, subprogram or task in which the exception occurred; if no exception handler has been specified then execution of the block, subprogram or task in which the exception occurred is terminated. However, the statement in which the exception occurred can be re-executed by enclosing the statement in a block with a local exception handler and enclosing the block in a loop.

Sometimes errors (i.e., exceptions) in interacting with input and output devices, such as tape drives, are caused by transient conditions such as those resulting from electrical noise. In these cases it often suffices to retry the unsuccessful operation a few times until it works right. In other situations it may be desirable to retry an operation after the exception handler has rectified some of the conditions that may have caused the exception. For example an operation may result in the exception STORAGE_ERROR, because no more free storage is available. The operation is retried after storage is freed in the exception handler, by explicitly deallocating storage or by calling a garbage collector.

The following program segment [ICH80] illustrates how an attempt is made to read a tape 10 times before giving up, assuming that the tape drive malfunction is not due to transient errors.

```
——in case of errors try again to read the tape
——but give up after 10 attempts

for I in 1..10 loop
   begin
      READ_TAPE(BLOCK);
      exit;
           ——an appropriate use of the exit statement
   exception
      when TAPE_ERROR =>
         if I = 10 then
            raise TAPE_DRIVE_MALFUNCTION;
         else
            BACK_SPACE;    ——back up to beginning of last block
         end if;
   end;
end loop;
```

8. Suppressing Exceptions [11.7]

Normally, exceptions are automatically raised when detected, but the raising of some predefined exceptions may be suppressed by requesting the compiler to not check for certain conditions (e.g., division by zero or uninitialized variables). The pragma SUPPRESS is used to make requests for suppressing checks. The compiler may choose to ignore the request if the suppression of the specified check is impossible or too expensive.

Suppression of checks may lead to a program that will run faster and use less storage, since code for performing the checks need not be inserted into the program. For example, the code to check whether or not array subscripts are legal may be left out if the check INDEX_CHECK is suppressed. *The user must be very careful, especially in critical applications, of the ramifications of suppressing checks.* Checks should be suppressed only after ensuring that the corresponding conditions will not arise during program execution.

The scope of suppressing the checks is the block, the body of the subprogram, the package or the task in whose declarative part the SUPPRESS pragma appears. The SUPPRESS pragma has the form

pragma SUPPRESS(check_name [,[ON =>] name]);

The second parameter is an object or type name for which the check is to be suppressed. If the second parameter is left out then the check specified will be suppressed throughout the unit containing the pragma.

Checks that can be suppressed and the associated exceptions are given in the table below:

Check Suppressed	Exception Affected
ACCESS_CHECK DISCRIMINANT_CHECK INDEX_CHECK LENGTH_CHECK RANGE_CHECK	CONSTRAINT_ERROR
DIVISION_CHECK OVERFLOW_CHECK	NUMERIC_ERROR
ELABORATION_CHECK	PROGRAM_ERROR
STORAGE_CHECK	STORAGE_ERROR

9. Examples

The examples in this section illustrate the handling of exceptions in the context of packages, subprograms and tasks. The first example discusses how package FIFO, declared in Chapter 3 on Packages, can be modified to handle limiting conditions by the use of exceptions. The next example illustrates the differences, with respect to exceptions, between an iterative and a recursive formulation of a program to compute factorials. The next two examples illustrate the use of exceptions in tasks monitoring a nuclear reactor for overheating or overcooling and a house for fires and break-ins. The example on merging two sorted files shows the use of exceptions in file handling, how a program should clean up after handling an exception and how to identify the operation raising a predefined exception. The next example illustrates how subprograms may be written so that they can express their *last wishes* before being terminated, because of the occurrence of an exception. Finally, there is an example from parsing that shows the use of a user-defined exception to abandon execution of the parser when the parser cannot continue in a meaningful way.

9.1 The package FIFO (from the Set of Priority Queues example given in Chapter 3 on Packages)

The problem is to modify the package FIFO used in the *Set of Priority Queues* example so that appropriate exceptions are raised when an attempt is made to add an item to a full queue or to remove an item from an empty queue.

The following changes are made to the package FIFO to handle the limiting conditions:

1. The exceptions FULL and EMPTY are declared in the specification of FIFO.

2. The procedures Q_ADD and Q_FIRST are modified by replacing the *if* statements printing messages that the queue is full or the queue is empty by *if* statements raising the appropriate exceptions. For example, the *if* statement

```
if Q.CUR_SIZE = MAX_SIZE then
    PUT("ERROR: Queue Full");
    NEW_LINE;
    return;
end if;
```

in Q_ADD is replaced by the *if* statement

```
if Q.CUR_SIZE = MAX_SIZE then
    raise FULL;
end if;
```

Of course, it is the responsibility of the user of FIFO (the package PRIORITY_QUEUES in this case) to handle the exceptions FIFO.FULL and FIFO.EMPTY. For example, procedure ADD in the body of the package PRIORITY_QUEUES

```
procedure ADD(P: in PRIORITY; J: in JOB_ID) is
begin
    Q_ADD(P_Q(P), J);
end ADD;
```

is modified to

```
procedure ADD(P: in PRIORITY; J: in JOB_ID) is
begin
   Q_ADD(P_Q(P), J);
exception
   when FULL =>
            --take appropriate actions to handle the case
            --when the queue is full
end ADD;
```

9.2 Factorial

The problem is to write a function that computes the factorial of a number n
($\geqslant 0$). This function must return the largest value of type INTEGER if the
exception NUMERIC_ERROR is raised, because the factorial is too large.

The iterative version FACT_ITER is

```
function FACT_ITER(N: NATURAL) return INTEGER is
   FACT: INTEGER := 1;
begin
   for I in 2..N loop
      FACT := FACT * I;
   end loop;
   return FACT;
exception
   when NUMERIC_ERROR => return INTEGER'LAST;
end FACT_ITER;
```

The recursive version FACT_REC is

```
function FACT_REC(N: NATURAL) return INTEGER is
begin
   if N = 0 then
      return 1;
   else
      return N * FACT_REC(N - 1);
   end if;
exception
   when NUMERIC_ERROR => return INTEGER'LAST;
end FACT_REC;
```

The raising and handling of exceptions in the iterative and recursive versions of
the function to compute the factorial differ in an interesting way. In case of
FACT_ITER, as soon as overflow occurs the exception NUMERIC_ERROR is
raised, execution of the normal part of FACT_ITER is abandoned and
INTEGER'LAST returned via the exception handler.

On the other hand, in case of FACT_REC, the currently active instantiation of FACT_REC is abandoned as soon as overflow occurs with INTEGER'LAST returned to the previous activation. Overflow occurs again causing the exception NUMERIC_ERROR to be raised again. This exception raising cascades to the first activation, which eventually returns INTEGER'LAST as the factorial of N.

The number of times the exception NUMERIC_ERROR is raised in the iterative version is at most one, while in case of the recursive version it can be raised several times.[43]

9.3 Controlling a Nuclear Reactor

The problem is to design a task VESSEL_MONITOR that monitors and controls the temperature of the walls of the pressure vessel of a nuclear reactor. This task is given control of the pressure vessel (i.e., the task is activated) by a startup task, called START_REACTOR, but only after the pressure vessel has reached a steady state and its temperature is near the optimal operating temperature T_OPT.

The temperature of the pressure vessel must be maintained between T_MIN and T_MAX, and as close to T_OPT as possible (T_MIN < T_OPT < T_MAX). *If the pressure vessel temperature goes outside these limits, the reactor must be shut down first and questions asked and answered later.*

The pressure vessel temperature can be increased or decreased by an amount DELTA_T by decreasing or increasing the coolant flow by an amount DELTA_F. Larger changes in the pressure vessel temperature can be obtained by increasing or decreasing the coolant flow by a proportionally larger amount.

A package PRESSURE_VESSEL is available with procedures to control the coolant flow around the pressure vessel, read the latest pressure vessel temperature and so on. It also has the appropriate constant definitions. The specification of PRESSURE_VESSEL is

---

43. Up to N−7 times if 16 bit words are used to implement values of type INTEGER with one bit being reserved for the sign, and up to N−12 times if a 32 bit word is used.

```
package PRESSURE_VESSEL is

    subtype TEMPERATURE is FLOAT;

    DELTA_F: constant := 1000.0;
    DELTA_T: constant TEMPERATURE := 1.0;
        --A unit change in temperature is caused by changing the
        --coolant flow by DELTA_F/DELTA_T. The temperature
        --change is negative or positive depending on whether the
        --coolant flow change is positive or negative

    T_MIN: constant TEMPERATURE := 400.0;
    T_MAX: constant TEMPERATURE := 500.0;
    T_OPT: constant TEMPERATURE := 450.0;

    procedure CHANGE_FLOW(F: in FLOAT);
        --To change the temperature by an amount T the
        --flow should be changed by an amount equal to
        --T * (-DELTA_F/DELTA_T).
        --The - sign indicates that the flow is to be decreased
        --when T is positive and increased when T is negative

    --specifications of other procedures such as START_FLOW
    --and STOP_FLOW to start and stop the coolant flow
    procedure READ_TEMP(T: out TEMPERATURE);

end PRESSURE_VESSEL;
```

Task START_REACTOR takes care of the pressure vessel until it reaches a steady state and then hands over control of the pressure vessel to the task VESSEL_MONITOR. VESSEL_MONITOR is defined abstractly as

```
Wait until START_REACTOR gives the go ahead
loop
    Read the temperature
    if The temperature is not within the limits then
        First initiate reactor shut down by raising the
        exception TEMP_OUTSIDE_LIMITS.
        Follow up by appropriate messages
    end if;
    Adjust coolant flow so as to move the vessel temperature
        toward the optimum temperature
end loop;
```

These two tasks are enclosed in a procedure RUN_REACTOR declared as

```
with PRESSURE_VESSEL, TEXT_IO;
use PRESSURE_VESSEL, TEXT_IO;
procedure RUN_REACTOR is
    pragma PRIORITY(10);
        --highest priority provided by the implementation
        --is given to executing this task
    task START_REACTOR is
      .
      .
    end START_REACTOR;

    task VESSEL_MONITOR is
        entry START;
    end VESSEL_MONITOR;

    task body START_REACTOR is
      .
      .
    begin
      .
      .
        VESSEL_MONITOR.START;
      .
      .
    end START_REACTOR;

        --body of the task VESSEL_MONITOR is placed here
begin
    null;
                --a procedure must have one statement even
                --even if it is the null statement
end RUN_REACTOR;
```

The procedure RUN_REACTOR has been given the highest priority supported by an implementation, because it is of the utmost important that such a critical program be scheduled before all the other programs or tasks. It would be desirable if no other task or program on the system were given this high priority. It would be better if a computer were dedicated to running the program RUN_REACTOR. Of course, if the computer is dedicated to running RUN_REACTOR then the specification of the priority will not make any difference.

The body of the task VESSEL_MONITOR is

```
task body VESSEL_MONITOR is
   T: TEMPERATURE;
   TEMP_OUTSIDE_LIMITS: exception;
   DELTA_FT: constant FLOAT := - DELTA_F/DELTA_T;
         --flow decrease required per unit temperature increase;
         --the flow increase required for a unit
         --temperature decrease is -DELTA_FT
begin
   accept START;
   loop
      READ_TEMP(T);
      if T >= T_MIN and T <= T_MAX then
         CHANGE_FLOW((T_OPT-T) * DELTA_FT);
                     --move temperature toward T_OPT
      else
         raise TEMP_OUTSIDE_LIMITS;
      end if;
   end loop;
exception
   when TEMP_OUTSIDE_LIMITS =>

      --call the appropriate procedures to initiate
      --IMMEDIATE SHUT DOWN of the reactor

      if T < T_MIN then
            --note that any identifier accessible in the
            --main program is accessible here
         PUT("SHUT DOWN => Vessel OVERCOOLING");
      else
         PUT("SHUT DOWN => Vessel OVERHEATING");
      end if;

      --Task terminates after the exception is handled
   end VESSEL_MONITOR;
```

9.4 Home Fire/Energy/Security Monitoring

The use of computers at home is becoming common. One of their uses will be to monitor the state of a house, which includes routine tasks such as keeping track of the energy usage, and being on the alert for exceptional situations like fires and break-ins. The computer will be programmed to respond to exceptional situations.

This example illustrates a task ALARM that is used to monitor fires or break-ins. The presence of a fire or break-in is indicated by interrupts at locations 8#100# and 8#110# by the heat sensors and the movement detectors. The interrupts supply an integer value (of subtype LOCATION) identifying the location in the house where the fire or break-in has been detected. If there are no interrupts, thus indicating that everything is fine, then the task ALARM informs a task STATUS that all is well by calling its entry NO_FIRE_OR_BURGLAR at least once every 5 seconds. The task STATUS may be executing on a computer different from the one running ALARM. In this case, not getting an entry call from ALARM within 5 seconds could imply that the computer running the task ALARM has failed or been tampered with and that these possibilities should be checked.

The specification of the task ALARM is

```
task ALARM is
    entry HEAT_SENSOR(I: in LOCATION);
    entry MOVEMENT_DETECTOR(I: in LOCATION);

    for HEAT_SENSOR use at 8#100#;
    for MOVEMENT_DETECTOR use at 8#110#;
end ALARM;
```

ALARM implements the abstract algorithm

```
loop
    select
        Sound the fire alarm if the temperature of some part
            of the house has exceeded the ignition point
    or
        Sound the burglar alarm if suspicious movement
            has been detected
    else
        Wait for 4.5 seconds and signal all is well
    end select
end loop
```

The body of the task ALARM is

```
      task body ALARM is
        X: LOCATION;
        FIRE, BREAK_IN: exception;
      begin
        loop
          select
            accept HEAT_SENSOR(I: in LOCATION) do
              X := I;
            end HEAT_SENSOR;
            raise FIRE;
          or
            accept MOVEMENT_DETECTOR(I: in LOCATION) do
              X := I;
            end MOVEMENT_DETECTOR;
            raise BREAK_IN;
          or
            delay 4.5;    --Must acknowledge within 5 second intervals
            STATUS.NO_FIRE_OR_BURGLAR;
          end select;
        end loop;
      exception
        when FIRE =>
          --SOUND the FIRE ALARM and call the fire department
          --with the address of the house and the location of fire
        when BREAK_IN =>
          --SOUND the BURGLAR ALARM and call the police with
          --the address of the house and the location of the burglar
      end ALARM;
```

The task ALARM is terminated after it finishes handling the FIRE or BREAK_IN exception. ALARM must be restarted.

9.5 Merging Sorted Files

This example illustrates how subprograms *clean up* after an exception has been raised and how programs can be written to identify the statements that caused a predefined exception to be raised. Also illustrated in this example is the use of files and the exceptions raised by file operations.

The problem is to write a subprogram that merges two non-empty files, sorted in increasing order, to produce another file also sorted in increasing order. The input files have the *external* names A and B while the output file is named C (external names are the system names). Each of the files A and B contains elements of the type STUDENT_DATA. The comparison operation "<" is defined for elements of type STUDENT_DATA and is available in the context of the subprogram MERGE_SORT.

There are quite a few problems in writing MERGE_SORT. For example, occasionally an empty file is mistakenly given as input, which causes the exception END_ERROR to be raised. The underlying hardware (e.g., a tape drive) may malfunction, causing the exception DEVICE_ERROR to be raised. Also, there is some possibility that the files may contain elements of the wrong type (i.e., not STUDENT_DATA), which causes the exception DATA_ERROR to be raised. These exceptions are all raised when trying to read a tape. *When any of these exceptions is raised, prior to abandoning the sort, all the open files must be closed and appropriate error messages printed.*

The algorithm for merging two sorted files A and B to produce a sorted file C can be abstractly described as

```
Name the files P, Q, and R and open them
READ(P, X); READ(Q, Y);
loop
  if X < Y then
     WRITE(R, X);
     if file P is empty then
        WRITE(R, Y);
        Copy rest of Q onto R
        exit;
            ——an appropriate use of the exit statement
     end if;
     READ(P, X);
  else
     WRITE(R, Y);
     if file Q is empty then
        WRITE(R, X);
        Copy rest of P onto R
        exit;
     end if;
     READ(Q, Y);
  end if;
end loop;
```

In procedure MERGE_SORT, an instantiation of the predefined generic package SEQUENTIAL_IO [14.2.3] will be used for reading and writing elements of type STUDENT_DATA. This will allow the declaration of files with elements of type STUDENT_DATA and will also supply the file operations, such as OPEN, CLOSE, READ and END_OF_FILE.

```
with SEQUENTIAL_IO, TEXT_IO;
with STUDENT; use STUDENT;
      --package STUDENT contains type declarations
      --relevant to students such as STUDENT_DATA
      --and appropriate operations
procedure MERGE_SORT(A, B, C: STRING) is
   package STUDENT_DATA_IO is
                  new SEQUENTIAL_IO(STUDENT_DATA);
   use STUDENT_DATA_IO;

   P, Q, R: FILE_TYPE;
             --internal files corresponding to the external
             --files A, B, C

   X, Y: STUDENT_DATA;

begin
   --associate the internal names for the files with the external ones
   --and specify their modes
      OPEN(FILE => P, MODE=IN_FILE, NAME => A);
                  --named notation used
      OPEN(Q, IN_FILE, B); OPEN(R, OUT_FILE, C);
                  --positional notation used for illustration

   READ(P, X); READ(Q, Y);
                  --exception END_ERROR will be raised if
                  --either P or Q is empty to start with

   loop
      if X < Y then
         WRITE(R, X);
         if END_OF_FILE(P) then
            WRITE(R, Y);
            while not END_OF_FILE(Q) loop
               READ(Q, Y);
               WRITE(R, Y);
            end loop;
            exit;
         end if;
         READ(P, X);
      else
         WRITE(R, Y);
         if END_OF_FILE(Q) then
            WRITE(R, X);
```

```
                    while not END_OF_FILE(P) loop
                        READ(P, X);
                        WRITE(R, X);
                    end loop;
                    exit;
                end if;
                READ(Q, Y);
            end if;
        end loop;

    exception
        when END_ERROR =>
            TEXT_IO.PUT("ERROR: One of the files "
                    & A & " or " & B & " was empty");
            CLOSE(P); CLOSE(Q); CLOSE(R);
        when DEVICE_ERROR =>
            TEXT_IO.PUT("ERROR: hardware device with files "
                    & A & " or " & B & " malfunctioning");
            CLOSE(P); CLOSE(Q); CLOSE(R);
        when DATA_ERROR =>
            TEXT_IO.PUT("ERROR: One of the files "
                    & A & " or " & B & " has bad data");
            CLOSE(P); CLOSE(Q); CLOSE(R);
    end MERGE_SORT;
```

The problem with Ada's treatment of exceptions is that it is not easy to pinpoint the statement that causes an exception to be raised. For example, in the above program it cannot be determined which read operation raised the exception, so the bad file or the malfunctioning device cannot be pinpointed.

This problem can be solved by modifying MERGE_SORT as follows:

1. Encapsulate the READ operation in a procedure, say CLEAR_READ which does its own exception handling. Procedure CLEAR_READ is

```
procedure CLEAR_READ(F: in IN_FILE;
                     V: out STUDENT_DATA) is
begin
    READ(F, V);
exception
    when END_ERROR =>
        TEXT_IO.PUT("ERROR: File "
                        & NAME(F) & " was empty");
        raise;
    when DEVICE_ERROR =>
        TEXT_IO.PUT("ERROR: hardware device with file "
                        & NAME(F) & " malfunctioning");
        raise;
    when DATA_ERROR =>
        TEXT_IO.PUT("ERROR: File "
                        & NAME(F) & " has bad data");
        raise;
end CLEAR_READ;
```

An exception in CLEAR_READ is handled by CLEAR_READ itself. Since the name of the file involved in the read operation is known there is no problem in identifying the file (or the device it is on) that caused the exception to be raised. CLEAR_READ raises the exception again for the benefit of MERGE_SORT, which can then close all the files.

2. Replace all calls to READ by calls to CLEAR_READ.

3. Change the *exception* section of MERGE_SORT to contain just the following exception handler.

```
when END_ERROR | DEVICE_ERROR | DATA_ERROR =>
    CLOSE(P); CLOSE(Q); CLOSE(R);
```

This example also illustrated an appropriate use of the *exit* statement. The program could have been written without the *exit* statement,[44] albeit inelegantly, by using one of the alternative formulations:

1. Using a *while* loop along with some additional BOOLEAN variables.

2. Allowing the READ statements in the loop to raise END_ERROR exception and do all the final processing in the corresponding exception

---

44. As an *exit* statement is a restricted form of the *goto* statement, a programmer should justify each use of *exit*.

handler (copying one of the non-empty input files to the output file and closing the files). This would, of course, require explicit checks for empty input files. This solution moves some of the normal computation, i.e., the final processing occurs when the end of one of the two input files has been reached, into the exception handler. Using exception handlers to do the final processing in a program is not good style, because an exception handler is meant processing exceptional situations only.

An elegant and succinct solution, that does not require the use of *exit* statements, can be easily arrived at in a language like Pascal [JEN74] that provides the user with a one element look-ahead for all input files.[45]

while neither file P nor Q is empty **loop**

P and Q are the look-ahead variables associated with files P and Q.
Set H to be the appropriate of P or Q and advance
the file (this advancing is the read but it is done
after examining the variable)

Write H on the output file R

end loop;

Copy the rest of the non-empty file (one of P or Q) to R

9.6 Example Illustrating the Last Wishes of a Subprogram [DOD79b]

Suppose that during execution of a subprogram several exceptions may occur which are not handled locally but are propagated to the caller. Prior to termination, the subprogram should have an opportunity to fulfill its last wishes, such as cleaning up and undoing the unwanted effects caused by its partial execution. This opportunity can be given to the subprogram by incorporating in it an exception handler with the choice **others**. The handler will contain the last wishes of the subprogram followed by the *raise* statement to propagate the exception to the caller of the subprogram.

Assume that the generic package DIRECT_IO has been appropriately instantiated and its entities made directly visible by a *use* clause. Now consider, as an example, the subprogram FILE_PROCESS that is used to process a file in some way:

---

45. This look ahead strategy causes problems when doing interactive input [FEU82].

```
procedure FILE_PROCESS(FILE_NAME: STRING) is
    F: FILE_TYPE;
begin
    Initial actions
    OPEN(F, INOUT_FILE, FILE_NAME);
    Process file
    CLOSE(F);
    Final actions
end FILE_PROCESS;
```

An exception occurring during the processing of the file will cause it to be left in the open state, since execution of the operation FILE_PROCESS will be immediately terminated, with the exception being propagated to the caller of FILE_PROCESS. Before terminating, operation FILE_PROCESS, as its last wish, would like to close the input file. Execution of last wishes can provided by writing FILE_PROCESS as the subprogram SAFE_FILE_PROCESS:

```
procedure SAFE_FILE_PROCESS(FILE_NAME: STRING) is
    F: FILE_TYPE;
begin
    Initial actions
    OPEN(F, INOUT_FILE, FILE_NAME);
    begin
        Process file
    exception
        when others =>
            CLOSE(F);
            raise;
    end;
    CLOSE(F);
    Final actions
end SAFE_FILE_PROCESS;
```

All exceptions that occur during the execution of SAFE_FILE_PROCESS are propagated to its caller. Exceptions that occur during the processing of the file are first handled locally. The local handler closes the file and reraises the exception for the caller.

9.7 An Example from Parsing

In parsing, situations arise when the parser is no longer able to make head or tail of the input program, because of the large number of errors present in the program. In these cases the parser gives up further analysis of the input program and quits. The skeleton of a parsing procedure PARSE shows that the exception CANNOT_RECOVER is raised when there is no point continuing the parse. The exception handler for CANNOT_RECOVER closes the files and prints appropriate messages.

```
procedure PARSE is
    .
    .
    CANNOT_RECOVER: exception;
    .
    .
begin
    .
    .
    if Error then
        if Can recover then
            Recover correcting error in best possible way
        else
            raise CANNOT_RECOVER;
        end if;
    end if;
    .
    .
exception
    .
    .
    when CANNOT_RECOVER =>
        Print messages including one indicating where the parsing
        was abandoned, close all files, ...
    .
    .
end PARSE;
```

Chapter 6: **Generic Facilities** [12]

1. Introduction

Subprograms and packages in Ada can be generic, that is, they can be templates of ordinary subprograms and packages. Generic subprograms and packages are often parameterized and can accept, in addition to normal parameters, types and subprograms as parameters. Generic subprograms and packages constitute the fourth form of a program unit from which programs are composed—the others being subprograms, packages and tasks.

Generic subprograms and packages have two parts—a generic specification and a body. They are specified by means of a generic declaration. A generic declaration consists of a generic part, where the generic formal parameters are declared, followed by the specification of the subprogram or the package. The body of a generic subprogram or a package has the same form as the body of an ordinary subprogram or a package.

Generic subprograms and packages cannot be used directly, since they are templates from which usable subprograms and packages are created. A generic subprogram or a package must first be instantiated (by means of a declaration) for some set of generic actual parameters. The instantiation creates a new subprogram or package, which can then be used just like any other subprogram or package. Many such instantiations can be created.

Generic subprograms and packages simplify some of the tedious aspects of programming. As an example, suppose we have to sort several arrays each with elements of a different type, e.g., reals, enumeration types, integers and characters. Without generic facilities, a sort procedure has to be written for each element type. With generic facilities, one sort procedure can be written to sort all arrays regardless of their element type. The generic sort procedure will have the array element type, the array type and the comparison operator < (defined for the array element type) as its formal parameters. This generic procedure can be instantiated for any element type that has < defined for it.

The advantages of having generic facilities in a programming language include [GEH80, GRI77]

1. *Reduced Programming Effort*: Only one generic subprogram or package need be written for subprograms and packages that are identical except for the types of their formal parameters and associated local variables, and the subprograms used by them.

2. *More Manageable Programs*: Program listings become smaller and less storage is required for the source code, since there will be fewer subprograms and packages. Program correctness proofs also become smaller, but these proofs, unlike those for normal subprograms and packages, must also take into consideration the restrictions and conditions on the generic formal parameters of the generic subprograms or packages being verified.

3. *Abstraction*: Generic subprograms and packages are abstractions of ordinary subprograms and packages. Generic facilities are therefore in accordance with the strategy of developing programs using stepwise refinement. Stepwise refinement encourages the programmer to concentrate on the algorithm without worrying about the details. In this case, the details are the actual types and subprograms used in the generic subprogram or the package body.

4. *Portability Across Types*: Changes to type declarations in a program will not require any changes to the generic subprogram or package, provided the subprograms used in the generic program unit are declared for the modified types. For example, suppose a program uses an instantiation of the generic sort procedure to sort an array with elements of type T. Type T was initially declared to be an integer but is now modified to be a real. As a result of this modification, no change is necessary for the generic subprogram or its instantiation for sorting an array with elements of type T.

2. Generic Specifications and Bodies [12.1-2]

A generic subprogram or package specification has the form

generic
     generic formal parameters
  subprogram or package specification

A generic formal parameter can be an ordinary parameter declaration, a generic type definition, or a generic formal subprogram. Generic subprograms or packages are not required to have any parameters. Some examples of generic declarations are

```
generic
    type ELEM is private;
            −−The generic actual parameter corresponding to ELEM
            −−cannot be a limited private type, since it would not have
            −−the assignment and equality operations. The assignment
            −−operation will be used in sorting
    type VECTOR is array(INTEGER range < >) of ELEM;
    with function ">"(A, B: in ELEM) return BOOLEAN is < >;
            −−the box < > allows for an identical subprogram visible
            −−at the point of instantiation to be used if this generic
            −−actual parameter is not supplied

    procedure INSERTION_SORT_G(A: in out VECTOR);
```

A normal (nongeneric) sort procedure is derived from the generic procedure INSERTION_SORT_G by instantiating it with three generic actual parameters−the element type, the array type and the comparison function ">":

```
    procedure BOOLEAN_SORT is new
                INSERTION_SORT_G(BOOLEAN,
                    BOOLEAN_ARRAY, ">");
```

Another example is the specification of a generic package STACK_G that implements a stack [DOD83]:

```
    generic
        SIZE: POSITIVE;
        type ELEM is private;
    package STACK_G is
        procedure PUSH(E: in ELEM);
        procedure POP(E: out ELEM);
        STACK_OVERFLOW, STACK_UNDERFLOW: exception;
    end STACK_G;
```

STACK_G is instantiated with two generic actual parameters−the size of the desired stack and the type of the stack elements.

The specification of a generic subprogram, unlike for ordinary subprograms, must always be given. For ordinary subprograms, the subprogram body can also act as the specification of the subprogram. As another example, consider the following generic procedure SWAP_G, which is a generic version of procedure SWAP given in Chapter 1. The specification of SWAP_G is

```
    generic
        type ELEM is private;
    procedure SWAP_G(X, Y: in out ELEM);
```

As mentioned before, bodies of generic subprograms and packages are similar
to those of ordinary subprograms and bodies. For example, the body of
SWAP_G is

```
procedure SWAP_G(X, Y: in out ELEM) is
    T: ELEM;    --ELEM is the generic formal parameter type
begin
    T := X;
    X := Y;
    Y := T;
end SWAP_G;
```

2.1 Generic Subprogram Names

Within the body of a generic subprogram, its name can be used in a
subprogram call—a recursive call to the current instantiation of the generic
subprogram.

3. Generic Formal Parameters [12.1.1-3]

Generic formal parameters can be ordinary parameters but their modes are
restricted to **in** or **in out**. The default mode is **in**. A generic formal parameter
with the mode **in** behaves as a constant. On the other hand, a generic formal
parameter with the mode **in out** renames the corresponding generic actual
parameter.

A generic formal parameter type definition can be one of

1. an array type,

2. an access type,

3. a private type definition,

4. any discrete type (denoted ($<>$)),

5. any integer type (denoted **range** $<>$),

6. any floating point type (denoted **digits** $<>$),

7. any fixed point type (denoted **delta** $<>$).

Some examples of generic type declarations are

```
type ELEM is private;
type BUFFER(LENGTH: POSITIVE) is limited private;
type ELEM is (<>);
type VECTOR is array (INTEGER range <>) of ELEM;
```

In Ada, subprograms cannot be passed as ordinary parameters. However, the
same effect can be achieved by using generic facilities and specifying a

subprogram to be a generic formal parameter, as is illustrated by generic function INTEGRATE_G:

> **generic**
>   **type** REAL **is digits** <>;
>   **with function** F(X: **in** REAL) **return** REAL;
>   **procedure** INTEGRATE_G(A, B, EPS: **in** REAL);

A subprogram corresponding to a generic formal subprogram parameter need not be supplied when instantiating a generic subprogram or package provided that

1. the generic formal subprogram declaration is followed by the keyword **is** and the name of a subprogram, in which case this subprogram is used by default, or

2. the generic formal subprogram declaration is followed by the keyword **is** and a *box* (i.e., <>). Then, by default, a subprogram with the same name as the generic formal subprogram is taken from the context in which the generic formal subprogram or package is instantiated. Such a subprogram must exist in the context of the instantiation; otherwise there is an error.

An example of generic formal parameter with a default value is

> **with function** ">"(A, B: **in** ELEM) **return** BOOLEAN **is** <>;

4. Instantiation of Generic Subprograms and Packages [12.3]

Generic subprograms and packages must be instantiated with actual parameters that match the generic formal parameters prior to being used. An instantiation is a declaration of the form

> [**procedure** | **function** | **package**] name **is**
>   **new** generic_name [(generic actual parameter list)] ;

where *name* is the name given to the instantiation and *generic_name* is the name of the generic subprogram or package instantiated. The name associated with the instantiation can be an operator [6.7] if a generic function with one or two formal parameters (the ordinary parameters and not the generic parameters) is being instantiated. The generic actual parameters may be specified using the positional or named notation as in subprogram calls. A generic actual parameter can be an expression, a variable name, a subprogram name, an entry name, a type name or a subtype name.

Some examples of instantiation are

procedure INTEGER_SORT **is new**
        INSERTION_SORT_G(ELEM => INTEGER,
        VECTOR => INTEGER_ARRAY);
           --named parameter notation is used;
           --the comparison operator > for type INTEGER
           --must be present in the context of the instantiation,
           --since it has not been explicitly supplied

procedure MATRIX_SWAP **is new** SWAP_G(MATRIX);
           --positional parameter notation is used

package INTEGER_STACK **is new** STACK_G(100, INTEGER);

Each instantiation of a generic subprogram or package results in a new set of declarations for the instantiation (including exceptions).

5. Generic Packages Without Parameters

Package ORDERED_SET given in Chapter 3 on Packages provided only one ordered set to the user. To circumvent this limitation it was reimplemented as package ORDERED_SET2 with limited private type ORD_SET. More than one ordered set could then be declared by just declaring objects of type ORD_SET. The generic facilities can also be used to create more than one instance of an object being implemented by a package. For example, by declaring ORDERED_SET as a generic package without parameters, ORDERED_SET_G, more than one set can be instantiated:

generic
package ORDERED_SET_G **is**
    --same specifications for N, INSERT, SMALLEST and EMPTY
    --as given in ORDERED_SET
end ORDERED_SET_G;

More than one set is created by simply instantiating ORDERED_SET_G the desired number of times as shown below:

package SET_1 **is new** ORDERED_SET_G;
package SET_2 **is new** ORDERED_SET_G;

The set operations are referred to by qualifying the operations with the name of the instantiated package. For example, the functions named EMPTY associated with the packages SET_1 and SET_2 are referred to as

    SET_1.EMPTY

and

SET_2.EMPTY

Many instances of an object implemented by a package can be declared either by implementing the package as a generic package without parameters or by using limited private types. How do these two approaches differ? Analyzing the differences between these two approaches is left as an exercise for the reader. *Hint*: Analyze the visibility rules and how the operations provided by the two implementations are referenced.

6. Matching Rules for Generic Formal Parameters [12.3.1]

The following rules must be obeyed in matching generic formal parameters with the corresponding actual parameters when instantiating a generic subprogram or package:

1. *Ordinary Parameters*—The type of the generic actual parameter must match the type of the generic formal parameter and satisfy any associated constraints.

2. *Formal Private Types*—A formal private type can be matched by any actual type subject to the following conditions. If the formal private type

   a. is a limited private type then it can be matched by any type including a task type.

   b. is not a limited private type then it can be matched by any actual type for which the assignment, equality and inequality operations are available.

   c. has discriminants then these must match the discriminants of the actual type.

3. *Formal Scalar Types*—A formal scalar type specified as

   a. (<>)   matches any discrete type

   b. **range** <> matches any integer type

   c. **digits** <> matches any floating point type

   d. **delta** <> matches any fixed point type

4. *Formal Array Types*—The actual parameter type must have the same number of indices as the generic formal type. Then, after substituting any generic types in the formal array type by the corresponding actual type, the array types must have the same component and index types (in the same order), and the same constraints. If either the generic formal array type or the corresponding actual parameter is unconstrained then the other must also be unconstrained.

5. *Formal Access Types*—If the object type in the generic formal access type is generic, then it is first replaced by the corresponding actual type. After the substitution has been done, the generic formal access type and the actual access type must have the same object type.

6. *Formal Subprograms*—If there are any generic types in the formal generic subprogram they are first replaced by the corresponding actual types. After the substitution has been performed, the generic formal subprogram and the actual subprogram must be such that the corresponding parameters have the same type, the same mode and the same constraints. If the formal subprogram is a function, then the generic formal and actual result types and the constraints on them must also be the same.

An operator can be passed as a generic actual parameter for a generic formal function subprogram parameter. Similarly, a function can be passed as a generic actual parameter for a generic formal parameter that is an operator.

An entry can be passed as a generic actual parameter for a generic formal procedure subprogram parameter.

7. Examples

The first example is a generic package that can be used to instantiate stacks of any size and element type. This example is followed by a generic sort procedure, which can be used to sort arrays of any element type, such as employee records, provided the comparison operator is defined for the type. Subprograms cannot be passed as ordinary parameters in Ada (as is possible in many languages, e.g., Pascal and Algol 60). The generic facilities can be used to accomplish passing of subprograms as parameters as is illustrated by the generic integration procedure. The next example is a generic package that can be used to create sets with different element types. The last two examples illustrate how the generic facilities can be used to implement classes of operations, such as general array operations and the MAPLIST function of Lisp.

7.1 Stacks

The problem is to implement a generic stack package that can be used to instantiate stacks of different sizes and element types. The specification of such a package, STACK_G, given earlier, is reproduced here:

```
generic
   SIZE: POSITIVE;
   type ELEM is private;
package STACK_G is
   procedure PUSH(E: in ELEM);
   procedure POP(E: out ELEM);
   STACK_OVERFLOW, STACK_UNDERFLOW: exception;
end STACK_G;
```

The body of generic package STACK_G is

```
package body STACK_G is
   SPACE: array(1..SIZE) of ELEM;
         --SIZE and ELEM are the generic formal parameters
   INDEX: INTEGER range 0..SIZE := 0;

   procedure PUSH(E: in ELEM) is
   begin
      if INDEX = SIZE then
         raise STACK_OVERFLOW;
      end if;
      INDEX := INDEX + 1;
      SPACE(INDEX) := E;
   end PUSH;

   procedure POP(E: out ELEM) is
   begin
      if INDEX = 0 then
         raise STACK_UNDERFLOW;
      end if;
      E := SPACE(INDEX);
      INDEX := INDEX - 1;
   end POP;
end STACK_G;
```

Any exceptions raised by calls to PUSH and POP are propagated to the caller. Looking at just the body of STACK_G (and ignoring the comments), it is not possible to say whether STACK_G is the body of an ordinary or generic package.

7.2 Generic Insertion Sort

The insertion sort procedure given in Chapter 1 is now modified to make it generic. The specification of the generic version, INSERTION_SORT_G, is

```
generic
    type ELEM is private;
    type VECTOR is array(INTEGER range <>) of ELEM;
    with function ">"(A, B: in ELEM) return BOOLEAN is <>;
            --if the comparison operator > for elements of type ELEM
            --is not supplied when instantiating then such an operator
            --must be present in the context of the instantiation
procedure INSERTION_SORT_G(A: in out VECTOR);
```

Generic procedure INSERTION_SORT_G can be used to instantiate procedures that sort arrays with integer subscripts only. This restriction can be removed by making the index type of the array to be sorted a generic parameter as shown by the specification of the generic procedure GENERAL_INSERTION_SORT_G:

```
generic
    type ELEM is private;
    type INDEX is (<>);    --any discrete type
    type VECTOR is array(INDEX) of ELEM;
    with function ">"(A, B: in ELEM) return BOOLEAN is <>;
procedure GENERAL_INSERTION_SORT_G(A: in out VECTOR);
```

Although the information supplied by the third generic parameter can be derived from the first two parameters, the treatment of types requires the presence of the third parameter.

The body of INSERTION_SORT_G is

```
procedure INSERTION_SORT_G(A: in out VECTOR) is

    I, J: A'RANGE;
    T: ELEM;
                --type of temporary variable T is the generic
                --formal type ELEM
    L: INTEGER := A'FIRST;
    U: INTEGER := A'LAST;

begin
    I := L;
    while I /= U loop
      T := A(I+1);
      J := I+1;
      while J /= L and then A(J-1) > T loop
        A(J) := A(J-1);
        J := J-1;
      end loop;
      A(J) := T;
      I := I+1;
    end loop;
end INSERTION_SORT_G;
```

Suppose the following declarations are in effect when instantiating INSERTION_SORT_G:

```
type BOOLEAN_ARRAY is array(INTEGER range <>)
                                    of BOOLEAN;

type EMPLOYEE is
  record
    NAME: STRING(1..40);
    ID: INTEGER;
  end RECORD;

type EMPLOYEE_ARRAY is array(INTEGER range <>)
                                    of EMPLOYEE;

function ">"(A, B: in EMPLOYEE) return BOOLEAN is
begin
  return A.ID > B.ID;
end ">";
```

Sorting routines for arrays with elements of type BOOLEAN and EMPLOYEE are instantiated as

```
procedure BOOLEAN_SORT is
    new INSERTION_SORT_G(ELEM => BOOLEAN,
            VECTOR => BOOLEAN_ARRAY, ">" => ">");
        --the generic formal parameter representing the greater
        --than operation has the same name as the generic actual
        --parameter, that is, the symbol >
```

```
procedure EMPLOYEE_SORT is
    new INSERTION_SORT_G(ELEM => EMPLOYEE,
            VECTOR => EMPLOYEE_ARRAY, ">" => ">");
```

If the comparison operator had not been given in the instantiation BOOLEAN_SORT

```
procedure BOOLEAN_SORT is
    new INSERTION_SORT_G(ELEM => BOOLEAN,
            VECTOR => BOOLEAN_ARRAY);
```

then by default a comparison operator from the context of the instantiation would have been used if one existed. Otherwise, the instantiation would have resulted in a compile time error.

In the above instantiation of EMPLOYEE_SORT named parameter notation was used. Positional parameter notation could also have been used. For example,

```
procedure EMPLOYEE_SORT is
    new INSERTION_SORT_G(EMPLOYEE,
            EMPLOYEE_ARRAY, ">");
```

A function with an identifier for its name, instead of an operator symbol, and with two formal parameters can also be supplied as a generic actual parameter for a generic formal parameter that is an operator. For example, function GREATER_THAN, declared as

```
function GREATER_THAN(A, B: EMPLOYEE) return BOOLEAN is
begin
    return A.ID > B.ID;
end GREATER_THAN;
```

is used as the generic actual parameter in the instantiation EMPLOYEE_SORT2

```
procedure EMPLOYEE_SORT2 is
    new INSERTION_SORT_G(EMPLOYEE,
            EMPLOYEE_ARRAY, GREATER_THAN);
```

The types of the formal parameters and result type of the operator ">" in the generic procedure INSERTION_SORT_G must, of course, match those of the function GREATER_THAN.

The generic procedure INSERTION_SORT_G sorts according to the generic operator ">" which normally stands for greater than. If x and y are elements of the array to be sorted and $x > y$ is TRUE then x will appear after y in the sorted array. Thus the array will be sorted in increasing order. Supplying the operator "<" when instantiating INSERTION_SORT_G will produce an instantiation that will sort the array in decreasing order. For example, the instantiation DECREASING_BOOLEAN_SORT will sort the elements of a BOOLEAN array in decreasing order:

> **procedure** DECREASING_BOOLEAN_SORT **is**
>   **new** INSERTION_SORT_G(BOOLEAN,
>   BOOLEAN_ARRAY, "<");

7.3 Integration via the Trapezoidal Rule

Write a generic function INTEGRATE_G that finds the definite integral of a function f: real $\rightarrow$ real between the limits a and b

$$I = \int_{i=a}^{i=b} f(x)$$

using the trapezoidal rule. It should be possible to instantiate the generic function INTEGRATE_G for different functions f.

The trapezoidal rule approximates the integral of a function between the two limits a and b by the area of the trapezoid with base b—a and heights f(a) and f(b).

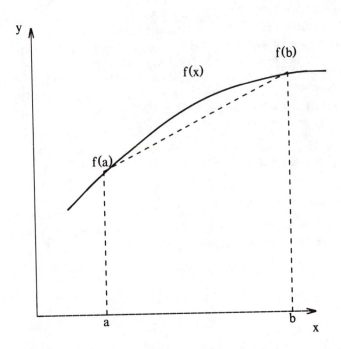

Approximating the integral of function f using one interval

This approximation can be improved by dividing a and b into two equal subintervals, taking the area of the two resulting trapezoids and adding them up. Each of these subintervals can be further divided into two more equal subintervals and the process repeated.

The approximate integral I_n of a function f between the limits a and b using n subintervals

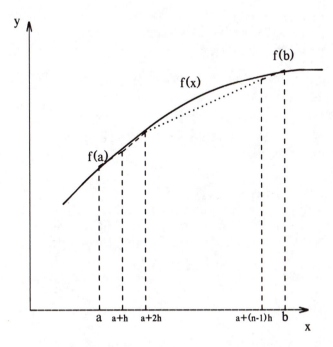

Approximating the integral of function f using on intervals

is given by the equation

$$I_n = h(\frac{f(a)}{2}+f(a+h)+f(a+2h)+ \cdots +f(a+(n-1)h)+\frac{f(b)}{2})$$

where h, the width of the interval, is given by

$$h = \frac{(b-a)}{n}$$

The subdividing process is repeated until two successive approximations of the integral of the function f as calculated by the trapezoidal rule differ in absolute value by less than EPS (EPS > 0), the desired stopping tolerance.

The trapezoidal integration algorithm can be described abstractly as

```
NEW_APPROX := 0;
FINISHED := FALSE;
while not FINISHED loop
    PREVIOUS_APPROX := NEW_APPROX;
    Calculate NEW_APPROX
    FINISHED :=
        abs (NEW_APPROX - PREVIOUS_APPROX) < EPS;
    Divide each subinterval into two equal subintervals
end loop;
```

The specification of generic function INTEGRATE_G implementing the trapezoidal integration algorithm is

```
generic
    type REAL is digits <>;
    with function F(X: in REAL) return REAL;
            --the function F must be supplied when instantiating
function INTEGRATE_G(A, B, EPS: in REAL) return REAL;
```

The body of the generic function INTEGRATE_G is

```
function INTEGRATE_G(A, B, EPS: in REAL) return REAL is
   NEW_APPROX: REAL := 0.0;    --random initial value
   PREVIOUS_APPROX: REAL;
   FINISHED: BOOLEAN := FALSE; --not finished to start with
   N: INTEGER;    --number of intervals
   H: REAL;          --interval size
   SUM: REAL;      --temporary variable
begin
   N := INTEGER(10.0 * (B − A)) + 1;
         --N should be such that the interval size is relatively
         --small; conversion of a real value to an integer
         --involves rounding

   H := (B − A)/REAL(N);     --initial interval size
   while not FINISHED loop
      PREVIOUS_APPROX := NEW_APPROX;
      --calculate NEW_APPROX
      SUM := F(A)/2.0;
      for I in 1..N−1 loop
         SUM := SUM + F(A + REAL(I) * H);
      end loop;
      SUM := SUM + F(B)/2.0;
      NEW_APPROX := SUM * H;
      FINISHED :=
         abs (NEW_APPROX − PREVIOUS_APPROX) < EPS;
      N := N * 2;
                  --number of intervals for next approximation
      H := H / 2.0;
                  --size of interval for next approximation
   end loop;
   return NEW_APPROX;
end INTEGRATE_G;
```

INTEGRATE_G does not work correctly if the first approximation of the integral of F is within EPS of 0.0, the random initial value assigned to NEW_APPROX. This problem can be solved by forcing the computation of at least two approximations or by initializing NEW_APPROX to an approximation of the integral instead of an arbitrary value:

```
NEW_APPROX: REAL := (F(A) + F(B))/2.0;
      --the area under the curve approximated as one big
      --trapezoid, i.e., N=1
```

7.4 Sets

In this example, sets are implemented using a generic package SET_G. Each instantiation of SET_G creates a new set. Operations are provided to add and remove an element, take the union or difference of two sets, determine if a set is empty and get a null (empty set). Type SET is designated as a private type so that sets can be assigned to objects of type SET and be compared for equality or inequality.

The specification of package SET_G is

```
    generic
       type ELEM is (<>);      --any discrete type
    package SET_G is

       type SET is private;

       procedure ADD(S: in out SET; E: in ELEM);
       procedure REMOVE(S: in out SET; E: in ELEM);
       function EMPTY(S: in SET) return BOOLEAN;
       function "+"(X, Y: in SET) return SET;    --set union
       function "-"(X, Y: in SET) return SET;
                   --set difference; returns a set that contains all
                   --the elements of X except those also present in Y
       function NULL_SET return SET;

    private
       type SET_ARRAY is array(ELEM) of BOOLEAN;
       type SET is
          record
             A: SET_ARRAY := (ELEM => FALSE);
          end record;
               --sets will be given the null (empty) set value when
               --created. Only a record type can have a default
               --initial value associated with it; this value applies
               --to all objects of that type. This reason is why
               --the BOOLEAN array A implementing the set has been
               --enclosed in a record. The default initial value can
               --be overridden by an explicit initialization

    end SET_G;
```

The implementation of SET_G is straightforward:

```
package body SET_G is

    procedure ADD(S: in out SET; E: in ELEM) is
    begin
        S.A(E) := TRUE;
    end ADD;

    procedure REMOVE(S: in out SET; E: in ELEM) is
    begin
        S.A(E) := FALSE;
    end REMOVE;

    function EMPTY(S: in SET) return BOOLEAN is
    begin
        for I in ELEM loop
            if S.A(I) then
                return FALSE;
            end if;
        end loop;
        return TRUE;
    end EMPTY;

    function "+"(X, Y: in SET) return SET is
        RESULT: SET;
                --initial value of RESULT is the empty set
    begin
        for I in ELEM loop
            RESULT.A(I) := X.A(I) or Y.A(I);
        end loop;
        return RESULT;
    end "+";

    function "-"(X, Y: in SET) return SET is
        RESULT: SET;
    begin
        for I in ELEM loop
            RESULT.A(I) := X.A(I) and not Y.A(I);
        end loop;
        return RESULT;
    end "-";
```

```
function NULL_SET return SET is
    RESULT: SET;
begin
    return RESULT;    --is null on declaration
end NULL_SET;

end SET_G;
```

Some examples of the use of package SET_G are

```
package INT_SET is new SET_G(SMALL_INT);
package CHAR_SET is new SET_G(CHARACTER);

A, B: INT_SET.SET;
X, Y: CHAR_SET.SET;
```

Implementing sets by using a boolean value for each element to indicate its presence or absence results in fast set operations. However, such an implementation does not make very efficient use of storage, especially if the number of elements in a set at any given time is small compared to the maximum number of possible elements that can be in the set. How can sets be implemented so that storage is used efficiently? Investigation of this problem is left to the reader. *Hint*: Implement the set as a list. Compare this implementation with the boolean array implementation with respect to the execution speed of the operations and the storage used for the set elements. What is the impact of ordering the elements of the list? Is there some other more complicated data structure that results in faster operations than those got by using lists but requires less space than boolean arrays?

7.5 General Operations on Arrays

The generic facilities in Ada can be used to define classes of operations. Examples of these operations are given for one-dimensional and two-dimensional arrays:

7.5.1 One-Dimensional Arrays: This example illustrates that several operations on a one-dimensional array, such as computing the maximum of all the elements and the product of all the elements, can be abstracted and written as one generic function VECTOR_OPERATION. This example also illustrates the versatility and the power of the generic facilities in Ada.

Assuming that VECTOR_OPERATION is instantiated as the function THETA_VECTOR for the operator θ, THETA_VECTOR(A) computes the value

$$a_1 \theta a_2 \theta \cdots \theta a_n$$

where a$_i$ are the elements of the array A.[46]

VECTOR_OPERATION has the specification

```
generic
   type ELEM is private;
   type INDEX is (<>);
               −−all operations of a discrete type are available
   type VECTOR is array(INDEX range <>) of ELEM;
               −−array operations such as indexing and slicing
               −−are available
   with function F(A, B: in ELEM) return ELEM;
   function VECTOR_OPERATION(A: in VECTOR) return ELEM;
```

The body of VECTOR_OPERATION is

```
function VECTOR_OPERATION(A: in VECTOR) return ELEM is
   RESULT: ELEM;    −−A should not be a null array
begin
   RESULT := A(A'FIRST);
   for I in INDEX'SUCC(A'FIRST) .. A'LAST loop
      RESULT := F(RESULT, A(I));
   end loop;
end VECTOR_OPERATION;
```

By instantiating VECTOR_OPERATION with different values of the generic formal parameters, different operations on arrays can be derived. For example,

---

46. VECTOR_OPERATION provides a facility similar to the *reduction* operator in APL.

```
function MAX_FLOAT_VECTOR is
    new VECTOR_OPERATION(ELEM => FLOAT,
        INDEX => INTEGER,
        VECTOR => FLOAT_ARRAY, F => MAX_FLOAT);

function MIN_FLOAT_VECTOR is
    new VECTOR_OPERATION(ELEM => FLOAT,
        INDEX => INTEGER,
        VECTOR => FLOAT_ARRAY, F => MIN_FLOAT);

function SUM_FLOAT_VECTOR is
    new VECTOR_OPERATION(ELEM => FLOAT,
        INDEX => INTEGER,
        VECTOR => FLOAT_ARRAY, F => "+");

function PROD_FLOAT_VECTOR is
    new VECTOR_OPERATION(ELEM => FLOAT,
        INDEX => INTEGER,
        VECTOR => FLOAT_ARRAY, F => "*");

function OR_BOOLEAN_VECTOR is
    new VECTOR_OPERATION(ELEM => BOOLEAN,
        INDEX => INTEGER,
        VECTOR => BOOLEAN_ARRAY, F => "or");

function AND_BOOLEAN_VECTOR is
    new VECTOR_OPERATION(ELEM => BOOLEAN,
        INDEX => INTEGER,
        VECTOR => BOOLEAN_ARRAY, F => "and");
```

FLOAT_ARRAY and BOOLEAN_ARRAY are unconstrained arrays with elements of type FLOAT and BOOLEAN, respectively, and both having indices of type INTEGER. Similar operations can be defined for other unconstrained arrays.

7.5.2 Two-Dimensional Arrays—Generalized Matrix Product: The product of two matrices A (size m × n) and B (size n × p) is given by the matrix C (size m × p) defined as

$$C_{i,j} = \sum_{k=L}^{k=U} A_{i,k} * B_{k,j}$$

$$= A_{i,L} * B_{L,j} + A_{i,L+1} * B_{L+1,j} + \cdots + A_{i,U} * B_{U,j}$$

where L and U are the lower and upper bounds of the second dimension of A and the first dimension of B (U−L+1 = n), respectively.

Procedure MAT_MULT, given in Chapter 1, computed the above product for matrices with floating point elements and indices of type INTEGER only. From this procedure, the element type, the index type, and the operations * and + are abstracted to get a generic procedure that computes the generalized matrix product. Generalized matrix multiplication is implemented by the generic procedure GEN_MATRIX_PRODUCT whose specification is

```
generic
    type ELEM is private;
    type INDEX is (<>);
    type MATRIX is array(INDEX range <>, INDEX range <>)
                                     of ELEM;
    with function "+"(A, B: in ELEM) return ELEM is <>;
    with function "*"(A, B: in ELEM) return ELEM is <>;
procedure GEN_MATRIX_PRODUCT(A, B: in MATRIX;
                                     C: out MATRIX);
```

The body of GEN_MATRIX_PRODUCT is

```
procedure GEN_MATRIX_PRODUCT(A, B: in MATRIX;
                              C: out MATRIX) is
--the array bounds of A, B and C must be appropriate.
--If desired, a check could be prior to computing the
--matrix product

    L: INDEX := A'FIRST(2);    --index of first column of A
begin
    for I in C'RANGE(1) loop
        for J in C'RANGE(2) loop

            --initialize C(I, J) to the product of the first pair of
            --elements; cannot initialize it to 0.0, because ELEM type
            --is generic and the type of the generic actual parameter
            --corresponding to it is not known. For example, it could
            --be INTEGER, REAL or BOOLEAN

            C(I, J) :=  A(I, L) * B(L, J);

            for K in INDEX'SUCC(L) .. A'LAST(2) loop
                C(I, J) := C(I, J) + A(I, K) * B(K, J);
            end loop;

        end loop;
    end loop;
end GEN_MATRIX_PRODUCT;
```

The generic procedure GEN_MATRIX_PRODUCT is now instantiated to produce some interesting operations. All the matrices used in the instantiation must have unconstrained index types. The declarations of the matrix types used are not given, but their declarations are clearly suggested by their names.

```
procedure FLOAT_MATRIX_PROD is
        new GEN_MATRIX_PRODUCT(FLOAT,
                            INTEGER, FLOAT_MATRIX);
        --the operations * and + for floating
        --point will be picked up from the environment

procedure CONNECTED_2 is
        new GEN_MATRIX_PRODUCT(BOOLEAN, INTEGER,
                            BOOLEAN_MATRIX, "or", "and");
        --if the element POINTS(I, J) has the value TRUE
        --when point I is directly connected to J and FALSE
        --otherwise, then the procedure call
        --CONNECTED_2(POINTS, POINTS, RESULT) will
        --update matrix RESULT so that RESULT(I, J)
        --will be TRUE if one can get from I to J
        --directly or via one intermediate point at
        --most (path of length 2).

procedure SHORTEST_DISTANCE_2 is
        new GEN_MATRIX_PRODUCT(FLOAT, INTEGER,
                            FLOAT_MATRIX, MIN, "+");
        --if the element (I, J) of matrix D contains the
        --distance of a point I from a point J then the
        --procedure call SHORTEST_DISTANCE_2(D, D, RESULT)
        --will produce a matrix RESULT such that an element
        --I, J of RESULT will contain the shortest distance
        --from I to J via at most one intermediate point
        --(path of length 2).
```

As an exercise for the reader, the problem of writing a generic function that traverses a tree in some order is suggested. Among other things, it should take a function F as an actual parameter. Instantiations of this generic function with appropriate functions can be used to produce functions to count the number of nodes in a tree, determine the depth of a tree, determine the width of the tree and so on.

7.6 MAPLIST

Suppose that functions on values of type T are to be extended to operate on lists of elements of type T. The extended functions take as actual parameters a value of type LIST, which is a list of elements of type T, and produce a result of type LIST. The generic function used in producing these extended functions is similar to function MAPLIST in Lisp. MAPLIST takes as actual parameters a function F and a list L. It applies the function F to all the elements of the list L, returning a list of the resulting values, i.e.,

$$\text{MAPLIST}(F, L) = (F(L_1), F(L_2), ..., F(L_N))$$

where L is the list $(L_1, L_2, ..., L_N)$.

An ordinary function cannot be written for MAPLIST, because subprograms cannot be passed as parameters in Ada. However, a generic function MAPLIST can be written that must be instantiated for every combination of the function F and the list type L. The difference between the Lisp version and ours is that, in the case of the Lisp MAPLIST, function F need not be known until run time, whereas in our case it must be known at compile time and is specified when instantiating our MAPLIST. This restriction is not really a problem, since functions cannot be manipulated or created at run time in Ada as is possible in Lisp. Moreover, in Lisp all lists are of one type, whereas in Ada lists can be of different types (e.g., those with different element types), as a consequence of which MAPLIST will be have to be instantiated for each type of list to be passed as a parameter.

MAPLIST has the specification

```
generic
     type LIST is private;
     type ELEM is private;

  with function F(E: in ELEM) return ELEM;
          --this is the function that is being extended

     --the following operations for values of the type LIST must
     --be supplied or be available in the context of the instantiation
     --since they are necessary for extending the function F

        with function HEAD(L: in LIST) return ELEM is <>;
                --first element of the list L
        with procedure ADD_LAST(L: in out LIST; X: in ELEM) is <>;
        with function TAIL(L: in LIST) return LIST is <>;
                --the list that is the same as L
                --but minus the first element
        with function EMPTY(L: in LIST) return BOOLEAN is <>;
        with function CREATE return LIST is <>;
                --an empty list
  function MAPLIST(L: in LIST) return LIST;
```

The body of MAPLIST is

```
function MAPLIST(L: in LIST) return LIST is
   A, RESULT: LIST;
begin
   A := L;
   RESULT := CREATE;   --the empty list
   while not EMPTY(A) loop
      ADD_LAST(RESULT, F(HEAD(A)));
      A := TAIL(A);
   end loop;
   return RESULT;
end MAPLIST;
```

The generic function MAPLIST may be instantiated for a list of integers and the function SQUARE as

```
function SQUARE_INTEGER_LIST is
        new MAPLIST(INTEGER_LIST, INTEGER, SQUARE);
```

Of course, the function SQUARE should take an INTEGER parameter and return an INTEGER value, and the appropriate functions for lists of type INTEGER_LIST should be available in the environment of the instantiation, since they have not been explicitly specified.

Chapter 7: **Program Structure and Separate Compilation** [10]

1. Introduction

Large programs are different from small programs, because they are software systems consisting of many components or modules (themselves small programs) and are usually written by different people. A programming language should support both *programming-in-the-small* (as is done by most existing languages such as Pascal and PL/I) and *programming-in-the-large*. Programming-in-the-large is supported by providing facilities for writing modules, information hiding, controlling visibility of objects and specifying dependencies between the modules [DER76].

Ada provides several facilities that support the construction and management of large software projects. It supports both programming-in-the-small and programming-in-the-large. In Ada, for example, program components (such as declarations and bodies of subprograms and packages, and task bodies) can be compiled *separately* and programs can be developed either *bottom up* or *top down*.

1.1 Separate Compilation

The ability to independently compile components of a program is important for constructing large programs and creating libraries of precompiled programs.[47] However, in *independent compilation* no checking is performed to determine whether the program component being compiled is consistent with the program components that have been already compiled. For example, the types of actual parameters in a call to an independently compiled subprogram are not checked to determine whether they match the types of corresponding formal parameters.

The notion of independent compilation was rejected in languages such as Pascal and Algol 68 on the grounds that the lack of type checking during independent compilation would defeat their strong typing mechanisms. Compilation of the whole program, which is safer than independent compilation, was suggested as a better alternative. However, this alternative is not very attractive in terms of cost and time, especially in the development of large programs. The whole

---

47. Independent compilation is one of the reasons for the success of FORTRAN.

255

program must be recompiled whenever any change, however small, is made. Components of programs cannot be compiled on their own, thus preventing the development of a large program by developing its components, compiling them and testing them, and putting them together at the end to get the final program. Another major disadvantage with this approach is that precompiled libraries of routines cannot be provided.[48]

Independent compilation is a practical necessity, but the lack of consistency checking is a serious problem. The solution adopted in Ada, called *separate compilation*, incorporates consistency checking into independent compilation. A record is kept of the properties of every program component that has been compiled. Whenever a new component of a program is compiled, the record is used to ensure that the new component is consistent with the program components that have been compiled previously.

1.2 Compilation and Library Units [10.1]

An Ada program can be compiled in one compilation by submitting all its text together to the compiler or alternatively, in several compilations by compiling its components separately. *Compilation units* are components of programs, preceded by contextual information, that can be compiled separately. Compilation units have the form

> context library_unit | context secondary_unit

where a *library_unit* is a

> subprogram_declaration
> | package_declaration
> | generic_declaration
> | generic_instantiation
> | subprogram_body

a *secondary_unit* is a

> library_unit_body | subunit

and a *library_unit_body* is a

---

48. The lack of a facility to compile components of a program independently or separately is another one of Pascal's weak points. It is a serious impediment to the usability of Pascal and has led to implementations providing their own nonstandard versions of independent compilation.

subprogram_body | package_body

A *subunit* is the body of a subprogram, a package or a task declared in the outermost part of another compilation unit, with a *body stub* given for it there. A body stub specifies that the corresponding body will be compiled later and that the environment present at the body stub will be used in the compilation.

All library units of a program must have unique names (except, of course, the corresponding declarations and bodies of subprograms or packages). Compiling a subprogram or package declaration establishes it as a library unit.

The *context* portion of a compilation unit consists of *with* clauses that specify the library units upon which the program component being compiled depends, that is, the library units used by the program component. These library units are directly visible inside the program component. The context may also contain *use* clauses which make the components of the specified library units directly visible inside the program component.

1.3 Order of Compilation [10.3]

Compilation units can be compiled in any order subject to the following restrictions, which are imposed to allow checking of consistency between the units and code generation:

1. The specification of a subprogram or package must be compiled before its body (the specification of a nongeneric subprogram can be omitted—the subprogram body may act as its own declaration).

2. A compilation unit, C, can be compiled only after all the compilation units (at least their declarations) used by it have been compiled. These compilation units are specified in the *with* clauses in the context portion of C.

3. A subunit cannot be compiled before the compilation unit containing its body stub.

1.4 Recompilation

The whole program does not have to be recompiled when a compilation unit is modified and recompiled. Recompilation of a

1. compilation unit that consists of a declaration requires the recompilation of all the compilation units that use (i.e., depend upon) this compilation unit.

2. compilation unit that consists of a package body or a subprogram body requires recompilation of only the subunits declared within it. Other compilation units that use the modified compilation unit do not have to be recompiled, since they do not depend upon the internals of a package or subprogram body (the internals being hidden from the user).

3.   subunit does not require the recompilation of any other subunit.

2. Program Development [10.1.1, 10.2]

Discovering the structure of a nontrivial problem and then designing the program to reflect this structure is a hard task. Designing programs so that they reflect the problem structure, i.e., *structured programming*, leads to programs that are readable, understandable, provable and modifiable [DAH72]. Most programming languages discourage the accurate recording of this structure by not providing any recording facilities. Ada, however, provides some recording facilities that support the (partial) preservation of this structure. These facilities support both bottom up and top down development of programs.

Bottom up program development is the construction of a program by first building and testing its components. Such an approach is appropriate for making good use of software tools [KER76] and program libraries available at an implementation. The *with* clause supports the construction of a program using components available as *library units*.

Top down program development is the same as program development by stepwise refinement. By providing facilities in a programming language to support stepwise refinement, the language allows the preservation of the some of the structure of the program development process. Ada supports top down programming in a limited way through the use of body stubs. The bodies of subprograms, packages and tasks in the outermost level of a compilation unit may be compiled separately as subunits by giving body stubs for them. Body stubs have the form

>   subprogram_specification **is separate**;
>
> | **package body** identifier **is separate**;
>
> | **task body** identifier **is separate**;

Bodies corresponding to the stubs are compiled as *subunits*, which have the form

>   **separate**(parent_unit_name) body

Each body being compiled in a subunit must be preceded by the name of the *parent* compilation unit *parent_unit_name* in which its body stub was given. If the parent is a subunit itself then the name must include the name of its parent and so on. The name must be given in full as a selected component starting with the first ancestor that is not a subunit.

Everything visible at a body stub is visible in the corresponding subunit along with any additional context that is specified in the subunit.

2.1 Development of Large Programs

Large programs are generally developed by a combination of top down and bottom up development. The top down approach allows the programmer to start with an overview of the problem while the bottom up approach allows the programmer to try and use the tools (programs) already available in libraries on the system. Also, programs are often developed using primarily a top down approach, but with code written and tested using a bottom up approach.

3. Examples

Two example programs are given—one illustrating facilities in Ada that support the bottom up program development and the other illustrating facilities supporting top down development. Throughout the book, examples have been developed using top down program development but the program development structure is not explicitly reflected by the final versions of the programs. In the second example given here, some of the development structure is recorded in the final version of the program, using the facilities provided by Ada.

The first program computes some statistics about a list of numbers. This program makes use of several programs that were developed earlier. The second program is a package that keeps track of planes in a radar surveillance system. Several body stubs are given in the package and the corresponding bodies are developed later. This program also illustrates dynamic task creation (using access types), unchecked storage deallocation, mutual exclusion, and the interaction between exceptions and tasks.

3.1 Bottom Up Program Development

As an illustration of the bottom up approach, a program that reads in a list of at most 500 integers and computes their mean, median and mode (the most frequently occurring value) is developed.

The generic subprograms INSERTION_SORT_G, VECTOR_OPERATION are available as library units (see sections 7.2 and 7.5.1 of Chapter 6 on Generic Facilities) along with a generic version of subprogram MODE, whose specification is

```
generic
    type ELEM is private;
    type VECTOR is array(INTEGER range < >) of ELEM;
    procedure MODE_G(A: VECTOR; MV: ELEM; MF: out INTEGER);
```

Procedure STATISTICS, which computes the required statistics and does its own input and output, uses instantiations of these generic procedures:

```
with INSERTION_SORT_G, VECTOR_OPERATION, MODE_G;
with TEXT_IO; use TEXT_IO;
procedure STATISTICS is
    package IO_INTEGER is new INTEGER_IO(NUM =>INTEGER);
    use IO_INTEGER;

    type INT_ARRAY is array(INTEGER range <>) of INTEGER;
    A: INT_ARRAY(1..500);
    MV, MF: INTEGER;    --mode value and frequency
    N: INTEGER := 0;        --number of values read in

    procedure SORT is
            new INSERTION_SORT_G(ELEM => INTEGER,
                    VECTOR => INT_ARRAY);
    function SUM is
            new VECTOR_OPERATION(ELEM => INTEGER,
                    INDEX => INTEGER,
                    VECTOR => INT_ARRAY, F => "+");
    procedure MODE is
            new MODE_G(ELEM => INTEGER,
                    VECTOR => INT_ARRAY);

begin
    --read in the values
    while not END_OF_FILE(STANDARD_INPUT) loop
        N := N + 1;
        GET(A(N));
    end loop;

    if N /= 0 then
        SORT(A(1..N));
                --note that in a slice, copies of the array elements
                --are not made; it is the array elements that are
                --passed as parameters; only the elements of A in
                --the slice A(1..N) will be sorted.

        PUT("Number of values read = "); PUT(N); NEW_LINE;
        PUT("Mean is "); PUT(SUM(A(1..N))/N); NEW_LINE;
        PUT("Median is "); PUT(A((N+1)/2)); NEW_LINE;

        MODE(A(1..N), MF, MV);

        PUT("Mode value and frequency are ");
        PUT(MV); PUT(" "); PUT(MF);
```

```
    else
        PUT("No Data => No Results");
    end if;
    NEW_LINE;
end STATISTICS;
```

3.2 Top Down Program Development

The problem is to write a package PLANE_TRACKER which is part of a complex real-time radar surveillance system that keeps track of plane positions.[49] This package should be able to handle up to 512 planes at a time. Subprograms are to be provided so that plane positions and velocity (three-dimensional vector of speed with direction) can be updated and queried. More than one task, from the rest of the radar surveillance system, will interact with this package. While waiting for external updates of plane positions and their velocities, the package should update the position of each plane on its own using the plane's old coordinates and velocity.

Every time a new plane is detected by radar the package PLANE_TRACKER is instructed to initiate tracking of the plane. Package PLANE_TRACKER is also informed when a plane is no longer detectable by radar, so that the tracking of the plane may be discontinued. PLANE_TRACKER should tell its users by means of exceptions when it cannot handle any more planes or when a plane is referenced that it is not tracking.

3.2.1 The Solution: The top down program construction facilities provided by Ada are used in developing this program. In addition to separate compilation, the program illustrates, dynamic task creation, storage deallocation, serializing concurrent executions of an operation to make them mutually exclusive, and raising and propagation of exceptions during task communication.

Although more than one task can try to query a plane position simultaneously, the solution presented allows only one task to do this at a time. The primary task communication facility in Ada is the rendezvous mechanism, which allows only one pair of tasks, at a time, to communicate with each other. To allow concurrent queries of the plane position, from several tasks, the data associated with a plane, instead of being part of the task tracking the plane, can be kept outside it, with the task acting as a manager, giving permission to tasks desiring to access this data and keeping track of the tasks accessing the data. More than one task can now be given permission to query this data. Of course, only one task at a time will be allowed to update the data.

---

49. This problem is adapted from DOD79b.

Every time a new plane is to be tracked, a new task is dynamically allocated and initialized with the observed coordinates and velocity. Storage to track 512 planes simultaneously is reserved (i.e., enough to allocate one tracking task for each plane). Requests to track more than 512 planes result in the exception STORAGE_ERROR being raised. This exception is handled within package PLANE_TRACKER and the exception TOO_MANY_PLANES raised and propagated to the user.

Queries and updates of a plane's position are directed to the task tracking the plane in question. At intervals of approximately one second, this task, on its own, updates the location of the plane based on its old location, its velocity and elapsed time. The tracking task is terminated when tracking the plane is no longer necessary. Exception TASKING_ERROR is raised when an attempt is made to query or update information of a plane that is no longer being tracked or on a plane that was never tracked. This exception is handled within package PLANE_TRACKER and the exception ILLEGAL_PLANE is propagated to the user.

An external identification for each plane being tracked is provided to the users. The access value indicating the storage area where the task is allocated is used as the internal identification of the plane. This value is not used as the external identification, because of the following problem. Suppose it is no longer necessary to track plane A and the task tracking it is deallocated. The storage freed may now be allocated to a new task assigned to track a new plane B. References to plane A, which are now illegal, now become references to plane B, and this cannot be checked. To avoid this problem, external names or external identification values are chosen from a large set of values such that the values are repeated only after long intervals. This solution allows the detection of illegal references. The mapping between the external and internal names will be provided by package ACTIVE_PLANES (which also provides the external names).

The specification of PLANE_TRACKER is submitted as a compilation unit to the Ada compiler, so that other parts of the radar surveillance program can be compiled without the body of PLANE_TRACKER. The specification of PLANE_TRACKER is

```
with CALENDAR;
package PLANE_TRACKER is

    type MILES is new FLOAT;

    type PLANE_INFO is
        record
            X, Y, Z: MILES;
            VX, VY, VZ: MILES;
                --velocity also has type MILES for convenience; really
                --it should be some type MILES_PER_HOUR
            T: CALENDAR.TIME;
        end record;

    type PLANE_ID is limited private;

    procedure CREATE_PLANE(I: PLANE_INFO;
                              ID: out PLANE_ID);
    procedure REMOVE_PLANE(ID: in out PLANE_ID);
    procedure UPDATE_PLANE(ID: PLANE_ID; I: PLANE_INFO);
    function READ_PLANE(ID: PLANE_ID) return PLANE_INFO;
        --read the latest position of the plane ID

    ILLEGAL_PLANE, TOO_MANY_PLANES: exception;
        --ILLEGAL_PLANE is raised when a reference is made to a
        --plane that never existed or is no longer being tracked;
        --TOO_MANY_PLANES is raised when a request is made to
        --handle the 513th plane

private

    type PLANE_ID is new INTEGER;

end PLANE_TRACKER;
```

The body of PLANE_TRACKER is compiled by itself. Several body stubs are used in it to specify the subunits that will be submitted for compilation later on. The body of PLANE_TRACKER is

```ada
with UNCHECKED_DEALLOCATION;
    --to deallocate storage occupied by the tasks that are no
    --longer needed and have terminated
package body PLANE_TRACKER is

    MAX_PLANES : constant := 512;
            --maximum number of planes at any instant

    task type TRACKER is
      --each instance keeps track of one plane
      entry INITIALIZE(I: PLANE_INFO);
      entry DIE;
      entry UPDATE(I: PLANE_INFO);
      entry READ(I: out PLANE_INFO);
    end TRACKER;

    type PLANE is access TRACKER;

    package ACTIVE_PLANES is
            --Keep track of all the active planes and provides
            --a mapping between the internal and external names
            --i.e., between PLANE and PLANE_ID.
            --Planes are added and removed one at a time.
            --Mutual exclusion is obtained by using tasks
    procedure ADD(P: PLANE; ID: out PLANE_ID);
            --Add a plane to the set of active planes.
            --Only MAX_PLANES planes can be handled.
            --Returns an external id for the plane (values
            --will repeat very infrequently)

        procedure DELETE(ID: PLANE_ID);
        function INTERNAL_NAME(ID: PLANE_ID) return PLANE;
          --raises exception ILLEGAL_PLANE when ID does
          --not correspond to an active plane
    end ACTIVE_PLANES;

    use ACTIVE_PLANES;
    for PLANE'STORAGE'SIZE
            use MAX_PLANES*TRACKER'STORAGE_SIZE;
            --reserve space for MAX_PLANES; this reservation
            --of space is discussed in the next chapter


    task body TRACKER is separate;
```

```
package body ACTIVE_PLANES is separate;
procedure CREATE_PLANE(I: PLANE_INFO; ID: out PLANE_ID)
                                                is separate;
procedure REMOVE_PLANE(ID: in out PLANE_ID) is separate;


procedure UPDATE_PLANE(ID: PLANE_ID; I: PLANE_INFO) is
begin
    INTERNAL_NAME(ID).UPDATE(I);
exception
    when TASKING_ERROR => raise ILLEGAL_PLANE;
end UPDATE_PLANE;

function READ_PLANE(ID: PLANE_ID) return PLANE_INFO is
    I: PLANE_INFO;
begin
    INTERNAL_NAME(ID).READ(I);
    return I;
exception
    when TASKING_ERROR => raise ILLEGAL_PLANE;
end READ_PLANE;


end PLANE_TRACKER;
```

The procedure initiating the tracking of a plane, CREATE_PLANE, is now compiled separately as

```
separate(PLANE_TRACKER)
            --makes available the environment present at
            --the body stub for CREATE_PLANE
procedure CREATE_PLANE(I: PLANE_INFO;
                            ID: out PLANE_ID) is
    P: PLANE;
begin
    P := new TRACKER;
    ADD(P, ID);
            --add plane P to the set of active planes and
            --return its external ID
    P.INITIALIZE(I);
exception
    when TASKING_ERROR => raise ILLEGAL_PLANE;
    when STORAGE_ERROR => raise TOO_MANY_PLANES;
end CREATE_PLANE;
```

A problem occurs if execution of the allocation operation is not mutually exclusive [BRI73] (Ada does not say anything about this), since multiple tasks calling CREATE_PLANE and executing *new* at the same time may end up with identical values for supposedly different dynamic objects. The solution is to force the allocation of the new tracking tasks to be done in a sequential manner. Sequential allocation is accomplished by putting the task allocation in a task ALLOCATOR with allocation requested by an entry call. Multiple entry calls are queued and accepted serially, one at a time. Two modifications are made to the package PLANE_TRACKER:

1. Task ALLOCATOR is declared in the body of PLANE_TRACKER:

```
task ALLOCATOR is
    entry NEW_PLANE(P: out PLANE);
end ALLOCATOR;

task body ALLOCATOR is
begin
    loop
        begin     --begin a block
            accept NEW_PLANE(P: out PLANE) do
                P := new TRACKER;
            end NEW_PLANE;
                --only one entry call is accepted at a time thus
                --effectively making the allocate operation atomic
        exception
            when STORAGE_ERROR => null;
        end;
    end loop;
end ALLOCATOR;
```

Note that the *accept* statement has been put in a block. When an exception occurs in an *accept* statement it is also propagated to the rendezvousing task. If the exception were not handled locally in the block, the task would terminate as a result of the exception is being raised. ALLOCATOR should, of course, not terminate when a request is made to handle the 513th plane.

2. The call to the allocator in CREATE_PLANE is replaced by the entry call[50]

---

50. During the ANSI standardization process, one modification proposed for Ada would have required the propagation of TASKING_ERROR to the calling task, instead of the exception actually raised, if an exception occurred during rendezvous. This modification was eventually *not* incorporated into Ada.

```
        ALLOCATOR.NEW_PLANE(P);
```

The procedure to end tracking a plane, REMOVE_PLANE, is compiled as

```
separate(PLANE_TRACKER)
procedure REMOVE_PLANE(ID: in out PLANE_ID) is
   procedure FREE is
            new UNCHECKED_DEALLOCATION(TRACKER, PLANE);
   P: PLANE;
begin
   P := INTERNAL_NAME(ID);
   P.DIE;
   DELETE(ID);
            --delete plane from the set of active planes
   FREE(P);
            --deallocate the task after plane is deleted
exception
   when TASKING_ERROR => raise ILLEGAL_PLANE;
end REMOVE_PLANE;
```

The body of task type TRACKER, which was represented by a body stub in the compilation unit PLANE_TRACKER, is now submitted to the compiler. It contains the body stub of procedure UPDATE_POSITION:

Had Ada been modified as suggested above, ALLOCATOR would have had to be called differently. Incorporation of this modification would result in exception TASKING_ERROR being propagated to the calling task, instead of the exception STORAGE_ERROR. This change would require that TASKING_ERROR be handled locally, right at the entry call, so that it could be determined when a call to ALLOCATOR results in TASKING_ERROR being propagated back. Exception TOO_MANY_PLANES would then be raised and propagated to the task requesting tracking of a new plane. Raising exception TOO_MANY_PLANES in the calling task can be accomplished by surrounding the call to the entry NEW_PLANE in a block:

```
begin
   ALLOCATOR.NEW_PLANE(P);
exception
   when TASKING_ERROR => raise TOO_MANY_PLANES;
end;
```

```
separate(PLANE_TRACKER)
task body TRACKER is
  DATA: PLANE_INFO;
  procedure UPDATE_POSITION is separate;
          --update the coordinates of the plane position
          --based on its velocity, old coordinates and time
          --elapsed since the last update
begin
  accept INITIALIZE(I: PLANE_INFO) do
    DATA := I;
  end INITIALIZE;
  loop
    select
      accept DIE; exit;
    or when DIE'COUNT = 0 =>
        accept UPDATE(I: PLANE_INFO) do
          DATA := I;
        end UPDATE;
    or when DIE'COUNT = 0 and UPDATE'COUNT = 0 =>
        accept READ(I: out PLANE_INFO) do
          I := DATA;
        end READ;
    or delay 1.0;
        UPDATE_POSITION;
    end select;
  end loop;
end TRACKER;
```

The body of procedure UPDATE_POSITION is now given:

```
  use CALENDAR;
  separate(PLANE_TRACKER.TRACKER)
        --selected component notation used to specify the
        --unit containing the body stub
  procedure UPDATE_POSITION is
     NEW_TIME: TIME := CLOCK;
     DELTA_TIME: DURATION := NEW_TIME - DATA.T;
     -- * is defined to multiply velocity and time to give distance
        function "*"(DT: DURATION; V: MILES) return MILES is
        begin
           return MILES(DT) * V;
        end "*";
  begin
     DATA.X := DATA.X + DELTA_TIME * DATA.VX;
     DATA.Y := DATA.Y + DELTA_TIME * DATA.VY;
     DATA.Z := DATA.Z + DELTA_TIME * DATA.VZ;
     DATA.T := NEW_TIME;
  end UPDATE_POSITION;
```

The implementation of ACTIVE_PLANES is left to the reader.

Chapter 8: **Representation Clauses and** [13] **Implementation Dependent Features**

1. Introduction

The primary benefit of using a suitable high level language lies in the possibility of defining abstract algorithms in a precise manner that is reasonably independent of the underlying machine characteristics [WIR77a] and independent of the representation of the data types used by an implementation. However, access to the characteristics of the underlying machine and the data type representations used is essential for writing systems programs such as device drivers, process control systems, interrupt handlers, storage allocators and other programs where efficiency is critical, i.e., where every available bit of storage and execution cycle must be used effectively. For example, in a typewriter keyboard driver program, it is necessary to access the keyboard hardware buffer and associate actions with its interrupt vector.

Consequently, a systems programming language should have facilities for dealing with objects at two levels:

1. The abstract level, where only the logical properties are important.

2. The physical level, which is concerned with the details of the machine and the representation.

Facilities for operating at these two levels should be kept separate and be clearly identifiable, because otherwise

1. programs will be harder to understand, since the logical properties of programs will be intermingled with the physical details.

2. changes in data type representations will require modifications to much of the program, instead of just small and isolated portions.

3. it will be hard to move programs from one machine to another, since the physical details, which need to be modified, will not be clearly discernible or separate from the rest of the program.

4. access to the physical level, which is both low level and dangerous, will probably violate the discipline being enforced by the high level language, such as strong typing, to provide error checking. Consequently, it is imperative that facilities allowing access to the physical level be kept separate from the rest of the program and a warning sign be posted.

Ada provides facilities for specifying the logical and physical properties of objects, and these have been kept separate and distinct from each other. The logical properties of objects in a program are specified by their declarations. The program relies on these properties to accomplish its objective. The physical details of these objects and interface of the program with the external environment may be specified explicitly by the programmer using the separate facilities provided especially for this purpose. If the physical details are not specified explicitly by the user then appropriate physical details are supplied by the Ada compiler. Ada allows the specification of physical details such as data type representations, interface with hardware interrupts, machine code insertion, allocation of objects at specific addresses in memory, deallocation of storage and breach of strong typing—all necessary for systems programming.

Most of these facilities should be used only when necessary and with the utmost caution, especially by the novice programmer, since their usage subverts the error checking built into the language.

Ada's facilities for interfacing with the hardware are called *representation clauses* of which there are two kinds—*type representation* clauses and *address* clauses.

2. Type Representation Clauses [13.1-13.4]

Data type representations will normally be selected by the compiler, since in most cases the programmer will be content with the default data type implementations. In the infrequent cases when the programmer is not satisfied with the data type representations selected by the compiler, the programmer has the following options:

1. The programmer can guide the compiler in selecting an appropriate representation by using predefined pragmas. For example, the pragma PACK can be used to indicate to the compiler that storage used in implementing the specified record or array type should be kept to a minimum.

2. The programmer can use a *type representation clause* to specify the actual mapping between a data type and features of the underlying machine by specifying the representation to be used, e.g., the amount of storage to be used, the internal representation of an enumeration type and the layout of a record type.

These pragmas and the representation clauses may be given in a declarative part or in the specification of a task or package. However, the pragmas must precede the representation clauses.

There are three kinds of type representation clauses—*length*, *enumeration representation* and *record representation*.

2.1 Length Clause [13.2]

The amount of storage to be associated with an entity is specified by means of a length clause. It has the form

    for attribute **use** amount;

where *amount* is an integer expression specifying the maximum amount of storage to be associated with the entity specified in the *attribute*. The term *storage unit* will be used to refer to the basic unit of storage allocation for the Ada implementation, e.g, byte or word. The attributes that can be specified are

Object Size	The *size* attribute of a type T (T'SIZE) is used to specify the maximum amount of storage (in bits) to be allocated for objects of type T. The number of bits specified should not be less than the minimum number of bits required to implement an object of type T. If a length clause is not specified, the compiler may allocate some convenient amount of storage. For example, objects of an integer type having the values from 0 to 3 may be allocated one whole byte or one whole word of storage so that the objects can be manipulated easily even though two bits would be sufficient.
Collection Size	The *collection size* attribute of an access type T (T'STORAGE_SIZE) is used to specify the total amount of storage (in storage units) to be reserved for the collection of objects associated with access type T. This attribute allows a programmer to put an upper bound on the number of objects designated by the access type T that can be created (or are allocated at any instant; this assumes that storage occupied by discarded objects is automatically reclaimed by the system or has been explicitly freed by the programmer).
Task Storage	The maximum amount of storage (in storage units) to be allocated for the activation of a task T or for activation of tasks of type T is specified by means of the *task storage* attribute (T'STORAGE_SIZE). The storage specified is the storage that will be used for the data area of T and not for the code generated for T.

Small

Specification of the maximum storage that a task can use prevents the task from using more than its share of storage.

The value of *small* that is to be used for implementing a fixed point type T is specified by using the attribute T'SMALL.

Exception STORAGE_ERROR may be raised if the space reserved by a length clause is exceeded.

2.2 Enumeration Representation Clause [13.3]

The internal representation used for an enumeration type can be specified by giving the internal codes (which must be integers) for the literals of the enumeration type. Such a specification may be necessary when interfacing with external files and devices. As an example, consider a program that uses the enumeration type DAY declared as

type DAY **is** (MON, TUE, WED, THU, FRI, SAT, SUN);

Values of type DAY are to be read in from a external binary file,[51] on which these values are represented by the integers 1 to 7 on the file. These integer values may not correspond to the internal representation used for DAY by an Ada compiler. For example, the internal representation used by an Ada compiler for type DAY may be the integers 0 to 6. This problem is easily solved by instructing the compiler that the integer values 1 to 7 are to be used for DAY. The compiler is instructed as follows:

for DAY **use** (MON => 1, TUE => 2, WED => 3,
             THU => 4, FRI => 5, SAT => 6, SUN => 7);

Another example is a program that generates object code for some computer [DOD79b] and in which the operation codes are defined to be values of enumeration type OP_CODE, which is declared as

type OP_CODE **is** (ADD, SUB, MUL, DIV, MOVE, JMP);

---

51. Values on a binary file are the internal representations of the values of the objects written to the file. All files, except text files, are binary files. This form of a file is more efficient for input and output when compared to text files, since the values on these files being internal representations of the objects, obviate the conversion that would have been required to output these values in a human readable form. A similar conversion is also avoided when reading these values.

It is necessary to map the symbolic operation codes represented by the enumeration literals into the actual operation codes of the computer. The actual operation codes corresponding to the operations ADD, SUB, MUL, DIV, MOVE and JMP for the computer in question are 1, 2, 5, 6, 10 and 12 respectively. The desired mapping is specified by the following representation of the enumeration type OP_CODE:

   for OP_CODE **use** (ADD => 1, SUB => 2, MUL => 5,
                         DIV => 6, MOVE => 10, JMP => 12);

The internal representation of an enumeration type does not have to consist of contiguous values.

2.3 Record Representation Clause [13.4]

The alignment of a record, and the order, position and size of its components can be specified by means of the *record representation clause*. The allocation of each record can be forced to a starting address that is a multiple of a specified value by using the *alignment clause*. The location of each record component is specified as an offset from the beginning of the first storage unit (numbered zero) allocated to the record. The ordering of the bits, i.e., left to right or right to left, is machine dependent. The number of bits occupied by a component is specified by identifying the first and last bits. The number of bits in a storage unit of a machine is given by the implementation dependent constant SYSTEM.STORAGE_UNIT.

As an example, consider the representation of program status words in an IBM 360-like computer [DOD83]. The program status word occupies two words (each word consists of four bytes) and is used to keep the status of the program with which it is associated. The program status word must be allocated at a double word boundary (i.e., starting at an even word address).

Objects representing program status words are declared to have type PROGRAM_STATUS_WORD, which is declared below, along with some related declarations:

   WORD: **constant** := 4;   −−4 bytes per word

   type STATE **is** (A, M, W, P);
   type MODE **is** (FIX, DEC, EXP, SIGNIF);
   type BYTE_MASK **is array**(0..7) **of** BOOLEAN;
   type STATE_MASK **is array**(STATE) **of** BOOLEAN;
   type MODE_MASK **is array**(MODE) **of** BOOLEAN;

```
type PROGRAM_STATUS_WORD is
  record
      SYSTEM_MASK: BYTE_MASK;
      PROTECTION_KEY: INTEGER range 0..3;
      MACHINE_STATE: STATE_MASK;
      INTERRUPT_CAUSE: INTERRUPTION_CODE;
      ILC: INTEGER range 0..3;
      CC: INTEGER range 0..3;
      PROGRAM_MASK: MODE_MASK;
      INST_ADDRESS: ADDRESS;
  end record;
```

Objects of type PROGRAM_STATUS_WORD are mapped to the underlying machine according to the following record representation and length clauses:

```
for PROGRAM_STATUS_WORD use
  record at mod 8;    ——align at even (8 byte) addresses
      SYSTEM_MASK at 0*WORD range 0..7;
                      ——allocate the first 8 bits of the first word
                      ——for the component SYSTEM_MASK
              ——bits 8 and 9 not used
      PROTECTION_KEY at 0*WORD range 10..11;
      MACHINE_STATE at 0*WORD range 12..15;
      INTERRUPT_CAUSE at 0*WORD range 16..31;
      ILC at 1*WORD range 0..1;
                      ——allocate the first 2 bits of the second word
                      ——for the component ILC
      CC at 1*WORD range 2..3;
      PROGRAM_MASK at 1*WORD range 4..7;
      INST_ADDRESS at 1*WORD range 8..31;
  end record;


for PROGRAM_STATUS_WORD'SIZE use 2 * SYSTEM.STORAGE_U
      ——allocate exactly two words for each program status word
```

3. Address Clause [13.5]

An *address clause* is used to

1. specify the starting address of an object in memory. With this mechanism, program objects can be associated with hardware objects such as device registers and hardware buffers.

2. specify that a subprogram, package or task is to be allocated starting at a specific memory location. Address specification is useful, since some machines and operating systems require that certain programs must be

allocated in specific parts of the memory. For example, if code is being generated for a machine with no memory management, then the locations where the code is to placed in the physical memory must be indicated to the compiler.

3. associate a hardware interrupt with an entry (cannot be an entry family). The occurrence of an interrupt causes a call to the associated entry to be issued. The priority of such calls is higher than that of calls issued by any user-defined tasks.

The address clause has the form

for name **use at** address;

where *name* is the program entity that is being associated with the memory location *address*. Some examples are

      for HARDWARE_BUFFER **use at** 8#177562#;
               −−the hardware buffer of a device at location
               −−8#177562# can now be accessed via the program
               −−variable HARDWARE_BUFFER

      for PUT **use at** 8#60#;
               −−interrupt at location 8#60# is associated with
               −−the entry PUT. This specification results in
               −−the entry call PUT being issued whenever the
               −−interrupt occurs

4. Change of Representation [13.6]

Ada allows only one representation to be specified for a data type. However, multiple representations may be desirable under certain circumstances, such as

1. enumeration type representations on different external media correspond to different internal representations.

2. one internal representation each may be used for compact storage and fast access.

It should also be possible to convert back and forth between the different representations.[52]

---

52. In Pascal [JEN74], the user can instruct the compiler to store an array in a packed form to economize on storage. However, accessing individual components of the packed arrays is costly and the programmer is advised to unpack the array before accessing it and to pack it afterward. For this purpose, Pascal provides the standard procedures *pack* and *unpack*.

Multiple representations for a type T are implemented by deriving new types from T and associating an internal representation with T and each of the types derived from it. A value is assigned to an object of the type with the desired internal representation. Representation changes are carried out by means of explicit type conversions.

As an example, suppose there are a large number of records of type DESCRIPTOR. To save storage, they are to be stored in a packed or compact form, but before being accessed they should be converted to the unpacked form for fast access.[53] A type PACKED_DESCRIPTOR is derived from DESCRIPTOR and a compact representation specified for it.

```
type DESCRIPTOR is
    record
        --components of descriptor
    end record;


type PACKED_DESCRIPTOR is new DESCRIPTOR;


type PACKED_DESCRIPTOR is
    record
        --compact representation to be used for the components
    end record;
```

DESCRIPTOR and PACKED_DESCRIPTOR have the same logical characteristics, although they have different physical representations. The representation of DESCRIPTOR was implicitly supplied by the compiler, while the representation for PACKED_DESCRIPTOR was explicitly supplied by the user. Changes in representation are accomplished by means of explicit type conversions. For example, the following statements first unpack an object P of type PACKED_DESCRIPTOR to an object D of type DESCRIPTOR and then pack D back into P.

```
D := DESCRIPTOR(P);              --unpack
P := PACKED_DESCRIPTOR(D);       --pack
```

---

53. Accessing record components stored in a packed form is slow, since several components may be packed into one storage unit (i.e., machine word). For example, updating a value that does not occupy an addressable storage unit may require that this value be extracted from the storage unit containing it, put by itself into a storage unit, the extracted value updated and, finally, this updated value put back into the packed form.

5. Implementation Dependent Configuration Features and Constants [13.7]

Ada allows the programmer to specify configuration dependent features in a program to help the Ada compiler exploit these features when generating code and yet not violate the restrictions imposed by them. Configuration dependent features such as

1. the computer make and model number,

2. the operating system,

,   the amount of memory available and

4. special hardware options.

can be specified. These features are specified by means of implementation dependent pragmas. Some examples are

```
pragma SYSTEM_NAME(UNIX);
pragma STORAGE_UNIT(32);
pragma MEMORY_SIZE(262144);
pragma MACHINE_NAME(VAX11_780);
```

Ada also allows the programmer to access implementation dependent constants known to the compiler by means of constants provided in the package SYSTEM (declared in the predefined package STANDARD). Some of the constants available in the package SYSTEM are

ADDRESS	the type of addresses provided in address clauses; it is also the type of the value returned by the attribute ADDRESS (X'ADDRESS is the starting address of object, program unit, label or entry X)
SYSTEM_NAME	the system name
STORAGE_UNIT	the number of bits per storage unit
MEMORY_SIZE	the total number of available storage units in memory
MIN_INT	the smallest integer supported by the implementation
MAX_INT	the largest integer supported by the implementation.
TICK	the basic clock period, in seconds

An example of the need to access these constants is a user-defined low level input/output routine that invokes different routines depending upon the operating system. This need is illustrated by the following program fragment:

```
case SYSTEM.SYSTEM_NAME is
   when UNIX =>
      code with appropriate calls to UNIX routines
   when MULTICS =>
      code with appropriate calls to MULTICS routines
   when VS_370 =>
      code with appropriate calls to VS_370 routines
end case;
```

The above *case* statement may as an optimization be conditionally compiled (i.e., evaluated at compile time), but this is left to the Ada compiler.

6. Machine Code Insertion [13.8]

Ada provides a facility to insert machine code instructions directly within a program. This facility can cause many problems and errors and should be used rarely. Some situations where it may be desirable to insert machine code in program are

- executing special machine dependent instructions,

- accessing registers which cannot be addressed like memory locations,

- fine tuning a program for very critical efficiency reasons and

- performing hardware functions.[54]

7. Interface to Other Languages [13.9]

One of the problems involved in changing from one language to another is what to do with all the existing software. The cost of rewriting the software in the new language may be prohibitive enough to prevent the switch over to the new language and thus force the continued use of the outdated programming language, despite the fact that it is technically inferior to a new programming language. Ada alleviates the need for rewriting software to some degree by providing a pragma that allows Ada programs to interface with subprograms written in another language. This pragma has the form

pragma INTERFACE(language_name, subprogram_name);

---

54. For example, the UNIX™ operating system kernel consists of about 10,000 lines of code written in the systems programming language C and about 1000 lines of assembly code. 800 lines of this assembly code could have been written in C, but were not for efficiency reasons, and the remaining *had to be written* in assembly language to perform hardware functions that are not possible in C [THO78].

The following example [DOD83] illustrates how two subprograms SQRT and EXP written in FORTRAN can be accessed from Ada programs:

```
package FORT_LIB is
    --the Ada specifications of SQRT and EXP
        function SQRT(X: FLOAT) return FLOAT;
        function EXP(X: FLOAT) return FLOAT;
private
    --these subprograms are implemented in FORTRAN
        pragma INTERFACE(FORTRAN, SQRT);
        pragma INTERFACE(FORTRAN, EXP);
end FORT_LIB;
```

8. Unchecked Storage Deallocation [13.10, 13.10.1]

Ada provides a generic subprogram UNCHECKED_DEALLOCATION for explicitly deallocating or reclaiming storage that has been allocated to access variables. Explicit deallocation of dynamic objects may be necessary if an Ada implementation does not provide a garbage collector and/or explicit memory management is explicitly desired. It is the programmer's responsibility to ensure that only storage that is no longer needed is deallocated.

The generic subprogram UNCHECKED_DEALLOCATION has the specification

```
generic
    type OBJECT is limited private;
    type NAME is access OBJECT;
procedure UNCHECKED_DEALLOCATION(X: in out NAME);
```

Suppose that two access variables X and Y designate the same object and FREE is an appropriate instantiation of the generic procedure UNCHECKED_DEALLOCATION. Then accessing this object using the access variable Y after the statement

```
FREE(X);
```

has been executed is an error, since the space previously occupied by this object has been deallocated and contains a value of some unknown type. It is the programmer's responsibility to ensure that such situations will not occur.

9. Unchecked Type Conversions [13.10, 13.10.2]

Representation viewing, which is called unchecked conversion in Ada, can be achieved by using the generic subprogram UNCHECKED_CONVERSION. Representation viewing allows any bit pattern in storage to be viewed as a value of any desired type. It is the programmer's responsibility to ensure that the bit pattern viewed as a value of some desired type constitutes a meaningful value of that type. Such unchecked conversions may be needed for user-defined storage allocation and deallocation procedures; integers representing memory addresses must be converted to access values of the appropriate type and vice versa.[55]

The specification of the generic subprogram UNCHECKED_CONVERSION is

```
generic
    type SOURCE is limited private;
    type TARGET is limited private;
    function UNCHECKED_CONVERSION(S: SOURCE) return TARGET;
```

10. Examples

The use of representation specifications is illustrated by two examples. The first example is a program that reads characters from the typewriter keyboard and outputs them via the typewriter printer. It illustrates the association of program variables with hardware buffers and entries with hardware interrupts. The second program illustrates how a user-defined storage allocator can be written easily in Ada—a program that is hard or impossible to write in strongly typed languages, such as Pascal, that do not provide facilities for bypassing the strong typing mechanism.

10.1 Typewriter Input and Output

The problem is to write a package TYPEWRITER for a PDP/11 computer that provides the user (most likely a systems programmer) with procedures to read a character from the keyboard and to write a character via the typewriter printer.[56] The relevant hardware specifications of the typewriter are

---

55. Another example of the use of unchecked conversion is the implementation of records with only variants in FORTRAN (actually FORTRAN does not even have records). To define a stack whose elements can be either integers or reals, an array of integers is declared. Elements of this array are viewed directly as integers or viewed indirectly as reals by means of the EQUIVALENCE statement. This approach is error prone, since integers can be mistakenly viewed as reals and vice versa, but the programmer has no choice, since FORTRAN does not have records with variants or an equivalent facility.

56. This problem is adaptation of the example in WIR77a.

Keyboard hardware buffer address	8#177562#
Keyboard interrupt address	8#60#
Printer hardware buffer address	8#177566#
Printer interrupt address	8#64#
Interrupt priority	4

The keyboard interrupt occurs after the hardware buffer has been filled with a new character.[57] The printer interrupt occurs after the character put into the hardware buffer has been printed.

One driver task will be defined for the typewriter keyboard and one for the printer. The keyboard driver will have an internal buffer of 64 characters and will be willing to accept characters from the keyboard as long as the buffer is not full. It is from this buffer that the user can read characters using the procedure READ_CHAR. The printer driver has a similar structure.

The specification of the package TYPEWRITER is

```
package TYPEWRITER is
    procedure READ_CHAR(C: out CHARACTER);
    procedure WRITE_CHAR(C: in CHARACTER);
end TYPEWRITER;
```

and its body is

---

57. The character in the hardware buffer should be retrieved before the next character arrives, since otherwise the first one will be lost. We will assume that the task reading characters from the hardware buffer will be able to respond with the required speed to avoid the loss of any characters. It is a consequence of the priority rules that an accept statement executed in response to an interrupt has a higher precedence over those that are to be executed in response to normal entry calls.

```
package body TYPEWRITER is

    task KEYBOARD is
        pragma PRIORITY(4);
                --must have at least the priority of the interrupt
        entry GET(C: out CHARACTER);
        entry PUT;
        for PUT use at 8#60#;
    end KEYBOARD;

    task PRINTER is
        pragma PRIORITY(4);
                --must have at least the priority of the interrupt
        entry GET;
        entry PUT(C: in CHARACTER);
        for GET use at 8#64#;
    end PRINTER;

    procedure READ_CHAR(C: out CHARACTER) is
    begin
        KEYBOARD.GET(C);
    end READ_CHAR;

    procedure WRITE_CHAR(C: in CHARACTER) is
    begin
        PRINTER.PUT(C);
    end WRITE_CHAR;

    task body KEYBOARD is separate;
    task body PRINTER is separate;

end TYPEWRITER;
```

The bodies of the two tasks KEYBOARD and PRINTER, whose stubs were given in the package TYPEWRITER, are

```
    separate(TYPEWRITER)
    task body KEYBOARD is
       MAX: constant := 64;    --internal buffer size
       A: array(1..MAX) of CHARACTER;    --internal buffer
       INB, OUTB: INTEGER := 1;    --buffer pointers
       N: INTEGER := 0;    --buffer count

       HARDWARE_BUFFER: CHARACTER;
       for HARDWARE_BUFFER use at 8#177562#;
    begin
       loop
          select
             when N > 0 =>
                accept GET(C: out CHARACTER) do
                   C := A(OUTB);
                end GET;
                OUTB := OUTB mod MAX + 1;
                N := N - 1;
          or
             when N < MAX =>
                accept PUT do
                   A(INB) := HARDWARE_BUFFER;
                end PUT;
                INB := INB mod MAX + 1;
                N := N + 1;
          end select;
       end loop;
    end KEYBOARD;


and
```

```
separate(TYPEWRITER)
task body PRINTER is
   MAX: constant := 64;    --internal buffer size
   A: array(1..MAX) of CHARACTER;    --internal buffer
   INB, OUTB: INTEGER := 1;    --buffer pointers
   N: INTEGER := 0;    --buffer count

   HARDWARE_BUFFER: CHARACTER;
   for HARDWARE_BUFFER use at 8#177566#;
   HARDWARE_BUFFER_EMPTY: BOOLEAN := TRUE;
begin
   loop
      select
         accept GET;    --character printed
         if N > 0 then
            HARDWARE_BUFFER := A(OUTB);
            OUTB := OUTB mod MAX + 1;
            N := N - 1;
         else
            HARDWARE_BUFFER_EMPTY := TRUE;
         end if;
      or
         when N < MAX =>
            accept PUT(C: in CHARACTER) do
               A(INB) := C;
            end PUT;
            INB := INB mod MAX + 1;
            N := N + 1;
            if HARDWARE_BUFFER_EMPTY then
               HARDWARE_BUFFER := A(OUTB);
               OUTB := OUTB mod MAX + 1;
               N := N - 1;
               HARDWARE_BUFFER_EMPTY := FALSE;
            end if;
      end select;
   end loop;
end PRINTER;
```

Tasks declared in the package TYPEWRITER, once activated, can only be terminated by aborting them.

10.2 Storage Allocator

The problem is to write a general purpose storage allocator ALLOCATE similar to the allocator *new* provided in Ada. It is assumed that the implementation dependent package SYSTEM (declared in the predefined package STANDARD) contains the procedure MORE_MEMORY that allocates raw (untyped) memory.[58] Procedure MORE_MEMORY has the specifications

> **procedure** MORE_MEMORY(N: **in** INTEGER;
> ADDR: **out** INTEGER);

where N is the number of bits to be allocated, and ADDR is the address of the first storage unit (bytes or words) of the storage allocated. An integer number of storage units, containing at least N bits, will be allocated.

ADDR is of type INTEGER and this must be converted to the access type for which storage is being allocated so as to conform to the strong typing rules of Ada. This conversion will be done using the generic function UNCHECKED_CONVERSION.

ALLOCATE will be declared as a generic procedure with generic formal parameters—the access type PT and the type of objects T designated by variables of type PT. The specification of ALLOCATE is

> **with** UNCHECKED_CONVERSION;
> **generic**
>   **type** T **is limited private**;
>   **type** PT **is private**;   ——designates objects of type T
> **procedure** ALLOCATE(X: **out** PT);

The body of ALLOCATE is

---

58. Writing ALLOCATE depends upon the facilities provided by the Ada implementation for Ada programs to interface with the underlying machine. For example, instead of the procedure MORE_MEMORY, the package SYSTEM may provide constants defining the lower and upper bounds for memory that can be used for user-defined storage allocation. In this case, a procedure similar to MORE_MEMORY must be written by the user.

```
procedure ALLOCATE(X: out PT) is
   A: INTEGER;   --will contain the integer version of the address
   function CONVERT is
         new UNCHECKED_CONVERSION(INTEGER, PT);
   use SYSTEM;
begin
   MORE_MEMORY(T'SIZE, A);
   X := CONVERT(A);
end ALLOCATE;
```

Appendix: Stepwise Refinement [GEH81][59]

1. Some Requirements for a Good Programming Methodology

A programming methodology should

1. help the programmer master the complexity of the problem being solved and give some guidelines on how to formulate the problem solution.

2. require the programmer to keep a written record of the program design process. This design can then be read by others and the decisions made appreciated and constructively criticized.

3. result in programs that are understandable.

4. lead to programs whose correctness can be verified by means of proofs. Since proofs are difficult, the methodology should allow for a systematic approach to program testing.

5. be generally applicable and not restricted to one class of problems.

6. allow for the production of efficient programs.

7. allow for the production of programs that can be modified in a systematic fashion.

2. Stepwise Refinement

Stepwise refinement is a top down design approach to program development (first advocated by Wirth [WIR71]) that meets the above criteria. Wirth really gave a systematic formulation and description to what many programmers were previously doing intuitively. Stepwise refinement is considered by many computer scientists to be the most important new programming formalization of the 1970s [BRO75]. This approach is applicable not only to program design, but also to the design of complex systems.

In a top down approach, the problem to be solved is decomposed or refined into subproblems, which are then solved. The decomposition or refinement should be such that

---

59. © 1981 American Telephone and Telegraph Company. Excerpted with permission.

1. the subproblems are solvable,

2. a subproblem should be solvable with as little impact on the other subproblems as possible,

3. the solution of each subproblem should involve less effort than the original problem,

4. once the subproblems are solved, the solution of the problem should not require much additional effort.

This process is repeated on the subproblems; of course, if the solution of a problem is obvious or trivial then there is no need to go through with the decomposition process.

If P_0 is the initial problem formulation/solution, then the final problem formulation/solution P_n (an executable program) is arrived at after a series of gradual "refinement" steps.

$$P_0 => P_1 => P_2 => \cdots => P_n$$

The refinement P_{i+1} of P_i is produced by supplying more details for the problem formulation/solution P_i. The refinements $P_0,...,P_n$ represent different levels of abstraction. P_0 may be said to give the most abstract view of the problem solution P_n while P_n represents a detailed version of the solution for P_0.

Each refinement P_i consists of a sequence of instructions and data description P_{ij}

$$P_{i1}$$
.
.
.
$$P_{in_i}$$

In each refinement step more details on how each P_i is to be implemented are provided. The refinement process stops when all the instructions can be either executed directly on a computer or easily translated into instructions executable by a computer.

3. Suggestions for Refinement

Stepwise refinement is an iterative process. If a refinement solution does not turn out to be appropriate, then the refinement process is repeated using the additional knowledge derived from the previous attempt. For large or complex problems, several iterations may be required before a programmer is satisfied with the correctness, elegance and efficiency of the solution. Some suggestions for developing a program by stepwise refinement are

1. The program should be developed in a gradual sequence of small steps. In each step, one or more instructions of the current refinement are refined. The refinement process terminates when the instructions have been expressed in the desired programming language or when they can be mechanically translated to the programming language.

2. Refinements should reflect the instructions they represent in detailed form.

3. Abstract instructions may be invented as desired. However, they must eventually be translatable to an executable form.

4. Information about the problem and its domain should be used in the formulation of abstract instructions.

5. Notation natural to the problem domain should be used.

6. Every refinement represents some implicit design decision. The programmer should be aware of this and should have considered alternative solutions. A written record of the major decisions made should be kept along with the refinements.

7. Recursion should be used when appropriate. Even if the language does not support recursion, recursive solutions should still be considered and, if selected, systematically converted to nonrecursive solutions.

8. Data types should be refined just as the instructions are refined. The programmer should recognize abstract data types and separate their refinements from the rest of the program, i.e., do not refine the data type operations in line—use procedure calls.

9. Data representation should be postponed as long as possible. This minimizes modifications to the design when an alternative representation is used instead of the original one.

10. If an instruction appears more than once, then the programmer ought to consider making it a procedure call. The instruction is then refined only once. Procedure calls should also be used when they clarify program structure.

11. The programmer should try to use loop invariants when developing program segments containing loops. Loop invariants give a good idea of the instructions that will constitute the body of the loop and also of the terminating condition for the loop.

Annotated Bibliography

AHO75   Aho, A. V., J. E. Hopcroft and J. D. Ullman. *The Design and Analysis of Computer Algorithms.* Addison-Wesley Publishing Company, 1975.

BAC82   Bach, I. On the Type Concept of Ada. *Ada Letters*, vII, no. 3, November-December 1982. Points out some dangers of Ada's derived type mechanism and some drawbacks of private types.

BAR80   Barnes, J. P. G. An Overview of Ada. *Software —Practice and Experience*, v10, pp. 851-887, 1980. Describes the development of Ada. Presents an informal description of the language. Points out the differences between the pre-ANSI and preliminary versions of Ada.

BAR82   Barnes, J. P. G. *Programming in Ada.* Addison-Wesley Publishing Co., 1982. Contains a fairly complete description of pre-ANSI Ada.

BLA80   Black, A. P. Exception Handling and Data Abstractions. Research Report RC 8059, IBM, T. J. Watson Research Center, Yorktown Heights, N. Y. 10598. Presents a simple treatment of exceptions in the context of formal (algebraic) specifications of abstract data types.

BRI73   Brinch Hansen, P. Concurrent Programming Concepts. *Computing Surveys*, v6, no. 4, December 1973. Discusses the advantages of high level features for concurrency in programming languages so that concurrent programs can be more readily understood and so that assertions in a program can be stated and checked automatically. Features from event queues and semaphores to critical regions and monitors are discussed. Contains many examples.

BRI77   Brinch Hansen, P. *The Architecture of Concurrent Programs.* Prentice-Hall, 1977. Contains a discussion of how to construct concurrent programs systematically using monitors. The development of an operating system called Solo is described. The programming language Concurrent Pascal is used.

BRI78   Brinch Hansen, P. Distributed Processes: A Concurrent
            Programming Concept. *CACM*, v21, no. 11, November
            1978. Brinch Hansen proposes that processes communicate and
            synchronize by means of procedure calls and guarded regions.

BRO75   Brooks, F. P. *The Mythical Man Month*. Addison-
            Wesley, Reading, Massachusetts, 1975. The book contains
            essays on software engineering, which I found to be enjoyable
            reading. In these essays the author discusses the management of
            large software projects based on his experiences in managing the
            development of IBM System/360 and its operating system
            OS/360.

BRO76   Bron, C., M. M. Fokkinga and A. C. M. De Haas. A
            Proposal for Dealing with Abnormal Termination of
            Programs. Mem. Nr. 150, November 1976, Twente
            University of Technology, The Netherlands.

BRO81   Brown, W. S. A Simple but Realistic Model of Floating
            Point Computation. *ACM Transactions on Mathematical
            Software*, v7, no. 4, pp. 445-480, December 1981. The
            semantics of real arithmetic is based on a model of real (actually
            floating point) arithmetic developed by Stan Brown and described
            in this paper. According to Stan Brown, the model of floating
            point computation is intended as a basis for developing efficient
            portable software. The model can be expressed in terms of four
            environmental parameters. Using appropriate values for these
            parameters, a program can be tailored to its host computer.

BRO82   Brosgol, B. Summary of Ada Language Changes. *Ada
            Letters*, v1, no.3, March-April 1982. As a result of the
            ANSI Canvass Approval process for Ada, a procedure required
            for approving Ada as an ANSI standard, revisions to Ada
            [DOD80b] have been recommended. These revisions consist of
            many small and localized modifications.

COM81   Special issue on Ada of the IEEE *Computer*, June 1981.
            Contains introductory articles on Ada, the Ada Environment, an
            Ada Language System, Ada for the Intel 432 Microcomputer and
            the Ada Compiler Validation Capability.

CON73   Conway, R. and D. Gries. *An Introduction to
            Programming*. Winthrop, 1973. Introductory book on PL/I
            and PL/C. Emphasis is on the development of correct and
            understandable programs. Programs are developed and explained
            using stepwise refinement (called *top down program
            development*).

COX80   Cox, M. G. and S. J. Hammarling. Evaluation of the Language Ada for use in Numerical Computations. Report DNACS 30/80, National Physical Laboratory, Teddington, Middlesex, U.K., July 1980. Discusses the suitability of the preliminary version of Ada for numerical computations. Plus points of preliminary Ada (that apply to the pre-ANSI version of Ada—array slicing, array assignment, strong typing, range constraints and exceptions. Minus points—storage order of arrays is unspecified (they would like the order to be specified so that this information can be used to improve program efficiency), restrictions on parameters to prevent aliasing.

DAH72   Dahl, O. J., E. W. Dijkstra and C. A. R. Hoare. *Structured Programming*. Academic Press, 1972. A classic book on the disciplined and methodological approach to programming that has come to be known as *structured programming*.

The book contains three articles. In the first article, "Notes on Structured Programming", Dijkstra outlines the methods and discipline used by him in programming. Abstraction is a very powerful tool in mastering complexity and should be used in the design of programs. Programs are developed using *invariants* and stepwise refinement using the three types of decomposition—*concatenation*, *selection* and *repetition*.

Hoare, in the second article titled "Notes on Data Structuring", applies the above principles to the design of data structures. The abstract versions of the program should rely only on the logical properties of the abstract versions of the data structures and not on details of the implementations of the abstract data structures. Implementation details of the abstract data structures should be postponed as long as possible, preferably until the writing of code, since this helps make a program independent of its implementation.

In the final article, "Hierarchical Program Structures", Hoare and Dahl talk about the connection between the design of data structures and the design of programs. The *class* concept of Simula 67 and coroutines are advocated as important program development ideas.

DAH74   Dahlquist, G., Å. Björck and N. Anderson. *Numerical Methods*. Prentice-Hall, 1974.

DAV81   Davis, J. S. Ada—A Suitable Replacement for COBOL. Technical Report, Army Institute for Research in

Management Information and Computer Science, Georgia Institute of Technology, Atlanta, Georgia 30332. The authors are of the opinion that Ada is superior to COBOL in facilitating good software development and maintenance practices. Ada does not provide built-in features for data formating and input/output. Ada may reduce total life cycle cost, but conversion from COBOL to Ada is not recommended for the near future.

DEN75   Dennis, Jack B. An Example of Programming with Abstract Data Types. *Sigplan Notices*, v10, July 1975.

DER76   DeRemer, F. and H. H. Kron. Programming-in-the-large Versus Programming-in-the-small. *IEEE Transactions on Software Engineering*, vSE-2, pp. 80-86, June 1976. Existing programming languages do not support the development of large programs. Large programs are systems that are composed of modules or small programs which are usually written by different people. A language for programming-in-the-large should support the definition of modules, support information hiding and allow the specification of the dependencies between the modules. The ideas presented in this paper are the forerunners of the concept of packages in Ada

DIJ68a   Dijkstra, E. W. Cooperating Sequential Processes. In *Programming Languages* edited by F. Genuys, Academic Press, 1968. The concepts of concurrent statements, semaphores and critical regions are introduced and mutual exclusion is discussed.

DIJ68b   Dijkstra, E. W. Goto Statement Considered Harmful. *CACM*, v11, pp. 147-148, March 1968. Dijkstra argues that the good programming constructs are those that allow the understanding of a program in time proportional to its length. In trying to understand a program containing *goto*s used in an undisciplined manner, the reader of the program is forced to repeatedly jump from one part of a program to another; the reader must follow the execution path of the program to understand the program. This slows program understanding. Constructs such as the *if-then-else* statement and the *while* loop do not cause such slowdowns.

DIJ76   Dijkstra, E. W. *A Discipline of Programming*. Prentice-Hall, 1976. A classic book in which Dijkstra explains a programming methodology based on the idea of statements being considered as predicate or specification transformers. Programs are constructed side by side with proofs of their correctness.

DIJ82   Dijkstra, E. W. *Selected Writings on Computing: A Personal Perspective*. Springer-Verlag, 1982.

DOD79a   *Preliminary Ada Reference Manual. Sigplan Notices*, v14, no. 6, part A, June 1979. The suitability of Ada was tested by using this definition to write many large and complex programs. Based on the experience gained by this testing and evaluation, the definition of Ada was modified resulting in its pre-ANSI form [DOD80b].

DOD79b   *Rationale for the Design of the Ada Programming Language. Sigplan Notices*, v14, no. 6, part B, June 1979. A comprehensive document that provides justification for the design of the preliminary version of Ada. This document is a must for all those interested in language design and those who want to know more about Ada.

DOD80a   *Requirements for Ada Programming Support Environments (Stoneman)*. United States Department of Defense, February 1980. In addition to specifying the requirements for an Ada Programming Support Environment (ASPE), it provides criteria for assessment and evaluation for ASPE designs and offers guidance for ASPE designers and implementors.

DOD80b   *Reference Manual for the Ada Programming Language*. United States Department of Defense, July 1980. Also published by Springer-Verlag, 1981. This document is the official document defining pre-ANSI Ada. Differences between this version of Ada (as defined here) and the preliminary version of Ada [DOD79b] are informally summarized by Barnes [BAR80] and informally detailed by Winkler [WIN81].

DOD82   *Reference Manual for the Ada Programming Language*. United States Department of Defense, 1982. In July 1982, the United States Department of Defense released for editorial review a revised *Reference Manual for the Ada Programming Language*. The revised manual incorporates changes to Ada made in the process of getting it adopted as an ANSI standard. This book reflects these changes to Ada. Adoption of Ada as an ANSI standard is expected by the end of 1982. Although some editorial changes to the *Reference Manual for the Ada Programming Language* are likely, no further changes to Ada itself are expected. In any case, if there are any changes to Ada, they are likely to be esoteric in nature, addressing pathological issues, and will, in all probability, have no impact on the material presented in this book.

(Ada was adopted as an ANSI standard in February 1983.)

DOD83   *Reference Manual for the Ada Programming Language.* United States Department of Defense, January 1983. ANSI standard Ada.

ECO81   Esperanto for Computers. Science brief in *The Economist*, September 12, 1981. Overview of developments leading to the design of Ada. Also contains a discussion of the programming languages that have preceded Ada and of Ada's chances of success.

FEU82   Feuer, A. and N. Gehani. A Comparison of the Programming Languages C and Pascal. *ACM Computing Surveys*, v14, no. 1, March 1982. The definition of *strong typing* in this paper is due to Narain Gehani and Charles Wetherell.

FIS78   Fisher, D. A. DoD's Common Programming Language Effort. *Computer*, pp. 24-23, March 1978. Describes the background, scope and goals of the project that lead to the design of Ada. Contains brief synopsis of the various versions of the requirements—Strawman, Woodenman, Tinman and Ironman. Discusses the philosophy underlying the technical requirements.

GAN77   Gannon, J. D. An Experimental Evaluation of Data Type Conventions. *CACM*, v20, no. 8, August 1977. Experimental evidence that strong typing in programming languages leads to increased program reliability and clarity. Fewer debugging runs are required than in the case of programming languages that are not strongly typed.

GEH77   Gehani, N. H. Units of Measure as a Data Attribute. *Computer Languages*, v2, pp. 93-111, 1977. Proposes the incorporation of units of measure in a programming language in a manner analogous to the specification of the types of objects. Specification of units allows the automatic detection of a class of errors not normally detectable in existing programming languages. It also results in better error correction, better program documentation and automatic conversion between different but equivalent set of units.

GEH80   Gehani, N. H. Generic Procedures: An Implementation and an Undecidability Result. *Computer Languages*, v5, pp. 155-161, December 1980. Points out the advantages of generic procedures and proposes a simple but powerful notation for incorporating generic procedures in a language along with an efficient implementation technique.

GEH81   Gehani, N. H. Program Development by Stepwise Refinement and Related Topics. *BSTJ*, v60, no. 3, March 1981. Takes another look at stepwise refinement in the context of recent developments in programming languages and programming methodology such as abstract data types, formal specifications, and multiversion programs. Offers explicit suggestions for the refinement process.

GEH82a   Gehani, N. H. Concurrency in Ada and Multicomputers. *Computer Languages*, v7, no. 1, 1982. Points out the problems that will arise in implementing Ada on a network of computers with no shared memory. The problems result from the fact that tasks can share data using global variables and pointers.

GEH82b   Gehani, N. H. Databases and Units of Measure. *IEEE Transactions on Software Engineering*, vSE-8, no. 6, pp. 605-611, November 1982. A serious impediment to the integrated use of databases across international boundaries, scientific disciplines and application areas is the use of different units of measure, e.g., dollars and rupees for currency, and miles and kilometers for distance. This impediment is eliminated by extending data definition languages to allow the units of measure to be specified. Conversions are performed automatically along with the detection of inconsistent usage.

GEHA82c Gehani, N. H. Ada's Derived Types and Units of Measure. Submitted for publication. Types in programming languages cannot model many properties of real world objects and quantities. Consequently errors resulting from the inconsistent usage of program objects representing real world quantities cannot be detected automatically. Two solutions to tackle this problem—*derived* types in Ada and *units of measure*—are compared and analyzed. The conclusion is that the units of measure approach is better than the derived types approach, since it ensures that objects are used consistently with respect to their units, detects more errors, does not prevent meaningful uses of objects, is convenient and elegant.

GOO75   Goodenough, J. Exception Handling: Issues and a Proposed Notation. *CACM*, v18, no. 12, pp. 683-696, December 1976. Detailed discussion on how exception handling should be incorporated into programming languages.

GOO80   Goodenough, J. et al. Ada Compiler Validation
         Implementors' Guide. Softech, 460 Totten Pond Road,
         Waltham, MA 02154. Attempts to find all the holes, even the
         minute ones, in Ada. This guide is especially important for the
         implementor. Testing suggestions for the implementor are also
         provided.

GRI71   Gries, D. *Compiler Construction for Digital Computers*.
         Wiley, New York, 1971. Classic book, slightly outdated but
         still worth reading, on the practical aspects of compiler
         construction.

GRI75   Gries, D. Recursion as a Programming Tool. Technical
         Report TR75-234, Department of Computer Science,
         Cornell University, Ithaca, N. Y. 14853, April 1975.

GRI76   Gries, D. An Illustration of Current Ideas on the
         Derivation of Correctness Proofs and Correct Programs.
         IEEE Transactions on Software Engineering v2, no. 4, pp.
         238-243, 1976. Explains how to develop correct programs. A
         non-trivial example (a line justifier) is developed hand in hand
         with its correctness proof.

GRI77   Gries, D. and N. Gehani. Some Ideas on Data Types in
         High Level Languages. *CACM* v20, no. 6, June 1977.
         Also presented at the *ACM Conference on Data* in Salt
         Lake City, Utah, March 1976.

GRI79   Gries, D. **cand** and **cor** before **and then or else** in Ada.
         Technical Report TR79-402, Department of Computer
         Science, Cornell University, Ithaca, N. Y. 14853, 1979.
         Criticizes the semantics of the **and then** and **or else** operators in
         the preliminary version of Ada. The semantics have since been
         corrected.

GRI81   Gries, D. *The Science of Programming*. Springer-Verlag,
         1981. Teaches the development of correct programs in
         conjunction with their correctness proofs. The program
         development approach used is based on Dijkstra's predicate
         transformers [DIJ76].

HAL80   Halloran, R. Pentagon Pins its Hopes on Ada; Just ask
         any Computer. *The New York Times*, p18E, November
         30, 1980.

HAM82   Hammarling, S. J. and B. A. Wichmann. Numerical
         Packages in Ada. In *The Relationship between Numerical
         Computation and Programming Languages* edited by J. K.

Reid, pp. 225-344, North-Holland Publishing Company, 1982. Although Ada was not designed for numerical computation, it meets most of the needs of numerical computation. This paper discusses the suitability of Ada in implementing numerical packages and libraries.

HIB81   Hibbard, P., A. Higen, J. Rosenberg, M. Shaw and M. Sherman. *Studies in Ada Style*. Springer-Verlag, 1981. Contains a reprint of an article by M. Shaw on the impact of ideas on abstraction in modern programming languages. This article is followed by a set of five Ada program written by the other four authors. The style of the solutions, represented by the Ada programs, is said to be influenced by the facilities in Ada.

HOA62   Hoare, C. A. R. Quicksort. *Computer Journal*, v5, no. 1, 1962.

HOA74   Hoare, C. A. R. Monitors: An Operating System Concept. *CACM*, v17, no. 10, October 1974. The monitor is proposed as a method of structuring an operating system. Contains several excellent illustrative examples.

HOA78   Hoare, C. A. R. Communicating Sequential Processes. *CACM*, v21, no. 8, pp. 666-677, August 1978. Ada's tasks are based on Hoare's proposal that parallel processes should communicate using input and output commands. Combined with Dijkstra's guarded commands, this idea becomes very powerful and versatile. Structuring programs as a composition of communicating sequential processes is advocated by Hoare as fundamental. Contains many excellent examples.

HOA81   Hoare, C. A. R. The Emperor's Old Clothes. *The 1980 ACM Turing Award Lecture, .CACM* v24, no. 2, pp. 75-83, February 1981. The author recounts his experiences in the design, implementation and standardization of programming languages and issues a warning for the future. He urges that Ada, which is a large and complex language containing unnecessary and dangerous features (e.g., exception handling), not be used for applications where reliability is critical, e.g., nuclear reactors and cruise missiles. Hoare takes this view, because he believes that it will be hard to implement a reliable compiler for Ada and write reliable programs in Ada.

HON79   Set of Sample Problems for the DoD High Order Language Program. Honeywell, Inc., Systems and Research Center, 2600 Ridgway Parkway, Minneapolis, MN 55412. Solutions to some programming problems in the language GREEN (the name initially given to the preliminary version of Ada).

HOR79   Horning, J. J. Effects of Programming Languages on Reliability. In *Computing Systems Reliability* edited by T. Anderson and B. Randell, Cambridge University Press, 1979. The first part of the paper is a comprehensive survey of programming language features (e.g., types and the treatment of types) that aid in the development of correct programs. Acknowledging the fact that faults and exceptional situations are inevitable in real programs, the author discusses language features (e.g., exception handling) for writing fault tolerant programs in the second part. The final part of the paper is a discussion of language features that encourage program correctness proofs.

HUS80   Huskey, V. R. and H. D. Huskey. Lady Lovelace and Charles Babbage. *Annals of the History of Computing*, v2, no. 4, pp. 299-329. This paper reports the correspondence between them.

IBM70   PL/I (F) Language Reference Manual, Form GC28-8201, IBM Corporation, 1970.

ICH80   Ichbiah, J. View-graphs for Jean Ichbiah's Presentation. In *Proceedings of the Ada Debut*, Defense Advanced Research Projects Agency, Arlington, VA 22209, September 1980. Contains a set of view-graphs that give an overview of Ada.

ISO81   Second Draft Proposal of the ISO Pascal Standard (January 1981). *Pascal News*, no.20.

JEN74   Jensen, K. and N. Wirth. *The Pascal User Manual and Report*. Springer Verlag, 1974. The user manual includes details of the implementation of Pascal on the CDC 6000 by Wirth. The report contains the definition of Pascal and is considered to be the de facto Pascal standard. It is small (about 75 pages) and, perhaps, because of this smallness there are some ambiguities and several details missing.

KER76   Kernighan, B. W. and P. J. Plauger. *Software Tools*. Addison-Wesley Publishing Co., 1976. The book explains how to write good programs that make good tools. These tools are intended for use in the construction of other programs. Real nontrivial examples are given.

KER81   Kernighan, B. W. and P. J. Plauger. *Software Tools in Pascal*. Addison-Wesley Publishing Co., 1981. See KER76.

KID81   Kidman, B. P. The Type Concept in Ada. *Australian Computer Science Communication*, v3, no. 1a, pp. . 74-84, May 1981. Examination of the treatment of types in Ada. The author considers this part of the design of Ada as being successful.

KNU73   Knuth, D. E. *Sorting and Searching*. Addison-Wesley, Publishing Co., 1973.

KNU74   Knuth, D. E. Structured Programming with **goto** Statements. *Computing Surveys*, v6, no. 4, pp. 261-301, December 1974.

LAM83   Lamb, D. A. and P. N. Hilfinger. Simulation of Procedure Variables Using Ada Tasks. *IEEE Transactions on Software Engineering*, vSE-9, no. 1, pp. 13-15, January 1983. Ada does not allow the declaration of objects of type procedure (similar to the declaration of objects of types integer, real, array, task and so on). Tasks, which are similar to procedures, syntactically more than semantically, are used to simulate procedure variables.

LEB82   LeBlanc, R. J. and J. J. Goda. Ada and Software Development Support: A New Concept in Language Design. *Computer*, pp. 75-81, May 1982. Ada has excellent facilities for the development of large scale software. Much of Ada's complexity is due to these features. Ada is unfairly criticized as being complex in comparison with languages, such as Pascal, which have no facilities for large scale software development.

LED81   Ledgard, H. *ADA: An Introduction*. Springer-Verlag, 1981. A brief introduction to a subset of pre-ANSI Ada. Also contains the full pre-ANSI Ada Reference Manual [DOD80b].

LED82   Ledgard, H. and A. Singer. Scaling Down Ada (or Towards a Standard Ada Subset). *CACM*, v25, no. 2, pp. 121-125, February 1982. Authors make suggestions for trimming and streamlining Ada with the intention of reducing its size and complexity which, they claim, is the most significant technical obstacle to its success.

LEV77   Levin, R. Programming Structures for Exception Condition Handling. Ph. D. Thesis, Computer Science Department, Carnegie Mellon University, 1977.

Programming methodologies have failed to address a crucial aspect of program construction—exceptions. Surveys exception handling facilities in languages that preceded Ada, e.g., PL/I and Bliss. Proposes an exception handling mechanism for programming languages that has been designed taking into account issues of verifiability, uniformity, adequacy and practicality.

LIS74   Liskov, B. H. and S. N. Zilles. Programming with Abstract Data Types. *Sigplan Notices*, v9, no. 4, April 1974.

LIS76   Liskov, B. H. Discussion in the *Design and Implementation of Programming Languages* edited by J. H. Williams and D. A. Fisher, p25, Springer-Verlag, 1976.

LIS77   Liskov, B. H. et al. Abstraction Mechanisms in CLU. *CACM*, v20, pp. 564-576, August 1977.

LUC80   Luckham, D. C. and W. Polak. Ada Exception Handling: An Axiomatic Approach. *ACM Transactions on Programming Languages and Systems*, v2, no. 2, April 1980. The exception handling of preliminary Ada is considered.

MCC79   McCorduck, P. *Machines Who Think*. W. H. Freeman and Company, 1979. A personal inquiry into the history and prospects of artificial intelligence.

MCG82   McGettrick, A. D. *Program Verification Using Ada.* Cambridge University Press, 1982.

MOO77   Moore, L. D. *Ada: Countess of Lovelace—Byron's Legitimate Daughter*. John Murray, 1977. The first full biography of Ada. I found it somewhat boring. The article titled *Lady Lovelace and Charles Babbage* [HUS80] is much shorter and more interesting.

MOR73   Morris, J. H., Jr. Types are not Sets. *ACM Symposium on Principles of Programming Languages*. Boston, MA, 1973. Introduces the notion that types are sets of values plus a set of operations.

MOR81   Morris, A. H., Jr. Can Ada Replace FORTRAN for Numerical Computation? *Sigplan Notices*, v16, no. 12, pp. 10-13, December 1981. Unconvincing arguments for concluding that Ada is not suitable as a replacement for FORTRAN.

NIS81   Nissen, J. C. D., P. Wallis, B. A. Wichmann and others. Ada Europe Guidelines for the Portability of Ada Programs. Technical Report, National Physical Laboratory, Teddington, Middlesex, TW11 0LW, UK. Guide to aid programmers in designing and coding portable programs.

PAR72   Parnas, D. On the Criteria to be used in Decomposing Systems into Modules. *CACM*, v15, pp. 1053-1058, December 1972. The advantages of composing a system from modules are widely recognized. Suggests rules for decomposing a system into modules by comparing two decompositions of a software system—one composed of modules representing execution steps and the other representing logical functions. The second formulation uses the *principle of information hiding*, i.e., only information relevant to the user of the module should be available to the user and all other information should be hidden. The second formulation is easier to modify and understand than the first one.

PRA75   Pratt, T. W. *Programming Languages: Design and Implementation.* Prentice-Hall, 1975.

PYL81   Pyle, I. C. *The Ada Programming Language.* Prentice-Hall International, 1981. This book is a fairly comprehensive introduction to Ada. It contains brief, but not exhaustive, notes for FORTRAN and Pascal programmers interested in Ada.

ROB81   Roberts, E. S., E. M. Clarke, A. Evans, Jr. and C. R. Morgan. Task Mangement in Ada: A Critical Evaluation for Real-Time Multiprocessors. *Software—Practice & Experience*, v11, no. 10, October 1981. Preliminary Ada is used in the discussion.

SCH80   Schwartz, R. L. and P. M. Melliar-Smith. On the Suitability of Ada for Artificial Intelligence Applications. SRI International, 333 Ravenswood Avenue, Menlo Park, California 94205, July 1980. The preliminary version of Ada is considered to analyze its suitability for programming artificial intelligence (AI) applications. Although a useful proportion of AI programs can be written in Ada, the authors do not feel that preliminary Ada is suitable as a general research programming language for AI.

SKE82   Skelly, P. G. The ACM Position on the Standardization of the Ada Language. *CACM*, v25, no. 2, pp. 118-120, February 1982. Adoption of Ada as an ANSI standard involves a *canvass process*. 96 organizations responded to the canvass, out of which 66 favored the adoption of Ada as an ANSI standard, 23 objected and 7 abstained. ACM objected to the standardization of Ada based on its present specification [DOD80b]. This report contains the reasons for the objection and the DoD's response. The ACM objection was based on a membership response—72 no votes, 39 yes votes and 4 abstentions.

SYM80   *Proceedings of the ACM-SIGPLAN Symposium on the Ada Programming Language*, Boston, Massachusetts, December 1980. Contains technical papers discussing experiences in using Ada, writing Ada compilers, issues in implementing different aspects of Ada and so on.

THO78   Thompson, K. UNIX Implementation. *BSTJ*, v57, no. 6, part 2, pp. 1931-1946, July-August 1978.

WAS80   Wasserman, A. I. *Tutorial: Programming Language Design*. IEEE Computer Society, 1980 Contains reprints of articles on various aspects of programming language design— design philosophy, control structures, data types, the designs of Pascal and Ada, exception handling and programming language design experience. In particular, it contains the document describing the final requirements (called *Steelman*) which formed the basis for the design of Ada.

WEG80   Wegner, P. *Programming with Ada: An Introduction by Means of Graduated Examples*. Prentice-Hall, 1980. Introduction to the preliminary version of Ada.

WEG81   Wegner, P. A Self-Assessment Procedure Dealing with the Programming Language Ada. *CACM*, v24, no. 10, pp. 647-677, October 1981. A set of short mechanisms to help readers assess and develop their knowledge of Ada.

WEG83   Wegner, P. On the Unification of Data and Program Abstraction in Ada. Conference Record of the *Tenth Annual ACM Symposium on Principles of Programming Languages*, pp. 256-264, Austin, Texas, January 1983. Ada provides two equivalent mechanisms for hiding data representations called *data abstraction* and *program abstraction* and related to the type and generic mechanisms, respectively. Data abstraction is used to provide the user with a private type and operations on objects of this type. Program abstraction (instantiation of a generic package) provides a user with operations on an object hidden from the user. Providing two different abstraction mechanisms increases Ada's complexity. Unification of these two abstraction mechanisms is proposed. Author claims that it is not too early to start thinking of redesigning Ada with the view of producing a successor to Ada.

WEL77   Welsh, J., M. J. Sneeringer and C. A. R. Hoare. Ambiguities and Insecurities in Pascal. *Software — Practice and Experience*, v7, no. 6, pp. 685-696, November 1977. Contains a discussion of the issue of type equivalence. Type equivalence is classified into two categories—name and structural.

WEL81   Welsh, J. and A. Lister. A Comparative Study of Task Communication in Ada. *Software — Practice and Experience*, v11, pp. 257-290, 1981. Compares the mechanism for process communication in Ada with those in Hoare's communicating sequential processes and Brinch Hansen's distributed processes.

WET81   Wetherell, C. S. Problems with the Ada Reference Grammar. *Sigplan Notices*, v16, no. 9, pp. 90-104, September 1981. The Ada Grammar in the Ada Reference Manual is not quite complete and is not suitable for use in the automatic generation of parsers. A revised grammar is presented.

WET83   Wetherell, C. S. Private Communication. February 28 and March 18, 1983.

WIC81   Wichmann, B. A. Tutorial Material on the Real Data-Types in Ada. Technical Report, National Physical Laboratory, Teddington, Middlesex, TW11 0LW, UK. Introduces the novel features of Ada in the area of numerics to programmers familiar with numeric computations but not with Ada.

WIN81   Winkler, J. F. H. Differences between Preliminary Ada and Final Ada. *Sigplan Notices*, v16, no. 8, pp. 69-81, August 1981. Listing of the main differences between the preliminary version of Ada [DOD79a] and the pre-ANSI version of Ada [DOD80b].

WIR71   Wirth, N. Program Development by Stepwise Refinement. *CACM*, v14, no. 4, 1971. Classic paper on stepwise refinement. F. P. Brooks in his book *The Mythical Man — Month* calls stepwise refinement the most important programming formalization of the 1970s.

WIR73   Wirth, N. *Systematic Programming: An Introduction.*
             Prentice-Hall, 1973.

WIR76   Wirth, N. *Algorithms + Data Structures = Programs.*
             Prentice-Hall, 1976.

WIR77a   Wirth,   N.   Modula: A   Language   for   Modular
             Multiprogramming. *Software—Practice and Experience*,
             v7, 1977 The high level language Modula is an attempt to break
             one of the last holds of assembly language programming, viz.,
             machine dependent system programming such as device drivers.
             Modula   is   a   Pascal   descendant.   It   has   facilities   for
             multiprogramming and has been designed specifically for the
             PDP-11 computers. It introduces the concept of the module
             (similar to the Ada package) and has the concepts of processes,
             interface modules and signals.

WIR77b   Wirth, N. The Use of Modula. *Software—Practice and
             Experience*, v7, 1977.

WIR77c   Wirth,   N.   Design   and   Implementation   of   Modula.
             Software—Practice and Experience, v7, 1977.

WIR80   Wirth, N. Modula-2. Technical Report #36, Institut fur
             Informatik, ETH, CH-8092 Zurich. Modula-2 is the result
             of experience gained by Wirth from designing, implementing and
             using Modula. The concept of processes has been replaced by the
             lower level notion of coroutines. The advantage of this is that
             now the programmer can write any desired scheduling algorithm
             and not be forced to use the one built into the language for the
             scheduling of processes as in Modula. Modula-2 also supports
             the notion of programming in the large by providing separate
             definition and implementation modules. The language is tailored
             to the PDP-11 series of computers (as was Modula).

WIR82   Wirth, N. *Programming in Modula-2*. Springer-Verlag,
             1982.

ZUC81   Zuckerman, S. L. Problems with the Multitasking
             Facilities in the Ada Programming Language. Technical
             Note, Defense Communications Engineering Center,
             Reston, Virginia. Author claims that Ada's unconventional
             multitasking facilities do not provide capabilities equivalent to
             multitasking facilities in existing languages.

Index

C

E

F

G

H

I

U

V

W

X

REFERENCE MANUAL FOR THE

Ada®

PROGRAMMING LANGUAGE

ANSI/MIL-STD-1815 A

United States Department of Defense

Foreword

Ada is the result of a collective effort to design a common language for programming large scale and real-time systems.

The common high order language program began in 1974. The requirements of the United States Department of Defense were formalized in a series of documents which were extensively reviewed by the Services, industrial organizations, universities, and foreign military departments. The Ada language was designed in accordance with the final (1978) form of these requirements, embodied in the Steelman specification.

The Ada design team was led by Jean D. Ichbiah and has included Bernd Krieg-Brueckner, Brian A. Wichmann, Henry F. Ledgard, Jean-Claude Heliard, Jean-Loup Gailly, Jean-Raymond Abrial, John G.P. Barnes, Mike Woodger, Olivier Roubine, Paul N. Hilfinger, and Robert Firth.

At various stages of the project, several people closely associated with the design team made major contributions. They include J.B. Goodenough, R.F. Brender, M.W. Davis, G. Ferran, K. Lester, L. MacLaren, E. Morel, I.R. Nassi, I.C. Pyle, S.A. Schuman, and S.C. Vestal.

Two parallel efforts that were started in the second phase of this design had a deep influence on the language. One was the development of a formal definition using denotational semantics, with the participation of V. Donzeau-Gouge, G. Kahn, and B. Lang. The other was the design of a test translator with the participation of K. Ripken, P. Boullier, P. Cadiou, J. Holden, J.F. Hueras, R.G. Lange, and D.T. Cornhill. The entire effort benefitted from the dedicated assistance of Lyn Churchill and Marion Myers, and the effective technical support of B. Gravem, W.L. Heimerdinger, and P. Cleve. H.G. Schmitz served as program manager.

Over the five years spent on this project, several intense week-long design reviews were conducted, with the participation of P. Belmont, B. Brosgol, P. Cohen, R. Dewar, A. Evans, G. Fisher, H. Harte, A.L. Hisgen, P. Knueven, M. Kronental, N. Lomuto, E. Ploedereder, G. Seegmueller, V. Stenning, D. Taffs, and also F. Belz, R. Converse, K. Correll, A.N. Habermann, J. Sammet, S. Squires, J. Teller, P. Wegner, and P.R. Wetherall.

Several persons had a constructive influence with their comments, criticisms and suggestions. They include P. Brinch Hansen, G. Goos, C.A.R. Hoare, Mark Rain, W.A. Wulf, and also E. Boebert, P. Bonnard, H. Clausen, M. Cox, G. Dismukes, R. Eachus, T. Froggatt, H. Ganzinger, C. Hewitt, S. Kamin, R. Kotler, O. Lecarme, J.A.N. Lee, J.L. Mansion, F. Minel, T. Phinney, J. Roehrich, V. Schneider, A. Singer, D. Slosberg, I.C. Wand, the reviewers of Ada-Europe, AdaTEC, Afcet, those of the LMSC review team, and those of the Ada Tokyo Study Group.

These reviews and comments, the numerous evaluation reports received at the end of the first and second phase, the nine hundred language issue reports and test and evaluation reports received from fifteen different countries during the third phase of the project, the thousands of comments received during the ANSI Canvass, and the on-going work of the IFIP Working Group 2.4 on system implementation languages and that of the Purdue Europe LTPL-E committee, all had a substantial influence on the final definition of Ada.

The Military Departments and Agencies have provided a broad base of support including funding, extensive reviews, and countless individual contributions by the members of the High Order Language Working Group and other interested personnel. In particular, William A. Whitaker provided leadership for the program during the formative stages. David A. Fisher was responsible for the successful development and refinement of the language requirement documents that led to the Steelman specification.

This language definition was developed by Cii Honeywell Bull and later Alsys, and by Honeywell Systems and Research Center, under contract to the United States Department of Defense. William E. Carlson, and later Larry E. Druffel and Robert F. Mathis, served as the technical representatives of the United States Government and effectively coordinated the efforts of all participants in the Ada program.

Table of Contents

1. Introduction

Ada is a programming language designed in accordance with requirements defined by the United States Department of Defense: the so-called Steelman requirements. Overall, these requirements call for a language with considerable expressive power covering a wide application domain. As a result, the language includes facilities offered by classical languages such as Pascal as well as facilities often found only in specialized languages. Thus the language is a modern algorithmic language with the usual control structures, and with the ability to define types and subprograms. It also serves the need for modularity, whereby data, types, and subprograms can be packaged. It treats modularity in the physical sense as well, with a facility to support separate compilation.

In addition to these aspects, the language covers real-time programming, with facilities to model parallel tasks and to handle exceptions. It also covers systems programming; this requires precise control over the representation of data and access to system-dependent properties. Finally, both application-level and machine-level input-output are defined.

1.1 Scope of the Standard

This standard specifies the form and meaning of program units written in Ada. Its purpose is to promote the portability of Ada programs to a variety of data processing systems.

1.1.1 Extent of the Standard

This standard specifies:

(a) The form of a program unit written in Ada.

(b) The effect of translating and executing such a program unit.

(c) The manner in which program units may be combined to form Ada programs.

(d) The predefined program units that a conforming implementation must supply.

(e) The permissible variations within the standard, and the manner in which they must be specified.

(f) Those violations of the standard that a conforming implementation is required to detect, and the effect of attempting to translate or execute a program unit containing such violations.

(g) Those violations of the standard that a conforming implementation is not required to detect.

This standard does not specify:

(h)   The means whereby a program unit written in Ada is transformed into object code executable by a processor.

(i)   The means whereby translation or execution of program units is invoked and the executing units are controlled.

(j)   The size or speed of the object code, or the relative execution speed of different language constructs.

(k)   The form or contents of any listings produced by implementations; in particular, the form or contents of error or warning messages.

(l)   The effect of executing a program unit that contains any violation that a conforming implementation is not required to detect.

(m)   The size of a program or program unit that will exceed the capacity of a particular conforming implementation.

Where this standard specifies that a program unit written in Ada has an exact effect, this effect is the operational meaning of the program unit and must be produced by all conforming implementations. Where this standard specifies permissible variations in the effects of constituents of a program unit written in Ada, the operational meaning of the program unit as a whole is understood to be the range of possible effects that result from all these variations, and a conforming implementation is allowed to produce any of these possible effects. Examples of permissible variations are:

● The represented values of fixed or floating numeric quantities, and the results of operations upon them.

● The order of execution of statements in different parallel tasks, in the absence of explicit synchronization.

1.1.2 Conformity of an Implementation with the Standard

A conforming implementation is one that:

(a)   Correctly translates and executes legal program units written in Ada, provided that they are not so large as to exceed the capacity of the implementation.

(b)   Rejects all program units that are so large as to exceed the capacity of the implementation.

(c)   Rejects all program units that contain errors whose detection is required by the standard.

(d)   Supplies all predefined program units required by the standard.

(e)   Contains no variations except where the standard permits.

(f)   Specifies all such permitted variations in the manner prescribed by the standard.

1.2 Structure of the Standard

This reference manual contains fourteen chapters, three annexes, three appendices, and an index.

Each chapter is divided into sections that have a common structure. Each section introduces its subject, gives any necessary syntax rules, and describes the semantics of the corresponding language constructs. Examples and notes, and then references, may appear at the end of a section.

Examples are meant to illustrate the possible forms of the constructs described. Notes are meant to emphasize consequences of the rules described in the section or elsewhere. References are meant to attract the attention of readers to a term or phrase having a technical meaning defined in another section.

The standard definition of the Ada programming language consists of the fourteen chapters and the three annexes, subject to the following restriction: the material in each of the items listed below is informative, and not part of the standard definition of the Ada programming language:

- Section 1.3 Design goals and sources

- Section 1.4 Language summary

- The examples, notes, and references given at the end of each section

- Each section whose title starts with the word "Example" or "Examples"

1.3 Design Goals and Sources

Ada was designed with three overriding concerns: program reliability and maintenance, programming as a human activity, and efficiency.

The need for languages that promote reliability and simplify maintenance is well established. Hence emphasis was placed on program readability over ease of writing. For example, the rules of the language require that program variables be explicitly declared and that their type be specified. Since the type of a variable is invariant, compilers can ensure that operations on variables are compatible with the properties intended for objects of the type. Furthermore, error-prone notations have been avoided, and the syntax of the language avoids the use of encoded forms in favor of more English-like constructs. Finally, the language offers support for separate compilation of program units in a way that facilitates program development and maintenance, and which provides the same degree of checking between units as within a unit.

Concern for the human programmer was also stressed during the design. Above all, an attempt was made to keep the language as small as possible, given the ambitious nature of the application domain. We have attempted to cover this domain with a small number of underlying concepts integrated in a consistent and systematic way. Nevertheless we have tried to avoid the pitfalls of excessive involution, and in the constant search for simpler designs we have tried to provide language constructs that correspond intuitively to what the users will normally expect.

Like many other human activities, the development of programs is becoming ever more decentralized and distributed. Consequently, the ability to assemble a program from independently produced software components has been a central idea in this design. The concepts of packages, of private types, and of generic units are directly related to this idea, which has ramifications in many other aspects of the language.

Design Goals and Sources 1.3

No language can avoid the problem of efficiency. Languages that require over-elaborate compilers, or that lead to the inefficient use of storage or execution time, force these inefficiencies on all machines and on all programs. Every construct of the language was examined in the light of present implementation techniques. Any proposed construct whose implementation was unclear or that required excessive machine resources was rejected.

None of the above design goals was considered as achievable after the fact. The design goals drove the entire design process from the beginning.

A perpetual difficulty in language design is that one must both identify the capabilities required by the application domain and design language features that provide these capabilities. The difficulty existed in this design, although to a lesser degree than usual because of the Steelman requirements. These requirements often simplified the design process by allowing it to concentrate on the design of a given system providing a well defined set of capabilities, rather than on the definition of the capabilities themselves.

Another significant simplification of the design work resulted from earlier experience acquired by several successful Pascal derivatives developed with similar goals. These are the languages Euclid, Lis, Mesa, Modula, and Sue. Many of the key ideas and syntactic forms developed in these languages have counterparts in Ada. Several existing languages such as Algol 68 and Simula, and also recent research languages such as Alphard and Clu, influenced this language in several respects, although to a lesser degree than did the Pascal family.

Finally, the evaluation reports received on an earlier formulation (the Green language), and on alternative proposals (the Red, Blue, and Yellow languages), the language reviews that took place at different stages of this project, and the thousands of comments received from fifteen different countries during the preliminary stages of the Ada design and during the ANSI canvass, all had a significant impact on the standard definition of the language.

1.4 Language Summary

An Ada program is composed of one or more program units. These program units can be compiled separately. Program units may be subprograms (which define executable algorithms), package units (which define collections of entities), task units (which define parallel computations), or generic units (which define parameterized forms of packages and subprograms). Each unit normally consists of two parts: a specification, containing the information that must be visible to other units, and a body, containing the implementation details, which need not be visible to other units.

This distinction of the specification and body, and the ability to compile units separately, allows a program to be designed, written, and tested as a set of largely independent software components.

An Ada program will normally make use of a library of program units of general utility. The language provides means whereby individual organizations can construct their own libraries. The text of a separately compiled program unit must name the library units it requires.

Program Units

A subprogram is the basic unit for expressing an algorithm. There are two kinds of subprograms: procedures and functions. A procedure is the means of invoking a series of actions. For example, it may read data, update variables, or produce some output. It may have parameters, to provide a controlled means of passing information between the procedure and the point of call.

A function is the means of invoking the computation of a value. It is similar to a procedure, but in addition will return a result.

A package is the basic unit for defining a collection of logically related entities. For example, a package can be used to define a common pool of data and types, a collection of related subprograms, or a set of type declarations and associated operations. Portions of a package can be hidden from the user, thus allowing access only to the logical properties expressed by the package specification.

A task unit is the basic unit for defining a task whose sequence of actions may be executed in parallel with those of other tasks. Such tasks may be implemented on multicomputers, multiprocessors, or with interleaved execution on a single processor. A task unit may define either a single executing task or a task type permitting the creation of any number of similar tasks.

Declarations and Statements

The body of a program unit generally contains two parts: a declarative part, which defines the logical entities to be used in the program unit, and a sequence of statements, which defines the execution of the program unit.

The declarative part associates names with declared entities. For example, a name may denote a type, a constant, a variable, or an exception. A declarative part also introduces the names and parameters of other nested subprograms, packages, task units, and generic units to be used in the program unit.

The sequence of statements describes a sequence of actions that are to be performed. The statements are executed in succession (unless an exit, return, or goto statement, or the raising of an exception, causes execution to continue from another place).

An assignment statement changes the value of a variable. A procedure call invokes execution of a procedure after associating any actual parameters provided at the call with the corresponding formal parameters.

Case statements and if statements allow the selection of an enclosed sequence of statements based on the value of an expression or on the value of a condition.

The loop statement provides the basic iterative mechanism in the language. A loop statement specifies that a sequence of statements is to be executed repeatedly as directed by an iteration scheme, or until an exit statement is encountered.

A block statement comprises a sequence of statements preceded by the declaration of local entities used by the statements.

Certain statements are only applicable to tasks. A delay statement delays the execution of a task for a specified duration. An entry call statement is written as a procedure call statement; it specifies that the task issuing the call is ready for a rendezvous with another task that has this entry. The called task is ready to accept the entry call when its execution reaches a corresponding accept statement, which specifies the actions then to be performed. After completion of the rendezvous, both the calling task and the task having the entry may continue their execution in parallel. One form of the select statement allows a selective wait for one of several alternative rendezvous. Other forms of the select statement allow conditional or timed entry calls.

Execution of a program unit may encounter error situations in which normal program execution cannot continue. For example, an arithmetic computation may exceed the maximum allowed value of a number, or an attempt may be made to access an array component by using an incorrect index value. To deal with such error situations, the statements of a program unit can be textually followed by exception handlers that specify the actions to be taken when the error situation arises. Exceptions can be raised explicitly by a raise statement.

Data Types

Every object in the language has a type, which characterizes a set of values and a set of applicable operations. The main classes of types are scalar types (comprising enumeration and numeric types), composite types, access types, and private types.

An enumeration type defines an ordered set of distinct enumeration literals, for example a list of states or an alphabet of characters. The enumeration types BOOLEAN and CHARACTER are predefined.

Numeric types provide a means of performing exact or approximate numerical computations. Exact computations use integer types, which denote sets of consecutive integers. Approximate computations use either fixed point types, with absolute bounds on the error, or floating point types, with relative bounds on the error. The numeric types INTEGER, FLOAT, and DURATION are predefined.

Composite types allow definitions of structured objects with related components. The composite types in the language provide for arrays and records. An array is an object with indexed components of the same type. A record is an object with named components of possibly different types. The array type STRING is predefined.

A record may have special components called discriminants. Alternative record structures that depend on the values of discriminants can be defined within a record type.

Access types allow the construction of linked data structures created by the evaluation of allocators. They allow several variables of an access type to designate the same object, and components of one object to designate the same or other objects. Both the elements in such a linked data structure and their relation to other elements can be altered during program execution.

Private types can be defined in a package that conceals structural details that are externally irrelevant. Only the logically necessary properties (including any discriminants) are made visible to the users of such types.

The concept of a type is refined by the concept of a subtype, whereby a user can constrain the set of allowed values of a type. Subtypes can be used to define subranges of scalar types, arrays with a limited set of index values, and records and private types with particular discriminant values.

Other Facilities

Representation clauses can be used to specify the mapping between types and features of an underlying machine. For example, the user can specify that objects of a given type must be represented with a given number of bits, or that the components of a record are to be represented using a given storage layout. Other features allow the controlled use of low level, nonportable, or implementation-dependent aspects, including the direct insertion of machine code.

Input-output is defined in the language by means of predefined library packages. Facilities are provided for input-output of values of user-defined as well as of predefined types. Standard means of representing values in display form are also provided.

Finally, the language provides a powerful means of parameterization of program units, called generic program units. The generic parameters can be types and subprograms (as well as objects) and so allow general algorithms to be applied to all types of a given class.

1.5 Method of Description and Syntax Notation

The form of Ada program units is described by means of a context-free syntax together with context-dependent requirements expressed by narrative rules.

The meaning of Ada program units is described by means of narrative rules defining both the effects of each construct and the composition rules for constructs. This narrative employs technical terms whose precise definition is given in the text (references to the section containing the definition of a technical term appear at the end of each section that uses the term).

All other terms are in the English language and bear their natural meaning, as defined in Webster's Third New International Dictionary of the English Language.

The context-free syntax of the language is described using a simple variant of Backus-Naur-Form. In particular,

(a) Lower case words, some containing embedded underlines, are used to denote syntactic categories, for example:

   adding_operator

Whenever the name of a syntactic category is used apart from the syntax rules themselves, spaces take the place of the underlines (thus: adding operator).

(b) Boldface words are used to denote reserved words, for example:

   array

(c) Square brackets enclose optional items. Thus the two following rules are equivalent.

   return_statement ::= **return** [expression];
   return_statement ::= **return**; | **return** expression;

(d) Braces enclose a repeated item. The item may appear zero or more times; the repetitions occur from left to right as with an equivalent left-recursive rule. Thus the two following rules are equivalent.

   term ::= factor {multiplying_operator factor}
   term ::= factor | term multiplying_operator factor

(e) A vertical bar separates alternative items unless it occurs immediately after an opening brace, in which case it stands for itself:

```
letter_or_digit ::= letter | digit
component_association ::= [choice {| choice} =>] expression
```

(f) If the name of any syntactic category starts with an italicized part, it is equivalent to the category name without the italicized part. The italicized part is intended to convey some semantic information. For example *type*_name and *task*_name are both equivalent to name alone.

Note:

The syntax rules describing structured constructs are presented in a form that corresponds to the recommended paragraphing. For example, an if statement is defined as

```
if_statement ::=
    if condition then
        sequence_of_statements
    { elsif condition then
        sequence_of_statements}
    [ else
        sequence_of_statements]
    end if;
```

Different lines are used for parts of a syntax rule if the corresponding parts of the construct described by the rule are intended to be on different lines. Indentation in the rule is a recommendation for indentation of the corresponding part of the construct. It is recommended that all indentations be by multiples of a basic step of indentation (the number of spaces for the basic step is not defined). The preferred places for other line breaks are after semicolons. On the other hand, if a complete construct can fit on one line, this is also allowed in the recommended paragraphing.

1.6 Classification of Errors

The language definition classifies errors into several different categories:

(a) Errors that must be detected at compilation time by every Ada compiler.

These errors correspond to any violation of a rule given in this reference manual, other than the violations that correspond to (b) or (c) below. In particular, violation of any rule that uses the terms *must, allowed, legal,* or *illegal* belongs to this category. Any program that contains such an error is not a legal Ada program; on the other hand, the fact that a program is legal does not mean, per se, that the program is free from other forms of error.

(b) Errors that must be detected at run time by the execution of an Ada program.

The corresponding error situations are associated with the names of the predefined exceptions. Every Ada compiler is required to generate code that raises the corresponding exception if such an error situation arises during program execution. If an exception is certain to be raised in every execution of a program, then compilers are allowed (although not required) to report this fact at compilation time.

(c) Erroneous execution.

The language rules specify certain rules to be obeyed by Ada programs, although there is no requirement on Ada compilers to provide either a compilation-time or a run-time detection of the violation of such rules. The errors of this category are indicated by the use of the word *erroneous* to qualify the execution of the corresponding constructs. The effect of erroneous execution is unpredictable.

(d) Incorrect order dependences.

Whenever the reference manual specifies that different parts of a given construct are to be executed *in some order that is not defined by the language*, this means that the implementation is allowed to execute these parts in any given order, following the rules that result from that given order, but not in parallel. Furthermore, the construct is incorrect if execution of these parts in a different order would have a different effect. Compilers are not required to provide either compilation-time or run-time detection of incorrect order dependences. The foregoing is expressed in terms of the process that is called execution; it applies equally to the processes that are called evaluation and elaboration.

If a compiler is able to recognize at compilation time that a construct is erroneous or contains an incorrect order dependence, then the compiler is allowed to generate, in place of the code otherwise generated for the construct, code that raises the predefined exception PROGRAM_ERROR. Similarly, compilers are allowed to generate code that checks at run time for erroneous constructs, for incorrect order dependences, or for both. The predefined exception PROGRAM_ERROR is raised if such a check fails.

2. Lexical Elements

The text of a program consists of the texts of one or more compilations. The text of a compilation is a sequence of lexical elements, each composed of characters; the rules of composition are given in this chapter. Pragmas, which provide certain information for the compiler, are also described in this chapter.   1

References: character 2.1, compilation 10.1, lexical element 2.2, pragma 2.8   2

2.1 Character Set

The only characters allowed in the text of a program are the graphic characters and format effectors. Each graphic character corresponds to a unique code of the *ISO* seven-bit coded character set (*ISO* standard 646), and is represented (visually) by a graphical symbol. Some graphic characters are represented by different graphical symbols in alternative national representations of the *ISO* character set. The description of the language definition in this standard reference manual uses the *ASCII* graphical symbols, the *ANSI* graphical representation of the *ISO* character set.   1

    graphic_character ::= basic_graphic_character
      | lower_case_letter | other_special_character   2

    basic_graphic_character ::=
        upper_case_letter | digit
      | special_character | space_character

    basic_character ::=
        basic_graphic_character | format_effector

The basic character set is sufficient for writing any program. The characters included in each of the categories of basic graphic characters are defined as follows: 3

(a) upper case letters
     A B C D E F G H I J K L M N O P Q R S T U V W X Y Z   4

(b) digits
     0 1 2 3 4 5 6 7 8 9   5

(c) special characters
     " # & ' ( ) * + , - . / : ; < = > _ | 6

(d) the space character   7

Format effectors are the *ISO* (and *ASCII*) characters called horizontal tabulation, vertical tabulation, carriage return, line feed, and form feed.   8

9   The characters included in each of the remaining categories of graphic characters are defined as follows:

10   (e)   lower case letters
      a b c d e f g h i j k l m n o p q r s t u v w x y z

11   (f)   other special characters
      ! $ % ? @ [\ ] ^ ` { } ~

12   Allowable replacements for the special characters vertical bar (|), sharp (#), and quotation (") are defined in section 2.10.

Notes:

13   The *ISO* character that corresponds to the sharp graphical symbol in the *ASCII* representation appears as a pound sterling symbol in the French, German, and United Kingdom standard national representations. In any case, the font design of graphical symbols (for example, whether they are in italic or bold typeface) is not part of the *ISO* standard.

14   The meanings of the acronyms used in this section are as follows: *ANSI* stands for American National Standards Institute, *ASCII* stands for American Standard Code for Information Interchange, and *ISO* stands for International Organization for Standardization.

15   The following names are used when referring to special characters and other special characters:

symbol	name	symbol	name
"	quotation	>	greater than
#	sharp	_	underline
&	ampersand	|	vertical bar
'	apostrophe	!	exclamation mark
(	left parenthesis	$	dollar
)	right parenthesis	%	percent
*	star, multiply	?	question mark
+	plus	@	commercial at
,	comma	[	left square bracket
-	hyphen, minus	\	back-slash
.	dot, point, period	]	right square bracket
/	slash, divide	^	circumflex
:	colon	`	grave accent
;	semicolon	{	left brace
<	less than	}	right brace
=	equal	~	tilde

2.2   Lexical Elements, Separators, and Delimiters

1   The text of a program consists of the texts of one or more compilations. The text of each compilation is a sequence of separate lexical elements. Each lexical element is either a delimiter, an identifier (which may be a reserved word), a numeric literal, a character literal, a string literal, or a comment. The effect of a program depends only on the particular sequences of lexical elements that form its compilations, excluding the comments, if any.

In some cases an explicit *separator* is required to separate adjacent lexical elements (namely, when without separation, interpretation as a single lexical element is possible). A separator is any of a space character, a format effector, or the end of a line. A space character is a separator except within a comment, a string literal, or a space character literal. Format effectors other than horizontal tabulation are always separators. Horizontal tabulation is a separator except within a comment.

The end of a line is always a separator. The language does not define what causes the end of a line. However if, for a given implementation, the end of a line is signified by one or more characters, then these characters must be format effectors other than horizontal tabulation. In any case, a sequence of one or more format effectors other than horizontal tabulation must cause at least one end of line.

One or more separators are allowed between any two adjacent lexical elements, before the first of each compilation, or after the last. At least one separator is required between an identifier or a numeric literal and an adjacent identifier or numeric literal.

A *delimiter* is either one of the following special characters (in the basic character set)

     & ' ( ) * + , - . / : ; < = > |

or one of the following *compound delimiters* each composed of two adjacent special characters

    =>   ..   **   :=   /=   >=   <=   <<   >>   <>

Each of the special characters listed for single character delimiters is a single delimiter except if this character is used as a character of a compound delimiter, or as a character of a comment, string literal, character literal, or numeric literal.

The remaining forms of lexical element are described in other sections of this chapter.

Notes:

Each lexical element must fit on one line, since the end of a line is a separator. The quotation, sharp, and underline characters, likewise two adjacent hyphens, are not delimiters, but may form part of other lexical elements.

The following names are used when referring to compound delimiters:

delimiter	name
=>	arrow
..	double dot
**	double star, exponentiate
:=	assignment (pronounced: "becomes")
/=	inequality (pronounced: "not equal")
>=	greater than or equal
<=	less than or equal
<<	left label bracket
>>	right label bracket
<>	box

References: character literal 2.5, comment 2.7, compilation 10.1, format effector 2.1, identifier 2.3, numeric literal 2.4, reserved word 2.9, space character 2.1, special character 2.1, string literal 2.6

2.3 Identifiers

1   Identifiers are used as names and also as reserved words.

2
```
identifier ::=
    letter {[underline] letter_or_digit}

letter_or_digit ::= letter | digit

letter ::= upper_case_letter | lower_case_letter
```

3   All characters of an identifier are significant, including any underline character inserted between a letter or digit and an adjacent letter or digit. Identifiers differing only in the use of corresponding upper and lower case letters are considered as the same.

4   *Examples:*

COUNT	X	get_symbol	Ethelyn	Marion
SNOBOL_4	X1	PageCount	STORE_NEXT_ITEM	

Note:

5   No space is allowed within an identifier since a space is a separator.

6   *References:* digit 2.1, lower case letter 2.1, name 4.1, reserved word 2.9, separator 2.2, space character 2.1, upper case letter 2.1

2.4 Numeric Literals

1   There are two classes of numeric literals: real literals and integer literals. A real literal is a numeric literal that includes a point; an integer literal is a numeric literal without a point. Real literals are the literals of the type *universal_real*. Integer literals are the literals of the type *universal_integer*.

2
```
numeric_literal ::= decimal_literal | based_literal
```

3   *References:* literal 4.2, universal_integer type 3.5.4, universal_real type 3.5.6

2.4.1 Decimal Literals

1   A decimal literal is a numeric literal expressed in the conventional decimal notation (that is, the base is implicitly ten).

2
```
decimal_literal ::= integer [.integer] [exponent]

integer ::= digit {[underline] digit}

exponent ::= E [+] integer | E - integer
```

An underline character inserted between adjacent digits of a decimal literal does not affect the   3
value of this numeric literal. The letter E of the exponent, if any, can be written either in lower case
or in upper case, with the same meaning.

An exponent indicates the power of ten by which the value of the decimal literal without the expo-   4
nent is to be multiplied to obtain the value of the decimal literal with the exponent. An exponent for
an integer literal must not have a minus sign.

Examples: 5

12	0	1E6	123_456	--	integer literals
12.0	0.0	0.456	3.14159_26	--	real literals
1.34E-12	1.0E+6	--	real literals with exponent		

Notes:

Leading zeros are allowed. No space is allowed in a numeric literal, not even between constituents   6
of the exponent, since a space is a separator. A zero exponent is allowed for an integer literal.

References: digit 2.1, lower case letter 2.1, numeric literal 2.4, separator 2.2, space character 2.1, upper case letter   7
2.1

2.4.2 Based Literals

A based literal is a numeric literal expressed in a form that specifies the base explicitly. The base   1
must be at least two and at most sixteen.

```
based_literal ::=
    base # based_integer [.based_integer] # [exponent]

base ::= integer

based_integer ::=
    extended_digit {[underline] extended_digit}

extended_digit ::= digit | letter
```

An underline character inserted between adjacent digits of a based literal does not affect the value   3
of this numeric literal. The base and the exponent, if any, are in decimal notation. The only letters
allowed as extended digits are the letters A through F for the digits ten through fifteen. A letter in a
based literal (either an extended digit or the letter E of an exponent) can be written either in lower
case or in upper case, with the same meaning.

The conventional meaning of based notation is assumed; in particular the value of each extended   4
digit of a based literal must be less than the base. An exponent indicates the power of the base by
which the value of the based literal without the exponent is to be multiplied to obtain the value of
the based literal with the exponent.

5   *Examples:*

```
2#1111_1111#      16#FF#         016#0FF#      --  integer literals of value 255
16#E#E1           2#1110_0000#                 --  integer literals of value 224
16#F.FF#E+2       2#1.1111_1111_111#E11        --  real literals of value 4095.0
```

6   *References:* digit 2.1, exponent 2.4.1, letter 2.3, lower case letter 2.1, numeric literal 2.4, upper case letter 2.1

2.5 Character Literals

1   A character literal is formed by enclosing one of the 95 graphic characters (including the space) between two apostrophe characters. A character literal has a value that belongs to a character type.

2   character_literal ::= 'graphic_character'

3   *Examples:*

'A'   '*'   '''   ' '

4   *References:* character type 3.5.2, graphic character 2.1, literal 4.2, space character 2.1

2.6 String Literals

1   A string literal is formed by a sequence of graphic characters (possibly none) enclosed between two quotation characters used as *string brackets*.

2   string_literal ::= "{graphic_character}"

3   A string literal has a value that is a sequence of character values corresponding to the graphic characters of the string literal apart from the quotation character itself. If a quotation character value is to be represented in the sequence of character values, then a pair of adjacent quotation characters must be written at the corresponding place within the string literal. (This means that a string literal that includes two adjacent quotation characters is never interpreted as two adjacent string literals.)

4   The *length* of a string literal is the number of character values in the sequence represented. (Each doubled quotation character is counted as a single character.)

5   *Examples:*

"Message of the day:"

""   -- an empty string literal
" "   "A"   """"   -- three string literals of length 1

"Characters such as $, %, and } are allowed in string literals"

Note:

A string literal must fit on one line since it is a lexical element (see 2.2). Longer sequences of graphic character values can be obtained by catenation of string literals. Similarly catenation of constants declared in the package ASCII can be used to obtain sequences of character values that include nongraphic character values (the so-called control characters). Examples of such uses of catenation are given below: 6

```
"FIRST PART OF A SEQUENCE OF CHARACTERS " &
"THAT CONTINUES ON THE NEXT LINE"

"sequence that includes the" & ASCII.ACK & "control character"
```

References: ascii predefined package C, catenation operation 4.5.3, character value 3.5.2, constant 3.2.1, declaration 3.1, end of a line 2.2, graphic character 2.1, lexical element 2.2   7

2.7 Comments

A comment starts with two adjacent hyphens and extends up to the end of the line. A comment can appear on any line of a program. The presence or absence of comments has no influence on whether a program is legal or illegal. Furthermore, comments do not influence the effect of a program; their sole purpose is the enlightenment of the human reader.   1

Examples: 2

```
--  the last sentence above echoes the Algol 68 report

end;  --  processing of LINE is complete

--  a long comment may be split onto
--  two or more consecutive lines

----------------  the first two hyphens start the comment
```

Note:

Horizontal tabulation can be used in comments, after the double hyphen, and is equivalent to one or more spaces (see 2.2).   3

References: end of a line 2.2, illegal 1.6, legal 1.6, space character 2.1   4

2.8 Pragmas

A pragma is used to convey information to the compiler. A pragma starts with the reserved word **pragma** followed by an identifier that is the name of the pragma.   1

```
pragma ::=
    pragma identifier [(argument_association {, argument_association})];

argument_association ::=
      [argument_identifier =>] name
    | [argument_identifier =>] expression
```
2

3   Pragmas are only allowed at the following places in a program:

4   ● After a semicolon delimiter, but not within a formal part or discriminant part.

5   ● At any place where the syntax rules allow a construct defined by a syntactic category whose name ends with "declaration", "statement", "clause", or "alternative", or one of the syntactic categories variant and exception handler; but not in place of such a construct. Also at any place where a compilation unit would be allowed.

6   Additional restrictions exist for the placement of specific pragmas.

7   Some pragmas have arguments. Argument associations can be either positional or named as for parameter associations of subprogram calls (see 6.4). Named associations are, however, only possible if the argument identifiers are defined. A name given in an argument must be either a name visible at the place of the pragma or an identifier specific to the pragma.

8   The pragmas defined by the language are described in Annex B: they must be supported by every implementation. In addition, an implementation may provide implementation-defined pragmas, which must then be described in Appendix F. An implementation is not allowed to define pragmas whose presence or absence influences the legality of the text outside such pragmas. Consequently, the legality of a program does not depend on the presence or absence of implementation-defined pragmas.

9   A pragma that is not language-defined has no effect if its identifier is not recognized by the (current) implementation. Furthermore, a pragma (whether language-defined or implementation-defined) has no effect if its placement or its arguments do not correspond to what is allowed for the pragma. The region of text over which a pragma has an effect depends on the pragma.

10   *Examples:*

```
pragma LIST(OFF);
pragma OPTIMIZE(TIME);
pragma INLINE(SETMASK);
pragma SUPPRESS(RANGE_CHECK, ON => INDEX);
```

Note:

11   It is recommended (but not required) that implementations issue warnings for pragmas that are not recognized and therefore ignored.

12   *References:* compilation unit 10.1, delimiter 2.2, discriminant part 3.7.1, exception handler 11.2, expression 4.4, formal part 6.1, identifier 2.3, implementation-defined pragma F, language-defined pragma B, legal 1.6, name 4.1, reserved word 2.9, statement 5, static expression 4.9, variant 3.7.3, visibility 8.3

13   *Categories ending with "declaration" comprise:* basic declaration 3.1, component declaration 3.7, entry declaration 9.5, generic parameter declaration 12.1

14   *Categories ending with "clause" comprise:* alignment clause 13.4, component clause 13.4, context clause 10.1.1, representation clause 13.1, use clause 8.4, with clause 10.1.1

15   *Categories ending with "alternative" comprise:* accept alternative 9.7.1, case statement alternative 5.4, delay alternative 9.7.1, select alternative 9.7.1, selective wait alternative 9.7.1, terminate alternative 9.7.1

2.9 Reserved Words

The identifiers listed below are called *reserved words* and are reserved for special significance in   1
the language. For readability of this manual, the reserved words appear in lower case boldface.

					2
abort	**declare**	**generic**	**of**	**select**	
abs	**delay**	**goto**	**or**	**separate**	
accept	**delta**		**others**	**subtype**	
access	**digits**	**if**	**out**		
all	**do**	**in**		**task**	
and		**is**	**package**	**terminate**	
array			**pragma**	**then**	
at	**else**		**private**	**type**	
	elsif	**limited**	**procedure**		
	end	**loop**			
begin	**entry**		**raise**	**use**	
body	**exception**		**range**		
	exit	**mod**	**record**	**when**	
			rem	**while**	
		new	**renames**	**with**	
case	**for**	**not**	**return**		
constant	**function**	**null**	**reverse**	**xor**	

A reserved word must not be used as a declared identifier.   3

Notes:

Reserved words differing only in the use of corresponding upper and lower case letters are con-   4
sidered as the same (see 2.3). In some attributes the identifier that appears after the apostrophe is
identical to some reserved word.

References: attribute 4.1.4, declaration 3.1, identifier 2.3, lower case letter 2.1, upper case letter 2.1   5

2.10 Allowable Replacements of Characters

The following replacements are allowed for the vertical bar, sharp, and quotation basic characters: 1

- A vertical bar character (|) can be replaced by an exclamation mark (!) where used as a   2
  delimiter.

- The sharp characters (#) of a based literal can be replaced by colons (:) provided that the   3
  replacement is done for both occurrences.

- The quotation characters (") used as string brackets at both ends of a string literal can be   4
  replaced by percent characters (%) provided that the enclosed sequence of characters contains no quotation character, and provided that both string brackets are replaced. Any percent
  character within the sequence of characters must then be doubled and each such doubled
  percent character is interpreted as a single percent character value.

5   These replacements do not change the meaning of the program.

Notes:

6   It is recommended that use of the replacements for the vertical bar, sharp, and quotation characters be restricted to cases where the corresponding graphical symbols are not available. Note that the vertical bar appears as a broken bar on some equipment; replacement is not recommended in this case.

7   The rules given for identifiers and numeric literals are such that lower case and upper case letters can be used indifferently; these lexical elements can thus be written using only characters of the basic character set. If a string literal of the predefined type STRING contains characters that are not in the basic character set, the same sequence of character values can be obtained by catenating string literals that contain only characters of the basic character set with suitable character constants declared in the predefined package ASCII. Thus the string literal "AB $CD" could be replaced by "AB" & ASCII.DOLLAR & "CD". Similarly, the string literal "ABcd" with lower case letters could be replaced by "AB" & ASCII.LC_C & ASCII.LC_D.

8   *References:* ascii predefined package C, based literal 2.4.2, basic character 2.1, catenation operation 4.5.3, character value 3.5.2, delimiter 2.2, graphic character 2.1, graphical symbol 2.1, identifier 2.3, lexical element 2.2, lower case letter 2.1, numeric literal 2.4, string bracket 2.6, string literal 2.6, upper case letter 2.1

3. Declarations and Types

This chapter describes the types in the language and the rules for declaring constants, variables, and named numbers.   1

3.1 Declarations

The language defines several kinds of entities that are declared, either explicitly or implicitly, by declarations. Such an entity can be a numeric literal, an object, a discriminant, a record compo- nent, a loop parameter, an exception, a type, a subtype, a subprogram, a package, a task unit, a generic unit, a single entry, an entry family, a formal parameter (of a subprogram, entry, or generic subprogram), a generic formal parameter, a named block or loop, a labeled statement, or an opera- tion (in particular, an attribute or an enumeration literal; see 3.3.3).   1

There are several forms of declaration. A basic declaration is a form of declaration defined as fol- lows.   2

```
basic_declaration ::=
      object_declaration        |  number_declaration
    | type_declaration          |  subtype_declaration
    | subprogram_declaration    |  package_declaration
    | task_declaration          |  generic_declaration
    | exception_declaration     |  generic_instantiation
    | renaming_declaration      |  deferred_constant_declaration
```
3

Certain forms of declaration always occur (explicitly) as part of a basic declaration; these forms are discriminant specifications, component declarations, entry declarations, parameter specifications, generic parameter declarations, and enumeration literal specifications. A loop parameter specifica- tion is a form of declaration that occurs only in certain forms of loop statement.   4

The remaining forms of declaration are implicit: the name of a block, the name of a loop, and a statement label are implicitly declared. Certain operations are implicitly declared (see 3.3.3).   5

For each form of declaration the language rules define a certain region of text called the *scope* of the declaration (see 8.2). Several forms of declaration associate an identifier with a declared entity. Within its scope, and only there, there are places where it is possible to use the identifier to refer to the associated declared entity; these places are defined by the visibility rules (see 8.3). At such places the identifier is said to be a *name* of the entity (its simple name); the name is said to *denote* the associated entity.   6

Certain forms of enumeration literal specification associate a character literal with the cor- responding declared entity. Certain forms of declaration associate an operator symbol or some other notation with an explicitly or implicitly declared operation.   7

The process by which a declaration achieves its effect is called the *elaboration* of the declaration; this process happens during program execution.   8

9 After its elaboration, a declaration is said to be *elaborated*. Prior to the completion of its elaboration (including before the elaboration), the declaration is not yet elaborated. The elaboration of any declaration has always at least the effect of achieving this change of state (from not yet elaborated to elaborated). The phrase *"the elaboration has no other effect"* is used in this manual whenever this change of state is the only effect of elaboration for some form of declaration. An elaboration process is also defined for declarative parts, declarative items, and compilation units (see 3.9 and 10.5).

10 Object, number, type, and subtype declarations are described here. The remaining basic declarations are described in later chapters.

Note:

11 The syntax rules use the term *identifier* for the first occurrence of an identifier in some form of declaration; the term *simple name* is used for any occurrence of an identifier that already denotes some declared entity.

12 *References:* attribute 4.1.4, block name 5.6, block statement 5.6, character literal 2.5, component declaration 3.7, declarative item 3.9, declarative part 3.9, deferred constant declaration 7.4, discriminant specification 3.7.1, elaboration 3.9, entry declaration 9.5, enumeration literal specification 3.5.1, exception declaration 11.1, generic declaration 12.1, generic instantiation 12.3, generic parameter declaration 12.1, identifier 2.3, label 5.1, loop name 5.5, loop parameter specification 5.5, loop statement 5.5, name 4.1, number declaration 3.2.2, numeric literal 2.4, object declaration 3.2.1, operation 3.3, operator symbol 6.1, package declaration 7.1, parameter specification 6.1, record component 3.7, renaming declaration 8.5, representation clause 13.1, scope 8.2, simple name 4.1, subprogram body 6.3, subprogram declaration 6.1, subtype declaration 3.3.2, task declaration 9.1, type declaration 3.3.1, visibility 8.3

3.2 Objects and Named Numbers

1 An *object* is an entity that contains (has) a value of a given type. An object is one of the following:

2 ● an object declared by an object declaration or by a single task declaration,

3 ● a formal parameter of a subprogram, entry, or generic subprogram,

4 ● a generic formal object,

5 ● a loop parameter,

6 ● an object designated by a value of an access type,

7 ● a component or a slice of another object.

8 A number declaration is a special form of object declaration that associates an identifier with a value of type *universal_integer* or *universal_real*.

9
```
object_declaration ::=
        identifier_list : [constant] subtype_indication [:= expression];
    |   identifier_list : [constant] constrained_array_definition [:= expression];

number_declaration ::=
        identifier_list : constant := universal_static_expression;

identifier_list ::=   identifier {, identifier}
```

An object declaration is called a *single object declaration* if its identifier list has a single identifier; it is called a *multiple object declaration* if the identifier list has two or more identifiers. A multiple object declaration is equivalent to a sequence of the corresponding number of single object declarations. For each identifier of the list, the equivalent sequence has a single object declaration formed by this identifier, followed by a colon and by whatever appears at the right of the colon in the multiple object declaration; the equivalent sequence is in the same order as the identifier list.

A similar equivalence applies also for the identifier lists of number declarations, component declarations, discriminant specifications, parameter specifications, generic parameter declarations, exception declarations, and deferred constant declarations.

In the remainder of this reference manual, explanations are given for declarations with a single identifier; the corresponding explanations for declarations with several identifiers follow from the equivalence stated above.

Example:

```
--   the multiple object declaration

JOHN, PAUL : PERSON_NAME := new PERSON(SEX => M);   --   see 3.8.1

--   is equivalent to the two single object declarations in the order given

JOHN  : PERSON_NAME := new PERSON(SEX => M);
PAUL  : PERSON_NAME := new PERSON(SEX => M);
```

References: access type 3.8, constrained array definition 3.6, component 3.3, declaration 3.1, deferred constant declaration 7.4, designate 3.8, discriminant specification 3.7.1, entry 9.5, exception declaration 11.1, expression 4.4, formal parameter 6.1, generic formal object 12.1.1, generic parameter declaration 12.1, generic unit 12, generic subprogram 12.1, identifier 2.3, loop parameter 5.5, numeric type 3.5, parameter specification 6.1, scope 8.2, simple name 4.1, single task declaration 9.1, slice 4.1.2, static expression 4.9, subprogram 6, subtype indication 3.3.2, type 3.3, universal_integer type 3.5.4, universal_real type 3.5.6

3.2.1 Object Declarations

An object declaration declares an object whose type is given either by a subtype indication or by a constrained array definition. If the object declaration includes the assignment compound delimiter followed by an expression, the expression specifies an initial value for the declared object; the type of the expression must be that of the object.

The declared object is a *constant* if the reserved word **constant** appears in the object declaration; the declaration must then include an explicit initialization. The value of a constant cannot be modified after initialization. Formal parameters of mode **in** of subprograms and entries, and generic formal parameters of mode **in**, are also constants; a loop parameter is a constant within the corresponding loop; a subcomponent or slice of a constant is a constant.

An object that is not a constant is called a *variable* (in particular, the object declared by an object declaration that does not include the reserved word **constant** is a variable). The only ways to change the value of a variable are either directly by an assignment, or indirectly when the variable is updated (see 6.2) by a procedure or entry call statement (this action can be performed either on the variable itself, on a subcomponent of the variable, or on another variable that has the given variable as subcomponent).

4   The elaboration of an object declaration proceeds as follows:

5   (a) The subtype indication or the constrained array definition is first elaborated. This establishes the subtype of the object.

6   (b) If the object declaration includes an explicit initialization, the initial value is obtained by evaluating the corresponding expression. Otherwise any implicit initial values for the object or for its subcomponents are evaluated.

7   (c) The object is created.

8   (d) Any initial value (whether explicit or implicit) is assigned to the object or to the corresponding subcomponent.

9   Implicit initial values are defined for objects declared by object declarations, and for components of such objects, in the following cases:

10   ● If the type of an object is an access type, the implicit initial value is the null value of the access type.

11   ● If the type of an object is a task type, the implicit initial (and only) value designates a corresponding task.

12   ● If the type of an object is a type with discriminants and the subtype of the object is constrained, the implicit initial (and only) value of each discriminant is defined by the subtype of the object.

13   ● If the type of an object is a composite type, the implicit initial value of each component that has a default expression is obtained by evaluation of this expression, unless the component is a discriminant of a constrained object (the previous case).

14   In the case of a component that is itself a composite object and whose value is defined neither by an explicit initialization nor by a default expression, any implicit initial values for components of the composite object are defined by the same rules as for a declared object.

15   The steps (a) to (d) are performed in the order indicated. For step (b), if the default expression for a discriminant is evaluated, then this evaluation is performed before that of default expressions for subcomponents that depend on discriminants, and also before that of default expressions that include the name of the discriminant. Apart from the previous rule, the evaluation of default expressions is performed in some order that is not defined by the language.

16   The initialization of an object (the declared object or one of its subcomponents) checks that the initial value belongs to the subtype of the object; for an array object declared by an object declaration, an implicit subtype conversion is first applied as for an assignment statement, unless the object is a constant whose subtype is an unconstrained array type. The exception CONSTRAINT_ERROR is raised if this check fails.

17   The value of a scalar variable is undefined after elaboration of the corresponding object declaration unless an initial value is assigned to the variable by an initialization (explicitly or implicitly).

18   If the operand of a type conversion or qualified expression is a variable that has scalar subcomponents with undefined values, then the values of the corresponding subcomponents of the result are undefined. The execution of a program is erroneous if it attempts to evaluate a scalar variable with an undefined value. Similarly, the execution of a program is erroneous if it attempts to apply a predefined operator to a variable that has a scalar subcomponent with an undefined value.

3.2.1 Object Declarations   **3-4**

Examples of variable declarations: [19]

```
COUNT, SUM    : INTEGER;
SIZE          : INTEGER range 0 .. 10_000 := 0;
SORTED        : BOOLEAN := FALSE;
COLOR_TABLE   : array(1 .. N) of COLOR;
OPTION        : BIT_VECTOR(1 .. 10) := (others => TRUE);
```

Examples of constant declarations: [20]

```
LIMIT       : constant INTEGER  := 10_000;
LOW_LIMIT   : constant INTEGER  := LIMIT/10;
TOLERANCE   : constant REAL := DISPERSION(1.15);
```

Note:

The expression initializing a constant object need not be a static expression (see 4.9). In the above [21] examples, LIMIT and LOW_LIMIT are initialized with static expressions, but TOLERANCE is not if DISPERSION is a user-defined function.

References: access type 3.8, assignment 5.2, assignment compound delimiter 5.2, component 3.3, composite type [22] 3.3, constrained array definition 3.6, constrained subtype 3.3, constraint_error exception 11.1, conversion 4.6, declaration 3.1, default expression for a discriminant 3.7, default initial value for an access type 3.8, depend on a discriminant 3.7.1, designate 3.8, discriminant 3.3, elaboration 3.9, entry 9.5, evaluation 4.5, expression 4.4, formal parameter 6.1, generic formal parameter 12.1 12.3, generic unit 12, in some order 1.6, limited type 7.4.4, mode in 6.1, package 7, predefined operator 4.5, primary 4.4, private type 7.4, qualified expression 4.7, reserved word 2.9, scalar type 3.5, slice 4.1.2, subcomponent 3.3, subprogram 6, subtype 3.3, subtype indication 3.3.2, task 9, task type 9.2, type 3.3, visible part 7.2

3.2.2 Number Declarations

A number declaration is a special form of constant declaration. The type of the static expression [1] given for the initialization of a number declaration must be either the type *universal_integer* or the type *universal_real*. The constant declared by a number declaration is called a *named number* and has the type of the static expression.

Note:

The rules concerning expressions of a universal type are explained in section 4.10. It is a conse- [2] quence of these rules that if every primary contained in the expression is of the type *univer-sal_integer*, then the named number is also of this type. Similarly, if every primary is of the type *universal_real*, then the named number is also of this type.

Examples of number declarations: [3]

```
PI              : constant := 3.14159_26536;   -- a real number
TWO_PI          : constant := 2.0*PI;          -- a real number
MAX             : constant := 500;             -- an integer number
POWER_16        : constant := 2**16;           -- the integer 65_536
ONE, UN, EINS   : constant := 1;               -- three different names for 1
```

References: identifier 2.3, primary 4.4, static expression 4.9, type 3.3, universal_integer type 3.5.4, universal_real [4] type 3.5.6, universal type 4.10

3.3 Types and Subtypes

1   A type is characterized by a set of values and a set of operations.

2   There exist several *classes* of types. *Scalar* types are integer types, real types, and types defined by enumeration of their values; values of these types have no components. *Array* and *record* types are composite; a value of a composite type consists of *component* values. An *access* type is a type whose values provide access to objects. *Private* types are types for which the set of possible values is well defined, but not directly available to the users of such types. Finally, there are *task* types. (Private types are described in chapter 7, task types are described in chapter 9, the other classes of types are described in this chapter.)

3   Certain record and private types have special components called *discriminants* whose values distinguish alternative forms of values of one of these types. If a private type has discriminants, they are known to users of the type. Hence a private type is only known by its name, its discriminants if any, and by the corresponding set of operations.

4   The set of possible values for an object of a given type can be subjected to a condition that is called a *constraint* (the case where the constraint imposes no restriction is also included); a value is said to *satisfy* a constraint if it satisfies the corresponding condition. A *subtype* is a type together with a constraint; a value is said to *belong to a subtype* of a given type if it belongs to the type and satisfies the constraint; the given type is called the *base type* of the subtype. A type is a subtype of itself; such a subtype is said to be *unconstrained*: it corresponds to a condition that imposes no restriction. The base type of a type is the type itself.

5   The set of operations defined for a subtype of a given type includes the operations that are defined for the type; however the assignment operation to a variable having a given subtype only assigns values that belong to the subtype. Additional operations, such as qualification (in a qualified expression), are implicitly defined by a subtype declaration.

6   Certain types have *default initial values* defined for objects of the type; certain other types have *default expressions* defined for some or all of their components. Certain operations of types and subtypes are called *attributes*; these operations are denoted by the form of name described in section 4.1.4.

7   The term *subcomponent* is used in this manual in place of the term component to indicate either a component, or a component of another component or subcomponent. Where other subcomponents are excluded, the term component is used instead.

8   A given type must not have a subcomponent whose type is the given type itself.

9   The name of a class of types is used in this manual as a qualifier for objects and values that have a type of the class considered. For example, the term "array object" is used for an object whose type is an array type; similarly, the term "access value" is used for a value of an access type.

Note:

10   The set of values of a subtype is a subset of the values of the base type. This subset need not be a proper subset; it can be an empty subset.

11   *References:* access type 3.8, array type 3.6, assignment 5.2, attribute 4.1.4, component of an array 3.6, component of a record 3.7, discriminant constraint 3.7.2, enumeration type 3.5.1, integer type 3.5.4, object 3.2.1, private type 7.4, qualified expression 4.7, real type 3.5.6, record type 3.7, subtype declaration 3.3.2, task type 9.1, type declaration 3.3.1

3.3.1 Type Declarations

A type declaration declares a type.   1

```
type_declaration ::=  full_type_declaration                                       2
    |  incomplete_type_declaration | private_type_declaration

full_type_declaration ::=
    type identifier [discriminant_part] is type_definition;

type_definition ::=
    enumeration_type_definition  | integer_type_definition
    |  real_type_definition        | array_type_definition
    |  record_type_definition      | access_type_definition
    |  derived_type_definition
```

The elaboration of a full type declaration consists of the elaboration of the discriminant part, if any   3
(except in the case of the full type declaration for an incomplete or private type declaration), and of
the elaboration of the type definition.

The types created by the elaboration of distinct type definitions are distinct types. Moreover, the   4
elaboration of the type definition for a numeric or derived type creates both a base type and a subtype of the base type; the same holds for a constrained array definition (one of the two forms of
array type definition).

The simple name declared by a full type declaration denotes the declared type, unless the type   5
declaration declares both a base type and a subtype of the base type, in which case the simple
name denotes the subtype, and the base type is anonymous. A type is said to be *anonymous* if it
has no simple name. For explanatory purposes, this reference manual sometimes refers to an
anonymous type by a pseudo-name, written in italics, and uses such pseudo-names at places
where the syntax normally requires an identifier.

Examples of type definitions: 6

```
(WHITE, RED, YELLOW, GREEN, BLUE, BROWN, BLACK)
range 1 .. 72
array(1 .. 10) of INTEGER
```

Examples of type declarations: 7

```
type COLOR    is (WHITE, RED, YELLOW, GREEN, BLUE, BROWN, BLACK);
type COLUMN   is range 1 .. 72;
type TABLE    is array(1 .. 10) of INTEGER;
```

Notes:

Two type definitions always define two distinct types, even if they are textually identical. Thus, the   8
array type definitions given in the declarations of A and B below define distinct types.

```
A  : array(1 .. 10) of BOOLEAN;
B  : array(1 .. 10) of BOOLEAN;
```

If A and B are declared by a multiple object declaration as below, their types are nevertheless dif-   9
ferent, since the multiple object declaration is equivalent to the above two single object declarations.

```
A, B : array(1 .. 10) of BOOLEAN;
```

10   Incomplete type declarations are used for the definition of recursive and mutually dependent types (see 3.8.1). Private type declarations are used in package specifications and in generic parameter declarations (see 7.4 and 12.1).

11   *References:* access type definition 3.8, array type definition 3.6, base type 3.3, constrained array definition 3.6, constrained subtype 3.3, declaration 3.1, derived type 3.4, derived type definition 3.4, discriminant part 3.7.1, elaboration 3.9, enumeration type definition 3.5.1, identifier 2.3, incomplete type declaration 3.8.1, integer type definition 3.5.4, multiple object declaration 3.2, numeric type 3.5, private type declaration 7.4, real type definition 3.5.6, reserved word 2.9, type 3.3

3.3.2 Subtype Declarations

1   A subtype declaration declares a subtype.

2
```
subtype_declaration ::=
    subtype identifier is subtype_indication;

subtype_indication ::=   type_mark [constraint]

type_mark ::= type_name | subtype_name

constraint ::=
      range_constraint    | floating_point_constraint | fixed_point_constraint
    | index_constraint    | discriminant_constraint
```

3   A type mark denotes a type or a subtype. If a type mark is the name of a type, the type mark denotes this type and also the corresponding unconstrained subtype. The *base type of a type mark* is, by definition, the base type of the type or subtype denoted by the type mark.

4   A subtype indication defines a subtype of the base type of the type mark.

5   If an index constraint appears after a type mark in a subtype indication, the type mark must not already impose an index constraint. Likewise for a discriminant constraint, the type mark must not already impose a discriminant constraint.

6   The elaboration of a subtype declaration consists of the elaboration of the subtype indication. The elaboration of a subtype indication creates a subtype. If the subtype indication does not include a constraint, the subtype is the same as that denoted by the type mark. The elaboration of a subtype indication that includes a constraint proceeds as follows:

7   (a) The constraint is first elaborated.

8   (b) A check is then made that the constraint is *compatible* with the type or subtype denoted by the type mark.

9   The condition imposed by a constraint is the condition obtained after elaboration of the constraint. (The rules of constraint elaboration are such that the expressions and ranges of constraints are evaluated by the elaboration of these constraints.) The rules defining compatibility are given for each form of constraint in the appropriate section. These rules are such that if a constraint is compatible with a subtype, then the condition imposed by the constraint cannot contradict any condition already imposed by the subtype on its values. The exception CONSTRAINT_ERROR is raised if any check of compatibility fails.

Examples of subtype declarations: 10

```
subtype RAINBOW    is COLOR range RED .. BLUE;        -- see 3.3.1
subtype RED_BLUE   is RAINBOW;
subtype INT        is INTEGER;
subtype SMALL_INT  is INTEGER range -10 .. 10;
subtype UP_TO_K    is COLUMN range 1 .. K;           -- see 3.3.1
subtype SQUARE     is MATRIX(1 .. 10, 1 .. 10);      -- see 3.6
subtype MALE       is PERSON(SEX => M);              -- see 3.8
```

Note:

A subtype declaration does not define a new type.   11

References: base type 3.3, compatibility of discriminant constraints 3.7.2, compatibility of fixed point constraints   12
3.5.9, compatibility of floating point constraints 3.5.7, compatibility of index constraints 3.6.1, compatibility of range
constraints 3.5, constraint_error exception 11.1, declaration 3.1, discriminant 3.3, discriminant constraint 3.7.2,
elaboration 3.9, evaluation 4.5, expression 4.4, floating point constraint 3.5.7, fixed point constraint 3.5.9, index constraint 3.6.1, range constraint 3.5, reserved word 2.9, subtype 3.3, type 3.3, type name 3.3.1, unconstrained subtype
3.3

3.3.3 Classification of Operations

The set of operations of a type includes the explicitly declared subprograms that have a parameter   1
or result of the type; such subprograms are necessarily declared after the type declaration.

The remaining operations are each implicitly declared for a given type declaration, immediately   2
after the type definition. These implicitly declared operations comprise the *basic* operations, the
predefined operators (see 4.5), and enumeration literals. In the case of a derived type declaration,
the implicitly declared operations include any derived subprograms. The operations implicitly
declared for a given type declaration occur after the type declaration and before the next explicit
declaration, if any. The implicit declarations of derived subprograms occur last.

A basic operation is an operation that is inherent in one of the following: 3

- An assignment (in assignment statements and initializations), an allocator, a membership test,   4
  or a short-circuit control form.

- A selected component, an indexed component, or a slice.   5

- A qualification (in qualified expressions), an explicit type conversion, or an implicit type con-   6
  version of a value of type *universal_integer* or *universal_real* to the corresponding value of
  another numeric type.

- A numeric literal (for a universal type), the literal **null** (for an access type), a string literal, an   7
  aggregate, or an attribute.

For every type or subtype T, the following attribute is defined: 8

T'BASE   The base type of T. This attribute is allowed only as the prefix of the name of   9
           another attribute: for example, T'BASE'FIRST.

                                                                       Classification of Operations 3.3.3

Note:

10 Each literal is an operation whose evaluation yields the corresponding value (see 4.2). Likewise, an aggregate is an operation whose evaluation yields a value of a composite type (see 4.3). Some operations of a type *operate on* values of the type, for example, predefined operators and certain subprograms and attributes. The evaluation of some operations of a type *returns* a value of the type, for example, literals and certain functions, attributes, and predefined operators. Assignment is an operation that operates on an object and a value. The evaluation of the operation corresponding to a selected component, an indexed component, or a slice, yields the object or value denoted by this form of name.

11 *References:* aggregate 4.3, allocator 4.8, assignment 5.2, attribute 4.1.4, character literal 2.5, composite type 3.3, conversion 4.6, derived subprogram 3.4, enumeration literal 3.5.1, formal parameter 6.1, function 6.5, indexed component 4.1.1, initial value 3.2.1, literal 4.2, membership test 4.5 4.5.2, null literal 3.8, numeric literal 2.4, numeric type 3.5, object 3.2.1, 6.1, predefined operator 4.5, qualified expression 4.7, selected component 4.1.3, short-circuit control form 4.5 4.5.1, slice 4.1.2, string literal 2.6, subprogram 6, subtype 3.3, type 3.3, type declaration 3.3.1, universal_integer type 3.5.4, universal_real type 3.5.6, universal type 4.10

3.4 Derived Types

1 A derived type definition defines a new (base) type whose characteristics are derived from those of a *parent type*; the new type is called a *derived type*. A derived type definition further defines a *derived subtype*, which is a subtype of the derived type.

2   derived_type_definition ::= **new** subtype_indication

3 The subtype indication that occurs after the reserved word **new** defines the *parent subtype*. The parent type is the base type of the parent subtype. If a constraint exists for the parent subtype, a similar constraint exists for the derived subtype; the only difference is that for a range constraint, and likewise for a floating or fixed point constraint that includes a range constraint, the value of each bound is replaced by the corresponding value of the derived type. The characteristics of the derived type are defined as follows:

4 • The derived type belongs to the same class of types as the parent type. The set of possible values for the derived type is a copy of the set of possible values for the parent type. If the parent type is composite, then the same components exist for the derived type, and the subtype of corresponding components is the same.

5 • For each basic operation of the parent type, there is a corresponding basic operation of the derived type. Explicit type conversion of a value of the parent type into the corresponding value of the derived type is allowed and vice versa as explained in section 4.6.

6 • For each enumeration literal or predefined operator of the parent type there is a corresponding operation for the derived type.

7 • If the parent type is a task type, then for each entry of the parent type there is a corresponding entry for the derived type.

8 • If a default expression exists for a component of an object having the parent type, then the same default expression is used for the corresponding component of an object having the derived type.

- If the parent type is an access type, then the parent and the derived type share the same collection; there is a null access value for the derived type and it is the default initial value of that type.   9

- If an explicit representation clause exists for the parent type and if this clause appears before the derived type definition, then there is a corresponding representation clause (an implicit one) for the derived type.   10

- Certain subprograms that are operations of the parent type are said to be *derivable*. For each derivable subprogram of the parent type, there is a corresponding derived subprogram for the derived type. Two kinds of derivable subprograms exist. First, if the parent type is declared immediately within the visible part of a package, then a subprogram that is itself explicitly declared immediately within the visible part becomes derivable after the end of the visible part, if it is an operation of the parent type. (The explicit declaration is by a subprogram declaration, a renaming declaration, or a generic instantiation.) Second, if the parent type is itself a derived type, then any subprogram that has been derived by this parent type is further derivable, unless the parent type is declared in the visible part of a package and the derived subprogram is hidden by a derivable subprogram of the first kind.   11

Each operation of the derived type is implicitly declared at the place of the derived type declaration. The implicit declarations of any derived subprograms occur last.   12

The specification of a derived subprogram is obtained implicitly by systematic replacement of the parent type by the derived type in the specification of the derivable subprogram. Any subtype of the parent type is likewise replaced by a subtype of the derived type with a similar constraint (as for the transformation of a constraint of the parent subtype into the corresponding constraint of the derived subtype). Finally, any expression of the parent type is made to be the operand of a type conversion that yields a result of the derived type.   13

Calling a derived subprogram is equivalent to calling the corresponding subprogram of the parent type, in which each actual parameter that is of the derived type is replaced by a type conversion of this actual parameter to the parent type (this means that a conversion to the parent type happens before the call for the modes **in** and **in out**; a reverse conversion to the derived type happens after the call for the modes **in out** and **out**, see 6.4.1). In addition, if the result of a called function is of the parent type, this result is converted to the derived type.   14

If a derived or private type is declared immediately within the visible part of a package, then, within this visible part, this type must not be used as the parent type of a derived type definition. (For private types, see also section 7.4.1.)   15

For the elaboration of a derived type definition, the subtype indication is first elaborated, the derived type is then created, and finally, the derived subtype is created.   16

Examples: 17

```
type LOCAL_COORDINATE is new COORDINATE;    --  two different types
type MIDWEEK is new DAY range TUE .. THU;    --  see 3.5.1
type COUNTER is new POSITIVE;                --  same range as POSITIVE

type SPECIAL_KEY is new KEY_MANAGER.KEY;     --  see 7.4.2
-- the derived subprograms have the following specifications:

-- procedure GET_KEY(K : out SPECIAL_KEY);
-- function "<"(X,Y : SPECIAL_KEY) return BOOLEAN;
```

Notes:

18   The rules of derivation of basic operations and enumeration literals imply that the notation for any literal or aggregate of the derived type is the same as for the parent type; such literals and aggregates are said to be *overloaded*. Similarly, it follows that the notation for denoting a component, a discriminant, an entry, a slice, or an attribute is the same for the derived type as for the parent type.

19   Hiding of a derived subprogram is allowed even within the same declarative region (see 8.3). A derived subprogram hides a predefined operator that has the same parameter and result type profile (see 6.6).

20   A generic subprogram declaration is not derivable since it declares a generic unit rather than a subprogram. On the other hand, an instantiation of a generic subprogram is a (nongeneric) subprogram, which is derivable if it satisfies the requirements for derivability of subprograms.

21   If the parent type is a boolean type, the predefined relational operators of the derived type deliver a result of the predefined type BOOLEAN (see 4.5.2).

22   If a representation clause is given for the parent type but appears after the derived type declaration, then no corresponding representation clause applies to the derived type; hence an explicit representation clause for such a derived type is allowed.

23   For a derived subprogram, if a parameter belongs to the derived type, the subtype of this parameter need not have any value in common with the derived subtype.

24   *References:* access value 3.8, actual parameter 6.4.1, aggregate 4.3, attribute 4.1.4, base type 3.3, basic operation 3.3.3, boolean type 3.5.3, bound of a range 3.5, class of type 3.3, collection 3.8, component 3.3, composite type 3.3, constraint 3.3, conversion 4.6, declaration 3.1, declarative region 8.1, default expression 3.2.1, default initial value for an access type 3.8, discriminant 3.3, elaboration 3.9, entry 9.5, enumeration literal 3.5.1, floating point constraint 3.5.7, fixed point constraint 3.5.9, formal parameter 6.1, function call 6.4, generic declaration 12.1, immediately within 8.1, implicit declaration 3.1, literal 4.2, mode 6.1, overloading 6.6 8.7, package 7, package specification 7.1, parameter association 6.4, predefined operator 4.5, private type 7.4, procedure 6, procedure call statement 6.4, range constraint 3.5, representation clause 13.1, reserved word 2.9, slice 4.1.2, subprogram 6, subprogram specification 6.1, subtype indication 3.3.2, subtype 3.3, type 3.3, type definition 3.3.1, visible part 7.2

3.5 Scalar Types

1   Scalar types comprise enumeration types, integer types, and real types. Enumeration types and integer types are called *discrete* types; each value of a discrete type has a position number which is an integer value. Integer types and real types are called *numeric* types. All scalar types are ordered, that is, all relational operators are predefined for their values.

2   range_constraint ::= **range** range

    range ::= *range*_attribute
       | simple_expression .. simple_expression

A range specifies a subset of values of a scalar type. The range L .. R specifies the values from L to   3
R inclusive if the relation L <= R is true. The values L and R are called the *lower bound* and *upper bound* of the range, respectively. A value V is said to *satisfy* a range constraint if it belongs to the range; the value V is said to *belong* to the range if the relations L <= V and V <= R are both TRUE. A *null* range is a range for which the relation R < L is TRUE; no value belongs to a null range. The operators <= and < in the above definitions are the predefined operators of the scalar type.

If a range constraint is used in a subtype indication, either directly or as part of a floating or fixed   4
point constraint, the type of the simple expressions (likewise, of the bounds of a range attribute) must be the same as the base type of the type mark of the subtype indication. A range constraint is *compatible* with a subtype if each bound of the range belongs to the subtype, or if the range constraint defines a null range; otherwise the range constraint is not compatible with the subtype.

The elaboration of a range constraint consists of the evaluation of the range. The evaluation of a   5
range defines its lower bound and its upper bound. If simple expressions are given to specify the bounds, the evaluation of the range evaluates these simple expressions in some order that is not defined by the language.

Attributes   6

For any scalar type T or for any subtype T of a scalar type, the following attributes are defined: 7

T'FIRST   Yields the lower bound of T. The value of this attribute has the same type as T.   8

T'LAST   Yields the upper bound of T. The value of this attribute has the same type as T.   9

Note:

Indexing and iteration rules use values of discrete types.   10

References: attribute 4.1.4, constraint 3.3, enumeration type 3.5.1, erroneous 1.6, evaluation 4.5, fixed point   11
constraint 3.5.9, floating point constraint 3.5.7, index 3.6, integer type 3.5.4, loop statement 5.5, range attribute 3.6.2, real type 3.5.6, relational operator 4.5 4.5.2, satisfy a constraint 3.3, simple expression 4.4, subtype indication 3.3.2, type mark 3.3.2

3.5.1 Enumeration Types

An enumeration type definition defines an enumeration type.   1

    enumeration_type_definition ::=   2
        (enumeration_literal_specification {, enumeration_literal_specification})

    enumeration_literal_specification ::=   enumeration_literal

    enumeration_literal ::=   identifier | character_literal

The identifiers and character literals listed by an enumeration type definition must be distinct. Each   3
enumeration literal specification is the declaration of the corresponding enumeration literal: this declaration is equivalent to the declaration of a parameterless function, the designator being the enumeration literal, and the result type being the enumeration type. The elaboration of an enumeration type definition creates an enumeration type; this elaboration includes that of every enumeration literal specification.

4 Each enumeration literal yields a different enumeration value. The predefined order relations between enumeration values follow the order of corresponding position numbers. The position number of the value of the first listed enumeration literal is zero; the position number for each other enumeration literal is one more than for its predecessor in the list.

5 If the same identifier or character literal is specified in more than one enumeration type definition, the corresponding literals are said to be *overloaded*. At any place where an overloaded enumeration literal occurs in the text of a program, the type of the enumeration literal must be determinable from the context (see 8.7).

6 *Examples:*

```
type DAY     is (MON, TUE, WED, THU, FRI, SAT, SUN);
type SUIT    is (CLUBS, DIAMONDS, HEARTS, SPADES);
type GENDER  is (M, F);
type LEVEL   is (LOW, MEDIUM, URGENT);
type COLOR   is (WHITE, RED, YELLOW, GREEN, BLUE, BROWN, BLACK);
type LIGHT   is (RED, AMBER, GREEN); -- RED and GREEN are overloaded

type HEXA    is ('A', 'B', 'C', 'D', 'E', 'F');
type MIXED   is ('A', 'B', '*', B, NONE, '?', '%');

subtype WEEKDAY is DAY    range MON .. FRI;
subtype MAJOR   is SUIT   range HEARTS .. SPADES;
subtype RAINBOW is COLOR  range RED .. BLUE;  --   the color RED, not the light
```

Note:

7 If an enumeration literal occurs in a context that does not otherwise suffice to determine the type of the literal, then qualification by the name of the enumeration type is one way to resolve the ambiguity (see 8.7).

8 *References:* character literal 2.5, declaration 3.1, designator 6.1, elaboration 3.9, 6.1, function 6.5, identifier 2.3, name 4.1, overloading 6.6 8.7, position number 3.5, qualified expression 4.7, relational operator 4.5 4.5.2, type 3.3, type definition 3.3.1

3.5.2 Character Types

1 An enumeration type is said to be a character type if at least one of its enumeration literals is a character literal. The predefined type CHARACTER is a character type whose values are the 128 characters of the *ASCII* character set. Each of the 95 graphic characters of this character set is denoted by the corresponding character literal.

2 *Example:*

```
type ROMAN_DIGIT is ('I', 'V', 'X', 'L', 'C', 'D', 'M');
```

Notes:

3 The predefined package ASCII includes the declaration of constants denoting control characters and of constants denoting graphic characters that are not in the basic character set.

A conventional character set such as *EBCDIC* can be declared as a character type; the internal codes of the characters can be specified by an enumeration representation clause as explained in section 13.3.

References: ascii predefined package C, basic character 2.1, character literal 2.5, constant 3.2.1, declaration 3.1, enumeration type 3.5.1, graphic character 2.1, identifier 2.3, literal 4.2, predefined type C, type 3.3

3.5.3 Boolean Types

There is a predefined enumeration type named BOOLEAN. It contains the two literals FALSE and TRUE ordered with the relation FALSE < TRUE. A boolean type is either the type BOOLEAN or a type that is derived, directly or indirectly, from a boolean type.

References: derived type 3.4, enumeration literal 3.5.1, enumeration type 3.5.1, relational operator 4.5 4.5.2, type 3.3

3.5.4 Integer Types

An integer type definition defines an integer type whose set of values includes at least those of the specified range.

    integer_type_definition ::= range_constraint

If a range constraint is used as an integer type definition, each bound of the range must be defined by a static expression of some integer type, but the two bounds need not have the same integer type. (Negative bounds are allowed.)

A type declaration of the form:

    type T is range L .. R;

is, by definition, equivalent to the following declarations:

    type integer_type is new predefined_integer_type;
    subtype T is integer_type range integer_type(L) .. integer_type(R);

where *integer_type* is an anonymous type, and where the predefined integer type is implicitly selected by the implementation, so as to contain the values L to R inclusive. The integer type declaration is illegal if none of the predefined integer types satisfies this requirement, excepting *universal_integer*. The elaboration of the declaration of an integer type consists of the elaboration of the equivalent type and subtype declarations.

The predefined integer types include the type INTEGER. An implementation may also have predefined types such as SHORT_INTEGER and LONG_INTEGER, which have (substantially) shorter and longer ranges, respectively, than INTEGER. The range of each of these types must be symmetric about zero, excepting an extra negative value which may exist in some implementations. The base type of each of these types is the type itself.

8   Integer literals are the literals of an anonymous predefined integer type that is called *univer-sal_integer* in this reference manual. Other integer types have no literals. However, for each integer type there exists an implicit conversion that converts a *universal_integer* value into the corresponding value (if any) of the integer type. The circumstances under which these implicit conversions are invoked are described in section 4.6.

9   The position number of an integer value is the corresponding value of the type *universal_integer*.

10   The same arithmetic operators are predefined for all integer types (see 4.5). The exception NUMERIC_ERROR is raised by the execution of an operation (in particular an implicit conversion) that cannot deliver the correct result (that is, if the value corresponding to the mathematical result is not a value of the integer type). However, an implementation is not required to raise the exception NUMERIC_ERROR if the operation is part of a larger expression whose result can be computed correctly, as described in section 11.6.

11   *Examples:*

```
type PAGE_NUM   is range  1  ..  2_000;
type LINE_SIZE  is range  1  ..  MAX_LINE_SIZE;

subtype SMALL_INT    is INTEGER   range -10 ..  10;
subtype COLUMN_PTR   is LINE_SIZE range  1  ..  10;
subtype BUFFER_SIZE  is INTEGER   range  0  ..  MAX;
```

Notes:

12   The name declared by an integer type declaration is a subtype name. On the other hand, the predefined operators of an integer type deliver results whose range is defined by the parent predefined type; such a result need not belong to the declared subtype, in which case an attempt to assign the result to a variable of the integer subtype raises the exception CONSTRAINT_ERROR.

13   The smallest (most negative) value supported by the predefined integer types of an implementation is the named number SYSTEM.MIN_INT and the largest (most positive) value is SYSTEM.MAX_INT (see 13.7).

14   *References:* anonymous type 3.3.1, belong to a subtype 3.3, bound of a range 3.5, constraint_error exception 11.1, conversion 4.6, identifier 2.3, integer literal 2.4, literal 4.2, numeric_error exception 11.1, parent type 3.4, predefined operator 4.5, range constraint 3.5, static expression 4.9, subtype declaration 3.3.2, system predefined package 13.7, type 3.3, type declaration 3.3.1, type definition 3.3.1, universal type 4.10

3.5.5 Operations of Discrete Types

1   The basic operations of a discrete type include the operations involved in assignment, the membership tests, and qualification; for a boolean type they include the short-circuit control forms; for an integer type they include the explicit conversion of values of other numeric types to the integer type, and the implicit conversion of values of the type *universal_integer* to the type.

2   Finally, for every discrete type or subtype T, the basic operations include the attributes listed below. In this presentation, T is referred to as being a subtype (the subtype T) for any property that depends on constraints imposed by T; other properties are stated in terms of the base type of T.

The first group of attributes yield characteristics of the subtype T. This group includes the attribute BASE (see 3.3.2), the attributes FIRST and LAST (see 3.5), the representation attribute SIZE (see 13.7.2), and the attribute WIDTH defined as follows:

T'WIDTH   Yields the maximum image length over all values of the subtype T (the *image* is the sequence of characters returned by the attribute IMAGE, see below). Yields zero for a null range. The value of this attribute is of the type *universal_integer*.

All attributes of the second group are functions with a single parameter. The corresponding actual parameter is indicated below by X.

T'POS   This attribute is a function. The parameter X must be a value of the base type of T. The result type is the type *universal_integer*. The result is the position number of the value of the parameter.

T'VAL   This attribute is a special function with a single parameter which can be of any integer type. The result type is the base type of T. The result is the value whose position number is the *universal_integer* value corresponding to X. The exception CONSTRAINT_ERROR is raised if the *universal_integer* value corresponding to X is not in the range T'POS(T'BASE'FIRST) .. T'POS(T'BASE'LAST).

T'SUCC   This attribute is a function. The parameter X must be a value of the base type of T. The result type is the base type of T. The result is the value whose position number is one greater than that of X. The exception CONSTRAINT_ERROR is raised if X equals T'BASE'LAST.

T'PRED   This attribute is a function. The parameter X must be a value of the base type of T. The result type is the base type of T. The result is the value whose position number is one less than that of X. The exception CONSTRAINT_ERROR is raised if X equals T'BASE'FIRST.

T'IMAGE   This attribute is a function. The parameter X must be a value of the base type of T. The result type is the predefined type STRING. The result is the *image* of the value of X, that is, a sequence of characters representing the value in display form. The image of an integer value is the corresponding decimal literal; without underlines, leading zeros, exponent, or trailing spaces; but with a single leading character that is either a minus sign or a space. The lower bound of the image is one.

The image of an enumeration value is either the corresponding identifier in upper case or the corresponding character literal (including the two apostrophes); neither leading nor trailing spaces are included. The image of a character C, other than a graphic character, is implementation-defined; the only requirement is that the image must be such that C equals CHARACTER'VALUE (CHARACTER'IMAGE (C)).

T'VALUE   This attribute is a function. The parameter X must be a value of the predefined type STRING. The result type is the base type of T. Any leading and any trailing spaces of the sequence of characters that corresponds to the parameter are ignored.

For an enumeration type, if the sequence of characters has the syntax of an enumeration literal and if this literal exists for the base type of T, the result is the corresponding enumeration value. For an integer type, if the sequence of characters has the syntax of an integer literal, with an optional single leading character that is a plus or minus sign, and if there is a corresponding value in the base type of T, the result is this value. In any other case,, the exception CONSTRAINT_ERROR is raised.

Operations of Discrete Types 3.5.5

14 In addition, the attributes A'SIZE and A'ADDRESS are defined for an object A of a discrete type (see 13.7.2).

15 Besides the basic operations, the operations of a discrete type include the predefined relational operators. For enumeration types, operations include enumeration literals. For boolean types, operations include the predefined unary logical negation operator **not**, and the predefined logical operators. For integer types, operations include the predefined *arithmetic* operators: these are the binary and unary adding operators - and +, all multiplying operators, the unary operator **abs**, and the exponentiating operator.

16 The operations of a subtype are the corresponding operations of its base type except for the following: assignment, membership tests, qualification, explicit type conversions, and the attributes of the first group; the effect of each of these operations depends on the subtype (assignments, membership tests, qualifications, and conversions involve a subtype check; attributes of the first group yield a characteristic of the subtype).

Notes:

17 For a subtype of a discrete type, the results delivered by the attributes SUCC, PRED, VAL, and VALUE need not belong to the subtype; similarly, the actual parameters of the attributes POS, SUCC, PRED, and IMAGE need not belong to the subtype. The following relations are satisfied (in the absence of an exception) by these attributes:

$$T'POS(T'SUCC(X)) = T'POS(X) + 1$$
$$T'POS(T'PRED(X)) = T'POS(X) - 1$$

$$T'VAL(T'POS(X)) = X$$
$$T'POS(T'VAL(N)) = N$$

18 *Examples:*

```
--  For the types and subtypes declared in section 3.5.1 we have:

--  COLOR'FIRST     = WHITE,    COLOR'LAST      = BLACK
--  RAINBOW'FIRST  = RED,      RAINBOW'LAST   = BLUE

--  COLOR'SUCC(BLUE)  = RAINBOW'SUCC(BLUE) = BROWN
--  COLOR'POS(BLUE)   = RAINBOW'POS(BLUE)  = 4
--  COLOR'VAL(0)      = RAINBOW'VAL(0)     = WHITE
```

19 *References:* abs operator 4.5 4.5.6, assignment 5.2, attribute 4.1.4, base type 3.3, basic operation 3.3.3, binary adding operator 4.5 4.5.3, boolean type 3.5.3, bound of a range 3.5, character literal 2.5, constraint 3.3, constraint_error exception 11.1, conversion 4.6, discrete type 3.5, enumeration literal 3.5.1, exponentiating operator 4.5 4.5.6, function 6.5, graphic character 2.1, identifier 2.3, integer type 3.5.4, logical operator 4.5 4.5.1, membership test 4.5 4.5.2, multiplying operator 4.5 4.5.5, not operator 4.5 4.5.6, numeric literal 2.4, numeric type 3.5, object 3.2, operation 3.3, position number 3.5, predefined operator 4.5, predefined type C, qualified expression 4.7, relational operator 4.5 4.5.2, short-circuit control form 4.5 4.5.1, string type 3.6.3, subtype 3.3, type 3.3, unary adding operator 4.5 4.5.4, universal_integer type 3.5.4, universal type 4.10

3.5.6 Real Types

Real types provide approximations to the real numbers, with relative bounds on errors for floating point types, and with absolute bounds for fixed point types.   1

    real_type_definition ::=
        floating_point_constraint | fixed_point_constraint   2

A set of numbers called *model numbers* is associated with each real type. Error bounds on the predefined operations are given in terms of the model numbers. An implementation of the type must include at least these model numbers and represent them exactly.   3

An implementation-dependent set of numbers, called the *safe numbers*, is also associated with each real type. The set of safe numbers of a real type must include at least the set of model numbers of the type. The range of safe numbers is allowed to be larger than the range of model numbers, but error bounds on the predefined operations for safe numbers are given by the same rules as for model numbers. Safe numbers therefore provide guaranteed error bounds for operations on an implementation-dependent range of numbers; in contrast, the range of model numbers depends only on the real type definition and is therefore independent of the implementation.   4

Real literals are the literals of an anonymous predefined real type that is called *universal_real* in this reference manual. Other real types have no literals. However, for each real type, there exists an implicit conversion that converts a *universal_real* value into a value of the real type. The conditions under which these implicit conversions are invoked are described in section 4.6.   If the *universal_real* value is a safe number, the implicit conversion delivers the corresponding value; if it belongs to the range of safe numbers but is not a safe number, then the converted value can be any value within the range defined by the safe numbers next above and below the *universal_real* value.   5

The execution of an operation that yields a value of a real type may raise the exception NUMERIC_ERROR, as explained in section 4.5.7, if it cannot deliver a correct result (that is, if the value corresponding to one of the possible mathematical results does not belong to the range of safe numbers); in particular, this exception can be raised by an implicit conversion. However, an implementation is not required to raise the exception NUMERIC_ERROR if the operation is part of a larger expression whose result can be computed correctly (see 11.6).   6

The elaboration of a real type definition includes the elaboration of the floating or fixed point constraint and creates a real type.   7

Note:

An algorithm written to rely only upon the minimum numerical properties guaranteed by the type definition for model numbers will be portable without further precautions.   8

References: conversion 4.6, elaboration 3.9, fixed point constraint 3.5.9, floating point constraint 3.5.7, literal 4.2, numeric_error exception 11.1, predefined operation 3.3.3, real literal 2.4, type 3.3, type definition 3.3.1, universal type 4.10   9

3.5.7 Floating Point Types

1   For floating point types, the error bound is specified as a relative precision by giving the required minimum number of significant decimal digits.

2
```
floating_point_constraint ::=
    floating_accuracy_definition [range_constraint]

floating_accuracy_definition ::=  digits static_simple_expression
```

3   The minimum number of significant decimal digits is specified by the value of the static simple expression of the floating accuracy definition. This value must belong to some integer type and must be positive (nonzero); it is denoted by D in the remainder of this section. If the floating point constraint is used as a real type definition and includes a range constraint, then each bound of the range must be defined by a static expression of some real type, but the two bounds need not have the same real type.

4   For a given *radix*, the following canonical form is defined for any floating point model number other than zero:

$$sign * mantissa * (radix ** exponent)$$

5   In this form: *sign* is either +1 or -1; *mantissa* is expressed in a number base given by *radix*; and *exponent* is an integer number (possibly negative) such that the integer part of mantissa is zero and the first digit of its fractional part is not a zero.

6   The specified number D is the minimum number of decimal digits required after the point in the decimal mantissa (that is, if *radix* is ten). The value of D in turn determines a corresponding number B that is the minimum number of binary digits required after the point in the binary mantissa (that is, if *radix* is two). The number B associated with D is the smallest value such that the relative precision of the binary form is no less than that specified for the decimal form. (The number B is the integer next above (D*log(10)/log(2)) + 1.)

7   The model numbers defined by a floating accuracy definition comprise zero and all numbers whose binary canonical form has exactly B digits after the point in the mantissa and an exponent in the range -4*B .. +4*B. The guaranteed minimum accuracy of operations of a floating point type is defined in terms of the model numbers of the floating point constraint that forms the corresponding real type definition (see 4.5.7).

8   The predefined floating point types include the type FLOAT. An implementation may also have predefined types such as SHORT_FLOAT and LONG_FLOAT, which have (substantially) less and more accuracy, respectively, than FLOAT. The base type of each predefined floating point type is the type itself. The model numbers of each predefined floating point type are defined in terms of the number D of decimal digits returned by the attribute DIGITS (see 3.5.8).

9   For each predefined floating point type (consequently also for each type derived therefrom), a set of safe numbers is defined as follows. The safe numbers have the same number B of mantissa digits as the model numbers of the type and have an exponent in the range -E .. +E where E is implementation-defined and at least equal to the 4*B of model numbers. (Consequently, the safe numbers include the model numbers.) The rules defining the accuracy of operations with model and safe numbers are given in section 4.5.7. The safe numbers of a subtype are those of its base type.

A floating point type declaration of one of the two forms (that is, with or without the optional range constraint indicated by the square brackets): 10

```
type T is digits D [range L .. R];
```

is, by definition, equivalent to the following declarations: 11

```
type floating_point_type is new predefined_floating_point_type;
subtype T is floating_point_type digits D
    [range floating_point_type(L) .. floating_point_type(R)];
```

where *floating_point_type* is an anonymous type, and where the predefined floating point type is implicitly selected by the implementation so that its model numbers include the model numbers defined by D; furthermore, if a range L .. R is supplied, then both L and R must belong to the range of safe numbers. The floating point declaration is illegal if none of the predefined floating point types satisfies these requirements, excepting *universal_real*. The maximum number of digits that can be specified in a floating accuracy definition is given by the system-dependent named number SYSTEM.MAX_DIGITS (see 13.7.1). 12

The elaboration of a floating point type declaration consists of the elaboration of the equivalent type and subtype declarations. 13

If a floating point constraint follows a type mark in a subtype indication, the type mark must denote a floating point type or subtype. The floating point constraint is *compatible* with the type mark only if the number D specified in the floating accuracy definition is not greater than the corresponding number D for the type or subtype denoted by the type mark. Furthermore, if the floating point constraint includes a range constraint, the floating point constraint is compatible with the type mark only if the range constraint is, itself, compatible with the type mark. 14

The elaboration of such a subtype indication includes the elaboration of the range constraint, if there is one; it creates a floating point subtype whose model numbers are defined by the corresponding floating accuracy definition. A value of a floating point type belongs to a floating point subtype if and only if it belongs to the range defined by the subtype. 15

The same arithmetic operators are predefined for all floating point types (see 4.5). 16

Notes:

A range constraint is allowed in a floating point subtype indication, either directly after the type mark, or as part of a floating point constraint. In either case the bounds of the range must belong to the base type of the type mark (see 3.5). The imposition of a floating point constraint on a type mark in a subtype indication cannot reduce the allowed range of values unless it includes a range constraint (the range of model numbers that correspond to the specified number of digits can be smaller than the range of numbers of the type mark). A value that belongs to a floating point subtype need not be a model number of the subtype. 17

Examples:
18

```
type COEFFICIENT is digits 10 range -1.0 .. 1.0;

type REAL   is digits 8;
type MASS is digits 7 range 0.0 .. 1.0E35;

subtype SHORT_COEFF is COEFFICIENT digits 5;    --  a subtype with less accuracy
subtype PROBABILITY is REAL range 0.0 .. 1.0;   --  a subtype with a smaller range
```

Notes on the examples:

19   The implemented accuracy for COEFFICIENT is that of a predefined type having at least 10 digits of precision. Consequently the specification of 5 digits of precision for the subtype SHORT_COEFF is allowed. The largest model number for the type MASS is approximately 1.27E30 and hence less than the specified upper bound (1.0E35). Consequently the declaration of this type is legal only if this upper bound is in the range of the safe numbers of a predefined floating point type having at least 7 digits of precision.

20   *References:* anonymous type 3.3.1, arithmetic operator 3.5.5 4.5, based literal 2.4.2, belong to a subtype 3.3, bound of a range 3.5, compatible 3.3.2, derived type 3.4, digit 2.1, elaboration 3.1 3.9, error bound 3.5.6, exponent 2.4.1 integer type 3.5.4, model number 3.5.6, operation 3.3, predefined operator 4.5, predefined type C, range constraint 3.5, real type 3.5.6, real type definition 3.5.6, safe number 3.5.6, simple expression 4.4, static expression 4.9, subtype declaration 3.3.2, subtype indication 3.3.2, subtype 3.3, type 3.3, type declaration 3.3.1, type mark 3.3.2

3.5.8 Operations of Floating Point Types

1   The basic operations of a floating point type include the operations involved in assignment, membership tests, qualification, the explicit conversion of values of other numeric types to the floating point type, and the implicit conversion of values of the type *universal_real* to the type.

2   In addition, for every floating point type or subtype T, the basic operations include the attributes listed below. In this presentation, T is referred to as being a subtype (the subtype T) for any property that depends on constraints imposed by T; other properties are stated in terms of the base type of T.

3   The first group of attributes yield characteristics of the subtype T. The attributes of this group are the attribute BASE (see 3.3.2), the attributes FIRST and LAST (see 3.5), the representation attribute SIZE (see 13.7.2), and the following attributes:

4   T'DIGITS   Yields the number of decimal digits in the decimal mantissa of model numbers of the subtype T. (This attribute yields the number D of section 3.5.7.) The value of this attribute is of the type *universal_integer*.

5   T'MANTISSA   Yields the number of binary digits in the binary mantissa of model numbers of the subtype T. (This attribute yields the number B of section 3.5.7.) The value of this attribute is of the type *universal_integer*.

6   T'EPSILON   Yields the absolute value of the difference between the model number 1.0 and the next model number above, for the subtype T. The value of this attribute is of the type *universal_real*.

7   T'EMAX   Yields the largest exponent value in the binary canonical form of model numbers of the subtype T. (This attribute yields the product 4∗B of section 3.5.7.) The value of this attribute is of the type *universal_integer*.

8   T'SMALL   Yields the smallest positive (nonzero) model number of the subtype T. The value of this attribute is of the type *universal_real*.

9   T'LARGE   Yields the largest positive model number of the subtype T. The value of this attribute is of the type *universal_real*.

The attributes of the second group include the following attributes which yield characteristics of the safe numbers: [10]

T'SAFE_EMAX   Yields the largest exponent value in the binary canonical form of safe numbers of the base type of T. (This attribute yields the number E of section 3.5.7.) The value of this attribute is of the type *universal_integer*. [11]

T'SAFE_SMALL   Yields the smallest positive (nonzero) safe number of the base type of T. The value of this attribute is of the type *universal_real*. [12]

T'SAFE_LARGE   Yields the largest positive safe number of the base type of T. The value of this attribute is of the type *universal_real*. [13]

In addition, the attributes A'SIZE and A'ADDRESS are defined for an object A of a floating point type (see 13.7.2). Finally, for each floating point type there are machine-dependent attributes that are not related to model numbers and safe numbers. They correspond to the attribute designators MACHINE_RADIX, MACHINE_MANTISSA, MACHINE_EMAX, MACHINE_EMIN, MACHINE_ROUNDS, and MACHINE_OVERFLOWS (see 13.7.3). [14]

Besides the basic operations, the operations of a floating point type include the relational operators, and the following predefined arithmetic operators: the binary and unary adding operators - and +, the multiplying operators * and /, the unary operator **abs**, and the exponentiating operator. [15]

The operations of a subtype are the corresponding operations of the type except for the following: assignment, membership tests, qualification, explicit conversion, and the attributes of the first group; the effects of these operations are redefined in terms of the subtype. [16]

Notes:

The attributes EMAX, SMALL, LARGE, and EPSILON are provided for convenience. They are all related to MANTISSA by the following formulas: [17]

```
T'EMAX      = 4*T'MANTISSA
T'EPSILON   = 2.0**(1 - T'MANTISSA)
T'SMALL     = 2.0**(-T'EMAX - 1)
T'LARGE     = 2.0**T'EMAX * (1.0 - 2.0**(-T'MANTISSA))
```

The attribute MANTISSA, giving the number of binary digits in the mantissa, is itself related to DIGITS. The following relations hold between the characteristics of the model numbers and those of the safe numbers: [18]

```
T'BASE'EMAX    <=  T'SAFE_EMAX
T'BASE'SMALL   >=  T'SAFE_SMALL
T'BASE'LARGE   <=  T'SAFE_LARGE
```

The attributes T'FIRST and T'LAST need not yield model or safe numbers. If a certain number of digits is specified in the declaration of a type or subtype T, the attribute T'DIGITS yields this number. [19]

References: abs operator 4.5 4.5.6, arithmetic operator 3.5.5 4.5, assignment 5.2, attribute 4.1.4, base type 3.3, basic operation 3.3.3, binary adding operator 4.5 4.5.3, bound of a range 3.5, constraint 3.3, conversion 4.6, digit 2.1, exponentiating operator 4.5 4.5.6, floating point type 3.5.7, membership test 4.5 4.5.2, model number 3.5.6, multiplying operator 4.5 4.5.5, numeric type 3.5, object 3.2, operation 3.3, predefined operator 4.5, qualified expression 4.7, relational operator 4.5 4.5.2, safe number 3.5.6, subtype 3.3, type 3.3, unary adding operator 4.5 4.5.4, universal type 4.10, universal_integer type 3.5.4, universal_real type 3.5.6 [20]

Operations of Floating Point Types 3.5.8

3.5.9 Fixed Point Types

1   For fixed point types, the error bound is specified as an absolute value, called the *delta* of the fixed point type.

2
```
fixed_point_constraint ::=
    fixed_accuracy_definition [range_constraint]

fixed_accuracy_definition ::=   delta static_simple_expression
```

3   The delta is specified by the value of the static simple expression of the fixed accuracy definition. This value must belong to some real type and must be positive (nonzero). If the fixed point constraint is used as a real type definition, then it must include a range constraint; each bound of the specified range must be defined by a static expression of some real type but the two bounds need not have the same real type. If the fixed point constraint is used in a subtype indication, the range constraint is optional.

4   A canonical form is defined for any fixed point model number other than zero. In this form: *sign* is either +1 or -1; *mantissa* is a positive (nonzero) integer; and any model number is a multiple of a certain positive real number called *small*, as follows:

   sign ∗ *mantissa* ∗ *small*

5   For the model numbers defined by a fixed point constraint, the number *small* is chosen as the largest power of two that is not greater than the delta of the fixed accuracy definition. Alternatively, it is possible to specify the value of *small* by a length clause (see 13.2), in which case model numbers are multiples of the specified value. The guaranteed minimum accuracy of operations of a fixed point type is defined in terms of the model numbers of the fixed point constraint that forms the corresponding real type definition (see 4.5.7).

6   For a fixed point constraint that includes a range constraint, the model numbers comprise zero and all multiples of *small* whose *mantissa* can be expressed using exactly B binary digits, where the value of B is chosen as the smallest integer number for which each bound of the specified range is either a model number or lies at most *small* distant from a model number. For a fixed point constraint that does not include a range constraint (this is only allowed after a type mark, in a subtype indication), the model numbers are defined by the delta of the fixed accuracy definition and by the range of the subtype denoted by the type mark.

7   An implementation must have at least one anonymous predefined fixed point type. The base type of each such fixed point type is the type itself. The model numbers of each predefined fixed point type comprise zero and all numbers for which *mantissa* (in the canonical form) has the number of binary digits returned by the attribute MANTISSA, and for which the number *small* has the value returned by the attribute SMALL.

8   A fixed point type declaration of the form:

   type T **is delta** D **range** L .. R;

9   is, by definition, equivalent to the following declarations:

```
type fixed_point_type is new predefined_fixed_point_type;
subtype T is fixed_point_type
    range fixed_point_type(L) .. fixed_point_type(R);
```

In these declarations, *fixed_point_type* is an anonymous type, and the predefined fixed point type is implicitly selected by the implementation so that its model numbers include the model numbers defined by the fixed point constraint (that is, by D, L, and R, and possibly by a length clause specifying *small*). **10**

The fixed point declaration is illegal if no predefined type satisfies these requirements. The safe numbers of a fixed point type are the model numbers of its base type. **11**

The elaboration of a fixed point type declaration consists of the elaboration of the equivalent type and subtype declarations. **12**

If the fixed point constraint follows a type mark in a subtype indication, the type mark must denote a fixed point type or subtype. The fixed point constraint is *compatible* with the type mark only if the delta specified by the fixed accuracy definition is not smaller than the delta for the type or subtype denoted by the type mark. Furthermore, if the fixed point constraint includes a range constraint, the fixed point constraint is compatible with the type mark only if the range constraint is, itself, compatible with the type mark. **13**

The elaboration of such a subtype indication includes the elaboration of the range constraint, if there is one; it creates a fixed point subtype whose model numbers are defined by the corresponding fixed point constraint and also by the length clause specifying small, if there is one. A value of a fixed point type belongs to a fixed point subtype if and only if it belongs to the range defined by the subtype. **14**

The same arithmetic operators are predefined for all fixed point types (see 4.5). Multiplication and division of fixed point values deliver results of an anonymous predefined fixed point type that is called *universal_fixed* in this reference manual; the accuracy of this type is arbitrarily fine. The values of this type must be converted explicitly to some numeric type. **15**

Notes:

If S is a subtype of a fixed point type or subtype T, then the set of model numbers of S is a subset of those of T. If a length clause has been given for T, then both S and T have the same value for *small*. Otherwise, since *small* is a power of two, the *small* of S is equal to the *small* of T multiplied by a nonnegative power of two. **16**

A range constraint is allowed in a fixed point subtype indication, either directly after the type mark, or as part of a fixed point constraint. In either case the bounds of the range must belong to the base type of the type mark (see 3.5). **17**

Examples: **18**

```
type VOLT is delta 0.125 range 0.0 .. 255.0;
subtype ROUGH_VOLTAGE is VOLT delta 1.0;  --   same range as VOLT

--  A pure fraction which requires all the available space in a word
--  on a two's complement machine can be declared as the type FRACTION:

DEL : constant := 1.0/2**(WORD_LENGTH - 1);
type FRACTION is delta DEL range -1.0 .. 1.0 - DEL;
```

References: anonymous type 3.3.1, arithmetic operator 3.5.5 4.5, base type 3.3, belong to a subtype 3.3, bound of a range 3.5, compatible 3.3.2, conversion 4.6, elaboration 3.9, error bound 3.5.6, length clause 13.2, model number 3.5.6, numeric type 3.5, operation 3.3, predefined operator 4.5, range constraint 3.5, real type 3.5.6, real type definition 3.5.6, safe number 3.5.6, simple expression 4.4, static expression 4.9, subtype 3.3, subtype declaration 3.3.2, subtype indication 3.3.2, type 3.3, type declaration 3.3.1, type mark 3.3.2 **19**

3.5.10 Operations of Fixed Point Types

1   The basic operations of a fixed point type include the operations involved in assignment, membership tests, qualification, the explicit conversion of values of other numeric types to the fixed point type, and the implicit conversion of values of the type *universal_real* to the type.

2   In addition, for every fixed point type or subtype T the basic operations include the attributes listed below. In this presentation T is referred to as being a subtype (the subtype T) for any property that depends on constraints imposed by T; other properties are stated in terms of the base type of T.

3   The first group of attributes yield characteristics of the subtype T. The attributes of this group are the attributes BASE (see 3.3.2), the attributes FIRST and LAST (see 3.5), the representation attribute SIZE (see 13.7.2) and the following attributes:

4   T'DELTA   Yields the value of the delta specified in the fixed accuracy definition for the subtype T. The value of this attribute is of the type *universal_real*.

5   T'MANTISSA   Yields the number of binary digits in the mantissa of model numbers of the subtype T. (This attribute yields the number B of section 3.5.9.) The value of this attribute is of the type *universal_integer*.

6   T'SMALL   Yields the smallest positive (nonzero) model number of the subtype T. The value of this attribute is of the type *universal_real*.

7   T'LARGE   Yields the largest positive model number of the subtype T. The value of this attribute is of the type *universal_real*.

8   T'FORE   Yields the minimum number of characters needed for the integer part of the decimal representation of any value of the subtype T, assuming that the representation does not include an exponent, but includes a one-character prefix that is either a minus sign or a space. (This minimum number does not include superfluous zeros or underlines, and is at least two.) The value of this attribute is of the type *universal_integer*.

9   T'AFT   Yields the number of decimal digits needed after the point to accommodate the precision of the subtype T, unless the delta of the subtype T is greater than 0.1, in which case the attribute yields the value one. (T'AFT is the smallest positive integer N for which $(10**N)*$T'DELTA is greater than or equal to one.) The value of this attribute is of the type *universal_integer*.

10   The attributes of the second group include the following attributes which yield characteristics of the safe numbers:

11   T'SAFE_SMALL Yields the smallest positive (nonzero) safe number of the base type of T. The value of this attribute is of the type *universal_real*.

12   T'SAFE_LARGE Yields the largest positive safe number of the base type of T. The value of this attribute is of the type *universal_real*.

13   In addition, the attributes A'SIZE and A'ADDRESS are defined for an object A of a fixed point type (see 13.7.2). Finally, for each fixed point type or subtype T, there are the machine-dependent attributes T'MACHINE_ROUNDS and T'MACHINE_OVERFLOWS (see 13.7.3).

Besides the basic operations, the operations of a fixed point type include the relational operators, and the following predefined arithmetic operators: the binary and unary adding operators - and +, the multiplying operators ∗ and /, and the operator **abs**. 14

The operations of a subtype are the corresponding operations of the type except for the following: 15
assignment, membership tests, qualification, explicit conversion, and the attributes of the first group; the effects of these operations are redefined in terms of the subtype.

Notes:

The value of the attribute T'FORE depends only on the range of the subtype T. The value of the 16
attribute T'AFT depends only on the value of T'DELTA. The following relations exist between attributes of a fixed point type:

```
T'LARGE        = (2**T'MANTISSA  -  1)  ∗  T'SMALL
T'SAFE_LARGE   = T'BASE'LARGE
T'SAFE_SMALL   = T'BASE'SMALL
```

References: abs operator 4.5 4.5.6, arithmetic operator 3.5.5 4.5, assignment 5.2, base type 3.3, basic operation 17
3.3.3, binary adding operator 4.5 4.5.3, bound of a range 3.5, conversion 4.6, delta 3.5.9, fixed point type 3.5.9,
membership test 4.5 4.5.2, model number 3.5.6, multiplying operator 4.5 4.5.5, numeric type 3.5, object 3.2, operation 3.3, qualified expression 4.7, relational operator 4.5 4.5.2, safe number 3.5.6, subtype 3.3, unary adding operator
4.5 4.5.4, universal_integer type 3.5.4, universal_real type 3.5.6

3.6 Array Types

An array object is a composite object consisting of components that have the same subtype. The 1
name for a component of an array uses one or more index values belonging to specified discrete types. The value of an array object is a composite value consisting of the values of its components.

```
array_type_definition  ::=                                                             2
    unconstrained_array_definition | constrained_array_definition

unconstrained_array_definition  ::=
    array(index_subtype_definition {, index_subtype_definition}) of
            component_subtype_indication

constrained_array_definition  ::=
    array index_constraint of component_subtype_indication

index_subtype_definition  ::= type_mark range <>

index_constraint  ::=  (discrete_range {, discrete_range})

discrete_range  ::= discrete_subtype_indication | range
```

An array object is characterized by the number of indices (the *dimensionality* of the array), the type 3
and position of each index, the lower and upper bounds for each index, and the type and possible constraint of the components. The order of the indices is significant.

4   A one-dimensional array has a distinct component for each possible index value. A multidimensional array has a distinct component for each possible sequence of index values that can be formed by selecting one value for each index position (in the given order). The possible values for a given index are all the values between the lower and upper bounds, inclusive; this range of values is called the *index range*.

5   An unconstrained array definition defines an array type. For each object that has the array type, the number of indices, the type and position of each index, and the subtype of the components are as in the type definition; the values of the lower and upper bounds for each index belong to the corresponding index subtype, except for null arrays as explained in section 3.6.1. The *index subtype* for a given index position is, by definition, the subtype denoted by the type mark of the corresponding index subtype definition. The compound delimiter <> (called a *box*) of an index subtype definition stands for an undefined range (different objects of the type need not have the same bounds). The elaboration of an unconstrained array definition creates an array type; this elaboration includes that of the component subtype indication.

6   A constrained array definition defines both an array type and a subtype of this type:

7   ● The array type is an implicitly declared anonymous type; this type is defined by an (implicit) unconstrained array definition, in which the component subtype indication is that of the constrained array definition, and in which the type mark of each index subtype definition denotes the subtype defined by the corresponding discrete range.

8   ● The array subtype is the subtype obtained by imposition of the index constraint on the array type.

9   If a constrained array definition is given for a type declaration, the simple name declared by this declaration denotes the array subtype.

10   The elaboration of a constrained array definition creates the corresponding array type and array subtype. For this elaboration, the index constraint and the component subtype indication are elaborated. The evaluation of each discrete range of the index constraint and the elaboration of the component subtype indication are performed in some order that is not defined by the language.

11   *Examples of type declarations with unconstrained array definitions:*

```
type VECTOR      is array(INTEGER   range <>) of REAL;
type MATRIX      is array(INTEGER   range <>, INTEGER range <>) of REAL;
type BIT_VECTOR  is array(INTEGER   range <>) of BOOLEAN;
type ROMAN       is array(POSITIVE  range <>) of ROMAN_DIGIT;
```

12   *Examples of type declarations with constrained array definitions:*

```
type TABLE     is array(1 .. 10) of INTEGER;
type SCHEDULE  is array(DAY) of BOOLEAN;
type LINE      is array(1 .. MAX_LINE_SIZE) of CHARACTER;
```

13   *Examples of object declarations with constrained array definitions:*

```
GRID  : array(1 .. 80, 1 .. 100) of BOOLEAN;
MIX   : array(COLOR range RED .. GREEN) of BOOLEAN;
PAGE  : array(1 .. 50) of LINE;   --  an array of arrays
```

Note:

For a one-dimensional array, the rule given means that a type declaration with a constrained array   14
definition such as

    type T **is array**(POSITIVE **range** MIN .. MAX) **of** COMPONENT;

is equivalent (in the absence of an incorrect order dependence) to the succession of declarations   15

    subtype *index_subtype* **is** POSITIVE **range** MIN .. MAX;
    type *array_type* **is array**(*index_subtype* **range** <>) **of** COMPONENT;
    subtype T **is** *array_type*(*index_subtype*);

where *index_subtype* and *array_type* are both anonymous. Consequently, T is the name of a sub-   16
type and all objects declared with this type mark are arrays that have the same bounds. Similar
transformations apply to multidimensional arrays.

A similar transformation applies to an object whose declaration includes a constrained array defini-   17
tion. A consequence of this is that no two such objects have the same type.

References: anonymous type 3.3.1, bound of a range 3.5, component 3.3, constraint 3.3, discrete type 3.5,   18
elaboration 3.1 3.9, in some order 1.6, name 4.1, object 3.2, range 3.5, subtype 3.3, subtype indication 3.3.2, type
3.3, type declaration 3.3.1, type definition 3.3.1, type mark 3.3.2

3.6.1 Index Constraints and Discrete Ranges

An index constraint determines the range of possible values for every index of an array type, and   1
thereby the corresponding array bounds.

For a discrete range used in a constrained array definition and defined by a range, an implicit con-   2
version to the predefined type INTEGER is assumed if each bound is either a numeric literal, a
named number, or an attribute, and the type of both bounds (prior to the implicit conversion) is the
type *universal_integer*. Otherwise, both bounds must be of the same discrete type, other than
universal_integer; this type must be determinable independently of the context, but using the fact
that the type must be discrete and that both bounds must have the same type. These rules apply
also to a discrete range used in an iteration rule (see 5.5) or in the declaration of a family of entries
(see 9.5).

If an index constraint follows a type mark in a subtype indication, then the type or subtype denoted   3
by the type mark must not already impose an index constraint. The type mark must denote either
an unconstrained array type or an access type whose designated type is such an array type. In
either case, the index constraint must provide a discrete range for each index of the array type and
the type of each discrete range must be the same as that of the corresponding index.

An index constraint is *compatible* with the type denoted by the type mark if and only if the con-   4
straint defined by each discrete range is compatible with the corresponding index subtype. If any of
the discrete ranges defines a null range, any array thus constrained is a *null array*, having no components. An array value *satisfies* an index constraint if at each index position the array value and
the index constraint have the same index bounds. (Note, however, that assignment and certain
other operations on arrays involve an implicit subtype conversion.)

5   The bounds of each array object are determined as follows:

6   ● For a variable declared by an object declaration, the subtype indication of the corresponding object declaration must define a constrained array subtype (and, thereby, the bounds). The same requirement exists for the subtype indication of a component declaration, if the type of the record component is an array type; and for the component subtype indication of an array type definition, if the type of the array components is itself an array type.

7   ● For a constant declared by an object declaration, the bounds of the constant are defined by the initial value if the subtype of the constant is unconstrained; they are otherwise defined by this subtype (in the latter case, the initial value is the result of an implicit subtype conversion). The same rule applies to a generic formal parameter of mode **in**.

8   ● For an array object designated by an access value, the bounds must be defined by the allocator that creates the array object. (The allocated object is constrained with the corresponding values of the bounds.)

9   ● For a formal parameter of a subprogram or entry, the bounds are obtained from the corresponding actual parameter. (The formal parameter is constrained with the corresponding values of the bounds.)

10   ● For a renaming declaration and for a generic formal parameter of mode **in out**, the bounds are those of the renamed object or of the corresponding generic actual parameter.

11   For the elaboration of an index constraint, the discrete ranges are evaluated in some order that is not defined by the language.

12   *Examples of array declarations including an index constraint:*

```
BOARD        : MATRIX(1 .. 8,   1 .. 8);   --  see 3.6
RECTANGLE    : MATRIX(1 .. 20,  1 .. 30);
INVERSE      : MATRIX(1 .. N,   1 .. N);   --  N need not be static

FILTER       : BIT_VECTOR(0 .. 31);
```

13   *Example of array declaration with a constrained array subtype:*

```
MY_SCHEDULE : SCHEDULE;   --  all arrays of type SCHEDULE have the same bounds
```

14   *Example of record type with a component that is an array:*

```
type VAR_LINE(LENGTH : INTEGER) is
   record
      IMAGE : STRING(1 .. LENGTH);
   end record;

NULL_LINE : VAR_LINE(0);   --  NULL_LINE.IMAGE is a null array
```

Notes:

15   The elaboration of a subtype indication consisting of a type mark followed by an index constraint checks the compatibility of the index constraint with the type mark (see 3.3.2).

16   All components of an array have the same subtype. In particular, for an array of components that are one-dimensional arrays, this means that all components have the same bounds and hence the same length.

References: access type 3.8, access type definition 3.8, access value 3.8, actual parameter 6.4.1, allocator 4.8, array   17
bound 3.6, array component 3.6, array type 3.6, array type definition 3.6, bound of a range 3.5, compatible 3.3.2,
component declaration 3.7, constant 3.2.1, constrained array definition 3.6, constrained array subtype 3.6, conversion
4.6, designate 3.8, designated type 3.8, discrete range 3.6, entry 9.5, entry family declaration 9.5, expression 4.4, formal parameter 6.1, function 6.5, generic actual parameter 12.3, generic formal parameter 12.1 12.3, generic
parameter 12.1, index 3.6, index constraint 3.6.1, index subtype 3.6, initial value 3.2.1, integer literal 2.4, integer type
3.5.4, iteration rule 5.5, mode 12.1.1, name 4.1, null range 3.5, object 3.2, object declaration 3.2.1, predefined type
C, range 3.5, record component 3.7, renaming declaration 8.5, result subtype 6.1, satisfy 3.3, subprogram 6, subtype
conversion 4.6, subtype indication 3.3.2, type mark 3.3.2, unconstrained array type 3.6, unconstrained subtype 3.3,
universal type 4.10, universal_integer type 3.5.4, variable 3.2.1

3.6.2 Operations of Array Types

The basic operations of an array type include the operations involved in assignment and   1
aggregates (unless the array type is limited), membership tests, indexed components, qualification,
and explicit conversion; for one-dimensional arrays the basic operations also include the operations involved in slices, and also string literals if the component type is a character type.

If A is an array object, an array value, or a constrained array subtype, the basic operations also   2
include the attributes listed below. These attributes are not allowed for an unconstrained array
type. The argument N used in the attribute designators for the N-th dimension of an array must be
a static expression of type *universal_integer*. The value of N must be positive (nonzero) and no
greater than the dimensionality of the array.

A'FIRST	Yields the lower bound of the first index range. The value of this attribute has the same type as this lower bound.	3
A'FIRST(N)	Yields the lower bound of the N-th index range. The value of this attribute has the same type as this lower bound.	4
A'LAST	Yields the upper bound of the first index range. The value of this attribute has the same type as this upper bound.	5
A'LAST(N)	Yields the upper bound of the N-th index range. The value of this attribute has the same type as this upper bound.	6
A'RANGE	Yields the first index range, that is, the range A'FIRST .. A'LAST .	7
A'RANGE(N)	Yields the N-th index range, that is, the range A'FIRST (N) .. A'LAST (N).	8
A'LENGTH	Yields the number of values of the first index range (zero for a null range). The value of this attribute is of the type *universal_integer*.	9
A'LENGTH(N)	Yields the number of values of the N-th index range (zero for a null range). The value of this attribute is of the type *universal_integer*.	10

In addition, the attribute T'BASE is defined for an array type or subtype T (see 3.3.3); the attribute   11
T'SIZE is defined for an array type or subtype T, and the attributes A'SIZE and A'ADDRESS are
defined for an array object A (see 13.7.2).

12 Besides the basic operations, the operations of an array type include the predefined comparison for equality and inequality, unless the array type is limited. For one-dimensional arrays, the operations include catenation, unless the array type is limited; if the component type is a discrete type, the operations also include all predefined relational operators; if the component type is a boolean type, then the operations also include the unary logical negation operator **not**, and the logical operators.

13 *Examples (using arrays declared in the examples of section 3.6.1):*

```
--  FILTER'FIRST        =    0   FILTER'LAST        =   31   FILTER'LENGTH   =
--  RECTANGLE'LAST(1)   =   20   RECTANGLE'LAST(2)  =   30
```

Notes:

14 The attributes A'FIRST and A'FIRST(1) yield the same value. A similar relation exists for the attributes A'LAST, A'RANGE, and A'LENGTH. The following relations are satisfied (except for a null array) by the above attributes if the index type is an integer type:

```
A'LENGTH    = A'LAST    - A'FIRST    + 1
A'LENGTH(N) = A'LAST(N) - A'FIRST(N) + 1
```

15 An array type is limited if its component type is limited (see 7.4.4).

16 *References:* aggregate 4.3, array type 3.6, assignment 5.2, attribute 4.1.4, basic operation 3.3.3, bound of a range 3.5, catenation operator 4.5 4.5.3, character type 3.5.2, constrained array subtype 3.6, conversion 4.6, designator 6.1, dimension 3.6, index 3.6, indexed component 4.1.1, limited type 7.4.4, logical operator 4.5 4.5.1, membership test 4.5 4.5.2, not operator 4.5 4.5.6, null range 3.5, object 3.2, operation 3.3, predefined operator 4.5, qualified expression 4.7, relational operator 4.5 4.5.2, slice 4.1.2, static expression 4.9, string literal 2.6, subcomponent 3.3, type 3.3, unconstrained array type 3.6, universal type 4.10, universal_integer type 3.5.4

3.6.3 The Type String

1 The values of the predefined type STRING are one-dimensional arrays of the predefined type CHARACTER, indexed by values of the predefined subtype POSITIVE:

```
subtype POSITIVE is INTEGER range 1 .. INTEGER'LAST;
type STRING is array(POSITIVE range <>) of CHARACTER;
```

2 *Examples:*

```
STARS        : STRING(1 .. 120)  := (1 .. 120 => '*' );
QUESTION     : constant STRING   := "HOW MANY CHARACTERS?";
--  QUESTION'FIRST = 1, QUESTION'LAST = 20 (the number of characters)

ASK_TWICE    : constant STRING   := QUESTION & QUESTION;
NINETY_SIX   : constant ROMAN    := "XCVI";           -- see 3.6
```

Notes:

3 String literals (see 2.6 and 4.2) are basic operations applicable to the type STRING and to any other one-dimensional array type whose component type is a character type. The catenation operator is a predefined operator for the type STRING and for one-dimensional array types; it is represented as &. The relational operators <, <=, >, and >= are defined for values of these types, and correspond to lexicographic order (see 4.5.2).

References: aggregate 4.3, array 3.6, catenation operator 4.5 4.5.3, character type 3.5.2, component type (of an ⁴ array) 3.6, dimension 3.6, index 3.6, lexicographic order 4.5.2, positional aggregate 4.3, predefined operator 4.5, predefined type C, relational operator 4.5 4.5.2, string literal 2.6, subtype 3.3, type 3.3

3.7 Record Types

A record object is a composite object consisting of named components. The value of a record ₁ object is a composite value consisting of the values of its components.

```
record_type_definition ::=                                                         2
    record
        component_list
    end record

component_list ::=
        component_declaration {component_declaration}
    | {component_declaration} variant_part
    | null;

component_declaration ::=
    identifier_list : component_subtype_definition [:= expression];

.component_subtype_definition ::=  subtype_indication
```

Each component declaration declares a component of the record type. Besides components ₃ declared by component declarations, the components of a record type include any components declared by discriminant specifications of the record type declaration. The identifiers of all components of a record type must be distinct. The use of a name that denotes a record component other than a discriminant is not allowed within the record type definition that declares the component.

A component declaration with several identifiers is equivalent to a sequence of single component ₄ declarations, as explained in section 3.2. Each single component declaration declares a record component whose subtype is specified by the component subtype definition.

If a component declaration includes the assignment compound delimiter followed by an expres- ₅ sion, the expression is the default expression of the record component; the default expression must be of the type of the component. Default expressions are not allowed for components that are of a limited type.

If a record type does not have a discriminant part, the same components are present in all values ₆ of the type. If the component list of a record type is defined by the reserved word **null** and there is no discriminant part, then the record type has no components and all records of the type are *null* records.

The elaboration of a record type definition creates a record type; it consists of the elaboration of ₇ any corresponding (single) component declarations, in the order in which they appear, including any component declaration in a variant part. The elaboration of a component declaration consists of the elaboration of the component subtype definition.

For the elaboration of a component subtype definition, if the constraint does not depend on a dis- ₈ criminant (see 3.7.1), then the subtype indication is elaborated. If, on the other hand, the constraint depends on a discriminant, then the elaboration consists of the evaluation of any included expression that is not a discriminant.

9 *Examples of record type declarations:*

```
type DATE is
   record
      DAY    : INTEGER range 1 .. 31;
      MONTH  : MONTH_NAME;
      YEAR   : INTEGER range 0 .. 4000;
   end record;

type COMPLEX is
   record
      RE  : REAL := 0.0;
      IM  : REAL := 0.0;
   end record;
```

10 *Examples of record variables:*

```
TOMORROW, YESTERDAY : DATE;
A, B, C : COMPLEX;
```

-- both components of A, B, and C are implicitly initialized to zero

Notes:

11 The default expression of a record component is implicitly evaluated by the elaboration of the declaration of a record object, in the absence of an explicit initialization (see 3.2.1). If a component declaration has several identifiers, the expression is evaluated once for each such component of the object (since the declaration is equivalent to a sequence of single component declarations).

12 Unlike the components of an array, the components of a record need not be of the same type.

13 *References:* assignment compound delimiter 2.2, component 3.3, composite value 3.3, constraint 3.3, declaration 3.1, depend on a discriminant 3.7.1, discriminant 3.3, discriminant part 3.7 3.7.1, elaboration 3.9, expression 4.4, identifier 2.3, identifier list 3.2, limited type 7.4.4, name 4.1, object 3.2, subtype 3.3, type 3.3, type mark 3.3.2, variant part 3.7.3

3.7.1 Discriminants

1 A discriminant part specifies the discriminants of a type. A discriminant of a record is a component of the record. The type of a discriminant must be discrete.

2
```
discriminant_part ::=
    (discriminant_specification {; discriminant_specification})

discriminant_specification ::=
    identifier_list : type_mark [:= expression]
```

3 A discriminant part is only allowed in the type declaration for a record type, in a private type declaration or an incomplete type declaration (the corresponding full declaration must then declare a record type), and in the generic parameter declaration for a formal private type.

A discriminant specification with several identifiers is equivalent to a sequence of single discriminant specifications, as explained in section 3.2. Each single discriminant specification declares a discriminant. If a discriminant specification includes the assignment compound delimiter followed by an expression, the expression is the default expression of the discriminant; the default expression must be of the type of the discriminant. Default expressions must be provided either for all or for none of the discriminants of a discriminant part.

The use of the name of a discriminant is not allowed in default expressions of a discriminant part if the specification of the discriminant is itself given in the discriminant part.

Within a record type definition the only allowed uses of the name of a discriminant of the record type are: in the default expressions for record components; in a variant part as the discriminant name; and in a component subtype definition, either as a bound in an index constraint, or to specify a discriminant value in a discriminant constraint. A discriminant name used in these component subtype definitions must appear by itself, not as part of a larger expression. Such component subtype definitions and such constraints are said to *depend on a discriminant*.

A component is said to *depend on a discriminant* if it is a record component declared in a variant part, or a record component whose component subtype definition depends on a discriminant, or finally, one of the subcomponents of a component that itself depends on a discriminant.

Each record value includes a value for each discriminant specified for the record type; it also includes a value for each record component that does not depend on a discriminant. The values of the discriminants determine which other component values are in the record value.

Direct assignment to a discriminant of an object is not allowed; furthermore a discriminant is not allowed as an actual parameter of mode **in out** or **out**, or as a generic actual parameter of mode **in out**. The only allowed way to change the value of a discriminant of a variable is to assign a (complete) value to the variable itself. Similarly, an assignment to the variable itself is the only allowed way to change the constraint of one of its components, if the component subtype definition depends on a discriminant of the variable.

The elaboration of a discriminant part has no other effect.

Examples:

```
type BUFFER(SIZE : BUFFER_SIZE := 100) is          -- see 3.5.4
   record
      POS    : BUFFER_SIZE := 0;
      VALUE  : STRING(1 .. SIZE);
   end record;

type SQUARE(SIDE : INTEGER) is
   record
      MAT : MATRIX(1 .. SIDE, 1 .. SIDE);           -- see 3.6
   end record;

type DOUBLE_SQUARE(NUMBER : INTEGER) is
   record
      LEFT   : SQUARE (NUMBER);
      RIGHT  : SQUARE (NUMBER);
   end record;
```

```
type ITEM(NUMBER : POSITIVE) is
   record
      CONTENT : INTEGER;
      --  no component depends on the discriminant
   end record;
```

12   *References:* assignment 5.2, assignment compound delimiter 2.2, bound of a range 3.5, component 3.3, component declaration 3.7, component of a record 3.7, declaration 3.1, discrete type 3.5, discriminant 3.3, discriminant constraint 3.7.2, elaboration 3.9, expression 4.4, generic formal type 12.1, generic parameter declaration 12.1, identifier 2.3, identifier list 3.2, incomplete type declaration 3.8.1, index constraint 3.6.1, name 4.1, object 3.2, private type 7.4, private type declaration 7.4, record type 3.7, scope 8.2, simple name 4.1, subcomponent 3.3, subtype indication 3.3.2, type declaration 3.3.1, type mark 3.3.2, variant part 3.7.3

3.7.2 Discriminant Constraints

1   A discriminant constraint is only allowed in a subtype indication, after a type mark. This type mark must denote either a type with discriminants, or an access type whose designated type is a type with discriminants. A discriminant constraint specifies the values of these discriminants.

2
```
discriminant_constraint ::=
   (discriminant_association {, discriminant_association})

discriminant_association ::=
   [discriminant_simple_name {| discriminant_simple_name} =>] expression
```

3   Each discriminant association associates an expression with one or more discriminants. A discriminant association is said to be *named* if the discriminants are specified explicitly by their names; it is otherwise said to be *positional*. For a positional association, the (single) discriminant is implicitly specified by position, in textual order. Named associations can be given in any order, but if both positional and named associations are used in the same discriminant constraint, then positional associations must occur first, at their normal position. Hence once a named association is used, the rest of the discriminant constraint must use only named associations.

4   For a named discriminant association, the discriminant names must denote discriminants of the type for which the discriminant constraint is given. A discriminant association with more than one discriminant name is only allowed if the named discriminants are all of the same type. Furthermore, for each discriminant association (whether named or positional), the expression and the associated discriminants must have the same type. A discriminant constraint must provide exactly one value for each discriminant of the type.

5   A discriminant constraint is compatible with the type denoted by a type mark, if and only if each discriminant value belongs to the subtype of the corresponding discriminant. In addition, for each subcomponent whose component subtype specification depends on a discriminant, the discriminant value is substituted for the discriminant in this component subtype specification and the compatibility of the resulting subtype indication is checked.

6   A composite value satisfies a discriminant constraint if and only if each discriminant of the composite value has the value imposed by the discriminant constraint.

The initial values of the discriminants of an object of a type with discriminants are determined as follows: 7

- For a variable declared by an object declaration, the subtype indication of the corresponding   8
  object declaration must impose a discriminant constraint unless default expressions exist for
  the discriminants; the discriminant values are defined either by the constraint or, in its
  absence, by the default expressions. The same requirement exists for the subtype indication of
  a component declaration, if the type of the record component has discriminants; and for the
  component subtype indication of an array type, if the type of the array components is a type
  with discriminants.

- For a constant declared by an object declaration, the values of the discriminants are those of   9
  the initial value if the subtype of the constant is unconstrained; they are otherwise defined by
  this subtype (in the latter case, an exception is raised if the initial value does not belong to this
  subtype). The same rule applies to a generic parameter of mode **in**.

- For an object designated by an access value, the discriminant values must be defined by the   10
  allocator that creates the object. (The allocated object is constrained with the corresponding
  discriminant values.)

- For a formal parameter of a subprogram or entry, the discriminants of the formal parameter   11
  are initialized with those of the corresponding actual parameter. (The formal parameter is
  constrained if the corresponding actual parameter is constrained, and in any case if the mode
  is **in** or if the subtype of the formal parameter is constrained.)

- For a renaming declaration and for a generic formal parameter of mode **in out**, the discrimi-   12
  nants are those of the renamed object or of the corresponding generic actual parameter.

For the elaboration of a discriminant constraint, the expressions given in the discriminant associa-   13
tions are evaluated in some order that is not defined by the language; the expression of a named
association is evaluated once for each named discriminant.

Examples (using types declared in the previous section):   14

```
LARGE    : BUFFER(200);   --   constrained, always 200 characters (explicit discriminant value)
MESSAGE  : BUFFER;        --   unconstrained, initially 100 characters (default discriminant value)

BASIS    : SQUARE(5);     --   constrained, always 5 by 5
ILLEGAL  : SQUARE;        --   illegal, a SQUARE must be constrained
```

Note:

The above rules and the rules defining the elaboration of an object declaration (see 3.2) ensure   15
that discriminants always have a value. In particular, if a discriminant constraint is imposed on an
object declaration, each discriminant is initialized with the value specified by the constraint.
Similarly, if the subtype of a component has a discriminant constraint, the discriminants of the
component are correspondingly initialized.

References: access type 3.8, access type definition 3.8, access value 3.8, actual parameter 6.4.1, allocator 4.8, array   16
type definition 3.6, bound of a range 3.5, compatible 3.3.2, component 3.3, component declaration 3.7, component
subtype indication 3.7, composite value 3.3, constant 3.2.1, constrained subtype 3.3, constraint 3.3, declaration 3.1,
default expression for a discriminant 3.7, depend on a discriminant 3.7.1, designate 3.8, designated type 3.8, discriminant 3.3, elaboration 3.9, entry 9.5, evaluation 4.5, expression 4.4, formal parameter 6.1, generic actual parameter
12.3, generic formal parameter 12.1 12.3, mode in 6.1, mode in out 6.1, name 4.1, object 3.2, object declaration
3.2.1, renaming declaration 8.5, reserved word 2.9, satisfy 3.3, simple name 4.1, subcomponent 3.3, subprogram 6,
subtype 3.3, subtype indication 3.3.2, type 3.3, type mark 3.3.2, variable 3.2.1

Discriminant Constraints 3.7.2

3.7.3 Variant Parts

1. A record type with a variant part specifies alternative lists of components. Each variant defines the components for the corresponding value or values of the discriminant.

2.
```
variant_part ::=
    case discriminant_simple_name is
        variant
        { variant }
    end case;

variant ::=
    when choice {| choice} =>
        component_list

choice ::= simple_expression
    | discrete_range | others | component_simple_name
```

3. Each variant starts with a list of choices which must be of the same type as the discriminant of the variant part. The type of the discriminant of a variant part must not be a generic formal type. If the subtype of the discriminant is static, then each value of this subtype must be represented once and only once in the set of choices of the variant part, and no other value is allowed. Otherwise, each value of the (base) type of the discriminant must be represented once and only once in the set of choices.

4. The simple expressions and discrete ranges given as choices in a variant part must be static. A choice defined by a discrete range stands for all values in the corresponding range (none if a null range). The choice **others** is only allowed for the last variant and as its only choice; it stands for all values (possibly none) not given in the choices of previous variants. A component simple name is not allowed as a choice of a variant (although it is part of the syntax of choice).

5. A record value contains the values of the components of a given variant if and only if the discriminant value is equal to one of the values specified by the choices of the variant. This rule applies in turn to any further variant that is, itself, included in the component list of the given variant. If the component list of a variant is specified by **null**, the variant has no components.

6. *Example of record type with a variant part:*

```
type DEVICE is (PRINTER, DISK, DRUM);
type STATE  is (OPEN, CLOSED);

type PERIPHERAL(UNIT : DEVICE := DISK) is
    record
        STATUS : STATE;
        case UNIT is
            when PRINTER =>
                LINE_COUNT : INTEGER range 1 .. PAGE_SIZE;
            when others =>
                CYLINDER   : CYLINDER_INDEX;
                TRACK      : TRACK_NUMBER;
        end case;
    end record;
```

Examples of record subtypes: 7

```
subtype DRUM_UNIT  is  PERIPHERAL(DRUM);
subtype DISK_UNIT  is  PERIPHERAL(DISK);
```

Examples of constrained record variables: 8

```
WRITER  : PERIPHERAL(UNIT => PRINTER);
ARCHIVE : DISK_UNIT;
```

Note:

Choices with discrete values are also used in case statements and in array aggregates. Choices 9
with component simple names are used in record aggregates.

References: array aggregate 4.3.2, base type 3.3, component 3.3, component list 3.7, discrete range 3.6, 10
discriminant 3.3, generic formal type 12.1.2, null range 3.5, record aggregate 4.3.1, range 3.5, record type 3.7, simple
expression 4.4, simple name 4.1, static discrete range 4.9, static expression 4.9, static subtype 4.9, subtype 3.3

3.7.4 Operations of Record Types

The basic operations of a record type include the operations involved in assignment and 1
aggregates (unless the type is limited), membership tests, selection of record components,
qualification, and type conversion (for derived types).

For any object A of a type with discriminants, the basic operations also include the following 2
attribute:

A'CONSTRAINED   Yields the value TRUE if a discriminant constraint applies to the object A, 3
or if the object is a constant (including a formal parameter or generic for-
mal parameter of mode **in**); yields the value FALSE otherwise. If A is a
generic formal parameter of mode **in out**, or if A is a formal parameter of
mode **in out** or **out** and the type mark given in the corresponding
parameter specification denotes an unconstrained type with discriminants, then the value of this attribute is obtained from that of the corresponding actual parameter. The value of this attribute is of the
predefined type BOOLEAN.

In addition, the attributes T'BASE and T'SIZE are defined for a record type or subtype T (see 3.3.3); 4
the attributes A'SIZE and A'ADDRESS are defined for a record object A (see 13.7.2).

Besides the basic operations, the operations of a record type include the predefined comparison 5
for equality and inequality, unless the type is limited.

Note:

A record type is limited if the type of any of its components is limited (see 7.4.4). 6

References: actual parameter 6.4.1, aggregate 4.3, assignment 5.2, attribute 4.1.4, basic operation 3.3.3, boolean 7
type 3.5.3, constant 3.2.1, conversion 4.6, derived type 3.4, discriminant 3.3, discriminant constraint 3.7.2, formal
parameter 6.1, generic actual parameter 12.3, generic formal parameter 12.1 12.3, limited type 7.4.4, membership
test 4.5 4.5.2, mode 6.1, object 3.2.1, operation 3.3, predefined operator 4.5, predefined type C, qualified expression
4.7, record type 3.7, relational operator 4.5 4.5.2, selected component 4.1.3, subcomponent 3.3, subtype 3.3, type
3.3

3.8 Access Types

1 An object declared by an object declaration is created by the elaboration of the object declaration and is denoted by a simple name or by some other form of name. In contrast, there are objects that are created by the evaluation of *allocators* (see 4.8) and that have no simple name. Access to such an object is achieved by an *access value* returned by an allocator; the access value is said to *designate* the object.

2
    access_type_definition ::= **access** subtype_indication

3 For each access type, there is a literal **null** which has a null access value designating no object at all. The null value of an access type is the default initial value of the type. Other values of an access type are obtained by evaluation of a special operation of the type, called an allocator. Each such access value designates an object of the subtype defined by the subtype indication of the access type definition; this subtype is called the *designated subtype*; the base type of this subtype is called the *designated type*. The objects designated by the values of an access type form a *collection* implicitly associated with the type.

4 The elaboration of an access type definition consists of the elaboration of the subtype indication and creates an access type.

5 If an access object is constant, the contained access value cannot be changed and always designates the same object. On the other hand, the value of the designated object need not remain the same (assignment to the designated object is allowed unless the designated type is limited).

6 The only forms of constraint that are allowed after the name of an access type in a subtype indication are index constraints and discriminant constraints. (See sections 3.6.1 and 3.7.2 for the rules applicable to these subtype indications.) An access value *belongs* to a corresponding subtype of an access type either if the access value is the null value or if the value of the designated object satisfies the constraint.

7 *Examples:*

        type FRAME **is access** MATRIX;   -- see 3.6

        type BUFFER_NAME **is access** BUFFER;   -- see 3.7.1

Notes:

8 An access value delivered by an allocator can be assigned to several access objects. Hence it is possible for an object created by an allocator to be designated by more than one variable or constant of the access type. An access value can only designate an object created by an allocator; in particular, it cannot designate an object declared by an object declaration.

9 If the type of the objects designated by the access values is an array type or a type with discriminants, these objects are constrained with either the array bounds or the discriminant values supplied implicitly or explicitly for the corresponding allocators (see 4.8).

10 Access values are called *pointers* or *references* in some other languages.

11 *References:* allocator 4.8, array type 3.6, assignment 5.2, belong to a subtype 3.3, constant 3.2.1, constraint 3.3, discriminant constraint 3.7.2, elaboration 3.9, index constraint 3.6.1, index specification 3.6, limited type 7.4.4, literal 4.2, name 4.1, object 3.2.1, object declaration 3.2.1, reserved word 2.9, satisfy 3.3, simple name 4.1, subcomponent 3.3, subtype 3.3, subtype indication 3.3.2, type 3.3, variable 3.2.1

3.8.1 Incomplete Type Declarations

There are no particular limitations on the designated type of an access type. In particular, the type of a component of the designated type can be another access type, or even the same access type. This permits mutually dependent and recursive access types. Their declarations require a prior incomplete (or private) type declaration for one or more types.

    incomplete_type_declaration ::= **type** identifier [discriminant_part]; 2

For each incomplete type declaration, there must be a corresponding declaration of a type with the 3 same identifier. The corresponding declaration must be either a full type declaration or the declaration of a task type. In the rest of this section, explanations are given in terms of full type declarations; the same rules apply also to declarations of task types. If the incomplete type declaration occurs immediately within either a declarative part or the visible part of a package specification, then the full type declaration must occur later and immediately within this declarative part or visible part. If the incomplete type declaration occurs immediately within the private part of a package, then the full type declaration must occur later and immediately within either the private part itself, or the declarative part of the corresponding package body.

A discriminant part must be given in the full type declaration if and only if one is given in the 4 incomplete type declaration; if discriminant parts are given, then they must conform (see 6.3.1 for the conformance rules). Prior to the end of the full type declaration, the only allowed use of a name that denotes a type declared by an incomplete type declaration is as the type mark in the subtype indication of an access type definition; the only form of constraint allowed in this subtype indication is a discriminant constraint.

The elaboration of an incomplete type declaration creates a type. If the incomplete type declara- 5 tion has a discriminant part, this elaboration includes that of the discriminant part: in such a case, the discriminant part of the full type declaration is not elaborated.

Example of a recursive type: 6

```
type CELL;  --  incomplete type declaration
type LINK is access CELL;

type CELL is
   record
      VALUE  : INTEGER;
      SUCC   : LINK;
      PRED   : LINK;
   end record;

HEAD  : LINK := new CELL'(0, null, null);
NEXT  : LINK := HEAD.SUCC;
```

Examples of mutually dependent access types: 7

```
type PERSON(SEX : GENDER);   --  incomplete type declaration
type CAR;                     --  incomplete type declaration

type PERSON_NAME  is access PERSON;
type CAR_NAME      is access CAR;

type CAR is
   record
      NUMBER   : INTEGER;
      OWNER    : PERSON_NAME;
   end record;
```

```
type PERSON(SEX : GENDER) is
  record
    NAME     : STRING(1 .. 20);
    BIRTH    : DATE;
    AGE      : INTEGER range 0 .. 130;
    VEHICLE  : CAR_NAME;
    case SEX is
      when M  => WIFE      : PERSON_NAME(SEX => F);
      when F  => HUSBAND   : PERSON_NAME(SEX => M);
    end case;
  end record;

MY_CAR, YOUR_CAR, NEXT_CAR : CAR_NAME;  --  implicitly initialized with null value
```

8   *References:* access type 3.8, access type definition 3.8, component 3.3, conform 6.3.1, constraint 3.3, declaration 3.1, declarative item 3.9, designate 3.8, discriminant constraint 3.7.2, discriminant part 3.7.1, elaboration 3.9, identifier 2.3, name 4.1, subtype indication 3.3.2, type 3.3, type mark 3.3.2

3.8.2 Operations of Access Types

1   The basic operations of an access type include the operations involved in assignment, allocators for the access type, membership tests, qualification, explicit conversion, and the literal **null**. If the designated type is a type with discriminants, the basic operations include the selection of the corresponding discriminants; if the designated type is a record type, they include the selection of the corresponding components; if the designated type is an array type, they include the formation of indexed components and slices; if the designated type is a task type, they include selection of entries and entry families. Furthermore, the basic operations include the formation of a selected component with the reserved word **all** (see 4.1.3).

2   If the designated type is an array type, the basic operations include the attributes that have the attribute designators FIRST, LAST, RANGE, and LENGTH (likewise, the attribute designators of the N-th dimension). The prefix of each of these attributes must be a value of the access type. These attributes yield the corresponding characteristics of the designated object (see 3.6.2).

3   If the designated type is a task type, the basic operations include the attributes that have the attribute designators TERMINATED and CALLABLE (see 9.9). The prefix of each of these attributes must be a value of the access type. These attributes yield the corresponding characteristics of the designated task objects.

4   In addition, the attribute T'BASE (see 3.3.3) and the representation attributes T'SIZE and T'STORAGE_SIZE (see 13.7.2) are defined for an access type or subtype T; the attributes A'SIZE and A'ADDRESS are defined for an access object A (see 13.7.2).

5   Besides the basic operations, the operations of an access type include the predefined comparison for equality and inequality.

6   *References:* access type 3.8, allocator 4.8, array type 3.6, assignment 5.2, attribute 4.1.4, attribute designator 4.1.4, base type 3.3, basic operation 3.3.3, collection 3.8, constrained array subtype 3.6, conversion 4.6, designate 3.8, designated subtype 3.8, designated type 3.8, discriminant 3.3, indexed component 4.1.1, literal 4.2, membership test 4.5 4.5.2, object 3.2.1, operation 3.3, private type 7.4, qualified expression 4.7, record type 3.7, selected component 4.1.3, slice 4.1.2, subtype 3.3, task type 9.1, type 3.3

3.9 Declarative Parts

A declarative part contains declarative items (possibly none).   1

```
declarative_part ::=                                                              2
    {basic_declarative_item} {later_declarative_item}

basic_declarative_item ::= basic_declaration
    | representation_clause | use_clause

later_declarative_item ::= body
    | subprogram_declaration  | package_declaration
    | task_declaration        | generic_declaration
    | use_clause              | generic_instantiation

body ::= proper_body | body_stub

proper_body ::= subprogram_body | package_body | task_body
```

The elaboration of a declarative part consists of the elaboration of the declarative items, if any, in   3
the order in which they are given in the declarative part. After its elaboration, a declarative item is
said to be *elaborated*. Prior to the completion of its elaboration (including before the elaboration),
the declarative item is not yet elaborated.

For several forms of declarative item, the language rules (in particular scope and visibility rules) are   4
such that it is either impossible or illegal to use an entity before the elaboration of the declarative
item that declares this entity. For example, it is not possible to use the name of a type for an object
declaration if the corresponding type declaration is not yet elaborated. In the case of bodies, the
following checks are performed:

- For a subprogram call, a check is made that the body of the subprogram is already elaborated.   5

- For the activation of a task, a check is made that the body of the corresponding task unit is   6
  already elaborated.

- For the instantiation of a generic unit that has a body, a check is made that this body is   7
  already elaborated.

The exception PROGRAM_ERROR is raised if any of these checks fails.   8

If a subprogram declaration, a package declaration, a task declaration, or a generic declaration is a   9
declarative item of a given declarative part, then the body (if there is one) of the program unit
declared by the declarative item must itself be a declarative item of this declarative part (and must
appear later). If the body is a body stub, then a separately compiled subunit containing the corresponding proper body is required for the program unit (see 10.2).

References: activation 9.3, instantiation 12.3, program_error exception 11.1, scope 8.2, subprogram call 6.4, type   10
3.3, visibility 8.3

Elaboration of declarations: 3.1, component declaration 3.7, deferred constant declaration 7.4.3, discriminant   11
specification 3.7.1, entry declaration 9.5, enumeration literal specification 3.5.1, generic declaration 12.1, generic
instantiation 12.3, incomplete type declaration 3.8.1, loop parameter specification 5.5, number declaration 3.2.2,
object declaration 3.2.1, package declaration 7.2, parameter specification 6.1, private type declaration 7.4.1, renaming declaration 8.5, subprogram declaration 6.1, subtype declaration 3.3.2, task declaration 9.1, type declaration 3.3.1

12   *Elaboration of type definitions:*   3.3.1, access type definition 3.8, array type definition 3.6, derived type definition 3.4, enumeration type definition 3.5.1, integer type definition 3.5.4, real type definition 3.5.6, record type definition 3.7

13   *Elaboration of other constructs:*   context clause 10.1, body stub 10.2, compilation unit 10.1, discriminant part 3.7.1, generic body 12.2, generic formal parameter 12.1 12.3, library unit 10.5, package body 7.1, representation clause 13.1, subprogram body 6.3, subunit 10.2, task body 9.1, task object 9.2, task specification 9.1, use clause 8.4, with clause 10.1.1

4. Names and Expressions

The rules applicable to the different forms of name and expression, and to their evaluation, are given in this chapter. 1

4.1 Names

Names can denote declared entities, whether declared explicitly or implicitly (see 3.1). Names can also denote objects designated by access values; subcomponents and slices of objects and values; single entries, entry families, and entries in families of entries. Finally, names can denote attributes of any of the foregoing. 1

```
name ::= simple_name
     | character_literal    | operator_symbol
     | indexed_component    | slice
     | selected_component   | attribute

simple_name ::= identifier

prefix ::= name | function_call
```
2

A simple name for an entity is either the identifier associated with the entity by its declaration, or another identifier associated with the entity by a renaming declaration. 3

Certain forms of name (indexed and selected components, slices, and attributes) include a *prefix* that is either a name or a function call. If the type of a prefix is an access type, then the prefix must not be a name that denotes a formal parameter of mode **out** or a subcomponent thereof. 4

If the prefix of a name is a function call, then the name denotes a component, a slice, an attribute, an entry, or an entry family, either of the result of the function call, or (if the result is an access value) of the object designated by the result. 5

A prefix is said to be *appropriate for a type* in either of the following cases: 6

- The type of the prefix is the type considered. 7

- The type of the prefix is an access type whose designated type is the type considered. 8

The evaluation of a name determines the entity denoted by the name. This evaluation has no other effect for a name that is a simple name, a character literal, or an operator symbol. 9

The evaluation of a name that has a prefix includes the evaluation of the prefix, that is, of the corresponding name or function call. If the type of the prefix is an access type, the evaluation of the prefix includes the determination of the object designated by the corresponding access value; the exception CONSTRAINT_ERROR is raised if the value of the prefix is a null access value, except in the case of the prefix of a representation attribute (see 13.7.2). 10

11   *Examples of simple names:*

PI	--	the simple name of a number	(see 3.2.2)
LIMIT	--	the simple name of a constant	(see 3.2.1)
COUNT	--	the simple name of a scalar variable	(see 3.2.1)
BOARD	--	the simple name of an array variable	(see 3.6.1)
MATRIX	--	the simple name of a type	(see 3.6)
RANDOM	--	the simple name of a function	(see 6.1)
ERROR	--	the simple name of an exception	(see 11.1)

12   *References:* access type 3.8, access value 3.8, attribute 4.1.4, belong to a type 3.3, character literal 2.5, component 3.3, constraint_error exception 11.1, declaration 3.1, designate 3.8, designated type 3.8, entity 3.1, entry 9.5, entry family 9.5, evaluation 4.5, formal parameter 6.1, function call 6.4, identifier 2.3, indexed component 4.1.1, mode 6.1, null access value 3.8, object 3.2.1, operator symbol 6.1, raising of exceptions 11, renaming declarations 8.5, selected component 4.1.3, slice 4.1.2, subcomponent 3.3, type 3.3

4.1.1 Indexed Components

1   An indexed component denotes either a component of an array or an entry in a family of entries.

2   indexed_component ::= prefix(expression {, expression})

3   In the case of a component of an array, the prefix must be appropriate for an array type. The expressions specify the index values for the component; there must be one such expression for each index position of the array type. In the case of an entry in a family of entries, the prefix must be a name that denotes an entry family of a task object, and the expression (there must be exactly one) specifies the index value for the individual entry.

4   Each expression must be of the type of the corresponding index. For the evaluation of an indexed component, the prefix and the expressions are evaluated in some order that is not defined by the language. The exception CONSTRAINT_ERROR is raised if an index value does not belong to the range of the corresponding index of the prefixing array or entry family.

5   *Examples of indexed components:*

MY_SCHEDULE(SAT)	--	a component of a one-dimensional array	(see 3.6.1)
PAGE(10)	--	a component of a one-dimensional array	(see 3.6)
BOARD(M, J + 1)	--	a component of a two-dimensional array	(see 3.6.1)
PAGE(10)(20)	--	a component of a component	(see 3.6)
REQUEST(MEDIUM)	--	an entry in a family of entries	(see 9.5)
NEXT_FRAME(L)(M, N)	--	a component of a function call	(see 6.1)

Notes on the examples:

6   Distinct notations are used for components of multidimensional arrays (such as BOARD) and arrays of arrays (such as PAGE). The components of an array of arrays are arrays and can therefore be indexed. Thus PAGE (10)(20) denotes the 20th component of PAGE (10). In the last example NEXT_FRAME(L) is a function call returning an access value which designates a two-dimensional array.

7   *References:* appropriate for a type 4.1, array type 3.6, component 3.3, component of an array 3.6, constraint_error exception 11.1, dimension 3.6, entry 9.5, entry family 9.5, evaluation 4.5, expression 4.4, function call 6.4, in some order 1.6, index 3.6, name 4.1, prefix 4.1, raising of exceptions 11, returned value 5.8 6.5, task object 9.2

4.1.2 Slices

A slice denotes a one-dimensional array formed by a sequence of consecutive components of a one-dimensional array. A slice of a variable is a variable; a slice of a constant is a constant; a slice of a value is a value.

```
slice ::= prefix(discrete_range)
```

The prefix of a slice must be appropriate for a one-dimensional array type. The type of the slice is the base type of this array type. The bounds of the discrete range define those of the slice and must be of the type of the index; the slice is a *null slice* denoting a null array if the discrete range is a null range.

For the evaluation of a name that is a slice, the prefix and the discrete range are evaluated in some order that is not defined by the language. The exception CONSTRAINT_ERROR is raised by the evaluation of a slice, other than a null slice, if any of the bounds of the discrete range does not belong to the index range of the prefixing array. (The bounds of a null slice need not belong to the subtype of the index.)

Examples of slices:

```
STARS(1 .. 15)            -- a slice of 15 characters          (see 3.6.3)
PAGE(10 .. 10 + SIZE)     -- a slice of 1 + SIZE components    (see 3.6 and 3.2.1)
PAGE(L)(A .. B)           -- a slice of the array PAGE(L)      (see 3.6)
STARS(1 .. 0)             -- a null slice                      (see 3.6.3)
MY_SCHEDULE(WEEKDAY)      -- bounds given by subtype           (see 3.6 and 3.5.1)
STARS(5 .. 15)(K)         -- same as STARS(K)                  (see 3.6.3)
                          -- provided that K is in 5 .. 15
```

Notes:

For a one-dimensional array A, the name A(N .. N) is a slice of one component; its type is the base type of A. On the other hand, A(N) is a component of the array A and has the corresponding component type.

References: appropriate for a type 4.1, array 3.6, array type 3.6, array value 3.8, base type 3.3, belong to a subtype 3.3, bound of a discrete range 3.6.1, component 3.3, component type 3.3, constant 3.2.1, constraint 3.3, constraint_error exception 11.1, dimension 3.6, discrete range 3.6, evaluation 4.5, index 3.6, index range 3.6, name 4.1, null array 3.6.1, null range 3.5, prefix 4.1, raising of exceptions 11, type 3.3, variable 3.2.1

4.1.3 Selected Components

Selected components are used to denote record components, entries, entry families, and objects designated by access values; they are also used as *expanded names* as described below.

```
selected_component ::= prefix.selector
```

```
selector ::= simple_name
    | character_literal | operator_symbol | all
```

3   The following four forms of selected components are used to denote a discriminant, a record component, an entry, or an object designated by an access value:

4   (a) A discriminant:

5   The selector must be a simple name denoting a discriminant of an object or value. The prefix must be appropriate for the type of this object or value.

6   (b) A component of a record:

7   The selector must be a simple name denoting a component of a record object or value. The prefix must be appropriate for the type of this object or value.

8   For a component of a variant, a check is made that the values of the discriminants are such that the record has this component. The exception CONSTRAINT_ERROR is raised if this check fails.

9   (c) A single entry or an entry family of a task:

10   The selector must be a simple name denoting a single entry or an entry family of a task. The prefix must be appropriate for the type of this task.

11   (d) An object designated by an access value:

12   The selector must be the reserved word **all**. The value of the prefix must belong to an access type.

13   A selected component of one of the remaining two forms is called an *expanded name*. In each case the selector must be either a simple name, a character literal, or an operator symbol. A function call is not allowed as the prefix of an expanded name. An expanded name can denote:

14   (e) An entity declared in the visible part of a package:

15   The prefix must denote the package. The selector must be the simple name, character literal, or operator symbol of the entity.

16   (f) An entity whose declaration occurs immediately within a named construct:

17   The prefix must denote a construct that is either a program unit, a block statement, a loop statement, or an accept statement. In the case of an accept statement, the prefix must be either the simple name of the entry or entry family, or an expanded name ending with such a simple name (that is, no index is allowed). The selector must be the simple name, character literal, or operator symbol of an entity whose declaration occurs immediately within the construct.

18   This form of expanded name is only allowed within the construct itself (including the body and any subunits, in the case of a program unit). A name declared by a renaming declaration is not allowed as the prefix. If the prefix is the name of a subprogram or accept statement and if there is more than one visible enclosing subprogram or accept statement of this name, the expanded name is ambiguous, independently of the selector.

19   If, according to the visibility rules, there is at least one possible interpretation of the prefix of a selected component as the name of an enclosing subprogram or accept statement, then the only interpretations considered are those of rule (f), as expanded names (no interpretations of the prefix as a function call are then considered).

The evaluation of a name that is a selected component includes the evaluation of the prefix.   20

Examples of selected components: 21

```
TOMORROW.MONTH        --  a record component              (see 3.7)
NEXT_CAR.OWNER        --  a record component              (see 3.8.1)
NEXT_CAR.OWNER.AGE    --  a record component              (see 3.8.1)
WRITER.UNIT           --  a record component (a discriminant)  (see 3.7.3)
MIN_CELL(H).VALUE     --  a record component of the result  (see 6.1 and 3.8.1)
                      --  of the function call MIN_CELL(H)

CONTROL.SEIZE         --  an entry of the task CONTROL     (see 9.1 and 9.2)
POOL(K).WRITE         --  an entry of the task POOL(K)     (see 9.1 and 9.2)

NEXT_CAR.all          --  the object designated by
                      --  the access variable NEXT_CAR    (see 3.8.1)
```

Examples of expanded names: 22

```
TABLE_MANAGER.INSERT  --  a procedure of the visible part of a package  (see 7.5)
KEY_MANAGER."<"       --  an operator of the visible part of a package   (see 7.4.2)

DOT_PRODUCT.SUM       --  a variable declared in a procedure body  (see 6.5)
BUFFER.POOL           --  a variable declared in a task unit       (see 9.12)
BUFFER.READ           --  an entry of a task unit                  (see 9.12)
SWAP.TEMP             --  a variable declared in a block statement  (see 5.6)
STANDARD.BOOLEAN      --  the name of a predefined type             (see 8.6 and C)
```

Note:

For a record with components that are other records, the above rules imply that the simple name   23
must be given at each level for the name of a subcomponent. For example, the name
NEXT_CAR.OWNER.BIRTH.MONTH cannot be shortened (NEXT_CAR.OWNER.MONTH is not
allowed).

References: accept statement 9.5, access type 3.8, access value 3.8, appropriate for a type 4.1, block statement 5.6,   24
body of a program unit 3.9, character literal 2.5, component of a record 3.7, constraint_error exception 11.1, declaration 3.1, designate 3.8, discriminant 3.3, entity 3.1, entry 9.5, entry family 9.5, function call 6.4, index 3.6, loop statement 5.5, object 3.2.1, occur immediately within 8.1, operator 4.5, operator symbol 6.1, overloading 8.3, package 7,
predefined type C, prefix 4.1, procedure body 6.3, program unit 6, raising of exceptions 11, record 3.7, record component 3.7, renaming declaration 8.5, reserved word 2.9, simple name 4.1, subprogram 6, subunit 10.2, task 9, task
object 9.2, task unit 9, variable 3.7.3, variant 3.7.3, visibility 8.3, visible part 3.7.3

4.1.4 Attributes

An attribute denotes a basic operation of an entity given by a prefix.   1

    attribute ::= prefix'attribute_designator   2

    attribute_designator ::= simple_name [(*universal_static_*expression)]

The applicable attribute designators depend on the prefix. An attribute can be a basic operation   3
delivering a value; alternatively it can be a function, a type, or a range. The meaning of the prefix of
an attribute must be determinable independently of the attribute designator and independently of
the fact that it is the prefix of an attribute.

4 The attributes defined by the language are summarized in Annex A. In addition, an implementation may provide implementation-defined attributes; their description must be given in Appendix F. The attribute designator of any implementation-defined attribute must not be the same as that of any language-defined attribute.

5 The evaluation of a name that is an attribute consists of the evaluation of the prefix.

Notes:

6 The attribute designators DIGITS, DELTA, and RANGE have the same identifier as a reserved word. However, no confusion is possible since an attribute designator is always preceded by an apostrophe. The only predefined attribute designators that have a universal expression are those for certain operations of array types (see 3.6.2).

7 *Examples of attributes:*

COLOR'FIRST	-- minimum value of the enumeration type COLOR	(see 3.3.1 3.5)
RAINBOW'BASE'FIRST	-- same as COLOR'FIRST	(see 3.3.2 3.3.3)
REAL'DIGITS	-- precision of the type REAL	(see 3.5.7 3.5.8)
BOARD'LAST(2)	-- upper bound of the second dimension of BOARD	(see 3.6.1 3.6.2)
BOARD'RANGE(1)	-- index range of the first dimension of BOARD	(see 3.6.1 3.6.2)
POOL(K)'TERMINATED	-- TRUE if task POOL(K) is terminated	(see 9.2 9.9)
DATE'SIZE	-- number of bits for records of type DATE	(see 3.7 13.7.2)
MESSAGE'ADDRESS	-- address of the record variable MESSAGE	(see 3.7.2 13.7.2)

8 *References:* appropriate for a type 4.1, basic operation 3.3.3, declared entity 3.1, name 4.1, prefix 4.1, reserved word 2.9, simple name 4.1, static expression 4.9, type 3.3, universal expression 4.10

4.2 Literals

1 A literal is either a numeric literal, an enumeration literal, the literal **null**, or a string literal. The evaluation of a literal yields the corresponding value.

2 Numeric literals are the literals of the types *universal_integer* and *universal_real*. Enumeration literals include character literals and yield values of the corresponding enumeration types. The literal **null** yields a null access value which designates no objects at all.

3 A string literal is a basic operation that combines a sequence of characters into a value of a one-dimensional array of a character type; the bounds of this array are determined according to the rules for positional array aggregates (see 4.3.2). For a null string literal, the upper bound is the predecessor, as given by the PRED attribute, of the lower bound. The evaluation of a null string literal raises the exception CONSTRAINT_ERROR if the lower bound does not have a predecessor (see 3.5.5).

4 The type of a string literal and likewise the type of the literal **null** must be determinable solely from the context in which this literal appears, excluding the literal itself, but using the fact that the literal **null** is a value of an access type, and similarly that a string literal is a value of a one-dimensional array type whose component type is a character type.

5 The character literals corresponding to the graphic characters contained within a string literal must be visible at the place of the string literal (although these characters themselves are not used to determine the type of the string literal).

Examples:

```
3.14159_26536    --   a real literal
1_345            --   an integer literal
CLUBS            --   an enumeration literal
'A'              --   a character literal
"SOME TEXT"      --   a string literal
```

References: access type 3.8, aggregate 4.3, array 3.6, array bound 3.6, array type 3.6, character literal 2.5, character type 3.5.2, component type 3.3, constraint_error exception 11.1, designate 3.8, dimension 3.6, enumeration literal 3.5.1, graphic character 2.1, integer literal 2.4, null access value 3.8, null literal 3.8, numeric literal 2.4, object 3.2.1, real literal 2.4, string literal 2.6, type 3.3, universal_integer type 3.5.4, universal_real type 3.5.6, visibility 8.3

4.3 Aggregates

An aggregate is a basic operation that combines component values into a composite value of a record or array type.

```
aggregate ::=
   (component_association  {, component_association})

component_association ::=
   [choice {| choice} => ] expression
```

Each component association associates an expression with components (possibly none). A component association is said to be *named* if the components are specified explicitly by choices; it is otherwise said to be *positional*. For a positional association, the (single) component is implicitly specified by position, in the order of the corresponding component declarations for record components, in index order for array components.

Named associations can be given in any order (except for the choice **others**), but if both positional and named associations are used in the same aggregate, then positional associations must occur first, at their normal position. Hence once a named association is used, the rest of the aggregate must use only named associations. Aggregates containing a single component association must always be given in named notation. Specific rules concerning component associations exist for record aggregates and array aggregates.

Choices in component associations have the same syntax as in variant parts (see 3.7.3). A choice that is a component simple name is only allowed in a record aggregate. For a component association, a choice that is a simple expression or a discrete range is only allowed in an array aggregate; a choice that is a simple expression specifies the component at the corresponding index value; similarly a discrete range specifies the components at the index values in the range. The choice **others** is only allowed in a component association if the association appears last and has this single choice; it specifies all remaining components, if any.

Each component of the value defined by an aggregate must be represented once and only once in the aggregate. Hence each aggregate must be complete and a given component is not allowed to be specified by more than one choice.

The type of an aggregate must be determinable solely from the context in which the aggregate appears, excluding the aggregate itself, but using the fact that this type must be composite and not limited. The type of an aggregate in turn determines the required type for each of its components.

Notes:

8   The above rule implies that the determination of the type of an aggregate cannot use any information from within the aggregate. In particular, this determination cannot use the type of the expression of a component association, or the form or the type of a choice. An aggregate can always be distinguished from an expression enclosed by parentheses: this is a consequence of the fact that named notation is required for an aggregate with a single component.

9   *References:* array aggregate 4.3.2, array type 3.6, basic operation 3.3.3, choice 3.7.3, component 3.3, composite type 3.3, composite value 3.3, discrete range 3.6, expression 4.4, index 3.6, limited type 7.4.4, primary 4.4, record aggregate 4.3.1, record type 3.7, simple expression 4.4, simple name 4.1, type 3.3, variant part 3.7.3

4.3.1 Record Aggregates

1   If the type of an aggregate is a record type, the component names given as choices must denote components (including discriminants) of the record type. If the choice **others** is given as a choice of a record aggregate, it must represent at least one component. A component association with the choice **others** or with more than one choice is only allowed if the represented components are all of the same type. The expression of a component association must have the type of the associated record components.

2   The value specified for a discriminant that governs a variant part must be given by a static expression (note that this value determines which dependent components must appear in the record value).

3   For the evaluation of a record aggregate, the expressions given in the component associations are evaluated in some order that is not defined by the language. The expression of a named association is evaluated once for each associated component. A check is made that the value of each subcomponent of the aggregate belongs to the subtype of this subcomponent. The exception CONSTRAINT_ERROR is raised if this check fails.

4   *Example of a record aggregate with positional associations:*

        (4, JULY, 1776)   -- see 3.7

5   *Examples of record aggregates with named associations:*

        (DAY => 4, MONTH => JULY, YEAR => 1776)
        (MONTH => JULY, DAY => 4, YEAR => 1776)

        (DISK, CLOSED, TRACK => 5, CYLINDER => 12)   -- see 3.7.3
        (UNIT => DISK, STATUS => CLOSED, CYLINDER => 9, TRACK => 1)

6   *Example of component association with several choices:*

        (VALUE => 0, SUCC|PRED => **new** CELL'(0, **null**, **null**))   -- see 3.8.1
        -- The allocator is evaluated twice: SUCC and PRED designate different cells

Note:

7   For an aggregate with positional associations, discriminant values appear first since the discriminant part is given first in the record type declaration; they must be in the same order as in the discriminant part.

References: aggregate 4.3, allocator 4.8, choice 3.7.3, component association 4.3, component name 3.7, constraint 3.3, constraint_error exception 11.1, depend on a discriminant 3.7.1, discriminant 3.3, discriminant part 3.7.1, evaluate 4.5, expression 4.4, in some order 1.6, program 10, raising of exceptions 11, record component 3.7, record type 3.7, satisfy 3.3, static expression 4.9, subcomponent 3.3, subtype 3.3.2, type 3.3, variant part 3.7.3 8

4.3.2 Array Aggregates

If the type of an aggregate is a one-dimensional array type, then each choice must specify values of the index type, and the expression of each component association must be of the component type. 1

If the type of an aggregate is a multidimensional array type, an n-dimensional aggregate is written as a one-dimensional aggregate, in which the expression specified for each component association is itself written as an (n-1)-dimensional aggregate which is called a *subaggregate*; the index subtype of the one-dimensional aggregate is given by the first index position of the array type. The same rule is used to write a subaggregate if it is again multidimensional, using successive index positions. A string literal is allowed in a multidimensional aggregate at the place of a one-dimensional array of a character type. In what follows, the rules concerning array aggregates are formulated in terms of one-dimensional aggregates. 2

Apart from a final component association with the single choice **others**, the rest (if any) of the component associations of an array aggregate must be either all positional or all named. A named association of an array aggregate is only allowed to have a choice that is not static, or likewise a choice that is a null range, if the aggregate includes a single component association and this component association has a single choice. An **others** choice is static if the applicable index constraint is static. 3

The bounds of an array aggregate that has an **others** choice are determined by the applicable index constraint. An **others** choice is only allowed if the aggregate appears in one of the following contexts (which defines the applicable index constraint): 4

(a) The aggregate is an actual parameter, a generic actual parameter, the result expression of a function, or the expression that follows an assignment compound delimiter. Moreover, the subtype of the corresponding formal parameter, generic formal parameter, function result, or object is a constrained array subtype. 5

For an aggregate that appears in such a context and contains an association with an **others** choice, named associations are allowed for other associations only in the case of a (nongeneric) actual parameter or function result. If the aggregate is a multidimensional array, this restriction also applies to each of its subaggregates. 6

(b) The aggregate is the operand of a qualified expression whose type mark denotes a constrained array subtype. 7

(c) The aggregate is the expression of the component association of an enclosing (array or record) aggregate. Moreover, if this enclosing aggregate is a multidimensional array aggregate then it is itself in one of these three contexts. 8

The bounds of an array aggregate that does not have an **others** choice are determined as follows. For an aggregate that has named associations, the bounds are determined by the smallest and largest choices given. For a positional aggregate, the lower bound is determined by the applicable index constraint if the aggregate appears in one of the contexts (a) through (c); otherwise, the lower bound is given by S'FIRST where S is the index subtype; in either case, the upper bound is determined by the number of components. 9

10 The evaluation of an array aggregate that is not a subaggregate proceeds in two steps. First, th
choices of this aggregate and of its subaggregates, if any, are evaluated in some order that is no
defined by the language. Second, the expressions of the component associations of the arra
aggregate are evaluated in some order that is not defined by the language; the expression of
named association is evaluated once for each associated component. The evaluation of a subagg
gregate consists of this second step (the first step is omitted since the choices have already beer
evaluated).

11 For the evaluation of an aggregate that is not a null array, a check is made that the index value
defined by choices belong to the corresponding index subtypes, and also that the value of eacl
subcomponent of the aggregate belongs to the subtype of this subcomponent. For an n
dimensional multidimensional aggregate, a check is made that all (n-1)-dimensional subaggrega
tes have the same bounds. The exception CONSTRAINT_ERROR is raised if any of these check
fails.

Note:

12 The allowed contexts for an array aggregate including an **others** choice are such that the bounds o
such an aggregate are always known from the context.

13 *Examples of array aggregates with positional associations:*

```
(7, 9, 5, 1, 3, 2, 4, 8, 6, 0)
TABLE'(5, 8, 4, 1, others => 0)   --  see 3.6
```

14 *Examples of array aggregates with named associations:*

```
(1 .. 5 => (1 .. 8 => 0.0))      --  two-dimensional
(1 .. N => new CELL)             --  N new cells, in particular for N = 0

TABLE'(2 | 4 | 10 =>   1, others   => 0)
SCHEDULE'(MON .. FRI => TRUE,   others => FALSE)   --  see 3.6
SCHEDULE'(WED | SUN => FALSE,   others =>  TRUE )
```

15 *Examples of two-dimensional array aggregates:*

```
-- Three aggregates for the same value of type MATRIX (see 3.6):

((1.1, 1.2, 1.3), (2.1, 2.2, 2.3))
(1 => (1.1, 1.2, 1.3), 2 => (2.1, 2.2, 2.3))
(1 => (1 => 1.1, 2 => 1.2, 3 => 1.3), 2 => (1 => 2.1, 2 => 2.2, 3 => 2.3
```

16 *Examples of aggregates as initial values:*

```
A : TABLE := (7, 9, 5, 1, 3, 2, 4, 8, 6, 0);          -- A(1)=7, A(10)=0
B : TABLE := TABLE'(2 | 4 | 10 => 1, others => 0);  -- B(1)=0, B(10)=1
C : constant MATRIX := (1 .. 5 => (1 .. 8 => 0.0));  -- C'FIRST(1)=1, C'LAST(2)=8

D : BIT_VECTOR(M .. N) := (M .. N => TRUE);  -- see 3.6
E : BIT_VECTOR(M .. N) := (others  => TRUE);
F : STRING(1 .. 1) := (1 => 'F');  -- a one component aggregate: same as "F"
```

17 *References:* actual parameter 6.4.1, aggregate 4.3, array type 3.6, assignment compound delimiter 5.2, choice 3.7.3
component 3.3, component association 4.3, component type 3.3, constrained array subtype 3.6, constraint 3.3, con-
straint_error exception 11.1, dimension 3.6, evaluate 4.5, expression 4.4, formal parameter 6.1, function 6.5, in some
order 1.6, index constraint 3.6.1, index range 3.6, index subtype 3.6, index type 3.6, named component association
4.3, null array 3.6.1, object 3.2, positional component association 4.3, qualified expression 4.7, raising of exceptions
11, static expression 4.9, subcomponent 3.3, type 3.3

4.4 Expressions

An expression is a formula that defines the computation of a value.

```
expression ::=
      relation {and relation}  |  relation {and then relation}
   |  relation {or relation}   |  relation {or else relation}
   |  relation {xor relation}

relation ::=
      simple_expression [relational_operator simple_expression]
   |  simple_expression [not] in range
   |  simple_expression [not] in type_mark

simple_expression ::= [unary_adding_operator] term {binary_adding_operator term}

term ::= factor {multiplying_operator factor}

factor ::= primary [** primary]  |  abs primary  |  not primary

primary ::=
      numeric_literal | null | aggregate | string_literal | name | allocator
   |  function_call | type_conversion | qualified_expression | (expression)
```

Each primary has a value and a type. The only names allowed as primaries are named numbers; attributes that yield values; and names denoting objects (the value of such a primary is the value of the object) or denoting values. Names that denote formal parameters of mode **out** are not allowed as primaries; names of their subcomponents are only allowed in the case of discriminants.

The type of an expression depends only on the type of its constituents and on the operators applied; for an overloaded constituent or operator, the determination of the constituent type, or the identification of the appropriate operator, depends on the context. For each predefined operator, the operand and result types are given in section 4.5.

Examples of primaries:

```
4.0                     --  real literal
PI                      --  named number
(1 .. 10 => 0)          --  array aggregate
SUM                     --  variable
INTEGER'LAST            --  attribute
SINE(X)                 --  function call
COLOR'(BLUE)            --  qualified expression
REAL(M*N)               --  conversion
(LINE_COUNT + 10)       --  parenthesized expression
```

Examples of expressions:

```
VOLUME                  --  primary
not DESTROYED           --  factor
2*LINE_COUNT            --  term
-4.0                    --  simple expression
-4.0 + A                --  simple expression
B**2 - 4.0*A*C          --  simple expression
PASSWORD(1 .. 3) = "BWV"   --  relation
COUNT in SMALL_INT      --  relation
COUNT not in SMALL_INT  --  relation
INDEX = 0 or ITEM_HIT   --  expression
(COLD and SUNNY) or WARM   --  expression (parentheses are required)
A**(B**C)               --  expression (parentheses are required)
```

7   *References:* aggregate 4.3, allocator 4.8, array aggregate 4.3.2, attribute 4.1.4, binary adding operator 4.5 4.5.3, context of overload resolution 8.7, exponentiating operator 4.5 4.5.6, function call 6.4, multiplying operator 4.5 4.5.5, name 4.1, named number 3.2, null literal 3.8, numeric literal 2.4, object 3.2, operator 4.5, overloading 8.3, overloading an operator 6.7, qualified expression 4.7, range 3.5, real literal 2.4, relation 4.5.1, relational operator 4.5 4.5.2, result type 6.1, string literal 2.6, type 3.3, type conversion 4.6, type mark 3.3.2, unary adding operator 4.5 4.5.4, variable 3.2.1

4.5 Operators and Expression Evaluation

1   The language defines the following six classes of operators. The corresponding operator symbols (except /=), and only those, can be used as designators in declarations of functions for user-defined operators. They are given in the order of increasing precedence.

2 | | | |
|---|---|---|
| logical_operator | ::= | **and** \| **or** \| **xor** |
| relational_operator | ::= | = \| /= \| < \| <= \| > \| >= |
| binary_adding_operator | ::= | + \| - \| & |
| unary_adding_operator | ::= | + \| - |
| multiplying_operator | ::= | * \| / \| **mod** \| **rem** |
| highest_precedence_operator | ::= | ** \| **abs** \| **not** |

3   The short-circuit control forms **and then** and **or else** have the same precedence as logical operators. The membership tests **in** and **not in** have the same precedence as relational operators.

4   For a term, simple expression, relation, or expression, operators of higher precedence are associated with their operands before operators of lower precedence. In this case, for a sequence of operators of the same precedence level, the operators are associated in textual order from left to right; parentheses can be used to impose specific associations.

5   The operands of a factor, of a term, of a simple expression, or of a relation, and the operands of an expression that does not contain a short-circuit control form, are evaluated in some order that is not defined by the language (but before application of the corresponding operator). The right operand of a short-circuit control form is evaluated if and only if the left operand has a certain value (see 4.5.1).

6   For each form of type declaration, certain of the above operators are *predefined*, that is, they are implicitly declared by the type declaration. For each such implicit operator declaration, the names of the parameters are LEFT and RIGHT for binary operators; the single parameter is called RIGHT for unary adding operators and for the unary operators **abs** and **not**. The effect of the predefined operators is explained in subsections 4.5.1 through 4.5.7.

7   The predefined operations on integer types either yield the mathematically correct result or raise the exception NUMERIC_ERROR. A predefined operation that delivers a result of an integer type (other than *universal_integer*) can only raise the exception NUMERIC_ERROR if the mathematical result is not a value of the type. The predefined operations on real types yield results whose accuracy is defined in section 4.5.7. A predefined operation that delivers a result of a real type (other than *universal_real*) can only raise the exception NUMERIC_ERROR if the result is not within the range of the safe numbers of the type, as explained in section 4.5.7.

Examples of precedence:

```
not SUNNY or WARM     --   same as (not SUNNY) or WARM
X > 4.0 and Y > 0.0   --   same as (X > 4.0) and (Y > 0.0)

-4.0*A**2             --   same as -(4.0 * (A**2))
abs(1 + A) + B        --   same as (abs (1 + A)) + B
Y**(-3)               --   parentheses are necessary
A / B * C             --   same as (A/B)*C
A + (B + C)           --   evaluate B + C before adding it to A
```

References: designator 6.1, expression 4.4, factor 4.4, implicit declaration 3.1, in some order 1.6, integer type 3.5.4, membership test 4.5.2, name 4.1, numeric_error exception 11.1, overloading 6.6 8.7, raising of an exception 11, range 3.5, real type 3.5.6, relation 4.4, safe number 3.5.6, short-circuit control form 4.5 4.5.1, simple expression 4.4, term 4.4, type 3.3, type declaration 3.3.1, universal_integer type 3.5.4, universal_real type 3.5.6

4.5.1 Logical Operators and Short-circuit Control Forms

The following logical operators are predefined for any boolean type and any one-dimensional array type whose components are of a boolean type; in either case the two operands have the same type.

Operator	Operation	Operand type	Result type
and	conjunction	any boolean type array of boolean components	same boolean type same array type
or	inclusive disjunction	any boolean type array of boolean components	same boolean type same array type
xor	exclusive disjunction	any boolean type array of boolean components	same boolean type same array type

The operations on arrays are performed on a component-by-component basis on matching components, if any (as for equality, see 4.5.2). The bounds of the resulting array are those of the left operand. A check is made that for each component of the left operand there is a matching component of the right operand, and vice versa. The exception CONSTRAINT_ERROR is raised if this check fails.

The short-circuit control forms **and then** and **or else** are defined for two operands of a boolean type and deliver a result of the same type. The left operand of a short-circuit control form is always evaluated first. If the left operand of an expression with the control form **and then** evaluates to FALSE, the right operand is not evaluated and the value of the expression is FALSE. If the left operand of an expression with the control form **or else** evaluates to TRUE, the right operand is not evaluated and the value of the expression is TRUE. If both operands are evaluated, **and then** delivers the same result as **and**, and **or else** delivers the same result as **or**.

Note: The conventional meaning of the logical operators is given by the following truth table:

A	B	A **and** B	A **or** B	A **xor** B
TRUE	TRUE	TRUE	TRUE	FALSE
TRUE	FALSE	FALSE	TRUE	TRUE
FALSE	TRUE	FALSE	TRUE	TRUE
FALSE	FALSE	FALSE	FALSE	FALSE

7   *Examples of logical operators:*

    SUNNY **or** WARM
    FILTER(1 .. 10) **and** FILTER(15 .. 24)   --   see 3.6.1

8   *Examples of short-circuit control forms:*

    NEXT_CAR.OWNER /= **null and then** NEXT_CAR.OWNER.AGE > 25   --   see 3.8.1
    N = 0 **or else** A(N) = HIT_VALUE

9   *References:* array type 3.6, boolean type 3.5.3, bound of an index range 3.6.1, component of an array 3.6, constraint_error exception 11.1, dimension 3.6, false boolean value 3.5.3, index subtype 3.6, matching components of arrays 4.5.2, null array 3.6.1, operation 3.3, operator 4.5, predefined operator 4.5, raising of exceptions 11, true boolean value 3.5.3, type 3.3

4.5.2 Relational Operators and Membership Tests

1   The equality and inequality operators are predefined for any type that is not limited. The other relational operators are the ordering operators < (less than), <= (less than or equal), > (greater than), and >= (greater than or equal). The ordering operators are predefined for any scalar type, and for any discrete array type, that is, a one-dimensional array type whose components are of a discrete type. The operands of each predefined relational operator have the same type. The result type is the predefined type BOOLEAN.

2   The relational operators have their conventional meaning: the result is equal to TRUE if the corresponding relation is satisfied; the result is FALSE otherwise. The inequality operator gives the complementary result to the equality operator: FALSE if equal, TRUE if not equal.

3
Operator	Operation	Operand type	Result type
= /=	equality and inequality	any type	BOOLEAN
< <= > >=	test for ordering	any scalar type	BOOLEAN
		discrete array type	BOOLEAN

4   Equality for the discrete types is equality of the values. For real operands whose values are *nearly equal*, the results of the predefined relational operators are given in section 4.5.7. Two access values are equal either if they designate the same object, or if both are equal to the null value of the access type.

5   For two array values or two record values of the same type, the left operand is equal to the right operand if and only if for each component of the left operand there is a *matching component* of the right operand and vice versa; and the values of matching components are equal, as given by the predefined equality operator for the component type. In particular, two null arrays of the same type are always equal; two null records of the same type are always equal.

6   For comparing two records of the same type, *matching components* are those which have the same component identifier.

7   For comparing two one-dimensional arrays of the same type, *matching components* are those (if any) whose index values match in the following sense: the lower bounds of the index ranges are defined to match, and the successors of matching indices are defined to match. For comparing two multidimensional arrays, matching components are those whose index values match in successive index positions.

If equality is explicitly defined for a limited type, it does not extend to composite types having sub-components of the limited type (explicit definition of equality is allowed for such composite types).   8

The ordering operators <, <=, >, and >= that are defined for discrete array types correspond to   9
lexicographic order using the predefined order relation of the component type. A null array is lex-icographically less than any array having at least one component. In the case of nonnull arrays, the left operand is lexicographically less than the right operand if the first component of the left operand is less than that of the right; otherwise the left operand is lexicographically less than the right operand only if their first components are equal and the tail of the left operand is lex-icographically less than that of the right (the tail consists of the remaining components beyond the first and can be null).

The membership tests **in** and **not in** are predefined for all types. The result type is the predefined   10
type BOOLEAN. For a membership test with a range, the simple expression and the bounds of the range must be of the same scalar type; for a membership test with a type mark, the type of the simple expression must be the base type of the type mark. The evaluation of the membership test **in** yields the result TRUE if the value of the simple expression is within the given range, or if this value belongs to the subtype denoted by the given type mark; otherwise this evaluation yields the result FALSE (for a value of a real type, see 4.5.7). The membership test **not in** gives the complementary result to the membership test **in**.

Examples: 11

```
X /= Y

""  <  "A"  and  "A"  <  "AA"        --    TRUE
"AA"  <  "B"  and  "A"  <  "A    "    --    TRUE

MY_CAR  =  null                  -- true if MY_CAR has been set to null  (see 3.8.1)
MY_CAR  =  YOUR_CAR              -- true if we both share the same car
MY_CAR.all  =  YOUR_CAR.all      -- true if the two cars are identical

N not in 1 .. 10        -- range membership test
TODAY in MON .. FRI     -- range membership test
TODAY in WEEKDAY        -- subtype membership test  (see 3.5.1)
ARCHIVE in DISK_UNIT    -- subtype membership test  (see 3.7.3)
```

Notes:

No exception is ever raised by a predefined relational operator or by a membership test, but an   12
exception can be raised by the evaluation of the operands.

If a record type has components that depend on discriminants, two values of this type have mat-   13
ching components if and only if their discriminants are equal. Two nonnull arrays have matching components if and only if the value of the attribute LENGTH(N) for each index position N is the same for both.

References: access value 3.8, array type 3.6, base type 3.3, belong to a subtype 3.3, boolean predefined type 3.5.3,   14
bound of a range 3.5, component 3.3, component identifier 3.7, component type 3.3, composite type 3.3, designate 3.8, dimension 3.6, discrete type 3.5, evaluation 4.5, exception 11, index 3.6, index range 3.6, limited type 7.4.4, null access value 3.8, null array 3.6.1, null record 3.7, object 3.2.1, operation 3.3, operator 4.5, predefined operator 4.5, raising of exceptions 11, range 3.5, record type 3.7, scalar type 3.5, simple expression 4.4, subcomponent 3.3, successor 3.5.5, type 3.3, type mark 3.3.2

4.5.3 Binary Adding Operators

1 The binary adding operators + and - are predefined for any numeric type and have their conventional meaning. The catenation operators & are predefined for any one-dimensional array type that is not limited.

2

Operator	Operation	Left operand type	Right operand type	Result type
+	addition	any numeric type	same numeric type	same numeric type
-	subtraction	any numeric type	same numeric type	same numeric type
&	catenation	any array type	same array type	same array type
		any array type	the component type	same array type
		the component type	any array type	same array type
		the component type	the component type	any array type

3 For real types, the accuracy of the result is determined by the operand type (see 4.5.7).

4 If both operands are one-dimensional arrays, the result of the catenation is a one-dimensional array whose length is the sum of the lengths of its operands, and whose components comprise the components of the left operand followed by the components of the right operand. The lower bound of this result is the lower bound of the left operand, unless the left operand is a null array, in which case the result of the catenation is the right operand.

5 If either operand is of the component type of an array type, the result of the catenation is given by the above rules, using in place of this operand an array having this operand as its only component and having the lower bound of the index subtype of the array type as its lower bound.

6 The exception CONSTRAINT_ERROR is raised by catenation if the upper bound of the result exceeds the range of the index subtype, unless the result is a null array. This exception is also raised if any operand is of the component type but has a value that does not belong to the component subtype.

7 *Examples:*

```
Z + 0.1        --  Z must be of a real type

"A" & "BCD"    --  catenation of two string literals
'A' & "BCD"    --  catenation of a character literal and a string literal
'A' & 'A'      --  catenation of two character literals
```

8 *References:* array type 3.6, character literal 2.5, component type 3.3, constraint_error exception 11.1, dimension 3.6, index subtype 3.6, length of an array 3.6.2, limited type 7.4.4, null array 3.6.1, numeric type 3.5, operation 3.3, operator 4.5, predefined operator 4.5, raising of exceptions 11, range of an index subtype 3.6.1, real type 3.5.6, string literal 2.6, type 3.3

4.5.4 Unary Adding Operators

1 The unary adding operators + and - are predefined for any numeric type and have their conventional meaning. For each of these operators, the operand and the result have the same type.

Operator	Operation	Operand type	Result type	
+	identity	any numeric type	same numeric type	2
-	negation	any numeric type	same numeric type	

References: numeric type 3.5, operation 3.3, operator 4.5, predefined operator 4.5, type 3.3   3

4.5.5 Multiplying Operators

The operators * and / are predefined for any integer and any floating point type and have their con-   1
ventional meaning; the operators **mod** and **rem** are predefined for any integer type. For each of
these operators, the operands and the result have the same base type. For floating point types, the
accuracy of the result is determined by the operand type (see 4.5.7).

Operator	Operation	Operand type	Result type	
*	multiplication	any integer type any floating point type	same integer type same floating point type	2
/	integer division floating division	any integer type any floating point type	same integer type same floating point type	
mod	modulus	any integer type	same integer type	
rem	remainder	any integer type	same integer type	

Integer division and remainder are defined by the relation   3

$$A = (A/B)*B + (A \text{ rem } B)$$

where (A **rem** B) has the sign of A and an absolute value less than the absolute value of B. Integer   4
division satisfies the identity

$$(-A)/B = -(A/B) = A/(-B)$$

The result of the modulus operation is such that (A **mod** B) has the sign of B and an absolute value   5
less than the absolute value of B; in addition, for some integer value N, this result must satisfy the
relation

$$A = B*N + (A \text{ mod } B)$$

For each fixed point type, the following multiplication and division operators, with an operand of   6
the predefined type INTEGER , are predefined.

Operator	Operation	Left operand type	Right operand type	Result type	
*	multiplication	any fixed point type INTEGER	INTEGER any fixed point type	same as left same as right	7
/	division	any fixed point type	INTEGER	same as left	

Multiplying Operators 4.5.5

8   Integer multiplication of fixed point values is equivalent to repeated addition. Division of a fixed point value by an integer does not involve a change in type but is approximate (see 4.5.7).

9   Finally, the following multiplication and division operators are declared in the predefined package STANDARD. These two special operators apply to operands of all fixed point types (it is a consequence of other rules that they cannot be renamed or given as generic actual parameters).

10
Operator	Operation	Left operand type	Right operand type	Result type
*	multiplication	any fixed point type	any fixed point type	universal_fixed
/	division	any fixed point type	any fixed point type	universal_fixed

11   Multiplication of operands of the same or of different fixed point types is exact and delivers a result of the anonymous predefined fixed point type *universal_fixed* whose delta is arbitrarily small. The result of any such multiplication must always be explicitly converted to some numeric type. This ensures explicit control of the accuracy of the computation. The same considerations apply to division of a fixed point value by another fixed point value. No other operators are defined for the type *universal_fixed*.

12   The exception NUMERIC_ERROR is raised by integer division, **rem**, and **mod** if the right operand is zero.

13   *Examples:*

```
I   :  INTEGER := 1;
J   :  INTEGER := 2;
K   :  INTEGER := 3;

X   :  REAL digits 6 := 1.0;          --      see 3.5.7
Y   :  REAL digits 6 := 2.0;

F   :  FRACTION delta 0.0001 := 0.1;  --      see 3.5.9
G   :  FRACTION delta 0.0001 := 0.1;
```

Expression	Value	Result Type
I*J	2	same as I and J, that is, INTEGER
K/J	1	same as K and J, that is, INTEGER
K **mod** J	1	same as K and J, that is, INTEGER
X/Y	0.5	same as X and Y, that is, REAL
F/2	0.05	same as F, that is, FRACTION
3*F	0.3	same as F, that is, FRACTION
F*G	0.01	*universal_fixed*, conversion needed
FRACTION(F*G)	0.01	FRACTION, as stated by the conversion
REAL(J)*Y	4.0	REAL, the type of both operands after conversion of J

Notes:

For positive A and B, A/B is the quotient and A **rem** B is the remainder when A is divided by B. The
following relations are satisfied by the **rem** operator:

```
A    rem  (-B)  =     A  rem  B
(-A)  rem   B   =    -(A  rem  B)
```

For any integer K, the following identity holds:

$$A \textbf{ mod } B \quad = \quad (A + K{*}B) \textbf{ mod } B$$

The relations between integer division, remainder, and modulus are illustrated by the following
table:

A	B	A/B	A rem B	A mod B	A	B	A/B	A rem B	A mod B
10	5	2	0	0	-10	5	-2	0	0
11	5	2	1	1	-11	5	-2	-1	4
12	5	2	2	2	-12	5	-2	-2	3
13	5	2	3	3	-13	5	-2	-3	2
14	5	2	4	4	-14	5	-2	-4	1
10	-5	-2	0	0	-10	-5	2	0	0
11	-5	-2	1	-4	-11	-5	2	-1	-1
12	-5	-2	2	-3	-12	-5	2	-2	-2
13	-5	-2	3	-2	-13	-5	2	-3	-3
14	-5	-2	4	-1	-14	-5	2	-4	-4

References: actual parameter 6.4.1, base type 3.3, declaration 3.1, delta of a fixed point type 3.5.9, fixed point type
3.5.9, floating point type 3.5.7, generic formal subprogram 12.1, integer type 3.5.4, numeric type 3.5, numeric_error
exception 11.1, predefined operator 4.5, raising of exceptions 11, renaming declaration 8.5, standard predefined
package 8.6, type conversion 4.6

4.5.6 Highest Precedence Operators

The highest precedence unary operator **abs** is predefined for any numeric type. The highest
precedence unary operator **not** is predefined for any boolean type and any one-dimensional array
type whose components have a boolean type.

Operator	Operation	Operand type	Result type
abs	absolute value	any numeric type	same numeric type
not	logical negation	any boolean type array of boolean components	same boolean type same array type

The operator **not** that applies to a one-dimensional array of boolean components yields a one-
dimensional boolean array with the same bounds; each component of the result is obtained by
logical negation of the corresponding component of the operand (that is, the component that has
the same index value).

4   The highest precedence *exponentiating* operator ∗∗ is predefined for each integer type and for each floating point type. In either case the right operand, called the exponent, is of the predefined type INTEGER.

5

Operator	Operation	Left operand type	Right operand type	Result type
∗∗	exponentiation	any integer type	INTEGER	same as left
		any floating point type	INTEGER	same as left

6   Exponentiation with a positive exponent is equivalent to repeated multiplication of the left operand by itself, as indicated by the exponent and from left to right. For an operand of a floating point type, the exponent can be negative, in which case the value is the reciprocal of the value with the positive exponent. Exponentiation by a zero exponent delivers the value one. Exponentiation of a value of a floating point type is approximate (see 4.5.7). Exponentiation of an integer raises the exception CONSTRAINT_ERROR for a negative exponent.

7   *References:* array type 3.6, boolean type 3.5.3, bound of an array 3.6.1, component of an array 3.6, constraint_error exception 11.1, dimensionality 3.6, floating point type 3.5.9, index 3.6, integer type 3.5.4, multiplication operation 4.5.5, predefined operator 4.5, raising of exceptions 11

4.5.7 Accuracy of Operations with Real Operands

1   A real subtype specifies a set of model numbers. Both the accuracy required from any basic or predefined operation giving a real result, and the result of any predefined relation between real operands are defined in terms of these model numbers.

2   A *model interval* of a subtype is any interval whose bounds are model numbers of the subtype. The model interval associated with a value that belongs to a real subtype is the smallest model interval (of the subtype) that includes the value. (The model interval associated with a model number of a subtype consists of that number only.)

3   For any basic operation or predefined operator that yields a result of a real subtype, the required bounds on the result are given by a model interval defined as follows:

4   • The result model interval is the smallest model interval (of the result subtype) that includes the minimum and the maximum of all the values obtained by applying the (exact) mathematical operation, when each operand is given any value of the model interval (of the operand subtype) defined for the operand.

5   • The model interval of an operand that is itself the result of an operation, other than an implicit conversion, is the result model interval of this operation.

6   • The model interval of an operand whose value is obtained by implicit conversion of a universal expression is the model interval associated with this value within the operand subtype.

7   The result model interval is undefined if the absolute value of one of the above mathematical results exceeds the largest safe number of the result type. Whenever the result model interval is undefined, it is highly desirable that the exception NUMERIC_ERROR be raised if the implementation cannot produce an actual result that is in the range of safe numbers. This is, however, not required by the language rules, in recognition of the fact that certain target machines do not permit easy detection of overflow situations. The value of the attribute MACHINE_OVERFLOWS indicates whether the target machine raises the exception NUMERIC_ERROR in overflow situations (see 13.7.3).

The safe numbers of a real type are defined (see 3.5.6) as a superset of the model numbers, for 8
which error bounds follow the same rules as for model numbers. Any definition given in this section in terms of model intervals can therefore be extended to safe intervals of safe numbers. A consequence of this extension is that an implementation is not allowed to raise the exception NUMERIC_ERROR when the result interval is a safe interval.

For the result of exponentiation, the model interval defining the bounds on the result is obtained by 9
applying the above rules to the sequence of multiplications defined by the exponent, and to the final division in the case of a negative exponent.

For the result of a relation between two real operands, consider for each operand the model inter- 10
val (of the operand subtype) defined for the operand; the result can be any value obtained by applying the mathematical comparison to values arbitrarily chosen in the corresponding operand model intervals. If either or both of the operand model intervals is undefined (and if neither of the operand evaluations raises an exception) then the result of the comparison is allowed to be any possible value (that is, either TRUE or FALSE).

The result of a membership test is defined in terms of comparisons of the operand value with the 11
lower and upper bounds of the given range or type mark (the usual rules apply to these comparisons).

Note:

For a floating point type the numbers 15.0, 3.0, and 5.0 are always model numbers. Hence X/Y 12
where X equals 15.0 and Y equals 3.0 yields exactly 5.0 according to the above rules. In the general case, division does not yield model numbers and in consequence one cannot assume that $(1.0/X)*X = 1.0$.

References: attribute 4.1.4, basic operation 3.3.3, bound of a range 3.5, error bound 3.5.6, exponentiation operation 13
4.5.6, false boolean value 3.5.3, floating point type 3.5.9, machine_overflows attribute 13.7.1, membership test
4.5.2, model number 3.5.6, multiplication operation 4.5.5, numeric_error exception 11.1, predefined operation 3.3.3,
raising of exceptions 11, range 3.5, real type 3.5.6, relation 4.4, relational operator 4.5.2 4.5, safe number 3.5.6, subtype 3.3, true boolean value 3.5.3, type conversion 4.6, type mark 3.3.2, universal expression 4.10

4.6 Type Conversions

The evaluation of an explicit type conversion evaluates the expression given as the operand, and 1
converts the resulting value to a specified *target* type. Explicit type conversions are allowed between closely related types as defined below.

    type_conversion ::= type_mark(expression) 2

The target type of a type conversion is the base type of the type mark. The type of the operand of a 3
type conversion must be determinable independently of the context (in particular, independently of the target type). Furthermore, the operand of a type conversion is not allowed to be a literal **null**, an allocator, an aggregate, or a string literal; an expression enclosed by parentheses is allowed as the operand of a type conversion only if the expression alone is allowed.

A conversion to a subtype consists of a conversion to the target type followed by a check that the 4
result of the conversion belongs to the subtype. A conversion of an operand of a given type to the type itself is allowed.

5   The other allowed explicit type conversions correspond to the following three cases:

6   (a) Numeric types

7   The operand can be of any numeric type; the value of the operand is converted to the target
         type which must also be a numeric type. For conversions involving real types, the result is
         within the accuracy of the specified subtype (see 4.5.7). The conversion of a real value to an
         integer type rounds to the nearest integer; if the operand is halfway between two integers
         (within the accuracy of the real subtype) rounding may be either up or down.

8   (b) Derived types

9   The conversion is allowed if one of the target type and the operand type is derived from the
         other, directly or indirectly, or if there exists a third type from which both types are derived,
         directly or indirectly.

10   (c) Array types

11   The conversion is allowed if the operand type and the target type are array types that satisfy
         the following conditions: both types must have the same dimensionality; for each index posi-
         tion the index types must either be the same or be convertible to each other; the component
         types must be the same; finally, if the component type is a type with discriminants or an
         access type, the component subtypes must be either both constrained or both unconstrained.
         If the type mark denotes an unconstrained array type, then, for each index position, the
         bounds of the result are obtained by converting the bounds of the operand to the cor-
         responding index type of the target type. If the type mark denotes a constrained array sub-
         type, then the bounds of the result are those imposed by the type mark. In either case, the
         value of each component of the result is that of the matching component of the operand (see
         4.5.2).

12   In the case of conversions of numeric types and derived types, the exception CONSTRAINT_ERROR
     is raised by the evaluation of a type conversion if the result of the conversion fails to satisfy a con-
     straint imposed by the type mark.

13   In the case of array types, a check is made that any constraint on the component subtype is the
     same for the operand array type as for the target array type. If the type mark denotes an
     unconstrained array type and if the operand is not a null array, then, for each index position, a
     check is made that the bounds of the result belong to the corresponding index subtype of the
     target type. If the type mark denotes a constrained array subtype, a check is made that for each
     component of the operand there is a matching component of the target subtype, and vice versa.
     The exception CONSTRAINT_ERROR is raised if any of these checks fails.

14   If a conversion is allowed from one type to another, the reverse conversion is also allowed. This
     reverse conversion is used where an actual parameter of mode **in out** or **out** has the form of a type
     conversion of a (variable) name as explained in section 6.4.1.

15   Apart from the explicit type conversions, the only allowed form of type conversion is the implicit
     conversion of a value of the type *universal_integer* or *universal_real* into another numeric type. An
     implicit conversion of an operand of type *universal_integer* to another integer type, or of an
     operand of type *universal_real* to another real type, can only be applied if the operand is either a
     numeric literal, a named number, or an attribute; such an operand is called a *convertible* universal
     operand in this section. An implicit conversion of a convertible universal operand is applied if and
     only if the innermost complete context (see 8.7) determines a unique (numeric) target type for the
     implicit conversion, and there is no legal interpretation of this context without this conversion.

Notes:

The rules for implicit conversions imply that no implicit conversion is ever applied to the operand of an explicit type conversion. Similarly, implicit conversions are not applied if both operands of a predefined relational operator are convertible universal operands. [15]

The language allows implicit subtype conversions in the case of array types (see 5.2.1). An explicit type conversion can have the effect of a change of representation (in particular see 13.6). Explicit conversions are also used for actual parameters (see 6.4). [16]

Examples of numeric type conversion: [17]

```
REAL(2*J)      --  value is converted to floating point
INTEGER(1.6)   --  value is 2
INTEGER(-0.4)  --  value is 0
```

Example of conversion between derived types: [18]

```
type A_FORM is new B_FORM;

X  : A_FORM;
Y  : B_FORM;

X  := A_FORM(Y);
Y  := B_FORM(X);  --  the reverse conversion
```

Examples of conversions between array types: [19]

```
type SEQUENCE is array (INTEGER range <>) of INTEGER;
subtype DOZEN is SEQUENCE(1 .. 12);
LEDGER : array(1 .. 100) of INTEGER;

SEQUENCE(LEDGER)          --  bounds are those of LEDGER
SEQUENCE(LEDGER(31 .. 42))  --  bounds are 31 and 42
DOZEN(LEDGER(31 .. 42))   --  bounds are those of DOZEN
```

Examples of implicit conversions: [20]

```
X : INTEGER := 2;

X + 1 + 2        --  implicit conversion of each integer literal
1 + 2 + X        --  implicit conversion of each integer literal
X + (1 + 2)      --  implicit conversion of each integer literal

2 = (1 + 1)      --  no implicit conversion:  the type is universal_integer
A'LENGTH = B'LENGTH  --  no implicit conversion:  the type is universal_integer
C : constant := 3 + 2;  --  no implicit conversion:  the type is universal_integer

X = 3 and 1 = 2  --  implicit conversion of 3, but not of 1 and 2
```

References: actual parameter 6.4.1, array type 3.6, attribute 4.1.4, base type 3.3, belong to a subtype 3.3, component 3.3, constrained array subtype 3.6, constraint_error exception 11.1, derived type 3.4, dimension 3.6, expression 4.4, floating point type 3.5.7, index 3.6, index subtype 3.6, index type 3.6, integer type 3.5.4, matching component 4.5.2, mode 6.1, name 4.1, named number 3.2, null array 3.6.1, numeric literal 2.4, numeric type 3.5, raising of exceptions 11, real type 3.5.6, representation 13.1, statement 5, subtype 3.3, type 3.3, type mark 3.3.2, unconstrained array type 3.6, universal_integer type 3.5.4, universal_real type 3.5.6, variable 3.2.1 [21]

4.7 Qualified Expressions

1 A qualified expression is used to state explicitly the type, and possibly the subtype, of an operand that is the given expression or aggregate.

2
```
qualified_expression ::=
    type_mark'(expression) | type_mark'aggregate
```

3 The operand must have the same type as the base type of the type mark. The value of a qualified expression is the value of the operand. The evaluation of a qualified expression evaluates the operand and checks that its value belongs to the subtype denoted by the type mark. The exception CONSTRAINT_ERROR is raised if this check fails.

4 *Examples:*

```
type MASK is (FIX, DEC, EXP, SIGNIF);
type CODE is (FIX, CLA, DEC, TNZ, SUB);

PRINT (MASK'(DEC));    --  DEC is of type MASK
PRINT (CODE'(DEC));    --  DEC is of type CODE

for J in CODE'(FIX) .. CODE'(DEC) loop ...  -- qualification needed for either FIX or DEC
for J in CODE range FIX .. DEC loop ...     -- qualification unnecessary
for J in CODE'(FIX) .. DEC loop ...         -- qualification unnecessary for DEC

DOZEN'(1 | 3 | 5 | 7 => 2, others => 0) -- see 4.6
```

Notes:

5 Whenever the type of an enumeration literal or aggregate is not known from the context, a qualified expression can be used to state the type explicitly. For example, an overloaded enumeration literal must be qualified in the following cases: when given as a parameter in a subprogram call to an overloaded subprogram that cannot otherwise be identified on the basis of remaining parameter or result types, in a relational expression where both operands are overloaded enumeration literals, or in an array or loop parameter range where both bounds are overloaded enumeration literals. Explicit qualification is also used to specify which one of a set of overloaded parameterless functions is meant, or to constrain a value to a given subtype.

6 *References:* aggregate 4.3, array 3.6, base type 3.3, bound of a range 3.5, constraint_error exception 11.1, context of overload resolution 8.7, enumeration literal 3.5.1, expression 4.4, function 6.5, loop parameter 5.5, overloading 8.5, raising of exceptions 11, range 3.3, relation 4.4, subprogram 6, subprogram call 6.4, subtype 3.3, type 3.3, type mark 3.3.2

4.8 Allocators

1 The evaluation of an allocator creates an object and yields an access value that designates the object.

2
```
allocator ::=
    new subtype_indication | new qualified_expression
```

The type of the object created by an allocator is the base type of the type mark given in either the subtype indication or the qualified expression. For an allocator with a qualified expression, this expression defines the initial value of the created object. The type of the access value returned by an allocator must be determinable solely from the context, but using the fact that the value returned is of an access type having the named designated type.   3

The only allowed forms of constraint in the subtype indication of an allocator are index and discriminant constraints. If an allocator includes a subtype indication and if the type of the object created is an array type or a type with discriminants that do not have default expressions, then the subtype indication must either denote a constrained subtype, or include an explicit index or discriminant constraint.   4

If the type of the created object is an array type or a type with discriminants, then the created object is always constrained. If the allocator includes a subtype indication, the created object is constrained either by the subtype or by the default discriminant values. If the allocator includes a qualified expression, the created object is constrained by the bounds or discriminants of the initial value. For other types, the subtype of the created object is the subtype defined by the subtype indication of the access type definition.   5

For the evaluation of an allocator, the elaboration of the subtype indication or the evaluation of the qualified expression is performed first. The new object is then created. Initializations are then performed as for a declared object (see 3.2.1); the initialization is considered explicit in the case of a qualified expression; any initializations are implicit in the case of a subtype indication. Finally, an access value that designates the created object is returned.   6

An implementation must guarantee that any object created by the evaluation of an allocator remains allocated for as long as this object or one of its subcomponents is accessible directly or indirectly, that is, as long as it can be denoted by some name. Moreover, if an object or one of its subcomponents belongs to a task type, it is considered to be accessible as long as the task is not terminated. An implementation may (but need not) reclaim the storage occupied by an object created by an allocator, once this object has become inaccessible.   7

When an application needs closer control over storage allocation for objects designated by values of an access type, such control may be achieved by one or more of the following means: 8

a) The total amount of storage available for the collection of objects of an access type can be set by means of a length clause (see 13.2).   9

b) The pragma CONTROLLED informs the implementation that automatic storage reclamation must not be performed for objects designated by values of the access type, except upon leaving the innermost block statement, subprogram body, or task body that encloses the access type declaration, or after leaving the main program.   10

pragma CONTROLLED (*access_type*_simple_name);

A pragma CONTROLLED for a given access type is allowed at the same places as a representation clause for the type (see 13.1). This pragma is not allowed for a derived type.   11

c) The explicit deallocation of the object designated by an access value can be achieved by calling a procedure obtained by instantiation of the predefined generic library procedure UNCHECKED_DEALLOCATION (see 13.10.1).   12

The exception STORAGE_ERROR is raised by an allocator if there is not enough storage. Note also that the exception CONSTRAINT_ERROR can be raised by the evaluation of the qualified expression, by the elaboration of the subtype indication, or by the initialization.   13

14   *Examples (for access types declared in section 3.8):*

```
new CELL'(O, null, null)                         -- initialized explicitly
new CELL'(VALUE => 0, SUCC => null, PRED => null) -- initialized explicitly
new CELL                                          -- not initialized

new MATRIX(1 .. 10, 1 .. 20)                      -- the bounds only are given
new MATRIX'(1 .. 10 => (1 .. 20 => 0.0))          -- initialized explicitly

new BUFFER(100)                                   -- the discriminant only is given

new BUFFER'(SIZE => 80, POS => 0, VALUE => (1 .. 80 => 'A'))  -- initialized explicitl
```

15   *References:* access type 3.8, access type definition 3.8, access value 3.8, array type 3.6, block statement 5.6, bound of an array 3.6.1, collection 3.8, constrained subtype 3.3, constraint 3.3, constraint_error exception 11.1, context o overload resolution 8.7, derived type 3.4, designate 3.8, discriminant 3.3, discriminant constraint 3.7.2, elaboration 3.9, evaluation of a qualified expression 4.7, generic procedure 12.1, index constraint 3.6.1, initial value 3.2.1 initialization 3.2.1, instantiation 12.3, length clause 13.2, library unit 10.1, main program 10.1, name 4.1, objec 3.2.1, object declaration 3.2.1, pragma 2.8, procedure 6, qualified expression 4.7, raising of exceptions 11, represen- tation clause 13.1, simple name 4.1, storage_error exception 11.1, subcomponent 3.3, subprogram body 6.3, subtype 3.3, subtype indication 3.3.2, task body 9.1, task type 9.2, terminated task 9.4, type 3.3, type declaration 3.3.1, type mark 3.3.2 type with discriminants 3.3

4.9 Static Expressions and Static Subtypes

1   Certain expressions of a scalar type are said to be *static*. Similarly, certain discrete ranges are said to be static, and the type marks of certain scalar subtypes are said to denote static subtypes.

2   An expression of a scalar type is said to be static if and only if every primary is one of those listed in (a) through (h) below, every operator denotes a predefined operator, and the evaluation of the expression delivers a value (that is, it does not raise an exception):

3   (a)   An enumeration literal (including a character literal).

4   (b)   A numeric literal.

5   (c)   A named number.

6   (d)   A constant explicitly declared by a constant declaration with a static subtype, and initialized with a static expression.

7   (e)   A function call whose function name is an operator symbol that denotes a predefined operator, including a function name that is an expanded name; each actual parameter must also be a static expression.

8   (f)   A language-defined attribute of a static subtype; for an attribute that is a function, the actual parameter must also be a static expression.

(g) A qualified expression whose type mark denotes a static subtype and whose operand is a   9
static expression.

(h) A static expression enclosed in parentheses.   10

A static range is a range whose bounds are static expressions. A static range constraint is a range   11
constraint whose range is static. A static subtype is either a scalar base type, other than a generic
formal type; or a scalar subtype formed by imposing on a static subtype either a static range constraint, or a floating or fixed point constraint whose range constraint, if any, is static. A static discrete range is either a static subtype or a static range. A static index constraint is an index constraint for which each index subtype of the corresponding array type is static, and in which each
discrete range is static. A static discriminant constraint is a discriminant constraint for which the
subtype of each discriminant is static, and in which each expression is static.

Notes:

The accuracy of the evaluation of a static expression having a real type is defined by the rules given   12
in section 4.5.7. If the result is not a model number (or a safe number) of the type, the value
obtained by this evaluation at compilation time need not be the same as the value that would be
obtained by an evaluation at run time.

Array attributes are not static: in particular, the RANGE attribute is not static.   13

References: actual parameter 6.4.1, attribute 4.1.4, base type 3.3, bound of a range 3.5, character literal 2.5,   14
constant 3.2.1, constant declaration 3.2.1, discrete range 3.6, discrete type 3.5, enumeration literal 3.5.1, exception
11, expression 4.4, function 6.5, generic actual parameter 12.3, generic formal type 12.1.2, implicit declaration 3.1,
initialize 3.2.1, model number 3.5.6, named number 3.2, numeric literal 2.4, predefined operator 4.5, qualified expression 4.7, raising of exceptions 11, range constraint 3.5, safe number 3.5.6, scalar type 3.5, subtype 3.3, type mark
3.3.2

4.10 Universal Expressions

A *universal_expression* is either an expression that delivers a result of type *universal_integer* or   1
one that delivers a result of type *universal_real*.

The same operations are predefined for the type *universal_integer* as for any integer type. The   2
same operations are predefined for the type *universal_real* as for any floating point type. In addition, these operations include the following multiplication and division operators:

Operator	Operation	Left operand type	Right operand type	Result type	3
*	multiplication	universal_real	universal_integer	universal_real	
		universal_integer	universal_real	universal_real	
/	division	universal_real	universal_integer	universal_real	

The accuracy of the evaluation of a universal expression of type *universal_real* is at least as good   4
as that of the most accurate predefined floating point type supported by the implementation, apart
from *universal_real* itself. Furthermore, if a universal expression is a static expression, then the
evaluation must be exact.

5   For the evaluation of an operation of a nonstatic universal expression, an implementation is allowed to raise the exception NUMERIC_ERROR only if the result of the operation is a real value whose absolute value exceeds the largest safe number of the most accurate predefined floating point type (excluding *universal_real*), or an integer value greater than SYSTEM.MAX_INT or less than SYSTEM.MIN_INT.

Note:

6   It is a consequence of the above rules that the type of a universal expression is *universal_integer* if every primary contained in the expression is of this type (excluding actual parameters of attributes that are functions, and excluding right operands of exponentiation operators) and that otherwise the type is *universal_real*.

7   *Examples:*

```
1 + 1      -- 2
abs(-10)*3   -- 30

KILO  : constant := 1000;
MEGA  : constant := KILO*KILO;   -- 1_000_000
LONG  : constant := FLOAT'DIGITS*2;

HALF_PI    : constant := PI/2;              -- see 3.2.2
DEG_TO_RAD : constant := HALF_PI/90;
RAD_TO_DEG : constant := 1.0/DEG_TO_RAD;  -- equivalent to 1.0/((3.14159_26536/2)/90)
```

8   *References:* actual parameter 6.4.1, attribute 4.1.4, evaluation of an expression 4.5, floating point type 3.5.9, function 6.5, integer type 3.5.4, multiplying operator 4.5 4.5.5, predefined operation 3.3.3, primary 4.4, real type 3.5.6, safe number 3.5.6, system.max_int 13.7, system.min_int 13.7, type 3.3, universal_integer type 3.5.4, universal_real type 3.5.6

5. Statements

A *statement* defines an action to be performed; the process by which a statement achieves its action is called *execution* of the statement. ₁

This chapter describes the general rules applicable to all statements. Some specific statements are discussed in later chapters. Procedure call statements are described in Chapter 6 on subprograms. Entry call, delay, accept, select, and abort statements are described in Chapter 9 on tasks. Raise statements are described in Chapter 11 on exceptions, and code statements in Chapter 13. The remaining forms of statements are presented in this chapter. ₂

References: abort statement 9.10, accept statement 9.5, code statement 13.8, delay statement 9.6, entry call statement 9.5, procedure call statement 6.4, raise statement 11.3, select statement 9.7 ₃

5.1 Simple and Compound Statements - Sequences of Statements

A statement is either simple or compound. A simple statement encloses no other statement. A compound statement can enclose simple statements and other compound statements. ₁

```
sequence_of_statements ::= statement {statement}                                ₂

statement ::=
   {label} simple_statement | {label} compound_statement

simple_statement ::= null_statement
   |   assignment_statement   |   procedure_call_statement
   |   exit_statement         |   return_statement
   |   goto_statement         |   entry_call_statement
   |   delay_statement        |   abort_statement
   |   raise_statement        |   code_statement

compound_statement ::=
       if_statement           |   case_statement
   |   loop_statement         |   block_statement
   |   accept_statement       |   select_statement

label ::= <<label_simple_name>>

null_statement ::= null;
```

A statement is said to be *labeled* by the label name of any label of the statement. A label name, and similarly a loop or block name, is implicitly declared at the end of the declarative part of the innermost block statement, subprogram body, package body, task body, or generic body that encloses the labeled statement, the named loop statement, or the named block statement, as the case may be. For a block statement without a declarative part, an implicit declarative part (and preceding **declare**) is assumed. ₃

4   The implicit declarations for different label names, loop names, and block names occur in the same order as the beginnings of the corresponding labeled statements, loop statements, and block statements. Distinct identifiers must be used for all label, loop, and block names that are implicitly declared within the body of a program unit, including within block statements enclosed by this body, but excluding within other enclosed program units (a program unit is either a subprogram, a package, a task unit, or a generic unit).

5   Execution of a null statement has no other effect than to pass to the next action.

6   The execution of a sequence of statements consists of the execution of the individual statements in succession until the sequence is completed, or a transfer of control takes place. A transfer of control is caused either by the execution of an exit, return, or goto statement; by the selection of a terminate alternative; by the raising of an exception; or (indirectly) by the execution of an abort statement.

7   *Examples of labeled statements:*

    <<HERE>> <<ICI>> <<AQUI>> <<HIER>> **null**;

    <<AFTER>> X := 1;

Note:

8   The scope of a declaration starts at the place of the declaration itself (see 8.2). In the case of a label, loop, or block name, it follows from this rule that the scope of the *implicit* declaration starts before the first *explicit* occurrence of the corresponding name, since this occurrence is either in a statement label, a loop statement, a block statement, or a goto statement. An implicit declaration in a block statement may hide a declaration given in an outer program unit or block statement (according to the usual rules of hiding explained in section 8.3).

9   *References:* abort statement 9.10, accept statement 9.5, assignment statement 5.2, block name 5.6, block statement 5.6, case statement 5.4, code statement 13.8, declaration 3.1, declarative part 3.9, delay statement 9.6, entry call statement 9.5, exception 11, exit statement 5.7, generic body 12.1, generic unit 12, goto statement 5.9, hiding 8.3, identifier 2.3, if statement 5.3, implicit declaration 3.1, loop name 5.5, loop statement 5.5, package 7, package body 7.1, procedure call statement 6.4, program unit 6, raise statement 11.3, raising of exceptions 11, return statement 5.8, scope 8.2, select statement 9.7, simple name 4.1, subprogram 6, subprogram body 6.3, task 9, task body 9.1, task unit 9.1, terminate alternative 9.7.1, terminated task 9.4

5.2 Assignment Statement

1   An assignment statement replaces the current value of a variable with a new value specified by an expression. The named variable and the right-hand side expression must be of the same type; this type must not be a limited type.

2   assignment_statement ::=
        *variable*_name := expression;

3   For the execution of an assignment statement, the variable name and the expression are first evaluated, in some order that is not defined by the language. A check is then made that the value of the expression belongs to the subtype of the variable, except in the case of a variable that is an array (the assignment then involves a subtype conversion as described in section 5.2.1). Finally, the value of the expression becomes the new value of the variable.

The exception CONSTRAINT_ERROR is raised if the above-mentioned subtype check fails; in such a case the current value of the variable is left unchanged. If the variable is a subcomponent that depends on discriminants of an unconstrained record variable, then the execution of the assignment is erroneous if the value of any of these discriminants is changed by this execution. [1]

Examples: [5]

```
VALUE  := MAX_VALUE - 1;
SHADE  := BLUE;

NEXT_FRAME(F)(M, N) := 2.5;        --  see 4.1.1
U := DOT_PRODUCT(V, W);            --  see 6.5

WRITER := (STATUS => OPEN, UNIT => PRINTER, LINE_COUNT => 60);  -- see 3.7.3
NEXT_CAR.all := (72074, null);        --  see 3.8.1
```

Examples of constraint checks: [6]

```
I, J  : INTEGER range 1 .. 10;
K     : INTEGER range 1 .. 20;

    ...

I  := J;   --  identical ranges
K  := J;   --  compatible ranges
J  := K;   --  will raise the exception CONSTRAINT_ERROR if K > 10
```

Notes:

The values of the discriminants of an object designated by an access value cannot be changed (not even by assigning a complete value to the object itself) since such objects, created by allocators, are always constrained (see 4.8); however, subcomponents of such objects may be unconstrained. [7]

If the right-hand side expression is either a numeric literal or named number, or an attribute that yields a result of type *universal_integer* or *universal_real*, then an implicit type conversion is performed, as described in section 4.6. [8]

The determination of the type of the variable of an assignment statement may require consideration of the expression if the variable name can be interpreted as the name of a variable designated by the access value returned by a function call, and similarly, as a component or slice of such a variable (see section 8.7 for the context of overload resolution). [9]

References: access type 3.8, allocator 4.8, array 3.6, array assignment 5.2.1, component 3.6 3.7, constraint_error [10] exception 11.1, designate 3.8, discriminant 3.7.1, erroneous 1.6, evaluation 4.5, expression 4.4, function call 6.4, implicit type conversion 4.6, name 4.1, numeric literal 2.4, object 3.2, overloading 6.6 8.7, slice 4.1.2, subcomponent 3.3, subtype 3.3, subtype conversion 4.6, type 3.3, universal_integer type 3.5.4, universal_real type 3.5.6, variable 3.2.1

5.2.1 Array Assignments

If the variable of an assignment statement is an array variable (including a slice variable), the value [1] of the expression is implicitly converted to the subtype of the array variable; the result of this subtype conversion becomes the new value of the array variable.

2 This means that the new value of each component of the array variable is specified by the matching component in the array value obtained by evaluation of the expression (see 4.5.2 for the definition of matching components). The subtype conversion checks that for each component of the array variable there is a matching component in the array value, and vice versa. The exception CONSTRAINT_ERROR is raised if this check fails; in such a case the value of each component of the array variable is left unchanged.

3 *Examples:*

```
A  : STRING(1 .. 31);
B  : STRING(3 .. 33);
   ...

A  := B;    --   same number of components

A(1 .. 9)  := "tar sauce";
A(4 .. 12) := A(1 .. 9);  --   A(1 .. 12) = "tartar sauce"
```

Notes:

4 Array assignment is defined even in the case of overlapping slices, because the expression on the right-hand side is evaluated before performing any component assignment. In the above example, an implementation yielding A(1 .. 12) = "tartartartar" would be incorrect.

5 The implicit subtype conversion described above for assignment to an array variable is performed only for the value of the right-hand side expression as a whole; it is not performed for subcomponents that are array values.

6 *References:* array 3.6, assignment 5.2, constraint_error exception 11.1, matching array components 4.5.2, slice 4.1.2, subtype conversion 4.6, type 3.3, variable 3.2.1

5.3 If Statements

1 An if statement selects for execution one or none of the enclosed sequences of statements, depending on the (truth) value of one or more corresponding conditions.

2
```
if_statement ::=
    if condition then
      sequence_of_statements
  { elsif condition then
      sequence_of_statements}
  [ else
      sequence_of_statements]
    end if;

condition ::= boolean_expression
```

3 An expression specifying a condition must be of a boolean type.

4 For the execution of an if statement, the condition specified after **if**, and any conditions specified after **elsif**, are evaluated in succession (treating a final **else** as **elsif** TRUE **then**), until one evaluates to TRUE or all conditions are evaluated and yield FALSE. If one condition evaluates to TRUE, then the corresponding sequence of statements is executed; otherwise none of the sequences of statements is executed.

Examples: 5

```
if MONTH = DECEMBER and DAY = 31 then
   MONTH := JANUARY;
   DAY   := 1;
   YEAR  := YEAR + 1;
end if;

if LINE_TOO_SHORT then
   raise LAYOUT_ERROR;
elsif LINE_FULL then
   NEW_LINE;
   PUT(ITEM);
else
   PUT(ITEM);
end if;

if MY_CAR.OWNER.VEHICLE /= MY_CAR then          -- see 3.8
   REPORT ("Incorrect data");
end if;
```

References: boolean type 3.5.3, evaluation 4.5, expression 4.4, sequence of statements 5.1   6

5.4 Case Statements

A case statement selects for execution one of a number of alternative sequences of statements;   1
the chosen alternative is defined by the value of an expression.

```
case_statement ::=
   case expression is
       case_statement_alternative
      { case_statement_alternative}
   end case;

case_statement_alternative ::=
   when choice {| choice } =>
      sequence_of_statements
```

The expression must be of a discrete type which must be determinable independently of the con-   3
text in which the expression occurs, but using the fact that the expression must be of a discrete
type. Moreover, the type of this expression must not be a generic formal type. Each choice in a
case statement alternative must be of the same type as the expression; the list of choices specifies
for which values of the expression the alternative is chosen.

If the expression is the name of an object whose subtype is static, then each value of this subtype   4
must be represented once and only once in the set of choices of the case statement, and no other
value is allowed; this rule is likewise applied if the expression is a qualified expression or type conversion whose type mark denotes a static subtype. Otherwise, for other forms of expression, each
value of the (base) type of the expression must be represented once and only once in the set of
choices, and no other value is allowed.

5 The simple expressions and discrete ranges given as choices in a case statement must be static. A choice defined by a discrete range stands for all values in the corresponding range (none if a null range). The choice **others** is only allowed for the last alternative and as its only choice; it stands for all values (possibly none) not given in the choices of previous alternatives. A component simple name is not allowed as a choice of a case statement alternative.

6 The execution of a case statement consists of the evaluation of the expression followed by the execution of the chosen sequence of statements.

7 *Examples:*

```
case SENSOR is
   when ELEVATION   => RECORD_ELEVATION (SENSOR_VALUE);
   when AZIMUTH     => RECORD_AZIMUTH   (SENSOR_VALUE);
   when DISTANCE    => RECORD_DISTANCE (SENSOR_VALUE);
   when others      => null;
end case;

case TODAY is
   when MON         => COMPUTE_INITIAL_BALANCE;
   when FRI         => COMPUTE_CLOSING_BALANCE;
   when TUE .. THU  => GENERATE_REPORT(TODAY);
   when SAT .. SUN  => null;
end case;

case BIN_NUMBER(COUNT) is
   when 1        => UPDATE_BIN(1);
   when 2        => UPDATE_BIN(2);
   when 3 | 4 =>
      EMPTY_BIN(1);
      EMPTY_BIN(2);
   when others  => raise ERROR;
end case;
```

Notes:

8 The execution of a case statement chooses one and only one alternative, since the choices are exhaustive and mutually exclusive. Qualification of the expression of a case statement by a static subtype can often be used to limit the number of choices that need be given explicitly.

9 An **others** choice is required in a case statement if the type of the expression is the type *universal_integer* (for example, if the expression is an integer literal), since this is the only way to cover all values of the type *universal_integer*.

10 *References:* base type 3.3, choice 3.7.3, context of overload resolution 8.7, discrete type 3.5, expression 4.4, function call 6.4, generic formal type 12.1, conversion 4.6, discrete type 3.5, enumeration literal 3.5.1, expression 4.4, name 4.1, object 3.2.1, overloading 6.6 8.7, qualified expression 4.7, sequence of statements 5.1, static discrete range 4.9, static subtype 4.9, subtype 3.3, type 3.3, type conversion 4.6, type mark 3.3.2

5.5 Loop Statements

A loop statement includes a sequence of statements that is to be executed repeatedly, zero or   1
more times.

```
loop_statement ::=                                            2
   [loop_simple_name:]
      [ iteration_scheme] loop
          sequence_of_statements
      end loop [loop_simple_name];

iteration_scheme ::= while condition
   | for loop_parameter_specification

loop_parameter_specification ::=
   identifier in [reverse] discrete_range
```

If a loop statement has a loop simple name, this simple name must be given both at the beginning   3
and at the end.

A loop statement without an iteration scheme specifies repeated execution of the sequence of   4
statements. Execution of the loop statement is complete when the loop is left as a consequence of
the execution of an exit statement, or as a consequence of some other transfer of control (see 5.1).

For a loop statement with a **while** iteration scheme, the condition is evaluated before each execu-   5
tion of the sequence of statements; if the value of the condition is TRUE , the sequence of
statements is executed, if FALSE the execution of the loop statement is complete.

For a loop statement with a **for** iteration scheme, the loop parameter specification is the declara-   6
tion of the *loop parameter* with the given identifier. The loop parameter is an object whose type is
the base type of the discrete range (see 3.6.1). Within the sequence of statements, the loop
parameter is a constant. Hence a loop parameter is not allowed as the (left-hand side) variable of
an assignment statement. Similarly the loop parameter must not be given as an **out** or **in out**
parameter of a procedure or entry call statement, or as an **in out** parameter of a generic instantiation.

For the execution of a loop statement with a **for** iteration scheme, the loop parameter specification   7
is first elaborated. This elaboration creates the loop parameter and evaluates the discrete range.

If the discrete range is a null range, the execution of the loop statement is complete. Otherwise,   8
the sequence of statements is executed once for each value of the discrete range (subject to the
loop not being left as a consequence of the execution of an exit statement or as a consequence of
some other transfer of control). Prior to each such iteration, the corresponding value of the discrete
range is assigned to the loop parameter. These values are assigned in increasing order unless the
reserved word **reverse** is present, in which case the values are assigned in decreasing order.

Example of a loop statement without an iteration scheme: 9

```
loop
   GET(CURRENT_CHARACTER);
   exit when CURRENT_CHARACTER = '*';
end loop;
```

10   *Example of a loop statement with a while iteration scheme:*

```
while  BID(N).PRICE  <  CUT_OFF.PRICE loop
   RECORD_BID(BID(N).PRICE);
   N := N + 1;
end loop;
```

11   *Example of a loop statement with a for iteration scheme:*

```
for  J  in  BUFFER'RANGE loop        --  legal  even  with  a  null  range
   if BUFFER(J) /= SPACE then
      PUT(BUFFER(J));
   end if;
end loop;
```

12   *Example of a loop statement with a loop simple name:*

```
SUMMATION:
   while NEXT /= HEAD loop           -- see 3.8
      SUM    := SUM + NEXT.VALUE;
      NEXT   := NEXT.SUCC;
   end loop SUMMATION;
```

Notes:

13   The scope of a loop parameter extends from the loop parameter specification to the end of the loop statement, and the visibility rules are such that a loop parameter is only visible within the sequence of statements of the loop.

14   The discrete range of a for loop is evaluated just once. Use of the reserved word **reverse** does not alter the discrete range, so that the following iteration schemes are not equivalent; the first has a null range.

```
for  J  in  reverse  1 .. 0
for  J  in  0 .. 1
```

15   Loop names are also used in exit statements, and in expanded names (in a prefix of the loop parameter).

16   *References:* actual parameter 6.4.1, assignment statement 5.2, base type 3.3, bound of a range 3.5, condition 5.3, constant 3.2.1, context of overload resolution 8.7, conversion 4.6, declaration 3.1, discrete range 3.6.1, elaboration 3.1, entry call statement 9.5, evaluation 4.5, exit statement 5.7, expanded name 4.1.3, false boolean value 3.5.3, generic actual parameter 12.3, generic instantiation 12.3, goto statement 5.9, identifier 2.3, integer type 3.5.4, null range 3.5, object 3.2.1, prefix 4.1, procedure call 6.4, raising of exceptions 11, reserved word 2.9, return statement 5.8, scope 8.2, sequence of statements 5.1, simple name 4.1, terminate alternative 9.7.1, true boolean value 3.5.3 3.5.4, visibility 8.3

5.6 Block Statements

A block statement encloses a sequence of statements optionally preceded by a declarative part   1
and optionally followed by exception handlers.

```
block_statement ::=
    [block_simple_name:]
        [ declare
                declarative_part]
        begin
                sequence_of_statements
        [ exception
                exception_handler
                { exception_handler}]
        end [block_simple_name];
```
   2

If a block statement has a block simple name, this simple name must be given both at the beginn-   3
ing and at the end.

The execution of a block statement consists of the elaboration of its declarative part (if any) fol-   4
lowed by the execution of the sequence of statements. If the block statement has exception
handlers, these service corresponding exceptions that are raised during the execution of the
sequence of statements (see 11.2).

Example: 5

```
SWAP:
    declare
        TEMP : INTEGER;
    begin
        TEMP := V; V := U; U := TEMP;
    end SWAP;
```

Notes:

If task objects are declared within a block statement whose execution is completed, the block   6
statement is not left until all its dependent tasks are terminated (see 9.4). This rule applies also to
a completion caused by an exit, return, or goto statement; or by the raising of an exception.

Within a block statement, the block name can be used in expanded names denoting local entities   7
such as SWAP.TEMP in the above example (see 4.1.3 (f)).

References: declarative part 3.9, dependent task 9.4, exception handler 11.2, exit statement 5.7, expanded name   8
4.1.3, goto statement 5.9, raising of exceptions 11, return statement 5.8, sequence of statements 5.1, simple name
4.1, task object 9.2

5.7 Exit Statements

1 An exit statement is used to complete the execution of an enclosing loop statement (called the loop in what follows); the completion is conditional if the exit statement includes a condition.

2
```
exit_statement ::=
    exit [loop_name] [when condition];
```

3 An exit statement with a loop name is only allowed within the named loop, and applies to that loop; an exit statement without a loop name is only allowed within a loop, and applies to the innermost enclosing loop (whether named or not). Furthermore, an exit statement that applies to a given loop must not appear within a subprogram body, package body, task body, generic body, or accept statement, if this construct is itself enclosed by the given loop.

4 For the execution of an exit statement, the condition, if present, is first evaluated. Exit from the loop then takes place if the value is TRUE or if there is no condition.

5 *Examples:*

```
for N in 1 .. MAX_NUM_ITEMS loop
    GET_NEW_ITEM(NEW_ITEM);
    MERGE_ITEM(NEW_ITEM, STORAGE_FILE);
    exit when NEW_ITEM = TERMINAL_ITEM;
end loop;

MAIN_CYCLE:
    loop
        --   initial statements
        exit MAIN_CYCLE when FOUND;
        --   final statements
    end loop MAIN_CYCLE;
```

Note:

6 Several nested loops can be exited by an exit statement that names the outer loop.

7 *References:* accept statement 9.5, condition 5.3, evaluation 4.5, generic body 12.1, loop name 5.5, loop statement 5.5, package body 7.1, subprogram body 6.3, true boolean value 3.5.3

5.8 Return Statements

1 A return statement is used to complete the execution of the innermost enclosing function, procedure, or accept statement.

2
```
return_statement ::= return [expression];
```

3 A return statement is only allowed within the body of a subprogram or generic subprogram, or within an accept statement, and applies to the innermost (enclosing) such construct; a return statement is not allowed within the body of a task unit, package, or generic package enclosed by this construct (on the other hand, it is allowed within a compound statement enclosed by this construct and, in particular, in a block statement).

A return statement for an accept statement or for the body of a procedure or generic procedure   4
must not include an expression. A return statement for the body of a function or generic function
must include an expression.

The value of the expression defines the result returned by the function. The type of this expression   5
must be the base type of the type mark given after the reserved word **return** in the specification of
the function or generic function (this type mark defines the result subtype).

For the execution of a return statement, the expression (if any) is first evaluated and a check is   6
made that the value belongs to the result subtype. The execution of the return statement is thereby
completed if the check succeeds; so also is the execution of the subprogram or of the accept
statement. The exception CONSTRAINT_ERROR is raised at the place of the return statement if the
check fails.

Examples: 7

```
return;                              -- in  a  procedure
return KEY_VALUE(LAST_INDEX);        -- in  a  function
```

Note:

If the expression is either a numeric literal or named number, or an attribute that yields a result of   8
type *universal_integer* or *universal_real*, then an implicit conversion of the result is performed as
described in section 4.6.

References: accept statement 9.5, attribute A, block statement 5.6, constraint_error exception 11.1, expression 4.4,   9
function body 6.3, function call 6.4, generic body 12.1, implicit type conversion 4.6, named number 3.2, numeric
literal 2.4, package body 7.1, procedure body 6.3, reserved word 2.9, result subtype 6.1, subprogram body 6.3, subprogram specification 6.1, subtype 3.3, task body 9.1, type mark 3.3.2, universal_integer type 3.5.4, universal_real
type 3.5.6

5.9 Goto Statements

A goto statement specifies an explicit transfer of control from this statement to a *target* statement   1
named by a label.

```
goto_statement ::= goto label_name;
```
    2

The innermost sequence of statements that encloses the target statement must also enclose the   3
goto statement (note that the goto statement can be a statement of an inner sequence). Furthermore, if a goto statement is enclosed by an accept statement or the body of a program unit, then
the target statement must not be outside this enclosing construct; conversely, it follows from the
previous rule that if the target statement is enclosed by such a construct, then the goto statement
cannot be outside.

The execution of a goto statement transfers control to the named target statement.   4

Note:

5 The above rules allow transfer of control to a statement of an enclosing sequence of statements but not the reverse. Similarly, they prohibit transfers of control such as between alternatives of a case statement, if statement, or select statement; between exception handlers; or from an exception handler of a frame back to the sequence of statements of this frame.

6 *Example:*

```
<<COMPARE>>
  if A(I) < ELEMENT then
    if LEFT(I) /= 0 then
      I := LEFT(I);
      goto COMPARE;
    end if;
    --   some statements
  end if;
```

7 *References:* accept statement 9.5, block statement 5.6, case statement 5.4, compound statement 5.1, exception handler 11.2, frame 11.2, generic body 12.1, if statement 5.3, label 5.1, package body 7.1, program unit 6, select statement 9.7, sequence of statements 5.1, statement 5.1, subprogram body 6.3, task body 9.1, transfer of control 5.1

6. Subprograms

Subprograms are one of the four forms of *program unit*, of which programs can be composed. The other forms are packages, task units, and generic units.

A subprogram is a program unit whose execution is invoked by a subprogram call. There are two forms of subprogram: procedures and functions. A procedure call is a statement; a function call is an expression and returns a value. The definition of a subprogram can be given in two parts: a subprogram declaration defining its calling conventions, and a subprogram body defining its execution.

References: function 6.5, function call 6.4, generic unit 12, package 7, procedure 6.1, procedure call 6.4, subprogram body 6.3, subprogram call 6.4, subprogram declaration 6.1, task unit 9

6.1 Subprogram Declarations

A subprogram declaration declares a procedure or a function, as indicated by the initial reserved word.

```
subprogram_declaration ::= subprogram_specification;

subprogram_specification ::=
     procedure identifier  [formal_part]
   |  function designator  [formal_part] return type_mark

designator ::= identifier | operator_symbol

operator_symbol ::= string_literal

formal_part ::=
     (parameter_specification {; parameter_specification})

parameter_specification ::=
     identifier_list : mode type_mark [:= expression]

mode ::= [in] | in out | out
```

The specification of a procedure specifies its identifier and its *formal parameters* (if any). The specification of a function specifies its designator, its formal parameters (if any) and the subtype of the returned value (the *result subtype*). A designator that is an operator symbol is used for the overloading of an operator. The sequence of characters represented by an operator symbol must be an operator belonging to one of the six classes of overloadable operators defined in section 4.5 (extra spaces are not allowed and the case of letters is not significant).

4 A parameter specification with several identifiers is equivalent to a sequence of single parameter specifications, as explained in section 3.2. Each single parameter specification declares a formal parameter. If no mode is explicitly given, the mode **in** is assumed. If a parameter specification ends with an expression, the expression is the *default expression* of the formal parameter. A default expression is only allowed in a parameter specification if the mode is **in** (whether this mode is indicated explicitly or implicitly). The type of a default expression must be that of the corresponding formal parameter.

5 The use of a name that denotes a formal parameter is not allowed in default expressions of a formal part if the specification of the parameter is itself given in this formal part.

6 The elaboration of a subprogram declaration elaborates the corresponding formal part. The elaboration of a formal part has no other effect.

7 *Examples of subprogram declarations:*

```
procedure TRAVERSE_TREE;
procedure INCREMENT(X : in out INTEGER);
procedure RIGHT_INDENT(MARGIN : out LINE_SIZE);      -- see 3.5.4
procedure SWITCH(FROM, TO : in out LINK);            -- see 3.8.1

function RANDOM return PROBABILITY;                  -- see 3.5.7

function MIN_CELL(X : LINK) return CELL;             -- see 3.8.1
function NEXT_FRAME(K : POSITIVE) return FRAME;      -- see 3.8
function DOT_PRODUCT(LEFT,RIGHT: VECTOR) return REAL; -- see 3.6

function "*"(LEFT,RIGHT : MATRIX) return MATRIX;     -- see 3.6
```

8 *Examples of in parameters with default expressions:*

```
procedure PRINT_HEADER(PAGES   : in NATURAL;
                       HEADER  : in LINE    := (1 .. LINE'LAST => ' ');  -- see 3
                       CENTER  : in BOOLEAN := TRUE);
```

Notes:

9 The evaluation of default expressions is caused by certain subprogram calls, as described in section 6.4.2 (default expressions are not evaluated during the elaboration of the subprogram declaration).

10 All subprograms can be called recursively and are reentrant.

11 *References:* declaration 3.1, elaboration 3.9, evaluation 4.5, expression 4.4, formal parameter 6.2, function 6.5, identifier 2.3, identifier list 3.2, mode 6.2, name 4.1, elaboration has no other effect 3.9, operator 4.5, overloading 6.6 8.7, procedure 6, string literal 2.6, subprogram call 6.4, type mark 3.3.2

6.2 Formal Parameter Modes

The value of an object is said to be *read* when this value is evaluated; it is also said to be read   1
when one of its subcomponents is read. The value of a variable is said to be *updated* when an
assignment is performed to the variable, and also (indirectly) when the variable is used as actual
parameter of a subprogram call or entry call statement that updates its value; it is also said to be
updated when one of its subcomponents is updated.

A formal parameter of a subprogram has one of the three following modes: 2

in   The formal parameter is a constant and permits only reading of the value of the   3
            associated actual parameter.

in out The formal parameter is a variable and permits both reading and updating of the value of the   4
            associated actual parameter.

out   The formal parameter is a variable and permits updating of the value of the associated actual   5
            parameter.

            The value of a scalar parameter that is not updated by the call is undefined upon return; the
            same holds for the value of a scalar subcomponent, other than a discriminant. Reading
            the bounds and discriminants of the formal parameter and of its subcomponents is allowed,
            but no other reading.

For a scalar parameter, the above effects are achieved by copy: at the start of each call, if the mode   6
is **in** or **in out**, the value of the actual parameter is copied into the associated formal parameter;
then after normal completion of the subprogram body, if the mode is **in out** or **out**, the value of the
formal parameter is copied back into the associated actual parameter. For a parameter whose
type is an access type, copy-in is used for all three modes, and copy-back for the modes **in out** and
out.

For a parameter whose type is an array, record, or task type, an implementation may likewise   7
achieve the above effects by copy, as for scalar types. In addition, if copy is used for a parameter of
mode **out**, then copy-in is required at least for the bounds and discriminants of the actual
parameter and of its subcomponents, and also for each subcomponent whose type is an access
type. Alternatively, an implementation may achieve these effects by reference, that is, by arranging
that every use of the formal parameter (to read or to update its value) be treated as a use of the
associated actual parameter, throughout the execution of the subprogram call. The language does
not define which of these two mechanisms is to be adopted for parameter passing, nor whether
different calls to the same subprogram are to use the same mechanism. The execution of a
program is erroneous if its effect depends on which mechanism is selected by the implementation.

For a parameter whose type is a private type, the above effects are achieved according to the rule   8
that applies to the corresponding full type declaration.

Within the body of a subprogram, a formal parameter is subject to any constraint resulting from   9
the type mark given in its parameter specification. For a formal parameter of an unconstrained
array type, the bounds are obtained from the actual parameter, and the formal parameter is constrained by these bounds (see 3.6.1). For a formal parameter whose declaration specifies an
unconstrained (private or record) type with discriminants, the discriminants of the formal
parameter are initialized with the values of the corresponding discriminants of the actual
parameter; the formal parameter is unconstrained if and only if the mode is **in out** or **out** and the
variable name given for the actual parameter denotes an unconstrained variable (see 3.7.1 and
6.4.1).

If the actual parameter of a subprogram call is a subcomponent that depends on discriminants of   10
an unconstrained record variable, then the execution of the call is erroneous if the value of any of
the discriminants of the variable is changed by this execution; this rule does not apply if the mode
is **in** and the type of the subcomponent is a scalar type or an access type.

Notes:

11   For parameters of array and record types, the parameter passing rules have these consequences:

12   ● If the execution of a subprogram is abandoned as a result of an exception, the final value of an actual parameter of such a type can be either its value before the call or a value assigned to the formal parameter during the execution of the subprogram.

13   ● If no actual parameter of such a type is accessible by more than one path, then the effect of a subprogram call (unless abandoned) is the same whether or not the implementation uses copying for parameter passing. If, however, there are multiple access paths to such a parameter (for example, if a global variable, or another formal parameter, refers to the same actual parameter), then the value of the formal is undefined after updating the actual other than by updating the formal. A program using such an undefined value is erroneous.

14   The same parameter modes are defined for formal parameters of entries (see 9.5) with the same meaning as for subprograms. Different parameter modes are defined for generic formal parameters (see 12.1.1).

15   For all modes, if an actual parameter designates a task, the associated formal parameter designates the same task; the same holds for a subcomponent of an actual parameter and the corresponding subcomponent of the associated formal parameter.

16   *References:* access type 3.8, actual parameter 6.4.1, array type 3.6, assignment 5.2, bound of an array 3.6.1, constraint 3.3, depend on a discriminant 3.7.1, discriminant 3.7.1, entry call statement 9.5, erroneous 1.6, evaluation 4.5, exception 11, expression 4.4, formal parameter 6.1, generic formal parameter 12.1, global 8.1, mode 6.1, null access value 3.8, object 3.2, parameter specification 6.1, private type 7.4, record type 3.7, scalar type 3.5, subcomponent 3.3, subprogram body 6.3, subprogram call statement 6.4, task 9, task type 9.2, type mark 3.3.2, unconstrained array type 3.6, unconstrained type with discriminants 3.7.1, unconstrained variable 3.2.1, variable 3.2.1

6.3 Subprogram Bodies

1   A subprogram body specifies the execution of a subprogram.

2
```
subprogram_body ::=
     subprogram_specification is
         [ declarative_part]
     begin
             sequence_of_statements
   [ exception
             exception_handler
           { exception_handler}]
     end [designator];
```

3   The declaration of a subprogram is optional. In the absence of such a declaration, the subprogram specification of the subprogram body (or body stub) acts as the declaration. For each subprogram declaration, there must be a corresponding body (except for a subprogram written in another language, as explained in section 13.9). If both a declaration and a body are given, the subprogram specification of the body must conform to the subprogram specification of the declaration (see section 6.3.1 for conformance rules).

If a designator appears at the end of a subprogram body, it must repeat the designator of the sub- 4
program specification.

The elaboration of a subprogram body has no other effect than to establish that the body can from 5
then on be used for the execution of calls of the subprogram.

The execution of a subprogram body is invoked by a subprogram call (see 6.4). For this execution, 6
after establishing the association between formal parameters and actual parameters, the
declarative part of the body is elaborated, and the sequence of statements of the body is then
executed. Upon completion of the body, return is made to the caller (and any necessary copying
back of formal to actual parameters occurs (see 6.2)). The optional exception handlers at the end
of a subprogram body handle exceptions raised during the execution of the sequence of statements of the subprogram body (see 11.4).

Note:

It follows from the visibility rules that if a subprogram declared in a package is to be visible outside 7
the package, a subprogram specification must be given in the visible part of the package. The same
rules dictate that a subprogram declaration must be given if a call of the subprogram occurs textually before the subprogram body (the declaration must then occur earlier than the call in the
program text). The rules given in sections 3.9 and 7.1 imply that a subprogram declaration and the
corresponding body must both occur immediately within the same declarative region.

Example of subprogram body: 8

```
procedure PUSH(E : in ELEMENT_TYPE; S : in out STACK) is
begin
   if S.INDEX = S.SIZE then
      raise STACK_OVERFLOW;
   else
      S.INDEX := S.INDEX + 1;
      S.SPACE(S.INDEX) := E;
   end if;
end PUSH;
```

References: actual parameter 6.4.1, body stub 10.2, conform 6.3.1, declaration 3.1, declarative part 3.9, declarative 9
region 8.1, designator 6.1, elaboration 3.9, elaboration has no other effect 3.1, exception 11, exception handler 11.2,
formal parameter 6.1, occur immediately within 8.1, package 7, sequence of statements 5.1, subprogram 6, subprogram call 6.4, subprogram declaration 6.1, subprogram specification 6.1, visibility 8.3, visible part 7.2

6.3.1 Conformance Rules

Whenever the language rules require or allow the specification of a given subprogram to be 1
provided in more than one place, the following variations are allowed at each place:

- A numeric literal can be replaced by a different numeric literal if and only if both have the 2
  same value.

- A simple name can be replaced by an expanded name in which this simple name is the selec- 3
  tor, if and only if at both places the meaning of the simple name is given by the same declaration.

- A string literal given as an operator symbol can be replaced by a different string literal if and 4
  only if both represent the same operator.

5 Two subprogram specifications are said to *conform* if, apart from comments and the above allowed variations, both specifications are formed by the same sequence of lexical elements, and corresponding lexical elements are given the same meaning by the visibility and overloading rules.

6 Conformance is likewise defined for formal parts, discriminant parts, and type marks (for deferred constants and for actual parameters that have the form of a type conversion (see 6.4.1)).

Notes:

7 A simple name can be replaced by an expanded name even if the simple name is itself the prefix of a selected component. For example, Q.R can be replaced by P.Q.R if Q is declared immediately within P.

8 The following specifications do not conform since they are not formed by the same sequence of lexical elements:

```
procedure P(X,Y : INTEGER)
procedure P(X : INTEGER; Y : INTEGER)
procedure P(X,Y : in INTEGER)
```

9 *References:* actual parameter 6.4 6.4.1, allow 1.6, comment 2.7, declaration 3.1, deferred constant 7.4.3, direct visibility 8.3, discriminant part 3.7.1, expanded name 4.1.3, formal part 6.1, lexical element 2, name 4.1, numeric literal 2.4, operator symbol 6.1, overloading 6.6 8.7, prefix 4.1, selected component 4.1.3, selector 4.1.3, simple name 4.1, subprogram specification 6.1, type conversion 4.6, visibility 8.3

6.3.2 Inline Expansion of Subprograms

1 The pragma INLINE is used to indicate that inline expansion of the subprogram body is desired for every call of each of the named subprograms. The form of this pragma is as follows:

```
pragma INLINE (name {, name});
```

2 Each name is either the name of a subprogram or the name of a generic subprogram. The pragma INLINE is only allowed at the place of a declarative item in a declarative part or package specification, or after a library unit in a compilation, but before any subsequent compilation unit.

3 If the pragma appears at the place of a declarative item, each name must denote a subprogram or a generic subprogram declared by an earlier declarative item of the same declarative part or package specification. If several (overloaded) subprograms satisfy this requirement, the pragma applies to all of them. If the pragma appears after a given library unit, the only name allowed is the name of this unit. If the name of a generic subprogram is mentioned in the pragma, this indicates that inline expansion is desired for calls of all subprograms obtained by instantiation of the named generic unit.

4 The meaning of a subprogram is not changed by the pragma INLINE. For each call of the named subprograms, an implementation is free to follow or to ignore the recommendation expressed by the pragma. (Note, in particular, that the recommendation cannot generally be followed for a recursive subprogram.)

5 *References:* allow 1.6, compilation 10.1, compilation unit 10.1, declarative item 3.9, declarative part 3.9, generic subprogram 12.1, generic unit 12 12.1, instantiation 12.3, library unit 10.1, name 4.1, overloading 6.6 8.7, package specification 7.1, pragma 2.8, subprogram 6, subprogram body 6.3, subprogram call 6.4

6.4 Subprogram Calls

A subprogram call is either a procedure call statement or a function call; it invokes the execution   1
of the corresponding subprogram body. The call specifies the association of the actual parameters,
if any, with formal parameters of the subprogram.

    procedure_call_statement ::=   2
        procedure_name [actual_parameter_part];

    function_call ::=
        function_name [actual_parameter_part]

    actual_parameter_part ::=
        (parameter_association {, parameter_association})

    parameter_association ::=
        [formal_parameter =>] actual_parameter

    formal_parameter ::= parameter_simple_name

    actual_parameter ::=
        expression | variable_name | type_mark(variable_name)

Each parameter association associates an actual parameter with a corresponding formal   3
parameter. A parameter association is said to be *named* if the formal parameter is named explicitly; it is otherwise said to be *positional*. For a positional association, the actual parameter corresponds to the formal parameter with the same position in the formal part.

Named associations can be given in any order, but if both positional and named associations are   4
used in the same call, positional associations must occur first, at their normal position. Hence
once a named association is used, the rest of the call must use only named associations.

For each formal parameter of a subprogram, a subprogram call must specify exactly one cor-   5
responding actual parameter. This actual parameter is specified either explicitly, by a parameter
association, or, in the absence of such an association, by a default expression (see 6.4.2).

The parameter associations of a subprogram call are evaluated in some order that is not defined by 6
the language. Similarly, the language rules do not define in which order the values of **in out** or **out**
parameters are copied back into the corresponding actual parameters (when this is done).

Examples of procedure calls: 7

    TRAVERSE_TREE;
    TABLE_MANAGER.INSERT(E);   -- see 6.1
    PRINT_HEADER(128, TITLE, TRUE);   -- see 7.5
                                                               -- see 6.1

    SWITCH(FROM => X, TO => NEXT);   -- see 6.1
    PRINT_HEADER(128, HEADER => TITLE, CENTER => TRUE);   -- see 6.1
    PRINT_HEADER(HEADER => TITLE, CENTER => TRUE, PAGES => 128); -- see 6.1

Examples of function calls: 8

    DOT_PRODUCT(U, V)   -- see 6.1 and 6.5
    CLOCK   -- see 9.6

9   *References:* default expression for a formal parameter 6.1, erroneous 1.6, expression 4.4, formal parameter 6.1, formal part 6.1, name 4.1, simple name 4.1, subprogram 6, type mark 3.3.2, variable 3.2.1

6.4.1 Parameter Associations

1   Each actual parameter must have the same type as the corresponding formal parameter.

2   An actual parameter associated with a formal parameter of mode **in** must be an expression; it is evaluated before the call.

3   An actual parameter associated with a formal parameter of mode **in out** or **out** must be either the name of a variable, or of the form of a type conversion whose argument is the name of a variable. In either case, for the mode **in out**, the variable must not be a formal parameter of mode **out** or a subcomponent thereof. For an actual parameter that has the form of a type conversion, the type mark must conform (see 6.3.1) to the type mark of the formal parameter; the allowed operand and target types are the same as for type conversions (see 4.6).

4   The variable name given for an actual parameter of mode **in out** or **out** is evaluated before the call. If the actual parameter has the form of a type conversion, then before the call, for a parameter of mode **in out**, the variable is converted to the specified type; after (normal) completion of the subprogram body, for a parameter of mode **in out** or **out**, the formal parameter is converted back to the type of the variable. (The type specified in the conversion must be that of the formal parameter.)

5   The following constraint checks are performed for parameters of scalar and access types:

6   ● Before the call: for a parameter of mode **in** or **in out**, it is checked that the value of the actual parameter belongs to the subtype of the formal parameter.

7   ● After (normal) completion of the subprogram body: for a parameter of mode **in out** or **out**, it is checked that the value of the formal parameter belongs to the subtype of the actual variable. In the case of a type conversion, the value of the formal parameter is converted back and the check applies to the result of the conversion.

8   In each of the above cases, the execution of the program is erroneous if the checked value is undefined.

9   For other types, for all modes, a check is made before the call as for scalar and access types; no check is made upon return.

10   The exception CONSTRAINT_ERROR is raised at the place of the subprogram call if either of these checks fails.

Note:

11   For array types and for types with discriminants, the check before the call is sufficient (a check upon return would be redundant) if the type mark of the formal parameter denotes a constrained subtype, since neither array bounds nor discriminants can then vary.

If this type mark denotes an unconstrained array type, the formal parameter is constrained with the bounds of the corresponding actual parameter and no check (neither before the call nor upon return) is needed (see 3.6.1). Similarly, no check is needed if the type mark denotes an unconstrained type with discriminants, since the formal parameter is then constrained exactly as the corresponding actual parameter (see 3.7.1).   12

References: actual parameter 6.4, array bound 3.6, array type 3.6, call of a subprogram 6.4, conform 6.3.1, constrained subtype 3.3, constraint 3.3, constraint_error exception 11.1, discriminant 3.7.1, erroneous 1.6, evaluation 4.5, evaluation of a name 4.1, expression 4.4, formal parameter 6.1, mode 6.1, name 4.1, parameter association 6.4, subtype 3.3, type 3.3, type conversion 4.6, type mark 3.3.2, unconstrained array type 3.6, unconstrained type with discriminants 3.7.1, undefined value 3.2.1, variable 3.2.1   13

6.4.2 Default Parameters

If a parameter specification includes a default expression for a parameter of mode **in**, then corresponding subprogram calls need not include a parameter association for the parameter. If a parameter association is thus omitted from a call, then the rest of the call, following any initial positional associations, must use only named associations.   1

For any omitted parameter association, the default expression is evaluated before the call and the resulting value is used as an implicit actual parameter.   2

Examples of procedures with default values: 3

```
procedure ACTIVATE( PROCESS  : in PROCESS_NAME;
                    AFTER     : in PROCESS_NAME := NO_PROCESS;
                    WAIT      : in DURATION := 0.0;
                    PRIOR     : in BOOLEAN := FALSE);

procedure PAIR(LEFT, RIGHT : PERSON_NAME := new PERSON);
```

Examples of their calls: 4

```
ACTIVATE(X);
ACTIVATE(X, AFTER => Y);
ACTIVATE(X, WAIT => 60.0, PRIOR => TRUE);
ACTIVATE(X, Y, 10.0, FALSE);

PAIR;
PAIR(LEFT => new PERSON, RIGHT => new PERSON);
```

Note:

If a default expression is used for two or more parameters in a multiple parameter specification, the default expression is evaluated once for each omitted parameter. Hence in the above examples, the two calls of PAIR are equivalent.   5

References: actual parameter 6.4.1, default expression for a formal parameter 6.1, evaluation 4.5, formal parameter 6.1, mode 6.1, named parameter association 6.4, parameter association 6.4, parameter specification 6.1, positional parameter association 6.4, subprogram call 6.4   6

6.5 Function Subprograms

1   A function is a subprogram that returns a value (the result of the function call). The specification of a function starts with the reserved word **function**, and the parameters, if any, must have the mode **in** (whether this mode is specified explicitly or implicitly). The statements of the function body (excluding statements of program units that are inner to the function body) must include one or more return statements specifying the returned value.

2   The exception PROGRAM_ERROR is raised if a function body is left otherwise than by a return statement. This does not apply if the execution of the function is abandoned as a result of an exception.

3   *Example:*

```
function DOT_PRODUCT(LEFT, RIGHT : VECTOR) return REAL is
   SUM : REAL := 0.0;
begin
   CHECK(LEFT'FIRST = RIGHT'FIRST and LEFT'LAST = RIGHT'LAST);
   for J in LEFT'RANGE loop
      SUM := SUM + LEFT(J)*RIGHT(J);
   end loop;
   return SUM;
end DOT_PRODUCT;
```

4   *References:* exception 11, formal parameter 6.1, function 6.1, function body 6.3, function call 6.4, function specification 6.1, mode 6.1, program_error exception 11.1, raising of exceptions 11, return statement 5.8, statement 5

6.6 Parameter and Result Type Profile - Overloading of Subprograms

1   Two formal parts are said to have the same *parameter type profile* if and only if they have the same number of parameters, and at each parameter position corresponding parameters have the same base type. A subprogram or entry has the same *parameter and result type profile* as another subprogram or entry if and only if both have the same parameter type profile, and either both are functions with the same result base type, or neither of the two is a function.

2   The same subprogram identifier or operator symbol can be used in several subprogram specifications. The identifier or operator symbol is then said to be *overloaded*; the subprograms that have this identifier or operator symbol are also said to be overloaded and to overload each other. As explained in section 8.3, if two subprograms overload each other, one of them can hide the other only if both subprograms have the same parameter and result type profile (see section 8.3 for the other requirements that must be met for hiding).

3   A call to an overloaded subprogram is ambiguous (and therefore illegal) if the name of the subprogram, the number of parameter associations, the types and the order of the actual parameters, the names of the formal parameters (if named associations are used), and the result type (for functions) are not sufficient to determine exactly one (overloaded) subprogram specification.

Examples of overloaded subprograms:

```
procedure PUT(X : INTEGER);
procedure PUT(X : STRING);
procedure SET(TINT    : COLOR);
procedure SET(SIGNAL  : LIGHT);
```

Examples of calls:

```
PUT(28);
PUT("no possible ambiguity here");

SET(TINT    => RED);
SET(SIGNAL  => RED);
SET(COLOR'(RED));

--  SET(RED) would be ambiguous since RED may
--  denote a value either of type COLOR or of type LIGHT
```

Notes:

The notion of parameter and result type profile does not include parameter names, parameter modes, parameter subtypes, default expressions and their presence or absence.

Ambiguities may (but need not) arise when actual parameters of the call of an overloaded subprogram are themselves overloaded function calls, literals, or aggregates. Ambiguities may also (but need not) arise when several overloaded subprograms belonging to different packages are visible. These ambiguities can usually be resolved in several ways: qualified expressions can be used for some or all actual parameters, and for the result, if any; the name of the subprogram can be expressed more explicitly as an expanded name; finally, the subprogram can be renamed.

References: actual parameter 6.4.1, aggregate 4.3, base type 3.3, default expression for a formal parameter 6.1, entry 9.5, formal parameter 6.1, function 6.5, function call 6.4, hiding 8.3, identifier 2.3, illegal 1.6, literal 4.2, mode 6.1, named parameter association 6.4, operator symbol 6.1, overloading 8.7, package 7, parameter of a subprogram 6.2, qualified expression 4.7, renaming declaration 8.5, result subtype 6.1, subprogram 6, subprogram specification 6.1, subtype 3.3, type 3.3

6.7 Overloading of Operators

The declaration of a function whose designator is an operator symbol is used to overload an operator. The sequence of characters of the operator symbol must be either a logical, a relational, a binary adding, a unary adding, a multiplying, or a highest precedence operator (see 4.5). Neither membership tests nor the short-circuit control forms are allowed as function designators.

The subprogram specification of a unary operator must have a single parameter. The subprogram specification of a binary operator must have two parameters; for each use of this operator, the first parameter takes the left operand as actual parameter, the second parameter takes the right operand. Similarly, a generic function instantiation whose designator is an operator symbol is only allowed if the specification of the generic function has the corresponding number of parameters. Default expressions are not allowed for the parameters of an operator (whether the operator is declared with an explicit subprogram specification or by a generic instantiation).

3 For each of the operators "+" and "-", overloading is allowed both as a unary and as a binary operator.

4 The explicit declaration of a function that overloads the equality operator "=", other than by a renaming declaration, is only allowed if both parameters are of the same limited type. An overloading of equality must deliver a result of the predefined type BOOLEAN; it also implicitly overloads the inequality operator "/=" so that this still gives the complementary result to the equality operator. Explicit overloading of the inequality operator is not allowed.

5 A renaming declaration whose designator is the equality operator is only allowed to rename another equality operator. (For example, such a renaming declaration can be used when equality is visible by selection but not directly visible.)

Note:

6 Overloading of relational operators does not affect basic comparisons such as testing for membership in a range or the choices in a case statement.

7 *Examples:*

```
function "+" (LEFT, RIGHT : MATRIX)   return MATRIX;
function "+" (LEFT, RIGHT : VECTOR)   return VECTOR;

--   assuming that A, B, and C are of the type VECTOR
--   the three following assignments are equivalent

A := B + C;

A := "+"(B, C);
A := "+"(LEFT => B, RIGHT => C);
```

8 *References:* allow 1.6, actual parameter 6.4.1, binary adding operator 4.5 4.5.3, boolean predefined type 3.5.3, character 2.1, complementary result 4.5.2, declaration 3.1, default expression for a formal parameter 6.1, designator 6.1, directly visible 8.3, equality operator 4.5, formal parameter 6.1, function declaration 6.1, highest precedence operator 4.5 4.5.6, implicit declaration 3.1, inequality operator 4.5.2, limited type 7.4.4, logical operator 4.5 4.5.1, membership test 4.5 4.5.2, multiplying operator 4.5 4.5.5, operator 4.5, operator symbol 6.1, overloading 6.6 8.7, relational operator 4.5 4.5.2, short-circuit control form 4.5 4.5.1, type definition 3.3.1, unary adding operator 4.5 4.5.4, visible by selection 8.3

7. Packages

Packages are one of the four forms of program unit, of which programs can be composed. The other forms are subprograms, task units, and generic units.

Packages allow the specification of groups of logically related entities. In their simplest form packages specify pools of common object and type declarations. More generally, packages can be used to specify groups of related entities including also subprograms that can be called from outside the package, while their inner workings remain concealed and protected from outside users.

References: generic unit 12, program unit 6, subprogram 6, task unit 9, type declaration 3.3.1

7.1 Package Structure

A package is generally provided in two parts: a package specification and a package body. Every package has a package specification, but not all packages have a package body.

```
package_declaration ::= package_specification;

package_specification ::=
    package identifier is
      {basic_declarative_item}
  [ private
      {basic_declarative_item}]
    end [package_simple_name]

package_body ::=
    package body package_simple_name is
        [ declarative_part]
  [ begin
          sequence_of_statements
  [ exception
          exception_handler
        { exception_handler}]]
    end [package_simple_name];
```

The simple name at the start of a package body must repeat the package identifier. Similarly if a simple name appears at the end of the package specification or body, it must repeat the package identifier.

If a subprogram declaration, a package declaration, a task declaration, or a generic declaration is a declarative item of a given package specification, then the body (if there is one) of the program unit declared by the declarative item must itself be a declarative item of the declarative part of the body of the given package.

Notes:

5 A simple form of package, specifying a pool of objects and types, does not require a package body. One of the possible uses of the sequence of statements of a package body is to initialize such objects. For each subprogram declaration there must be a corresponding body (except for a subprogram written in another language, as explained in section 13.9). If the body of a program unit is a body stub, then a separately compiled subunit containing the corresponding proper body is required for the program unit (see 10.2). A body is not a basic declarative item and so cannot appear in a package specification.

6 A package declaration is either a library package (see 10.2) or a declarative item declared within another program unit.

7 *References:* basic declarative item 3.9, body stub 10.2, declarative item 3.9, declarative part 3.9, exception handler 11.2, generic body 12.2, generic declaration 12.1, identifier 2.3, library unit 10.1, object 3.2, package body 7.3, program unit 6, proper body 3.9, sequence of statements 5.1, simple name 4.1, subprogram body 6.3, subprogram declaration 6.1, subunit 10.2, task body 9.1, task declaration 9.1, type 3.3

7.2 Package Specifications and Declarations

1 The first list of declarative items of a package specification is called the *visible part* of the package. The optional list of declarative items after the reserved word **private** is called the *private part* of the package.

2 An entity declared in the private part of a package is not visible outside the package itself (a name denoting such an entity is only possible within the package). In contrast, expanded names denoting entities declared in the visible part can be used even outside the package; furthermore, direct visibility of such entities can be achieved by means of use clauses (see 4.1.3 and 8.4).

3 The elaboration of a package declaration consists of the elaboration of its basic declarative items in the given order.

Notes:

4 The visible part of a package contains all the information that another program unit is able to know about the package. A package consisting of only a package specification (that is, without a package body) can be used to represent a group of common constants or variables, or a common pool of objects and types, as in the examples below.

5 *Example of a package describing a group of common variables:*

```
package PLOTTING_DATA is
   PEN_UP : BOOLEAN;

   CONVERSION_FACTOR,
   X_OFFSET, Y_OFFSET,
   X_MIN,     Y_MIN,
   X_MAX,     Y_MAX:  REAL;      -- see 3.5.7

   X_VALUE   : array (1 .. 500) of REAL;
   Y_VALUE   : array (1 .. 500) of REAL;
end PLOTTING_DATA;
```

Example of a package describing a common pool of objects and types:

```
package WORK_DATA is
    type DAY is (MON, TUE, WED, THU, FRI, SAT, SUN);
    type HOURS_SPENT is delta 0.25 range 0.0 .. 24.0;
    type TIME_TABLE    is array (DAY) of HOURS_SPENT;

    WORK_HOURS    : TIME_TABLE;
    NORMAL_HOURS  : constant TIME_TABLE :=
                    (MON .. THU => 8.25, FRI => 7.0, SAT | SUN => 0.0);
end WORK_DATA;
```

References: basic declarative item 3.9, constant 3.2.1, declarative item 3.9, direct visibility 8.3, elaboration 3.9,   7
expanded name 4.1.3, name 4.1, number declaration 3.2.2, object declaration 3.2.1, package 7, package declaration
7.1, package identifier 7.1, package specification 7.1, scope 8.2, simple name 4.1, type declaration 3.3.1, use clause
8.4, variable 3.2.1

7.3 Package Bodies

In contrast to the entities declared in the visible part of a package specification, the entities decla-   1
red in the package body are only visible within the package body itself. As a consequence, a package with a package body can be used for the construction of a group of related subprograms (a *pac-*
kage in the usual sense), in which the logical operations available to the users are clearly isolated
from the internal entities.

For the elaboration of a package body, its declarative part is first elaborated, and its sequence of   2
statements (if any) is then executed. The optional exception handlers at the end of a package body
service exceptions raised during the execution of the sequence of statements of the package body.

Notes:

A variable declared in the body of a package is only visible within this body and, consequently, its   3
value can only be changed within the package body. In the absence of local tasks, the value of
such a variable remains unchanged between calls issued from outside the package to subprograms
declared in the visible part. The properties of such a variable are similar to those of an "own"
variable of Algol 60.

The elaboration of the body of a subprogram declared in the visible part of a package is caused by   4
the elaboration of the body of the package. Hence a call of such a subprogram by an outside program unit raises the exception PROGRAM_ERROR if the call takes place before the elaboration of
the package body (see 3.9).

5   *Example of a package:*

```
package RATIONAL_NUMBERS is

   type RATIONAL is
      record
         NUMERATOR    : INTEGER;
         DENOMINATOR  : POSITIVE;
      end record;

   function EQUAL (X,Y : RATIONAL) return BOOLEAN;

   function "/"    (X,Y : INTEGER)   return RATIONAL;  --  to construct a rational number

   function "+"    (X,Y : RATIONAL) return RATIONAL;
   function "-"    (X,Y : RATIONAL) return RATIONAL;
   function "*"    (X,Y : RATIONAL) return RATIONAL;
   function "/"    (X,Y : RATIONAL) return RATIONAL;
end;

package body RATIONAL_NUMBERS is

   procedure SAME_DENOMINATOR (X,Y : in out RATIONAL) is
   begin
      --  reduces X and Y to the same denominator:
      ...
   end;

   function EQUAL(X,Y : RATIONAL) return BOOLEAN is
      U,V : RATIONAL;
   begin
      U := X;
      V := Y;
      SAME_DENOMINATOR (U,V);
      return U.NUMERATOR = V.NUMERATOR;
   end EQUAL;

   function "/" (X,Y : INTEGER) return RATIONAL is
   begin
      if Y > 0 then
         return (NUMERATOR => X,  DENOMINATOR => Y);
      else
         return (NUMERATOR => -X, DENOMINATOR => -Y);
      end if;
   end "/";

   function "+"  (X,Y : RATIONAL) return RATIONAL is ...  end "+";
   function "-"  (X,Y : RATIONAL) return RATIONAL is ...  end "-";
   function "*"  (X,Y : RATIONAL) return RATIONAL is ...  end "*";
   function "/"  (X,Y : RATIONAL) return RATIONAL is ...  end "/";

end RATIONAL_NUMBERS;
```

6   *References:* declaration 3.1, declarative part 3.9, elaboration 3.1 3.9, exception 11, exception handler 11.2, name 4.1, package specification 7.1, program unit 6, program_error exception 11.1, sequence of statements 5.1, subprogram 6, variable 3.2.1, visible part 7.2

7.4 Private Type and Deferred Constant Declarations

The declaration of a type as a private type in the visible part of a package serves to separate the [1] characteristics that can be used directly by outside program units (that is, the logical properties) from other characteristics whose direct use is confined to the package (the details of the definition of the type itself). Deferred constant declarations declare constants of private types.

    private_type_declaration ::=   [2]
        type identifier [discriminant_part] is [limited] private;

    deferred_constant_declaration ::=
        identifier_list : constant type_mark;

A private type declaration is only allowed as a declarative item of the visible part of a package, or [3] as the generic parameter declaration for a generic formal type in a generic formal part.

The type mark of a deferred constant declaration must denote a private type or a subtype of a pri- [4] vate type; a deferred constant declaration and the declaration of the corresponding private type must both be declarative items of the visible part of the same package. A deferred constant decla- ration with several identifiers is equivalent to a sequence of single deferred constant declarations as explained in section 3.2.

Examples of private type declarations: [5]

    type KEY is private;
    type FILE_NAME is limited private;

Example of deferred constant declaration: [6]

    NULL_KEY : constant KEY;

References: constant 3.2.1, declaration 3.1, declarative item 3.9, deferred constant 7.4.3, discriminant part 3.7.1, [7] generic formal part 12.1, generic formal type 12.1, generic parameter declaration 12.1, identifier 2.3, identifier list 3.2, limited type 7.4.4, package 7, private type 7.4.1, program unit 6, subtype 3.3, type 3.3, type mark 3.3.2, visible part 7.2

7.4.1 Private Types

If a private type declaration is given in the visible part of a package, then a corresponding declara- [1] tion of a type with the same identifier must appear as a declarative item of the private part of the package. The corresponding declaration must be either a full type declaration or the declaration of a task type. In the rest of this section explanations are given in terms of full type declarations; the same rules apply also to declarations of task types.

2 A private type declaration and the corresponding full type declaration define a single type. The private type declaration, together with the visible part, define the operations that are available to outside program units (see section 7.4.2 on the operations that are available for private types). On the other hand, the full type declaration defines other operations whose direct use is only possible within the package itself.

3 If the private type declaration includes a discriminant part, the full declaration must include a discriminant part that conforms (see 6.3.1 for the conformance rules) and its type definition must be a record type definition. Conversely, if the private type declaration does not include a discriminant part, the type declared by the full type declaration (the *full type*) must not be an unconstrained type with discriminants. The full type must not be an unconstrained array type. A limited type (in particular a task type) is allowed for the full type only if the reserved word **limited** appears in the private type declaration (see 7.4.4).

4 Within the specification of the package that declares a private type and before the end of the corresponding full type declaration, a restriction applies to the use of a name that denotes the private type or a subtype of the private type and, likewise, to the use of a name that denotes any type or subtype that has a subcomponent of the private type. The only allowed occurrences of such a name are in a deferred constant declaration, a type or subtype declaration, a subprogram specification, or an entry declaration; moreover, occurrences within derived type definitions or within simple expressions are not allowed.

5 The elaboration of a private type declaration creates a private type. If the private type declaration has a discriminant part, this elaboration includes that of the discriminant part. The elaboration of the full type declaration consists of the elaboration of the type definition; the discriminant part, if any, is not elaborated (since the conforming discriminant part of the private type declaration has already been elaborated).

Notes:

6 It follows from the given rules that neither the declaration of a variable of a private type, nor the creation by an allocator of an object of the private type are allowed before the full declaration of the type. Similarly before the full declaration, the name of the private type cannot be used in a generic instantiation or in a representation clause.

7 *References:* allocator 4.8, array type 3.6, conform 6.3.1, declarative item 3.9, deferred constant declaration 7.4.3, derived type 3.4, discriminant part 3.7.1, elaboration 3.9, entry declaration 9.5, expression 4.4, full type declaration 3.3.1, generic instantiation 12.3, identifier 2.3, incomplete type declaration 3.8.1, limited type 7.4.4, name 4.1, operation 3.3, package 7, package specification 7.1, private part 7.2, private type 7.4, private type declaration 7.4, record type definition 3.7, representation clause 13.1, reserved word 2.9, subcomponent 3.3, subprogram specification 6.1, subtype 3.3, subtype declaration 3.3.2, type 3.3, type declaration 3.3.1, type definition 3.3.1, unconstrained array type 3.6, variable 3.2.1, visible part 7.2

7.4.2 Operations of a Private Type

1 The operations that are implicitly declared by a private type declaration include basic operations. These are the operations involved in assignment (unless the reserved word **limited** appears in the declaration), membership tests, selected components for the selection of any discriminant, qualification, and explicit conversions.

For a private type T, the basic operations also include the attributes T'BASE (see 3.3.3) and T'SIZE   2
(see 13.7.2). For an object A of a private type, the basic operations include the attribute
A'CONSTRAINED if the private type has discriminants (see 3.7.4), and in any case, the attributes
A'SIZE and A'ADDRESS (see 13.7.2).

Finally, the operations implicitly declared by a private type declaration include the predefined com-   3
parison for equality and inequality unless the reserved word **limited** appears in the private type
declaration.

The above operations, together with subprograms that have a parameter or result of the private   4
type and that are declared in the visible part of the package, are the only operations from the
package that are available outside the package for the private type.

Within the package that declares the private type, the additional operations implicitly declared by   5
the full type declaration are also available. However, the redefinition of these implicitly declared
operations is allowed within the same declarative region, including between the private type
declaration and the corresponding full declaration. An explicitly declared subprogram hides an
implicitly declared operation that has the same parameter and result type profile (this is only possible if the implicitly declared operation is a derived subprogram or a predefined operator).

If a composite type has subcomponents of a private type and is declared outside the package that   6
declares the private type, then the operations that are implicitly declared by the declaration of the
composite type include all operations that only depend on the characteristics that result from the
private type declaration alone. (For example the operator $<$ is not included for a one-dimensional
array type.)

If the composite type is itself declared within the package that declares the private type (including   7
within an inner package or generic package), then additional operations that depend on the
characteristics of the full type are implicitly declared, as required by the rules applicable to the
composite type (for example the operator $<$ is declared for a one-dimensional array type if the full
type is discrete). These additional operations are implicitly declared at the earliest place within the
immediate scope of the composite type and after the full type declaration.

The same rules apply to the operations that are implicitly declared for an access type whose   8
designated type is a private type or a type declared by an incomplete type declaration.

For every private type or subtype T the following attribute is defined: 9

T'CONSTRAINED Yields the value FALSE if T denotes an unconstrained nonformal private type   10
with discriminants; also yields the value FALSE if T denotes a generic formal
private type, and the associated actual subtype is either an unconstrained type
with discriminants or an unconstrained array type; yields the value TRUE
otherwise. The value of this attribute is of the predefined type BOOLEAN.

Note:

A private type declaration and the corresponding full type declaration define two different views of   11
one and the same type. Outside of the defining package the characteristics of the type are those
defined by the visible part. Within these outside program units the type is just a private type and
any language rule that applies only to another class of types does not apply. The fact that the full
declaration might *implement* the private type with a type of a particular class (for example, as an
array type) is only relevant within the package itself.

12 The consequences of this actual implementation are, however, valid everywhere. For example: any default initialization of components takes place; the attribute SIZE provides the size of the full type; task dependence rules still apply to components that are task objects.

13 *Example:*

```
package KEY_MANAGER is
   type KEY is private;
   NULL_KEY : constant KEY;
   procedure GET_KEY(K : out KEY);
   function "<" (X, Y : KEY) return BOOLEAN;
private
   type KEY is new NATURAL;
   NULL_KEY : constant KEY := 0;
end;

package body KEY_MANAGER is
   LAST_KEY : KEY := 0;
   procedure GET_KEY(K : out KEY) is
   begin
      LAST_KEY := LAST_KEY + 1;
      K := LAST_KEY;
   end GET_KEY;

   function "<" (X, Y : KEY) return BOOLEAN is
   begin
      return INTEGER(X) < INTEGER(Y);
   end "<";
end KEY_MANAGER;
```

Notes on the example:

14 Outside of the package KEY_MANAGER, the operations available for objects of type KEY include assignment, the comparison for equality or inequality, the procedure GET_KEY and the operator "<"; they do not include other relational operators such as ">=", or arithmetic operators.

15 The explicitly declared operator "<" hides the predefined operator "<" implicitly declared by the full type declaration. Within the body of the function, an explicit conversion of X and Y to the type INTEGER is necessary to invoke the "<" operator of this type. Alternatively, the result of the function could be written as **not** (X >= Y), since the operator ">=" is not redefined.

16 The value of the variable LAST_KEY, declared in the package body, remains unchanged between calls of the procedure GET_KEY. (See also the Notes of section 7.3.)

17 *References:* assignment 5.2, attribute 4.1.4, basic operation 3.3.3, component 3.3, composite type 3.3, conversion 4.6. declaration 3.1, declarative region 8.1, derived subprogram 3.4, derived type 3.4, dimension 3.6, discriminant 3.3. equality 4.5.2, full type 7.4.1, full type declaration 3.3.1, hiding 8.3, immediate scope 8.2, implicit declaration 3.3, incomplete type declaration 3.8.1, membership test 4.5, operation 3.3, package 7, parameter of a subprogram 6.2, predefined function 8.6, predefined operator 4.5, private type 7.4, private type declaration 7.4, program unit 6, qualification 4.7, relational operator 4.5, selected component 4.1.3, subprogram 6, task dependence 9.4, visible part 7.2

7.4.3 Deferred Constants

If a deferred constant declaration is given in the visible part of a package then a constant declaration (that is, an object declaration declaring a constant object, with an explicit initialization) with the same identifier must appear as a declarative item of the private part of the package. This object declaration is called the *full* declaration of the deferred constant. The type mark given in the full declaration must conform to that given in the deferred constant declaration (see 6.3.1). Multiple or single declarations are allowed for the deferred and the full declarations, provided that the equivalent single declarations conform.

Within the specification of the package that declares a deferred constant and before the end of the corresponding full declaration, the use of a name that denotes the deferred constant is only allowed in the default expression for a record component or for a formal parameter (not for a generic formal parameter).

The elaboration of a deferred constant declaration has no other effect.

The execution of a program is erroneous if it attempts to use the value of a deferred constant before the elaboration of the corresponding full declaration.

Note:

The full declaration for a deferred constant that has a given private type must not appear before the corresponding full type declaration. This is a consequence of the rules defining the allowed uses of a name that denotes a private type (see 7.4.1).

References: conform 6.3.1, constant declaration 3.2.1, declarative item 3.9, default expression for a discriminant 3.7.1, deferred constant 7.4, deferred constant declaration 7.4, elaboration has no other effect 3.1, formal parameter 6.1, generic formal parameter 12.1 12.3, identifier 2.3, object declaration 3.2.1, package 7, package specification 7.1, private part 7.2, record component 3.7, type mark 3.3.2, visible part 7.2

7.4.4 Limited Types

A limited type is a type for which neither assignment nor the predefined comparison for equality and inequality is *implicitly* declared.

A private type declaration that includes the reserved word **limited** declares a limited type. A task type is a limited type. A type derived from a limited type is itself a limited type. Finally, a composite type is limited if the type of any of its subcomponents is limited.

The operations available for a private type that is limited are as given in section 7.4.2 for private types except for the absence of assignment and of a predefined comparison for equality and inequality.

For a formal parameter whose type is limited and whose declaration occurs in an explicit subprogram declaration, the mode **out** is only allowed if this type is private and the subprogram declaration occurs within the visible part of the package that declares the private type. The same holds for formal parameters of entry declarations and of generic procedure declarations. The corresponding full type must not be limited if the mode **out** is used for any such formal parameter. Otherwise, the corresponding full type is allowed (but not required) to be a limited type (in particular, it is allowed to be a task type). If the full type corresponding to a limited private type is not itself limited, then assignment for the type is available within the package, but not outside.

5 The following are consequences of the rules for limited types:

6 ● An explicit initialization is not allowed in an object declaration if the type of the object is limited.

7 ● A default expression is not allowed in a component declaration if the type of the record component is limited.

8 ● An explicit initial value is not allowed in an allocator if the designated type is limited.

9 ● A generic formal parameter of mode **in** must not be of a limited type.

Notes:

10 The above rules do not exclude a default expression for a formal parameter of a limited type; they do not exclude a deferred constant of a limited type if the full type is not limited. An explicit declaration of an equality operator is allowed for a limited type (see 6.7).

11 Aggregates are not available for a limited composite type (see 3.6.2 and 3.7.4). Catenation is not available for a limited array type (see 3.6.2).

12 *Example:*

```
package I_O_PACKAGE is
   type FILE_NAME is limited private;

   procedure OPEN  (F : in out FILE_NAME);
   procedure CLOSE (F : in out FILE_NAME);
   procedure READ  (F : in FILE_NAME; ITEM : out INTEGER);
   procedure WRITE (F : in FILE_NAME; ITEM : in  INTEGER);
private
   type FILE_NAME is
      record
         INTERNAL_NAME : INTEGER := 0;
      end record;
end I_O_PACKAGE;

package body I_O_PACKAGE is
   LIMIT : constant := 200;
   type FILE_DESCRIPTOR is record  ...  end record;
   DIRECTORY : array (1 .. LIMIT) of FILE_DESCRIPTOR;
   ...
   procedure OPEN  (F : in out FILE_NAME) is  ...  end;
   procedure CLOSE (F : in out FILE_NAME) is  ...  end;
   procedure READ  (F : in FILE_NAME; ITEM : out  INTEGER) is ... end;
   procedure WRITE (F : in FILE_NAME; ITEM : in   INTEGER) is ... end;
begin
   ...
end I_O_PACKAGE;
```

Notes on the example:

13 In the example above, an outside subprogram making use of I_O_PACKAGE may obtain a file name by calling OPEN and later use it in calls to READ and WRITE. Thus, outside the package, a file name obtained from OPEN acts as a kind of password; its internal properties (such as containing a numeric value) are not known and no other operations (such as addition or comparison of internal names) can be performed on a file name.

7.4.4 Limited Types   7-1

This example is characteristic of any case where complete control over the operations of a type is desired. Such packages serve a dual purpose. They prevent a user from making use of the internal structure of the type. They also implement the notion of an *encapsulated* data type where the only operations on the type are those given in the package specification. 14

References: aggregate 4.3, allocator 4.8, assignment 5.2, catenation operator 4.5, component declaration 3.7, component type 3.3, composite type 3.3, default expression for a discriminant 3.7, deferred constant 7.4.3, derived type 3.4, designate 3.8, discriminant specification 3.7.1, equality 4.5.2, formal parameter 6.1, full type 7.4.1, full type declaration 3.3.1, generic formal parameter 12.1 12.3, implicit declaration 3.1, initial value 3.2.1, mode 12.1.1, object 3.2, operation 3.3, package 7, predefined operator 4.5, private type 7.4, private type declaration 7.4, record component 3.7, record type 3.7, relational operator 4.5, subcomponent 3.3, subprogram 6, task type 9.1 9.2, type 3.3 15

7.5   Example of a Table Management Package

The following example illustrates the use of packages in providing high level procedures with a simple interface to the user. 1

The problem is to define a table management package for inserting and retrieving items. The items are inserted into the table as they are supplied. Each inserted item has an order number. The items are retrieved according to their order number, where the item with the lowest order number is retrieved first. 2

From the user's point of view, the package is quite simple. There is a type called ITEM designating table items, a procedure INSERT for inserting items, and a procedure RETRIEVE for obtaining the item with the lowest order number. There is a special item NULL_ITEM that is returned when the table is empty, and an exception TABLE_FULL which is raised by INSERT if the table is already full. 3

A sketch of such a package is given below. Only the specification of the package is exposed to the user. 4

```
package TABLE_MANAGER is

    type ITEM is
      record
        ORDER_NUM   : INTEGER;
        ITEM_CODE   : INTEGER;
        QUANTITY    : INTEGER;
        ITEM_TYPE   : CHARACTER;
      end record;

    NULL_ITEM : constant ITEM :=
      (ORDER_NUM | ITEM_CODE | QUANTITY => 0, ITEM_TYPE => ' ');

    procedure INSERT   (NEW_ITEM   : in    ITEM);
    procedure RETRIEVE (FIRST_ITEM : out   ITEM);

    TABLE_FULL : exception;   --   raised by INSERT when table full
    end;
```
5

6   The details of implementing such packages can be quite complex; in this case they involve a two way linked table of internal items. A local housekeeping procedure EXCHANGE is used to move a internal item between the busy and the free lists. The initial table linkages are established by the initialization part. The package body need not be shown to the users of the package.

7

```
package body TABLE_MANAGER is
    SIZE : constant := 2000;
    subtype INDEX is INTEGER range 0 .. SIZE;

    type INTERNAL_ITEM is
      record
        CONTENT  : ITEM;
        SUCC     : INDEX;
        PRED     : INDEX;
      end record;

    TABLE : array (INDEX) of INTERNAL_ITEM;
    FIRST_BUSY_ITEM  : INDEX := 0;
    FIRST_FREE_ITEM  : INDEX := 1;

    function FREE_LIST_EMPTY  return BOOLEAN is ... end;
    function BUSY_LIST_EMPTY  return BOOLEAN is ... end;
    procedure EXCHANGE (FROM : in INDEX; TO : in INDEX) is ... end;

    procedure INSERT (NEW_ITEM : in ITEM) is
    begin
      if FREE_LIST_EMPTY then
        raise TABLE_FULL;
      end if;
      --   remaining code for INSERT
    end INSERT;

    procedure RETRIEVE (FIRST_ITEM : out ITEM) is ... end;

begin
    --   initialization of the table linkages
end TABLE_MANAGER;
```

7.6   Example of a Text Handling Package

1   This example illustrates a simple text handling package. The users only have access to the visible part; the implementation is hidden from them in the private part and the package body (not shown).

2   From a user's point of view, a TEXT is a variable-length string. Each text object has a maximum length, which must be given when the object is declared, and a current value, which is a string of some length between zero and the maximum. The maximum possible length of a text object is an implementation-defined constant.

3   The package defines first the necessary types, then functions that return some characteristics of objects of the type, then the conversion functions between texts and the predefined CHARACTER and STRING types, and finally some of the standard operations on varying strings. Most operations are overloaded on strings and characters as well as on the type TEXT, in order to minimize the number of explicit conversions the user has to write.

```
package TEXT_HANDLER is                                                           4
    MAXIMUM : constant := SOME_VALUE;  --  implementation-defined
    subtype INDEX is INTEGER range 0 .. MAXIMUM;

    type TEXT(MAXIMUM_LENGTH : INDEX) is limited private;

    function LENGTH   (T : TEXT)  return INDEX;
    function VALUE    (T : TEXT)  return STRING;
    function EMPTY    (T : TEXT)  return BOOLEAN;

    function TO_TEXT (S : STRING;      MAX : INDEX) return TEXT;  --  maximum length MAX
    function TO_TEXT (C : CHARACTER; MAX : INDEX) return TEXT;
    function TO_TEXT (S : STRING)       return TEXT;  --  maximum length S'LENGTH
    function TO_TEXT (C : CHARACTER)   return TEXT;

    function "&" (LEFT : TEXT;       RIGHT : TEXT)      return TEXT;
    function "&" (LEFT : TEXT;       RIGHT : STRING)    return TEXT;
    function "&" (LEFT : STRING;    RIGHT : TEXT)       return TEXT;
    function "&" (LEFT : TEXT;       RIGHT : CHARACTER) return TEXT;
    function "&" (LEFT : CHARACTER; RIGHT : TEXT)       return TEXT;

    function "="   (LEFT : TEXT; RIGHT : TEXT) return BOOLEAN;
    function "<"   (LEFT : TEXT; RIGHT : TEXT) return BOOLEAN;
    function "<="  (LEFT : TEXT; RIGHT : TEXT) return BOOLEAN;
    function ">"   (LEFT : TEXT; RIGHT : TEXT) return BOOLEAN;
    function ">="  (LEFT : TEXT; RIGHT : TEXT) return BOOLEAN;

    procedure SET (OBJECT : in out TEXT; VALUE : in TEXT);
    procedure SET (OBJECT : in out TEXT; VALUE : in STRING);
    procedure SET (OBJECT : in out TEXT; VALUE : in CHARACTER);

    procedure APPEND (TAIL : in TEXT;       TO : in out TEXT);
    procedure APPEND (TAIL : in STRING;     TO : in out TEXT);
    procedure APPEND (TAIL : in CHARACTER; TO : in out TEXT);

    procedure AMEND (OBJECT : in out TEXT; BY : in TEXT;       POSITION : in INDEX);
    procedure AMEND (OBJECT : in out TEXT; BY : in STRING;     POSITION : in INDEX);
    procedure AMEND (OBJECT : in out TEXT; BY : in CHARACTER; POSITION : in INDEX);

    --  amend replaces part of the object by the given text, string, or character
    --  starting at the given position in the object

    function LOCATE (FRAGMENT : TEXT;       WITHIN : TEXT) return INDEX;
    function LOCATE (FRAGMENT : STRING;     WITHIN : TEXT) return INDEX;
    function LOCATE (FRAGMENT : CHARACTER; WITHIN : TEXT) return INDEX;

    --  all return 0 if the fragment is not located

private
    type TEXT(MAXIMUM_LENGTH : INDEX) is
      record
        POS    : INDEX := 0;
        VALUE  : STRING(1 .. MAXIMUM_LENGTH);
      end record;
end TEXT_HANDLER;
```

Example of a Text Handling Package 7.6

5   *Example of use of the text handling package:*

6   A program opens an output file, whose name is supplied by the string NAME. This string has th
    form

        [DEVICE :] [FILENAME [.EXTENSION]]

7   There are standard defaults for device, filename, and extension. The user-supplied name is passe
    to EXPAND_FILE_NAME as a parameter, and the result is the expanded version, with any necessar
    defaults added.

8
```
function EXPAND_FILE_NAME (NAME : STRING) return STRING is
   use TEXT_HANDLER;

   DEFAULT_DEVICE     : constant STRING := "SY:";
   DEFAULT_FILE_NAME  : constant STRING := "RESULTS";
   DEFAULT_EXTENSION  : constant STRING := ".DAT";

   MAXIMUM_FILE_NAME_LENGTH : constant INDEX := SOME_APPROPRIATE_VALUE;
   FILE_NAME : TEXT(MAXIMUM_FILE_NAME_LENGTH);

begin

   SET(FILE_NAME, NAME);

   if EMPTY(FILE_NAME) then
      SET(FILE_NAME, DEFAULT_FILE_NAME);
   end if;

   if LOCATE(':', FILE_NAME) = 0 then
      SET(FILE_NAME, DEFAULT_DEVICE & FILE_NAME);
   end if;

   if LOCATE('.', FILE_NAME) = 0 then
      APPEND(DEFAULT_EXTENSION, TO => FILE_NAME);
   end if;

   return VALUE(FILE_NAME);

end EXPAND_FILE_NAME;
```

8. Visibility Rules

The rules defining the scope of declarations and the rules defining which identifiers are visible at various points in the text of the program are described in this chapter. The formulation of these rules uses the notion of a declarative region. [1]

References: declaration 3.1, declarative region 8.1, identifier 2.3, scope 8.2, visibility 8.3 [2]

8.1 Declarative Region

A declarative region is a portion of the program text. A single declarative region is formed by the text of each of the following: [1]

- A subprogram declaration, a package declaration, a task declaration, or a generic declaration, together with the corresponding body, if any. If the body is a body stub, the declarative region also includes the corresponding subunit. If the program unit has subunits, they are also included. [2]

- An entry declaration together with the corresponding accept statements. [3]

- A record type declaration, together with a corresponding private or incomplete type declaration if any, and together with a corresponding record representation clause if any. [4]

- A renaming declaration that includes a formal part, or a generic parameter declaration that includes either a formal part or a discriminant part. [5]

- A block statement or a loop statement. [6]

In each of the above cases, the declarative region is said to be *associated* with the corresponding declaration or statement. A declaration is said to *occur immediately within* a declarative region if this region is the innermost region that encloses the declaration, not counting the declarative region (if any) associated with the declaration itself. [7]

A declaration that occurs immediately within a declarative region is said to be *local* to the region. Declarations in outer (enclosing) regions are said to be *global* to an inner (enclosed) declarative region. A local entity is one declared by a local declaration; a global entity is one declared by a global declaration. [8]

Some of the above forms of declarative region include several disjoint parts (for example, other declarative items can be between the declaration of a package and its body). Each declarative region is nevertheless considered as a (logically) continuous portion of the program text. Hence if any rule defines a portion of text as the text that *extends* from some specific point of a declarative region to the end of this region, then this portion is the corresponding subset of the declarative region (for example it does not include intermediate declarative items between the two parts of a package). [9]

Notes:

10   As defined in section 3.1, the term declaration includes basic declarations, implicit declarations, and those declarations that are part of basic declarations, for example, discriminant and parameter specifications. It follows from the definition of a declarative region that a discriminant specification occurs immediately within the region associated with the enclosing record type declaration. Similarly, a parameter specification occurs immediately within the region associated with the enclosing subprogram body or accept statement.

11   The package STANDARD forms a declarative region which encloses all library units: the implicit declaration of each library unit is assumed to occur immediately within this package (see sections 8.6 and 10.1.1).

12   Declarative regions can be nested within other declarative regions. For example, subprograms, packages, task units, generic units, and block statements can be nested within each other, and can contain record type declarations, loop statements, and accept statements.

13   *References:* accept statement 9.5, basic declaration 3.1, block statement 5.6, body stub 10.2, declaration 3.1, discriminant part 3.7.1, discriminant specification 3.7.1, entry declaration 9.5, formal part 6.1, generic body 12.2, generic declaration 12.1, generic parameter declaration 12.1, implicit declaration 3.1, incomplete type declaration 3.8.1, library unit 10.1, loop statement 5.5, package 7, package body 7.1, package declaration 7.1, parameter specification 6.1, private type declaration 7.4, record representation clause 13.4, record type 3.7, renaming declaration 8.5, standard package 8.6, subprogram body 6.3, subprogram declaration 6.1, subunit 10.2, task body 9.1, task declaration 9.1, task unit 9

8.2 Scope of Declarations

1   For each form of declaration, the language rules define a certain portion of the program text called the *scope* of the declaration. The scope of a declaration is also called the scope of any entity declared by the declaration. Furthermore, if the declaration associates some notation with a declared entity, this portion of the text is also called the scope of this notation (either an identifier, a character literal, an operator symbol, or the notation for a basic operation). Within the scope of an entity, and only there, there are places where it is legal to use the associated notation in order to refer to the declared entity. These places are defined by the rules of visibility and overloading.

2   The scope of a declaration that occurs immediately within a declarative region extends from the beginning of the declaration to the end of the declarative region; this part of the scope of a declaration is called the *immediate scope.* Furthermore, for any of the declarations listed below, the scope of the declaration extends beyond the immediate scope:

3   (a)   A declaration that occurs immediately within the visible part of a package declaration.

4   (b)   An entry declaration.

5   (c)   A component declaration.

6   (d)   A discriminant specification.

7   (e)   A parameter specification.

8   (f)   A generic parameter declaration.

In each of these cases, the given declaration occurs immediately within some enclosing declara- 9
tion, and the scope of the given declaration extends to the end of the scope of the enclosing
declaration.

In the absence of a subprogram declaration, the subprogram specification given in the subprogram 10
body or in the body stub acts as the declaration and rule (e) applies also in such a case.

Note:

The above scope rules apply to all forms of declaration defined by section 3.1; in particular, they 11
apply also to implicit declarations. Rule (a) applies to a package declaration and thus not to the
package specification of a generic declaration. For nested declarations, the rules (a) through (f)
apply at each level. For example, if a task unit is declared in the visible part of a package, the scope
of an entry of the task unit extends to the end of the scope of the task unit, that is, to the end of the
scope of the enclosing package. The scope of a use clause is defined in section 8.4.

References: basic operation 3.3.3, body stub 10.2, character literal 2.5, component declaration 3.7, declaration 3.1, 12
declarative region 8.1, discriminant specification 3.7.1, entry declaration 9.5, extends 8.1, generic declaration 12.1,
generic parameter declaration 12.1, identifier 2.3, implicit declaration 3.1, occur immediately within 8.1, operator
symbol 6.1, overloading 6.6 8.7, package declaration 7.1, package specification 7.1, parameter specification 6.1,
record type 3.7, renaming declaration 8.5, subprogram body 6.3, subprogram declaration 6.1, task declaration 9.1,
task unit 9, type declaration 3.3.1, use clause 8.4, visibility 8.3, visible part 7.2

8.3 Visibility

The meaning of the occurrence of an identifier at a given place in the text is defined by the visibility 1
rules and also, in the case of overloaded declarations, by the overloading rules. The identifiers considered in this chapter include any identifier other than a reserved word, an attribute designator, a
pragma identifier, the identifier of a pragma argument, or an identifier given as a pragma argument. The places considered in this chapter are those where a lexical element (such as an identifier) occurs. The overloaded declarations considered in this chapter are those for subprograms,
enumeration literals, and single entries.

For each identifier and at each place in the text, the visibility rules determine a set of declarations 2
(with this identifier) that define possible meanings of an occurrence of the identifier. A declaration
is said to be *visible* at a given place in the text when, according to the visibility rules, the declaration defines a possible meaning of this occurrence. Two cases arise.

- The visibility rules determine *at most one* possible meaning. In such a case the visibility rules 3
  are sufficient to determine the declaration defining the meaning of the occurrence of the identifier, or in the absence of such a declaration, to determine that the occurrence is not legal at
  the given point.

- The visibility rules determine *more than one* possible meaning. In such a case the occurrence 4
  of the identifier is legal at this point if and only if *exactly one* visible declaration is acceptable
  for the overloading rules in the given context (see section 6.6 for the rules of overloading and
  section 8.7 for the context used for overload resolution).

5   A declaration is only visible within a certain part of its scope; this part starts at the end of the declaration except in a package specification, in which case it starts at the reserved word **is** given after the identifier of the package specification. (This rule applies, in particular, for implicit declarations.)

6   Visibility is either by selection or direct. A declaration is visible *by selection* at places that are defined as follows.

7   (a)   For a declaration given in the visible part of a package declaration: at the place of the selector after the dot of an expanded name whose prefix denotes the package.

8   (b)   For an entry declaration of a given task type: at the place of the selector after the dot of a selected component whose prefix is appropriate for the task type.

9   (c)   For a component declaration of a given record type declaration: at the place of the selector after the dot of a selected component whose prefix is appropriate for the type; also at the place of a component simple name (before the compound delimiter =>) in a named component association of an aggregate of the type.

10   (d)   For a discriminant specification of a given type declaration: at the same places as for a component declaration; also at the place of a discriminant simple name (before the compound delimiter =>) in a named discriminant association of a discriminant constraint for the type.

11   (e)   For a parameter specification of a given subprogram specification or entry declaration: at the place of the formal parameter (before the compound delimiter =>) in a named parameter association of a corresponding subprogram or entry call.

12   (f)   For a generic parameter declaration of a given generic unit: at the place of the generic formal parameter (before the compound delimiter =>) in a named generic association of a corresponding generic instantiation.

13   Finally, within the declarative region associated with a construct other than a record type declaration, any declaration that occurs immediately within the region is visible by selection at the place of the selector after the dot of an expanded name whose prefix denotes the construct.

14   Where it is not visible by selection, a visible declaration is said to be *directly visible*. A declaration is directly visible within a certain part of its immediate scope; this part extends to the end of the immediate scope of the declaration, but excludes places where the declaration is hidden as explained below. In addition, a declaration occurring immediately within the visible part of a package can be made directly visible by means of a use clause according to the rules described in section 8.4. (See also section 8.6 for the visibility of library units.)

15   A declaration is said to be *hidden* within (part of) an inner declarative region if the inner region contains a homograph of this declaration; the outer declaration is then hidden within the immediate scope of the inner homograph. Each of two declarations is said to be a *homograph* of the other if both declarations have the same identifier and overloading is allowed for at most one of the two. If overloading is allowed for both declarations, then each of the two is a homograph of the other if they have the same identifier, operator symbol, or character literal, as well as the same parameter and result type profile (see 6.6).

16   Within the specification of a subprogram, every declaration with the same designator as the subprogram is hidden; the same holds within a generic instantiation that declares a subprogram, and within an entry declaration or the formal part of an accept statement; where hidden in this manner, a declaration is visible neither by selection nor directly.

Two declarations that occur immediately within the same declarative region must not be homographs, unless either or both of the following requirements are met: (a) exactly one of them is the implicit declaration of a predefined operation; (b) exactly one of them is the implicit declaration of a derived subprogram. In such cases, a predefined operation is always hidden by the other homograph; a derived subprogram hides a predefined operation, but is hidden by any other homograph. Where hidden in this manner, an implicit declaration is hidden within the entire scope of the other declaration (regardless of which declaration occurs first); the implicit declaration is visible neither by selection nor directly. 17

Whenever a declaration with a certain identifier is visible from a given point, the identifier and the declared entity (if any) are also said to be visible from that point. Direct visibility and visibility by selection are likewise defined for character literals and operator symbols. An operator is directly visible if and only if the corresponding operator declaration is directly visible. Finally, the notation associated with a basic operation is directly visible within the entire scope of this operation. 18

Example: 19

```
procedure P is
    A, B : BOOLEAN;

    procedure Q is
        C  : BOOLEAN;
        B  : BOOLEAN;   --  an inner homograph of B
    begin
        ...
        B  := A;   --   means Q.B := P.A;
        C  := P.B;   --   means Q.C := P.B;
    end;
begin
    ...
    A := B;  --   means P.A := P.B;
end;
```

Note on the visibility of library units:

The visibility of library units is determined by with clauses (see 10.1.1) and by the fact that library units are implicitly declared in the package STANDARD (see 8.6). 20

Note on homographs:

The same identifier may occur in different declarations and may thus be associated with different entities, even if the scopes of these declarations overlap. Overlap of the scopes of declarations with the same identifier can result from overloading of subprograms and of enumeration literals. Such overlaps can also occur for entities declared in package visible parts and for entries, record components, and parameters, where there is overlap of the scopes of the enclosing package declarations, task declarations, record type declarations, subprogram declarations, renaming declarations, or generic declarations. Finally overlapping scopes can result from nesting. 21

Note on immediate scope, hiding, and visibility:

The rules defining immediate scope, hiding, and visibility imply that a reference to an identifier within its own declaration is illegal (except for packages and generic packages). The identifier hides outer homographs within its immediate scope, that is, from the start of the declaration; on the other hand, the identifier is visible only after the end of the declaration. For this reason, all but the last of the following declarations are illegal: 22

```
K : INTEGER := K * K;          -- illegal
T : T;                         -- illegal
procedure P(X : P);            -- illegal
procedure Q(X : REAL := Q);    -- illegal, even if there is a function named Q
procedure R(R : REAL);  --  an inner declaration is legal (although confusing)
```

23 *References:* accept statement 9.5, aggregate 4.3, appropriate for a type 4.1, argument 2.8, basic operation 3.3.3, character literal 2.5, component association 4.3, component declaration 3.7, compound delimiter 2.2, declaration 3.1, declarative region 8.1, designate 3.8, discriminant constraint 3.7.2, discriminant specification 3.7.1, entry call 9.5, entry declaration 9.5, entry family 9.5, enumeration literal specification 3.5.1, expanded name 4.1.3, extends 8.1, formal parameter 6.1, generic association 12.3, generic formal parameter 12.1, generic instantiation 12.3, generic package 12.1, generic parameter declaration 12.1, generic unit 12, identifier 2.3, immediate scope 8.2, implicit declaration 3.1, lexical element 2.2, library unit 10.1, object 3.2, occur immediately within 8.1, operator 4.5, operator symbol 6.1, overloading 6.6 8.7, package 7, parameter 6.2, parameter association 6.4, parameter specification 6.1, pragma 2.8, program unit 6, record type 3.7, reserved word 2.9, scope 8.2, selected component 4.1.3, selector 4.1.3, simple name 4.1, subprogram 6, subprogram call 6.4, subprogram declaration 6.1, subprogram specification 6.1, task type 9.1, task unit 9, type 3.3, type declaration 3.3.1, use clause 8.4, visible part 7.2

8.4 Use Clauses

1 A use clause achieves direct visibility of declarations that appear in the visible parts of named packages.

2 use_clause ::= **use** *package*_name {, *package*_name};

3 For each use clause, there is a certain region of text called the *scope* of the use clause. This region starts immediately after the use clause. If a use clause is a declarative item of some declarative region, the scope of the clause extends to the end of the declarative region. If a use clause occurs within a context clause of a compilation unit, the scope of the use clause extends to the end of the declarative region associated with the compilation unit.

4 In order to define which declarations are made directly visible at a given place by use clauses, consider the set of packages named by all use clauses whose scopes enclose this place, omitting from this set any packages that enclose this place. A declaration that can be made directly visible by a use clause (a potentially visible declaration) is any declaration that occurs immediately within the visible part of a package of the set. A potentially visible declaration is actually made directly visible except in the following two cases:

5 ● A potentially visible declaration is not made directly visible if the place considered is within the immediate scope of a homograph of the declaration.

6 ● Potentially visible declarations that have the same identifier are not made directly visible unless each of them is either an enumeration literal specification or the declaration of a subprogram (by a subprogram declaration, a renaming declaration, a generic instantiation, or an implicit declaration).

7 The elaboration of a use clause has no other effect.

Note:

8 The above rules guarantee that a declaration that is made directly visible by a use clause cannot hide an otherwise directly visible declaration. The above rules are formulated in terms of the set of packages named by use clauses.

8.4 Use Clauses

Consequently, the following lines of text all have the same effect (assuming only one package P).   9

```
use P;
use P; use P, P;
```

Example of conflicting names in two packages: 10

```
procedure R is
  package TRAFFIC is
    type COLOR is (RED, AMBER, GREEN);
    ...
  end TRAFFIC;

  package WATER_COLORS is
    type COLOR is (WHITE, RED, YELLOW, GREEN, BLUE, BROWN, BLACK);
    ...
  end WATER_COLORS;

  use TRAFFIC;         --  COLOR, RED, AMBER, and GREEN are directly visible
  use WATER_COLORS;    --  two homographs of GREEN are directly visible
                       --  but COLOR is no longer directly visible

  subtype LIGHT   is TRAFFIC.COLOR;        -- Subtypes are used to resolve
  subtype SHADE   is WATER_COLORS.COLOR;   -- the conflicting type name COLOR

  SIGNAL : LIGHT;
  PAINT  : SHADE;
begin
  SIGNAL := GREEN;    --  that of TRAFFIC
  PAINT  := GREEN;    --  that of WATER_COLORS
end R;
```

Example of name identification with a use clause: 11

```
package D is
  T, U, V : BOOLEAN;
end D;

procedure P is
  package E is
    B, W, V : INTEGER;
  end E;

  procedure Q is
    T, X : REAL;
    use D, E;
  begin
    --  the name T    means Q.T, not D.T
    --  the name U    means D.U
    --  the name B    means E.B
    --  the name W    means E.W
    --  the name X    means Q.X
    --  the name V    is illegal : either D.V or E.V must be used
    ...
  end Q;
begin
  ...
end P;
```

12   *References:* compilation unit 10.1, context clause 10.1, declaration 3.1, declarative item 3.9, declarative region 8.1, direct visibility 8.3, elaboration 3.1 3.9, elaboration has no other effect 3.1, enumeration literal specification 3.5.1, extends 8.1, hiding 8.3, homograph 8.3, identifier 2.3, immediate scope 8.2, name 4.1, occur immediately within 8.1, package 7, scope 8.2, subprogram declaration 6.1, visible part 7.2

8.5 Renaming Declarations

1   A renaming declaration declares another name for an entity.

2
```
renaming_declaration ::=
      identifier : type_mark       renames object_name;
    | identifier : exception       renames exception_name;
    | package identifier           renames package_name;
    | subprogram_specification     renames subprogram_or_entry_name;
```

3   The elaboration of a renaming declaration evaluates the name that follows the reserved word **renames** and thereby determines the entity denoted by this name (the renamed entity). At any point where a renaming declaration is visible, the identifier, or operator symbol of this declaration denotes the renamed entity.

4   The first form of renaming declaration is used for the renaming of objects. The renamed entity must be an object of the base type of the type mark. The properties of the renamed object are not affected by the renaming declaration. In particular, its value and whether or not it is a constant are unaffected; similarly, the constraints that apply to an object are not affected by renaming (any constraint implied by the type mark of the renaming declaration is ignored). The renaming declaration is legal only if exactly one object has this type and can be denoted by the object name.

5   The following restrictions apply to the renaming of a subcomponent that depends on discriminants of a variable. The renaming is not allowed if the subtype of the variable, as defined in a corresponding object declaration, component declaration, or component subtype indication, is an unconstrained type; or if the variable is a generic formal object (of mode **in out**). Similarly if the variable is a formal parameter, the renaming is not allowed if the type mark given in the parameter specification denotes an unconstrained type whose discriminants have default expressions.

6   The second form of renaming declaration is used for the renaming of exceptions; the third form for the renaming of packages.

7   The last form of renaming declaration is used for the renaming of subprograms and entries. The renamed subprogram or entry and the subprogram specification given in the renaming declaration must have the same parameter and result type profile (see 6.6). The renaming declaration is legal only if exactly one visible subprogram or entry satisfies the above requirements and can be denoted by the given subprogram or entry name. In addition, parameter modes must be identical for formal parameters that are at the same parameter position.

8   The subtypes of the parameters and result (if any) of a renamed subprogram or entry are not affected by renaming. These subtypes are those given in the original subprogram declaration, generic instantiation, or entry declaration (not those of the renaming declaration); even for calls that use the new name. On the other hand, a renaming declaration can introduce parameter names and default expressions that differ from those of the renamed subprogram; named associations of calls with the new subprogram name must use the new parameter name; calls with the old subprogram name must use the old parameter names.

A procedure can only be renamed as a procedure. Either of a function or operator can be renamed as either of a function or operator; for renaming as an operator, the subprogram specification given in the renaming declaration is subject to the rules given in section 6.7 for operator declarations. Enumeration literals can be renamed as functions; similarly, attributes defined as functions (such as SUCC and PRED) can be renamed as functions. An entry can only be renamed as a procedure; the new name is only allowed to appear in contexts that allow a procedure name. An entry of a family can be renamed, but an entry family cannot be renamed as a whole. 9

Examples: 10

```
declare
   L : PERSON renames LEFTMOST_PERSON;  -- see 3.8.1
begin
   L.AGE := L.AGE + 1;
end;

FULL : exception renames TABLE_MANAGER.TABLE_FULL; -- see 7.5

package TM renames TABLE_MANAGER;

function REAL_PLUS(LEFT, RIGHT : REAL    ) return REAL    renames "+";
function INT_PLUS  (LEFT, RIGHT : INTEGER) return INTEGER renames "+";

function ROUGE return COLOR renames RED;  --   see 3.5.1
function ROT    return COLOR renames RED;
function ROSSO return COLOR renames ROUGE;

function NEXT(X : COLOR) return COLOR renames COLOR'SUCC; -- see 3.5.5
```

Example of a renaming declaration with new parameter names: 11

```
function "*" (X,Y : VECTOR) return REAL renames DOT_PRODUCT; -- see 6.1
```

Example of a renaming declaration with a new default expression: 12

```
function MINIMUM(L : LINK := HEAD) return CELL renames MIN_CELL; -- see 6.1
```

Notes:

Renaming may be used to resolve name conflicts and to act as a shorthand. Renaming with a different identifier or operator symbol does not hide the old name; the new name and the old name need not be visible at the same points. The attributes POS and VAL cannot be renamed since the corresponding specifications cannot be written; the same holds for the predefined multiplying operators with a *universal_fixed* result. 13

Calls with the new name of a renamed entry are procedure call statements and are not allowed at places where the syntax requires an entry call statement in conditional and timed entry calls; similarly, the COUNT attribute is not available for the new name. 14

A task object that is declared by an object declaration can be renamed as an object. However, a single task cannot be renamed since the corresponding task type is anonymous. For similar reasons, an object of an anonymous array type cannot be renamed. No syntactic form exists for renaming a generic unit. 15

A subtype can be used to achieve the effect of renaming a type (including a task type) as in 16

```
subtype MODE is TEXT_IO.FILE_MODE;
```

17 *References:* allow 1.6, attribute 4.1.4, base type 3.3, conditional entry call 9.7.2, constant 3.2.1, constrained subtype 3.3, constraint 3.3, declaration 3.1, default expression 6.1, depend on a discriminant 3.7.1, discriminant 3.7.1, elaboration 3.1 3.9, entry 9.5, entry call 9.5, entry call statement 9.5, entry declaration 9.5, entry family 9.5, enumeration literal 3.5.1, evaluation of a name 4.1, exception 11, formal parameter 6.1, function 6.5, identifier 2.3, legal 1.6, mode 6.1, name 4.1, object 3.2, object declaration 3.2, operator 6.7, operator declaration 6.7, operator symbol 6.1, package 7, parameter 6.2, parameter specification 6.1, procedure 6.1, procedure call statement 6.4, reserved word 2.9, subcomponent 3.3, subprogram 6, subprogram call 6.4, subprogram declaration 6.1, subprogram specification 6.1, subtype 3.3.2, task object 9.2, timed entry call 9.7.3, type 3.3, type mark 3.3.2, variable 3.2.1, visibility 8.3

8.6 The Package Standard

1 The predefined types (for example the types BOOLEAN, CHARACTER and INTEGER) are the types that are declared in a predefined package called STANDARD; this package also includes the declarations of their predefined operations. The package STANDARD is described in Annex C. Apart from the predefined numeric types, the specification of the package STANDARD must be the same for all implementations of the language.

2 The package STANDARD forms a declarative region which encloses every library unit and consequently the main program; the declaration of every library unit is assumed to occur immediately within this package. The implicit declarations of library units are assumed to be ordered in such a way that the scope of a given library unit includes any compilation unit that mentions the given library unit in a with clause. However, the only library units that are visible within a given compilation unit are as follows: they include the library units named by all with clauses that apply to the given unit, and moreover, if the given unit is a secondary unit of some library unit, they include this library unit.

Notes:

3 If all block statements of a program are named, then the name of each program unit can always be written as an expanded name starting with STANDARD (unless this package is itself hidden).

4 If a type is declared in the visible part of a library package, then it is a consequence of the visibility rules that a basic operation (such as assignment) for this type is directly visible at places where the type itself is not visible (whether by selection or directly). However this operation can only be applied to operands that are visible and the declaration of these operands requires the visibility of either the type or one of its subtypes.

5 *References:* applicable with clause 10.1.1, block name 5.6, block statement 5.6, declaration 3.1, declarative region 8.1, expanded name 4.1.3, hiding 8.3, identifier 2.3, implicit declaration 3.1, library unit 10.1, loop statement 5.5, main program 10.1, must 1.6, name 4.1, occur immediately within 8.1, operator 6.7, package 7, program unit 6 secondary unit 10.1, subtype 3.3, type 3.3, visibility 8.3, with clause 10.1.1

8.7 The Context of Overload Resolution

1 Overloading is defined for subprograms, enumeration literals, operators, and single entries, and also for the operations that are inherent in several basic operations such as assignment, membership tests, allocators, the literal **null**, aggregates, and string literals.

For overloaded entities, overload resolution determines the actual meaning that an occurrence of an identifier has, whenever the visibility rules have determined that more than one meaning is acceptable at the place of this occurrence; overload resolution likewise determines the actual meaning of an occurrence of an operator or some basic operation. `2`

At such a place all visible declarations are considered. The occurrence is only legal if there is exactly one interpretation of each constituent of the innermost complete context; a *complete context* is one of the following: `3`

- A declaration.

`4`

- A statement.

`5`

- A representation clause.

`6`

When considering possible interpretations of a complete context, the only rules considered are the syntax rules, the scope and visibility rules, and the rules of the form described below. `7`

(a) Any rule that requires a name or expression to have a certain type, or to have the same type as another name or expression. `8`

(b) Any rule that requires the type of a name or expression to be a type of a certain class; similarly, any rule that requires a certain type to be a discrete, integer, real, universal, character, boolean, or nonlimited type. `9`

(c) Any rule that requires a prefix to be appropriate for a certain type. `10`

(d) Any rule that specifies a certain type as the result type of a basic operation, and any rule that specifies that this type is of a certain class. `11`

(e) The rules that require the type of an aggregate or string literal to be determinable solely from the enclosing complete context (see 4.3 and 4.2). Similarly, the rules that require the type of the prefix of an attribute, the type of the expression of a case statement, or the type of the operand of a type conversion, to be determinable independently of the context (see 4.1.4, 5.4, 4.6, and 6.4.1). `12`

(f) The rules given in section 6.6, for the resolution of overloaded subprogram calls; in section 4.6, for the implicit conversions of universal expressions; in section 3.6.1, for the interpretation of discrete ranges with bounds having a universal type; and in section 4.1.3, for the interpretation of an expanded name whose prefix denotes a subprogram or an accept statement. `13`

Subprogram names used as pragma arguments follow a different rule: the pragma can apply to several overloaded subprograms, as explained in section 6.3.2 for the pragma INLINE, in section 11.7 for the pragma SUPPRESS, and in section 13.9 for the pragma INTERFACE. `14`

Similarly, the simple names given in context clauses (see 10.1.1) and in address clauses (see 13.5) follow different rules. `15`

Notes:

16   If there is only one possible interpretation, the identifier denotes the corresponding entity. However, this does not mean that the occurrence is necessarily legal since other requirements exist which are not considered for overload resolution; for example, the fact that an expression is static, the parameter modes, whether an object is constant, conformance rules, forcing occurrences for a representation clause, order of elaboration, and so on.

17   Similarly, subtypes are not considered for overload resolution (the violation of a constraint does not make a program illegal but raises an exception during program execution).

18   A loop parameter specification is a declaration, and hence a complete context.

19   Rules that require certain constructs to have the same parameter and result type profile fall under the category (a); the same holds for rules that require conformance of two constructs since conformance requires that corresponding names be given the same meaning by the visibility and overloading rules.

20   *References:* aggregate 4.3, allocator 4.8, assignment 5.2, basic operation 3.3.3, case statement 5.4, class of type 3.3, declaration 3.1, entry 9.5, enumeration literal 3.5.1, exception 11, expression 4.4, formal part 6.1, identifier 2.3, legal 1.6, literal 4.2, loop parameter specification 5.5, membership test 4.5.2, name 4.1, null literal 3.8, operation 3.3.3, operator 4.5, overloading 6.6, pragma 2.8, representation clause 13.1, statement 5, static expression 4.9, static subtype 4.9, subprogram 6, subtype 3.3, type conversion 4.6, visibility 8.3

21   *Rules of the form (a):* address clause 13.5, assignment 5.2, choice 3.7.3 4.3.2 5.4, component association 4.3.1 4.3.2, conformance rules 9.5, default expression 3.7 3.7.1 6.1 12.1.1, delay statement 9.6, discrete range 3.6.1 5.5 9.5, discriminant constraint 3.7.2, enumeration representation clause 13.3, generic parameter association 12.3.1, index constraint 3.6.1, index expression 4.1.1 4.1.2 9.5, initial value 3.2.1, membership test 4.5.2, parameter association 6.4.1, parameter and result type profile 8.5 12.3.6, qualified expression 4.7, range constraint 3.5, renaming of an object 8.5, result expression 5.8

22   *Rules of the form (b):* abort statement 9.10, assignment 5.2, case expression 5.4, condition 5.3 5.5 5.7 9.7.1, discrete range 3.6.1 5.5 9.5, fixed point type declaration 3.5.9, floating point type declaration 3.5.7, integer type declaration 3.5.4, length clause 13.2, membership test 4.4, number declaration 3.2.2, record representation clause 13.4, selected component 4.1.3, short-circuit control form 4.4, val attribute 3.5.5

23   *Rules of the form (c):* indexed component 4.1.1, selected component 4.1.3, slice 4.1.2

24   *Rules of the form (d):* aggregate 4.3, allocator 4.8, membership test 4.4, null literal 4.2, numeric literal 2.4, short-circuit control form 4.4, string literal 4.2

8.7 The Context of Overload Resolution

9. Tasks

The execution of a program that does not contain a task is defined in terms of a sequential execution of its actions, according to the rules described in other chapters of this manual. These actions can be considered to be executed by a single *logical processor*.

Tasks are entities whose executions proceed *in parallel* in the following sense. Each task can be considered to be executed by a logical processor of its own. Different tasks (different logical processors) proceed independently, except at points where they synchronize.

Some tasks have *entries*. An entry of a task can be *called* by other tasks. A task *accepts* a call of one of its entries by executing an accept statement for the entry. Synchronization is achieved by *rendezvous* between a task issuing an entry call and a task accepting the call. Some entries have parameters; entry calls and accept statements for such entries are the principal means of communicating values between tasks.

The properties of each task are defined by a corresponding *task unit* which consists of a *task specification* and a *task body*. Task units are one of the four forms of program unit of which programs can be composed. The other forms are subprograms, packages and generic units. The properties of task units, tasks, and entries, and the statements that affect the interaction between tasks (that is, entry call statements, accept statements, delay statements, select statements, and abort statements) are described in this chapter.

Note:

Parallel tasks (parallel logical processors) may be implemented on multicomputers, multiprocessors, or with interleaved execution on a single *physical processor*. On the other hand, whenever an implementation can detect that the same effect can be guaranteed if parts of the actions of a given task are executed by different physical processors acting in parallel, it may choose to execute them in this way; in such a case, several physical processors implement a single logical processor.

References: abort statement 9.10, accept statement 9.5, delay statement 9.6, entry 9.5, entry call statement 9.5, generic unit 12, package 7, parameter in an entry call 9.5, program unit 6, rendezvous 9.5, select statement 9.7, subprogram 6, task body 9.1, task specification 9.1

9.1 Task Specifications and Task Bodies

A task unit consists of a task specification and a task body. A task specification that starts with the reserved words **task type** declares a task type. The value of an object of a task type designates a task having the entries, if any, that are declared in the task specification; these entries are also called entries of this object. The execution of the task is defined by the corresponding task body.

2   A task specification without the reserved word **type** defines a *single task*. A task declaration with this form of specification is equivalent to the declaration of an anonymous task type immediately followed by the declaration of an object of the task type, and the task unit identifier names the object. In the remainder of this chapter, explanations are given in terms of task type declarations; the corresponding explanations for single task declarations follow from the stated equivalence.

3   task_declaration ::= task_specification;

task_specification ::=
  task [**type**] identifier [**is**
    {entry_declaration}
    {representation_clause}
  end [*task*_simple_name]]

task_body ::=
    task body *task*_simple_name **is**
      [declarative_part]
    begin
        sequence_of_statements
  [**exception**
      exception_handler
      { exception_handler}]
    end [*task*_simple_name];

4   The simple name at the start of a task body must repeat the task unit identifier. Similarly if a simple name appears at the end of the task specification or body, it must repeat the task unit identifier. Within a task body, the name of the corresponding task unit can also be used to refer to the task object that designates the task currently executing the body; furthermore, the use of this name as a type mark is not allowed within the task unit itself.

5   For the elaboration of a task specification, entry declarations and representation clauses, if any, are elaborated in the order given. Such representation clauses only apply to the entries declared in the task specification (see 13.5).

6   The elaboration of a task body has no other effect than to establish that the body can from then on be used for the execution of tasks designated by objects of the corresponding task type.

7   The execution of a task body is invoked by the activation of a task object of the corresponding type (see 9.3). The optional exception handlers at the end of a task body handle exceptions raised during the execution of the sequence of statements of the task body (see 11.4).

8   *Examples of specifications of task types:*

```
task type RESOURCE is
  entry SEIZE;
  entry RELEASE;
end RESOURCE;

task type KEYBOARD_DRIVER is
  entry READ (C : out  CHARACTER);
  entry WRITE(C : in    CHARACTER);
end KEYBOARD_DRIVER;
```

Tasks

Examples of specifications of single tasks:

```
task PRODUCER_CONSUMER is
   entry READ (V : out ITEM);
   entry WRITE (E : in   ITEM);
end;

task CONTROLLER is
   entry REQUEST(LEVEL)(D : ITEM);   --  a family of entries
end CONTROLLER;

task USER;  --  has no entries
```

Example of task specification and corresponding body:

```
task PROTECTED_ARRAY is
   --  INDEX and ITEM are global types
   entry READ (N : in INDEX; V : out ITEM);
   entry WRITE(N : in INDEX; E : in   ITEM);
end;

task body PROTECTED_ARRAY is
   TABLE : array(INDEX) of ITEM := (INDEX => NULL_ITEM);
begin
   loop
     select
       accept READ (N : in INDEX; V : out ITEM) do
         V := TABLE(N);
       end READ;
     or
       accept WRITE(N : in INDEX; E : in   ITEM) do
         TABLE(N) := E;
       end WRITE;
     end select;
   end loop;
end PROTECTED_ARRAY;
```

Note:

A task specification specifies the interface of tasks of the task type with other tasks of the same or of different types, and also with the main program.

11

References: declaration 3.1, declarative part 3.9, elaboration 3.9, entry 9.5, entry declaration 9.5, exception handler 11.2, identifier 2.3, main program 10.1, object 3.2, object declaration 3.2.1, representation clause 13.1, reserved word 2.9, sequence of statements 5.1, simple name 4.1, type 3.3, type declaration 3.3.1

9.2 Task Types and Task Objects

A task type is a limited type (see 7.4.4). Hence neither assignment nor the predefined comparison for equality and inequality are defined for objects of task types; moreover, the mode **out** is not allowed for a formal parameter whose type is a task type.

Task Types and Task Objects 9.2

2   A task object is an object whose type is a task type. The value of a task object designates a task that has the entries of the corresponding task type, and whose execution is specified by the corresponding task body. If a task object is the object, or a subcomponent of the object, declared by an object declaration, then the value of the task object is defined by the elaboration of the object declaration. If a task object is the object, or a subcomponent of the object, created by the evaluation of an allocator, then the value of the task object is defined by the evaluation of the allocator. For all parameter modes, if an actual parameter designates a task, the associated formal parameter designates the same task; the same holds for a subcomponent of an actual parameter and the corresponding subcomponent of the associated formal parameter; finally, the same holds for generic parameters.

3   *Examples:*

        CONTROL : RESOURCE;
        TELETYPE : KEYBOARD_DRIVER;
        POOL   : **array**(1 .. 10) **of** KEYBOARD_DRIVER;
        --   see also examples of declarations of single tasks in 9.1

4   *Example of access type designating task objects:*

        type KEYBOARD **is access** KEYBOARD_DRIVER;

        TERMINAL : KEYBOARD := **new** KEYBOARD_DRIVER;

Notes:

5   Since a task type is a limited type, it can appear as the definition of a limited private type in a private part, and as a generic actual parameter associated with a formal parameter whose type is a limited type. On the other hand, the type of a generic formal parameter of mode **in** must not be a limited type and hence cannot be a task type.

6   Task objects behave as constants (a task object always designates the same task) since their values are implicitly defined either at declaration or allocation, or by a parameter association, and since no assignment is available. However the reserved word **constant** is not allowed in the declaration of a task object since this would require an explicit initialization. A task object that is a formal parameter of mode **in** is a constant (as is any formal parameter of this mode).

7   If an application needs to store and exchange task identities, it can do so by defining an access type designating the corresponding task objects and by using access values for identification purposes (see above example). Assignment is available for such an access type as for any access type.

8   Subtype declarations are allowed for task types as for other types, but there are no constraints applicable to task types.

9   *References:* access type 3.8, actual parameter 6.4.1, allocator 4.8, assignment 5.2, component declaration 3.7, composite type 3.3, constant 3.2.1, constant declaration 3.2.1, constraint 3.3, designate 3.8 9.1, elaboration 3.9, entry 9.5, equality operator 4.5.2, formal parameter 6.2, formal parameter mode 6.2, generic actual parameter 12.3, generic association 12.3, generic formal parameter 12.1, generic formal parameter mode 12.1.1, generic unit 12, inequality operator 4.5.2, initialization 3.2.1, limited type 7.4.4, object 3.2, object declaration 3.2.1, parameter association 6.4, private part 7.2, private type 7.4, reserved word 2.9, subcomponent 3.3, subprogram 6, subtype declaration 3.3.2, task body 9.1, type 3.3

9.2 Task Types and Task Objects

9.3 Task Execution - Task Activation

A task body defines the execution of any task that is designated by a task object of the corresponding task type. The initial part of this execution is called the *activation* of the task object, and also that of the designated task; it consists of the elaboration of the declarative part, if any, of the task body. The execution of different tasks, in particular their activation, proceeds in parallel.

If an object declaration that declares a task object occurs immediately within a declarative part, then the activation of the task object starts after the elaboration of the declarative part (that is, after passing the reserved word **begin** following the declarative part); similarly if such a declaration occurs immediately within a package specification, the activation starts after the elaboration of the declarative part of the package body. The same holds for the activation of a task object that is a subcomponent of an object declared immediately within a declarative part or package specification. The first statement following the declarative part is executed only after conclusion of the activation of these task objects.

Should an exception be raised by the activation of one of these tasks, that task becomes a completed task (see 9.4); other tasks are not directly affected. Should one of these tasks thus become completed during its activation, the exception TASKING_ERROR is raised upon conclusion of the activation of all of these tasks (whether successfully or not); the exception is raised at a place that is immediately before the first statement following the declarative part (immediately after the reserved word **begin**). Should several of these tasks thus become completed during their activation, the exception TASKING_ERROR is raised only once.

Should an exception be raised by the elaboration of a declarative part or package specification, then any task that is created (directly or indirectly) by this elaboration and that is not yet activated becomes terminated and is therefore never activated (see section 9.4 for the definition of a terminated task).

For the above rules, in any package body without statements, a null statement is assumed. For any package without a package body, an implicit package body containing a single null statement is assumed. If a package without a package body is declared immediately within some program unit or block statement, the implicit package body occurs at the end of the declarative part of the program unit or block statement; if there are several such packages, the order of the implicit package bodies is undefined.

A task object that is the object, or a subcomponent of the object, created by the evaluation of an allocator is activated by this evaluation. The activation starts after any initialization for the object created by the allocator; if several subcomponents are task objects, they are activated in parallel. The access value designating such an object is returned by the allocator only after the conclusion of these activations.

Should an exception be raised by the activation of one of these tasks, that task becomes a completed task; other tasks are not directly affected. Should one of these tasks thus become completed during its activation, the exception TASKING_ERROR is raised upon conclusion of the activation of all of these tasks (whether successfully or not); the exception is raised at the place where the allocator is evaluated. Should several of these tasks thus become completed during their activation, the exception TASKING_ERROR is raised only once.

Should an exception be raised by the initialization of the object created by an allocator (hence before the start of any activation), any task designated by a subcomponent of this object becomes terminated and is therefore never activated.

9 *Example:*

```
procedure P is
    A, B : RESOURCE;    --  elaborate the task objects A, B
    C    : RESOURCE;    --  elaborate the task object C
begin
    --  the tasks A, B, C are activated in parallel before the first statement
    ...
end;
```

Notes:

10 An entry of a task can be called before the task has been activated. If several tasks are activated in parallel, the execution of any of these tasks need not await the end of the activation of the other tasks. A task may become completed during its activation either because of an exception or because it is aborted (see 9.10).

11 *References:* allocator 4.8, completed task 9.4, declarative part 3.9, elaboration 3.9, entry 9.5, exception 11, handling an exception 11.4, package body 7.1, parallel execution 9, statement 5, subcomponent 3.3, task body 9.1, task object 9.2, task termination 9.4, task type 9.1, tasking_error exception 11.1

9.4 Task Dependence - Termination of Tasks

1 Each task *depends* on at least one master. A *master* is a construct that is either a task, a currently executing block statement or subprogram, or a library package (a package declared within another program unit is not a master). The dependence on a master is a direct dependence in the following two cases:

2 (a) The task designated by a task object that is the object, or a subcomponent of the object, created by the evaluation of an allocator depends on the master that elaborates the corresponding access type definition.

3 (b) The task designated by any other task object depends on the master whose execution creates the task object.

4 Furthermore, if a task depends on a given master that is a block statement executed by another master, then the task depends also on this other master, in an indirect manner; the same holds if the given master is a subprogram called by another master, and if the given master is a task that depends (directly or indirectly) on another master. Dependences exist for objects of a private type whose full declaration is in terms of a task type.

5 A task is said to have *completed* its execution when it has finished the execution of the sequence of statements that appears after the reserved word **begin** in the corresponding body. Similarly a block or a subprogram is said to have completed its execution when it has finished the execution of the corresponding sequence of statements. For a block statement, the execution is also said to be completed when it reaches an exit, return, or goto statement transferring control out of the block. For a procedure, the execution is also said to be completed when a corresponding return statement is reached. For a function, the execution is also said to be completed after the evaluation of the result expression of a return statement. Finally the execution of a task, block statement, or subprogram is completed if an exception is raised by the execution of its sequence of statements and there is no corresponding handler, or, if there is one, when it has finished the execution of the corresponding handler.

If a task has no dependent task, its *termination* takes place when it has completed its execution. After its termination, a task is said to be *terminated*. If a task has dependent tasks, its termination takes place when the execution of the task is completed and all dependent tasks are terminated. A block statement or subprogram body whose execution is completed is not left until all of its dependent tasks are terminated.

Termination of a task otherwise takes place if and only if its execution has reached an open terminate alternative in a select statement (see 9.7.1), and the following conditions are satisfied:

- The task depends on some master whose execution is completed (hence not a library package).

- Each task that depends on the master considered is either already terminated or similarly waiting on an open terminate alternative of a select statement.

When both conditions are satisfied, the task considered becomes terminated, together with all tasks that depend on the master considered.

Example:

```
declare
   type GLOBAL is access RESOURCE;           --  see 9.1
   A, B  : RESOURCE;
   G     : GLOBAL;
begin
   --   activation of A and B
   declare
      type LOCAL is access RESOURCE;
      X  : GLOBAL := new RESOURCE;  --  activation of X.all
      L  : LOCAL  := new RESOURCE;  --  activation of L.all
      C  : RESOURCE;
   begin
      --   activation of C
      G := X;  --   both G and X designate the same task object
      ...
   end;   --   await termination of C and L.all (but not X.all)
   ...
end;   --   await termination of A, B, and G.all
```

Notes:

The rules given for termination imply that all tasks that depend (directly or indirectly) on a given master and that are not already terminated, can be terminated (collectively) if and only if each of them is waiting on an open terminate alternative of a select statement and the execution of the given master is completed.

The usual rules apply to the main program. Consequently, termination of the main program awaits termination of any dependent task even if the corresponding task type is declared in a library package. On the other hand, termination of the main program does not await termination of tasks that depend on library packages; the language does not define whether such tasks are required to terminate.

For an access type derived from another access type, the corresponding access type definition is that of the parent type; the dependence is on the master that elaborates the ultimate parent access type definition.

15   A renaming declaration defines a new name for an existing entity and hence creates no further dependence.

1C   *References:* access type 3.8, allocator 4.8, block statement 5.6, declaration 3.1, designate 3.8 9.1, exception 11, exception handler 11.2, exit statement 5.7, function 6.5, goto statement 5.9, library unit 10.1, main program 10.1, object 3.2, open alternative 9.7.1, package 7, program unit 6, renaming declaration 8.5, return statement 5.8, selective wait 9.7.1, sequence of statements 5.1, statement 5, subcomponent 3.3, subprogram body 6.3, subprogram call 6.4, task body 9.1, task object 9.2, terminate alternative 9.7.1

9.5 Entries, Entry Calls, and Accept Statements

1   Entry calls and accept statements are the primary means of synchronization of tasks, and of communicating values between tasks. An entry declaration is similar to a subprogram declaration and is only allowed in a task specification. The actions to be performed when an entry is called are specified by corresponding accept statements.

2

    entry_declaration ::=
      entry identifier [(discrete_range)] [formal_part];

    entry_call_statement ::= *entry*_name [actual_parameter_part];

    accept_statement ::=
      accept *entry*_simple_name [(entry_index)] [formal_part] [**do**
        sequence_of_statements
      end [*entry*_simple_name]];

    entry_index ::= expression

3   An entry declaration that includes a discrete range (see 3.6.1) declares a *family* of distinct entries having the same formal part (if any); that is, one such entry for each value of the discrete range. The term *single entry* is used in the definition of any rule that applies to any entry other than one of a family. The task designated by an object of a task type has (or owns) the entries declared in the specification of the task type.

4   Within the body of a task, each of its single entries or entry families can be named by the corresponding simple name. The name of an entry of a family takes the form of an indexed component, the family simple name being followed by the index in parentheses; the type of this index must be the same as that of the discrete range in the corresponding entry family declaration. Outside the body of a task an entry name has the form of a selected component, whose prefix denotes the task object, and whose selector is the simple name of one of its single entries or entry families.

5   A single entry overloads a subprogram, an enumeration literal, or another single entry if they have the same identifier. Overloading is not defined for entry families. A single entry or an entry of an entry family can be renamed as a procedure as explained in section 8.5.

6   The parameter modes defined for parameters of the formal part of an entry declaration are the same as for a subprogram declaration and have the same meaning (see 6.2). The syntax of an entry call statement is similar to that of a procedure call statement, and the rules for parameter associations are the same as for subprogram calls (see 6.4.1 and 6.4.2).

An accept statement specifies the actions to be performed at a call of a named entry (it can be an entry of a family). The formal part of an accept statement must conform to the formal part given in the declaration of the single entry or entry family named by the accept statement (see section 6.3.1 for the conformance rules). If a simple name appears at the end of an accept statement, it must repeat that given at the start.

An accept statement for an entry of a given task is only allowed within the corresponding task body; excluding within the body of any program unit that is, itself, inner to the task body; and excluding within another accept statement for either the same single entry or an entry of the same family. (One consequence of this rule is that a task can execute accept statements only for its own entries.) A task body can contain more than one accept statement for the same entry.

For the elaboration of an entry declaration, the discrete range, if any, is evaluated and the formal part, if any, is then elaborated as for a subprogram declaration.

Execution of an accept statement starts with the evaluation of the entry index (in the case of an entry of a family). Execution of an entry call statement starts with the evaluation of the entry name; this is followed by any evaluations required for actual parameters in the same manner as for a subprogram call (see 6.4). Further execution of an accept statement and of a corresponding entry call statement are synchronized.

If a given entry is called by only one task, there are two possibilities:

- If the calling task issues an entry call statement before a corresponding accept statement is reached by the task owning the entry, the execution of the calling task is *suspended*.

- If a task reaches an accept statement prior to any call of that entry, the execution of the task is suspended until such a call is received.

When an entry has been called and a corresponding accept statement has been reached, the sequence of statements, if any, of the accept statement is executed by the called task (while the calling task remains suspended). This interaction is called a *rendezvous*. Thereafter, the calling task and the task owning the entry continue their execution in parallel.

If several tasks call the same entry before a corresponding accept statement is reached, the calls are queued; there is one queue associated with each entry. Each execution of an accept statement removes one call from the queue. The calls are processed in the order of arrival.

An attempt to call an entry of a task that has completed its execution raises the exception TASKING_ERROR at the point of the call, in the calling task; similarly, this exception is raised at the point of the call if the called task completes its execution before accepting the call (see also 9.10 for the case when the called task becomes abnormal). The exception CONSTRAINT_ERROR is raised if the index of an entry of a family is not within the specified discrete range.

Examples of entry declarations:

```
entry READ(V : out ITEM);
entry SEIZE;
entry REQUEST(LEVEL)(D : ITEM);   --  a family of entries
```

Examples of entry calls:

```
CONTROL.RELEASE;                        --  see 9.2 and 9.1
PRODUCER_CONSUMER.WRITE(E);             --  see 9.1
POOL(5).READ(NEXT_CHAR);                --  see 9.2 and 9.1
CONTROLLER.REQUEST(LOW)(SOME_ITEM);     --  see 9.1
```

Entries, Entry Calls, and Accept Statements 9.5

19 *Examples of accept statements:*

```
accept SEIZE;

accept READ(V : out ITEM) do
   V := LOCAL_ITEM;
end READ;

accept REQUEST(LOW)(D : ITEM) do
   ...
end REQUEST;
```

Notes:

20 The formal part given in an accept statement is not elaborated; it is only used to identify the corresponding entry.

21 An accept statement can call subprograms that issue entry calls. An accept statement need not have a sequence of statements even if the corresponding entry has parameters. Equally, it can have a sequence of statements even if the corresponding entry has no parameters. The sequence of statements of an accept statement can include return statements. A task can call its own entries but it will, of course, deadlock. The language permits conditional and timed entry calls (see 9.7.2 and 9.7.3). The language rules ensure that a task can only be in one entry queue at a given time.

22 If the bounds of the discrete range of an entry family are integer literals, the index (in an entry name or accept statement) must be of the predefined type INTEGER (see 3.6.1).

23 *References:* abnormal task 9.10, actual parameter part 6.4, completed task 9.4, conditional entry call 9.7.2, conformance rules 6.3.1, constraint_error exception 11.1, designate 9.1, discrete range 3.6.1, elaboration 3.1 3.9, enumeration literal 3.5.1, evaluation 4.5, expression 4.4, formal part 6.1, identifier 2.3, indexed component 4.1.1, integer type 3.5.4, name 4.1, object 3.2, overloading 6.6 8.7, parallel execution 9, prefix 4.1, procedure 6, procedure call 6.4, renaming declaration 8.5, return statement 5.8, scope 8.2, selected component 4.1.3, selector 4.1.3, sequence of statements 5.1, simple expression 4.4, simple name 4.1, subprogram 6, subprogram body 6.3, subprogram declaration 6.1, task 9, task body 9.1, task specification 9.1, tasking_error exception 11.1, timed entry call 9.7.3

9.6 Delay Statements, Duration, and Time

1 The execution of a delay statement evaluates the simple expression, and suspends further execution of the task that executes the delay statement, for at least the duration specified by the resulting value.

2   delay_statement ::= **delay** simple_expression;

3 The simple expression must be of the predefined fixed point type DURATION; its value is expressed in seconds; a delay statement with a negative value is equivalent to a delay statement with a zero value.

4 Any implementation of the type DURATION must allow representation of durations (both positive and negative) up to at least 86400 seconds (one day); the smallest representable duration, DURATION'SMALL must not be greater than twenty milliseconds (whenever possible, a value not greater than fifty microseconds should be chosen). Note that DURATION'SMALL need not correspond to the basic clock cycle, the named number SYSTEM.TICK (see 13.7).

The definition of the type TIME is provided in the predefined library package CALENDAR. The function CLOCK returns the current value of TIME at the time it is called. The functions YEAR, MONTH, DAY and SECONDS return the corresponding values for a given value of the type TIME; the procedure SPLIT returns all four corresponding values. Conversely, the function TIME_OF combines a year number, a month number, a day number, and a duration, into a value of type TIME. The operators "+" and "-" for addition and subtraction of times and durations, and the relational operators for times, have the conventional meaning.

The exception TIME_ERROR is raised by the function TIME_OF if the actual parameters do not form a proper date. This exception is also raised by the operators "+" and "-" if, for the given operands, these operators cannot return a date whose year number is in the range of the corresponding subtype, or if the operator "-" cannot return a result that is in the range of the type DURATION.

```ada
package CALENDAR is
   type TIME is private;

   subtype YEAR_NUMBER   is INTEGER  range 1901 .. 2099;
   subtype MONTH_NUMBER  is INTEGER  range 1 .. 12;
   subtype DAY_NUMBER    is INTEGER  range 1 .. 31;
   subtype DAY_DURATION  is DURATION range 0.0 .. 86_400.0;

   function CLOCK return TIME;

   function YEAR    (DATE : TIME) return YEAR_NUMBER;
   function MONTH   (DATE : TIME) return MONTH_NUMBER;
   function DAY     (DATE : TIME) return DAY_NUMBER;
   function SECONDS (DATE : TIME) return DAY_DURATION;

   procedure SPLIT ( DATE    : in  TIME;
                     YEAR    : out YEAR_NUMBER;
                     MONTH   : out MONTH_NUMBER;
                     DAY     : out DAY_NUMBER;
                     SECONDS : out DAY_DURATION);

   function TIME_OF ( YEAR    : YEAR_NUMBER;
                      MONTH   : MONTH_NUMBER;
                      DAY     : DAY_NUMBER;
                      SECONDS : DAY_DURATION := 0.0) return TIME;


   function "+" (LEFT : TIME;     RIGHT : DURATION) return TIME;
   function "+" (LEFT : DURATION; RIGHT : TIME)     return TIME;
   function "-" (LEFT : TIME;     RIGHT : DURATION) return TIME;
   function "-" (LEFT : TIME;     RIGHT : TIME)     return DURATION;

   function "<"  (LEFT, RIGHT : TIME) return BOOLEAN;
   function "<=" (LEFT, RIGHT : TIME) return BOOLEAN;
   function ">"  (LEFT, RIGHT : TIME) return BOOLEAN;
   function ">=" (LEFT, RIGHT : TIME) return BOOLEAN;

   TIME_ERROR : exception;  -- can be raised by TIME_OF, "+", and "-"

private
   -- implementation-dependent
end;
```

8   *Examples:*

```
delay 3.0;  --  delay 3.0 seconds

declare
   use CALENDAR;
   --  INTERVAL is a global constant of type DURATION
   NEXT_TIME : TIME := CLOCK + INTERVAL;
begin
   loop
      delay NEXT_TIME - CLOCK;
      --  some actions
      NEXT_TIME := NEXT_TIME + INTERVAL;
   end loop;
end;
```

Notes:

9   The second example causes the loop to be repeated every INTERVAL seconds on average. This interval between two successive iterations is only approximate. However, there will be no cumulative drift as long as the duration of each iteration is (sufficiently) less than INTERVAL.

10   *References:* adding operator 4.5, duration C, fixed point type 3.5.9, function call 6.4, library unit 10.1, operator 4.5, package 7, private type 7.4, relational operator 4.5, simple expression 4.4, statement 5, task 9, type 3.3

9.7 Select Statements

1   There are three forms of select statements. One form provides a selective wait for one or more alternatives. The other two provide conditional and timed entry calls.

2
```
select_statement ::= selective_wait
   | conditional_entry_call | timed_entry_call
```

3   *References:* selective wait 9.7.1, conditional entry call 9.7.2, timed entry call 9.7.3

9.7.1 Selective Waits

1   This form of the select statement allows a combination of waiting for, and selecting from, one or more alternatives. The selection can depend on conditions associated with each alternative of the selective wait.

```
selective_wait ::=                                                               2
    select
       select_alternative
  { or
       select_alternative}
  [ else
       sequence_of_statements]
    end select;

select_alternative ::=
  [ when condition =>]
       selective_wait_alternative

selective_wait_alternative ::= accept_alternative
  | delay_alternative | terminate_alternative

accept_alternative  ::= accept_statement [sequence_of_statements]

delay_alternative    ::= delay_statement  [sequence_of_statements]

terminate_alternative ::= terminate;
```

A selective wait must contain at least one accept alternative. In addition a selective wait can con-   3
tain either a terminate alternative (only one), or one or more delay alternatives, or an else part;
these three possibilities are mutually exclusive.

A select alternative is said to be *open* if it does not start with **when** and a condition, or if the condi-   4
tion is TRUE. It is said to be *closed* otherwise.

For the execution of a selective wait, any conditions specified after **when** are evaluated in some   5
order that is not defined by the language; open alternatives are thus determined. For an open
delay alternative, the delay expression is also evaluated. Similarly, for an open accept alternative
for an entry of a family, the entry index is also evaluated. Selection and execution of one open
alternative, or of the else part, then completes the execution of the selective wait; the rules for this
selection are described below.

Open accept alternatives are first considered. Selection of one such alternative takes place   6
immediately if a corresponding rendezvous is possible, that is, if there is a corresponding entry call
issued by another task and waiting to be accepted. If several alternatives can thus be selected,
one of them is selected arbitrarily (that is, the language does not define which one). When such an
alternative is selected, the corresponding accept statement and possible subsequent statements
are executed. If no rendezvous is immediately possible and there is no else part, the task waits
until an open selective wait alternative can be selected.

Selection of the other forms of alternative or of an else part is performed as follows: 7

- An open delay alternative will be selected if no accept alternative can be selected before the   8
  specified delay has elapsed (immediately, for a negative or zero delay in the absence of
  queued entry calls); any subsequent statements of the alternative are then executed. If several
  delay alternatives can thus be selected (that is, if they have the same delay), one of them is
  selected arbitrarily.

- The else part is selected and its statements are executed if no accept alternative can be   9
  immediately selected, in particular, if all alternatives are closed.

- An open terminate alternative is selected if the conditions stated in section 9.4 are satisfied.   10
  It is a consequence of other rules that a terminate alternative cannot be selected while there is
  a queued entry call for any entry of the task.

Selective Waits 9.7.1

11   The exception PROGRAM_ERROR is raised if all alternatives are closed and there is no else part.

12   *Examples of a select statement:*

```
select
   accept DRIVER_AWAKE_SIGNAL;
or
   delay 30.0*SECONDS;
   STOP_THE_TRAIN;
end select;
```

13   *Example of a task body with a select statement:*

```
task body RESOURCE is
   BUSY : BOOLEAN := FALSE;
begin
   loop
      select
         when not BUSY =>
            accept SEIZE do
               BUSY := TRUE;
            end;
      or
         accept RELEASE do
            BUSY := FALSE;
         end;
      or
         terminate;
      end select;
   end loop;
end RESOURCE;
```

Notes:

14   A selective wait is allowed to have several open delay alternatives. A selective wait is allowed to have several open accept alternatives for the same entry.

15   *References:* accept statement 9.5, condition 5.3, declaration 3.1, delay expression 9.6, delay statement 9.6, duration 9.6, entry 9.5, entry call 9.5, entry index 9.5, program_error exception 11.1, queued entry call 9.5, rendezvous 9.5 select statement 9.7, sequence of statements 5.1, task 9

9.7.2 Conditional Entry Calls

1   A conditional entry call issues an entry call that is then canceled if a rendezvous is not immediately possible.

2
```
conditional_entry_call ::=
   select
      entry_call_statement
      [ sequence_of_statements]
   else
      sequence_of_statements
   end select;
```

For the execution of a conditional entry call, the entry name is first evaluated. This is followed by any evaluations required for actual parameters as in the case of a subprogram call (see 6.4).   3

The entry call is canceled if the execution of the called task has not reached a point where it is   4
ready to accept the call (that is, either an accept statement for the corresponding entry, or a select statement with an open accept alternative for the entry), or if there are prior queued entry calls for this entry. If the called task has reached a select statement, the entry call is canceled if an accept alternative for this entry is not selected.

If the entry call is canceled, the statements of the else part are executed. Otherwise, the rendez-   5
vous takes place; and the optional sequence of statements after the entry call is then executed.

The execution of a conditional entry call raises the exception TASKING_ERROR if the called task   6
has already completed its execution (see also 9.10 for the case when the called task becomes abnormal).

Example: 7

```
procedure SPIN(R : RESOURCE) is
begin
  loop
    select
        R.SEIZE;
        return;
    else
        null;  --  busy  waiting
    end select;
  end loop;
end;
```

References: abnormal task 9.10, accept statement 9.5, actual parameter part 6.4, completed task 9.4, entry call   8
statement 9.5, entry family 9.5, entry index 9.5, evaluation 4.5, expression 4.4, open alternative 9.7.1, queued entry call 9.5, rendezvous 9.5, select statement 9.7, sequence of statements 5.1, task 9, tasking_error exception 11.1

9.7.3 Timed Entry Calls

A timed entry call issues an entry call that is canceled if a rendezvous is not started within a given   1
delay.

```
timed_entry_call ::=                                    2
    select
        entry_call_statement
      [ sequence_of_statements]
    or
        delay_alternative
    end select;
```

3   For the execution of a timed entry call, the entry name is first evaluated. This is followed by any evaluations required for actual parameters as in the case of a subprogram call (see 6.4). The expression stating the delay is then evaluated, and the entry call is finally issued.

4   If a rendezvous can be started within the specified duration (or immediately, as for a conditional entry call, for a negative or zero delay), it is performed and the optional sequence of statements after the entry call is then executed. Otherwise, the entry call is canceled when the specified duration has expired, and the optional sequence of statements of the delay alternative is executed.

5   The execution of a timed entry call raises the exception TASKING_ERROR if the called task completes its execution before accepting the call (see also 9.10 for the case when the called task becomes abnormal).

6   *Example:*

```
select
    CONTROLLER.REQUEST(MEDIUM)(SOME_ITEM);
or
    delay  45.0;
    --  controller  too  busy,  try  something  else
end  select;
```

7   *References:* abnormal task 9.10, accept statement 9.5, actual parameter part 6.4, completed task 9.4, conditional entry call 9.7.2, delay expression 9.6, delay statement 9.6, duration 9.6, entry call statement 9.5, entry family 9.5, entry index 9.5, evaluation 4.5, expression 4.4, rendezvous 9.5, sequence of statements 5.1, task 9, tasking_error exception 11.1

9.8 Priorities

1   Each task may (but need not) have a priority, which is a value of the subtype PRIORITY (of the type INTEGER) declared in the predefined library package SYSTEM (see 13.7). A lower value indicates a lower degree of urgency; the range of priorities is implementation-defined. A priority is associated with a task if a pragma

      pragma PRIORITY (*static_*expression);

2   appears in the corresponding task specification; the priority is given by the value of the expression. A priority is associated with the main program if such a pragma appears in its outermost declarative part. At most one such pragma can appear within a given task specification or for a subprogram that is a library unit, and these are the only allowed places for this pragma. A pragma PRIORITY has no effect if it occurs in a subprogram other than the main program.

3   The specification of a priority is an indication given to assist the implementation in the allocation of processing resources to parallel tasks when there are more tasks eligible for execution than can be supported simultaneously by the available processing resources. The effect of priorities on scheduling is defined by the following rule:

4   If two tasks with different priorities are both eligible for execution and could sensibly be executed using the same physical processors and the same other processing resources, then it cannot be the case that the task with the lower priority is executing while the task with the higher priority is not.

For tasks of the same priority, the scheduling order is not defined by the language. For tasks without explicit priority, the scheduling rules are not defined, except when such tasks are engaged in a rendezvous. If the priorities of both tasks engaged in a rendezvous are defined, the rendezvous is executed with the higher of the two priorities. If only one of the two priorities is defined, the rendezvous is executed with at least that priority. If neither is defined, the priority of the rendezvous is undefined. 5

Notes:

The priority of a task is static and therefore fixed. However, the priority during a rendezvous is not necessarily static since it also depends on the priority of the task calling the entry. Priorities should be used only to indicate relative degrees of urgency; they should not be used for task synchronization. 6

References: declarative part 3.9, entry call statement 9.5, integer type 3.5.4, main program 10.1, package system 13.7, pragma 2.8, rendezvous 9.5, static expression 4.9, subtype 3.3, task 9, task specification 9.1 7

9.9 Task and Entry Attributes

For a task object or value T the following attributes are defined: 1

T'CALLABLE   Yields the value FALSE when the execution of the task designated by T is either completed or terminated, or when the task is abnormal. Yields the value TRUE otherwise. The value of this attribute is of the predefined type BOOLEAN. 2

T'TERMINATED   Yields the value TRUE if the task designated by T is terminated. Yields the value FALSE otherwise. The value of this attribute is of the predefined type BOOLEAN. 3

In addition, the representation attributes STORAGE_SIZE, SIZE, and ADDRESS are defined for a task object T or a task type T (see 13.7.2). 4

The attribute COUNT is defined for an entry E of a task unit T. The entry can be either a single entry or an entry of a family (in either case the name of the single entry or entry family can be either a simple or an expanded name). This attribute is only allowed within the body of T, but excluding within any program unit that is, itself, inner to the body of T. 5

E'COUNT   Yields the number of entry calls presently queued on the entry E (if the attribute is evaluated by the execution of an accept statement for the entry E, the count does not include the calling task). The value of this attribute is of the type *universal_integer*. 6

Note:

Algorithms interrogating the attribute E'COUNT should take precautions to allow for the increase of the value of this attribute for incoming entry calls, and its decrease, for example with timed entry calls. 7

References: abnormal task 9.10, accept statement 9.5, attribute 4.1.4, boolean type 3.5.3, completed task 9.4, designate 9.1, entry 9.5, false boolean value 3.5.3, queue of entry calls 9.5, storage unit 13.7, task 9, task object 9.2, task type 9.1, terminated task 9.4, timed entry call 9.7.3, true boolean value 3.5.3, universal_integer type 3.5.4 8

Task and Entry Attributes 9.9

9.10 Abort Statements

1 An abort statement causes one or more tasks to become *abnormal*, thus preventing any further rendezvous with such tasks.

2   abort_statement ::= **abort** *task*_name {, *task*_name};

3 The determination of the type of each task name uses the fact that the type of the name is a task type.

4 For the execution of an abort statement, the given task names are evaluated in some order that is not defined by the language. Each named task then becomes abnormal unless it is already terminated; similarly, any task that depends on a named task becomes abnormal unless it is already · terminated.

5 Any abnormal task whose execution is suspended at an accept statement, a select statement, or a delay statement becomes completed; any abnormal task whose execution is suspended at an entry call, and that is not yet in a corresponding rendezvous, becomes completed and is removed from the entry queue; any abnormal task that has not yet started its activation becomes completed (and hence also terminated). This completes the execution of the abort statement.

6 The completion of any other abnormal task need not happen before completion of the abort statement. It must happen no later than when the abnormal task reaches a synchronization point that is one of the following: the end of its activation; a point where it causes the activation of another task; an entry call; the start or the end of an accept statement; a select statement; a delay statement; an exception handler; or an abort statement. If a task that calls an entry becomes abnormal while in a rendezvous, its termination does not take place before the completion of the rendezvous (see 11.5).

7 The call of an entry of an abnormal task raises the exception TASKING_ERROR at the place of the call. Similarly, the exception TASKING_ERROR is raised for any task that has called an entry of an abnormal task, if the entry call is still queued or if the rendezvous is not yet finished (whether the entry call is an entry call statement, or a conditional or timed entry call); the exception is raised no later than the completion of the abnormal task. The value of the attribute CALLABLE is FALSE for any task that is abnormal (or completed).

8 If the abnormal completion of a task takes place while the task updates a variable, then the value of this variable is undefined.

9 *Example:*

       abort USER , TERMINAL.**all**, POOL(3);

Notes:

10 An abort statement should be used only in extremely severe situations requiring unconditional termination. A task is allowed to abort any task, including itself.

11 *References:* abnormal in rendezvous 11.5, accept statement 9.5, activation 9.3, attribute 4.1.4, callable (predefined attribute) 9.9, conditional entry call 9.7.2, delay statement 9.6, dependent task 9.4, entry call statement 9.5, evaluation of a name 4.1, exception handler 11.2, false boolean value 3.5.3, name 4.1, queue of entry calls 9.5, rendezvous 9.5, select statement 9.7, statement 5, task 9, tasking_error exception 11.1, terminated task 9.4, timed entry call 9.7.3

9.11 Shared Variables

The normal means of communicating values between tasks is by entry calls and accept statements.

If two tasks read or update a *shared* variable (that is, a variable accessible by both), then neither of them may assume anything about the order in which the other performs its operations, except at the points where they synchronize. Two tasks are synchronized at the start and at the end of their rendezvous. At the start and at the end of its activation, a task is synchronized with the task that causes this activation. A task that has completed its execution is synchronized with any other task.

For the actions performed by a program that uses shared variables, the following assumptions can always be made:

- If between two synchronization points of a task, this task reads a shared variable whose type is a scalar or access type, then the variable is not updated by any other task at any time between these two points.

- If between two synchronization points of a task, this task updates a shared variable whose type is a scalar or access type, then the variable is neither read nor updated by any other task at any time between these two points.

The execution of the program is erroneous if any of these assumptions is violated.

If a given task reads the value of a shared variable, the above assumptions allow an implementation to maintain local copies of the value (for example, in registers or in some other form of temporary storage); and for as long as the given task neither reaches a synchronization point nor updates the value of the shared variable, the above assumptions imply that, for the given task, reading a local copy is equivalent to reading the shared variable itself.

Similarly, if a given task updates the value of a shared variable, the above assumptions allow an implementation to maintain a local copy of the value, and to defer the effective store of the local copy into the shared variable until a synchronization point, provided that every further read or update of the variable by the given task is treated as a read or update of the local copy. On the other hand, an implementation is not allowed to introduce a store, unless this store would also be executed in the canonical order (see 11.6).

The pragma SHARED can be used to specify that every read or update of a variable is a synchronization point for that variable; that is, the above assumptions always hold for the given variable (but not necessarily for other variables). The form of this pragma is as follows:

pragma SHARED(*variable*_simple_name);

This pragma is allowed only for a variable declared by an object declaration and whose type is a scalar or access type; the variable declaration and the pragma must both occur (in this order) immediately within the same declarative part or package specification; the pragma must appear before any occurrence of the name of the variable, other than in an address clause.

An implementation must restrict the objects for which the pragma SHARED is allowed to objects for which each of direct reading and direct updating is implemented as an indivisible operation.

References: accept statement 9.5, activation 9.3, assignment 5.2, canonical order 11.6, declarative part 3.9, entry call statement 9.5, erroneous 1.6, global 8.1, package specification 7.1, pragma 2.8, read a value 6.2, rendezvous 9.5, simple name 3.1 4.1, task 9, type 3.3, update a value 6.2, variable 3.2.1

9.12 Example of Tasking

1   The following example defines a buffering task to smooth variations between the speed of output of a producing task and the speed of input of some consuming task. For instance, the producing task may contain the statements

2
```
loop
    --   produce the next character CHAR
    BUFFER.WRITE(CHAR);
    exit when CHAR = ASCII.EOT;
end loop;
```

3   and the consuming task may contain the statements

4
```
loop
    BUFFER.READ(CHAR);
    -- consume the character CHAR
    exit when CHAR = ASCII.EOT;
end loop;
```

5   The buffering task contains an internal pool of characters processed in a round-robin fashion. The pool has two indices, an IN_INDEX denoting the space for the next input character and an OUT_INDEX denoting the space for the next output character.

6
```
task BUFFER is
    entry READ (C : out  CHARACTER);
    entry WRITE (C : in   CHARACTER);
end;

task body BUFFER is
    POOL_SIZE : constant INTEGER := 100;
    POOL        : array(1 .. POOL_SIZE) of CHARACTER;
    COUNT        : INTEGER range 0 .. POOL_SIZE := 0;
    IN_INDEX, OUT_INDEX : INTEGER range 1 .. POOL_SIZE := 1;
begin
    loop
        select
            when COUNT < POOL_SIZE =>
                accept WRITE(C : in CHARACTER) do
                    POOL(IN_INDEX) := C;
                end;
                IN_INDEX := IN_INDEX mod POOL_SIZE + 1;
                COUNT    := COUNT + 1;
        or when COUNT > 0 =>
                accept READ(C : out CHARACTER) do
                    C := POOL(OUT_INDEX);
                end;
                OUT_INDEX := OUT_INDEX mod POOL_SIZE + 1;
                COUNT     := COUNT - 1;
        or
                terminate;
        end select;
    end loop;
end BUFFER;
```

10. Program Structure and Compilation Issues

The overall structure of programs and the facilities for separate compilation are described in this chapter. A program is a collection of one or more compilation units submitted to a compiler in one or more compilations. Each compilation unit specifies the separate compilation of a construct which can be a subprogram declaration or body, a package declaration or body, a generic declaration or body, or a generic instantiation. Alternatively this construct can be a subunit, in which case it includes the body of a subprogram, package, task unit, or generic unit declared within another compilation unit.

References: compilation 10.1, compilation unit 10.1, generic body 12.2, generic declaration 12.1, generic instantiation 12.3, package body 7.1, package declaration 7.1, subprogram body 6.3, subprogram declaration 6.1, subunit 10.2, task body 9.1, task unit 9

10.1 Compilation Units - Library Units

The text of a program can be submitted to the compiler in one or more compilations. Each compilation is a succession of compilation units.

```
compilation  ::=  {compilation_unit}

compilation_unit  ::=
      context_clause library_unit  |  context_clause secondary_unit

library_unit  ::=
      subprogram_declaration   |  package_declaration
    |  generic_declaration      |  generic_instantiation
    |  subprogram_body

secondary_unit  ::=  library_unit_body  |  subunit

library_unit_body  ::=  subprogram_body  |  package_body
```

The compilation units of a program are said to belong to a *program library*. A compilation unit defines either a library unit or a secondary unit. A secondary unit is either the separately compiled proper body of a library unit, or a subunit of another compilation unit. The designator of a separately compiled subprogram (whether a library unit or a subunit) must be an identifier. Within a program library the simple names of all library units must be distinct identifiers.

The effect of compiling a library unit is to define (or redefine) this unit as one that belongs to the program library. For the visibility rules, each library unit acts as a declaration that occurs immediately within the package STANDARD.

The effect of compiling a secondary unit is to define the body of a library unit, or in the case of a subunit, to define the proper body of a program unit that is declared within another compilation unit.

6   A subprogram body given in a compilation unit is interpreted as a secondary unit if the program library already contains a library unit that is a subprogram with the same name; it is otherwise interpreted both as a library unit and as the corresponding library unit body (that is, as a secondary unit).

7   The compilation units of a compilation are compiled in the given order. A pragma that applies to the whole of a compilation must appear before the first compilation unit of that compilation.

8   A subprogram that is a library unit can be used as a *main program* in the usual sense. Each main program acts as if called by some environment task; the means by which this execution is initiated are not prescribed by the language definition. An implementation may impose certain requirements on the parameters and on the result, if any, of a main program (these requirements must be stated in Appendix F). In any case, every implementation is required to allow, at least, main programs that are parameterless procedures, and every main program must be a subprogram that is a library unit.

Notes:

9   A simple program may consist of a single compilation unit. A compilation need not have any compilation units; for example, its text can consist of pragmas.

10   The designator of a library function cannot be an operator symbol, but a renaming declaration is allowed to rename a library function as an operator. Two library subprograms must have distinct simple names and hence cannot overload each other. However, renaming declarations are allowed to define overloaded names for such subprograms, and a locally declared subprogram is allowed to overload a library subprogram. The expanded name STANDARD.L can be used for a library unit L (unless the name STANDARD is hidden) since library units act as declarations that occur immediately within the package STANDARD.

11   *References:* allow 1.6, context clause 10.1.1, declaration 3.1, designator 6.1, environment 10.4, generic declaration 12.1, generic instantiation 12.3, hiding 8.3, identifier 2.3, library unit 10.5, local declaration 8.1, must 1.6, name 4.1, occur immediately within 8.1, operator 4.5, operator symbol 6.1, overloading 6.6 8.7, package body 7.1, package declaration 7.1, parameter of a subprogram 6.2, pragma 2.8, procedure 6.1, program unit 6, proper body 3.9, renaming declaration 8.5, simple name 4.1, standard package 8.6, subprogram 6, subprogram body 6.3, subprogram declaration 6.1, subunit 10.2, task 9, visibility 8.3

10.1.1 Context Clauses - With Clauses

1   A context clause is used to specify the library units whose names are needed within a compilation unit.

2   context_clause ::= {with_clause {use_clause}}

     with_clause ::= **with** *unit*_simple_name {, *unit*_simple_name};

3   The names that appear in a context clause must be the simple names of library units. The simple name of any library unit is allowed within a with clause. The only names allowed in a use clause of a context clause are the simple names of library packages mentioned by previous with clauses of the context clause. A simple name declared by a renaming declaration is not allowed in a context clause.

4   The with clauses and use clauses of the context clause of a library unit *apply* to this library unit and also to the secondary unit that defines the corresponding body (whether such a clause is repeated or not for this unit). Similarly, the with clauses and use clauses of the context clause of a compilation unit *apply* to this unit and also to its subunits, if any.

f a library unit is named by a with clause that applies to a compilation unit, then this library unit is   5
directly visible within the compilation unit, except where hidden; the library unit is visible as if
declared immediately within the package STANDARD (see 8.6).

Dependences among compilation units are defined by with clauses; that is, a compilation unit that   6
mentions other library units in its with clauses *depends* on those library units. These dependences
between units are taken into account for the determination of the allowed order of compilation
(and recompilation) of compilation units, as explained in section 10.3, and for the determination of
the allowed order of elaboration of compilation units, as explained in section 10.5.

Notes:

A library unit named by a with clause of a compilation unit is visible (except where hidden) within   7
the compilation unit and hence can be used as a corresponding program unit. Thus within the
compilation unit, the name of a library package can be given in use clauses and can be used to
form expanded names; a library subprogram can be called; and instances of a library generic unit
can be declared.

The rules given for with clauses are such that the same effect is obtained whether the name of a   8
library unit is mentioned once or more than once by the applicable with clauses, or even within a
given with clause.

Example 1 : A main program:

The following is an example of a main program consisting of a single compilation unit: a procedure   9
for printing the real roots of a quadratic equation. The predefined package TEXT_IO and a user-
defined package REAL_OPERATIONS (containing the definition of the type REAL and of the
packages REAL_IO and REAL_FUNCTIONS) are assumed to be already present in the program
library. Such packages may be used by other main programs.

```
    with TEXT_IO, REAL_OPERATIONS; use REAL_OPERATIONS;                                    10
    procedure QUADRATIC_EQUATION is
      A, B, C, D : REAL;
      use  REAL_IO,          --  achieves direct visibility of GET and PUT for REAL
           TEXT_IO,          --  achieves direct visibility of PUT for strings and of NEW_LINE
           REAL_FUNCTIONS;   --  achieves direct visibility of SQRT
    begin
      GET(A); GET(B); GET(C);
      D := B**2 - 4.0*A*C;
      if  D < 0.0 then
        PUT("Imaginary Roots.");
      else
        PUT("Real Roots : X1 = ");
        PUT((-B - SQRT(D))/(2.0*A)); PUT(" X2 = ");
        PUT((-B + SQRT(D))/(2.0*A));
      end if;
      NEW_LINE;
    end QUADRATIC_EQUATION;
```

Notes on the example:

The with clauses of a compilation unit need only mention the names of those library subprograms   11
and packages whose visibility is actually necessary within the unit. They need not (and should not)
mention other library units that are used in turn by some of the units named in the with clauses,
unless these other library units are also used directly by the current compilation unit. For example,
the body of the package REAL_OPERATIONS may need elementary operations provided by other
packages. The latter packages should not be named by the with clause of QUADRATIC_EQUATION
since these elementary operations are not directly called within its body.

12   *References:* allow 1.6, compilation unit 10.1, direct visibility 8.3, elaboration 3.9, generic body 12.2, generic unit 12.1, hiding 8.3, instance 12.3, library unit 10.1, main program 10.1, must 1.6, name 4.1, package 7, package body 7.1, package declaration 7.1, procedure 6.1, program unit 6, secondary unit 10.1, simple name 4.1, standard predefined package 8.6, subprogram body 6.3, subprogram declaration 6.1, subunit 10.2, type 3.3, use clause 8.4, visibility 8.3

10.1.2 Examples of Compilation Units

1   A compilation unit can be split into a number of compilation units. For example, consider the following program.

2
```
procedure PROCESSOR is

    SMALL  : constant   := 20;
    TOTAL  : INTEGER    := 0;

    package STOCK is
        LIMIT  : constant := 1000;
        TABLE : array (1 .. LIMIT) of INTEGER;
        procedure RESTART;
    end STOCK;

    package body STOCK is
        procedure RESTART is
        begin
            for N in 1 .. LIMIT loop
                TABLE(N) := N;
            end loop;
        end;
    begin
        RESTART;
    end STOCK;

    procedure UPDATE(X : INTEGER) is
        use STOCK;
    begin
        ...
        TABLE(X) := TABLE(X) + SMALL;
        ...
    end UPDATE;

begin
    ...
    STOCK.RESTART;   -- reinitializes TABLE
    ...
end PROCESSOR;
```

3   The following three compilation units define a program with an effect equivalent to the above example (the broken lines between compilation units serve to remind the reader that these units need not be contiguous texts).

Example 2 : Several compilation units:

4

```
package STOCK is
   LIMIT : constant := 1000;
   TABLE : array (1 .. LIMIT) of INTEGER;
   procedure RESTART;
end STOCK;
```

5

```
package body STOCK is
   procedure RESTART is
   begin
      for N in 1 .. LIMIT loop
         TABLE(N) := N;
      end loop;
   end;
begin
   RESTART;
end STOCK;
```

6

```
with STOCK;
procedure PROCESSOR is

   SMALL : constant := 20;
   TOTAL : INTEGER := 0;

   procedure UPDATE(X : INTEGER) is
      use STOCK;
   begin
      ...
      TABLE(X) := TABLE(X) + SMALL;
      ...
   end UPDATE;
begin
   ...
   STOCK.RESTART;   -- reinitializes TABLE
   ...
end PROCESSOR;
```

7

Note that in the latter version, the package STOCK has no visibility of outer identifiers other than the predefined identifiers (of the package STANDARD). In particular, STOCK does not use any identifier declared in PROCESSOR such as SMALL or TOTAL; otherwise STOCK could not have been extracted from PROCESSOR in the above manner. The procedure PROCESSOR, on the other hand, depends on STOCK and mentions this package in a with clause. This permits the inner occurrences of STOCK in the expanded name STOCK.RESTART and in the use clause.

8

These three compilation units can be submitted in one or more compilations. For example, it is possible to submit the package specification and the package body together and in this order in a single compilation.

9

References: compilation unit 10.1, declaration 3.1, identifier 2.3, package 7, package body 7.1, package specification 7.1, program 10, standard package 8.6, use clause 8.4, visibility 8.3, with clause 10.1.1

10

Examples of Compilation Units 10.1.2

10.2 Subunits of Compilation Units

1   A subunit is used for the separate compilation of the proper body of a program unit declared within another compilation unit. This method of splitting a program permits hierarchical program development.

2

```
body_stub ::=
    subprogram_specification is separate;
  | package body package_simple_name is separate;
  | task body task_simple_name is separate;

subunit ::=
    separate (parent_unit_name) proper_body
```

3   A body stub is only allowed as the body of a program unit (a subprogram, a package, a task unit, or a generic unit) if the body stub occurs immediately within either the specification of a library package or the declarative part of another compilation unit.

4   If the body of a program unit is a body stub, a separately compiled subunit containing the corresponding proper body is required. In the case of a subprogram, the subprogram specifications given in the proper body and in the body stub must conform (see 6.3.1).

5   Each subunit mentions the name of its *parent unit*, that is, the compilation unit where the corresponding body stub is given. If the parent unit is a library unit, it is called the *ancestor* library unit. If the parent unit is itself a subunit, the parent unit name must be given in full as an expanded name, starting with the simple name of the ancestor library unit. The simple names of all subunits that have the same ancestor library unit must be distinct identifiers.

6   Visibility within the proper body of a subunit is the visibility that would be obtained at the place of the corresponding body stub (within the parent unit) if the with clauses and use clauses of the subunit were appended to the context clause of the parent unit. If the parent unit is itself a subunit, then the same rule is used to define the visibility within the proper body of the parent unit.

7   The effect of the elaboration of a body stub is to elaborate the proper body of the subunit.

Notes:

8   Two subunits of different library units in the same program library need not have distinct identifiers. In any case, their full expanded names are distinct, since the simple names of library units are distinct and since the simple names of all subunits that have a given library unit as ancestor unit are also distinct. By means of renaming declarations, overloaded subprogram names that rename (distinct) subunits can be introduced.

9   A library unit that is named by the with clause of a subunit can be hidden by a declaration (with the same identifier) given in the proper body of the subunit. Moreover, such a library unit can even be hidden by a declaration given within a parent unit since a library unit acts as if declared in STANDARD; this however does not affect the interpretation of the with clauses themselves, since only names of library units can appear in with clauses.

References: compilation unit 10.1, conform 6.3.1, context clause 10.1.1, declaration 3.1, declarative part 3.9, direct 10
visibility 8.3, elaboration 3.9, expanded name 4.1.3, generic body 12.2, generic unit 12, hidden declaration 8.3, identifier 2.3, library unit 10.1, local declaration 8.1, name 4.1, occur immediately within 8.1, overloading 8.3, package 7,
package body 7.1, package specification 7.1, program 10, program unit 6, proper body 3.9, renaming declaration 8.5,
separate compilation 10.1, simple name 4.1, subprogram 6, subprogram body 6.3, subprogram specification 6.1, task
9, task body 9.1, task unit 9.1, use clause 8.4, visibility 8.3, with clause 10.1.1

10.2.1 Examples of Subunits

The procedure TOP is first written as a compilation unit without subunits.   1

```
with  TEXT_IO;                                                                               2
procedure  TOP  is

    type  REAL  is  digits  10;
    R, S : REAL := 1.0;

    package  FACILITY  is
        PI : constant := 3.14159_26536;
        function     F (X : REAL) return REAL;
        procedure    G (Y, Z : REAL);
    end  FACILITY;

    package  body  FACILITY  is
        --   some  local  declarations  followed  by

        function F(X : REAL) return REAL is
        begin
            --   sequence of statements of F
            ...
        end  F;

        procedure G(Y, Z : REAL) is
            --   local  procedures  using  TEXT_IO
            ...
        begin
            --   sequence of statements of G
            ...
        end  G;
    end  FACILITY;

    procedure TRANSFORM(U : in out  REAL) is
        use FACILITY;
    begin
        U := F(U);
        ...
    end TRANSFORM;
begin -- TOP
    TRANSFORM(R);
    ...
    FACILITY.G(R, S);
end TOP;
```

3   The body of the package FACILITY and that of the procedure TRANSFORM can be made into separate subunits of TOP. Similarly, the body of the procedure G can be made into a subunit of FACILITY as follows.

4   *Example 3:*

5
```
procedure TOP is

    type REAL is digits 10;
    R, S : REAL := 1.0;

    package FACILITY is
        PI : constant := 3.14159_26536;
        function    F (X : REAL) return REAL;
        procedure   G (Y, Z : REAL);
    end FACILITY;

    package body FACILITY is separate;                      --  stub of FACILITY
    procedure TRANSFORM(U : in out REAL) is separate;       --  stub of TRANSFORM

begin  --  TOP
    TRANSFORM(R);
    ...
    FACILITY.G(R, S);
end TOP;
```

6
```
separate (TOP)
procedure TRANSFORM(U : in out REAL) is
    use FACILITY;
begin
    U := F(U);
    ...
end TRANSFORM;
```

7
```
separate (TOP)
package body FACILITY is
    --  some local declarations followed by

    function F(X : REAL) return REAL is
    begin
        --  sequence of statements of F
        ...
    end F;

    procedure G(Y, Z : REAL) is separate;                  -- stub of G
end FACILITY;
```

```
with TEXT_IO;
separate (TOP.FACILITY)                         -- full name of FACILITY
procedure G(Y, Z : REAL) is
    --  local procedures using TEXT_IO
    ...
begin
    --  sequence of statements of G
    ...
end  G;
```
8

In the above example TRANSFORM and FACILITY are subunits of TOP, and G is a subunit of FACILITY. The visibility in the split version is the same as in the initial version except for one change: since TEXT_IO is only used within G, the corresponding with clause is written for G instead of for TOP. Apart from this change, the same identifiers are visible at corresponding program points in the two versions. For example, all of the following are (directly) visible within the proper body of the subunit G: the procedure TOP, the type REAL, the variables R and S, the package FACILITY and the contained named number PI and subprograms F and G.
9

References: body stub 10.2, compilation unit 10.1, identifier 2.3, local declaration 8.1, named number 3.2, package 7, package body 7.1, procedure 6, procedure body 6.3, proper body 3.9, subprogram 6, type 3.3, variable 3.2.1, visibility 8.3, with clause 10.1.1
10

10.3 Order of Compilation

The rules defining the order in which units can be compiled are direct consequences of the visibility rules and, in particular, of the fact that any library unit that is mentioned by the context clause of a compilation unit is visible in the compilation unit.
1

A compilation unit must be compiled after all library units named by its context clause. A secondary unit that is a subprogram or package body must be compiled after the corresponding library unit. Any subunit of a parent compilation unit must be compiled after the parent compilation unit.
2

If any error is detected while attempting to compile a compilation unit, then the attempted compilation is rejected and it has no effect whatsoever on the program library; the same holds for recompilations (no compilation unit can become obsolete because of such a recompilation).
3

The order in which the compilation units of a program are compiled must be consistent with the partial ordering defined by the above rules.
4

Similar rules apply for recompilations. A compilation unit is potentially affected by a change in any library unit named by its context clause. A secondary unit is potentially affected by a change in the corresponding library unit. The subunits of a parent compilation unit are potentially affected by a change of the parent compilation unit. If a compilation unit is successfully recompiled, the compilation units potentially affected by this change are obsolete and must be recompiled unless they are no longer needed. An implementation may be able to reduce the compilation costs if it can deduce that some of the potentially affected units are not actually affected by the change.
5

6   The subunits of a unit can be recompiled without affecting the unit itself. Similarly, changes in a subprogram or package body do not affect other compilation units (apart from the subunits of the body) since these compilation units only have access to the subprogram or package specification. An implementation is only allowed to deviate from this rule for inline inclusions, for certain compiler optimizations, and for certain implementations of generic program units, as described below.

7   ● If a pragma INLINE is applied to a subprogram declaration given in a package specification, inline inclusion will only be achieved if the package body is compiled before units calling the subprogram. In such a case, inline inclusion creates a *dependence* of the calling unit on the package body, and the compiler must recognize this dependence when deciding on the need for recompilation. If a calling unit is compiled before the package body, the pragma may be ignored by the compiler for such calls (a warning that inline inclusion was not achieved may be issued). Similar considerations apply to a separately compiled subprogram for which an INLINE pragma is specified.

8   ● For optimization purposes, an implementation may compile several units of a given compilation in a way that creates further dependences among these compilation units. The compiler must then take these dependences into account when deciding on the need for recompilations.

9   ● An implementation may require that a generic declaration and the corresponding proper body be part of the same compilation, whether the generic unit is itself separately compiled or is local to another compilation unit. An implementation may also require that subunits of a generic unit be part of the same compilation.

10   *Examples of Compilation Order:*

11   (a)   In example 1 (see 10.1.1): The procedure QUADRATIC_EQUATION must be compiled after the library packages TEXT_IO and REAL_OPERATIONS since they appear in its with clause.

12   (b)   In example 2 (see 10.1.2): The package body STOCK must be compiled after the corresponding package specification.

13   (c)   In example 2 (see 10.1.2): The specification of the package STOCK must be compiled before the procedure PROCESSOR. On the other hand, the procedure PROCESSOR can be compiled either before or after the package body STOCK.

14   (d)   In example 3 (see 10.2.1): The procedure G must be compiled after the package TEXT_IO since this package is named by the with clause of G. On the other hand, TEXT_IO can be compiled either before or after TOP.

15   (e)   In example 3 (see 10.2.1): The subunits TRANSFORM and FACILITY must be compiled after the main program TOP. Similarly, the subunit G must be compiled after its parent unit FACILITY.

Notes:

16   For library packages, it follows from the recompilation rules that a package body is made obsolete by the recompilation of the corresponding specification. If the new package specification is such that a package body is not required (that is, if the package specification does not contain the declaration of a program unit), then the recompilation of a body for this package is not required. In any case, the obsolete package body must not be used and can therefore be deleted from the program library.

References: compilation 10.1, compilation unit 10.1, context clause 10.1.1, elaboration 3.9, generic body 12.2,   17
generic declaration 12.1, generic unit 12, library unit 10.1, local declaration 8.1, name 4.1, package 7, package body
7.1, package specification 7.1, parent unit 10.2, pragma inline 6.3.2, procedure 6.1, procedure body 6.3, proper body
3.9, secondary unit 10.1, subprogram body 6.3, subprogram declaration 6.1, subprogram specification 6.1, subunit
10.2, type 3.3, variable 3.2.1, visibility 8.3, with clause 10.1.1

10.4 The Program Library

Compilers are required to enforce the language rules in the same manner for a program consisting   1
of several compilation units (and subunits) as for a program submitted as a single compilation.
Consequently, a library file containing information on the compilation units of the program library
must be maintained by the compiler or compiling environment. This information may include symbol tables and other information pertaining to the order of previous compilations.

A normal submission to the compiler consists of the compilation unit(s) and the library file. The   2
latter is used for checks and is updated for each compilation unit successfully compiled.

Notes:

A single program library is implied for the compilation units of a compilation. The possible   3
existence of different program libraries and the means by which they are named are not concerns
of the language definition; they are concerns of the programming environment.

There should be commands for creating the program library of a given program or of a given family   4
of programs. These commands may permit the reuse of units of other program libraries. Finally,
there should be commands for interrogating the status of the units of a program library. The form
of these commands is not specified by the language definition.

References: compilation unit 10.1, context clause 10.1.1, order of compilation 10.3, program 10.1, program library   5
10.1, subunit 10.2, use clause 8.4, with clause 10.1.1

10.5 Elaboration of Library Units

Before the execution of a main program, all library units needed by the main program are   1
elaborated, as well as the corresponding library unit bodies, if any. The library units needed by the
main program are: those named by with clauses applicable to the main program, to its body, and
to its subunits; those named by with clauses applicable to these library units themselves, to the
corresponding library unit bodies, and to their subunits; and so on, in a transitive manner.

The elaboration of these library units and of the corresponding library unit bodies is performed in   2
an order consistent with the partial ordering defined by the with clauses (see 10.3). In addition, a
library unit mentioned by the context clause of a subunit must be elaborated before the body of the
ancestor library unit of the subunit.

An order of elaboration that is consistent with this partial ordering does not always ensure that   3
each library unit body is elaborated before any other compilation unit whose elaboration neces-
sitates that the library unit body be already elaborated. If the prior elaboration of library unit
bodies is needed, this can be requested by a pragma ELABORATE. The form of this pragma is as
follows:

    pragma ELABORATE (*library_unit*_simple_name {, *library_unit*_simple_name});

                                                         Elaboration of Library Units 10.5

4 These pragmas are only allowed immediately after the context clause of a compilation unit (before the subsequent library unit or secondary unit). Each argument of such a pragma must be the simple name of a library unit mentioned by the context clause, and this library unit must have a library unit body. Such a pragma specifies that the library unit body must be elaborated before the given compilation unit. If the given compilation unit is a subunit, the library unit body must be elaborated before the body of the ancestor library unit of the subunit.

5 The program is illegal if no consistent order can be found (that is, if a circularity exists). The elaboration of the compilation units of the program is performed in some order that is otherwise not defined by the language.

6 *References:* allow 1.6, argument of a pragma 2.8, compilation unit 10.1, context clause 10.1.1, dependence between compilation units 10.3, elaboration 3.9, illegal 1.6, in some order 1.6, library unit 10.1, name 4.1, main program 10.1, pragma 2.8, secondary unit 10.1, separate compilation 10.1, simple name 4.1, subunit 10.2, with clause 10.1.1

10.6 Program Optimization

1 Optimization of the elaboration of declarations and the execution of statements may be performed by compilers. In particular, a compiler may be able to optimize a program by evaluating certain expressions, in addition to those that are static expressions. Should one of these expressions, whether static or not, be such that an exception would be raised by its evaluation, then the code in that path of the program can be replaced by code to raise the exception; the same holds for exceptions raised by the evaluation of names and simple expressions. (See also section 11.6.)

2 A compiler may find that some statements or subprograms will never be executed, for example, if their execution depends on a condition known to be FALSE. The corresponding object machine code can then be omitted. This rule permits the effect of *conditional compilation* within the language.

Note:

3 An expression whose evaluation is known to raise an exception need not represent an error if it occurs in a statement or subprogram that is never executed. The compiler may warn the programmer of a potential error.

4 *References:* condition 5.3, declaration 3.1, elaboration 3.9, evaluation 4.5, exception 11, expression 4.4, false boolean value 3.5.3, program 10, raising of exceptions 11.3, statement 5, static expression 4.9, subprogram 6

11. Exceptions

This chapter defines the facilities for dealing with errors or other exceptional situations that arise during program execution. Such a situation is called an *exception*. To *raise* an exception is to abandon normal program execution so as to draw attention to the fact that the corresponding situation has arisen. Executing some actions, in response to the arising of an exception, is called *handling* the exception.

An exception declaration declares a name for an exception. An exception can be raised by a raise statement, or it can be raised by another statement or operation that *propagates* the exception. When an exception arises, control can be transferred to a user-provided exception handler at the end of a block statement or at the end of the body of a subprogram, package, or task unit.

References: block statement 5.6, error situation 1.6, exception handler 11.2, name 4.1, package body 7.1, propagation of an exception 11.4.1 11.4.2, raise statement 11.3, subprogram body 6.3, task body 9.1

11.1 Exception Declarations

An exception declaration declares a name for an exception. The name of an exception can only be used in raise statements, exception handlers, and renaming declarations.

```
exception_declaration ::= identifier_list : exception;
```

An exception declaration with several identifiers is equivalent to a sequence of single exception declarations, as explained in section 3.2. Each single exception declaration declares a name for a different exception. In particular, if a generic unit includes an exception declaration, the exception declarations implicitly generated by different instantiations of the generic unit refer to distinct exceptions (but all have the same identifier). The particular exception denoted by an exception name is determined at compilation time and is the same regardless of how many times the exception declaration is elaborated. Hence, if an exception declaration occurs in a recursive subprogram, the exception name denotes the same exception for all invocations of the recursive subprogram.

The following exceptions are predefined in the language; they are raised when the situations described are detected.

CONSTRAINT_ERROR   This exception is raised in any of the following situations: upon an attempt to violate a range constraint, an index constraint, or a discriminant constraint; upon an attempt to use a record component that does not exist for the current discriminant values; and upon an attempt to use a selected component, an indexed component, a slice, or an attribute, of an object designated by an access value, if the object does not exist because the access value is null.

6   NUMERIC_ERROR   This exception is raised by the execution of a predefined numeric operation that cannot deliver a correct result (within the declared accuracy for real types); this includes the case where an implementation uses a predefined numeric operation for the execution, evaluation, or elaboration of some construct. The rules given in section 4.5.7 define the cases in which an implementation is not required to raise this exception when such an error situation arises; see also section 11.6.

7   PROGRAM_ERROR   This exception is raised upon an attempt to call a subprogram, to activate a task, or to elaborate a generic instantiation, if the body of the corresponding unit has not yet been elaborated. This exception is also raised if the end of a function is reached (see 6.5); or during the execution of a selective wait that has no else part, if this execution determines that all alternatives are closed (see 9.7.1). Finally, depending on the implementation, this exception may be raised upon an attempt to execute an action that is erroneous, and for incorrect order dependences (see 1.6).

8   STORAGE_ERROR   This exception is raised in any of the following situations: when the dynamic storage allocated to a task is exceeded; during the evaluation of an allocator, if the space available for the collection of allocated objects is exhausted; or during the elaboration of a declarative item, or during the execution of a subprogram call, if storage is not sufficient.

9   TASKING_ERROR   This exception is raised when exceptions arise during intertask communication (see 9 and 11.5).

Note:

10   The situations described above can arise without raising the corresponding exceptions, if the pragma SUPPRESS has been used to give permission to omit the corresponding checks (see 11.7).

11   *Examples of user-defined exception declarations:*

```
SINGULAR   : exception;
ERROR      : exception;
OVERFLOW, UNDERFLOW : exception;
```

12   *References:* access value 3.8, collection 3.8, declaration 3.1, exception 11, exception handler 11.2, generic body 12.2, generic instantiation 12.3, generic unit 12, identifier 2.3, implicit declaration 12.3, instantiation 12.3, name 4.1, object 3.2, raise statement 11.3, real type 3.5.6, record component 3.7, return statement 5.8, subprogram 6, subprogram body 6.3, task 9, task body 9.1

13   *Constraint_error exception contexts:* aggregate 4.3.1 4.3.2, allocator 4.8, assignment statement 5.2 5.2.1, constraint 3.3.2, discrete type attribute 3.5.5, discriminant constraint 3.7.2, elaboration of a generic formal parameter 12.3.1 12.3.2 12.3.4 12.3.5, entry index 9.5, exponentiating operator 4.5.6, index constraint 3.6.1, indexed component 4.1.1, logical operator 4.5.1, null access value 3.8, object declaration 3.2.1, parameter association 6.4.1, qualified expression 4.7, range constraint 3.5, selected component 4.1.3, slice 4.1.2, subtype indication 3.3.2, type conversion 4.6

14   *Numeric_error exception contexts:* discrete type attribute 3.5.5, implicit conversion 3.5.4 3.5.6 4.6, numeric operation 3.5.5 3.5.8 3.5.10, operator of a numeric type 4.5 4.5.7

15   *Program_error exception contexts:* collection 3.8, elaboration 3.9, elaboration check 3.9 7.3 9.3 12.2, erroneous 1.6, incorrect order dependence 1.6, leaving a function 6.5, selective wait 9.7.1

Storage_error exception contexts: allocator 4.8   16

Tasking error exception contexts: abort statement 9.10, entry call 9.5 9.7.2 9.7.3, exceptions during task   17
communication 11.5, task activation 9.3

11.2 Exception Handlers

The response to one or more exceptions is specified by an exception handler.   1

```
exception_handler ::=                                                        2
    when exception_choice {| exception_choice} =>
        sequence_of_statements
```

```
exception_choice ::= exception_name | others
```

An exception handler occurs in a construct that is either a block statement or the body of a sub-   3
program, package, task unit, or generic unit. Such a construct will be called a *frame* in this
chapter. In each case the syntax of a frame that has exception handlers includes the following
part:

```
begin                                                                        4
    sequence_of_statements
exception
    exception_handler
  {exception_handler}
end
```

The exceptions denoted by the exception names given as exception choices of a frame must all be   5
distinct. The exception choice **others** is only allowed for the last exception handler of a frame and
as its only exception choice; it stands for all exceptions not listed in previous handlers of the frame,
including exceptions whose names are not visible at the place of the exception handler.

The exception handlers of a frame handle exceptions that are raised by the execution of the   6
sequence of statements of the frame. The exceptions handled by a given exception handler are
those named by the corresponding exception choices.

Example: 7

```
begin
    --   sequence of statements
exception
    when SINGULAR | NUMERIC_ERROR =>
        PUT(" MATRIX IS SINGULAR ");
    when others =>
        PUT(" FATAL ERROR ");
        raise ERROR;
end;
```

Note:

The same kinds of statement are allowed in the sequence of statements of each exception handler   8
as are allowed in the sequence of statements of the frame. For example, a return statement is
allowed in a handler within a function body.

9   *References:* block statement 5.6, declarative part 3.9, exception 11, exception handling 11.4, function body 6.3, generic body 12.2, generic unit 12.1, name 4.1, package body 7.1, raise statement 11.3, return statement 5.8, sequence of statements 5.1, statement 5, subprogram body 6.3, task body 9.1, task unit 9 9.1, visibility 8.3

11.3 Raise Statements

1   A raise statement raises an exception.

2   raise_statement ::= **raise** [*exception*_name];

3   For the execution of a raise statement with an exception name, the named exception is raised. A raise statement without an exception name is only allowed within an exception handler (but not within the sequence of statements of a subprogram, package, task unit, or generic unit, enclosed by the handler); it raises again the exception that caused transfer to the innermost enclosing handler.

4   *Examples:*

    raise SINGULAR;
    raise NUMERIC_ERROR;   -- explicitly raising a predefined exception

    raise;   -- only within an exception handler

5   *References:* exception 11, generic unit 12, name 4.1, package 7, sequence of statements 5.1, subprogram 6, task unit 9

11.4 Exception Handling

1   When an exception is raised, normal program execution is abandoned and control is transferred to an exception handler. The selection of this handler depends on whether the exception is raised during the execution of statements or during the elaboration of declarations.

2   *References:* declaration 3.1, elaboration 3.1 3.9, exception 11, exception handler 11.2, raising of exceptions 11.3, statement 5

11.4.1 Exceptions Raised During the Execution of Statements

1   The handling of an exception raised by the execution of a sequence of statements depends on whether the innermost frame or accept statement that encloses the sequence of statements is a frame or an accept statement. The case where an accept statement is innermost is described in section 11.5. The case where a frame is innermost is presented here.

Different actions take place, depending on whether or not this frame has a handler for the exception, and on whether the exception is raised in the sequence of statements of the frame or in that of an exception handler. 2

If an exception is raised in the sequence of statements of a frame that has a handler for the exception, execution of the sequence of statements of the frame is abandoned and control is transferred to the exception handler. The execution of the sequence of statements of the handler completes the execution of the frame (or its elaboration if the frame is a package body). 3

If an exception is raised in the sequence of statements of a frame that does not have a handler for the exception, execution of this sequence of statements is abandoned. The next action depends on the nature of the frame: 4

(a) For a subprogram body, the same exception is raised again at the point of call of the subprogram, unless the subprogram is the main program itself, in which case execution of the main program is abandoned. 5

(b) For a block statement, the same exception is raised again immediately after the block statement (that is, within the innermost enclosing frame or accept statement). 6

(c) For a package body that is a declarative item, the same exception is raised again immediately after this declarative item (within the enclosing declarative part). If the package body is that of a subunit, the exception is raised again at the place of the corresponding body stub. If the package is a library unit, execution of the main program is abandoned. 7

(d) For a task body, the task becomes completed. 8

An exception that is raised again (as in the above cases (a), (b), and (c)) is said to be *propagated*, either by the execution of the subprogram, the execution of the block statement, or the elaboration of the package body. No propagation takes place in the case of a task body. If the frame is a subprogram or a block statement and if it has dependent tasks, the propagation of an exception takes place only after termination of the dependent tasks. 9

Finally, if an exception is raised in the sequence of statements of an exception handler, execution of this sequence of statements is abandoned. Subsequent actions (including propagation, if any) are as in the cases (a) to (d) above, depending on the nature of the frame. 10

Example: 11

```
function FACTORIAL (N : POSITIVE) return FLOAT is
begin
  if N = 1 then
    return 1.0;
  else
    return FLOAT(N) * FACTORIAL(N-1);
  end if;
exception
  when NUMERIC_ERROR => return FLOAT'SAFE_LARGE;
end FACTORIAL;
```

If the multiplication raises NUMERIC_ERROR, then FLOAT'SAFE_LARGE is returned by the handler. This value will cause further NUMERIC_ERROR exceptions to be raised by the evaluation of the expression in each of the remaining invocations of the function, so that for large values of N the function will ultimately return the value FLOAT'SAFE_LARGE. 12

13 *Example:*

```
procedure P is
   ERROR : exception;
   procedure R;

   procedure Q is
   begin
      R;
      ...                    -- error situation (2)
   exception
      ...
      when ERROR =>    --  handler E2
      ...
   end Q;

   procedure R is
   begin
      ...                    -- error situation (3)
   end R;

begin
   ...                       -- error situation (1)
   Q;
   ...
exception
   ...
   when ERROR =>    --  handler E1
   ...
end P;
```

14 The following situations can arise:

15 (1) If the exception ERROR is raised in the sequence of statements of the outer procedure P, the handler E1 provided within P is used to complete the execution of P.

16 (2) If the exception ERROR is raised in the sequence of statements of Q, the handler E2 provided within Q is used to complete the execution of Q. Control will be returned to the point of call of Q upon completion of the handler.

17 (3) If the exception ERROR is raised in the body of R, called by Q, the execution of R is abandoned and the same exception is raised in the body of Q. The handler E2 is then used to complete the execution of Q, as in situation (2).

18 Note that in the third situation, the exception raised in R results in (indirectly) transferring control to a handler that is part of Q and hence not enclosed by R. Note also that if a handler were provided within R for the exception choice **others**, situation (3) would cause execution of this handler, rather than direct termination of R.

19 Lastly, if ERROR had been declared in R, rather than in P, the handlers E1 and E2 could not provide an explicit handler for ERROR since this identifier would not be visible within the bodies of P and Q. In situation (3), the exception could however be handled in Q by providing a handler for the exception choice **others**.

Notes:

The language does not define what happens when the execution of the main program is abandoned after an unhandled exception. [20]

The predefined exceptions are those that can be propagated by the basic operations and the predefined operators. [21]

The case of a frame that is a generic unit is already covered by the rules for subprogram and package bodies, since the sequence of statements of such a frame is not executed but is the template for the corresponding sequences of statements of the subprograms or packages obtained by generic instantiation. [22]

References: accept statement 9.5, basic operation 3.3.3, block statement 5.6, body stub 10.2, completion 9.4, declarative item 3.9, declarative part 3.9, dependent task 9.4, elaboration 3.1 3.9, exception 11, exception handler 11.2, frame 11.2, generic instantiation 12.3, generic unit 12, library unit 10.1, main program 10.1, numeric_error exception 11.1, package 7, package body 7.1, predefined operator 4.5, procedure 6.1, sequence of statements 5.1, statement 5, subprogram 6, subprogram body 6.3, subprogram call 6.4, subunit 10.2, task 9, task body 9.1 [23]

11.4.2 Exceptions Raised During the Elaboration of Declarations

If an exception is raised during the elaboration of the declarative part of a given frame, this elaboration is abandoned. The next action depends on the nature of the frame: [1]

(a) For a subprogram body, the same exception is raised again at the point of call of the subprogram, unless the subprogram is the main program itself, in which case execution of the main program is abandoned. [2]

(b) For a block statement, the same exception is raised again immediately after the block statement. [3]

(c) For a package body that is a declarative item, the same exception is raised again immediately after this declarative item, in the enclosing declarative part. If the package body is that of a subunit, the exception is raised again at the place of the corresponding body stub. If the package is a library unit, execution of the main program is abandoned. [4]

(d) For a task body, the task becomes completed, and the exception TASKING_ERROR is raised at the point of activation of the task, as explained in section 9.3. [5]

Similarly, if an exception is raised during the elaboration of either a package declaration or a task declaration, this elaboration is abandoned; the next action depends on the nature of the declaration. [6]

(e) For a package declaration or a task declaration, that is a declarative item, the exception is raised again immediately after the declarative item in the enclosing declarative part or package specification. For the declaration of a library package, the execution of the main program is abandoned. [7]

An exception that is raised again (as in the above cases (a), (b), (c) and (e)) is said to be *propagated*, either by the execution of the subprogram or block statement, or by the elaboration of the package declaration, task declaration, or package body. [8]

9   *Example of an exception in the declarative part of a block statement (case (b)):*

```
procedure P is
    ...
begin
    declare
        N : INTEGER := F;      -- the function F may raise ERROR
    begin
        ...
    exception
        when ERROR =>          -- handler E1
    end;
    ...
exception
    when ERROR =>              -- handler E2
end P;

-- if the exception ERROR is raised in the declaration of N, it is handled by E2
```

10   *References:* activation 9.3, block statement 5.6, body stub 10.2, completed task 9.4, declarative item 3.9, declarative part 3.9, elaboration 3.1 3.9, exception 11, frame 11.2, library unit 10.1, main program 10.1, package body 7.1, package declaration 7.1, package specification 7.1, subprogram 6, subprogram body 6.3, subprogram call 6.4, subunit 10.2, task 9, task body 9.1, task declaration 9.1, tasking_error exception 11.1

11.5 Exceptions Raised During Task Communication

1   An exception can be propagated to a task communicating, or attempting to communicate, with another task. An exception can also be propagated to a calling task if the exception is raised during a rendezvous.

2   When a task calls an entry of another task, the exception TASKING_ERROR is raised in the calling task, at the place of the call, if the called task is completed before accepting the entry call or is already completed at the time of the call.

3   A rendezvous can be completed abnormally in two cases:

4   (a) When an exception is raised within an accept statement, but not handled within an inner frame. In this case, the execution of the accept statement is abandoned and the same exception is raised again immediately after the accept statement within the called task; the exception is also propagated to the calling task at the point of the entry call.

5   (b) When the task containing the accept statement is completed abnormally as the result of an abort statement. In this case, the exception TASKING_ERROR is raised in the calling task at the point of the entry call.

6   On the other hand, if a task issuing an entry call becomes abnormal (as the result of an abort statement) no exception is raised in the called task. If the rendezvous has not yet started, the entry call is cancelled. If the rendezvous is in progress, it completes normally, and the called task is unaffected.

References: abnormal task 9.10, abort statement 9.10, accept statement 9.5, completed task 9.4, entry call 9.5,   7
exception 11, frame 11.2, rendezvous 9.5, task 9, task termination 9.4, tasking_error exception 11.1

11.6 Exceptions and Optimization

The purpose of this section is to specify the conditions under which an implementation is allowed   1
to perform certain actions either earlier or later than specified by other rules of the language.

In general, when the language rules specify an order for certain actions (the *canonical order*), an   2
implementation may only use an alternative order if it can guarantee that the effect of the program
is not changed by the reordering. In particular, no exception should arise for the execution of the
reordered program if none arises for the execution of the program in the canonical order. When,
on the other hand, the order of certain actions is not defined by the language, any order can be
used by the implementation. (For example, the arguments of a predefined operator can be evaluated in any order since the rules given in section 4.5 do not require a specific order of evaluation.)

Additional freedom is left to an implementation for reordering actions involving predefined opera-   3
tions that are either predefined operators or basic operations other than assignments. This
freedom is left, as defined below, even in the case where the execution of these predefined operations may propagate a (predefined) exception:

(a) For the purpose of establishing whether the same effect is obtained by the execution of cer-   4
     tain actions in the canonical and in an alternative order, it can be assumed that none of the
     predefined operations invoked by these actions propagates a (predefined) exception, provided
     that the two following requirements are met by the alternative order: first, an operation must
     not be invoked in the alternative order if it is not invoked in the canonical order; second, for
     each operation, the innermost enclosing frame or accept statement must be the same in the
     alternative order as in the canonical order, and the same exception handlers must apply.

(b) Within an expression, the association of operators with operands is specified by the syntax.   5
     However, for a sequence of predefined operators of the same precedence level (and in the
     absence of parentheses imposing a specific association), any association of operators with
     operands is allowed if it satisfies the following requirement: an integer result must be equal to
     that given by the canonical left-to-right order; a real result must belong to the result model
     interval defined for the canonical left-to-right order (see 4.5.7). Such a reordering is allowed
     even if it may remove an exception, or introduce a further predefined exception.

Similarly, additional freedom is left to an implementation for the evaluation of numeric simple   6
expressions. For the evaluation of a predefined operation, an implementation is allowed to use the
operation of a type that has a range wider than that of the base type of the operands, provided that
this delivers the exact result (or a result within the declared accuracy, in the case of a real type),
even if some intermediate results lie outside the range of the base type. The exception
NUMERIC_ERROR need not be raised in such a case. In particular, if the numeric expression is an
operand of a predefined relational operator, the exception NUMERIC_ERROR need not be raised by
the evaluation of the relation, provided that the correct BOOLEAN result is obtained.

A predefined operation need not be invoked at all, if its only possible effect is to propagate a prede-   7
fined exception. Similarly, a predefined operation need not be invoked if the removal of subsequent
operations by the above rule renders this invocation ineffective.

                                                                             Exceptions and Optimization 11.6

Notes:

8 Rule (b) applies to predefined operators but not to the short-circuit control forms.

9 The expression SPEED < 300_000.0 can be replaced by TRUE if the value 300_000.0 lies outside the base type of SPEED, even though the implicit conversion of the numeric literal would raise the exception NUMERIC_ERROR.

10 *Example:*

```
declare
   N : INTEGER;
begin
   N := 0;                    -- (1)
   for J in 1 .. 10 loop
      N := N + J**A(K);    -- A and K are global variables
   end loop;
   PUT(N);
exception
   when others => PUT("Some error arose"); PUT(N);
end;
```

11 The evaluation of A(K) may be performed before the loop, and possibly immediately before the assignment statement (1) even if this evaluation can raise an exception. Consequently, within the exception handler, the value of N is either the undefined initial value or a value later assigned. On the other hand, the evaluation of A(K) cannot be moved before **begin** since an exception would then be handled by a different handler. For this reason, the initialization of N in the declaration itself would exclude the possibility of having an undefined initial value of N in the handler.

12 *References:* accept statement 9.5, accuracy of real operations 4.5.7, assignment 5.2, base type 3.3, basic operation 3.3.3, conversion 4.6, error situation 11, exception 11, exception handler 11.2, frame 11.2, numeric_error exception 11.1, predefined operator 4.5, predefined subprogram 8.6, propagation of an exception 11.4, real type 3.5.6, undefined value 3.2.1

11.7 Suppressing Checks

1 The presence of a SUPPRESS pragma gives permission to an implementation to omit certain run-time checks. The form of this pragma is as follows:

pragma SUPPRESS (identifier [, [ON =>] name]);

2 The identifier is that of the check that can be omitted. The name (if present) must be either a simple name or an expanded name and it must denote either an object, a type or subtype, a task unit, or a generic unit; alternatively the name can be a subprogram name, in which case it can stand for several visible overloaded subprograms.

A pragma SUPPRESS is only allowed immediately within a declarative part or immediately within 3
a package specification. In the latter case, the only allowed form is with a name that denotes an
entity (or several overloaded subprograms) declared immediately within the package specification.
The permission to omit the given check extends from the place of the pragma to the end of the
declarative region associated with the innermost enclosing block statement or program unit. For a
pragma given in a package specification, the permission extends to the end of the scope of the
named entity.

If the pragma includes a name, the permission to omit the given check is further restricted: it is 4
given only for operations on the named object or on all objects of the base type of a named type or
subtype; for calls of a named subprogram; for activations of tasks of the named task type; or for
instantiations of the given generic unit.

The following checks correspond to situations in which the exception CONSTRAINT_ERROR may 5
be raised; for these checks, the name (if present) must denote either an object or a type.

ACCESS_CHECK   When accessing a selected component, an indexed component, a 6
                       slice, or an attribute, of an object designated by an access value,
                       check that the access value is not null.

DISCRIMINANT_CHECK   Check that a discriminant of a composite value has the value imposed 7
                       by a discriminant constraint. Also, when accessing a record compo-
                       nent, check that it exists for the current discriminant values.

INDEX_CHECK   Check that the bounds of an array value are equal to the cor- 8
                       responding bounds of an index constraint. Also, when accessing a
                       component of an array object, check for each dimension that the given
                       index value belongs to the range defined by the bounds of the array
                       object. Also, when accessing a slice of an array object, check that the
                       given discrete range is compatible with the range defined by the
                       bounds of the array object.

LENGTH_CHECK   Check that there is a matching component for each component of an 9
                       array, in the case of array assignments, type conversions, and logical
                       operators for arrays of boolean components.

RANGE_CHECK   Check that a value satisfies a range constraint. Also, for the elabora- 10
                       tion of a subtype indication, check that the constraint (if present) is
                       compatible with the type mark. Also, for an aggregate, check that an
                       index or discriminant value belongs to the corresponding subtype.
                       Finally, check for any constraint checks performed by a generic instan-
                       tiation.

The following checks correspond to situations in which the exception NUMERIC_ERROR is raised. 11
The only allowed names in the corresponding pragmas are names of numeric types.

DIVISION_CHECK   Check that the second operand is not zero for the operations /, **rem** 12
                       and **mod**.

OVERFLOW_CHECK   Check that the result of a numeric operation does not overflow. 13

The following check corresponds to situations in which the exception PROGRAM_ERROR is raised. 14
The only allowed names in the corresponding pragmas are names denoting task units, generic
units, or subprograms.

ELABORATION_CHECK   When either a subprogram is called, a task activation is accomplished, 15
                       or a generic instantiation is elaborated, check that the body of the cor-
                       responding unit has already been elaborated.

16   The following check corresponds to situations in which the exception STORAGE_ERROR is raised. The only allowed names in the corresponding pragmas are names denoting access types, task units, or subprograms.

17   STORAGE_CHECK   Check that execution of an allocator does not require more space than is available for a collection. Check that the space available for a task or subprogram has not been exceeded.

18   If an error situation arises in the absence of the corresponding run-time checks, the execution of the program is erroneous (the results are not defined by the language).

19   *Examples:*

```
pragma SUPPRESS(RANGE_CHECK);
pragma SUPPRESS(INDEX_CHECK, ON => TABLE);
```

Notes:

20   For certain implementations, it may be impossible or too costly to suppress certain checks. The corresponding SUPPRESS pragma can be ignored. Hence, the occurrence of such a pragma within a given unit does not guarantee that the corresponding exception will not arise; the exceptions may also be propagated by called units.

21   *References:* access type 3.8, access value 3.8, activation 9.3, aggregate 4.3, allocator 4.8, array 3.6, attribute 4.1.4, block statement 5.6, collection 3.8, compatible 3.3.2, component of an array 3.6, component of a record 3.7, composite type 3.3, constraint 3.3, constraint_error exception 11.1, declarative part 3.9, designate 3.8, dimension 3.6, discrete range 3.6, discriminant 3.7.1, discriminant constraint 3.7.2, elaboration 3.1 3.9, erroneous 1.6, error situation 11, expanded name 4.1.3, generic body 11.1, generic instantiation 12.3, generic unit 12, identifier 2.3, index 3.6, index constraint 3.6.1, indexed component 4.1.1, null access value 3.8, numeric operation 3.5.5 3.5.8 3.5.10, numeric type 3.5, numeric_error exception 11.1, object 3.2, operation 3.3.3, package body 7.1, package specification 7.1, pragma 2.8, program_error exception 11.1, program unit 6, propagation of an exception 11.4, range constraint 3.5, record type 3.7, simple name 4.1, slice 4.1.2, subprogram 6, subprogram body 6.3, subprogram call 6.4, subtype 3.3, subunit 10.2, task 9, task body 9.1, task type 9.1, task unit 9, type 3.3, type mark 3.3.2

12. Generic Units

A generic unit is a program unit that is either a generic subprogram or a generic package. A generic unit is a *template*, which is parameterized or not, and from which corresponding (nongeneric) subprograms or packages can be obtained. The resulting program units are said to be *instances* of the original generic unit.

A generic unit is declared by a generic declaration. This form of declaration has a generic formal part declaring any generic formal parameters. An instance of a generic unit is obtained as the result of a generic instantiation with appropriate generic actual parameters for the generic formal parameters. An instance of a generic subprogram is a subprogram. An instance of a generic package is a package.

Generic units are templates. As templates they do not have the properties that are specific to their nongeneric counterparts. For example, a generic subprogram can be instantiated but it cannot be called. In contrast, the instance of a generic subprogram is a nongeneric subprogram; hence, this instance can be called but it cannot be used to produce further instances.

References: declaration 3.1, generic actual parameter 12.3, generic declaration 12.1, generic formal parameter 12.1, generic formal part 12.1, generic instantiation 12.3, generic package 12.1, generic subprogram 12.1, instance 12.3, package 7, program unit 6, subprogram 6

12.1 Generic Declarations

A generic declaration declares a generic unit, which is either a generic subprogram or a generic package. A generic declaration includes a generic formal part declaring any generic formal parameters. A generic formal parameter can be an object; alternatively (unlike a parameter of a subprogram), it can be a type or a subprogram.

    generic_declaration ::= generic_specification;

    generic_specification ::=
        generic_formal_part subprogram_specification
      | generic_formal_part package_specification

    generic_formal_part ::= **generic** {generic_parameter_declaration}

    generic_parameter_declaration ::=
        identifier_list : [**in** [**out**]] type_mark [:= expression];
      | **type** identifier **is** generic_type_definition;
      | private_type_declaration
      | **with** subprogram_specification [**is** name];
      | **with** subprogram_specification [**is** <>];

    generic_type_definition ::=
        (<>) | **range** <> | **digits** <> | **delta** <>
      | array_type_definition | access_type_definition

3   The terms generic formal object (or simply, *formal object*), generic formal type (or simply, *formal type*), and generic formal subprogram (or simply, *formal subprogram*) are used to refer to corresponding generic formal parameters.

4   The only form of subtype indication allowed within a generic formal part is a type mark (that is, the subtype indication must not include an explicit constraint). The designator of a generic subprogram must be an identifier.

5   Outside the specification and body of a generic unit, the name of this program unit denotes the generic unit. In contrast, within the declarative region associated with a generic subprogram, the name of this program unit denotes the subprogram obtained by the current instantiation of the generic unit. Similarly, within the declarative region associated with a generic package, the name of this program unit denotes the package obtained by the current instantiation.

6   The elaboration of a generic declaration has no other effect.

7   *Examples of generic formal parts:*

```
generic      --  parameterless

generic
   SIZE : NATURAL; --  formal object

generic
   LENGTH   : INTEGER := 200;               -- formal object with a default expression
   AREA     : INTEGER := LENGTH*LENGTH; -- formal object with a default expression

generic
   type ITEM   is private;                          -- formal type
   type INDEX is (<>);                              -- formal type
   type ROW   is array(INDEX range <>) of ITEM; -- formal type
   with function "<"(X, Y : ITEM) return BOOLEAN;      -- formal subprogram
```

8   *Examples of generic declarations declaring generic subprograms:*

```
generic
   type ELEM is private;
procedure EXCHANGE(U, V : in out ELEM);

generic
   type ITEM is private;
   with function "*"(U, V : ITEM) return ITEM is <>;
function SQUARING(X : ITEM) return ITEM;
```

9   *Example of a generic declaration declaring a generic package:*

```
generic
   type ITEM      is private;
   type VECTOR is array (POSITIVE range <>) of ITEM;
   with function SUM(X, Y : ITEM) return ITEM;
package ON_VECTORS is
   function SUM   (A, B  : VECTOR) return VECTOR;
   function SIGMA (A      : VECTOR) return ITEM;
   LENGTH_ERROR : exception;
end;
```

Notes:

Within a generic subprogram, the name of this program unit acts as the name of a subprogram. Hence this name can be overloaded, and it can appear in a recursive call of the current instantiation. For the same reason, this name cannot appear after the reserved word **new** in a (recursive) generic instantiation.

An expression that occurs in a generic formal part is either the default expression for a generic formal object of mode **in**, or a constituent of an entry name given as default name for a formal subprogram, or the default expression for a parameter of a formal subprogram. Default expressions for generic formal objects and default names for formal subprograms are only evaluated for generic instantiations that use such defaults. Default expressions for parameters of formal subprograms are only evaluated for calls of the formal subprograms that use such defaults. (The usual visibility rules apply to any name used in a default expression: the denoted entity must therefore be visible at the place of the expression.)

Neither generic formal parameters nor their attributes are allowed constituents of static expressions (see 4.9).

References: access type definition 3.8, array type definition 3.6, attribute 4.1.4, constraint 3.3, declaration 3.1, designator 6.1, elaboration has no other effect 3.1, entity 3.1, expression 4.4, function 6.5, generic instantiation 12.3, identifier 2.3, identifier list 3.2, instance 12.3, name 4.1, object 3.2, overloading 6.6 8.7, package specification 7.1, parameter of a subprogram 6.2, private type definition 7.4, procedure 6.1, reserved word 2.9, static expression 4.9, subprogram 6, subprogram specification 6.1, subtype indication 3.3.2, type 3.3, type mark 3.3.2

12.1.1 Generic Formal Objects

The first form of generic parameter declaration declares generic formal objects. The type of a generic formal object is the base type of the type denoted by the type mark given in the generic parameter declaration. A generic parameter declaration with several identifiers is equivalent to a sequence of single generic parameter declarations, as explained in section 3.2.

A generic formal object has a mode that is either **in** or **in out**. In the absence of an explicit mode indication in a generic parameter declaration, the mode **in** is assumed; otherwise the mode is the one indicated. If a generic parameter declaration ends with an expression, the expression is the *default expression* of the generic formal parameter. A default expression is only allowed if the mode is **in** (whether this mode is indicated explicitly or implicitly). The type of a default expression must be that of the corresponding generic formal parameter.

A generic formal object of mode **in** is a constant whose value is a copy of the value supplied as the matching generic actual parameter in a generic instantiation, as described in section 12.3. The type of a generic formal object of mode **in** must not be a limited type; the subtype of such a generic formal object is the subtype denoted by the type mark given in the generic parameter declaration.

A generic formal object of mode **in out** is a variable and denotes the object supplied as the matching generic actual parameter in a generic instantiation, as described in section 12.3. The constraints that apply to the generic formal object are those of the corresponding generic actual parameter.

Note:

5   The constraints that apply to a generic formal object of mode **in out** are those of the corresponding generic actual parameter (not those implied by the type mark that appears in the generic parameter declaration). Whenever possible (to avoid confusion) it is recommended that the name of a base type be used for the declaration of such a formal object. If, however, the base type is anonymous, it is recommended that the subtype name defined by the type declaration for the base type be used.

6   *References:* anonymous type 3.3.1, assignment 5.2, base type 3.3, constant declaration 3.2, constraint 3.3, declaration 3.1, generic actual parameter 12.3, generic formal object 12.1, generic formal parameter 12.1, generic instantiation 12.3, generic parameter declaration 12.1, identifier 2.3, limited type 7.4.4, matching generic actual parameter 12.3, mode 6.1, name 4.1, object 3.2, simple name 4.1, subtype 3.3, type declaration 3.3, type mark 3.3.2, variable 3.2.1

12.1.2 Generic Formal Types

1   A generic parameter declaration that includes a generic type definition or a private type declaration declares a generic formal type. A generic formal type denotes the subtype supplied as the corresponding actual parameter in a generic instantiation, as described in 12.3(d). However, within a generic unit, a generic formal type is considered as being distinct from all other (formal or nonformal) types. The form of constraint applicable to a formal type in a subtype indication depends on the class of the type as for a nonformal type.

2   The only form of discrete range that is allowed within the declaration of a generic formal (constrained) array type is a type mark.

3   The discriminant part of a generic formal private type must not include a default expression for a discriminant. (Consequently, a variable that is declared by an object declaration must be constrained if its type is a generic formal type with discriminants.)

4   Within the declaration and body of a generic unit, the operations available for values of a generic formal type (apart from any additional operation specified by a generic formal subprogram) are determined by the generic parameter declaration for the formal type:

5   (a)   For a private type declaration, the available operations are those defined in section 7.4.2 (in particular, assignment, equality, and inequality are available for a private type unless it is limited).

6   (b)   For an array type definition, the available operations are those defined in section 3.6.2 (for example, they include the formation of indexed components and slices).

7   (c)   For an access type definition, the available operations are those defined in section 3.8.2 (for example, allocators can be used).

8   The four forms of generic type definition in which a *box* appears (that is, the compound delimiter <>) correspond to the following major forms of scalar type:

9   (d)   Discrete types: (<>)

     The available operations are the operations common to enumeration and integer types; these are defined in section 3.5.5.

(e) Integer types: **range** <>

The available operations are the operations of integer types defined in section 3.5.5.

(f) Floating point types: **digits** <>

The available operations are those defined in section 3.5.8.

(g) Fixed point types: **delta** <>

The available operations are those defined in section 3.5.10.

In all of the above cases (a) through (f), each operation implicitly associated with a formal type (that is, other than an operation specified by a formal subprogram) is implicitly declared at the place of the declaration of the formal type. The same holds for a formal fixed point type, except for the multiplying operators that deliver a result of the type *universal_fixed* (see 4.5.5), since these special operators are declared in the package STANDARD.

For an instantiation of the generic unit, each of these operations is the corresponding basic operation or predefined operator of the matching actual type. For an operator, this rule applies even if the operator has been redefined for the actual type or for some parent type of the actual type.

Examples of generic formal types:

```
type ITEM is private;
type BUFFER(LENGTH : NATURAL) is limited private;

type ENUM    is (<>);
type INT     is range <>;
type ANGLE   is delta <>;
type MASS    is digits <>;

type TABLE is array (ENUM) of ITEM;
```

Example of a generic formal part declaring a formal integer type:

```
generic
    type RANK is range <>;
    FIRST    : RANK := RANK'FIRST;
    SECOND   : RANK := FIRST + 1;   --   the operator "+" of the type RANK
```

References: access type definition 3.8, allocator 4.8, array type definition 3.6, assignment 5.2, body of a generic unit 12.2, class of type 3.3, constraint 3.3, declaration 3.1, declaration of a generic unit 12.1, discrete range 3.6, discrete type 3.5, discriminant part 3.7.1, enumeration type 3.5.1, equality 4.5.2, fixed point type 3.5.9, floating point type 3.5.7, generic actual type 12.3, generic formal part 12.1, generic formal subprogram 12.1.3, generic formal type 12.1, generic parameter declaration 12.1, generic type definition 12.1, indexed component 4.1.1, instantiation 12.3, integer type 3.5.4, limited private type 7.4.4, matching generic actual type 12.3.2 12.3.3 12.3.4 12.3.5, multiplying operator 4.5 4.5.5, operation 3.3, operator 4.5, parent type 3.4, private type definition 7.4, scalar type 3.5, slice 4.1.2, standard package 8.6 C, subtype indication 3.3.2, type mark 3.3.2, universal_fixed 3.5.9

12.1.3 Generic Formal Subprograms

1 A generic parameter declaration that includes a subprogram specification declares a generic formal subprogram.

2 Two alternative forms of defaults can be specified in the declaration of a generic formal subprogram. In these forms, the subprogram specification is followed by the reserved word **is** and either a box or the name of a subprogram or entry. The matching rules for these defaults are explained in section 12.3.6.

3 A generic formal subprogram denotes the subprogram, enumeration literal, or entry supplied as the corresponding generic actual parameter in a generic instantiation, as described in section 12.3(f).

4 *Examples of generic formal subprograms:*

```
with function INCREASE(X : INTEGER) return INTEGER;
with function SUM(X, Y : ITEM) return ITEM;

with function "+"(X, Y : ITEM) return ITEM is <>;
with function IMAGE(X : ENUM) return STRING is ENUM'IMAGE;

with procedure UPDATE is DEFAULT_UPDATE;
```

Notes:

5 The constraints that apply to a parameter of a formal subprogram are those of the corresponding parameter in the specification of the matching actual subprogram (not those implied by the corresponding type mark in the specification of the formal subprogram). A similar remark applies to the result of a function. Whenever possible (to avoid confusion), it is recommended that the name of a base type be used rather than the name of a subtype in any declaration of a formal subprogram. If, however, the base type is anonymous, it is recommended that the subtype name defined by the type declaration be used.

6 The type specified for a formal parameter of a generic formal subprogram can be any visible type, including a generic formal type of the same generic formal part.

7 *References:* anonymous type 3.3.1, base type 3.3, box delimiter 12.1.2, constraint 3.3, designator 6.1, generic actual parameter 12.3, generic formal function 12.1, generic formal subprogram 12.1, generic instantiation 12.3, generic parameter declaration 12.1, identifier 2.3, matching generic actual subprogram 12.3.6, operator symbol 6.1, parameter of a subprogram 6.2, renaming declaration 8.5, reserved word 2.9, scope 8.2, subprogram 6, subprogram specification 6.1, subtype 3.3.2, type 3.3, type mark 3.3.2

12.2 Generic Bodies

1 The body of a generic subprogram or generic package is a template for the bodies of the corresponding subprograms or packages obtained by generic instantiations. The syntax of a generic body is identical to that of a nongeneric body.

2 For each declaration of a generic subprogram, there must be a corresponding body.

The elaboration of a generic body has no other effect than to establish that the body can from then on be used as the template for obtaining the corresponding instances. 3

Example of a generic procedure body: 4

```
procedure EXCHANGE(U, V : in out ELEM) is     --  see example in 12.1
   T : ELEM;  --  the generic formal type
begin
   T := U;
   U := V;
   V := T;
end EXCHANGE;
```

Example of a generic function body: 5

```
function SQUARING(X : ITEM) return ITEM is     --  see example in 12.1
begin
   return X*X; --  the formal operator "*"
end;
```

Example of a generic package body: 6

```
package body ON_VECTORS is    --  see example in 12.1

   function SUM(A, B : VECTOR) return VECTOR is
      RESULT   : VECTOR(A'RANGE);       --  the formal type VECTOR
      BIAS     : constant INTEGER := B'FIRST - A'FIRST;
   begin
      if A'LENGTH /= B'LENGTH then
         raise LENGTH_ERROR;
      end if;

      for N in A'RANGE loop
         RESULT(N) := SUM(A(N), B(N + BIAS));      --  the formal function SUM
      end loop;
      return RESULT;
   end;

   function SIGMA(A : VECTOR) return ITEM is
      TOTAL : ITEM := A(A'FIRST);               --  the formal type ITEM
   begin
      for N in A'FIRST + 1 .. A'LAST loop
         TOTAL := SUM(TOTAL, A(N));             --  the formal function SUM
      end loop;
      return TOTAL;
   end;
end;
```

References: body 3.9, elaboration 3.9, generic body 12.1, generic instantiation 12.3, generic package 12.1, generic subprogram 12.1, instance 12.3, package body 7.1, package 7, subprogram 6, subprogram body 6.3 7

12.3 Generic Instantiation

1   An instance of a generic unit is declared by a generic instantiation.

2
```
generic_instantiation  ::=
    package identifier is
        new generic_package_name [generic_actual_part];
    | procedure identifier is
        new generic_procedure_name [generic_actual_part];
    | function designator is
        new generic_function_name [generic_actual_part];

generic_actual_part  ::=
    (generic_association  {, generic_association})

generic_association  ::=
    [generic_formal_parameter =>] generic_actual_parameter

generic_formal_parameter  ::=  parameter_simple_name | operator_symbol

generic_actual_parameter  ::= expression | variable_name
    | subprogram_name | entry_name | type_mark
```

3   An explicit generic actual parameter must be supplied for each generic formal parameter, unless the corresponding generic parameter declaration specifies that a default can be used. Generic associations can be either positional or named, in the same manner as parameter associations of subprogram calls (see 6.4). If two or more formal subprograms have the same designator, then named associations are not allowed for the corresponding generic parameters.

4   Each generic actual parameter must *match* the corresponding generic formal parameter. An expression can match a formal object of mode **in**; a variable name can match a formal object of mode **in out**; a subprogram name or an entry name can match a formal subprogram; a type mark can match a formal type. The detailed rules defining the allowed matches are given in sections 12.3.1 to 12.3.6; these are the only allowed matches.

5   The instance is a copy of the generic unit, apart from the generic formal part; thus the instance of a generic package is a package, that of a generic procedure is a procedure, and that of a generic function is a function. For each occurrence, within the generic unit, of a name that denotes a given entity, the following list defines which entity is denoted by the corresponding occurrence within the instance.

6   (a) For a name that denotes the generic unit: The corresponding occurrence denotes the instance.

7   (b) For a name that denotes a generic formal object of mode **in**:   The corresponding name denotes a constant whose value is a copy of the value of the associated generic actual parameter.

8   (c) For a name that denotes a generic formal object of mode **in out**:   The corresponding name denotes the variable named by the associated generic actual parameter.

9   (d) For a name that denotes a generic formal type: The corresponding name denotes the subtype named by the associated generic actual parameter (the actual subtype).

10   (e) For a name that denotes a discriminant of a generic formal type: The corresponding name denotes the corresponding discriminant (there must be one) of the actual type associated with the generic formal type.

(f) For a name that denotes a generic formal subprogram: The corresponding name denotes the subprogram, enumeration literal, or entry named by the associated generic actual parameter (the actual subprogram). 11

(g) For a name that denotes a formal parameter of a generic formal subprogram: The corresponding name denotes the corresponding formal parameter of the actual subprogram associated with the formal subprogram. 12

(h) For a name that denotes a local entity declared within the generic unit: The corresponding name denotes the entity declared by the corresponding local declaration within the instance. 13

(i) For a name that denotes a global entity declared outside of the generic unit: The corresponding name denotes the same global entity. 14

Similar rules apply to operators and basic operations: in particular, formal operators follow a rule similar to rule (f), local operations follow a rule similar to rule (h), and operations for global types follow a rule similar to rule (i). In addition, if within the generic unit a predefined operator or basic operation of a formal type is used, then within the instance the corresponding occurrence refers to the corresponding predefined operation of the actual type associated with the formal type. 15

The above rules apply also to any type mark or (default) expression given within the generic formal part of the generic unit. 16

For the elaboration of a generic instantiation, each expression supplied as an explicit generic actual parameter is first evaluated, as well as each expression that appears as a constituent of a variable name or entry name supplied as an explicit generic actual parameter; these evaluations proceed in some order that is not defined by the language. Then, for each omitted generic association (if any), the corresponding default expression or default name is evaluated; such evaluations are performed in the order of the generic parameter declarations. Finally, the implicitly generated instance is elaborated. The elaboration of a generic instantiation may also involve certain constraint checks as described in later subsections. 17

Recursive generic instantiation is not allowed in the following sense: if a given generic unit includes an instantiation of a second generic unit, then the instance generated by this instantiation must not include an instance of the first generic unit (whether this instance is generated directly, or indirectly by intermediate instantiations). 18

Examples of generic instantiations (see 12.1): 19

```
procedure  SWAP  is new  EXCHANGE(ELEM => INTEGER);
procedure  SWAP  is new  EXCHANGE(CHARACTER);  —  SWAP is overloaded

function SQUARE is new SQUARING (INTEGER);   --  "*" of INTEGER used by default
function SQUARE is new SQUARING (ITEM => MATRIX, "*" => MATRIX_PRODUCT);
function SQUARE is new SQUARING (MATRIX, MATRIX_PRODUCT); -- same as previous

package INT_VECTORS is new ON_VECTORS(INTEGER, TABLE, "+");
```

Examples of uses of instantiated units: 20

```
SWAP(A, B);
A := SQUARE(A);

T  : TABLE(1 .. 5) := (10, 20, 30, 40, 50);
N  : INTEGER := INT_VECTORS.SIGMA(T);   --  150 (see 12.2 for the body of SIGMA)

use INT_VECTORS;
M : INTEGER := SIGMA(T);   --  150
```

Notes:

21   Omission of a generic actual parameter is only allowed if a corresponding default exists. If default expressions or default names (other than simple names) are used, they are evaluated in the order in which the corresponding generic formal parameters are declared.

22   If two overloaded subprograms declared in a generic package specification differ only by the (formal) type of their parameters and results, then there exist legal instantiations for which all calls of these subprograms from outside the instance are ambiguous. For example:

```
generic
   type A is (<>);
   type B is private;
package G is
   function NEXT(X : A)  return A;
   function NEXT(X : B)  return B;
end;

package P is new G(A => BOOLEAN, B => BOOLEAN);
-- calls of P.NEXT are ambiguous
```

23   *References:* declaration 3.1, designator 6.1, discriminant 3.7.1, elaboration 3.1 3.9, entity 3.1, entry name 9.5, evaluation 4.5, expression 4.4, generic formal object 12.1, generic formal parameter 12.1, generic formal subprogram 12.1, generic formal type 12.1, generic parameter declaration 12.1, global declaration 8.1, identifier 2.3, implicit declaration 3.1, local declaration 8.1, mode in 12.1.1, mode in out 12.1.1, name 4.1, operation 3.3, operator symbol 6.1, overloading 6.6 8.7, package 7, simple name 4.1, subprogram 6, subprogram call 6.4, subprogram name 6.1, subtype declaration 3.3.2, type mark 3.3.2, variable 3.2.1, visibility 8.3

12.3.1 Matching Rules for Formal Objects

1   A generic formal parameter of mode **in** of a given type is matched by an expression of the same type. If a generic unit has a generic formal object of mode **in**, a check is made that the value of the expression belongs to the subtype denoted by the type mark, as for an explicit constant declaration (see 3.2.1). The exception CONSTRAINT_ERROR is raised if this check fails.

2   A generic formal parameter of mode **in out** of a given type is matched by the name of a variable of the same type. The variable must not be a formal parameter of mode **out** or a subcomponent thereof. The name must denote a variable for which renaming is allowed (see 8.5).

Notes:

3   The type of a generic actual parameter of mode **in** must not be a limited type. The constraints that apply to a generic formal parameter of mode **in out** are those of the corresponding generic actual parameter (see 12.1.1).

4   *References:* constraint 3.3, constraint_error exception 11.1, expression 4.4, formal parameter 6.1, generic actual parameter 12.3, generic formal object 12.1.1, generic formal parameter 12.1, generic instantiation 12.3, generic unit 12.1, limited type 7.4.4, matching generic actual parameter 12.3, mode in 12.1.1, mode in out 12.1.1, mode out 6.2, name 4.1, raising of exceptions 11, satisfy 3.3, subcomponent 3.3, type 3.3, type mark 3.3.2, variable 3.2.1

12.3.2 Matching Rules for Formal Private Types

A generic formal private type is matched by any type or subtype (the actual subtype) that satisfies the following conditions:

- If the formal type is not limited, the actual type must not be a limited type. (If, on the other hand, the formal type is limited, no such condition is imposed on the corresponding actual type, which can be limited or not limited.)

- If the formal type has a discriminant part, the actual type must be a type with the same number of discriminants; the type of a discriminant that appears at a given position in the discriminant part of the actual type must be the same as the type of the discriminant that appears at the same position in the discriminant part of the formal type; and the actual subtype must be unconstrained. (If, on the other hand, the formal type has no discriminants, the actual type is allowed to have discriminants.)

Furthermore, consider any occurrence of the name of the formal type at a place where this name is used as an unconstrained subtype indication. The actual subtype must not be an unconstrained array type or an unconstrained type with discriminants, if any of these occurrences is at a place where either a constraint or default discriminants would be required for an array type or for a type with discriminants (see 3.6.1 and 3.7.2). The same restriction applies to occurrences of the name of a subtype of the formal type, and to occurrences of the name of any type or subtype derived, directly or indirectly, from the formal type.

If a generic unit has a formal private type with discriminants, the elaboration of a corresponding generic instantiation checks that the subtype of each discriminant of the actual type is the same as the subtype of the corresponding discriminant of the formal type. The exception CONSTRAINT_ERROR is raised if this check fails.

References: array type 3.6, constraint 3.3, constraint_error exception 11.1, default expression for a discriminant 3.7.1, derived type 3.4, discriminant 3.7.1, discriminant part 3.7.1, elaboration 3.9, generic actual type 12.3, generic body 12.2, generic formal type 12.1.2, generic instantiation 12.3, generic specification 12.1, limited type 7.4.4, matching generic actual parameter 12.3, name 4.1, private type 7.4, raising of exceptions 11, subtype 3.3, subtype indication 3.3.2, type 3.3, type with discriminants 3.3, unconstrained array type 3.6, unconstrained subtype 3.3

12.3.3 Matching Rules for Formal Scalar Types

A generic formal type defined by (<>) is matched by any discrete subtype (that is, any enumeration or integer subtype). A generic formal type defined by **range** <> is matched by any integer subtype. A generic formal type defined by **digits** <> is matched by any floating point subtype. A generic formal type defined by **delta** <> is matched by any fixed point subtype. No other matches are possible for these generic formal types.

References: box delimiter 12.1.2, discrete type 3.5, enumeration type 3.5.1, fixed point type 3.5.9, floating point type 3.5.7, generic actual type 12.3, generic formal type 12.1.2, generic type definition 12.1, integer type 3.5.4, matching generic actual parameter 12.3, scalar type 3.5

12.3.4 Matching Rules for Formal Array Types

1 A formal array type is matched by an actual array subtype that satisfies the following conditions:

2 • The formal array type and the actual array type must have the same dimensionality; the formal type and the actual subtype must be either both constrained or both unconstrained.

3 • For each index position, the index type must be the same for the actual array type as for the formal array type.

4 • The component type must be the same for the actual array type as for the formal array type. If the component type is other than a scalar type, then the component subtypes must be either both constrained or both unconstrained.

5 If a generic unit has a formal array type, the elaboration of a corresponding instantiation checks that the constraints (if any) on the component type are the same for the actual array type as for the formal array type, and likewise that for any given index position the index subtypes or the discrete ranges have the same bounds. The exception CONSTRAINT_ERROR is raised if this check fails.

6 *Example:*

```
-- given the generic package

generic
    type ITEM      is private;
    type INDEX     is (<>);
    type VECTOR    is array (INDEX range <>) of ITEM;
    type TABLE     is array (INDEX) of ITEM;
package P is
    ...
end;

-- and the types

type MIX      is array (COLOR range <>) of BOOLEAN;
type OPTION   is array (COLOR) of BOOLEAN;

-- then MIX can match VECTOR and OPTION can match TABLE

package R is new P(ITEM     => BOOLEAN, INDEX => COLOR,
                   VECTOR   => MIX,      TABLE => OPTION);

-- Note that MIX cannot match TABLE and OPTION cannot match VECTOR
```

Note:

7 For the above rules, if any of the index or component types of the formal array type is itself a formal type, then within the instance its name denotes the corresponding actual subtype (see 12.3(d)).

8 *References:* array type 3.6, array type definition 3.6, component of an array 3.6, constrained array type 3.6, constraint 3.3, constraint_error exception 11.1, elaboration 3.9, formal type 12.1, generic formal type 12.1.2, generic instantiation 12.3, index 3.6, index constraint 3.6.1, matching generic actual parameter 12.3, raise statement 11.3, subtype 3.3, unconstrained array type 3.6

12.3.5 Matching Rules for Formal Access Types

A formal access type is matched by an actual access subtype if the type of the designated objects [1]
is the same for the actual type as for the formal type. If the designated type is other than a scalar
type, then the designated subtypes must be either both constrained or both unconstrained.

If a generic unit has a formal access type, the elaboration of a corresponding instantiation checks [2]
that any constraints on the designated objects are the same for the actual access subtype as for
the formal access type. The exception CONSTRAINT_ERROR is raised if this check fails.

Example: [3]

```
--   the formal types of the generic package

generic
   type NODE  is private;
   type LINK   is access NODE;
package P is
   ...
end;

--   can be matched by the actual types

type CAR;
type CAR_NAME is access CAR;

type CAR is
   record
      PRED, SUCC : CAR_NAME;
      NUMBER      : LICENSE_NUMBER;
      OWNER       : PERSON;
   end record;


--   in the following generic instantiation

package R is new P(NODE => CAR, LINK => CAR_NAME);
```

Note:

For the above rules, if the designated type is itself a formal type, then within the instance its name [4]
denotes the corresponding actual subtype (see 12.3(d)).

References: access type 3.8, access type definition 3.8, constraint 3.3, constraint_error exception 11.1, designate [5]
3.8, elaboration 3.9, generic formal type 12.1.2, generic instantiation 12.3, matching generic actual parameter 12.3,
object 3.2, raise statement 11.3, value of access type 3.8

12.3.6 Matching Rules for Formal Subprograms

1 A formal subprogram is matched by an actual subprogram, enumeration literal, or entry if both have the same parameter and result type profile (see 6.6); in addition, parameter modes must be identical for formal parameters that are at the same parameter position.

2 If a generic unit has a default subprogram specified by a name, this name must denote a subprogram, an enumeration literal, or an entry, that matches the formal subprogram (in the above sense). The evaluation of the default name takes place during the elaboration of each instantiation that uses the default, as defined in section 12.3.

3 If a generic unit has a default subprogram specified by a box, the corresponding actual parameter can be omitted if a subprogram, enumeration literal, or entry matching the formal subprogram, and with the same designator as the formal subprogram, is directly visible at the place of the generic instantiation; this subprogram, enumeration literal, or entry is then used by default (there must be exactly one subprogram, enumeration literal, or entry satisfying the previous conditions).

4 *Example:*

```
-- given the generic function specification

generic
    type ITEM is private;
    with function "*" (U, V : ITEM) return ITEM is <>;
function SQUARING(X : ITEM) return ITEM;

-- and the function

function MATRIX_PRODUCT(A, B : MATRIX) return MATRIX;

-- the following instantiation is possible

function SQUARE is new SQUARING(MATRIX, MATRIX_PRODUCT);

-- the following instantiations are equivalent

function SQUARE is new SQUARING(ITEM => INTEGER, "*" => "*");
function SQUARE is new SQUARING(INTEGER, "*");
function SQUARE is new SQUARING(INTEGER);
```

Notes:

5 The matching rules for formal subprograms state requirements that are similar to those applying to subprogram renaming declarations (see 8.5). In particular, the name of a parameter of the formal subprogram need not be the same as that of the corresponding parameter of the actual subprogram; similarly, for these parameters, default expressions need not correspond.

6 A formal subprogram is matched by an attribute of a type if the attribute is a function with a matching specification. An enumeration literal of a given type matches a parameterless formal function whose result type is the given type.

7 *References:* attribute 4.1.4, box delimiter 12.1.2, designator 6.1, entry 9.5, function 6.5, generic actual type 12.3, generic formal subprogram 12.1.3, generic formal type 12.1.2, generic instantiation 12.3, matching generic actual parameter 12.3, name 4.1, parameter and result type profile 6.3, subprogram 6, subprogram specification 6.1, subtype 3.3, visibility 8.3

12.4 Example of a Generic Package

The following example provides a possible formulation of stacks by means of a generic package.   1
The size of each stack and the type of the stack elements are provided as generic parameters.

```
generic                                                                            2
  SIZE : POSITIVE;
  type ITEM is private;
package STACK is
  procedure PUSH (E : in    ITEM);
  procedure POP  (E : out  ITEM);
  OVERFLOW, UNDERFLOW : exception;
end STACK;

package body STACK is

  type TABLE is array (POSITIVE range <>) of ITEM;
  SPACE  : TABLE(1 .. SIZE);
  INDEX  : NATURAL := 0;

  procedure PUSH(E : in ITEM) is
  begin
    if INDEX >= SIZE then
      raise OVERFLOW;
    end if;
    INDEX := INDEX + 1;
    SPACE(INDEX) := E;
  end PUSH;

  procedure POP(E : out ITEM) is
  begin
    if INDEX = 0 then
      raise UNDERFLOW;
    end if;
    E := SPACE(INDEX);
    INDEX := INDEX - 1;
  end POP;

end STACK;
```

Instances of this generic package can be obtained as follows: 3

```
package STACK_INT   is new STACK(SIZE => 200, ITEM => INTEGER);
package STACK_BOOL  is new STACK(100, BOOLEAN);
```

Thereafter, the procedures of the instantiated packages can be called as follows: 4

```
STACK_INT.PUSH(N);
STACK_BOOL.PUSH(TRUE);
```

5   Alternatively, a generic formulation of the type STACK can be given as follows (package body omitted):

```
generic
    type ITEM is private;
package ON_STACKS is
    type STACK(SIZE : POSITIVE) is limited private;
    procedure PUSH (S : in out STACK; E : in    ITEM);
    procedure POP  (S : in out STACK; E : out   ITEM);
    OVERFLOW, UNDERFLOW : exception;
private
    type TABLE is array (POSITIVE range <>) of ITEM;
    type STACK(SIZE : POSITIVE) is
        record
            SPACE  : TABLE(1 .. SIZE);
            INDEX  : NATURAL := 0;
        end record;
end;
```

6   In order to use such a package, an instantiation must be created and thereafter stacks of the corresponding type can be declared:

```
declare
    package STACK_REAL is new ON_STACKS(REAL); use STACK_REAL;
    S : STACK(100);
begin
    ...
    PUSH(S, 2.54);
    ...
end;
```

13. Representation Clauses and Implementation-Dependent Features

This chapter describes representation clauses, certain implementation-dependent features, and other features that are used in system programming. 1

13.1 Representation Clauses

Representation clauses specify how the types of the language are to be mapped onto the underlying machine. They can be provided to give more efficient representation or to interface with features that are outside the domain of the language (for example, peripheral hardware). 1

```
representation_clause ::=
    type_representation_clause | address_clause
```
2

```
type_representation_clause ::= length_clause
    | enumeration_representation_clause | record_representation_clause
```

A type representation clause applies either to a type or to a *first named subtype* (that is, to a subtype declared by a type declaration, the base type being therefore anonymous). Such a representation clause applies to all objects that have this type or this first named subtype. At most one enumeration or record representation clause is allowed for a given type: an enumeration representation clause is only allowed for an enumeration type; a record representation clause, only for a record type. (On the other hand, more than one length clause can be provided for a given type; moreover, both a length clause and an enumeration or record representation clause can be provided.) A length clause is the only form of representation clause allowed for a type derived from a parent type that has (user-defined) derivable subprograms. 3

An address clause applies either to an object; to a subprogram, package, or task unit; or to an entry. At most one address clause is allowed for any of these entities. 4

A representation clause and the declaration of the entity to which the clause applies must both occur immediately within the same declarative part, package specification, or task specification; the declaration must occur before the clause. In the absence of a representation clause for a given declaration, a default representation of this declaration is determined by the implementation. Such a default determination occurs no later than the end of the immediately enclosing declarative part, package specification, or task specification. For a declaration given in a declarative part, this default determination occurs before any enclosed body. 5

In the case of a type, certain occurrences of its name imply that the representation of the type must already have been determined. Consequently these occurrences force the default determination of any aspect of the representation not already determined by a prior type representation clause. This default determination is also forced by similar occurrences of the name of a subtype of the type, or of the name of any type or subtype that has subcomponents of the type. A forcing occurrence is any occurrence other than in a type or subtype declaration, a subprogram specification, an entry declaration, a deferred constant declaration, a pragma, or a representation clause for the type itself. In any case, an occurrence within an expression is always forcing. 6

13-1

7   A representation clause for a given entity must not appear after an occurrence of the name of the entity if this occurrence forces a default determination of representation for the entity.

8   Similar restrictions exist for address clauses. For an object, any occurrence of its name (after the object declaration) is a forcing occurrence. For a subprogram, package, task unit, or entry, any occurrence of a representation attribute of such an entity is a forcing occurrence.

9   The effect of the elaboration of a representation clause is to define the corresponding aspects of the representation.

10   The interpretation of some of the expressions that appear in representation clauses is implementation-dependent, for example, expressions specifying addresses. An implementation may limit its acceptance of representation clauses to those that can be handled simply by the underlying hardware. If a representation clause is accepted by an implementation, the compiler must guarantee that the net effect of the program is not changed by the presence of the clause, except for address clauses and for parts of the program that interrogate representation attributes. If a program contains a representation clause that is not accepted, the program is illegal. For each implementation, the allowed representation clauses, and the conventions used for implementation-dependent expressions, must be documented in Appendix F of the reference manual.

11   Whereas a representation clause is used to impose certain characteristics of the mapping of an entity onto the underlying machine, pragmas can be used to provide an implementation with criteria for its selection of such a mapping. The pragma PACK specifies that storage minimization should be the main criterion when selecting the representation of a record or array type. Its form is as follows:

   pragma PACK (*type*_simple_name);

12   Packing means that gaps between the storage areas allocated to consecutive components should be minimized. It need not, however, affect the mapping of each component onto storage. This mapping can itself be influenced by a pragma (or controlled by a representation clause) for the component or component type. The position of a PACK pragma, and the restrictions on the named type, are governed by the same rules as for a representation clause; in particular, the pragma must appear before any use of a representation attribute of the packed entity.

13   The pragma PACK is the only language-defined representation pragma. Additional representation pragmas may be provided by an implementation; these must be documented in Appendix F. (In contrast to representation clauses, a pragma that is not accepted by the implementation is ignored.)

Note:

14   No representation clause is allowed for a generic formal type.

15   *References:* address clause 13.5, allow 1.6, body 3.9, component 3.3, declaration 3.1, declarative part 3.9, default expression 3.2.1, deferred constant declaration 7.4, derivable subprogram 3.4, derived type 3.4, entity 3.1, entry 9.5, enumeration representation clause 13.3, expression 4.4, generic formal type 12.1.2, illegal 1.6, length clause 13.2, must 1.6, name 4.1, object 3.2, occur immediately within 8.1, package 7, package specification 7.1, parent type 3.4, pragma 2.8, record representation clause 13.4, representation attribute 13.7.2 13.7.3, subcomponent 3.3, subprogram 6, subtype 3.3, subtype declaration 3.3.2, task specification 9.1, task unit 9, type 3.3, type declaration 3.3.1

13.2 Length Clauses

A length clause specifies an amount of storage associated with a type.   1

    length_clause ::= **for** attribute **use** simple_expression;   2

The expression must be of some numeric type and is evaluated during the elaboration of the length   3
clause (unless it is a static expression). The prefix of the attribute must denote either a type or a
first named subtype. The prefix is called T in what follows. The only allowed attribute designators
in a length clause are SIZE, STORAGE_SIZE, and SMALL. The effect of the length clause depends
on the attribute designator:

(a) Size specification: T'SIZE   4

    The expression must be a static expression of some integer type. The value of the expression   5
    specifies an upper bound for the number of bits to be allocated to objects of the type or first
    named subtype T. The size specification must allow for enough storage space to accom-
    modate every allowable value of these objects. A size specification for a composite type may
    affect the size of the gaps between the storage areas allocated to consecutive components.
    On the other hand, it need not affect the size of the storage area allocated to each component.

    The size specification is only allowed if the constraints on T and on its subcomponents (if any)   6
    are static. In the case of an unconstrained array type, the index subtypes must also be static.

(b) Specification of collection size: T'STORAGE_SIZE   7

    The prefix T must denote an access type. The expression must be of some integer type (but   8
    need not be static); its value specifies the number of storage units to be reserved for the col-
    lection, that is, the storage space needed to contain all objects designated by values of the
    access type and by values of other types derived from the access type, directly or indirectly.
    This form of length clause is not allowed for a type derived from an access type.

(c) Specification of storage for a task activation: T'STORAGE_SIZE   9

    The prefix T must denote a task type. The expression must be of some integer type (but need   10
    not be static); its value specifies the number of storage units to be reserved for an activation
    (not the code) of a task of the type.

(d) Specification of *small* for a fixed point type: T'SMALL   11

    The prefix T must denote the first named subtype of a fixed point type. The expression must   12
    be a static expression of some real type; its value must not be greater than the delta of the
    first named subtype. The effect of the length clause is to use this value of *small* for the
    representation of values of the fixed point base type. (The length clause thereby also affects
    the amount of storage for objects that have this type.)

Notes:

A size specification is allowed for an access, task, or fixed point type, whether or not another form 13
of length clause is also given for the type.

14 What is considered to be part of the storage reserved for a collection or for an activation of a task is implementation-dependent. The control afforded by length clauses is therefore relative to the implementation conventions. For example, the language does not define whether the storage reserved for an activation of a task includes any storage needed for the collection associated with an access type declared within the task body. Neither does it define the method of allocation for objects denoted by values of an access type. For example, the space allocated could be on a stack; alternatively, a general dynamic allocation scheme or fixed storage could be used.

15 The objects allocated in a collection need not have the same size if the designated type is an unconstrained array type or an unconstrained type with discriminants. Note also that the allocator itself may require some space for internal tables and links. Hence a length clause for the collection of an access type does not always give precise control over the maximum number of allocated objects.

16 *Examples:*

```
--  assumed declarations:

type MEDIUM is range  0 .. 65000;
type SHORT  is delta  0.01  range -100.0  .. 100.0;
type DEGREE is delta  0.1   range -360.0  .. 360.0;

BYTE : constant := 8;
PAGE : constant := 2000;

--  length clauses:

for COLOR'SIZE     use 1*BYTE;  --  see 3.5.1
for MEDIUM'SIZE    use 2*BYTE;
for SHORT'SIZE     use 15;

for CAR_NAME'STORAGE_SIZE use  --  approximately 2000 cars
        2000*((CAR'SIZE/SYSTEM.STORAGE_UNIT) + 1);

for KEYBOARD_DRIVER'STORAGE_SIZE use 1*PAGE;

for DEGREE'SMALL use 360.0/2**(SYSTEM.STORAGE_UNIT - 1);
```

17 *Notes on the examples:*

In the length clause for SHORT, fifteen bits is the minimum necessary, since the type definition requires SHORT'SMALL = 2.0**(-7) and SHORT'MANTISSA = 14. The length clause for DEGREE forces the model numbers to exactly span the range of the type.

18 *References:* access type 3.8, allocator 4.8, allow 1.6, array type 3.6, attribute 4.1.4, collection 3.8, composite type 3.3, constraint 3.3, delta of a fixed point type 3.5.9, derived type 3.4, designate 3.8, elaboration 3.9, entity 3.1, evaluation 4.5, expression 4.4, first named subtype 13.1, fixed point type 3.5.9, index subtype 3.6, integer type 3.5.4, must 1.6, numeric type 3.5, object 3.2, real type 3.5.6, record type 3.7, small of a fixed point type 3.5.10, static constraint 4.9, static expression 4.9, static subtype 4.9, storage unit 13.7, subcomponent 3.3, system package 13.7, task 9, task activation 9.3, task specification 9.1, task type 9.2, type 3.3, unconstrained array type 3.6

13.3 Enumeration Representation Clauses

An enumeration representation clause specifies the internal codes for the literals of the enumeration type that is named in the clause.   1

enumeration_representation_clause ::= **for** *type*_simple_name **use** aggregate;   2

The aggregate used to specify this mapping is written as a one-dimensional aggregate, for which the index subtype is the enumeration type and the component type is *universal_integer*.   3

All literals of the enumeration type must be provided with distinct integer codes, and all choices and component values given in the aggregate must be static. The integer codes specified for the enumeration type must satisfy the predefined ordering relation of the type.   4

Example: 5

```
type MIX_CODE is (ADD, SUB, MUL, LDA, STA, STZ);

for MIX_CODE use
   (ADD => 1, SUB => 2, MUL => 3, LDA => 8, STA => 24, STZ => 33);
```

Notes:

The attributes SUCC, PRED, and POS are defined even for enumeration types with a noncontiguous representation; their definition corresponds to the (logical) type declaration and is not affected by the enumeration representation clause. In the example, because of the need to avoid the omitted values, these functions are likely to be less efficiently implemented than they could be in the absence of a representation clause. Similar considerations apply when such types are used for indexing.   6

References: aggregate 4.3, array aggregate 4.3.2, array type 3.6, attribute of an enumeration type 3.5.5, choice 3.7.3, component 3.3, enumeration literal 3.5.1, enumeration type 3.5.1, function 6.5, index 3.6, index subtype 3.6, literal 4.2, ordering relation of an enumeration type 3.5.1, representation clause 13.1, simple name 4.1, static expression 4.9, type 3.3, type declaration 3.3.1, universal_integer type 3.5.4   7

13.4 Record Representation Clauses

A record representation clause specifies the storage representation of records, that is, the order, position, and size of record components (including discriminants, if any).   1

```
record_representation_clause ::=
   for type_simple_name use
      record [alignment_clause]
         {component_clause}
      end record;
```
   2

alignment_clause ::= **at mod** *static*_simple_expression;

component_clause ::=
   *component*_name **at** *static*_simple_expression **range** *static*_range;

3   The simple expression given after the reserved words **at mod** in an alignment clause, or after the reserved word **at** in a component clause, must be a static expression of some integer type. If the bounds of the range of a component clause are defined by simple expressions, then each bound of the range must be defined by a static expression of some integer type, but the two bounds need not have the same integer type.

4   An alignment clause forces each record of the given type to be allocated at a starting address that is a multiple of the value of the given expression (that is, the address modulo the expression must be zero). An implementation may place restrictions on the allowable alignments.

5   A component clause specifies the *storage place* of a component, relative to the start of the record. The integer defined by the static expression of a component clause is a relative address expressed in storage units. The range defines the bit positions of the storage place, relative to the storage unit. The first storage unit of a record is numbered zero. The first bit of a storage unit is numbered zero. The ordering of bits in a storage unit is machine-dependent and may extend to adjacent storage units. (For a specific machine, the size in bits of a storage unit is given by the configuration-dependent named number SYSTEM.STORAGE_UNIT.) Whether a component is allowed to overlap a storage boundary, and if so, how, is implementation-defined.

6   At most one component clause is allowed for each component of the record type, including for each discriminant (component clauses may be given for some, all, or none of the components). If no component clause is given for a component, then the choice of the storage place for the component is left to the compiler. If component clauses are given for all components, the record representation clause completely specifies the representation of the record type and must be obeyed exactly by the compiler.

7   Storage places within a record variant must not overlap, but overlap of the storage for distinct variants is allowed. Each component clause must allow for enough storage space to accommodate every allowable value of the component. A component clause is only allowed for a component if any constraint on this component or on any of its subcomponents is static.

8   An implementation may generate names that denote implementation-dependent components (for example, one containing the offset of another component). Such implementation-dependent names can be used in record representation clauses (these names need not be simple names; for example, they could be implementation-dependent attributes).

9   *Example:*

```
WORD : constant := 4;  --  storage unit is byte, 4 bytes per word

type STATE         is (A, M, W, P);
type MODE          is (FIX, DEC, EXP, SIGNIF);

type BYTE_MASK   is array (0 .. 7) of BOOLEAN;
type STATE_MASK  is array (STATE) of BOOLEAN;
type MODE_MASK   is array (MODE) of BOOLEAN;

type PROGRAM_STATUS_WORD is
  record
      SYSTEM_MASK      : BYTE_MASK;
      PROTECTION_KEY   : INTEGER range 0 .. 3;
      MACHINE_STATE    : STATE_MASK;
      INTERRUPT_CAUSE  : INTERRUPTION_CODE;
      ILC              : INTEGER range 0 .. 3;
      CC               : INTEGER range 0 .. 3;
      PROGRAM_MASK     : MODE_MASK;
      INST_ADDRESS     : ADDRESS;
  end record;
```

13.4 Record Representation Clauses

```
for PROGRAM_STATUS_WORD use
    record at mod 8;
        SYSTEM_MASK         at 0*WORD   range 0    .. 7;
        PROTECTION_KEY      at 0*WORD   range 10   .. 11;    -- bits 8, 9 unused
        MACHINE_STATE       at 0*WORD   range 12   .. 15;
        INTERRUPT_CAUSE     at 0*WORD   range 16   .. 31;
        ILC                 at 1*WORD   range 0    .. 1;     -- second word
        CC                  at 1*WORD   range 2    .. 3;
        PROGRAM_MASK        at 1*WORD   range 4    .. 7;
        INST_ADDRESS        at 1*WORD   range 8    .. 31;
    end record;

for PROGRAM_STATUS_WORD'SIZE use 8*SYSTEM.STORAGE_UNIT;
```

Note on the example:

The record representation clause defines the record layout. The length clause guarantees that   10
exactly eight storage units are used.

References: allow 1.6, attribute 4.1.4, constant 3.2.1, constraint 3.3, discriminant 3.7.1, integer type 3.5.4, must   11
1.6, named number 3.2, range 3.5, record component 3.7, record type 3.7, simple expression 4.4, simple name 4.1,
static constraint 4.9, static expression 4.9, storage unit 13.7, subcomponent 3.3, system package 13.7, variant 3.7.3

13.5 Address Clauses

An address clause specifies a required address in storage for an entity.   1

    address_clause ::= **for** simple_name **use at** simple_expression;   2

The expression given after the reserved word **at** must be of the type ADDRESS defined in the   3
package SYSTEM (see 13.7); this package must be named by a with clause that applies to the
compilation unit in which the address clause occurs. The conventions that define the interpretation
of a value of the type ADDRESS as an address, as an interrupt level, or whatever it may be, are
implementation-dependent. The allowed nature of the simple name and the meaning of the corresponding address are as follows:

(a) Name of an object: the address is that required for the object (variable or constant).   4

(b) Name of a subprogram, package, or task unit: the address is that required for the machine   5
    code associated with the body of the program unit.

(c) Name of a single entry: the address specifies a hardware interrupt to which the single entry is   6
    to be linked.

If the simple name is that of a single task, the address clause is understood to refer to the task unit   7
and not to the task object. In all cases, the address clause is only legal if exactly one declaration
with this identifier occurs earlier, immediately within the same declarative part, package specification, or task specification. A name declared by a renaming declaration is not allowed as the simple
name.

Address clauses should not be used to achieve overlays of objects or overlays of program units.   8
Nor should a given interrupt be linked to more than one entry. Any program using address clauses
to achieve such effects is erroneous.

9   *Example:*

   for CONTROL **use at** 16#0020#;   --   assuming that SYSTEM.ADDRESS is an integer type

   Notes:

10   The above rules imply that if two subprograms overload each other and are visible at a given point, an address clause for any of them is not legal at this point. Similarly if a task specification declares entries that overload each other, they cannot be interrupt entries. The syntax does not allow an address clause for a library unit. An implementation may provide pragmas for the specification of program overlays.

11   *References:* address predefined type 13.7, apply 10.1.1, compilation unit 10.1, constant 3.2.1, entity 3.1, entry 9.5, erroneous 1.6, expression 4.4, library unit 10.1, name 4.1, object 3.2, package 7, pragma 2.8, program unit 6, reserved word 2.9, simple expression 4.4, simple name 4.1, subprogram 6, subprogram body 6.3, system package 13.7, task body 9.1, task object 9.2, task unit 9, type 3.3, variable 3.2.1, with clause 10.1.1

13.5.1 Interrupts

1   An address clause given for an entry associates the entry with some device that may cause an interrupt; such an entry is referred to in this section as an *interrupt entry*. If control information is supplied upon an interrupt, it is passed to an associated interrupt entry as one or more parameters of mode **in**; only parameters of this mode are allowed.

2   An interrupt acts as an entry call issued by a hardware task whose priority is higher than the priority of the main program, and also higher than the priority of any user-defined task (that is, any task whose type is declared by a task unit in the program). The entry call may be an ordinary entry call, a timed entry call, or a conditional entry call, depending on the kind of interrupt and on the implementation.

3   If a select statement contains both a terminate alternative and an accept alternative for an interrupt entry, then an implementation may impose further requirements for the selection of the terminate alternative in addition to those given in section 9.4.

4   *Example:*

```
task INTERRUPT_HANDLER is
   entry DONE;
   for DONE use at 16#40#;   -- assuming that SYSTEM.ADDRESS is an integer type
end INTERRUPT_HANDLER;
```

   Notes:

5   Interrupt entry calls need only have the semantics described above; they may be implemented by having the hardware directly execute the appropriate accept statements.

6   Queued interrupts correspond to ordinary entry calls. Interrupts that are lost if not immediately processed correspond to conditional entry calls. It is a consequence of the priority rules that an accept statement executed in response to an interrupt takes precedence over ordinary, user-defined tasks, and can be executed without first invoking a scheduling action.

One of the possible effects of an address clause for an interrupt entry is to specify the priority of   7
the interrupt (directly or indirectly). Direct calls to an interrupt entry are allowed.

References: accept alternative 9.7.1, accept statement 9.5, address predefined type 13.7, allow 1.6, conditional   8
entry call 9.7.2, entry 9.5, entry call 9.5, mode 6.1, parameter of a subprogram 6.2, priority of a task 9.8, select alternative 9.7.1, select statement 9.7, system package 13.7, task 9, terminate alternative 9.7.1, timed entry call 9.7.3

13.6 Change of Representation

At most one representation clause is allowed for a given type and a given aspect of its representa-   1
tion. Hence, if an alternative representation is needed, it is necessary to declare a second type,
derived from the first, and to specify a different representation for the second type.

Example: 2

```
--   PACKED_DESCRIPTOR and DESCRIPTOR are two different types
--   with identical characteristics, apart from their representation

type DESCRIPTOR is
   record
      --   components of a descriptor
   end record;

type PACKED_DESCRIPTOR is new DESCRIPTOR;

for PACKED_DESCRIPTOR use
   record
      --   component clauses for some or for all components
   end record;
```

Change of representation can now be accomplished by assignment with explicit type conversions: 3

```
D  : DESCRIPTOR;
P  : PACKED_DESCRIPTOR;

P  := PACKED_DESCRIPTOR(D);   --   pack D
D  := DESCRIPTOR(P);          --   unpack P
```

References: assignment 5.2, derived type 3.4, type 3.3, type conversion 4.6, type declaration 3.1, representation   4
clause 13.1

13.7 The Package System

For each implementation there is a predefined library package called SYSTEM which includes the   1
definitions of certain configuration-dependent characteristics. The specification of the package
SYSTEM is implementation-dependent and must be given in Appendix F. The visible part of this
package must contain at least the following declarations.

2
```
package SYSTEM is
   type ADDRESS  is implementation_defined;
   type NAME     is implementation_defined_enumeration_type;

   SYSTEM_NAME    : constant NAME  := implementation_defined;

   STORAGE_UNIT   : constant := implementation_defined;
   MEMORY_SIZE    : constant := implementation_defined;

   --   System-Dependent Named Numbers:

   MIN_INT        : constant := implementation_defined;
   MAX_INT        : constant := implementation_defined;
   MAX_DIGITS     : constant := implementation_defined;
   MAX_MANTISSA   : constant := implementation_defined;
   FINE_DELTA     : constant := implementation_defined;
   TICK           : constant := implementation_defined;

   --   Other System-Dependent Declarations

   subtype PRIORITY is INTEGER range implementation_defined;

   ...
end SYSTEM ;
```

3 The type ADDRESS is the type of the addresses provided in address clauses; it is also the type of the result delivered by the attribute ADDRESS. Values of the enumeration type NAME are the names of alternative machine configurations handled by the implementation; one of these is the constant SYSTEM_NAME. The named number STORAGE_UNIT is the number of bits per storage unit; the named number MEMORY_SIZE is the number of available storage units in the configuration; these named numbers are of the type *universal_integer*.

4 An alternative form of the package SYSTEM, with given values for any of SYSTEM_NAME, STORAGE_UNIT, and MEMORY_SIZE, can be obtained by means of the corresponding pragmas. These pragmas are only allowed at the start of a compilation, before the first compilation unit (if any) of the compilation.

5 **pragma** SYSTEM_NAME (enumeration_literal);

6 The effect of the above pragma is to use the enumeration literal with the specified identifier for the definition of the constant SYSTEM_NAME. This pragma is only allowed if the specified identifier corresponds to one of the literals of the type NAME.

7 **pragma** STORAGE_UNIT (numeric_literal);

8 The effect of the above pragma is to use the value of the specified numeric literal for the definition of the named number STORAGE_UNIT.

9 **pragma** MEMORY_SIZE (numeric_literal);

10 The effect of the above pragma is to use the value of the specified numeric literal for the definition of the named number MEMORY_SIZE.

The compilation of any of these pragmas causes an implicit recompilation of the package SYSTEM. Consequently any compilation unit that names SYSTEM in its context clause becomes obsolete after this implicit recompilation. An implementation may impose further limitations on the use of these pragmas. For example, an implementation may allow them only at the start of the first compilation, when creating a new program library. 11

Note:

It is a consequence of the visibility rules that a declaration given in the package SYSTEM is not visible in a compilation unit unless this package is mentioned by a with clause that applies (directly or indirectly) to the compilation unit. 12

References: address clause 13.5, apply 10.1.1, attribute 4.1.4, compilation unit 10.1, declaration 3.1, enumeration 13
literal 3.5.1, enumeration type 3.5.1, identifier 2.3, library unit 10.1, must 1.6, named number 3.2, number declaration 3.2.2, numeric literal 2.4, package 7, package specification 7.1, pragma 2.8, program library 10.1, type 3.3, visibility 8.3, visible part 7.2, with clause 10.1.1

13.7.1 System-Dependent Named Numbers

Within the package SYSTEM, the following named numbers are declared. The numbers 1
FINE_DELTA and TICK are of the type *universal_real*; the others are of the type *universal_integer*.

MIN_INT   The smallest (most negative) value of all predefined integer types. 2

MAX_INT   The largest (most positive) value of all predefined integer types. 3

MAX_DIGITS   The largest value allowed for the number of significant decimal digits in a 4
floating point constraint.

MAX_MANTISSA The largest possible number of binary digits in the mantissa of model numbers 5
of a fixed point subtype.

FINE_DELTA   The smallest delta allowed in a fixed point constraint that has the range con- 6
straint -1.0 .. 1.0.

TICK   The basic clock period, in seconds. 7

References: allow 1.6, delta of a fixed point constraint 3.5.9, fixed point constraint 3.5.9, floating point constraint 8
3.5.7, integer type 3.5.4, model number 3.5.6, named number 3.2, package 7, range constraint 3.5, system package 13.7, type 3.3, universal_integer type 3.5.4, universal_real type 3.5.6

13.7.2 Representation Attributes

1   The values of certain implementation-dependent characteristics can be obtained by interrogating appropriate *representation attributes*. These attributes are described below.

2   For any object, program unit, label, or entry X:

3   X'ADDRESS   Yields the address of the first of the storage units allocated to X. For a sub-program, package, task unit or label, this value refers to the machine code associated with the corresponding body or statement. For an entry for which an address clause has been given, the value refers to the corresponding hardware interrupt. The value of this attribute is of the type ADDRESS defined in the package SYSTEM.

4   For any type or subtype X, or for any object X:

5   X'SIZE   Applied to an object, yields the number of bits allocated to hold the object. Applied to a type or subtype, yields the minimum number of bits that is needed by the implementation to hold any possible object of this type or sub-type. The value of this attribute is of the type *universal_integer*.

6   For the above two representation attributes, if the prefix is the name of a function, the attribute is understood to be an attribute of the function (not of the result of calling the function). Similarly, if the type of the prefix is an access type, the attribute is understood to be an attribute of the prefix (not of the designated object: attributes of the latter can be written with a prefix ending with the reserved word **all**).

7   For any component C of a record object R:

8   R.C'POSITION   Yields the offset, from the start of the first storage unit occupied by the record, of the first of the storage units occupied by C. This offset is measured in storage units. The value of this attribute is of the type *universal_integer*.

9   R.C'FIRST_BIT   Yields the offset, from the start of the first of the storage units occupied by C, of the first bit occupied by C. This offset is measured in bits. The value of this attribute is of the type *universal_integer*.

10   R.C'LAST_BIT   Yields the offset, from the start of the first of the storage units occupied by C, of the last bit occupied by C. This offset is measured in bits. The value of this attribute is of the type *universal_integer*.

11   For any access type or subtype T:

12   T'STORAGE_SIZE   Yields the total number of storage units reserved for the collection associated with the base type of T. The value of this attribute is of the type *universal_integer*.

13   For any task type or task object T:

14   T'STORAGE_SIZE   Yields the number of storage units reserved for each activation of a task of the type T or for the activation of the task object T. The value of this attribute is of the type *universal_integer*.

Notes:

For a task object X, the attribute X'SIZE gives the number of bits used to hold the object X, whereas X'STORAGE_SIZE gives the number of storage units allocated for the activation of the task designated by X. For a formal parameter X, if parameter passing is achieved by copy, then the attribute X'ADDRESS yields the address of the local copy; if parameter passing is by reference, then the address is that of the actual parameter.

15

References: access subtype 3.8, access type 3.8, activation 9.3, actual parameter 6.2, address clause 13.5, address predefined type 13.7, attribute 4.1.4, base type 3.3, collection 3.8, component 3.3, entry 9.5, formal parameter 6.1 6.2, label 5.1, object 3.2, package 7, package body 7.1, parameter passing 6.2, program unit 6, record object 3.7, statement 5, storage unit 13.7, subprogram 6, subprogram body 6.3, subtype 3.3, system predefined package 13.7, task 9, task body 9.1, task object 9.2, task type 9.2, task unit 9, type 3.3, universal_integer type 3.5.4

16

13.7.3 Representation Attributes of Real Types

For every real type or subtype T, the following machine-dependent attributes are defined, which are not related to the model numbers. Programs using these attributes may thereby exploit properties that go beyond the minimal properties associated with the numeric type (see section 4.5.7 for the rules defining the accuracy of operations with real operands). Precautions must therefore be taken when using these machine-dependent attributes if portability is to be ensured.

1

For both floating point and fixed point types:

2

T'MACHINE_ROUNDS   Yields the value TRUE if every predefined arithmetic operation on values of the base type of T either returns an exact result or performs rounding;   yields the value FALSE otherwise. The value of this attribute is of the predefined type BOOLEAN.

3

T'MACHINE_OVERFLOWS   Yields the value TRUE if every predefined operation on values of the base type of T either provides a correct result, or raises the exception NUMERIC_ERROR in overflow situations (see 4.5.7);   yields the value FALSE otherwise. The value of this attribute is of the predefined type BOOLEAN.

4

For floating point types, the following attributes provide characteristics of the underlying machine representation, in terms of the canonical form defined in section 3.5.7:

5

T'MACHINE_RADIX   Yields the value of the *radix* used by the machine representation of the base type of T. The value of this attribute is of the type *universal_integer.*

6

T'MACHINE_MANTISSA   Yields the number of digits in the *mantissa* for the machine representation of the base type of T (the digits are extended digits in the range 0 to T'MACHINE_RADIX -1). The value of this attribute is of the type *universal_integer.*

7

T'MACHINE_EMAX   Yields the largest value of *exponent* for the machine representation of the base type of T. The value of this attribute is of the type *universal_integer.*

8

T'MACHINE_EMIN   Yields the smallest (most negative) value of *exponent* for the machine representation of the base type of T. The value of this attribute is of the type *universal_integer.*

9

Note:

10   For many machines the largest machine representable number of type F is almost

(F'MACHINE_RADIX)**(F'MACHINE_EMAX),

11   and the smallest positive representable number is

F'MACHINE_RADIX ** (F'MACHINE_EMIN - 1)

12   *References:* arithmetic operator 4.5, attribute 4.1.4, base type 3.3, boolean predefined type 3.5.3, false boolean value 3.5.3, fixed point type 3.5.9, floating point type 3.5.7, model number 3.5.6, numeric type 3.5, numeric_error exception 11.1, predefined operation 3.3.3, radix 3.5.7, real type 3.5.6, subtype 3.3, true boolean value 3.5.3, type 3.3, universal_integer type 3.5.4

13.8 Machine Code Insertions

1   A machine code insertion can be achieved by a call to a procedure whose sequence of statements contains code statements.

2   code_statement ::= type_mark'*record*_aggregate;

3   A code statement is only allowed in the sequence of statements of a procedure body. If a procedure body contains code statements, then within this procedure body the only allowed form of statement is a code statement (labeled or not), the only allowed declarative items are use clauses, and no exception handler is allowed (comments and pragmas are allowed as usual).

4   Each machine instruction appears as a record aggregate of a record type that defines the corresponding instruction. The base type of the type mark of a code statement must be declared within the predefined library package called MACHINE_CODE; this package must be named by a with clause that applies to the compilation unit in which the code statement occurs. An implementation is not required to provide such a package.

5   An implementation is allowed to impose further restrictions on the record aggregates allowed in code statements. For example, it may require that expressions contained in such aggregates be static expressions.

6   An implementation may provide machine-dependent pragmas specifying register conventions and calling conventions. Such pragmas must be documented in Appendix F.

7   *Example:*

```
M : MASK;
procedure SET_MASK; pragma INLINE(SET_MASK);

procedure SET_MASK is
   use MACHINE_CODE;
begin
   SI_FORMAT'(CODE => SSM, B => M'BASE_REG, D => M'DISP);
   -- M'BASE_REG and M'DISP are implementation-specific predefined attributes
end;
```

References: allow 1.6, apply 10.1.1, comment 2.7, compilation unit 10.1, declarative item 3.9, exception handler   8
11.2, inline pragma 6.3.2, labeled statement 5.1, library unit 10.1, package 7, pragma 2.8, procedure 6 6.1, procedure
body 6.3, record aggregate 4.3.1, record type 3.7, sequence of statements 5.1, statement 5, static expression 4.9, use
clause 8.4, with clause 10.1.1

13.9 Interface to Other Languages

A subprogram written in another language can be called from an Ada program provided that all   1
communication is achieved via parameters and function results. A pragma of the form

>   **pragma** INTERFACE (*language_*name, *subprogram_*name);   2

must be given for each such subprogram; a subprogram name is allowed to stand for several   3
overloaded subprograms. This pragma is allowed at the place of a declarative item, and must apply
in this case to a subprogram declared by an earlier declarative item of the same declarative part or
package specification. The pragma is also allowed for a library unit; in this case the pragma must
appear   after the subprogram declaration, and before any subsequent compilation unit. The
pragma specifies the other language (and thereby the calling conventions) and informs the compiler that an object module will be supplied for the corresponding subprogram. A body is not
allowed for such a subprogram (not even in the form of a body stub) since the instructions of the
subprogram are written in another language.

This capability need not be provided by all implementations. An implementation may place   4
restrictions on the allowable forms and places of parameters and calls.

Example:
   5

```
package FORT_LIB is
    function SQRT (X : FLOAT) return FLOAT;
    function EXP   (X : FLOAT) return FLOAT;
private
    pragma INTERFACE(FORTRAN, SQRT);
    pragma INTERFACE(FORTRAN, EXP);
end FORT_LIB;
```

Notes:

The conventions used by other language processors that call Ada programs are not part of the Ada   6
language definition. Such conventions must be defined by these other language processors.

The pragma INTERFACE is not defined for generic subprograms.   7

References: allow 1.6, body stub 10.2, compilation unit 10.1, declaration 3.1, declarative item 3.9, declarative part   8
3.9, function result 6.5, library unit 10.1, must 1.6, name 4.1, overloaded subprogram 6.6, package specification 7.1,
parameter of a subprogram 6.2, pragma 2.8, subprogram 6, subprogram body 6.3, subprogram call 6.4, subprogram
declaration 6.1

13.10 Unchecked Programming

1   The predefined generic library subprograms UNCHECKED_DEALLOCATION and UNCHECKED_CONVERSION are used for unchecked storage deallocation and for unchecked type conversions.

2
```
generic
    type OBJECT  is limited private;
    type NAME    is access OBJECT;
procedure UNCHECKED_DEALLOCATION(X : in out NAME);
```

3
```
generic
    type SOURCE is limited private;
    type TARGET is limited private;
function UNCHECKED_CONVERSION(S : SOURCE) return TARGET;
```

4   *References:* generic subprogram 12.1, library unit 10.1, type 3.3

13.10.1 Unchecked Storage Deallocation

1   Unchecked storage deallocation of an object designated by a value of an access type is achieved by a call of a procedure that is obtained by instantiation of the generic procedure UNCHECKED_DEALLOCATION. For example:

```
procedure FREE is new UNCHECKED_DEALLOCATION (object_type_name, access_type_name);
```

2   Such a FREE procedure has the following effect:

3   (a) after executing FREE (X), the value of X is **null**;

4   (b) FREE (X), when X is already equal to **null**, has no effect;

5   (c) FREE (X), when X is not equal to **null**, is an indication that the object designated by X is no longer required, and that the storage it occupies is to be reclaimed.

6   If X and Y designate the same object, then accessing this object through Y is erroneous if this access is performed (or attempted) after the call FREE (X); the effect of each such access is not defined by the language.

7   *Notes:*

7   It is a consequence of the visibility rules that the generic procedure UNCHECKED_DEALLOCATION is not visible in a compilation unit unless this generic procedure is mentioned by a with clause that applies to the compilation unit.

8   If X designates a task object, the call FREE (X) has no effect on the task designated by the value of this task object. The same holds for any subcomponent of the object designated by X, if this subcomponent is a task object.

9   *References:* access type 3.8, apply 10.1.1, compilation unit 10.1, designate 3.8 9.1, erroneous 1.6, generic instantiation 12.3, generic procedure 12.1, generic unit 12, library unit 10.1, null access value 3.8, object 3.2, procedure 6, procedure call 6.4, subcomponent 3.3, task 9, task object 9.2, visibility 8.3, with clause 10.1.1

13.10.2 Unchecked Type Conversions

An unchecked type conversion can be achieved by a call of a function that is obtained by instantiation of the generic function UNCHECKED_CONVERSION. [1]

The effect of an unchecked conversion is to return the (uninterpreted) parameter value as a value [2] of the target type, that is, the bit pattern defining the source value is returned unchanged as the bit pattern defining a value of the target type. An implementation may place restrictions on unchecked conversions, for example, restrictions depending on the respective sizes of objects of the source and target type. Such restrictions must be documented in appendix F.

Whenever unchecked conversions are used, it is the programmer's responsibility to ensure that [3] these conversions maintain the properties that are guaranteed by the language for objects of the target type. Programs that violate these properties by means of unchecked conversions are erroneous.

Note:

It is a consequence of the visibility rules that the generic function UNCHECKED_CONVERSION is [4] not visible in a compilation unit unless this generic function is mentioned by a with clause that applies to the compilation unit.

References: apply 10.1.1, compilation unit 10.1, erroneous 1.6, generic function 12.1, instantiation 12.3, parameter [5] of a subprogram 6.2, type 3.3, with clause 10.1.1

14. Input-Output

Input-output is provided in the language by means of predefined packages. The generic packages SEQUENTIAL_IO and DIRECT_IO define input-output operations applicable to files containing elements of a given type. Additional operations for text input-output are supplied in the package TEXT_IO. The package IO_EXCEPTIONS defines the exceptions needed by the above three packages. Finally, a package LOW_LEVEL_IO is provided for direct control of peripheral devices.

References: direct_io package 14.2 14.2.4, io_exceptions package 14.5, low_level_io package 14.6, sequential_io package 14.2 14.2.2, text_io package 14.3

14.1 External Files and File Objects

Values input from the external environment of the program, or output to the environment, are considered to occupy *external files*. An external file can be anything external to the program that can produce a value to be read or receive a value to be written. An external file is identified by a string (the *name*). A second string (the *form*) gives further system-dependent characteristics that may be associated with the file, such as the physical organization or access rights. The conventions governing the interpretation of such strings must be documented in Appendix F.

Input and output operations are expressed as operations on objects of some *file type*, rather than directly in terms of the external files. In the remainder of this chapter, the term *file* is always used to refer to a file object; the term *external file* is used otherwise. The values transferred for a given file must all be of one type.

Input-output for sequential files of values of a single element type is defined by means of the generic package SEQUENTIAL_IO. The skeleton of this package is given below.

```
with IO_EXCEPTIONS;
generic
   type ELEMENT_TYPE is private;
package SEQUENTIAL_IO is
   type FILE_TYPE is limited private;

   type FILE_MODE is (IN_FILE, OUT_FILE);
   ...
   procedure OPEN (FILE : in out FILE_TYPE; ...);
   ...
   procedure READ  (FILE : in FILE_TYPE; ITEM : out ELEMENT_TYPE);
   procedure WRITE (FILE : in FILE_TYPE; ITEM : in ELEMENT_TYPE);
   ...
end SEQUENTIAL_IO;
```

In order to define sequential input-output for a given element type, an instantiation of this generic unit, with the given type as actual parameter, must be declared. The resulting package contains the declaration of a file type (called FILE_TYPE) for files of such elements, as well as the operations applicable to these files, such as the OPEN, READ, and WRITE procedures.

Input-output for direct access files is likewise defined by a generic package called DIRECT_IO. Input-output in human-readable form is defined by the (nongeneric) package TEXT_IO.

Before input or output operations can be performed on a file, the file must first be associated with an external file. While such an association is in effect, the file is said to be *open*, and otherwise the file is said to be *closed*.

The language does not define what happens to external files after the completion of the main program (in particular, if corresponding files have not been closed). The effect of input-output for access types is implementation-dependent.

An open file has a *current mode*, which is a value of one of the enumeration types

```
type FILE_MODE is (IN_FILE, INOUT_FILE, OUT_FILE);   --  for DIRECT_IO
type FILE_MODE is (IN_FILE, OUT_FILE);               --  for SEQUENTIAL_IO and TEXT_IO
```

These values correspond respectively to the cases where only reading, both reading and writing, or only writing are to be performed. The mode of a file can be changed.

Several file management operations are common to the three input-output packages. These operations are described in section 14.2.1 for sequential and direct files. Any additional effects concerning text input-output are described in section 14.3.1.

The exceptions that can be raised by a call of an input-output subprogram are all defined in the package IO_EXCEPTIONS; the situations in which they can be raised are described, either following the description of the subprogram (and in section 14.4), or in Appendix F in the case of error situations that are implementation-dependent.

Notes:

Each instantiation of the generic packages SEQUENTIAL_IO and DIRECT_IO declares a different type FILE_TYPE; in the case of TEXT_IO, the type FILE_TYPE is unique.

A bidirectional device can often be modeled as two sequential files associated with the device, one of mode IN_FILE, and one of mode OUT_FILE. An implementation may restrict the number of files that may be associated with a given external file. The effect of sharing an external file in this way by several file objects is implementation-dependent.

References: create procedure 14.2.1, current index 14.2, current size 14.2, delete procedure 14.2.1, direct access 14.2, direct file procedure 14.2, direct_io package 14.1 14.2, enumeration type 3.5.1, exception 11, file mode 14.2.3, generic instantiation 12.3, index 14.2, input file 14.2.2, io_exceptions package 14.5, open file 14.1, open procedure 14.2.1, output file 14.2.2, read procedure 14.2.4, sequential access 14.2, sequential file 14.2, sequential input-output 14.2.2, sequential_io package 14.2 14.2.2, string 3.6.3, text_io package 14.3, write procedure 14.2.4

14.2 Sequential and Direct Files

Two kinds of access to external files are defined: *sequential access* and *direct access*. The corresponding file types and the associated operations are provided by the generic packages SEQUENTIAL_IO and DIRECT_IO. A file object to be used for sequential access is called a *sequential file*, and one to be used for direct access is called a *direct file*.

For sequential access, the file is viewed as a sequence of values that are transferred in the order of their appearance (as produced by the program or by the environment). When the file is opened, transfer starts from the beginning of the file.

For direct access, the file is viewed as a set of elements occupying consecutive positions in linear order; a value can be transferred to or from an element of the file at any selected position. The position of an element is specified by its *index*, which is a number, greater than zero, of the implementation-defined integer type COUNT. The first element, if any, has index one; the index of the last element, if any, is called the *current size*; the current size is zero if there are no elements. The current size is a property of the external file.

An open direct file has a *current index*, which is the index that will be used by the next read or write operation. When a direct file is opened, the current index is set to one. The current index of a direct file is a property of a file object, not of an external file.

All three file modes are allowed for direct files. The only allowed modes for sequential files are the modes IN_FILE and OUT_FILE.

References: count type 14.3, file mode 14.1, in_file 14.1, out_file 14.1

14.2.1 File Management

The procedures and functions described in this section provide for the control of external files; their declarations are repeated in each of the three packages for sequential, direct, and text input-output. For text input-output, the procedures CREATE, OPEN, and RESET have additional effects described in section 14.3.1.

```
procedure CREATE(FILE : in out FILE_TYPE;
               MODE : in FILE_MODE := default_mode;
               NAME : in STRING := "";
               FORM : in STRING := "");
```

Establishes a new external file, with the given name and form, and associates this external file with the given file. The given file is left open. The current mode of the given file is set to the given access mode. The default access mode is the mode OUT_FILE for sequential and text input-output; it is the mode INOUT_FILE for direct input-output. For direct access, the size of the created file is implementation-dependent. A null string for NAME specifies an external file that is not accessible after the completion of the main program (a temporary file). A null string for FORM specifies the use of the default options of the implementation for the external file.

The exception STATUS_ERROR is raised if the given file is already open. The exception NAME_ERROR is raised if the string given as NAME does not allow the identification of an external file. The exception USE_ERROR is raised if, for the specified mode, the environment does not support creation of an external file with the given name (in the absence of NAME_ERROR) and form.

```
procedure OPEN( FILE : in out FILE_TYPE;
             MODE : in FILE_MODE;
             NAME : in STRING;
             FORM : in STRING := "");
```

Associates the given file with an existing external file having the given name and form, and sets the current mode of the given file to the given mode. The given file is left open.

The exception STATUS_ERROR is raised if the given file is already open. The exception NAME_ERROR is raised if the string given as NAME does not allow the identification of an external file; in particular, this exception is raised if no external file with the given name exists. The exception USE_ERROR is raised if, for the specified mode, the environment does not support opening for an external file with the given name (in the absence of NAME_ERROR) and form.

procedure CLOSE(FILE : **in out** FILE_TYPE);

> Severs the association between the given file and its associated external file. The given file is left closed.

> The exception STATUS_ERROR is raised if the given file is not open.

procedure DELETE(FILE : **in out** FILE_TYPE);

> Deletes the external file associated with the given file. The given file is closed, and the external file ceases to exist.

> The exception STATUS_ERROR is raised if the given file is not open. The exception USE_ERROR is raised if (as fully defined in Appendix F) deletion of the external file is not supported by the environment.

procedure RESET(FILE : **in out** FILE_TYPE; MODE : **in** FILE_MODE);
procedure RESET(FILE : **in out** FILE_TYPE);

> Resets the given file so that reading from or writing to its elements can be restarted from the beginning of the file; in particular, for direct access this means that the current index is set to one. If a MODE parameter is supplied, the current mode of the given file is set to the given mode.

> The exception STATUS_ERROR is raised if the file is not open. The exception USE_ERROR is raised if the environment does not support resetting for the external file and, also, if the environment does not support resetting to the specified mode for the external file.

function MODE(FILE : **in** FILE_TYPE) **return** FILE_MODE;

> Returns the current mode of the given file.

> The exception STATUS_ERROR is raised if the file is not open.

function NAME(FILE : **in** FILE_TYPE) **return** STRING;

> Returns a string which uniquely identifies the external file currently associated with the given file (and may thus be used in an OPEN operation). If an environment allows alternative specifications of the name (for example, abbreviations), the string returned by the function should correspond to a full specification of the name.

> The exception STATUS_ERROR is raised if the given file is not open.

function FORM(FILE : **in** FILE_TYPE) **return** STRING;

> Returns the form string for the external file currently associated with the given file. If an environment allows alternative specifications of the form (for example, abbreviations using default options), the string returned by the function should correspond to a full specification (that is, it should indicate explicitly all options selected, including default options).

> The exception STATUS_ERROR is raised if the given file is not open.

function IS_OPEN(FILE : **in** FILE_TYPE) **return** BOOLEAN;

> Returns TRUE if the file is open (that is, if it is associated with an external file), otherwise returns FALSE.

References: current mode 14.1, current size 14.1, closed file 14.1, direct access 14.2, external file 14.1, file 14.1, file_mode type 14.1, file_type type 14.1, form string 14.1, inout_file 14.2.4, mode 14.1, name string 14.1, name_error exception 14.4, open file 14.1, out_file 14.1, status_error exception 14.4, use_error exception 14.4

14.2.2 Sequential Input-Output

The operations available for sequential input and output are described in this section. The exception STATUS_ERROR is raised if any of these operations is attempted for a file that is not open.

procedure READ(FILE : **in** FILE_TYPE; ITEM : **out** ELEMENT_TYPE);

> Operates on a file of mode IN_FILE. Reads an element from the given file, and returns the value of this element in the ITEM parameter.

> The exception MODE_ERROR is raised if the mode is not IN_FILE. The exception END_ERROR is raised if no more elements can be read from the given file. The exception DATA_ERROR is raised if the element read cannot be interpreted as a value of the type ELEMENT_TYPE; however, an implementation is allowed to omit this check if performing the check is too complex.

procedure WRITE(FILE : **in** FILE_TYPE; ITEM : **in** ELEMENT_TYPE);

> Operates on a file of mode OUT_FILE. Writes the value of ITEM to the given file.

> The exception MODE_ERROR is raised if the mode is not OUT_FILE. The exception USE_ERROR is raised if the capacity of the external file is exceeded.

function END_OF_FILE(FILE : **in** FILE_TYPE) **return** BOOLEAN;

> Operates on a file of mode IN_FILE. Returns TRUE if no more elements can be read from the given file; otherwise returns FALSE.

> The exception MODE_ERROR is raised if the mode is not IN_FILE.

References: data_error exception 14.4, element 14.1, element_type 14.1, end_error exception 14.4, external file 14.1, file 14.1, file mode 14.1, file_type 14.1, in_file 14.1, mode_error exception 14.4, out_file 14.1, status_error exception 14.4, use_error exception 14.4

14.2.3 Specification of the Package Sequential_IO

```
with IO_EXCEPTIONS;
generic
   type ELEMENT_TYPE is private;
package SEQUENTIAL_IO is

   type FILE_TYPE   is limited private;

   type FILE_MODE is (IN_FILE, OUT_FILE);


   -- File management

   procedure CREATE (FILE    : in out FILE_TYPE;
                     MODE : in FILE_MODE := OUT_FILE;
                     NAME : in STRING := "";
                     FORM : in STRING := "");

   procedure OPEN   (FILE    : in out FILE_TYPE;
                     MODE : in FILE_MODE;
                     NAME : in STRING;
                     FORM : in STRING := "");

   procedure CLOSE  (FILE : in out FILE_TYPE);
   procedure DELETE (FILE : in out FILE_TYPE);
   procedure RESET  (FILE : in out FILE_TYPE; MODE : in FILE_MODE);
   procedure RESET  (FILE : in out FILE_TYPE);

   function MODE    (FILE : in FILE_TYPE) return FILE_MODE;
   function NAME    (FILE : in FILE_TYPE) return STRING;
   function FORM    (FILE : in FILE_TYPE) return STRING;

   function IS_OPEN (FILE : in FILE_TYPE) return BOOLEAN;

   -- Input and output operations

   procedure READ   (FILE : in FILE_TYPE; ITEM : out ELEMENT_TYPE);
   procedure WRITE  (FILE : in FILE_TYPE; ITEM : in ELEMENT_TYPE);

   function END_OF_FILE(FILE : in FILE_TYPE) return BOOLEAN;

   -- Exceptions

   STATUS_ERROR : exception renames IO_EXCEPTIONS.STATUS_ERROR;
   MODE_ERROR   : exception renames IO_EXCEPTIONS.MODE_ERROR;
   NAME_ERROR   : exception renames IO_EXCEPTIONS.NAME_ERROR;
   USE_ERROR    : exception renames IO_EXCEPTIONS.USE_ERROR;
   DEVICE_ERROR : exception renames IO_EXCEPTIONS.DEVICE_ERROR;
   END_ERROR    : exception renames IO_EXCEPTIONS.END_ERROR;
   DATA_ERROR   : exception renames IO_EXCEPTIONS.DATA_ERROR;

private
   -- implementation-dependent
end SEQUENTIAL_IO;
```

References: close procedure 14.2.1, create procedure 14.2.1, data_error exception 14.4, delete procedure 14.2.1, device_error exception 14.4, end_error exception 14.4, end_of_file function 14.2.2, file_mode 14.1, file_type 14.1, form function 14.2.1, in_file 14.1, io_exceptions 14.4, is_open function 14.2.1, mode function 14.2.1, mode_error exception 14.4, name function 14.2.1, name_error exception 14.4, open procedure 14.2.1, out_file 14.1, read procedure 14.2.2, reset procedure 14.2.1, sequential_io package 14.2 14.2.2, status_error exception 14.4, use_error exception 14.4, write procedure 14.2.2,

14.2.4 Direct Input-Output

The operations available for direct input and output are described in this section. The exception STATUS_ERROR is raised if any of these operations is attempted for a file that is not open.

> **procedure** READ(FILE : **in** FILE_TYPE; ITEM : **out** ELEMENT_TYPE;
> FROM : **in** POSITIVE_COUNT);
> **procedure** READ(FILE : **in** FILE_TYPE; ITEM : **out** ELEMENT_TYPE);

Operates on a file of mode IN_FILE or INOUT_FILE. In the case of the first form, sets the current index of the given file to the index value given by the parameter FROM. Then (for both forms) returns, in the parameter ITEM, the value of the element whose position in the given file is specified by the current index of the file; finally, increases the current index by one.

The exception MODE_ERROR is raised if the mode of the given file is OUT_FILE. The exception END_ERROR is raised if the index to be used exceeds the size of the external file. The exception DATA_ERROR is raised if the element read cannot be interpreted as a value of the type ELEMENT_TYPE; however, an implementation is allowed to omit this check if performing the check is too complex.

> **procedure** WRITE(FILE : **in** FILE_TYPE; ITEM : **in** ELEMENT_TYPE;
> TO   : **in** POSITIVE_COUNT);
> **procedure** WRITE(FILE : **in** FILE_TYPE; ITEM : **in** ELEMENT_TYPE);

Operates on a file of mode INOUT_FILE or OUT_FILE. In the case of the first form, sets the index of the given file to the index value given by the parameter TO. Then (for both forms) gives the value of the parameter ITEM to the element whose position in the given file is specified by the current index of the file; finally, increases the current index by one.

The exception MODE_ERROR is raised if the mode of the given file is IN_FILE. The exception USE_ERROR is raised if the capacity of the external file is exceeded.

> **procedure** SET_INDEX(FILE : **in** FILE_TYPE; TO : **in** POSITIVE_COUNT);

Operates on a file of any mode. Sets the current index of the given file to the given index value (which may exceed the current size of the file).

> **function** INDEX(FILE : **in** FILE_TYPE) **return** POSITIVE_COUNT;

Operates on a file of any mode. Returns the current index of the given file.

function SIZE(FILE : **in** FILE_TYPE) **return** COUNT;

>   Operates on a file of any mode. Returns the current size of the external file that is associated with the given file.

function END_OF_FILE(FILE : **in** FILE_TYPE) **return** BOOLEAN;

>   Operates on a file of mode IN_FILE or INOUT_FILE. Returns TRUE if the current index exceeds the size of the external file; otherwise returns FALSE.

>   The exception MODE_ERROR is raised if the mode of the given file is OUT_FILE.

References: count type 14.2, current index 14.2, current size 14.2, data_error exception 14.4, element 14.1, element_type 14.1, end_error exception 14.4, external file 14.1, file 14.1, file mode 14.1, file_type 14.1, in_file 14.1, index 14.2, inout_file 14.1, mode_error exception 14.4, open file 14.1, positive_count 14.3, status_error exception 14.4, use_error exception 14.4

14.2.5 Specification of the Package Direct_IO

```
with IO_EXCEPTIONS;
generic
   type ELEMENT_TYPE is private;
package DIRECT_IO is

   type FILE_TYPE   is limited private;

   type     FILE_MODE is (IN_FILE, INOUT_FILE, OUT_FILE);
   type     COUNT      is range 0 .. implementation_defined;
   subtype POSITIVE_COUNT is COUNT range 1 .. COUNT'LAST;


   -- File management

   procedure CREATE ( FILE   : in out FILE_TYPE;
                      MODE : in FILE_MODE := INOUT_FILE;
                      NAME : in STRING := "";
                      FORM : in STRING := "");

   procedure OPEN     ( FILE   : in out FILE_TYPE;
                        MODE : in FILE_MODE;
                        NAME : in STRING;
                        FORM : in STRING := "");

   procedure CLOSE  (FILE : in out FILE_TYPE);
   procedure DELETE (FILE : in out FILE_TYPE);
   procedure RESET  (FILE : in out FILE_TYPE; MODE : in FILE_MODE);
   procedure RESET  (FILE : in out FILE_TYPE);

   function MODE    (FILE : in FILE_TYPE) return FILE_MODE;
   function NAME    (FILE : in FILE_TYPE) return STRING;
   function FORM    (FILE : in FILE_TYPE) return STRING;

   function IS_OPEN (FILE : in FILE_TYPE) return BOOLEAN;
```

-- Input and output operations

procedure READ (FILE : **in** FILE_TYPE; ITEM : **out** ELEMENT_TYPE; FROM : POSITIVE_CO
procedure READ (FILE : **in** FILE_TYPE; ITEM : **out** ELEMENT_TYPE);

procedure WRITE (FILE : **in** FILE_TYPE; ITEM : **in** ELEMENT_TYPE; TO : POSITIVE_COUN
procedure WRITE (FILE : **in** FILE_TYPE; ITEM : **in** ELEMENT_TYPE);

procedure SET_INDEX(FILE : **in** FILE_TYPE; TO : **in** POSITIVE_COUNT);

function INDEX(FILE : **in** FILE_TYPE) **return** POSITIVE_COUNT;
function SIZE (FILE : **in** FILE_TYPE) **return** COUNT;

function END_OF_FILE (FILE : **in** FILE_TYPE) **return** BOOLEAN;

-- Exceptions

STATUS_ERROR : **exception renames** IO_EXCEPTIONS.STATUS_ERROR;
MODE_ERROR : **exception renames** IO_EXCEPTIONS.MODE_ERROR;
NAME_ERROR : **exception renames** IO_EXCEPTIONS.NAME_ERROR;
USE_ERROR : **exception renames** IO_EXCEPTIONS.USE_ERROR;
DEVICE_ERROR : **exception renames** IO_EXCEPTIONS.DEVICE_ERROR;
END_ERROR : **exception renames** IO_EXCEPTIONS.END_ERROR;
DATA_ERROR : **exception renames** IO_EXCEPTIONS.DATA_ERROR;

private
-- implementation-dependent
end DIRECT_IO;

References close procedure 14.2.1, count type 14.2, create procedure 14.2.1, data_error exception 14.4, default_mode 14.2.5, delete procedure 14.2.1, device_error exception 14.4, element_type 14.2.4, end_error exception 14.4, end_of_file function 14.2.4, file_mode 14.2.5, file_type 14.2.4, form function 14.2.1, in_file 14.2.4, index function 14.2.4, inout_file 14.2.4 14.2.1, io_exceptions package 14.4, is_open function 14.2.1, mode function 14.2.1, mode_error exception 14.4, name function 14.2.1, name_error exception 14.4, open procedure 14.2.1, out_file 14.2.1, read procedure 14.2.4, set_index procedure 14.2.4, size function 14.2.4, status_error exception 14.4, use_error exception 14.4, write procedure 14.2.4 14.2.1

14.3 Text Input-Output

This section describes the package TEXT_IO, which provides facilities for input and output in human-readable form. Each file is read or written sequentially, as a sequence of characters grouped into lines, and as a sequence of lines grouped into pages. The specification of the package is given below in section 14.3.10.

The facilities for file management given above, in sections 14.2.1 and 14.2.2, are available for text input-output. In place of READ and WRITE, however, there are procedures GET and PUT that input values of suitable types from text files, and output values to them. These values are provided to the PUT procedures, and returned by the GET procedures, in a parameter ITEM. Several overloaded procedures of these names exist, for different types of ITEM. These GET procedures analyze the input sequences of characters as lexical elements (see Chapter 2) and return the corresponding values; the PUT procedures output the given values as appropriate lexical elements. Procedures GET and PUT are also available that input and output individual characters treated as character values rather than as lexical elements.

In addition to the procedures GET and PUT for numeric and enumeration types of ITEM that operate on text files, analogous procedures are provided that read from and write to a parameter of type STRING. These procedures perform the same analysis and composition of character sequences as their counterparts which have a file parameter.

For all GET and PUT procedures that operate on text files, and for many other subprograms, there are forms with and without a file parameter. Each such GET procedure operates on an input file, and each such PUT procedure operates on an output file. If no file is specified, a default input file or a default output file is used.

At the beginning of program execution the default input and output files are the so-called standard input file and standard output file. These files are open, have respectively the current modes IN_FILE and OUT_FILE, and are associated with two implementation-defined external files. Procedures are provided to change the current default input file and the current default output file.

From a logical point of view, a text file is a sequence of pages, a page is a sequence of lines, and a line is a sequence of characters; the end of a line is marked by a *line terminator*; the end of a page is marked by the combination of a line terminator immediately followed by a *page terminator*; and the end of a file is marked by the combination of a line terminator immediately followed by a page terminator and then a *file terminator*. Terminators are generated during output; either by calls of procedures provided expressly for that purpose; or implicitly as part of other operations, for example, when a bounded line length, a bounded page length, or both, have been specified for a file.

The actual nature of terminators is not defined by the language and hence depends on the implementation. Although terminators are recognized or generated by certain of the procedures that follow, they are not necessarily implemented as characters or as sequences of characters. Whether they are characters (and if so which ones) in any particular implementation need not concern a user who neither explicitly outputs nor explicitly inputs control characters. The effect of input or output of control characters (other than horizontal tabulation) is not defined by the language.

The characters of a line are numbered, starting from one; the number of a character is called its *column number*. For a line terminator, a column number is also defined: it is one more than the number of characters in the line. The lines of a page, and the pages of a file, are similarly numbered. The *current column number* is the column number of the next character or line terminator to be transferred. The *current line number* is the number of the current line. The *current page number* is the number of the current page. These numbers are values of the subtype POSITIVE_COUNT of the type COUNT (by convention, the value zero of the type COUNT is used to indicate special conditions).

```
type COUNT is range 0 .. implementation_defined;
subtype POSITIVE_COUNT is COUNT range 1 .. COUNT'LAST;
```

For an output file, a *maximum line length* can be specified and a *maximum page length* can be specified. If a value to be output cannot fit on the current line, for a specified maximum line length, then a new line is automatically started before the value is output; if, further, this new line cannot fit on the current page, for a specified maximum page length, then a new page is automatically started before the value is output. Functions are provided to determine the maximum line length and the maximum page length. When a file is opened with mode OUT_FILE, both values are zero: by convention, this means that the line lengths and page lengths are unbounded. (Consequently, output consists of a single line if the subprograms for explicit control of line and page structure are not used.) The constant UNBOUNDED is provided for this purpose.

References: count type 14.3.10, default current input file 14.3.2, default current output file 14.3.2, external file 14.1, file 14.1, get procedure 14.3.5, in_file 14.1, out_file 14.1, put procedure 14.3.5, read 14.2.2, sequential access 14.1, standard input file 14.3.2, standard output file 14.3.2

14.3.1 File Management

The only allowed file modes for text files are the modes IN_FILE and OUT_FILE. The subprograms given in section 14.2.1 for the control of external files, and the function END_OF_FILE given in section 14.2.2 for sequential input-output, are also available for text files. There is also a version of END_OF_FILE that refers to the current default input file. For text files, the procedures have the following additional effects:

- For the procedures CREATE and OPEN: After opening a file with mode OUT_FILE, the page length and line length are unbounded (both have the conventional value zero). After opening a file with mode IN_FILE or OUT_FILE, the current column, current line, and current page numbers are set to one.

- For the procedure CLOSE: If the file has the current mode OUT_FILE, has the effect of calling NEW_PAGE, unless the current page is already terminated; then outputs a file terminator.

- For the procedure RESET: If the file has the current mode OUT_FILE, has the effect of calling NEW_PAGE, unless the current page is already terminated; then outputs a file terminator. If the new file mode is OUT_FILE, the page and line lengths are unbounded. For all modes, the current column, line, and page numbers are set to one.

The exception MODE_ERROR is raised by the procedure RESET upon an attempt to change the mode of a file that is either the current default input file, or the current default output file.

References: create procedure 14.2.1, current column number 14.3, current default input file 14.3, current line number 14.3, current page number 14.3, end_of_file 14.3, external file 14.1, file 14.1, file mode 14.1, file terminator 14.3, in_file 14.1, line length 14.3, mode_error exception 14.4, open procedure 14.2.1, out_file 14.1, page length 14.3, reset procedure 14.2.1

14.3.2 Default Input and Output Files

The following subprograms provide for the control of the particular default files that are used when a file parameter is omitted from a GET, PUT or other operation of text input-output described below.

> **procedure** SET_INPUT(FILE : **in** FILE_TYPE);
>
> > Operates on a file of mode IN_FILE. Sets the current default input file to FILE.
> >
> > The exception STATUS_ERROR is raised if the given file is not open. The exception MODE_ERROR is raised if the mode of the given file is not IN_FILE.

> **procedure** SET_OUTPUT(FILE : **in** FILE_TYPE);
>
> > Operates on a file of mode OUT_FILE. Sets the current default output file to FILE.
> >
> > The exception STATUS_ERROR is raised if the given file is not open. The exception MODE_ERROR is raised if the mode of the given file is not OUT_FILE.

function STANDARD_INPUT **return** FILE_TYPE;

> Returns the standard input file (see 14.3).

function STANDARD_OUTPUT **return** FILE_TYPE;

> Returns the standard output file (see 14.3).

function CURRENT_INPUT **return** FILE_TYPE;

> Returns the current default input file.

function CURRENT_OUTPUT **return** FILE_TYPE;

> Returns the current default output file.

Note:

The standard input and the standard output files cannot be opened, closed, reset, or deleted, because the parameter FILE of the corresponding procedures has the mode **in out**.

References: current default file 14.3, default file 14.3, file_type 14.1, get procedure 14.3.5, mode_error exception 14.4, put procedure 14.3.5, status_error exception 14.4

14.3.3 Specification of Line and Page Lengths

The subprograms described in this section are concerned with the line and page structure of a file of mode OUT_FILE. They operate either on the file given as the first parameter, or, in the absence of such a file parameter, on the current default output file. They provide for output of text with a specified maximum line length or page length. In these cases, line and page terminators are output implicitly and automatically when needed. When line and page lengths are unbounded (that is, when they have the conventional value zero), as in the case of a newly opened file, new lines and new pages are only started when explicitly called for.

In all cases, the exception STATUS_ERROR is raised if the file to be used is not open; the exception MODE_ERROR is raised if the mode of the file is not OUT_FILE.

procedure SET_LINE_LENGTH(FILE   : **in** FILE_TYPE; TO : **in** COUNT);
procedure SET_LINE_LENGTH(TO   : **in** COUNT);

> Sets the maximum line length of the specified output file to the number of characters specified by TO. The value zero for TO specifies an unbounded line length.

> The exception USE_ERROR is raised if the specified line length is inappropriate for the associated external file.

procedure SET_PAGE_LENGTH (FILE : **in** FILE_TYPE; TO : **in** COUNT);
procedure SET_PAGE_LENGTH (TO   : **in** COUNT);

Sets the maximum page length of the specified output file to the number of lines specified by TO. The value zero for TO specifies an unbounded page length.

The exception USE_ERROR is raised if the specified page length is inappropriate for the associated external file.

function LINE_LENGTH(FILE : **in** FILE_TYPE) **return** COUNT;
function LINE_LENGTH **return** COUNT;

Returns the maximum line length currently set for the specified output file, or zero if the line length is unbounded.

function PAGE_LENGTH(FILE : **in** FILE_TYPE) **return** COUNT;
function PAGE_LENGTH **return** COUNT;

Returns the maximum page length currently set for the specified output file, or zero if the page length is unbounded.

References: count type 14.3, current default output file 14.3, external file 14.1, file 14.1, file_type 14.1, line 14.3, line length 14.3, line terminator 14.3, maximum line length 14.3, maximum page length 14.3, mode_error exception 14.4, open file 14.1, out_file 14.1, page 14.3, page length 14.3, page terminator 14.3, status_error exception 14.4, unbounded page length 14.3, use_error exception 14.4

14.3.4 Operations on Columns, Lines, and Pages

The subprograms described in this section provide for explicit control of line and page structure; they operate either on the file given as the first parameter, or, in the absence of such a file parameter, on the appropriate (input or output) current default file. The exception STATUS_ERROR is raised by any of these subprograms if the file to be used is not open.

procedure NEW_LINE(FILE : **in** FILE_TYPE; SPACING : **in** POSITIVE_COUNT := 1);
procedure NEW_LINE(SPACING : **in** POSITIVE_COUNT := 1);

Operates on a file of mode OUT_FILE.

For a SPACING of one: Outputs a line terminator and sets the current column number to one. Then increments the current line number by one, except in the case that the current line number is already greater than or equal to the maximum page length, for a bounded page length; in that case a page terminator is output, the current page number is incremented by one, and the current line number is set to one.

For a SPACING greater than one, the above actions are performed SPACING times.

The exception MODE_ERROR is raised if the mode is not OUT_FILE.

```
procedure SKIP_LINE(FILE      : in  FILE_TYPE; SPACING : in  POSITIVE_COUNT := 1);
procedure SKIP_LINE(SPACING  : in  POSITIVE_COUNT := 1);
```

Operates on a file of mode IN_FILE.

For a SPACING of one: Reads and discards all characters until a line terminator has been read, and then sets the current column number to one. If the line terminator is not immediately followed by a page terminator, the current line number is incremented by one. Otherwise, if the line terminator is immediately followed by a page terminator, then the page terminator is skipped, the current page number is incremented by one, and the current line number is set to one.

For a SPACING greater than one, the above actions are performed SPACING times.

The exception MODE_ERROR is raised if the mode is not IN_FILE. The exception END_ERROR is raised if an attempt is made to read a file terminator.

```
function END_OF_LINE(FILE : in  FILE_TYPE) return BOOLEAN;
function END_OF_LINE return BOOLEAN;
```

Operates on a file of mode IN_FILE. Returns TRUE if a line terminator or a file terminator is next; otherwise returns FALSE.

The exception MODE_ERROR is raised if the mode is not IN_FILE.

```
procedure NEW_PAGE(FILE : in  FILE_TYPE);
procedure NEW_PAGE;
```

Operates on a file of mode OUT_FILE. Outputs a line terminator if the current line is not terminated, or if the current page is empty (that is, if the current column and line numbers are both equal to one). Then outputs a page terminator, which terminates the current page. Adds one to the current page number and sets the current column and line numbers to one.

The exception MODE_ERROR is raised if the mode is not OUT_FILE.

```
procedure SKIP_PAGE(FILE : in  FILE_TYPE);
procedure SKIP_PAGE;
```

Operates on a file of mode IN_FILE. Reads and discards all characters and line terminators until a page terminator has been read. Then adds one to the current page number, and sets the current column and line numbers to one.

The exception MODE_ERROR is raised if the mode is not IN_FILE. The exception END_ERROR is raised if an attempt is made to read a file terminator.

function END_OF_PAGE(FILE : **in** FILE_TYPE) **return** BOOLEAN;
function END_OF_PAGE **return** BOOLEAN;

Operates on a file of mode IN_FILE. Returns TRUE if the combination of a line terminator and a page terminator is next, or if a file terminator is next; otherwise returns FALSE.

The exception MODE_ERROR is raised if the mode is not IN_FILE.

function END_OF_FILE(FILE : **in** FILE_TYPE) **return** BOOLEAN;
function END_OF_FILE **return** BOOLEAN;

Operates on a file of mode IN_FILE. Returns TRUE if a file terminator is next, or if the combination of a line, a page, and a file terminator is next; otherwise returns FALSE.

The exception MODE_ERROR is raised if the mode is not IN_FILE.

The following subprograms provide for the control of the current position of reading or writing in a file. In all cases, the default file is the current output file.

procedure SET_COL(FILE : **in** FILE_TYPE; TO : **in** POSITIVE_COUNT);
procedure SET_COL(TO   : **in** POSITIVE_COUNT);

If the file mode is OUT_FILE :

If the value specified by TO is greater than the current column number, outputs spaces, adding one to the current column number after each space, until the current column number equals the specified value. If the value specified by TO is equal to the current column number, there is no effect. If the value specified by TO is less than the current column number, has the effect of calling NEW_LINE (with a spacing of one), then outputs (TO - 1) spaces, and sets the current column number to the specified value.

The exception LAYOUT_ERROR is raised if the value specified by TO exceeds LINE_LENGTH when the line length is bounded (that is, when it does not have the conventional value zero).

If the file mode is IN_FILE :

Reads (and discards) individual characters, line terminators, and page terminators, until the next character to be read has a column number that equals the value specified by TO ; there is no effect if the current column number already equals this value. Each transfer of a character or terminator maintains the current column, line, and page numbers in the same way as a GET procedure (see 14.3.5). (Short lines will be skipped until a line is reached that has a character at the specified column position.)

The exception END_ERROR is raised if an attempt is made to read a file terminator.

procedure SET_LINE(FILE   : **in** FILE_TYPE; TO : **in** POSITIVE_COUNT);
procedure SET_LINE(TO   : **in** POSITIVE_COUNT);

If the file mode is OUT_FILE :

If the value specified by TO is greater than the current line number, has the effect of repeatedly calling NEW_LINE (with a spacing of one), until the current line number equals the specified value. If the value specified by TO is equal to the current line number, there is no effect. If the value specified by TO is less than the current line number, has the effect of calling NEW_PAGE followed by a call of NEW_LINE with a spacing equal to (TO - 1).

The exception LAYOUT_ERROR is raised if the value specified by TO exceeds PAGE_LENGTH when the page length is bounded (that is, when it does not have the conventional value zero).

If the mode is IN_FILE :

Has the effect of repeatedly calling SKIP_LINE (with a spacing of one), until the current line number equals the value specified by TO ; there is no effect if the current line number already equals this value. (Short pages will be skipped until a page is reached that has a line at the specified line position.)

The exception END_ERROR is raised if an attempt is made to read a file terminator.

function COL(FILE : **in** FILE_TYPE) **return** POSITIVE_COUNT;
function COL **return** POSITIVE_COUNT;

Returns the current column number.

The exception LAYOUT_ERROR is raised if this number exceeds COUNT'LAST.

function LINE(FILE   : **in** FILE_TYPE) **return** POSITIVE_COUNT;
function LINE **return** POSITIVE_COUNT;

Returns the current line number.

The exception LAYOUT_ERROR is raised if this number exceeds COUNT'LAST.

function PAGE(FILE : **in** FILE_TYPE) **return** POSITIVE_COUNT;
function PAGE **return** POSITIVE_COUNT;

Returns the current page number.

The exception LAYOUT_ERROR is raised if this number exceeds COUNT'LAST.

The column number, line number, or page number are allowed to exceed COUNT'LAST (as a consequence of the input or output of sufficiently many characters, lines, or pages). These events do not cause any exception to be raised. However, a call of COL, LINE, or PAGE raises the exception LAYOUT_ERROR if the corresponding number exceeds COUNT'LAST.

14.3.4 Operations on Columns, Lines, and Pages   14-16

Note:

A page terminator is always skipped whenever the preceding line terminator is skipped. An implementation may represent the combination of these terminators by a single character, provided that it is properly recognized at input.

References: current column number 14.3, current default file 14.3, current line number 14.3, current page number 14.3, end_error exception 14.4, file 14.1, file terminator 14.3, get procedure 14.3.5, in_file 14.1, layout_error exception 14.4, line 14.3, line number 14.3, line terminator 14.3, maximum page length 14.3, mode_error exception 14.4, open file 14.1, page 14.3, page length 14.3, page terminator 14.3, positive count 14.3, status_error exception 14.4

14.3.5 Get and Put Procedures

The procedures GET and PUT for items of the types CHARACTER, STRING, numeric types, and enumeration types are described in subsequent sections. Features of these procedures that are common to most of these types are described in this section. The GET and PUT procedures for items of type CHARACTER and STRING deal with individual character values; the GET and PUT procedures for numeric and enumeration types treat the items as lexical elements.

All procedures GET and PUT have forms with a file parameter, written first. Where this parameter is omitted, the appropriate (input or output) current default file is understood to be specified. Each procedure GET operates on a file of mode IN_FILE. Each procedure PUT operates on a file of mode OUT_FILE.

All procedures GET and PUT maintain the current column, line, and page numbers of the specified file: the effect of each of these procedures upon these numbers is the resultant of the effects of individual transfers of characters and of individual output or skipping of terminators. Each transfer of a character adds one to the current column number. Each output of a line terminator sets the current column number to one and adds one to the current line number. Each output of a page terminator sets the current column and line numbers to one and adds one to the current page number. For input, each skipping of a line terminator sets the current column number to one and adds one to the current line number; each skipping of a page terminator sets the current column and line numbers to one and adds one to the current page number. Similar considerations apply to the procedures GET_LINE, PUT_LINE, and SET_COL.

Several GET and PUT procedures, for numeric and enumeration types, have *format* parameters which specify field lengths; these parameters are of the nonnegative subtype FIELD of the type INTEGER.

Input-output of enumeration values uses the syntax of the corresponding lexical elements. Any GET procedure for an enumeration type begins by skipping any leading blanks, or line or page terminators; a *blank* being defined as a space or a horizontal tabulation character. Next, characters are input only so long as the sequence input is an initial sequence of an identifier or of a character literal (in particular, input ceases when a line terminator is encountered). The character or line terminator that causes input to cease remains available for subsequent input.

For a numeric type, the GET procedures have a format parameter called WIDTH. If the value given for this parameter is zero, the GET procedure proceeds in the same manner as for enumeration types, but using the syntax of numeric literals instead of that of enumeration literals. If a nonzero value is given, then exactly WIDTH characters are input, or the characters up to a line terminator, whichever comes first; any skipped leading blanks are included in the count. The syntax used for numeric literals is an extended syntax that allows a leading sign (but no intervening blanks, or line or page terminators).

Any PUT procedure, for an item of a numeric or an enumeration type, outputs the value of the item as a numeric literal, identifier, or character literal, as appropriate. This is preceded by leading spaces if required by the format parameters WIDTH or FORE (as described in later sections), and then a minus sign for a negative value; for an enumeration type, the spaces follow instead of leading. The format given for a PUT procedure is overridden if it is insufficiently wide.

Two further cases arise for PUT procedures for numeric and enumeration types, if the line length of the specified output file is bounded (that is, if it does not have the conventional value zero). If the number of characters to be output does not exceed the maximum line length, but is such that they cannot fit on the current line, starting from the current column, then (in effect) NEW_LINE is called (with a spacing of one) before output of the item. Otherwise, if the number of characters exceeds the maximum line length, then the exception LAYOUT_ERROR is raised and no characters are output.

The exception STATUS_ERROR is raised by any of the procedures GET, GET_LINE, PUT, and PUT_LINE if the file to be used is not open. The exception MODE_ERROR is raised by the procedures GET and GET_LINE if the mode of the file to be used is not IN_FILE; and by the procedures PUT and PUT_LINE, if the mode is not OUT_FILE.

The exception END_ERROR is raised by a GET procedure if an attempt is made to skip a file terminator. The exception DATA_ERROR is raised by a GET procedure if the sequence finally input is not a lexical element corresponding to the type, in particular if no characters were input; for this test, leading blanks are ignored; for an item of a numeric type, when a sign is input, this rule applies to the succeeding numeric literal. The exception LAYOUT_ERROR is raised by a PUT procedure that outputs to a parameter of type STRING, if the length of the actual string is insufficient for the output of the item.

Examples:

In the examples, here and in sections 14.3.7 and 14.3.8, the string quotes and the lower case letter b are not transferred: they are shown only to reveal the layout and spaces.

```
N : INTEGER;
   ...
GET(N);
```

-- Characters at input	Sequence input	Value of N
-- bb-12535b	-12535	-12535
-- bb12_535E1b	12_535E1	125350
-- bb12_535E;	12_535E	(none) DATA_ERROR raised

Example of overridden width parameter:

```
PUT(ITEM => -23, WIDTH => 2);   --   "-23"
```

References: blank 14.3.9, column number 14.3, current default file 14.3, data_error exception 14.4, end_error exception 14.4, file 14.1, fore 14.3.8, get procedure 14.3.6 14.3.7 14.3.8 14.3.9, in_file 14.1, layout_error exception 14.4, line number 14.1, line terminator 14.1, maximum line length 14.3, mode 14.1, mode_error exception 14.4, new_file procedure 14.3.4, out_file 14.1, page number 14.1, page terminator 14.1, put procedure 14.3.6 14.3.7 14.3.8 14.3.9, skipping 14.3.7 14.3.8 14.3.9, status_error exception 14.4, width 14.3.5 14.3.7 14.3.9

14.3.6 Input-Output of Characters and Strings

For an item of type CHARACTER the following procedures are provided:

procedure GET(FILE   : **in** FILE_TYPE; ITEM : **out** CHARACTER);
procedure GET(ITEM : **out** CHARACTER);

> After skipping any line terminators and any page terminators, reads the next character from the specified input file and returns the value of this character in the **out** parameter ITEM .

> The exception END_ERROR is raised if an attempt is made to skip a file terminator.

procedure PUT(FILE   : **in** FILE_TYPE; ITEM : **in** CHARACTER);
procedure PUT(ITEM : **in** CHARACTER);

> If the line length of the specified output file is bounded (that is, does not have the conventional value zero), and the current column number exceeds it, has the effect of calling NEW_LINE with a spacing of one. Then, or otherwise, outputs the given character to the file.

For an item of type STRING the following procedures are provided:

procedure GET(FILE   : **in** FILE_TYPE; ITEM : **out** STRING);
procedure GET(ITEM : **out** STRING);

> Determines the length of the given string and attempts that number of GET operations for successive characters of the string (in particular, no operation is performed if the string is null).

procedure PUT(FILE   : **in** FILE_TYPE; ITEM : **in** STRING);
procedure PUT(ITEM : **in** STRING);

> Determines the length of the given string and attempts that number of PUT operations for successive characters of the string (in particular, no operation is performed if the string is null).

procedure GET_LINE(FILE : **in** FILE_TYPE; ITEM : **out** STRING; LAST : **out** NATURAL);
procedure GET_LINE(ITEM : **out** STRING; LAST : **out** NATURAL);

> Replaces successive characters of the specified string by successive characters read from the specified input file. Reading stops if the end of the line is met, in which case the procedure SKIP_LINE is then called (in effect) with a spacing of one; reading also stops if the end of the string is met. Characters not replaced are left undefined.

> If characters are read, returns in LAST the index value such that ITEM (LAST) is the last character replaced (the index of the first character replaced is ITEM'FIRST). If no characters are read, returns in LAST an index value that is one less than ITEM'FIRST.

> The exception END_ERROR is raised if an attempt is made to skip a file terminator.

Input-Output of Characters and Strings 14.3.6

```
procedure PUT_LINE(FILE : in FILE_TYPE; ITEM : in STRING);
procedure PUT_LINE(ITEM : in STRING);
```

Calls the procedure PUT for the given string, and then the procedure NEW_LINE with a spacing of one.

Notes:

In a literal string parameter of PUT, the enclosing string bracket characters are not output. Each doubled string bracket character in the enclosed string is output as a single string bracket character, as a consequence of the rule for string literals (see 2.6).

A string read by GET or written by PUT can extend over several lines.

References: current column number 14.3, end_error exception 14.4, file 14.1, file terminator 14.3, get procedure 14.3.5, line 14.3, line length 14.3, new_line procedure 14.3.4, page terminator 14.3, put procedure 14.3.4, skipping 14.3.5

14.3.7 Input-Output for Integer Types

The following procedures are defined in the generic package INTEGER_IO. This must be instantiated for the appropriate integer type (indicated by NUM in the specification).

Values are output as decimal or based literals, without underline characters or exponent, and preceded by a minus sign if negative. The format (which includes any leading spaces and minus sign) can be specified by an optional field width parameter. Values of widths of fields in output formats are of the nonnegative integer subtype FIELD. Values of bases are of the integer subtype NUMBER_BASE.

```
subtype NUMBER_BASE is INTEGER range 2 .. 16;
```

The default field width and base to be used by output procedures are defined by the following variables that are declared in the generic package INTEGER_IO :

```
DEFAULT_WIDTH  : FIELD := NUM'WIDTH;
DEFAULT_BASE   : NUMBER_BASE := 10;
```

The following procedures are provided:

```
procedure GET(FILE  : in FILE_TYPE; ITEM : out NUM; WIDTH : in FIELD := 0);
procedure GET(ITEM  : out NUM; WIDTH : in FIELD := 0);
```

If the value of the parameter WIDTH is zero, skips any leading blanks, line terminators, or page terminators, then reads a plus or a minus sign if present, then reads according to the syntax of an integer literal (which may be a based literal). If a nonzero value of WIDTH is supplied, then exactly WIDTH characters are input, or the characters (possibly none) up to a line terminator, whichever comes first; any skipped leading blanks are included in the count.

Returns, in the parameter ITEM, the value of type NUM that corresponds to the sequence input.

The exception DATA_ERROR is raised if the sequence input does not have the required syntax or if the value obtained is not of the subtype NUM.

```
procedure PUT(FILE  : in FILE_TYPE;
              ITEM  : in NUM;
              WIDTH : in FIELD := DEFAULT_WIDTH;
              BASE  : in NUMBER_BASE := DEFAULT_BASE);

procedure PUT(ITEM  : in NUM;
              WIDTH : in FIELD := DEFAULT_WIDTH;
              BASE  : in NUMBER_BASE := DEFAULT_BASE);
```

Outputs the value of the parameter ITEM as an integer literal, with no underlines, no exponent, and no leading zeros (but a single zero for the value zero), and a preceding minus sign for a negative value.

If the resulting sequence of characters to be output has fewer than WIDTH characters, then leading spaces are first output to make up the difference.

Uses the syntax for decimal literal if the parameter BASE has the value ten (either explicitly or through DEFAULT_BASE); otherwise, uses the syntax for based literal, with any letters in upper case.

```
procedure GET(FROM : in STRING; ITEM : out NUM; LAST : out POSITIVE);
```

Reads an integer value from the beginning of the given string, following the same rules as the GET procedure that reads an integer value from a file, but treating the end of the string as a file terminator. Returns, in the parameter ITEM, the value of type NUM that corresponds to the sequence input. Returns in LAST the index value such that FROM (LAST) is the last character read.

The exception DATA_ERROR is raised if the sequence input does not have the required syntax or if the value obtained is not of the subtype NUM.

```
procedure PUT(TO   : out STRING;
              ITEM : in NUM;
              BASE : in NUMBER_BASE := DEFAULT_BASE);
```

Outputs the value of the parameter ITEM to the given string, following the same rule as for output to a file, using the length of the given string as the value for WIDTH.

Examples:

```
package INT_IO is new INTEGER_IO(SMALL_INT); use INT_IO;
-- default format used at instantiation, DEFAULT_WIDTH = 4, DEFAULT_BASE = 10

PUT(126);                              -- "b126"
PUT(-126, 7);                          -- "bbb-126"
PUT(126, WIDTH => 13, BASE => 2);      -- "bbb2#1111110#"
```

References: based literal 2.4.2, blank 14.3.5, data_error exception 14.4, decimal literal 2.4.1, field subtype 14.3.5, file_type 14.1, get procedure 14.3.5, integer_io package 14.3.10, integer literal 2.4, layout_error exception 14.4, line terminator 14.3, put procedure 14.3.5, skipping 14.3.5, width 14.3.5

14.3.8 Input-Output for Real Types

1 The following procedures are defined in the generic packages FLOAT_IO and FIXED_IO, which must be instantiated for the appropriate floating point or fixed point type respectively (indicated by NUM in the specifications).

2 Values are output as decimal literals without underline characters. The format of each value output consists of a FORE field, a decimal point, an AFT field, and (if a nonzero EXP parameter is supplied) the letter E and an EXP field. The two possible formats thus correspond to:

        FORE . AFT

3 and to:

        FORE . AFT E EXP

without any spaces between these fields. The FORE field may include leading spaces, and a minus sign for negative values. The AFT field includes only decimal digits (possibly with trailing zeros). The EXP field includes the sign (plus or minus) and the exponent (possibly with leading zeros).

For floating point types, the default lengths of these fields are defined by the following variables that are declared in the generic package FLOAT_IO :

```
DEFAULT_FORE   : FIELD := 2;
DEFAULT_AFT    : FIELD := NUM'DIGITS-1;
DEFAULT_EXP    : FIELD := 3;
```

For fixed point types, the default lengths of these fields are defined by the following variables that are declared in the generic package FIXED_IO :

```
DEFAULT_FORE   : FIELD := NUM'FORE;
DEFAULT_AFT    : FIELD := NUM'AFT;
DEFAULT_EXP    : FIELD := 0;
```

The following procedures are provided:

```
procedure GET(FILE   : in FILE_TYPE; ITEM : out NUM; WIDTH : in FIELD := 0);
procedure GET(ITEM   : out NUM; WIDTH   : in FIELD := 0);
```

> If the value of the parameter WIDTH is zero, skips any leading blanks, line terminators, or page terminators, then reads a plus or a minus sign if present, then reads according to the syntax of a real literal (which may be a based literal). If a nonzero value of WIDTH is supplied, then exactly WIDTH characters are input, or the characters (possibly none) up to a line terminator, whichever comes first; any skipped leading blanks are included in the count.

> Returns, in the parameter ITEM, the value of type NUM that corresponds to the sequence input.

> The exception DATA_ERROR is raised if the sequence input does not have the required syntax or if the value obtained is not of the subtype NUM.

```
procedure PUT(FILE  : in FILE_TYPE;
              ITEM  : in NUM;
              FORE  : in FIELD := DEFAULT_FORE;
              AFT   : in FIELD := DEFAULT_AFT;
              EXP   : in FIELD := DEFAULT_EXP);

procedure PUT(ITEM  : in NUM;
              FORE  : in FIELD := DEFAULT_FORE;
              AFT   : in FIELD := DEFAULT_AFT;
              EXP   : in FIELD := DEFAULT_EXP);
```

Outputs the value of the parameter ITEM as a decimal literal with the format defined by FORE, AFT and EXP. If the value is negative, a minus sign is included in the integer part. If EXP has the value zero, then the integer part to be output has as many digits as are needed to represent the integer part of the value of ITEM, overriding FORE if necessary, or consists of the digit zero if the value of ITEM has no integer part.

If EXP has a value greater than zero, then the integer part to be output has a single digit, which is nonzero except for the value 0.0 of ITEM.

In both cases, however, if the integer part to be output has fewer than FORE characters, including any minus sign, then leading spaces are first output to make up the difference. The number of digits of the fractional part is given by AFT, or is one if AFT equals zero. The value is rounded; a value of exactly one half in the last place may be rounded either up or down.

If EXP has the value zero, there is no exponent part. If EXP has a value greater than zero, then the exponent part to be output has as many digits as are needed to represent the exponent part of the value of ITEM (for which a single digit integer part is used), and includes an initial sign (plus or minus). If the exponent part to be output has fewer than EXP characters, including the sign, then leading zeros precede the digits, to make up the difference. For the value 0.0 of ITEM, the exponent has the value zero.

```
procedure GET(FROM : in STRING; ITEM : out NUM; LAST : out POSITIVE);
```

Reads a real value from the beginning of the given string, following the same rule as the GET procedure that reads a real value from a file, but treating the end of the string as a file terminator. Returns, in the parameter ITEM, the value of type NUM that corresponds to the sequence input. Returns in LAST the index value such that FROM(LAST) is the last character read.

The exception DATA_ERROR is raised if the sequence input does not have the required syntax, or if the value obtained is not of the subtype NUM.

```
procedure PUT(TO   : out STRING;
              ITEM : in NUM;
              AFT  : in FIELD   := DEFAULT_AFT;
              EXP  : in INTEGER := DEFAULT_EXP);
```

Outputs the value of the parameter ITEM to the given string, following the same rule as for output to a file, using a value for FORE such that the sequence of characters output exactly fills the string, including any leading spaces.

Input-Output for Real Types 14.3.8

Examples:

```
package REAL_IO is new FLOAT_IO(REAL); use REAL_IO;
-- default format used at instantiation, DEFAULT_EXP = 3

X : REAL := -123.4567;   --   digits 8        (see 3.5.7)

PUT(X); -- default format                     "-1.2345670E+02"
PUT(X, FORE => 5, AFT => 3, EXP => 2);    --  "bbb-1.235E+2"
PUT(X, 5, 3, 0);                          --  "b-123.457"
```

Note:

For an item with a positive value, if output to a string exactly fills the string without leading spaces, then output of the corresponding negative value will raise LAYOUT_ERROR.

References: aft attribute 3.5.10, based literal 2.4.2, blank 14.3.5, data_error exception 14.3.5, decimal literal 2.4.1, field subtype 14.3.5, file_type 14.1, fixed_io package 14.3.10, floating_io package 14.3.10, fore attribute 3.5.10, get procedure 14.3.5, layout_error 14.3.5, line terminator 14.3.5, put procedure 14.3.5, real literal 2.4, skipping 14.3.5, width 14.3.5

14.3.9 Input-Output for Enumeration Types

The following procedures are defined in the generic package ENUMERATION_IO, which must be instantiated for the appropriate enumeration type (indicated by ENUM in the specification).

Values are output using either upper or lower case letters for identifiers. This is specified by the parameter SET, which is of the enumeration type TYPE_SET.

```
type TYPE_SET is (LOWER_CASE, UPPER_CASE);
```

The format (which includes any trailing spaces) can be specified by an optional field width parameter. The default field width and letter case are defined by the following variables that are declared in the generic package ENUMERATION_IO:

```
DEFAULT_WIDTH   : FIELD := 0;
DEFAULT_SETTING : TYPE_SET := UPPER_CASE;
```

The following procedures are provided:

```
procedure GET(FILE  : in FILE_TYPE; ITEM : out ENUM);
procedure GET(ITEM  : out ENUM);
```

> After skipping any leading blanks, line terminators, or page terminators, reads an identifier according to the syntax of this lexical element (lower and upper case being considered equivalent), or a character literal according to the syntax of this lexical element (including the apostrophes). Returns, in the parameter ITEM, the value of type ENUM that corresponds to the sequence input.

> The exception DATA_ERROR is raised if the sequence input does not have the required syntax, or if the identifier or character literal does not correspond to a value of the subtype ENUM.

```
procedure PUT( FILE   : in  FILE_TYPE;
             ITEM   : in  ENUM;
             WIDTH  : in  FIELD := DEFAULT_WIDTH;
             SET    : in  TYPE_SET := DEFAULT_SETTING);

procedure PUT( ITEM   : in  ENUM;
             WIDTH  : in  FIELD := DEFAULT_WIDTH;
             SET    : in  TYPE_SET := DEFAULT_SETTING);
```

Outputs the value of the parameter ITEM as an enumeration literal (either an identifier or a character literal). The optional parameter SET indicates whether lower case or upper case is used for identifiers; it has no effect for character literals. If the sequence of characters produced has fewer than WIDTH characters, then trailing spaces are finally output to make up the difference.

```
procedure GET( FROM : in  STRING; ITEM : out ENUM; LAST : out POSITIVE);
```

Reads an enumeration value from the beginning of the given string, following the same rule as the GET procedure that reads an enumeration value from a file, but treating the end of the string as a file terminator. Returns, in the parameter ITEM, the value of type ENUM that corresponds to the sequence input. Returns in LAST the index value such that FROM (LAST) is the last character read.

The exception DATA_ERROR is raised if the sequence input does not have the required syntax, or if the identifier or character literal does not correspond to a value of the subtype ENUM.

```
procedure PUT( TO   : out STRING;
             ITEM : in  ENUM;
             SET  : in  TYPE_SET := DEFAULT_SETTING);
```

Outputs the value of the parameter ITEM to the given string, following the same rule as for output to a file, using the length of the given string as the value for WIDTH.

Although the specification of the package ENUMERATION_IO would allow instantiation for an integer type, this is not the intended purpose of this generic package, and the effect of such instantiations is not defined by the language.

Notes:

There is a difference between PUT defined for characters, and for enumeration values. Thus

```
TEXT_IO.PUT('A');   --   outputs the character A

package CHAR_IO is new TEXT_IO.ENUMERATION_IO(CHARACTER);
CHAR_IO.PUT('A');   --   outputs the character 'A', between single quotes
```

The type BOOLEAN is an enumeration type, hence ENUMERATION_IO can be instantiated for this type.

References: blank 14.3.5, data_error 14.3.5, enumeration_io package 14.3.10, field subtype 14.3.5, file_type 14.1, get procedure 14.3.5, line terminator 14.3.5, put procedure 14.3.5, skipping 14.3.5, width 14.3.5

Input-Output for Enumeration Types 14.3.9

14.3.10 Specification of the Package Text_IO

```
with IO_EXCEPTIONS;
package TEXT_IO is

   type FILE_TYPE   is limited private;

   type FILE_MODE is (IN_FILE, OUT_FILE);

   type COUNT is range 0 .. implementation_defined;
   subtype POSITIVE_COUNT  is COUNT range 1 .. COUNT'LAST;
   UNBOUNDED : constant COUNT := 0; -- line and page length

   subtype FIELD          is INTEGER range 0 .. implementation_defined;
   subtype NUMBER_BASE is INTEGER range 2 .. 16;

   type TYPE_SET is (LOWER_CASE, UPPER_CASE);

   -- File Management

   procedure CREATE  ( FILE   : in out FILE_TYPE;
                       MODE : in FILE_MODE := OUT_FILE;
                       NAME : in STRING     := "";
                       FORM : in STRING     := "");

   procedure OPEN     ( FILE   : in out FILE_TYPE;
                        MODE : in FILE_MODE;
                        NAME : in STRING;
                        FORM : in STRING := "");

   procedure  CLOSE   (FILE : in out FILE_TYPE);
   procedure  DELETE  (FILE : in out FILE_TYPE);
   procedure  RESET   (FILE : in out FILE_TYPE; MODE : in FILE_MODE);
   procedure  RESET   (FILE : in out FILE_TYPE);

   function   MODE    (FILE : in FILE_TYPE) return FILE_MODE ;
   function   NAME    (FILE : in FILE_TYPE) return STRING;
   function   FORM    (FILE : in FILE_TYPE) return STRING;

   function   IS_OPEN(FILE : in FILE_TYPE) return BOOLEAN;

   -- Control of default input and output files

   procedure  SET_INPUT   (FILE : in FILE_TYPE);
   procedure  SET_OUTPUT (FILE : in FILE_TYPE);


   function   STANDARD_INPUT    return FILE_TYPE;
   function   STANDARD_OUTPUT  return FILE_TYPE;

   function   CURRENT_INPUT    return FILE_TYPE;
   function   CURRENT_OUTPUT  return FILE_TYPE;
```

-- Specification of line and page lengths

procedure SET_LINE_LENGTH   (FILE : **in** FILE_TYPE; TO : **in** COUNT);
procedure SET_LINE_LENGTH   (TO : **in** COUNT);

procedure SET_PAGE_LENGTH   (FILE : **in** FILE_TYPE; TO : **in** COUNT);
procedure SET_PAGE_LENGTH   (TO : **in** COUNT);

function LINE_LENGTH (FILE : **in** FILE_TYPE) **return** COUNT;
function LINE_LENGTH   **return** COUNT;

function PAGE_LENGTH (FILE : **in** FILE_TYPE) **return** COUNT;
function PAGE_LENGTH **return** COUNT;

-- Column, Line, and Page Control

procedure NEW_LINE   (FILE : **in** FILE_TYPE; SPACING : **in** POSITIVE_COUNT := 1);
procedure NEW_LINE   (SPACING : **in** POSITIVE_COUNT := 1);

procedure SKIP_LINE   (FILE : **in** FILE_TYPE; SPACING : **in** POSITIVE_COUNT := 1);
procedure SKIP_LINE   (SPACING : **in** POSITIVE_COUNT := 1);

function END_OF_LINE (FILE : **in** FILE_TYPE) **return** BOOLEAN;
function END_OF_LINE   **return** BOOLEAN;

procedure NEW_PAGE   (FILE : **in** FILE_TYPE);
procedure NEW_PAGE;

procedure SKIP_PAGE   (FILE : **in** FILE_TYPE);
procedure SKIP_PAGE;

function END_OF_PAGE (FILE : **in** FILE_TYPE) **return** BOOLEAN;
function END_OF_PAGE **return** BOOLEAN;

function END_OF_FILE (FILE : **in** FILE_TYPE) **return** BOOLEAN;
function END_OF_FILE   **return** BOOLEAN;

procedure SET_COL (FILE : **in** FILE_TYPE; TO : **in** POSITIVE_COUNT);
procedure SET_COL (TO   : **in** POSITIVE_COUNT);

procedure SET_LINE (FILE : **in** FILE_TYPE; TO : **in** POSITIVE_COUNT);
procedure SET_LINE (TO   : **in** POSITIVE_COUNT);

function COL   (FILE : **in** FILE_TYPE) **return** POSITIVE_COUNT;
function COL   **return** POSITIVE_COUNT;

function LINE (FILE : **in** FILE_TYPE) **return** POSITIVE_COUNT;
function LINE **return** POSITIVE_COUNT;

function PAGE (FILE : **in** FILE_TYPE) **return** POSITIVE_COUNT;
function PAGE **return** POSITIVE_COUNT;

-- Character Input-Output

```
procedure  GET(FILE   : in   FILE_TYPE; ITEM : out CHARACTER);
procedure  GET(ITEM   : out  CHARACTER);
procedure  PUT(FILE   : in   FILE_TYPE; ITEM : in CHARACTER);
procedure  PUT(ITEM   : in   CHARACTER);
```

-- String Input-Output

```
procedure  GET(FILE   : in   FILE_TYPE; ITEM : out STRING);
procedure  GET(ITEM   : out  STRING);
procedure  PUT(FILE   : in   FILE_TYPE; ITEM : in STRING);
procedure  PUT(ITEM   : in   STRING);

procedure  GET_LINE(FILE : in   FILE_TYPE;  ITEM : out STRING; LAST : out NATURAL);
procedure  GET_LINE(ITEM : out  STRING; LAST : out NATURAL);
procedure  PUT_LINE(FILE : in   FILE_TYPE; ITEM : in STRING);
procedure  PUT_LINE(ITEM : in   STRING);
```

-- Generic package for Input-Output of Integer Types

```
generic
   type NUM is range <>;
package INTEGER_IO is

  DEFAULT_WIDTH  : FIELD := NUM'WIDTH;
  DEFAULT_BASE   : NUMBER_BASE := 10;

  procedure GET(FILE   : in   FILE_TYPE; ITEM : out NUM; WIDTH : in FIELD := 0);
  procedure GET(ITEM   : out  NUM; WIDTH : in FIELD := 0);

  procedure PUT( FILE    : in FILE_TYPE;
                 ITEM    : in NUM;
                 WIDTH   : in FIELD := DEFAULT_WIDTH;
                 BASE    : in NUMBER_BASE := DEFAULT_BASE);
  procedure PUT(ITEM     : in NUM;
                 WIDTH   : in FIELD := DEFAULT_WIDTH;
                 BASE    : in NUMBER_BASE := DEFAULT_BASE);

  procedure GET( FROM  : in   STRING; ITEM : out NUM; LAST : out POSITIVE);
  procedure PUT(TO      : out STRING;
                 ITEM   : in NUM;
                 BASE   : in NUMBER_BASE := DEFAULT_BASE);

end INTEGER_IO;
```

```
-- Generic packages for Input-Output of Real Types

generic
  type NUM is digits <>;
package FLOAT_IO is

  DEFAULT_FORE  : FIELD := 2;
  DEFAULT_AFT   : FIELD := NUM'DIGITS-1;
  DEFAULT_EXP   : FIELD := 3;

  procedure  GET(FILE : in FILE_TYPE; ITEM : out NUM; WIDTH : in FIELD := 0);
  procedure  GET(ITEM : out NUM; WIDTH : in FIELD := 0);

  procedure PUT(FILE   : in FILE_TYPE;
                ITEM   : in NUM;
                FORE   : in FIELD := DEFAULT_FORE;
                AFT    : in FIELD := DEFAULT_AFT;
                EXP    : in FIELD := DEFAULT_EXP);
  procedure PUT(ITEM   : in NUM;
                FORE   : in FIELD := DEFAULT_FORE;
                AFT    : in FIELD := DEFAULT_AFT;
                EXP    : in FIELD := DEFAULT_EXP);

  procedure GET(FROM : in STRING; ITEM : out NUM; LAST : out POSITIVE);
  procedure PUT(TO    : out STRING;
                ITEM  : in NUM;
                AFT   : in FIELD := DEFAULT_AFT;
                EXP   : in FIELD := DEFAULT_EXP);
end FLOAT_IO;

generic
  type NUM is delta <>;
package FIXED_IO is

  DEFAULT_FORE   : FIELD := NUM'FORE;
  DEFAULT_AFT    : FIELD := NUM'AFT;
  DEFAULT_EXP    : FIELD := 0;

  procedure GET(FILE  : in FILE_TYPE; ITEM : out NUM; WIDTH : in FIELD := 0);
  procedure GET(ITEM  : out NUM; WIDTH : in FIELD := 0);

  procedure PUT(FILE   : in FILE_TYPE;
                ITEM   : in NUM;
                FORE   : in FIELD := DEFAULT_FORE;
                AFT    : in FIELD := DEFAULT_AFT;
                EXP    : in FIELD := DEFAULT_EXP);
  procedure PUT(ITEM   : in NUM;
                FORE   : in FIELD := DEFAULT_FORE;
                AFT    : in FIELD := DEFAULT_AFT;
                EXP    : in FIELD := DEFAULT_EXP);

  procedure GET(FROM : in  STRING; ITEM : out NUM; LAST : out POSITIVE);
  procedure PUT(TO    : out STRING;
                ITEM  : in NUM;
                AFT   : in FIELD := DEFAULT_AFT;
                EXP   : in FIELD := DEFAULT_EXP);

end FIXED_IO;
```

-- Generic package for Input-Output of Enumeration Types

generic
   type ENUM **is** (<>);
package ENUMERATION_IO **is**

   DEFAULT_WIDTH   : FIELD   := 0;
   DEFAULT_SETTING : TYPE_SET := UPPER_CASE;

   procedure GET(FILE   : **in** FILE_TYPE; ITEM : **out** ENUM);
   procedure GET(ITEM   : **out** ENUM);

   procedure PUT(FILE   : **in** FILE_TYPE;
              ITEM   : **in** ENUM;
              WIDTH : **in** FIELD   := DEFAULT_WIDTH;
              SET   : **in** TYPE_SET := DEFAULT_SETTING);
   procedure PUT(ITEM   : **in** ENUM;
              WIDTH : **in** FIELD   := DEFAULT_WIDTH;
              SET   : **in** TYPE_SET := DEFAULT_SETTING);

   procedure GET(FROM : **in**   STRING; ITEM : **out** ENUM; LAST : **out** POSITIVE);
   procedure PUT(TO   : **out** STRING;
            ITEM : **in**   ENUM;
            SET   : **in**   TYPE_SET := DEFAULT_SETTING);
end ENUMERATION_IO;

-- Exceptions

STATUS_ERROR : **exception renames** IO_EXCEPTIONS.STATUS_ERROR;
MODE_ERROR   : **exception renames** IO_EXCEPTIONS.MODE_ERROR;
NAME_ERROR   : **exception renames** IO_EXCEPTIONS.NAME_ERROR;
USE_ERROR   : **exception renames** IO_EXCEPTIONS.USE_ERROR;
DEVICE_ERROR : **exception renames** IO_EXCEPTIONS.DEVICE_ERROR;
END_ERROR   : **exception renames** IO_EXCEPTIONS.END_ERROR;
DATA_ERROR   : **exception renames** IO_EXCEPTIONS.DATA_ERROR;
LAYOUT_ERROR : **exception renames** IO_EXCEPTIONS.LAYOUT_ERROR;

private
   -- implementation-dependent
end TEXT_IO;

14.4 Exceptions in Input-Output

The following exceptions can be raised by input-output operations. They are declared in the package IO_EXCEPTIONS, defined in section 14.5; this package is named in the context clause for each of the three input-output packages. Only outline descriptions are given of the conditions under which NAME_ERROR, USE_ERROR, and DEVICE_ERROR are raised; for full details see Appendix F. If more than one error condition exists, the corresponding exception that appears earliest in the following list is the one that is raised.

The exception STATUS_ERROR is raised by an attempt to operate upon a file that is not open, and by an attempt to open a file that is already open.

The exception MODE_ERROR is raised by an attempt to read from, or test for the end of, a file whose current mode is OUT_FILE, and also by an attempt to write to a file whose current mode is IN_FILE. In the case of TEXT_IO, the exception MODE_ERROR is also raised by specifying a file whose current mode is OUT_FILE in a call of SET_INPUT, SKIP_LINE, END_OF_LINE, SKIP_PAGE, or END_OF_PAGE; and by specifying a file whose current mode is IN_FILE in a call of SET_OUTPUT, SET_LINE_LENGTH, SET_PAGE_LENGTH, LINE_LENGTH, PAGE_LENGTH, NEW_LINE, or NEW_PAGE.

The exception NAME_ERROR is raised by a call of CREATE or OPEN if the string given for the parameter NAME does not allow the identification of an external file. For example, this exception is raised if the string is improper, or, alternatively, if either none or more than one external file corresponds to the string.

The exception USE_ERROR is raised if an operation is attempted that is not possible for reasons that depend on characteristics of the external file. For example, this exception is raised by the procedure CREATE, among other circumstances, if the given mode is OUT_FILE but the form specifies an input only device, if the parameter FORM specifies invalid access rights, or if an external file with the given name already exists and overwriting is not allowed.

The exception DEVICE_ERROR is raised if an input-output operation cannot be completed because of a malfunction of the underlying system.

The exception END_ERROR is raised by an attempt to skip (read past) the end of a file.

The exception DATA_ERROR may be raised by the procedure READ if the element read cannot be interpreted as a value of the required type. This exception is also raised by a procedure GET (defined in the package TEXT_IO) if the input character sequence fails to satisfy the required syntax, or if the value input does not belong to the range of the required type or subtype.

The exception LAYOUT_ERROR is raised (in text input-output) by COL, LINE, or PAGE if the value returned exceeds COUNT'LAST. The exception LAYOUT_ERROR is also raised on output by an attempt to set column or line numbers in excess of specified maximum line or page lengths, respectively (excluding the unbounded cases). It is also raised by an attempt to PUT too many characters to a string.

References: col function 14.3.4, create procedure 14.2.1, end_of_line function 14.3.4, end_of_page function 14.3.4, external file 14.1, file 14.1, form string 14.1, get procedure 14.3.5, in_file 14.1, io_exceptions package 14.5, line function 14.3.4, line_length function 14.3.4, name string 14.1, new_line procedure 14.3.4, new_page procedure 14.3.4, open procedure 14.2.1, out_file 14.1, page function 14.3.4, page_length function 14.3.4, put procedure 14.3.5, read procedure 14.2.2 14.2.3, set_input procedure 14.3.2, set_line_length 14.3.3, set_page_length 14.3.3, set_output 14.3.2, skip_line procedure 14.3.4, skip_page procedure 14.3.4, text_io package 14.3

14.5 Specification of the Package IO_Exceptions

This package defines the exceptions needed by the packages SEQUENTIAL_IO, DIRECT_IO, and TEXT_IO.

```
package IO_EXCEPTIONS is

   STATUS_ERROR   : exception;
   MODE_ERROR     : exception;
   NAME_ERROR     : exception;
   USE_ERROR      : exception;
   DEVICE_ERROR   : exception;
   END_ERROR      : exception;
   DATA_ERROR     : exception;
   LAYOUT_ERROR   : exception;

end IO_EXCEPTIONS;
```

14.6 Low Level Input-Output

A low level input-output operation is an operation acting on a physical device. Such an operation is handled by using one of the (overloaded) predefined procedures SEND_CONTROL and RECEIVE_CONTROL.

A procedure SEND_CONTROL may be used to send control information to a physical device. A procedure RECEIVE_CONTROL may be used to monitor the execution of an input-output operation by requesting information from the physical device.

Such procedures are declared in the standard package LOW_LEVEL_IO and have two parameters identifying the device and the data. However, the kinds and formats of the control information will depend on the physical characteristics of the machine and the device. Hence, the types of the parameters are implementation-defined. Overloaded definitions of these procedures should be provided for the supported devices.

The visible part of the package defining these procedures is outlined as follows:

```
package LOW_LEVEL_IO is
   --  declarations of the possible types for DEVICE and DATA;
   --  declarations of overloaded procedures for these types:
   procedure SEND_CONTROL      (DEVICE : device_type; DATA : in out data_type);
   procedure RECEIVE_CONTROL   (DEVICE : device_type; DATA : in out data_type);
end;
```

The bodies of the procedures SEND_CONTROL and RECEIVE_CONTROL for various devices can be supplied in the body of the package LOW_LEVEL_IO. These procedure bodies may be written with code statements.

14.7 Example of Input-Output

The following example shows the use of some of the text input-output facilities in a dialogue with a user at a terminal. The user is prompted to type a color, and the program responds by giving the number of items of that color available in stock, according to an inventory. The default input and output files are used. For simplicity, all the requisite instantiations are given within one sub-program; in practice, a package, separate from the procedure, would be used.

```
with TEXT_IO; use TEXT_IO;
procedure DIALOGUE is
    type COLOR is (WHITE, RED, ORANGE, YELLOW, GREEN, BLUE, BROWN);
    package COLOR_IO is new ENUMERATION_IO(ENUM => COLOR);
    package NUMBER_IO is new INTEGER_IO(INTEGER);
    use COLOR_IO, NUMBER_IO;

    INVENTORY : array (COLOR) of INTEGER := (20, 17, 43, 10, 28, 173, 87);
    CHOICE : COLOR;

    procedure ENTER_COLOR (SELECTION : out COLOR) is
    begin
        loop
            begin
                PUT ("Color selected: ");    --  prompts user
                GET (SELECTION);             --  accepts color typed, or raises exception
                return;
            exception
                when DATA_ERROR =>
                    PUT("Invalid color, try again.  ");  --  user has typed new line
                    NEW_LINE(2);
                    --  completes execution of the block statement
            end;
        end loop;  --  repeats the block statement until color accepted
    end;
begin --  statements of DIALOGUE;

    NUMBER_IO.DEFAULT_WIDTH := 5;

    loop

        ENTER_COLOR(CHOICE);  --  user types color and new line

        SET_COL(5);    PUT(CHOICE); PUT(" items available:");
        SET_COL(40);   PUT(INVENTORY(CHOICE));  --  default width is 5
        NEW_LINE;
    end loop;
end DIALOGUE;
```

Example of an interaction (characters typed by the user are italicized):

```
Color selected:  Black
Invalid color, try again.

Color selected:  Blue
    BLUE  items  available:            173
Color selected:  Yellow
    YELLOW  items  available:          10
```

A. Predefined Language Attributes

This annex summarizes the definitions given elsewhere of the predefined language attributes. [1]

P'ADDRESS   For a prefix P that denotes an object, a program unit, a label, or an entry: [2]

Yields the address of the first of the storage units allocated to P. For a sub-program, package, task unit, or label, this value refers to the machine code associated with the corresponding body or statement. For an entry for which an address clause has been given, the value refers to the corresponding hardware interrupt. The value of this attribute is of the type ADDRESS defined in the package SYSTEM. (See 13.7.2.)

P'AFT   For a prefix P that denotes a fixed point subtype: [3]

Yields the number of decimal digits needed after the point to accommodate the precision of the subtype P, unless the delta of the subtype P is greater than 0.1, in which case the attribute yields the value one. (P'AFT is the smallest positive integer N for which $(10**N)*P'DELTA$ is greater than or equal to one.) The value of this attribute is of the type *universal_integer*. (See 3.5.10.)

P'BASE   For a prefix P that denotes a type or subtype: [4]

This attribute denotes the base type of P. It is only allowed as the prefix of the name of another attribute: for example, P'BASE'FIRST. (See 3.3.3.)

P'CALLABLE   For a prefix P that is appropriate for a task type: [5]

Yields the value FALSE when the execution of the task P is either completed or terminated, or when the task is abnormal; yields the value TRUE otherwise. The value of this attribute is of the predefined type BOOLEAN. (See 9.9.)

P'CONSTRAINED   For a prefix P that denotes an object of a type with discriminants: [6]

Yields the value TRUE if a discriminant constraint applies to the object P, or if the object is a constant (including a formal parameter or generic formal parameter of mode **in**); yields the value FALSE otherwise. If P is a generic formal parameter of mode **in out**, or if P is a formal parameter of mode **in out** or **out** and the type mark given in the corresponding parameter specification denotes an unconstrained type with discriminants, then the value of this attribute is obtained from that of the corresponding actual parameter. The value of this attribute is of the predefined type BOOLEAN. (See 3.7.4.)

7   P'CONSTRAINED   For a prefix P that denotes a private type or subtype:

Yields the value FALSE if P denotes an unconstrained nonformal private type with discriminants; also yields the value FALSE if P denotes a generic formal private type and the associated actual subtype is either an unconstrained type with discriminants or an unconstrained array type; yields the value TRUE otherwise. The value of this attribute is of the predefined type BOOLEAN. (See 7.4.2.)

8   P'COUNT   For a prefix P that denotes an entry of a task unit:

Yields the number of entry calls presently queued on the entry (if the attribute is evaluated within an accept statement for the entry P, the count does not include the calling task). The value of this attribute is of the type *universal_integer*. (See 9.9.)

9   P'DELTA   For a prefix P that denotes a fixed point subtype:

Yields the value of the delta specified in the fixed accuracy definition for the subtype P. The value of this attribute is of the type *universal_real*. (See 3.5.10.)

10   P'DIGITS   For a prefix P that denotes a floating point subtype:

Yields the number of decimal digits in the decimal mantissa of model numbers of the subtype P. (This attribute yields the number D of section 3.5.7.) The value of this attribute is of the type *universal_integer*. (See 3.5.8.)

11   P'EMAX   For a prefix P that denotes a floating point subtype:

Yields the largest exponent value in the binary canonical form of model numbers of the subtype P. (This attribute yields the product $4*B$ of section 3.5.7.) The value of this attribute is of the type *universal_integer*. (See 3.5.8.)

12   P'EPSILON   For a prefix P that denotes a floating point subtype:

Yields the absolute value of the difference between the model number 1.0 and the next model number above, for the subtype P. The value of this attribute is of the type *universal_real*. (See 3.5.8.)

13   P'FIRST   For a prefix P that denotes a scalar type, or a subtype of a scalar type:

Yields the lower bound of P. The value of this attribute has the same type as P. (See 3.5.)

14   P'FIRST   For a prefix P that is appropriate for an array type, or that denotes a constrained array subtype:

Yields the lower bound of the first index range. The value of this attribute has the same type as this lower bound. (See 3.6.2 and 3.8.2.)

P'FIRST(N)   For a prefix P that is appropriate for an array type, or that denotes a con-   15
               strained array subtype:

               Yields the lower bound of the N-th index range. The value of this attribute
               has the same type as this lower bound. The argument N must be a static
               expression of type *universal_integer*. The value of N must be positive
               (nonzero) and no greater than the dimensionality of the array. (See 3.6.2 and
               3.8.2.)

P'FIRST_BIT   For a prefix P that denotes a component of a record object: 16

               Yields the offset, from the start of the first of the storage units occupied by
               the component, of the first bit occupied by the component. This offset is
               measured in bits. The value of this attribute is of the type *universal_integer*.
               (See 13.7.2.)

P'FORE   For a prefix P that denotes a fixed point subtype: 17

               Yields the minimum number of characters needed for the integer part of the
               decimal representation of any value of the subtype P, assuming that the
               representation does not include an exponent, but includes a one-character
               prefix that is either a minus sign or a space. (This minimum number does not
               include superfluous zeros or underlines, and is at least two.) The value of
               this attribute is of the type *universal_integer*. (See 3.5.10.)

P'IMAGE   For a prefix P that denotes a discrete type or subtype: 18

               This attribute is a function with a single parameter. The actual parameter X
               must be a value of the base type of P. The result type is the predefined type
               STRING. The result is the *image* of the value of X, that is, a sequence of
               characters representing the value in display form. The image of an integer
               value is the corresponding decimal literal; without underlines, leading
               zeros, exponent, or trailing spaces; but with a one character prefix that is
               either a minus sign or a space.

               The image of an enumeration value is either the corresponding identifier in
               upper case or the corresponding character literal (including the two
               apostrophes); neither leading nor trailing spaces are included. The image of
               a character other than a graphic character is implementation-defined. (See
               3.5.5.)

P'LARGE   For a prefix P that denotes a real subtype: 19

               The attribute yields the largest positive model number of the subtype P. The
               value of this attribute is of the type *universal_real*. (See 3.5.8 and 3.5.10.)

P'LAST   For a prefix P that denotes a scalar type, or a subtype of a scalar type: 20

               Yields the upper bound of P. The value of this attribute has the same type as
               P. (See 3.5.)

P'LAST   For a prefix P that is appropriate for an array type, or that denotes a con-   21
               strained array subtype:

               Yields the upper bound of the first index range. The value of this attribute
               has the same type as this upper bound. (See 3.6.2 and 3.8.2.)

                                        A-3

22   P'LAST(N)   For a prefix P that is appropriate for an array type, or that denotes a constrained array subtype:

Yields the upper bound of the N-th index range. The value of this attribute has the same type as this upper bound. The argument N must be a static expression of type *universal_integer*. The value of N must be positive (nonzero) and no greater than the dimensionality of the array. (See 3.6.2 and 3.8.2.)

23   P'LAST_BIT   For a prefix P that denotes a component of a record object:

Yields the offset, from the start of the first of the storage units occupied by the component, of the last bit occupied by the component. This offset is measured in bits. The value of this attribute is of the type *universal_integer*. (See 13.7.2.)

24   P'LENGTH   For a prefix P that is appropriate for an array type, or that denotes a constrained array subtype:

Yields the number of values of the first index range (zero for a null range). The value of this attribute is of the type *universal_integer*. (See 3.6.2.)

25   P'LENGTH(N)   For a prefix P that is appropriate for an array type, or that denotes a constrained array subtype:

Yields the number of values of the N-th index range (zero for a null range). The value of this attribute is of the type *universal_integer*. The argument N must be a static expression of type *universal_integer*. The value of N must be positive (nonzero) and no greater than the dimensionality of the array. (See 3.6.2 and 3.8.2.)

26   P'MACHINE_EMAX   For a prefix P that denotes a floating point type or subtype:

Yields the largest value of *exponent* for the machine representation of the base type of P. The value of this attribute is of the type *universal_integer*. (See 13.7.3.)

27   P'MACHINE_EMIN   For a prefix P that denotes a floating point type or subtype:

Yields the smallest (most negative) value of *exponent* for the machine representation of the base type of P. The value of this attribute is of the type *universal_integer*. (See 13.7.3.)

28   P'MACHINE_MANTISSA   For a prefix P that denotes a floating point type or subtype:

Yields the number of digits in the *mantissa* for the machine representation of the base type of P (the digits are extended digits in the range 0 to P'MACHINE_RADIX - 1). The value of this attribute is of the type *universal_integer*. (See 13.7.3.)

P'MACHINE_OVERFLOWS   For a prefix P that denotes a real type or subtype: 29

Yields the value TRUE if every predefined operation on values of the base type of P either provides a correct result, or raises the exception NUMERIC_ERROR in overflow situations; yields the value FALSE otherwise. The value of this attribute is of the predefined type BOOLEAN. (See 13.7.3.)

P'MACHINE_RADIX   For a prefix P that denotes a floating point type or subtype: 30

Yields the value of the *radix* used by the machine representation of the base type of P. The value of this attribute is of the type *universal_integer*. (See 13.7.3.)

P'MACHINE_ROUNDS   For a prefix P that denotes a real type or subtype: 31

Yields the value TRUE if every predefined arithmetic operation on values of the base type of P either returns an exact result or performs rounding; yields the value FALSE otherwise. The value of this attribute is of the predefined type BOOLEAN. (See 13.7.3.)

P'MANTISSA   For a prefix P that denotes a real subtype: 32

Yields the number of binary digits in the binary mantissa of model numbers of the subtype P. (This attribute yields the number B of section 3.5.7 for a floating point type, or of section 3.5.9 for a fixed point type.) The value of this attribute is of the type *universal_integer*. (See 3.5.8 and 3.5.10.)

P'POS   For a prefix P that denotes a discrete type or subtype: 33

This attribute is a function with a single parameter. The actual parameter X must be a value of the base type of P. The result type is the type *universal_integer*. The result is the position number of the value of the actual parameter. (See 3.5.5.)

P'POSITION   For a prefix P that denotes a component of a record object: 34

Yields the offset, from the start of the first storage unit occupied by the record, of the first of the storage units occupied by the component. This offset is measured in storage units. The value of this attribute is of the type *universal_integer*. (See 13.7.2.)

P'PRED   For a prefix P that denotes a discrete type or subtype: 35

This attribute is a function with a single parameter. The actual parameter X must be a value of the base type of P. The result type is the base type of P. The result is the value whose position number is one less than that of X. The exception CONSTRAINT_ERROR is raised if X equals P'BASE'FIRST. (See 3.5.5.)

P'RANGE   For a prefix P that is appropriate for an array type, or that denotes a constrained array subtype: 36

Yields the first index range of P, that is, the range P'FIRST .. P'LAST. (See 3.6.2.)

37 **P'RANGE(N)**   For a prefix P that is appropriate for an array type, or that denotes a constrained array subtype:

Yields the N-th index range of P, that is, the range P'FIRST(N) .. P'LAST(N). (See 3.6.2.)

38 **P'SAFE_EMAX**   For a prefix P that denotes a floating point type or subtype:

Yields the largest exponent value in the binary canonical form of safe numbers of the base type of P. (This attribute yields the number E of section 3.5.7.) The value of this attribute is of the type *universal_integer*. (See 3.5.8.)

39 **P'SAFE_LARGE**   For a prefix P that denotes a real type or subtype:

Yields the largest positive safe number of the base type of P. The value of this attribute is of the type *universal_real*. (See 3.5.8 and 3.5.10.)

40 **P'SAFE_SMALL**   For a prefix P that denotes a real type or subtype:

Yields the smallest positive (nonzero) safe number of the base type of P. The value of this attribute is of the type *universal_real*. (See 3.5.8 and 3.5.10.)

41 **P'SIZE**   For a prefix P that denotes an object:

Yields the number of bits allocated to hold the object. The value of this attribute is of the type *universal_integer*. (See 13.7.2.)

42 **P'SIZE**   For a prefix P that denotes any type or subtype:

Yields the minimum number of bits that is needed by the implementation to hold any possible object of the type or subtype P. The value of this attribute is of the type *universal_integer*. (See 13.7.2.)

43 **P'SMALL**   For a prefix P that denotes a real subtype:

Yields the smallest positive (nonzero) model number of the subtype P. The value of this attribute is of the type *universal_real*. (See 3.5.8 and 3.5.10.)

44 **P'STORAGE_SIZE**   For a prefix P that denotes an access type or subtype:

Yields the total number of storage units reserved for the collection associated with the base type of P. The value of this attribute is of the type *universal_integer*. (See 13.7.2.)

45 **P'STORAGE_SIZE**   For a prefix P that denotes a task type or a task object:

Yields the number of storage units reserved for each activation of a task of the type P or for the activation of the task object P. The value of this attribute is of the type *universal_integer*. (See 13.7.2.)

P'SUCC   For a prefix P that denotes a discrete type or subtype: 46

This attribute is a function with a single parameter. The actual parameter
X must be a value of the base type of P. The result type is the base type
of P. The result is the value whose position number is one greater than
that of X. The exception CONSTRAINT_ERROR is raised if X equals
P'BASE'LAST. (See 3.5.5.)

P'TERMINATED   For a prefix P that is appropriate for a task type: 47

Yields the value TRUE if the task P is terminated; yields the value FALSE
otherwise. The value of this attribute is of the predefined type BOOLEAN.
(See 9.9.)

P'VAL   For a prefix P that denotes a discrete type or subtype: 48

This attribute is a special function with a single parameter X which can
be of any integer type. The result type is the base type of P. The result is
the value whose position number is the *universal_integer* value corresponding to X. The exception CONSTRAINT_ERROR is raised if the
universal_integer value corresponding to X is not in the range
P'POS (P'BASE'FIRST) .. P'POS (P'BASE'LAST). (See 3.5.5.)

P'VALUE   For a prefix P that denotes a discrete type or subtype: 49

This attribute is a function with a single parameter. The actual parameter
X must be a value of the predefined type STRING. The result type is the
base type of P. Any leading and any trailing spaces of the sequence of
characters that corresponds to X are ignored.

For an enumeration type, if the sequence of characters has the syntax of
an enumeration literal and if this literal exists for the base type of P, the
result is the corresponding enumeration value. For an integer type, if the
sequence of characters has the syntax of an integer literal, with an
optional single leading character that is a plus or minus sign, and if there
is a corresponding value in the base type of P, the result is this value. In
any other case, the exception CONSTRAINT_ERROR is raised. (See 3.5.5.)

P'WIDTH   For a prefix P that denotes a discrete subtype: 50

Yields the maximum image length over all values of the subtype P (the
image is the sequence of characters returned by the attribute IMAGE).
The value of this attribute is of the type *universal_integer*. (See 3.5.5.)

A-7

B. Predefined Language Pragmas

This annex defines the pragmas LIST, PAGE, and OPTIMIZE, and summarizes the definitions given elsewhere of the remaining language-defined pragmas.

Pragma	Meaning
CONTROLLED	Takes the simple name of an access type as the single argument. This pragma is only allowed immediately within the declarative part or package specification that contains the declaration of the access type; the declaration must occur before the pragma. This pragma is not allowed for a derived type. This pragma specifies that automatic storage reclamation must not be performed for objects designated by values of the access type, except upon leaving the innermost block statement, subprogram body, or task body that encloses the access type declaration, or after leaving the main program (see 4.8).
ELABORATE	Takes one or more simple names denoting library units as arguments. This pragma is only allowed immediately after the context clause of a compilation unit (before the subsequent library unit or secondary unit). Each argument must be the simple name of a library unit mentioned by the context clause. This pragma specifies that the corresponding library unit body must be elaborated before the given compilation unit. If the given compilation unit is a subunit, the library unit body must be elaborated before the body of the ancestor library unit of the subunit (see 10.5).
INLINE	Takes one or more names as arguments; each name is either the name of a subprogram or the name of a generic subprogram. This pragma is only allowed at the place of a declarative item in a declarative part or package specification, or after a library unit in a compilation, but before any subsequent compilation unit. This pragma specifies that the subprogram bodies should be expanded inline at each call whenever possible; in the case of a generic subprogram, the pragma applies to calls of its instantiations (see 6.3.2).
INTERFACE	Takes a language name and a subprogram name as arguments. This pragma is allowed at the place of a declarative item, and must apply in this case to a subprogram declared by an earlier declarative item of the same declarative part or package specification. This pragma is also allowed for a library unit; in this case the pragma must appear after the subprogram declaration, and before any subsequent compilation unit. This pragma specifies the other language (and thereby the calling conventions) and informs the compiler that an object module will be supplied for the corresponding subprogram (see 13.9).
LIST	Takes one of the identifiers ON or OFF as the single argument. This pragma is allowed anywhere a pragma is allowed. It specifies that listing of the compilation is to be continued or suspended until a LIST pragma with the opposite argument is given within the same compilation. The pragma itself is always listed if the compiler is producing a listing.
MEMORY_SIZE	Takes a numeric literal as the single argument. This pragma is only allowed at the start of a compilation, before the first compilation unit (if any) of the compilation. The effect of this pragma is to use the value of the specified numeric literal for the definition of the named number MEMORY_SIZE (see 13.7).

OPTIMIZE

Takes one of the identifiers TIME or SPACE as the single argument. This pragma is only allowed within a declarative part and it applies to the block or body enclosing the declarative part. It specifies whether time or space is the primary optimization criterion.

PACK

Takes the simple name of a record or array type as the single argument. The allowed positions for this pragma, and the restrictions on the named type, are governed by the same rules as for a representation clause. The pragma specifies that storage minimization should be the main criterion when selecting the representation of the given type (see 13.1).

PAGE

This pragma has no argument, and is allowed anywhere a pragma is allowed. It specifies that the program text which follows the pragma should start on a new page (if the compiler is currently producing a listing).

PRIORITY

Takes a static expression of the predefined integer subtype PRIORITY as the single argument. This pragma is only allowed within the specification of a task unit or immediately within the outermost declarative part of a main program. It specifies the priority of the task (or tasks of the task type) or the priority of the main program (see 9.8).

SHARED

Takes the simple name of a variable as the single argument. This pragma is allowed only for a variable declared by an object declaration and whose type is a scalar or access type; the variable declaration and the pragma must both occur (in this order) immediately within the same declarative part or package specification. This pragma specifies that every read or update of the variable is a synchronization point for that variable. An implementation must restrict the objects for which this pragma is allowed to objects for which each of direct reading and direct updating is implemented as an indivisible operation (see 9.11).

STORAGE_UNIT

Takes a numeric literal as the single argument. This pragma is only allowed at the start of a compilation, before the first compilation unit (if any) of the compilation. The effect of this pragma is to use the value of the specified numeric literal for the definition of the named number STORAGE_UNIT (see 13.7).

SUPPRESS

Takes as arguments the identifier of a check and optionally also the name of either an object, a type or subtype, a subprogram, a task unit, or a generic unit. This pragma is only allowed either immediately within a declarative part or immediately within a package specification. In the latter case, the only allowed form is with a name that denotes an entity (or several overloaded subprograms) declared immediately within the package specification. The permission to omit the given check extends from the place of the pragma to the end of the declarative region associated with the innermost enclosing block statement or program unit. For a pragma given in a package specification, the permission extends to the end of the scope of the named entity.

If the pragma includes a name, the permission to omit the given check is further restricted: it is given only for operations on the named object or on all objects of the base type of a named type or subtype; for calls of a named subprogram; for activations of tasks of the named task type; or for instantiations of the given generic unit (see 11.7).

SYSTEM_NAME

Takes an enumeration literal as the single argument. This pragma is only allowed at the start of a compilation, before the first compilation unit (if any) of the compilation. The effect of this pragma is to use the enumeration literal with the specified identifier for the definition of the constant SYSTEM_NAME. This pragma is only allowed if the specified identifier corresponds to one of the literals of the type NAME declared in the package SYSTEM (see 13.7).

C. Predefined Language Environment

This annex outlines the specification of the package STANDARD containing all predefined identifiers in the language. The corresponding package body is implementation-defined and is not shown.

The operators that are predefined for the types declared in the package STANDARD are given in comments since they are implicitly declared. Italics are used for pseudo-names of anonymous types (such as *universal_real*) and for undefined information (such as *implementation_defined* and *any_fixed_point_type*).

package STANDARD **is**

   type BOOLEAN **is** (FALSE, TRUE);

   -- The predefined relational operators for this type are as follows:

   -- **function** "="   (LEFT, RIGHT : BOOLEAN) **return** BOOLEAN;
   -- **function** "/=" (LEFT, RIGHT : BOOLEAN) **return** BOOLEAN;
   -- **function** "<"   (LEFT, RIGHT : BOOLEAN) **return** BOOLEAN;
   -- **function** "<=" (LEFT, RIGHT : BOOLEAN) **return** BOOLEAN;
   -- **function** ">"   (LEFT, RIGHT : BOOLEAN) **return** BOOLEAN;
   -- **function** ">=" (LEFT, RIGHT : BOOLEAN) **return** BOOLEAN;

   -- The predefined logical operators and the predefined logical negation operator are as follows:

   -- **function** "and" (LEFT, RIGHT : BOOLEAN) **return** BOOLEAN;
   -- **function** "or"   (LEFT, RIGHT : BOOLEAN) **return** BOOLEAN;
   -- **function** "xor" (LEFT, RIGHT : BOOLEAN) **return** BOOLEAN;

   -- **function** "not" (RIGHT : BOOLEAN) **return** BOOLEAN;

   -- The universal type *universal_integer* is predefined.

   type INTEGER **is** *implementation_defined*;

   -- The predefined operators for this type are as follows:

   -- **function** "="   (LEFT, RIGHT : INTEGER) **return** BOOLEAN;
   -- **function** "/=" (LEFT, RIGHT : INTEGER) **return** BOOLEAN;
   -- **function** "<"   (LEFT, RIGHT : INTEGER) **return** BOOLEAN;
   -- **function** "<=" (LEFT, RIGHT : INTEGER) **return** BOOLEAN;
   -- **function** ">"   (LEFT, RIGHT : INTEGER) **return** BOOLEAN;
   -- **function** ">=" (LEFT, RIGHT : INTEGER) **return** BOOLEAN;

```
-- function "+"    (RIGHT : INTEGER) return INTEGER;
-- function "-"    (RIGHT : INTEGER) return INTEGER;
-- function "abs"  (RIGHT : INTEGER) return INTEGER;


-- function "+"    (LEFT, RIGHT : INTEGER) return INTEGER;
-- function "-"    (LEFT, RIGHT : INTEGER) return INTEGER;
-- function "*"    (LEFT, RIGHT : INTEGER) return INTEGER;
-- function "/"    (LEFT, RIGHT : INTEGER) return INTEGER;
-- function "rem"  (LEFT, RIGHT : INTEGER) return INTEGER;
-- function "mod"  (LEFT, RIGHT : INTEGER) return INTEGER;


-- function "**"   (LEFT : INTEGER; RIGHT : INTEGER) return INTEGER;
```

7
-- An implementation may provide additional predefined integer types. It is recommended that the
-- names of such additional types end with INTEGER as in SHORT_INTEGER or LONG_INTEGER.
-- The specification of each operator for the type *universal_integer*, or for any additional
-- predefined integer type, is obtained by replacing INTEGER by the name of the type in the
-- specification of the corresponding operator of the type INTEGER, except for the right operand
-- of the exponentiating operator.

8
-- The universal type *universal_real* is predefined.

9
type FLOAT **is** *implementation_defined*;

-- The predefined operators for this type are as follows:

```
-- function "="    (LEFT, RIGHT : FLOAT) return BOOLEAN;
-- function "/="   (LEFT, RIGHT : FLOAT) return BOOLEAN;
-- function "<"    (LEFT, RIGHT : FLOAT) return BOOLEAN;
-- function "<="   (LEFT, RIGHT : FLOAT) return BOOLEAN;
-- function ">"    (LEFT, RIGHT : FLOAT) return BOOLEAN;
-- function ">="   (LEFT, RIGHT : FLOAT) return BOOLEAN;


-- function "+"    (RIGHT : FLOAT) return FLOAT;
-- function "-"    (RIGHT : FLOAT) return FLOAT;
-- function "abs"  (RIGHT : FLOAT) return FLOAT;


-- function "+"    (LEFT, RIGHT : FLOAT) return FLOAT;
-- function "-"    (LEFT, RIGHT : FLOAT) return FLOAT;
-- function "*"    (LEFT, RIGHT : FLOAT) return FLOAT;
-- function "/"    (LEFT, RIGHT : FLOAT) return FLOAT;


-- function "**"   (LEFT : FLOAT; RIGHT : INTEGER) return FLOAT;
```

10
-- An implementation may provide additional predefined floating point types. It is recom-
-- mended that the names of such additional types end with FLOAT as in SHORT_FLOAT or
-- LONG_FLOAT. The specification of each operator for the type *universal_real*, or for any
-- additional predefined floating point type, is obtained by replacing FLOAT by the name of the
-- type in the specification of the corresponding operator of the type FLOAT.

-- In addition, the following operators are predefined for universal types: 11

-- **function** "*" (LEFT : *universal_integer*; RIGHT : *universal_real*)   **return** *universal_real*;
-- **function** "*" (LEFT : *universal_real*;   RIGHT : *universal_integer*) **return** *universal_real*;
-- **function** "/"   (LEFT : *universal_real*;   RIGHT : *universal_integer*) **return** *universal_real*;

-- The type *universal_fixed* is predefined. The only operators declared for this type are

-- **function** "*" (LEFT : *any_fixed_point_type*; RIGHT : *any_fixed_point_type*) **return** *universal_fixed*;
-- **function** "/"   (LEFT : *any_fixed_point_type*; RIGHT : *any_fixed_point_type*) **return** *universal_fixed*;

-- The following characters form the standard ASCII character set. Character literals cor-   12
-- responding to control characters are not identifiers; they are indicated in italics in this definition.

type CHARACTER **is**   13

(*nul*,	*soh*,	*stx*,	*etx*,	*eot*,	*enq*,	*ack*,	*bel*,
bs,	*ht*,	*lf*,	*vt*,	*ff*,	*cr*,	*so*,	*si*,
dle,	*dc1*,	*dc2*,	*dc3*,	*dc4*,	*nak*,	*syn*,	*etb*,
can,	*em*,	*sub*,	*esc*,	*fs*,	*gs*,	*rs*,	*us*,
' ',	'!',	'"',	'#',	'$',	'%',	'&',	''',
'(',	')',	'*',	'+',	',',	'-',	'.',	'/',
'0',	'1',	'2',	'3',	'4',	'5',	'6',	'7',
'8',	'9',	':',	';',	'<',	'=',	'>',	'?',
'@',	'A',	'B',	'C',	'D',	'E',	'F',	'G',
'H',	'I',	'J',	'K',	'L',	'M',	'N',	'O',
'P',	'Q',	'R',	'S',	'T',	'U',	'V',	'W',
'X',	'Y',	'Z',	'[',	'\',	']',	'^',	'_',
'`',	'a',	'b',	'c',	'd',	'e',	'f',	'g',
'h',	'i',	'j',	'k',	'l',	'm',	'n',	'o',
'p',	'q',	'r',	's',	't',	'u',	'v',	'w',
'x',	'y',	'z',	'{',	'|',	'}',	'~',	*del*);

for CHARACTER **use** --   128 ASCII character set without holes
    (0, 1, 2, 3, 4, 5, ..., 125, 126, 127);

-- The predefined operators for the type CHARACTER are the same as for any enumeration type.   14

package ASCII **is**

  -- Control characters:

NUL	: **constant** CHARACTER := *nul*;	SOH	: **constant** CHARACTER := *soh*;
STX	: **constant** CHARACTER := *stx*;	ETX	: **constant** CHARACTER := *etx*;
EOT	: **constant** CHARACTER := *eot*;	ENQ	: **constant** CHARACTER := *enq*;
ACK	: **constant** CHARACTER := *ack*;	BEL	: **constant** CHARACTER := *bel*;
BS	: **constant** CHARACTER := *bs*;	HT	: **constant** CHARACTER := *ht*;
LF	: **constant** CHARACTER := *lf*;	VT	: **constant** CHARACTER := *vt*;
FF	: **constant** CHARACTER := *ff*;	CR	: **constant** CHARACTER := *cr*;
SO	: **constant** CHARACTER := *so*;	SI	: **constant** CHARACTER := *si*;
DLE	: **constant** CHARACTER := *dle*;	DC1	: **constant** CHARACTER := *dc1*;
DC2	: **constant** CHARACTER := *dc2*;	DC3	: **constant** CHARACTER := *dc3*;
DC4	: **constant** CHARACTER := *dc4*;	NAK	: **constant** CHARACTER := *nak*;
SYN	: **constant** CHARACTER := *syn*;	ETB	: **constant** CHARACTER := *etb*;
CAN	: **constant** CHARACTER := *can*;	EM	: **constant** CHARACTER := *em*;
SUB	: **constant** CHARACTER := *sub*;	ESC	: **constant** CHARACTER := *esc*;
FS	: **constant** CHARACTER := *fs*;	GS	: **constant** CHARACTER := *gs*;
RS	: **constant** CHARACTER := *rs*;	US	: **constant** CHARACTER := *us*;
DEL	: **constant** CHARACTER := *del*;		

  -- Other characters:

EXCLAM	: **constant** CHARACTER := '!';	QUOTATION	: **constant** CHARACTER := '"';
SHARP	: **constant** CHARACTER := '#';	DOLLAR	: **constant** CHARACTER := '$';
PERCENT	: **constant** CHARACTER := '%';	AMPERSAND	: **constant** CHARACTER := '&';
COLON	: **constant** CHARACTER := ':';	SEMICOLON	: **constant** CHARACTER := ';';
QUERY	: **constant** CHARACTER := '?';	AT_SIGN	: **constant** CHARACTER := '@';
L_BRACKET	: **constant** CHARACTER := '[';	BACK_SLASH	: **constant** CHARACTER := '\';
R_BRACKET	: **constant** CHARACTER := ']';	CIRCUMFLEX	: **constant** CHARACTER := '~';
UNDERLINE	: **constant** CHARACTER := '_';	GRAVE	: **constant** CHARACTER := '`';
L_BRACE	: **constant** CHARACTER := '{';	BAR	: **constant** CHARACTER := '	';
R_BRACE	: **constant** CHARACTER := '}';	TILDE	: **constant** CHARACTER := '~';

  -- Lower case letters:

  LC_A : **constant** CHARACTER := 'a';

  ...

  LC_Z : **constant** CHARACTER := 'z';

end ASCII;

-- Predefined subtypes:

subtype NATURAL **is** INTEGER **range** 0 .. INTEGER'LAST;
subtype POSITIVE **is** INTEGER **range** 1 .. INTEGER'LAST;

-- Predefined string type: 17

type STRING **is array**(POSITIVE **range** <>) **of** CHARACTER;

pragma PACK(STRING);

-- The predefined operators for this type are as follows: 18

```
-- function "="  (LEFT, RIGHT : STRING) return BOOLEAN;
-- function "/=" (LEFT, RIGHT : STRING) return BOOLEAN;
-- function "<"  (LEFT, RIGHT : STRING) return BOOLEAN;
-- function "<=" (LEFT, RIGHT : STRING) return BOOLEAN;
-- function ">"  (LEFT, RIGHT : STRING) return BOOLEAN;
-- function ">=" (LEFT, RIGHT : STRING) return BOOLEAN;
```

```
-- function "&" (LEFT : STRING;    RIGHT : STRING)    return STRING;
-- function "&" (LEFT : CHARACTER; RIGHT : STRING)    return STRING;
-- function "&" (LEFT : STRING;    RIGHT : CHARACTER) return STRING;
-- function "&" (LEFT : CHARACTER; RIGHT : CHARACTER) return STRING;
```

type DURATION **is delta** *implementation_defined* **range** *implementation_defined*;   19

-- The predefined operators for the type DURATION are the same as for any fixed point type.

-- The predefined exceptions: 20

```
CONSTRAINT_ERROR  : exception;
NUMERIC_ERROR     : exception;
PROGRAM_ERROR     : exception;
STORAGE_ERROR     : exception;
TASKING_ERROR     : exception;
```

end STANDARD;

Certain aspects of the predefined entities cannot be completely described in the language itself.   21
For example, although the enumeration type BOOLEAN can be written showing the two
enumeration literals FALSE and TRUE, the short-circuit control forms cannot be expressed in the
language.

Note:

The language definition predefines the following library units: 22

-	The package CALENDAR	(see 9.6)
-	The package SYSTEM	(see 13.7)
-	The package MACHINE_CODE (if provided)	(see 13.8)
-	The generic procedure UNCHECKED_DEALLOCATION	(see 13.10.1)
-	The generic function UNCHECKED_CONVERSION	(see 13.10.2)
-	The generic package SEQUENTIAL_IO	(see 14.2.3)
-	The generic package DIRECT_IO	(see 14.2.5)
-	The package TEXT_IO	(see 14.3.10)
-	The package IO_EXCEPTIONS	(see 14.5)
-	The package LOW_LEVEL_IO	(see 14.6)

D. Glossary

This appendix is informative and is not part of the standard definition of the Ada programming language. Italicized terms in the abbreviated descriptions below either have glossary entries themselves or are described in entries for related terms.

Accept statement. See *entry*.

Access type. A value of an access type (an *access value*) is either a null value, or a value that *designates* an *object* created by an *allocator*. The designated object can be read and updated via the access value. The definition of an access type specifies the type of the objects designated by values of the access type. See also *collection*.

Actual parameter. See *parameter*.

Aggregate. The evaluation of an aggregate yields a value of a *composite type*. The value is specified by giving the value of each of the *components*. Either *positional association* or *named association* may be used to indicate which value is associated with which component.

Allocator. The evaluation of an allocator creates an *object* and returns a new *access value* which *designates* the object.

Array type. A value of an array type consists of *components* which are all of the same *subtype* (and hence, of the same type). Each component is uniquely distinguished by an *index* (for a one-dimensional array) or by a sequence of indices (for a multidimensional array). Each index must be a value of a *discrete type* and must lie in the correct *index range*.

Assignment. Assignment is the *operation* that replaces the current value of a *variable* by a new value. An *assignment statement* specifies a variable on the left, and on the right, an *expression* whose value is to be the new value of the variable.

Attribute. The evaluation of an attribute yields a predefined characteristic of a named entity; some attributes are *functions*.

Block statement. A block statement is a single statement that may contain a sequence of statements. It may also include a *declarative part*, and *exception handlers*; their effects are local to the block statement.

Body. A body defines the execution of a *subprogram, package,* or *task*. A *body stub* is a form of body that indicates that this execution is defined in a separately compiled *subunit*.

Collection. A collection is the entire set of *objects* created by evaluation of *allocators* for an *access type*.

Compilation unit. A compilation unit is the *declaration* or the *body* of a *program unit*, presented for compilation as an independent text. It is optionally preceded by a *context clause*, naming other compilation units upon which it depends by means of one more *with* clauses.

Component. A component is a value that is a part of a larger value, or an *object* that is part of a larger object.

Composite type. A composite type is one whose values have *components*. There are two kinds of composite type: *array types* and *record types*.

Constant. See *object*.

Constraint. A constraint determines a subset of the values of a *type*. A value in that subset *satisfies* the constraint.

Context clause. See *compilation unit*.

Declaration. A declaration associates an identifier (or some other notation) with an entity. This association is in effect within a region of text called the *scope* of the declaration. Within the scope of a declaration, there are places where it is possible to use the identifier to refer to the associated declared entity. At such places the identifier is said to be a *simple name* of the entity; the *name* is said to *denote* the associated entity.

Declarative Part. A declarative part is a sequence of *declarations*. It may also contain related information such as *subprogram bodies* and *representation clauses*.

Denote. See *declaration*.

Derived Type. A derived type is a *type* whose operations and values are replicas of those of an existing type. The existing type is called the *parent type* of the derived type.

Designate. See *access type, task*.

Direct visibility. See *visibility*.

Discrete Type. A discrete type is a *type* which has an ordered set of distinct values. The discrete types are the *enumeration* and *integer types*. Discrete types are used for indexing and iteration, and for choices in case statements and record *variants*.

Discriminant. A discriminant is a distinguished *component* of an *object* or value of a *record type*. The *subtypes* of other components, or even their presence or absence, may depend on the value of the discriminant.

Discriminant constraint. A discriminant constraint on a *record type* or *private type* specifies a value for each *discriminant* of the type.

Elaboration. The elaboration of a *declaration* is the process by which the declaration achieves its effect (such as creating an *object*); this process occurs during program execution.

Entry. An entry is used for communication between *tasks*. Externally, an entry is called just as a *subprogram* is called; its internal behavior is specified by one or more *accept statements* specifying the actions to be performed when the entry is called.

Enumeration type. An enumeration type is a *discrete type* whose values are represented by enumeration literals which are given explicitly in the *type declaration*. These enumeration literals are either *identifiers* or *character literals*.

Evaluation. The evaluation of an *expression* is the process by which the value of the expression is computed. This process occurs during program execution.

Exception. An exception is an error situation which may arise during program execution. To *raise* an exception is to abandon normal program execution so as to signal that the error has taken place. An *exception handler* is a portion of program text specifying a response to the exception. Execution of such a program text is called *handling* the exception.

Expanded name. An expanded name *denotes* an entity which is *declared* immediately within some construct. An expanded name has the form of a *selected component*: the *prefix* denotes the construct (a *program unit*; or a *block*, loop, or *accept statement*); the *selector* is the *simple name* of the entity.

Expression. An expression defines the computation of a value.

Fixed point type. See *real type*.

Floating point type. See *real type*.

Formal parameter. See *parameter*.

Function. See *subprogram*.

Generic unit. A generic unit is a template either for a set of *subprograms* or for a set of *packages*. A subprogram or package created using the template is called an *instance* of the generic unit. A *generic instantiation* is the kind of *declaration* that creates an instance.

A generic unit is written as a subprogram or package but with the specification prefixed by a *generic formal part* which may declare *generic formal parameters*. A generic formal parameter is either a *type*, a *subprogram*, or an *object*. A generic unit is one of the kinds of *program unit*.

Handler. See *exception*.

Index. See *array type*.

Index constraint. An index constraint for an *array type* specifies the lower and upper bounds for each index *range* of the array type.

Indexed component. An indexed component *denotes* a *component* in an *array*. It is a form of *name* containing *expressions* which specify the values of the *indices* of the array component. An indexed component may also denote an *entry* in a family of entries.

Instance. See *generic unit*.

Integer type. An integer type is a *discrete type* whose values represent all integer numbers within a specific *range*.

Lexical element. A lexical element is an identifier, a *literal*, a delimiter, or a comment.

Limited type. A limited type is a *type* for which neither assignment nor the predefined comparison for equality is implicitly declared. All *task* types are limited. A *private type* can be defined to be limited. An equality operator can be explicitly declared for a limited type.

Literal. A literal represents a value literally, that is, by means of letters and other characters. A literal is either a numeric literal, an enumeration literal, a character literal, or a string literal.

Mode. See *parameter*.

Model number. A model number is an exactly representable value of a *real type*. *Operations* of a real type are defined in terms of operations on the model numbers of the type.

The properties of the model numbers and of their operations are the minimal properties preserved by all implementations of the real type.

Name. A name is a construct that stands for an entity: it is said that the name *denotes* the entity, and that the entity is the meaning of the name. See also *declaration*, *prefix*.

Named association. A named association specifies the association of an item with one or more positions in a list, by naming the positions.

Object. An object contains a value. A program creates an object either by *elaborating* an *object declaration* or by *evaluating* an *allocator*. The declaration or allocator specifies a *type* for the object: the object can only contain values of that type.

Operation. An operation is an elementary action associated with one or more *types*. It is either implicitly declared by the *declaration* of the type, or it is a *subprogram* that has a *parameter* or *result* of the type.

Operator. An operator is an operation which has one or two operands. A unary operator is written before an operand; a binary operator is written between two operands. This notation is a special kind of *function call*. An operator can be declared as a function. Many operators are implicitly declared by the *declaration* of a *type* (for example, most type declarations imply the declaration of the equality operator for values of the type).

Overloading. An identifier can have several alternative meanings at a given point in the program text: this property is called *overloading*. For example, an overloaded enumeration literal can be an identifier that appears in the definitions of two or more *enumeration types*. The effective meaning of an overloaded identifier is determined by the context. *Subprograms*, *aggregates*, *allocators*, and string *literals* can also be overloaded.

Package. A package specifies a group of logically related entities, such as *types*, *objects* of those types, and *subprograms* with *parameters* of those types. It is written as a *package declaration* and a *package body*. The package declaration has a *visible part*, containing the *declarations* of all entities that can be explicitly used outside the package. It may also have a *private part* containing structural details that complete the specification of the visible entities, but which are irrelevant to the user of the package. The *package body* contains implementations of *subprograms* (and possibly *tasks* as other *packages*) that have been specified in the package declaration. A package is one of the kinds of *program unit*.

Parameter. A parameter is one of the named entities associated with a *subprogram*, *entry*, or *generic unit*, and used to communicate with the corresponding subprogram body, *accept statement* or generic body. A *formal parameter* is an identifier used to denote the named entity within the body. An *actual parameter* is the particular entity associated with the corresponding formal parameter by a *subprogram call*, *entry call*, or *generic instantiation*. The *mode* of a formal parameter specifies whether the associated actual parameter supplies a value for the formal parameter, or the formal supplies a value for the actual parameter, or both. The association of actual parameters with formal parameters can be specified by *named associations*, by *positional associations*, or by a combination of these.

Parent type. See *derived type*.

Positional association. A positional association specifies the association of an item with a position in a list, by using the same position in the text to specify the item.

Pragma. A pragma conveys information to the compiler.

Prefix. A prefix is used as the first part of certain kinds of name. A prefix is either a *function call* or a *name*.

Private part. See *package*.

Private type. A private type is a *type* whose structure and set of values are clearly defined, but not directly available to the user of the type. A private type is known only by its *discriminants* (if any) and by the set of *operations* defined for it. A private type and its applicable operations are defined in the *visible part* of a *package*, or in a *generic formal part*. *Assignment*, equality, and inequality are also defined for private types, unless the private type is *limited*.

Procedure. See *subprogram*.

Program. A program is composed of a number of *compilation units*, one of which is a *subprogram* called the *main program*. Execution of the program consists of execution of the main program, which may invoke subprograms declared in the other compilation units of the program.

Program unit. A program unit is any one of a *generic unit*, *package*, *subprogram*, or *task unit*.

Qualified expression. A qualified expression is an *expression* preceded by an indication of its *type* or *subtype*. Such qualification is used when, in its absence, the expression might be ambiguous (for example as a consequence of *overloading*).

Raising an exception. See *exception*.

Range. A range is a contiguous set of values of a *scalar type*. A range is specified by giving the lower and upper bounds for the values. A value in the range is said to *belong* to the range.

Range constraint. A range constraint of a *type* specifies a *range*, and thereby determines the subset of the values of the type that *belong* to the range.

Real type. A real type is a *type* whose values represent approximations to the real numbers. There are two kinds of real type: *fixed point types* are specified by absolute error bound; *floating point types* are specified by a relative error bound expressed as a number of significant decimal digits.

Record type. A value of a record type consists of *components* which are usually of different *types* or *subtypes*. For each component of a record value or record *object*, the definition of the record type specifies an identifier that uniquely determines the component within the record.

Renaming declaration. A renaming declaration declares another *name* for an entity.

Rendezvous. A rendezvous is the interaction that occurs between two parallel *tasks* when one task has called an *entry* of the other task, and a corresponding *accept statement* is being executed by the other task on behalf of the calling task.

Representation clause. A representation clause directs the compiler in the selection of the mapping of a *type*, an *object*, or a *task* onto features of the underlying machine that executes a program. In some cases, representation clauses completely specify the mapping; in other cases, they provide criteria for choosing a mapping.

Satisfy. See *constraint, subtype*.

Scalar type. An *object* or value of a scalar *type* does not have *components*. A scalar type is either a *discrete type* or a *real type*. The values of a scalar type are ordered.

Scope. See *declaration*.

Selected component. A selected component is a *name* consisting of a *prefix* and of an identifier called the *selector*. Selected components are used to denote record components, *entries*, and *objects* designated by access values; they are also used as *expanded names*.

Selector. See *selected component*.

Simple name. See *declaration, name*.

Statement. A statement specifies one or more actions to be performed during the execution of a *program*.

Subcomponent. A subcomponent is either a *component*, or a component of another subcomponent.

Subprogram. A subprogram is either a *procedure* or a *function*. A procedure specifies a sequence of actions and is invoked by a *procedure call* statement. A function specifies a sequence of actions and also returns a value called the *result*, and so a *function call* is an *expression*. A subprogram is written as a *subprogram declaration*, which specifies its *name, formal parameters*, and (for a function) its result; and a *subprogram body* which specifies the sequence of actions. The subprogram call specifies the *actual parameters* that are to be associated with the formal parameters. A subprogram is one of the kinds of *program unit*.

Subtype. A subtype of a *type* characterizes a subset of the values of the type. The subset is determined by a *constraint* on the type. Each value in the set of values of a subtype *belongs* to the subtype and *satisfies* the constraint determining the subtype.

Subunit. See *body*.

Task. A task operates in parallel with other parts of the program. It is written as a *task specification* (which specifies the *name* of the task and the names and *formal parameters* of its entries), and a *task body* which defines its execution. A *task unit* is one of the kinds of *program unit*. A *task type* is a *type* that permits the subsequent *declaration* of any number of similar tasks of the type. A value of a task type is said to *designate* a task.

Type. A type characterizes both a set of values, and a set of *operations* applicable to those values. A *type definition* is a language construct that defines a type. A particular type is either an *access type*, an *array type*, a *private type*, a *record type*, a *scalar type*, or a *task type*.

Use clause. A use clause achieves *direct visibility* of *declarations* that appear in the *visible parts* of named *packages*.

Variable. See *object*.

Variant part. A variant part of a *record* specifies alternative record *components*, depending on a *discriminant* of the record. Each value of the discriminant establishes a particular alternative of the variant part.

Visibility. At a given point in a program text, the *declaration* of an entity with a certain identifier is said to be *visible* if the entity is an acceptable meaning for an occurrence at that point of the identifier. The declaration is *visible* by *selection* at the place of the *selector* in a *selected component* or at the place of the name in a *named association*. Otherwise, the declaration is *directly visible*, that is, if the identifier alone has that meaning.

Visible part. See *package*.

With clause. See *compilation unit*.

E. Syntax Summary

2.1

```
graphic_character ::= basic_graphic_character
    | lower_case_letter | other_special_character

basic_graphic_character ::=
        upper_case_letter | digit
    | special_character | space_character

basic_character ::=
        basic_graphic_character | format_effector
```

2.3

```
identifier ::=
    letter |[underline] letter_or_digit|

letter_or_digit ::= letter | digit

letter ::= upper_case_letter | lower_case_letter
```

2.4

```
numeric_literal ::= decimal_literal | based_literal
```

2.4.1

```
decimal_literal ::= integer [.integer] [exponent]

integer ::= digit |[underline] digit|

exponent ::= E [+] integer | E - integer
```

2.4.2

```
based_literal ::=
    base # based_integer [.based_integer] # [exponent]

base ::= integer

based_integer ::=
    extended_digit |[underline] extended_digit|

extended_digit ::= digit | letter
```

2.5

```
character_literal ::= 'graphic_character'
```

2.6

```
string_literal ::= "|graphic_character|"
```

2.8

```
pragma ::=
    pragma identifier [(argument_association
                        |, argument_association|)];

argument_association ::=
    [argument_identifier =>] name
    | [argument_identifier =>] expression
```

3.1

```
basic_declaration ::=
        object_declaration      | number_declaration
    | type_declaration          | subtype_declaration
    | subprogram_declaration    | package_declaration
    | task_declaration          | generic_declaration
    | exception_declaration     | generic_instantiation
    | renaming_declaration      | deferred_constant_declaration
```

3.2

```
object_declaration ::=
        identifier_list : [constant] subtype_indication [:= expression];
    | identifier_list : [constant] constrained_array_definition
                                                [:= expression];

number_declaration ::=
        identifier_list : constant := universal_static_expression;

identifier_list ::=   identifier |, identifier|
```

3.3.1

```
type_declaration ::=   full_type_declaration
    | incomplete_type_declaration | private_type_declaration

full_type_declaration ::=
    type identifier [discriminant_part] is type_definition;

type_definition ::=
        enumeration_type_definition | integer_type_definition
    | real_type_definition          | array_type_definition
    | record_type_definition        | access_type_definition
    | derived_type_definition
```

3.3.2

```
subtype_declaration ::=
    subtype identifier is subtype_indication;

subtype_indication ::=   type_mark [constraint]

type_mark ::= type_name | subtype_name

constraint ::=
        range_constraint        | floating_point_constraint
    | fixed_point_constraint    | index_constraint
    | discriminant_constraint
```

3.4

```
derived_type_definition ::= new subtype_indication
```

3.5

```
range_constraint ::=   range range

range ::=   range_attribute
    | simple_expression .. simple_expression
```

3.5.1

enumeration_type_definition ::=
　(enumeration_literal_specification
　　{, enumeration_literal_specification})

enumeration_literal_specification ::= enumeration_literal

enumeration_literal ::= identifier | character_literal

3.5.4

integer_type_definition ::= range_constraint

3.5.6

real_type_definition ::=
　floating_point_constraint | fixed_point_constraint

3.5.7

floating_point_constraint ::=
　floating_accuracy_definition [range_constraint]

floating_accuracy_definition ::=
　digits *static*_simple_expression

3.5.9

fixed_point_constraint ::=
　fixed_accuracy_definition [range_constraint]

fixed_accuracy_definition ::=
　delta *static*_simple_expression

3.6

array_type_definition ::=
　unconstrained_array_definition | constrained_array_definition

unconstrained_array_definition ::=
　array(index_subtype_definition {, index_subtype_definition}) **of**
　　*component*_subtype_indication

constrained_array_definition ::=
　array index_constraint **of** *component*_subtype_indication

index_subtype_definition ::= type_mark **range** <>

index_constraint ::= (discrete_range {, discrete_range})

discrete_range ::= *discrete*_subtype_indication | range

3.7

record_type_definition ::=
　record
　　component_list
　end record

component_list ::=
　　component_declaration {component_declaration}
　| {component_declaration} variant_part
　| **null**;

component_declaration ::=
　identifier_list : component_subtype_definition [:= expression];

component_subtype_definition ::= subtype_indication

3.7.1

discriminant_part ::=
　(discriminant_specification {; discriminant_specification})

discriminant_specification ::=
　identifier_list : type_mark [:= **expression**]

3.7.2

discriminant_constraint ::=
　(discriminant_association {, discriminant_association})

discriminant_association ::=
　[*discriminant*_simple_name {| *discriminant*_simple_name} =>]
　　expression

3.7.3

variant_part ::=
　case *discriminant*_simple_name **is**
　　variant
　　{ variant}
　end case;

variant ::=
　when choice {| choice} =>
　　component_list

choice ::= simple_expression
　| discrete_range | **others** | *component*_simple_name

3.8

access_type_definition ::= **access** subtype_indication

3.8.1

incomplete_type_declaration ::=
　type identifier [discriminant_part];

3.9

declarative_part ::=
　{basic_declarative_item} {later_declarative_item}

basic_declarative_item ::= basic_declaration
　| representation_clause | use_clause

later_declarative_item ::= body
　| subprogram_declaration　| package_declaration
　| task_declaration　　　 | generic_declaration
　| use_clause　　　　　　| generic_instantiation

body ::= proper_body | body_stub

proper_body ::=
　subprogram_body | package_body | task_body

Syntax Summary

4.1

```
name ::= simple_name
  | character_literal        | operator_symbol
  | indexed_component        | slice
  | selected_component       | attribute

simple_name ::= identifier

prefix ::= name | function_call
```

4.1.1

```
indexed_component ::= prefix(expression {, expression})
```

4.1.2

```
slice ::= prefix(discrete_range)
```

4.1.3

```
selected_component ::= prefix.selector

selector ::= simple_name
  | character_literal | operator_symbol | all
```

4.1.4

```
attribute ::= prefix'attribute_designator

attribute_designator ::=
  simple_name [(universal_static_expression)]
```

4.3

```
aggregate ::=
  (component_association {, component_association})

component_association ::=
  [choice {| choice} => ] expression
```

4.4

```
expression ::=
    relation {and relation}  | relation {and then relation}
  | relation {or relation}   | relation {or else relation}
  | relation {xor relation}

relation ::=
    simple_expression [relational_operator simple_expression]
  | simple_expression [not] in range
  | simple_expression [not] in type_mark

simple_expression ::=
  [unary_adding_operator] term {binary_adding_operator term}

term ::= factor {multiplying_operator factor}

factor ::= primary [** primary] | abs primary | not primary

primary ::=
    numeric_literal | null | aggregate | string_literal
  | name | allocator | function_call | type_conversion
  | qualified_expression | (expression)
```

4.5

```
logical_operator    ::=  and | or | xor

relational_operator  ::=  = | /= | < | <= | > | >=

binary_adding_operator  ::=  + | - | &

unary_adding_operator  ::=  + | -

multiplying_operator  ::=  * | / | mod | rem

highest_precedence_operator  ::=  ** | abs | not
```

4.6

```
type_conversion ::= type_mark(expression)
```

4.7

```
qualified_expression ::=
  type_mark'(expression) | type_mark'aggregate
```

4.8

```
allocator ::=
  new subtype_indication | new qualified_expression
```

5.1

```
sequence_of_statements ::= statement {statement}

statement ::=
  {label} simple_statement | {label} compound_statement

simple_statement ::= null_statement
  | assignment_statement   | procedure_call_statement
  | exit_statement         | return_statement
  | goto_statement         | entry_call_statement
  | delay_statement        | abort_statement
  | raise_statement        | code_statement

compound_statement ::=
    if_statement        | case_statement
  | loop_statement      | block_statement
  | accept_statement    | select_statement

label ::= <<label_simple_name>>

null_statement ::= null;
```

5.2

```
assignment_statement ::=
  variable_name := expression;
```

5.3

```
if_statement ::=
    if condition then
      sequence_of_statements
  {elsif condition then
      sequence_of_statements}
  [else
      sequence_of_statements]
    end if;

condition ::= boolean_expression
```

5.4

```
case_statement ::=
  case expression is
      case_statement_alternative
    { case_statement_alternative}
  end case;

case_statement_alternative ::=
  when choice {| choice } =>
      sequence_of_statements
```

5.5

```
loop_statement ::=
  [loop_simple_name:]
    [ iteration_scheme] loop
        sequence_of_statements
      end loop [loop_simple_name];

iteration_scheme ::= while condition
  |  for loop_parameter_specification

loop_parameter_specification ::=
    identifier in [reverse] discrete_range
```

5.6

```
block_statement ::=
  [block_simple_name:]
    [ declare
          declarative_part]
      begin
          sequence_of_statements
    [ exception
          exception_handler
        { exception_handler}]
      end [block_simple_name];
```

5.7

```
exit_statement ::=
  exit [loop_name] [when condition];
```

5.8

```
return_statement ::= return [expression];
```

5.9

```
goto_statement ::= goto label_name;
```

6.1

```
subprogram_declaration ::= subprogram_specification;

subprogram_specification ::=
      procedure identifier [formal_part]
  |  function designator [formal_part] return type_mark

designator ::= identifier | operator_symbol

operator_symbol ::= string_literal

formal_part ::=
    (parameter_specification {; parameter_specification})

parameter_specification ::=
    identifier_list : mode type_mark [:= expression]

mode ::= [in] | in out | out
```

6.3

```
subprogram_body ::=
    subprogram_specification is
        [ declarative_part]
      begin
          sequence_of_statements
    [ exception
          exception_handler
        { exception_handler}]
      end [designator];
```

6.4

```
procedure_call_statement ::=
    procedure_name [actual_parameter_part];

function_call ::=
    function_name [actual_parameter_part]

actual_parameter_part ::=
    (parameter_association {, parameter_association})

parameter_association ::=
    [ formal_parameter =>] actual_parameter

formal_parameter ::= parameter_simple_name

actual_parameter ::=
    expression | variable_name | type_mark(variable_name)
```

7.1

```
package_declaration ::= package_specification;

package_specification ::=
      package identifier is
        {basic_declarative_item}
    [ private
        {basic_declarative_item}]
      end [package_simple_name]

package_body ::=
      package body package_simple_name is
        [ declarative_part]
    [ begin
          sequence_of_statements
    [ exception
          exception_handler
        { exception_handler}]]
      end [package_simple_name];
```

7.4

```
private_type_declaration ::=
    type identifier [discriminant_part] is [limited] private;

deferred_constant_declaration ::=
    identifier_list : constant type_mark;
```

8.4

```
use_clause ::= use package_name {, package_name};
```

8.5

```
renaming_declaration ::=
      identifier : type_mark       renames object_name;
  |  identifier : exception       renames exception_name;
  |  package identifier           renames package_name;
  |  subprogram_specification     renames
                                  subprogram_or_entry_name;
```

9.1

task_declaration ::= task_specification;

task_specification ::=
  task [**type**] identifier [**is**
    {entry_declaration}
    {representation_clause}
  end [task_simple_name]]

task_body ::=
  task body task_simple_name **is**
    [declarative_part]
  begin
      sequence_of_statements
  [**exception**
      exception_handler
      { exception_handler}]
  end [task_simple_name];

9.5

entry_declaration ::=
  entry identifier [(discrete_range)] [formal_part];

entry_call_statement ::=
  entry_name [actual_parameter_part];

accept_statement ::=
  accept entry_simple_name [(entry_index)] [formal_part] [**do**
    sequence_of_statements
  end [entry_simple_name]];

entry_index ::= expression

9.6

delay_statement ::= **delay** simple_expression;

9.7

select_statement ::= selective_wait
  | conditional_entry_call | timed_entry_call

9.7.1

selective_wait ::=
  select
    select_alternative
  {**or**
    select_alternative}
  [**else**
    sequence_of_statements]
  end select;

select_alternative ::=
  [**when** condition =>]
    selective_wait_alternative

selective_wait_alternative ::= accept_alternative
  | delay_alternative | terminate_alternative

accept_alternative ::=
  accept_statement [sequence_of_statements]

delay_alternative ::=
  delay_statement [sequence_of_statements]

terminate_alternative ::= **terminate**;

9.7.2

conditional_entry_call ::=
  select
      entry_call_statement
    [sequence_of_statements]
  else
      sequence_of_statements
  end select;

9.7.3

timed_entry_call ::=
  select
      entry_call_statement
    [sequence_of_statements]
  or
      delay_alternative
  end select;

9.10

abort_statement ::= **abort** task_name {, task_name};

10.1

compilation ::= {compilation_unit}

compilation_unit ::=
      context_clause library_unit
  | context_clause secondary_unit

library_unit ::=
      subprogram_declaration | package_declaration
  | generic_declaration | generic_instantiation
  | subprogram_body

secondary_unit ::= library_unit_body | subunit

library_unit_body ::= subprogram_body | package_body

10.1.1

context_clause ::= {with_clause {use_clause}}

with_clause ::=
  with unit_simple_name {, unit_simple_name};

10.2

body_stub ::=
      subprogram_specification **is separate**;
  | **package body** package_simple_name **is separate**;
  | **task body** task_simple_name **is separate**;

subunit ::= **separate** (parent_unit_name) proper_body

11.1

exception_declaration ::= identifier_list : **exception**;

11.2

exception_handler ::=
  when exception_choice {| exception_choice} =>
    sequence_of_statements

exception_choice ::= exception_name | **others**

11.3

raise_statement ::= **raise** [exception_name];

12.1

generic_declaration ::= generic_specification;

generic_specification ::=
    generic_formal_part subprogram_specification
  | generic_formal_part package_specification

generic_formal_part ::= **generic** {generic_parameter_declaration}

generic_parameter_declaration ::=
    identifier_list : [**in** [**out**]] type_mark [:= expression];
  | **type** identifier **is** generic_type_definition;
  | private_type_declaration
  | **with** subprogram_specification [**is** name];
  | **with** subprogram_specification [**is** <>];

generic_type_definition ::=
    (<>) | **range** <> | **digits** <> | **delta** <>
  | array_type_definition | access_type_definition

12.3

generic_instantiation ::=
    package identifier **is**
      new *generic_package*_name [generic_actual_part];
  | **procedure** identifier **is**
      new *generic_procedure*_name [generic_actual_part];
  | **function** designator **is**
      new *generic_function*_name [generic_actual_part];

generic_actual_part ::=
  (generic_association {, generic_association})

generic_association ::=
  [generic_formal_parameter =>] generic_actual_parameter

generic_formal_parameter ::=
  *parameter*_simple_name | operator_symbol

generic_actual_parameter ::= expression | *variable*_name
  | *subprogram*_name | *entry*_name | type_mark

13.1

representation_clause ::=
    type_representation_clause | address_clause

type_representation_clause ::= length_clause
  | enumeration_representation_clause
  | record_representation_clause

13.2

length_clause ::= **for** attribute **use** simple_expression;

13.3

enumeration_representation_clause ::=
  for *type*_simple_name **use** aggregate;

13.4

record_representation_clause ::=
  for *type*_simple_name **use**
    record [alignment_clause]
      {component_clause}
    end record;

alignment_clause ::= **at mod** *static*_simple_expression;

component_clause ::=
  *component*_name **at** *static*_simple_expression
             range *static*_range;

13.5

address_clause ::=
  for simple_name **use at** simple_expression;

13.8

code_statement ::= type_mark'*record*_aggregate;

Syntax Cross Reference

In the list given below each syntactic category is followed by the section number where it is defined. For example:

adding_operator   4.5

In addition, each syntactic category is followed by the names of other categories in whose definition it appears. For example, adding_operator appears in the definition of simple_expression:

adding_operator   4.5
   simple_expression   4.4

An ellipsis (...) is used when the syntactic category is not defined by a syntax rule. For example:

lower_case_letter   ...

All uses of parentheses are combined in the term "()". The italicized prefixes used with some terms have been deleted here.

E-7

F. Implementation-Dependent Characteristics

The Ada language definition allows for certain machine-dependences in a controlled manner. No machine-dependent syntax or semantic extensions or restrictions are allowed. The only allowed implementation-dependences correspond to implementation-dependent pragmas and attributes, certain machine-dependent conventions as mentioned in chapter 13, and certain allowed restrictions on representation clauses.

The reference manual of each Ada implementation must include an appendix (called Appendix F) that describes all implementation-dependent characteristics. The appendix F for a given implementation must list in particular:

(1) The form, allowed places, and effect of every implementation-dependent pragma.

(2) The name and the type of every implementation-dependent attribute.

(3) The specification of the package SYSTEM (see 13.7).

(4) The list of all restrictions on representation clauses (see 13.1)

(5) The conventions used for any implementation-generated name denoting implementation-dependent components (see 13.4).

(6) The interpretation of expressions that appear in address clauses, including those for interrupts (see 13.5).

(7) Any restriction on unchecked conversions (see 13.10.2).

(8) Any implementation-dependent characteristics of the input-output packages (see 14).

Index

An entry exists in this index for each technical term or phrase that is defined in the reference manual. The term or phrase is in boldface and is followed by the section number where it is defined, also in boldface, for example:

Record aggregate 4.3.1

References to other sections that provide additional information are shown after a semicolon, for example:

Record aggregate 4.3.1; 4.3

References to other related entries in the index follow in brackets, and a line that is indented below a boldface entry gives the section numbers where particular uses of the term or phrase can be found; for example:

Record aggregate 4.3.1; 4.3
[see also: aggregate]
as a basic operation 3.3.3; 3.7.4
in a code statement 13.8

The index also contains entries for different parts of a phrase, entries that correct alternative terminology, and entries directing the reader to information otherwise hard to find, for example:

Check
[see: suppress pragma]

Accuracy
    of a numeric operation 4.5.7
    of a numeric operation of a universal type 4.10

Activation
    [see: task activation]

Actual object
    [see: generic actual object]

Actual parameter 6.4.1; D; (of an operator) 6.7; (of a sub-program) 6.4; 6.2, 6.3
    [see also: entry call, formal parameter, function call, procedure call statement, subprogram call]
    characteristics and overload resolution 6.6
    in a generic instantiation [see: generic actual parameter]
    of an array type 3.6.1
    of a record type 3.7.2
    of a task type 9.2
    that is an array aggregate 4.3.2
    that is a loop parameter 5.5

Actual parameter part 6.4
    in a conditional entry call 9.7.2
    in an entry call statement 9.5
    in a function call 6.4
    in a procedure call statement 6.4
    in a timed entry call 9.7.3

Actual part
    [see: actual parameter part, generic actual part]

Actual subprogram
    [see: generic actual subprogram]

Actual type
    [see: generic actual type]

Adding operator
    [see: binary adding operator, unary adding operator]

Addition operation 4.5.3
    accuracy for a real type 4.5.7

ADDRESS (predefined attribute) **13.7.2**; 3.5.5, 3.5.8, 3.5.10, 3.6.2, 3.7.4, 3.8.2, 7.4.2, 9.9, 13.7, A
    [see also: address clause, system.address]

ADDRESS (predefined type)
    [see: system.address]

Address clause 13.5; 13.1, 13.7
    [see also: storage address, system.address]
    as a representation clause 13.1
    for an entry 13.5.1

AFT (predefined attribute) for a fixed point type **3.5.10**; A

Aft field of text_io output **14.3.8**, **14.3.10**

Aggregate 4.3, D
    [see also: array aggregate, overloading of..., record aggregate]
    as a basic operation 3.3.3; 3.6.2, 3.7.4
    as a primary 4.4
    in an allocator 4.8
    in a code statement 13.8
    in an enumeration representation clause 13.3
    in a qualified expression 4.7
    must not be the argument of a conversion 4.6
    of a derived type 3.4

Alignment clause (in a record representation clause) **13.4**

All in a selected component **4.1.3**

Allocation of processing resources 9.8

Allocator 4.8; 3.8, D
    [see also: access type, collection, exception raised during..., initial value, object, overloading of...]
    as a basic operation 3.3.3; 3.8.2
    as a primary 4.4
    creating an object with a discriminant 4.8; 5.2
    for an array type 3.6.1
    for a generic formal access type 12.1.2
    for a private type 7.4.1
    for a record type 3.7.2
    for a task type 9.2; 9.3
    must not be the argument of a conversion 4.6
    raising storage_error due to the size of the collection being exceeded 11.1
    setting a task value 9.2
    without storage check 11.7

Allowed 1.6

Alternative
    [see: accept alternative, case statement alternative, closed alternative, delay alternative, open alternative, select alternative, selective wait, terminate alternative]

Ambiguity
    [see: overloading]

Ampersand
    [see: catenation]
    character 2.1
    delimiter 2.2

Ancestor library unit 10.2

And operator
    [see: logical operator]

And then control form
    [see: short circuit control form]

Anonymous type 3.3.1; 3.5.4, 3.5.7, 3.5.9, 3.6, 9.1
    anonymous base type [see: first named subtype]

ANSI (american national standards institute) **2.1**

Apostrophe character 2.1
    in a character literal 2.5

Apostrophe delimiter 2.2
    in an attribute 4.1.4
    of a qualified expression 4.7

Apply 10.1.1

Appropriate for a type **4.1**
    for an array type 4.1.1, 4.1.2
    for a record type 4.1.3
    for a task type 4.1.3

Arbitrary selection of select alternatives **9.7.1**

Argument association in a pragma **2.8**

Argument identifier in a pragma **2.8**

Arithmetic operator 4.5
    [see also: binary adding operator, exponentiating operator, multiplying operator, predefined operator, unary adding operator]
    as an operation of a fixed point type 3.5.10

as an operation of a floating point type 3.5.8
as an operation of an integer type 3.5.5
rounding for real types 13.7.3

Array aggregate 4.3.2; 4.3
[see also: aggregate]
as a basic operation 3.3.3; 3.6.2
in an enumeration representation clause 13.3

Array assignment 5.2.1

Array bounds
[see: bound of an array]

Array component
[see: array type, component, indexed component]

Array type 3.6; 3.3, D
[see also: component, composite type, constrained array, constrained..., index, matching components, null slice, slice, unconstrained...]
as a full type 7.4.1
as a generic formal type 12.1.2
as a generic parameter 12.3.4
as the type of a formal parameter 6.2
conversion 4.6
for a prefix of an indexed component 4.1.1
for a prefix of a slice 4.1.2
operation 3.6.2; 4.5.2, 4.5.3
operation on an array of boolean components 4.5.1, 4.5.6
with a component type with discriminants 3.7.2
with a limited component type 7.4.4

Array type definition 3.6; 3.3.1, 12.1.2, 12.3.4
[see also: constrained array definition, elaboration of..., unconstrained array definition]
as a generic type definition 12.1

Arrow compound delimiter 2.2

ASCII (american standard code for information interchange) **2.1**

ASCII (predefined library package) **3.5.2; 2.6, C**
[see also: graphical symbol]

Assignment compound delimiter 2.2; 5.2
in an object declaration 3.2.1

Assignment operation 5.2; D
[see also: initial value, limited type]
as a basic operation 3.3, 3.3.3; 3.5.5, 3.5.8, 3.5.10, 3.6.2, 3.7.4, 3.8.2, 7.4.2, 12.1.2
for a generic formal type 12.1.2
not available for a limited type 7.4.4
of an array aggregate 4.3.2
of an initial value to an object 3.2.1
to an array variable 5.2.1; 5.2
to a loop parameter 5.5
to an object designated by an access value 3.8
to a shared variable 9.11

Assignment statement 5.2; D
[see also: statement]
as a simple statement 5.1

Associated declarative region of a declaration or statement **8.1**

Association
[see: component association, discriminant association, generic association, parameter association]

Attribute 4.1.4; D
[see also: predefined attribute, representation attribute]
as a basic operation 3.3.3
as a name 4.1
as a primary 4.4
in a length clause 13.2
in a static expression in a generic unit 12.1
of an access type 3.5.8
of an array type 3.6.2
of a derived type 3.4
of a discrete type or subtype 3.5.5
of an entry 9.9
of a fixed point type 3.5.10
of a floating point type 3.5.8
of an object of a task type 9.9
of a private type 7.4.2; 3.7.4
of a record type 3.7.4
of a static subtype in a static expression 4.9
of a task type 9.9
of a type 3.3
of a type as a generic actual function 12.3.6
of a type with discriminants 3.7.4
renamed as a function 8.5
that is a function 3.5.5

Attribute designator 4.1.4

Bar
[see: vertical bar]

BASE (predefined attribute) **3.3.3; A**
for an access type 3.8.2
for an array type 3.6.2
for a discrete type 3.5.5
for a fixed point type 3.5.10
for a floating point type 3.5.8
for a private type 7.4.2
for a record type 3.7.4

Base type (of a subtype) **3.3**
as a static subtype 4.9
as target type of a conversion 4.6
due to elaboration of a type definition 3.3.1
name [see: name of a base type]
of an array type 3.6; 4.1.2
of a derived subtype 3.4
of a discriminant determining the set of choices of a variant part 3.7.3
of a fixed point type 3.5.9
of a floating point type 3.5.7
of a formal parameter of a generic formal subprogram 12.1.3
of an integer type 3.5.4
of a parent subtype 3.4
of a qualified expression 4.7
of a type mark 3.3.2
of a type mark in a membership test 4.5.2
of the discrete range in a loop parameter specification 5.5
of the expression in a case statement 5.4
of the result of a generic formal function 12.1.3
of the result subtype of a function 5.8
of the subtype indication in an access type definition 3.8
of the type in the declaration of a generic formal object 12.1.1
of the type mark in a renaming declaration 8.5

Based literal 2.4.2; 14.3.7
[see also: colon character, sharp character]
as a numeric literal 2.4

Basic character 2.1
[see also: basic graphic character, character]

Basic character set 2.1
is sufficient for a program text 2.10

Basic declaration 3.1
as a basic declarative item 3.9

Basic declarative item 3.9
in a package specification 7.1; 7.2

Basic graphic character 2.1
[see also: basic character, digit, graphic character, space character, special character, upper case letter]

Basic operation 3.3.3
[see also: operation, scope of..., visibility...]
accuracy for a real type 4.5.7
implicitly declared 3.1, 3.3.3
of an access type 3.8.2
of an array type 3.6.2
of a derived type 3.4
of a discrete type 3.5.5
of a fixed point type 3.5.10
of a floating point type 3.5.8
of a limited type 7.4.4
of a private type 7.4.2
of a record type 3.7.4
of a task type 9.9
propagating an exception 11.6
raising an exception 11.4.1
that is an attribute 4.1.4

Belong
to a range 3.5
to a subtype 3.3
to a subtype of an access type 3.8

Binary adding operator 4.5; 4.5.3, C
[see also: arithmetic operator, overloading of an operator]
for time predefined type 9.6
in a simple expression 4.4
overloaded 6.7

Binary operation 4.5

Bit
[see: storage bits]

Blank skipped by a text_io procedure **14.3.5**

Block name 5.6
declaration 5.1
implicitly declared 3.1

Block statement 5.6; D
[see also: completed block statement, statement]
as a compound statement 5.1
as a declarative region 8.1
entity denoted by an expanded name 4.1.3
having dependent tasks 9.4
including an exception handler 11.2; 11
including an implicit declaration 5.1
including a suppress pragma 11.7
raising an exception 11.4.1, 11.4.2

Body 3.9; D
[see also: declaration, generic body, generic package body, generic subprogram body, library unit, package body, proper body, subprogram body, task body]
as a later declarative item 3.9

Body stub 10.2; D
acting as a subprogram declaration 6.3
as a body 3.9
as a portion of a declarative region 8.1
must be in the same declarative region as the declaration 3.9, 7.1

BOOLEAN (predefined type) **3.5.3**; C
derived 3.4; 3.5.3
result of a condition 5.3
result of an explicitly declared equality operator 6.7

Boolean expression
[see: condition, expression]

Boolean operator
[see: logical operator]

Boolean type 3.5.3
[see also: derived type of a boolean type, predefined type]
operation 3.5.5; 4.5.1, 4.5.2, 4.5.6
operation comparing real operands 4.5.7

Bound
[see: error bound, first attribute, last attribute]

Bound of an array **3.6, 3.6.1**
[see also: index range, slice]
aggregate 4.3.2
ignored due to index_check suppression 11.7
initialization in an allocator constrains the allocated object 4.8
that is a formal parameter 6.2
that is the result of an operation 4.5.1, 4.5.3, 4.5.6

Bound of a range **3.5**; 3.5.4
of a discrete range in a slice 4.1.2
of a discrete range is of universal_integer type 3.6.1
of a static discrete range 4.9

Bound of a scalar type **3.5**

Bound of a slice **4.1.2**

Box compound delimiter 2.2
in a generic parameter declaration 12.1, 12.1.2, 12.1.3; 12.3.3
in an index subtype definition 3.6

Bracket
[see: label bracket, left parenthesis, parenthesized expression, right parenthesis, string bracket]

CALENDAR (predefined library package) **9.6**; C

Call
[see: conditional entry call, entry call statement, function call, procedure call statement, subprogram call, timed entry call]

CALLABLE (predefined attribute)
for an abnormal task 9.10
for a task object 9.9; A

Calling conventions
[see: subprogram declaration]
of a subprogram written in another language 13.9

Cancelation of an entry call statement **9.7.2, 9.7.3**

Compiler listing
[see: list pragma, page pragma]

Compiler optimization
[see: optimization, optimize pragma]

Completed block statement 9.4

Completed subprogram 9.4

Completed task 9.4; 9.9
[see also: tasking_error, terminated task]
  as recipient of an entry call 9.5, 9.7.2, 9.7.3
  becoming abnormal 9.10
  completion during activation 9.3
  due to an exception in the task body 11.4.1, 11.4.2

Component (of a composite type) **3.3**; 3.6, 3.7, D
[see also: component association, component clause,
component list, composite type, default expression,
dependence on a discriminant, discriminant, indexed component, object, record type, selected component, subcom-
ponent]
  combined by aggregate 4.3
  depending on a discriminant 3.7.1; 11.1
  name starting with a prefix 4.1
  of an array 3.6 [see also: array type]
  of a constant 3.2.1
  of a derived type 3.4
  of an object 3.2
  of a private type 7.4.2
  of a record 3.7 [see also: record type]
  of a variable 3.2.1
  simple name as a choice 3.7.3
  subtype 3.7
  subtype itself a composite type 3.6.1, 3.7.2
  that is a task object 9.3
  whose type is a limited type 7.4.4

Component association 4.3
  in an aggregate 4.3
  including an expression that is an array aggregate
  4.3.2
  named component association 4.3
  named component association for selective visibility
  8.3
  positional component association 4.3

Component clause (in a record representation clause) **13.4**

Component declaration 3.7
[see also: declaration, record type definition]
  as part of a basic declaration 3.1
  having an extended scope 8.2
  in a component list 3.7
  of an array object 3.6.1
  of a record object 3.7.2
  visibility 8.3

Component list 3.7
  in a record type definition 3.7
  in a variant 3.7.3

Component subtype definition 3.7
[see also: dependence on a discriminant]
  in a component declaration 3.7

Component type
  catenation with an array type 4.5.3
  object initialization [see: initial value]
  of an expression in an array aggregate 4.3.2
  of an expression in a record aggregate 4.3.1
  of a generic formal array type 12.3.4
  operation determining a composite type operation
  4.5.1, 4.5.2

Composite type 3.3; 3.6, 3.7, D
[see also: array type, class of type, component, discriminant, record type, subcomponent]
  including a limited subcomponent 7.4.4
  including a task subcomponent 9.2
  object initialization 3.2.1 [see also: initial value]
  of an aggregate 4.3
  with a private type component 7.4.2

Compound delimiter 2.2
[see also: arrow, assignment, box, delimiter, double dot,
double star, exponentiation, greater than or equal, inequality, left label bracket, less than or equal, right label bracket]
  names of delimiters 2.2

Compound statement 5.1
[see also: statement]
  including the destination of a goto statement 5.9

Concatenation
[see: catenation]

Condition 5.3
[see also: expression]
  determining an open alternative of a selective wait
  9.7.1
  in an exit statement 5.7
  in an if statement 5.3
  in a while iteration scheme 5.5

Conditional compilation 10.6

Conditional entry call 9.7.2; 9.7
  and renamed entries 8.5
  subject to an address clause 13.5.1

Conforming 6.3.1
  discriminant parts 6.3.1; 3.8.1, 7.4.1
  formal parts 6.3.1
  formal parts in entry declarations and accept statements 9.5
  subprogram specifications 6.3.1; 6.3
  subprogram specifications in body stub and subunit
  10.2
  type marks 6.3.1; 7.4.3

Conjunction
[see: logical operator]

Constant 3.2.1; D
[see also: deferred constant, loop parameter, object]
  access object 3.8
  formal parameter 6.2
  generic formal object 12.1.1, 12.3
  in a static expression 4.9
  renamed 8.5
  that is a slice 4.1.2

Constant declaration 3.2.1
[see also: deferred constant declaration]
  as a full declaration 7.4.3
  with an array type 3.6.1
  with a record type 3.7.2

CONSTRAINED (predefined attribute)
  for an object of a type with discriminants 3.7.4; A
  for a private type 7.4.2, A

Constrained array definition 3.6
  in an object declaration 3.2, 3.2.1

Constrained array type 3.6
[see also: array type, constraint]

Deallocation
[see: access type, unchecked_deallocation]

Decimal literal 2.4.1; 14.3.7, 14.3.8
    as a numeric literal 2.4

Decimal number (in text_io) **14.3.7**

Decimal point
[see: fixed point, floating point, point character]

Declaration 3.1; D
[see also: basic declaration, block name declaration, body, component declaration, constant declaration, deferred constant declaration, denote, discriminant specification, entry declaration, enumeration literal specification, exception declaration, exception raised during..., generic declaration, generic formal part, generic instantiation, generic parameter declaration, generic specification, hiding, implicit declaration, incomplete type declaration, label declaration, local declaration, loop name declaration, loop parameter specification, number declaration, object declaration, package declaration, package specification, parameter specification, private type declaration, renaming declaration, representation clause, scope of..., specification, subprogram declaration, subprogram specification, subtype declaration, task declaration, task specification, type declaration, visibility]
    as an overload resolution context 8.7
    determined by visibility from an identifier 8.3
    made directly visible by a use clause 8.4
    of an enumeration literal 3.5.1
    of a formal parameter 6.1
    of a loop parameter 5.5
    overloaded 6.6
    raising an exception 11.4.2; 11.4
    to which a representation clause applies 13.1

Declarative item 3.9
[see also: basic declarative item, later declarative item]
    in a code procedure body 13.8
    in a declarative part 3.9; 6.3.2
    in a package specification 6.3.2
    in a visible part 7.4
    that is a use clause 8.4

Declarative part 3.9; D
[see also: elaboration of...]
    in a block statement 5.6
    in a package body 7.1; 7.3
    in a subprogram body 6.3
    in a task body 9.1; 9.3
    including a generic declaration 12.2
    including an inline pragma 6.3.2
    including an interface pragma 13.9
    including a representation clause 13.1
    including a suppress pragma 11.7
    including a task declaration 9.3
    with implicit declarations 5.1

Declarative region 8.1; 8.2, 8.4
[see also: scope of...]
    determining the visibility of a declaration 8.3
    formed by the predefined package standard 8.6
    in which a declaration is hidden 8.3
    including a full type definition 7.4.2
    including a subprogram declaration 6.3

Declared immediately within
[see: occur immediately within]

Default determination of a representation for an entity **13.1**

Default expression
[see: default initial value, default initialization, discriminant specification, formal parameter, generic formal object, initial value]
    cannot include a forcing occurrence 13.1
    for a component 3.3; 7.4.3, 7.4.4
    for a component of a derived type object 3.4
    for a discriminant 3.7.1; 3.2.1, 3.7.2, 12.3.2
    for a formal parameter 6.1, 6.4.2; 6.4, 6.7, 7.4.3
    for a formal parameter of a generic formal subprogram 12.1; 7.4.3
    for a formal parameter of a renamed subprogram or entry 8.5
    for a generic formal object 12.1, 12.1.1; 12.3
    for the discriminants of an allocated object 4.8
    in a component declaration 3.7
    in a discriminant specification 3.7.1
    including the name of a private type 7.4.1

Default file 14.3.2; 14.3

Default generic formal subprogram 12.1; 12.1.3, 12.3.6

Default initial value (of a type) **3.3**
[see also: default expression, initial value]
    for an access type object 3.8; 3.2.1 [see also: null access value]
    for a record type object 3.7; 3.2.1

Default initialization (for an object) **3.2.1, 3.3**
[see also: default expression, default initial value, initial value]

Default mode (of a file) **14.2.1**; 14.2.3, 14.2.5, 14.3.10

Default_aft (field length)
    of fixed_io or float_io 14.3.8; 14.3.10

Default_base
    of integer_io 14.3.7; 14.3.10

Default_exp (field length)
    of fixed_io or float_io 14.3.8; 14.3.10

Default_fore (field length)
    of fixed_io or float_io 14.3.8; 14.3.10

Default_setting (letter case)
    of enumeration_io 14.3.9; 14.3.10

Default_width (field length)
    of enumeration_io 14.3.9; 14.3.10
    of integer_io 14.3.7; 14.3.10

Deferred constant 7.4.3
    of a limited type 7.4.4

Deferred constant declaration 7.4; 7.4.3
[see also: private part (of a package), visible part (of a package)]
    as a basic declaration 3.1
    is not a forcing occurrence 13.1

Definition
[see: access type definition, array type definition, component subtype definition, constrained array definition, derived type definition, enumeration type definition, generic type definition, index subtype definition, integer type definition, real type definition, record type definition, type definition, unconstrained array definition]

Delay alternative (of a selective wait) **9.7.1**

Delay expression 9.6; 9.7.1
[see also: duration]
    in a timed entry call 9.7.3

Delay statement 9.6
[see also: statement, task]
    as a simple statement 5.1
    in an abnormal task 9.10
    in a select alternative 9.7.1
    in a timed entry call 9.7.3

DELETE (input-output procedure)
    in an instance of direct_io 14.2.1; 14.2.5
    in an instance of sequential_io 14.2.1, 14.2.3
    in text_io 14.2.1; 14.3.10

Delimiter 2.2
[see also: ampersand, apostrophe, arrow, assignment, colon, compound delimiter, divide, dot, double dot, equal, exclamation mark, exponentiation, greater than or equal, greater than, inequality, label bracket, less than or equal, less than, minus, parenthesis, period, plus, point, semicolon, star, vertical bar]

Delta (of a fixed point type) **3.5.9**
[see also: fixed point type]
    of universal_fixed 4.5.5

DELTA (predefined attribute) **3.5.10**; 4.1.4, A

Denote an entity 3.1, 4.1; D
[see also: declaration, entity, name]

Dependence between compilation units **10.3**; 10.5
[see also: with clause]
    circularity implying illegality 10.5

Dependence on a discriminant **3.7.1**; 3.7
[see also: component subtype definition, component, constraint, discriminant constraint, discriminant, index constraint, subcomponent, subtype definition, variant part]
    affecting renaming 8.5
    by a subcomponent that is an actual parameter 6.2
    effect on compatibility 3.7.2
    effect on matching of components 4.5.2
    for an assignment 5.2

Dependent task 9.4
    delaying exception propagation 11.4.1
    of an abnormal task 9.10

Derivable subprogram 3.4
    prohibiting representation clauses 13.1

Derived subprogram 3.4
    as an operation 3.3.3
    implicitly declared 3.3.3

Derived type 3.4; D
[see also: parent type]
    conversion to or from a parent type or related type 4.6
    of an access type [see: access type, collection]
    of an access type designating a task type determining task dependence 9.4
    of a boolean type 3.4, 3.5.3
    of a limited type 7.4.4
    of a private type 7.4.1
    subject to a representation clause 13.1, 13.6

Derived type definition 3.4; 3.3.1
[see also: elaboration of...]

Designate 3.8, 9.1; D
[see also: access type, allocator, object designated by..., task designated by..., task object designated by ...]

Designated subtype (of an access type) **3.8**

Designated type (of an access type) **3.8**

Designator (of a function) **6.1**
[see also: attribute designator, operator, overloading of ...]
    in a function declaration 4.5
    in a subprogram body 6.3
    in a subprogram specification 6.1; 6.3
    of a generic formal subprogram 12.3.6; 12.1, 12.1.3

    of a library unit 10.1
    overloaded 6.6

DEVICE_ERROR (input-output exception) **14.4**; 14.2.3, 14.2.5, 14.3.10, 14.5

Digit 2.1
[see also: basic graphic character, extended digit, letter or digit]
    in a based literal 2.4.2
    in a decimal literal 2.4.1
    in an identifier 2.3

Digits (of a floating point type) **3.5.7**
[see also: floating point type]

DIGITS (predefined attribute) **3.5.8**; 4.1.4, A

Dimensionality of an array **3.6**

Direct access file 14.2; 14.1, 14.2.1

Direct input-output 14.2.4; 14.2.1

Direct visibility 8.3; D
[see also: basic operation, character literal, operation, operator symbol, selected component, visibility]
    due to a use clause 8.4
    of a library unit due to a with clause 10.1.1
    within a subunit 10.2

DIRECT_IO (predefined input-output generic package) **14.2, 14.2.4**; 14, 14.1, 14.2.5, C
    exceptions 14.4; 14.5
    specification 14.2.5

Discrete range 3.6, 3.6.1
[see also: range, static discrete range]
    as a choice 3.7.3
    as a choice in an aggregate 4.3
    for a loop parameter 5.5
    in a choice in a case statement 5.4
    in a generic formal array type declaration 12.1.2; 12.3.4
    in an index constraint 3.6
    in a loop parameter specification 5.5
    in a slice 4.1.2
    of entry indices in an entry declaration 9.5

Discrete type 3.5; D
[see also: basic operation of..., enumeration type, index, integer type, iteration scheme, operation of..., scalar type]
    as a generic actual parameter 12.3.3
    as a generic formal type 12.1.2
    expression in a case statement 5.4
    of a discriminant 3.7.1
    of a loop parameter 5.5
    of index values of an array 3.6
    operation 3.5.5; 4.5.2

Discriminant 3.3, 3.7.1; 3.7, D
[see also: component clause, component, composite type,
default expression, dependence on..., record type, selected
component, subcomponent]
    in a record aggregate 4.3.1
    initialization in an allocator constrains the allocated
    object 4.8
    of a derived type 3.4
    of a formal parameter 6.2
    of a generic actual type 12.3.2
    of a generic formal type 12.3, 12.3.2
    of an implicitly initialized object 3.2.1
    of an object designated by an access value 3.7.2;
    5.2
    of a private type 7.4.2; 3.3
    of a variant part must not be of a generic formal
    type 3.7.3
    simple name in a variant part 3.7.3
    subcomponent of an object 3.2.1
    with a default expression 3.7.1; 3.2.1

Discriminant association 3.7.2
    in a discriminant constraint 3.7.2
    named discriminant association 3.7.2
    named discriminant association for selective
    visibility 8.3
    positional discriminant association 3.7.2

Discriminant constraint 3.7.2; 3.3.2, D
[see also: dependence on a discriminant]
    ignored due to access_check suppression 11.7
    in an allocator 4.8
    on an access type 3.8
    violated 11.1

Discriminant part 3.7.1; 3.7
[see also: elaboration of...]
    absent from a record type declaration 3.7
    as a portion of a declarative region 8.1
    conforming to another 3.8.1, 6.3.1, 7.4.1
    in a generic formal type declaration 3.7.1; 12.1
    in an incomplete type declaration 3.8.1
    in a private type declaration 7.4, 7.4.1
    in a type declaration 3.3, 3.3.1
    must not include a pragma 2.8
    of a full type declaration is not elaborated 3.3.1

Discriminant specification 3.7.1
[see also: default expression]
    as part of a basic declaration 3.1
    declaring a component 3.7
    having an extended scope 8.2
    in a discriminant part 3.7.1
    visibility 8.3

Discriminant_check
[see: constraint_error, suppress]

Disjunction
[see: logical operator]

Divide
    character 2.1
    delimiter 2.2

Division operation 4.5.5
    accuracy for a real type 4.5.7

Division operator
[see: multiplying operator]

Division_check
[see: numeric_error, suppress]

Dot
[see: double dot]
    character 2.1 [see also: double dot, point character]
    delimiter 2.2
    delimiter of a selected component 8.3; 4.1.3

Double dot compound delimiter **2.2**

Double hyphen starting a comment **2.7**

Double star compound delimiter **2.2**
[see also: exponentiation compound delimiter]

DURATION (predefined type) **9.6**; C
[see also: delay expression, fixed point type]
    of alternative delay statements 9.7.1

Effect
[see: elaboration has no other effect]

ELABORATE (predefined pragma) **10.5**; B

Elaborated 3.9

Elaboration 3.9; 3.1, 3.3, 10.1, D
[see also: exception raised during..., order of elaboration]
    optimized 10.6

Elaboration has no other effect 3.1

Elaboration of
    an access type definition 3.8
    an array type definition 3.6
    a body stub 10.2
    a component declaration 3.7
    a component subtype definition 3.7
    a constrained array definition 3.6
    a declaration 3.1
    a declarative item 3.9
    a declarative part 3.9
    a deferred constant declaration 7.4.3
    a derived type definition 3.4
    a discriminant constraint 3.7.2
    a discriminant part 3.7.1
    a discriminant specification 3.7.1
    an entry declaration 9.5
    an enumeration literal specification 3.5.1
    an enumeration type definition 3.5.1
    a fixed point type declaration 3.5.9
    a floating point type declaration 3.5.7
    a formal part 6.1
    a full type declaration 3.3.1
    a generic body 12.2
    a generic declaration 12.1
    a generic instantiation 12.3
    an incomplete type declaration 3.8.1
    an index constraint 3.6.1
    an integer type definition 3.5.4
    a library unit 10.5
    a loop parameter specification 5.5
    an object declaration 3.2.1
    a package body 7.3
    a package declaration 7.2
    a parameter specification 6.1
    a private type declaration 7.4.1
    a range constraint 3.5
    a real type definition 3.5.6
    a record type definition 3.7
    a renaming declaration 8.5
    a representation clause 13.1

EPSILON (predefined attribute) **3.5.8**; A

Equal
> character 2.1
> delimiter 2.2

Equality operator 4.5; 4.5.2
> [see also: limited type, relational operator]
> explicitly declared 4.5.2, 6.7; 7.4.4
> for an access type 3.8.2
> for an array type 3.6.2
> for a generic formal type 12.1.2
> for a limited type 4.5.2, 7.4.4
> for a real type 4.5.7
> for a record type 3.7.4

Erroneous execution 1.6
> [see also: program_error]
> due to an access to a deallocated object 13.10.1
> due to an unchecked conversion violating properties of objects of the result type 13.10.2
> due to assignment to a shared variable 9.11
> due to changing of a discriminant value 5.2, 6.2
> due to dependence on parameter-passing mechanism 6.2
> due to multiple address clauses for overlaid entities 13.5
> due to suppression of an exception check 11.7
> due to use of an undefined value 3.2.1

Error bounds of a predefined operation of a real type **3.5.9**, **4.5.7**; 3.5.6, 3.5.7

Error detected at
> compilation time 1.6
> run time 1.6

Error situation 1.6, 11, 11.1; 11.6

Error that may not be detected **1.6**

Evaluation (of an expression) **4.5**; D
> [see also: compile time evaluation, expression]
> at compile time 4.9, 10.6
> of an actual parameter 6.4.1
> of an aggregate 4.3; 3.3.3
> of an allocator 4.8
> of an array aggregate 4.3.2
> of a condition 5.3, 5.5, 5.7, 9.7.1
> of a default expression 3.7.2
> of a default expression for a formal parameter 6.4.2; 6.1
> of a discrete range 3.5; 9.5
> of a discrete range used in an index constraint 3.6.1
> of an entry index 9.5
> of an expression in an assignment statement 5.2
> of an expression in a constraint 3.3.2
> of an expression in a generic actual parameter 12.3
> of an indexed component 4.1.1
> of an initial value [see: default expression]
> of a literal 4.2; 3.3.3
> of a logical operation 4.5.1
> of a name 4.1; 4.1.1, 4.1.2, 4.1.3, 4.1.4
> of a name in an abort statement 9.10
> of a name in a renaming declaration 8.5
> of a name of a variable 5.2, 6.4.1, 12.3
> of a primary 4.4
> of a qualified expression 4.7; 4.8
> of a range 3.5
> of a record aggregate 4.3.1
> of a short circuit control form 4.5.1
> of a static expression 4.9
> of a type conversion 4.6
> of a universal expression 4.10

> of the bounds of a loop parameter 5.5
> of the conditions of a selective wait 9.7.1

Evaluation order
> [see: order of evaluation]

Exception 11; 1.6, D
> [see also: constraint_error, numeric_error, predefined .., program_error, raise statement, raising of .., storage_error, tasking_error, time_error]
> causing a loop to be exited 5.5
> causing a transfer of control 5.1
> due to an expression evaluated at compile time 10.6
> implicitly declared in a generic instantiation 11.1
> in input-output 14.4; 14.5
> renamed 8.5
> suppress pragma 11.7

Exception choice 11.2

Exception declaration 11.1; 11
> as a basic declaration 3.1

Exception handler 11.2; D
> in an abnormal task 9.10
> in a block statement 5.6
> in a package body 7.1; 7.3
> in a subprogram body 6.3
> in a task body 9.1
> including a raise statement 11.3
> including the destination of a goto statement 5.9
> including the name of an exception 11.1
> not allowed in a code procedure body 13.8
> raising an exception 11.4.1
> selected to handle an exception 11.4.1; 11.6

Exception handling 11.4; 11.4.1, 11.4.2, 11.5

Exception propagation 11
> delayed by a dependent task 11.4.1
> from a declaration 11.4.2
> from a predefined operation 11.6
> from a statement 11.4.1
> to a communicating task 11.5

Exception raised during execution or elaboration of
> an accept statement 11.5
> an allocator of a task 9.3
> a conditional entry 9.7.2
> a declaration 11.4.2; 11.4
> a declarative part that declares tasks 9.3
> a generic instantiation 12.3.1, 12.3.2, 12.3.4, 12.3.5
> a selective wait 9.7.1
> a statement 11.4.1; 11.4
> a subprogram call 6.3; 6.2, 6.5
> a task 11.5
> a timed entry call 9.7.3
> task activation 9.3

Exceptions and optimization 11.6

Exclamation character 2.1
> replacing vertical bar 2.10

Exclusive disjunction
> [see: logical operator]

Execution
> [see: sequence of statements, statement, task body, task]

Exit statement 5.7
> [see also: statement]

accuracy of an operation 4.5.7
  as a generic actual type 12.3.3
  as a generic formal type 12.1.2
  error bounds 4.5.7; 3.5.6
  operation 3.5.10; 4.5.3, 4.5.4, 4.5.5
  result of an operation out of range of the type 4.5.7

FIXED_IO (text_io inner generic package) **14.3.8**; 14.3.10

FLOAT (predefined type) **3.5.7**; C

FLOAT_IO (text_io inner generic package) **14.3.8**; 14.3.10

Floating accuracy definition 3.5.7

Floating point constraint 3.5.7; 3.5.6
  on a derived subtype 3.4

Floating point predefined type
  [see: FLOAT, LONG_FLOAT, SHORT_FLOAT]

Floating point type 3.5.7; D
  [see also: numeric type, real type, scalar type,
system.max_digits]
      accuracy of an operation 4.5.7
      as a generic actual type 12.3.3
      as a generic formal type 12.1.2
      error bounds 4.5.7; 3.5.6
      operation 3.5.8; 4.5.3, 4.5.4, 4.5.5, 4.5.6
      result of an operation out of range of the type 4.5.7

Font design of graphical symbols **2.1**

For loop
  [see: loop statement]

Forcing occurrence (of a name leading to default determination of representation) **13.1**

FORE (predefined attribute) for a fixed point type **3.5.10**; A

Fore field of text_io input or output **14.3.8, 14.3.10**; 14.3.5

FORM (input-output function)
      in an instance of direct_io 14.2.1; 14.2.5
      in an instance of sequential_io 14.2.1, 14.2.3
      in text_io 14.2.1; 14.3.10
      raising an exception 14.4

Form feed format effector **2.1**

Form string of a file **14.1**; 14.2.1, 14.2.3, 14.2.5, 14.3.10

Formal object
  [see: generic formal object]

Formal parameter 6.1; D; (of an entry) 9.5; 3.2, 3.2.1; (of a function) 6.5; (of an operator) 6.7; (of a subprogram) 6.1, 6.2, 6.4; 3.2, 3.2.1, 6.3
  [see also: actual parameter, default expression, entry, generic formal parameter, mode, object, subprogram]
      as a constant 3.2.1
      as an object 3.2
      as a variable 3.2.1
      names and overload resolution 6.6
      of a derived subprogram 3.4
      of a generic formal subprogram 12.1, 12.1.3
      of a main program 10.1
      of an operation 3.3.3
      of a renamed entry or subprogram 8.5
      whose type is an array type 3.6.1
      whose type is a limited type 7.4.4
      whose type is a record type 3.7.2
      whose type is a task type 9.2

Formal part 6.1; 6.4
  [see also: generic formal part, parameter type profile]
      conforming to another 6.3.1
      in an accept statement 9.5
      in an entry declaration 9.5
      in a subprogram specification 6.1
      must not include a pragma 2.8

Formal subprogram
  [see: generic formal subprogram]

Formal type
  [see: generic formal type]

Format effector 2.1
  [see also: carriage return, form feed, horizontal tabulation, line feed, vertical tabulation]
      as a separator 2.2
      in an end of line 2.2

Format of text_io input or output **14.3.5, 14.3.7, 14.3.8, 14.3.9**

Formula
  [see: expression]

Frame 11.2
      and optimization 11.6
      in which an exception is raised 11.4.1, 11.4.2

Full declaration
      of a deferred constant 7.4.3

Full type declaration 3.3.1
      discriminant part is not elaborated 3.3.1
      of an incomplete type 3.8.1
      of a limited private type 7.4.4
      of a private type 7.4.1; 7.4.2

Function 6.1, 6.5; 6, 12.3, D
  [see also: operator, parameter and result type profile, parameter, predefined function, result subtype, return statement, subprogram]
      as a main program 10.1
      renamed 8.5
      result [see: returned value]
      that is an attribute 4.1.4; 12.3.6

Function body
  [see: subprogram body]

Function call 6.4; 6
  [see also: actual parameter, subprogram call]
      as a prefix 4.1, 4.1.3
      as a primary 4.4
      in a static expression 4.9
      with a parameter of a derived type 3.4
      with a result of a derived type 3.4

Function specification
  [see: subprogram specification]

Garbage collection 4.8

Generic actual object 12.3.1; 12.1.1
  [see also: generic actual parameter]

Generic actual parameter 12.3; 12
  [see also: generic actual object, generic actual subprogram, generic actual type, generic association, generic formal parameter, generic instantiation, matching]

Generic actual part • Generic specification

Generic subprogram 12.1; 12
    body 12.2; 12.1 [see also: subprogram body]
    instantiation 12.3; 12, 12.1 [see also: generic
    instantiation]
    interface pragma is not defined 13.9
    specification 12.1 [see also: generic specification]

Generic type definition 12.1; 12.1.2, 12.3.3, 12.3.4

Generic unit 12, 12.1; 12.2, 12.3, D
    [see also: generic declaration, program unit]
    including an exception declaration 11.1
    including a raise statement 11.3
    subject to a suppress pragma 11.7
    with a separately compiled body 10.2

Generic unit body
    [see: generic body]

Generic unit specification
    [see: generic specification]

GET (text_io procedure) **14.3.5**; 14.3, 14.3.2, 14.3.4,
14.3.10
    for character and string types 14.3.6
    for enumeration types 14.3.9
    for integer types 14.3.7
    for real types 14.3.8
    raising an exception 14.4

GET_LINE (text_io procedure) **14.3.6**; 14.3.10

Global declaration 8.1
    of a variable shared by tasks 9.11

Goto statement 5.9
    [see also: statement]
    as a simple statement 5.1
    causing a loop to be exited 5.5
    causing a transfer of control 5.1
    completing block statement execution 9.4

Graphic character 2.1
    [see also: basic graphic character, character, lower case
letter, other special character]
    in a character literal 2.5
    in a string literal 2.6

Graphical symbol 2.1
    [see also: ascii]
    not available 2.10

Greater than
    character 2.1
    delimiter 2.2
    operator [see: relational operator]

Greater than or equal
    compound delimiter 2.2
    operator [see: relational operator]

Handler
    [see: exception handler, exception handling]

Hiding (of a declaration) **8.3**
    [see also: visibility]
    and renaming 8.5
    and use clauses 8.4
    due to an implicit declaration 5.1
    of a generic unit 12.1
    of a library unit 10.1

    of a subprogram 6.6
    of or by a derived subprogram 3.4
    of the package standard 10.1
    within a subunit 10.2

Highest precedence operator 4.5
    [see also: abs, arithmetic operator, exponentiating
operator, not unary operator, overloading of an operator,
predefined operator]
    as an operation of a discrete type 3.5.5
    as an operation of a fixed point type 3.5.10
    as an operation of a floating point type 3.5.8
    overloaded 6.7

Homograph (declaration) **8.3**
    [see also: overloading]
    and use clauses 8.4

Horizontal tabulation
    as a separator 2.2
    character in a comment 2.7
    format effector 2.1
    in text_io input 14.3.5

Hyphen character 2.1
    [see also: minus character]
    starting a comment 2.7

Identifier 2.3; 2.2
    [see also: direct visibility, loop parameter, name,
overloading of..., scope of..., simple name, visibility]
    and an adjacent separator 2.2
    as an attribute designator 4.1.4
    as a designator 6.1
    as a reserved word 2.9
    as a simple name 4.1
    can be written in the basic character set 2.10
    denoting an object 3.2.1
    denoting a value 3.2.2
    in a deferred constant declaration 7.4.3
    in an entry declaration 9.5
    in an exception declaration 11.1
    in a generic instantiation 12.3
    in an incomplete type declaration 3.8.1
    in a number declaration 3.2.2
    in an object declaration 3.2
    in a package specification 7.1
    in a private type declaration 7.4; 7.4.1
    in a renaming declaration 8.5
    in a subprogram specification 6.1
    in a task specification 9.1
    in a type declaration 3.3.1; 7.4.1
    in its own declaration 8.3
    in pragma system_name 13.7
    of an argument of a pragma 2.8
    of an enumeration value 3.5.1
    of a formal parameter of a generic formal sub-
program 12.1.3
    of a generic formal object 12.1, 12.1.1
    of a generic formal subprogram 12.1; 12.1.3
    of a generic formal type 12.1; 12.1.2
    of a generic unit 12.1
    of a library unit 10.1
    of a pragma 2.8
    of a subprogram 6.1
    of a subtype 3.3.2
    of a subunit 10.2
    of homograph declarations 8.3
    overloaded 6.6
    versus simple name 3.1

Initial value (of an object) **3.2.1**
[see also: allocator, composite type, default expression,
default initial value, default initialization]
    in an allocator 4.8; 3.8, 7.4.4
    of an array object 3.6.1
    of a constant 3.2.1
    of a constant in a static expression 4.9
    of a discriminant of a formal parameter 6.2
    of a discriminant of an object 3.7.2
    of a limited private type object 7.4.4
    of an object declared in a package 7.1
    of an out mode formal parameter 6.2
    of a record object 3.7.2

Initialization
[see: assignment, default expression, default initialization,
initial value]

INLINE (predefined pragma) **6.3.2**; B
    creating recompilation dependence 10.3

INOUT_FILE (input-output file_mode enumeration literal)
14.1

Input-output **14**
[see also: direct_io, io_exceptions, low_level_io, sequen-
tial_io, text_io]
    at device level 14.6
    exceptions 14.4; 14.5
    with a direct access file 14.2.4
    with a sequential file 14.2.2
    with a text file 14.3

Instance
[see: generic instance]

Instantiation
[see: generic instantiation]

INTEGER (predefined type) **3.5.4**; C
    as base type of a loop parameter 5.5
    as default type for the bounds of a discrete range
    3.6.1; 9.5

Integer literal 2.4
[see also: based integer literal, universal_integer type]
    as a bound of a discrete range 9.5
    as a universal_integer literal 3.5.4
    in based notation 2.4.2
    in decimal notation 2.4.1

Integer part
    as a base of a based literal 2.4.2
    of a decimal literal 2.4.1

Integer predefined type 3.5.4
[see also: INTEGER, LONG_INTEGER, SHORT_INTEGER]

Integer subtype
[see: priority]
    due to an integer type definition 3.5.4

Integer type **3.5.4**; 3.3, 3.5, D
[see also: discrete type, numeric type, predefined type,
scalar type, system.max_int, system.min_int, univer-
sal_integer type]
    as a generic formal type 12.1.2
    as a generic parameter 12.3.3
    operation 3.5.5; 4.5.3, 4.5.4, 4.5.5, 4.5.6
    result of a conversion from a numeric type 4.6
    result of an operation out of range of the type 4.5

Integer type declaration
[see: integer type definition]

Integer type definition **3.5.4**; 3.3.1
    [see also: elaboration of...]

Integer type expression
    in a length clause 13.2
    in a record representation clause 13.4

INTEGER_IO (text_io inner generic package) **14.3.6**; 14.3.10

INTERFACE (predefined pragma) **13.9**; B

Interface to other languages **13.9**

Interrupt **13.5**

Interrupt entry **13.5.1**
    [see also: address attribute]

Interrupt queue
    [see: entry queue]

IO_EXCEPTIONS (predefined input-output package) **14.4**;
14, 14.1, 14.2.3, 14.2.5, 14.3.10, C
    specification 14.5

IS_OPEN (input-output function)
    in an instance of direct_io 14.2.1; 14.2.5
    in an instance of sequential_io 14.2.1; 14.2.3
    in text_io 14.2.1; 14.3.10

ISO (international organization for standardization) **2.1**

ISO seven bit coded character set **2.1**

Item
    [see: basic declarative item, later declarative item]

Iteration scheme **5.5**
    [see also: discrete type]

Label **5.1**
[see also: address attribute, name, statement]
    declaration 5.1
    implicitly declared 3.1
    target of a goto statement 5.9

Label bracket
    compound delimiter 2.2

Labeled statement **5.1**
    in a code statement 13.8

LARGE (predefined attribute) **3.5.8, 3.5.10**; A

LAST (predefined attribute) **A**
[see also: bound]
    for an access value 3.8.2
    for an array type 3.6.2
    for a scalar type 3.5

LAST_BIT (predefined attribute) **13.7.2**; A
    [see also: record representation clause]

Later declarative item **3.9**

Layout recommended
    [see: paragraphing recommended]

LAYOUT_ERROR (input-output exception) **14.4**; 14.3.4,
14.3.5, 14.3.7, 14.3.8, 14.3.9, 14.3.10, 14.5

Index

Leading zeros in a numeric literal **2.4.1**

Left label bracket compound delimiter **2.2**

Left parenthesis
    character 2.1
    delimiter 2.2

Legal **1.6**

LENGTH (predefined attribute) **3.6.2**; A
    for an access value 3.8.2

Length clause **13.2**
    as a representation clause 13.1
    for an access type 4.8
    specifying small of a fixed point type 13.2; 3.5.9

Length of a string literal **2.6**

Length of the result
    of an array comparison 4.5.1
    of an array logical negation 4.5.6
    of a catenation 4.5.3

Length_check
    [see: constraint_error, suppress]

Less than
    character 2.1
    delimiter 2.2
    operator [see: relational operator]

Less than or equal
    compound delimiter 2.2
    operator [see: relational operator]

Letter **2.3**
    [see also: lower case letter, upper case letter]
    e or E in a decimal literal 2.4.1
    in a based literal 2.4.2
    in an identifier 2.3

Letter_or_digit **2.3**

Lexical element 2, **2.2**; 2.4, 2.5, 2.6, D
    as a point in the program text 8.3
    in a conforming construct 6.3.1
    transferred by a text_io procedure 14.3, 14.3.5, 14.3.9

Lexicographic order **4.5.2**

Library package
    [see: library unit, package]
    having dependent tasks 9.4

Library package body
    [see: library unit, package body]
    raising an exception 11.4.1, 11.4.2

Library unit **10.1**; 10.5
    [see also: compilation unit, predefined package, predefined subprogram, program unit, secondary unit, standard predefined package, subunit]
    compiled before the corresponding body 10.3
    followed by an inline pragma 6.3.2
    included in the predefined package standard 8.6
    must not be subject to an address clause 13.5
    named in a use clause 10.5
    named in a with clause 10.1.1; 10.3, 10.5
    recompiled 10.3
    scope 8.2
    subject to an interface pragma 13.9

that is a package 7.1
visibility due to a with clause 8.3
whose name is needed in a compilation unit 10.1.1
with a body stub 10.2

Limited private type **7.4.4**
    [see also: private type]
    as a generic actual type 12.3.2
    as a generic formal type 12.1.2

Limited type **7.4.4**; 9.2, 12.3.1, D
    [see also: assignment, equality operator, inequality operator, predefined operator, task type]
    as a full type 7.4.1
    component of a record 3.7
    generic formal object 12.1.1
    in an object declaration 3.2.1
    limited record type 3.7.4
    operation 7.4.4; 4.5.2
    parameters for explicitly declared equality operators 6.7

Line **14.3**, **14.3.4**

LINE (text_io function) **14.3.4**; 14.3.10
    raising an exception 14.4

Line feed format effector 2.1

Line length **14.3**, **14.3.3**; 14.3.1, 14.3.4, 14.3.5, 14.3.6

Line terminator **14.3**; 14.3.4, 14.3.5, 14.3.6, 14.3.7, 14.3.8, 14.3.9

LINE_LENGTH (text_io function) **14.3.3**, **14.3.4**; 14.3.3, 14.3.10
    raising an exception 14.4

List
    [see: component list, identifier_list]

LIST (predefined pragma) **B**

Listing of program text
    [see: list pragma, page pragma]

Literal **4.2**; D
    [see also: based literal, character literal, decimal literal, enumeration literal, integer literal, null literal, numeric literal, overloading of..., real literal, string literal]
    as a basic operation 3.3.3
    of a derived type 3.4
    of universal_integer type 3.5.4
    of universal_real type 3.5.6
    specification [see: enumeration literal specification]

Local declaration **8.1**
    in a generic unit 12.3

Logical negation operation **4.5.6**

Logical operation **4.5.1**

Logical operator **4.5**; 4.4, 4.5.1, C
    [see also: overloading of an operator, predefined operator]
    as an operation of boolean type 3.5.5
    for an array type 3.6.2
    in an expression 4.4
    overloaded 6.7

Logical processor **9**

LONG_FLOAT (predefined type) **3.5.7**; C

LONG_INTEGER (predefined type) **3.5.4**; C

Loop name 5.5
> declaration 5.1
> implicitly declared 3.1
> in an exit statement 5.7

Loop parameter 5.5
> [see also: constant, object]
> as an object 3.2

Loop parameter specification 5.5
> [see also: elaboration of...]
> as an overload resolution context 8.7
> is a declaration 3.1

Loop statement 5.5
> [see also: statement]
> as a compound statement 5.1
> as a declarative region 8.1
> denoted by an expanded name 4.1.3
> including an exit statement 5.7

LOW_LEVEL_IO (predefined input-output package) **14.6**; 14, C

Lower bound
> [see: bound, first attribute]

Lower case letter 2.1
> [see also: graphic character]
> a to f in a based literal 2.4.2
> e in a decimal literal 2.4.1
> in an identifier 2.3

Machine code insertion 13.8

Machine dependent attribute 13.7.3

Machine representation
> [see: representation]

MACHINE_CODE (predefined package) **13.8**; C

MACHINE_EMAX (predefined attribute) **13.7.3**; 3.5.8, A

MACHINE_EMIN (predefined attribute) **13.7.3**; 3.5.8, A

MACHINE_MANTISSA (predefined attribute) **13.7.3**; 3.5.8, A

MACHINE_OVERFLOWS (predefined attribute) **13.7.3**; 3.5.8, 3.5.10, A

MACHINE_RADIX (predefined attribute) **13.7.3**; 3.5.8, A

MACHINE_ROUNDS (predefined attribute) **13.7.3**; 3.5.8, 3.5.10, A

Main program 10.1
> execution requiring elaboration of library units 10.5
> included in the predefined package standard 8.6
> including a priority pragma 9.8
> raising an exception 11.4.1, 11.4.2
> termination 9.4

MANTISSA (predefined attribute) **3.5.8, 3.5.10**; A

Mantissa
> of a fixed point number 3.5.9
> of a floating point number 3.5.7; 13.7.3

Mark
> [see: type_mark]

Master (task) **9.4**

Matching components
> of arrays 4.5.2; 4.5.1, 5.2.1
> of records 4.5.2

Matching generic formal
> and actual parameters 12.3
> access type 12.3.5
> array type 12.3.4
> default subprogram 12.3.6; 12.1.3
> object 12.3.1; 12.1.1
> private type 12.3.2
> scalar type 12.3.3
> subprogram 12.3.6; 12.1.3
> type 12.3.2, 12.3.3, 12.3.4, 12.3.5; 12.1.2

Mathematically correct result of a numeric operation **4.5**; 4.5.7

MAX_DIGITS
> [see: system.max_digits]

MAX_INT
> [see: system.max_int]

MAX_MANTISSA
> [see: system.max_mantissa]

Maximum line length 14.3

Maximum page length 14.3

Membership test 4.4, 4.5.2
> cannot be overloaded 6.7

Membership test operation 4.5
> [see also: overloading of...]
> as a basic operation 3.3.3; 3.3, 3.5.5, 3.5.8, 3.5.10, 3.6.2, 3.7.4, 3.8.2, 7.4.2
> for a real type 4.5.7

MEMORY_SIZE (predefined named number)
> [see: system.memory_size]

MEMORY_SIZE (predefined pragma) **13.7**; B

MIN_INT
> [see: system.min_int]

Minimization of storage
> [see: pack predefined pragma]

Minus
> character [see: hyphen character]
> character in an exponent of a numeric literal 2.4.1
> delimiter 2.2
> operator [see: binary adding operator, unary adding operator]
> unary operation 4.5.4

Mod operator 4.5.5
> [see also: multiplying operator]

MODE (input-output function)
> in an instance of direct_io 14.2.1; 14.2.5
> in an instance of sequential_io 14.2.1; 14.2.3
> in text_io 14.2.1; 14.3.3, 14.3.4, 14.3.10

Mode (of a file) **14.1**; 14.2.1
> of a direct access file 14.2; 14.2.5
> of a sequential access file 14.2; 14.2.3
> of a text_io file 14.3.1; 14.3.4

Mode (of a formal parameter) **6.2**; 6.1, D
[see also: formal parameter, generic formal parameter]
of a formal parameter of a derived subprogram 3.4
of a formal parameter of a renamed entry or subprogram 8.5
of a generic formal object 12.1.1

Mode in for a formal parameter **6.1, 6.2**; 3.2.1
of a function 6.5
of an interrupt entry 13.5.1

Mode in for a generic formal object **12.1.1**; 3.2.1, 12.3,
12.3.1

Mode in out for a formal parameter **6.1, 6.2**; 3.2.1
of a function is not allowed 6.5
of an interrupt entry is not allowed 13.5.1

Mode in out for a generic formal object **12.1.1**; 3.2.1, 12.3,
12.3.1

Mode out for a formal parameter **6.1, 6.2**
of a function is not allowed 6.5
of an interrupt entry is not allowed 13.5.1

MODE_ERROR (input-output exception) **14.4**; 14.2.2,
14.2.3, 14.2.4, 14.2.5, 14.3.1, 14.3.2, 14.3.3, 14.3.4,
14.3.5, 14.3.10, 14.5

Model interval of a subtype **4.5.7**

Model number (of a real type) **3.5.6**; D
[see also: real type, safe number]
accuracy of a real operation 4.5.7
of a fixed point type 3.5.9; 3.5.10
of a floating point type 3.5.7; 3.5.8

Modulus operation 4.5.5

MONTH (predefined function) **9.6**

Multidimensional array 3.6

Multiple
component declaration 3.7; 3.2
deferred constant declaration 7.4; 3.2
discriminant specification 3.7.1; 3.2
generic parameter declaration 12.1; 3.2
number declaration 3.2.2; 3.2
object declaration 3.2
parameter specification 6.1; 3.2

Multiplication operation 4.5.5
accuracy for a real type 4.5.7

Multiplying operator 4.5; 4.5.5, C
[see also: arithmetic operator, overloading of an operator]
in a term 4.4
overloaded 6.7

Must (legality requirement) **1.6**

Mutually recursive types 3.8.1; 3.3.1

NAME (input-output function)
in an instance of direct_io 14.2.1
in an instance of sequential_io 14.2.1
in text_io 14.2.1

NAME (predefined type)
[see: system.name]

Name (of an entity) **4.1**; 2.3, 3.1, D
[see also: attribute, block name, denote, designator,
evaluation of..., forcing occurrence, function call, identifier,
indexed component, label, loop name, loop parameter,
operator symbol, renaming declaration, selected component, simple name, slice, type_mark, visibility]
as a prefix 4.1
as a primary 4.4
as the argument of a pragma 2.8
as the expression in a case statement 5.4
conflicts 8.5
declared by renaming is not allowed as prefix of certain expanded names 4.1.3
declared in a generic unit 12.3
denoting an entity 4.1
denoting an object designated by an access value
4.1
generated by an implementation 13.4
starting with a prefix 4.1; 4.1.1, 4.1.2, 4.1.3, 4.1.4

Name string (of a file) **14.1**; 14.2.1, 14.2.3, 14.2.5, 14.3,
14.3.10, 14.4

NAME_ERROR (input-output exception) **14.4**; 14.2.1,
14.2.3, 14.2.5, 14.3.10, 14.5

Named association 6.4.2, D
[see also: component association, discriminant association, generic association, parameter association]

Named block statement
[see: block name]

Named loop statement
[see: loop name]

Named number 3.2; 3.2.2
as an entity 3.1
as a primary 4.4
in a static expression 4.9

NATURAL (predefined integer subtype) **C**

Negation
[see: logical negation operation]

Negation operation (numeric) **4.5.4**

Negative exponent
in a numeric literal 2.4.1
to an exponentiation operator 4.5.6

NEW_LINE (text_io procedure) **14.3.4**; 14.3.5, 14.3.6,
14.3.10
raising an exception 14.4

NEW_PAGE (text_io procedure) **14.3.4**; 14.3.10
raising an exception 14.4

No other effect
[see: elaboration has no other effect]

Not equal
compound delimiter [see: inequality compound
delimiter]
operator [see: relational operator]

Not in membership test
[see: membership test]

Not unary operator
[see: highest precedence operator]
as an operation of an array type 3.6.2
as an operation of boolean type 3.5.5
in a factor 4.4

Not yet elaborated 3.9

Null access value 3.8; 3.4, 4.2, 6.2, 11.1
[see also: default initial value of an access type object]
    causing constraint_error 4.1
    not causing constraint_error 11.7

Null array 3.6.1; 3.6
    aggregate 4.3.2
    and relational operation 4.5.2
    as an operand of a catenation 4.5.3

Null component list 3.7

Null literal 3.8, 4.2
[see also: overloading of...]
    as a basic operation 3.3.3; 3.8.2
    as a primary 4.4
    must not be the argument of a conversion 4.6

Null range 3.5
    as a choice of a variant part 3.7.3
    for a loop parameter 5.5

Null record 3.7
    and relational operation 4.5.2

Null slice 4.1.2
[see also: array type]

Null statement 5.1
[see also: statement]
    as a simple statement 5.1

Null string literal 2.6

Number
[see: based literal, decimal literal]

Number declaration 3.2, 3.2.2
    as a basic declaration 3.1

NUMBER_BASE (predefined integer subtype) **14.3.7**;
14.3.10

Numeric literal 2.4, 4.2; 2.2, 2.4.1, 2.4.2
[see also: universal type expression]
    and an adjacent separator 2.2
    as a basic operation 3.3.3
    as a primary 4.4
    as the parameter of value attribute 3.5.5
    as the result of image attribute 3.5.5
    assigned 5.2
    can be written in the basic character set 2.10
    in a conforming construct 6.3.1
    in a static expression 4.9
    in pragma memory_size 13.7
    in pragma storage_unit 13.7

Numeric operation of a universal type **4.10**

Numeric type 3.5
[see also: conversion, fixed point type, floating point type,
integer type, real type, scalar type]
    operation 4.5, 4.5.2, 4.5.3, 4.5.4, 4.5.5, 4.5.6

Numeric type expression
    in a length clause 13.2

Numeric value of a named number **3.2**

NUMERIC_ERROR (predefined exception) **11.1**
[see also: suppress pragma]
    not raised due to lost overflow conditions 13.7.3

    not raised due to optimization 11.6
    raised by a numeric operator 4.5
    raised by a predefined integer operation 3.5.4
    raised by a real result out of range of the safe
    numbers 4.5.7
    raised by a universal expression 4.10
    raised by integer division remainder or modulus
    4.5.5
    raised due to a conversion out of range 3.5.4, 3.5.6

Object 3.2; 3.2.1, D
[see also: address attribute, allocator, collection, component, constant, formal parameter, generic formal
parameter, initial value, loop parameter, size attribute,
storage bits allocated, subcomponent, variable]
    as an actual parameter 6.2
    as a generic formal parameter 12.1.1
    created by an allocator 4.8
    created by elaboration of an object declaration 3.2.1
    of an access type [see: access type object]
    of a file type [see: file]
    of a task type [see: task object]
    renamed 8.5
    subject to an address clause 13.5
    subject to a representation clause 13.1
    subject to a suppress pragma 11.7

Object declaration 3.2, 3.2.1
[see also: elaboration of..., generic parameter declaration]
    as a basic declaration 3.1
    as a full declaration 7.4.3
    implied by a task declaration 9.1
    in a package specification 7.1
    of an array object 3.6.1
    of a record object 3.7.2
    with a limited type 7.4.4
    with a task type 9.2; 9.3

Object designated
    by an access value 3.2, 3.8, 4.8; 4.1.3, 5.2, 9.2,
    11.1 [see also: task object designated...]
    by an access value denoted by a name 4.1
    by an access-to-array type 3.6.1
    by an access-to-record type 3.7.2
    by a generic formal access type value 12.3.5

Object module
    for a subprogram written in another language 13.9

Obsolete compilation unit (due to recompilation) **10.3**

Occur immediately within (a declarative region) **8.1**; 8.3,
8.4, 10.2

Omitted parameter association for a subprogram call **6.4.2**

OPEN (input-output procedure)
    in an instance of direct_io 14.2.1; 14.1, 14.2.5
    in an instance of sequential_io 14.2.1; 14.1, 14.2.3
    in text_io 14.2.1; 14.1, 14.3.1, 14.3.10
    raising an exception 14.4

Open alternative 9.7.1
[see also: alternative]
    accepting a conditional entry call 9.7.2
    accepting a timed entry call 9.7.3

Open file 14.1

Operation 3.3, 3.3.3; D
[see also: basic operation, direct visibility, operator,

Predefined operator 4.5, 8.6; C
[see also: abs, arithmetic operator, binary adding operator, catenation, equality, exponentiating operator, highest precedence operator, inequality, limited type, logical operator, multiplying operator, operator, predefined operation, relational operator, unary adding operator]
    applied to an undefined value 3.2.1
    as an operation 3.3.3
    for an access type 3.8.2
    for an array type 3.6.2
    for a record type 3.7.4
    implicitly declared 3.3.3
    in a static expression 4.9
    of a derived type 3.4
    of a fixed point type 3.5.9
    of a floating point type 3.5.7
    of an integer type 3.5.4
    raising an exception 11.4.1

Predefined package 8.6; C
[see also: ascii, library unit, predefined library package, standard]
    for input-output 14

Predefined pragma
[see: controlled, elaborate, inline, interface, list, memory_size, optimize, pack, page, priority, shared, storage_unit, suppress, system_name]

Predefined subprogram 8.6; C
[see also: input-output subprogram, library unit, predefined generic library subprogram]

Predefined subtype 8.6; C
[see also: field, natural, number_base, positive, priority]

Predefined type 8.6; C
[see also: boolean, character, count, duration, float, integer, long_float, long_integer, priority, short_float, short_integer, string, system.address, system .name, time, universal_integer, universal_real]

Prefix 4.1; D
[see also: appropriate for a type, function call, name, selected component, selector]
    in an attribute 4.1.4
    in an indexed component 4.1.1
    in a selected component 4.1.3
    in a slice 4.1.2
    that is a function call 4.1
    that is a name 4.1

Primary 4.4
    in a factor 4.4
    in a static expression 4.9

PRIORITY (predefined integer subtype) **9.8**; 13.7, C
[see also: Task priority]

PRIORITY (predefined pragma) **9.8**; 13.7, B
[see also: Task priority]

Private part (of a package) **7.2**; 7.4.1, 7.4.3, D
[see also: deferred constant declaration, private type declaration]

Private type 3.3, 7.4, 7.4.1; D
[see also: class of type, derived type of a private type, limited private type, type with discriminants]
    as a generic actual type 12.3.2
    as a generic formal type 12.1.2
    as a parent type 3.4
    corresponding full type declaration 3.3.1
    formal parameter 6.2

    of a deferred constant 7.4; 3.2.1
    operation 7.4.2

Private type declaration 7.4; 7.4.1, 7.4.2
[see also: private part (of a package), visible part (of a package)]
    as a generic type declaration 12.1
    as a portion of a declarative region 8.1
    including the word 'limited' 7.4.4

Procedure 6.1; 6, D
[see also: parameter and result type profile, parameter, subprogram]
    as a main program 10.1
    as a renaming of an entry 9.5
    renamed 8.5

Procedure body
[see: subprogram body]
    including code statements 13.8

Procedure call 6.4; 6, D
[see also: subprogram call]

Procedure call statement 6.4
[see also: actual parameter, statement]
    as a simple statement 5.1
    with a parameter of a derived type 3.4

Procedure specification
[see: subprogram specification]

Processor 9

Profile
[see: parameter and result type profile, parameter type profile]

Program 10; D
[see also: main program]

Program legality 1.6

Program library 10.1, 10.4; 10.5
    creation 10.4; 13.7
    manipulation and status 10.4

Program optimization 11.6; 10.6

Program text 2.2, 10.1; 2.10

Program unit 6, 7, 9, 12; D
[see also: address attribute, generic unit, library unit, package, subprogram, task unit]
    body separately compiled [see: subunit]
    including a declaration denoted by an expanded name 4.1.3
    including a suppress pragma 11.7
    subject to an address clause 13.5
    with a separately compiled body 10.2

PROGRAM_ERROR (predefined exception) **11.1**
[see also: erroneous execution, suppress pragma]
    raised by an erroneous program or incorrect order dependence 1.6; 11.1
    raised by a generic instantiation before elaboration of the body 3.9; 12.1, 12.2
    raised by a selective wait 9.7.1
    raised by a subprogram call before elaboration of the body 3.9; 7.3
    raised by a task activation before elaboration of the body 3.9
    raised by reaching the end of a function body 6.5

Recursive
  call of a subprogram 6.1, 12.1; 6.3.2
  generic instantiation 12.1, 12.3
  types 3.8.1; 3.3.1

Reentrant subprogram 6.1

Reference (parameter passing) **6.2**

Relation (in an expression) **4.4**

Relational expression
[see: relation, relational operator]

Relational operation 4.5.2
  of a boolean type 3.5.3
  of a discrete type 3.5.5
  of a fixed point type 3.5.10
  of a floating point type 3.5.8
  of a scalar type 3.5
  result for real operands 4.5.7

Relational operator 4.5; 4.5.2, C
[see also: equality operator, inequality operator, ordering
relation, overloading of an operator, predefined operator]
  for an access type 3.8.2
  for an array type 3.6.2
  for a private type 7.4.2
  for a record type 3.7.4
  for time predefined type 9.6
  in a relation 4.4
  overloaded 6.7

Relative address of a component within a record
[see: record representation clause]

Rem operator 4.5.5
[see also: multiplying operator]

Remainder operation 4.5.5

Renaming declaration 8.5; 4.1, 12.1.3, D
[see also: name]
  as a basic declaration 3.1
  as a declarative region 8.1
  cannot rename a universal_fixed operation 4.5.5
  for an array object 3.6.1
  for an entry 9.5
  for a record object 3.7.2
  name declared is not allowed as a prefix of certain
  expanded names 4.1.3
  to overload a library unit 10.1
  to overload a subunit 10.2
  to resolve an overloading ambiguity 6.6

Rendezvous (of tasks) **9.5**; 9, 9.7.1, 9.7.2, 9.7.3, D
  during which an exception is raised 11.5
  priority 9.8
  prohibited for an abnormal task 9.10

Replacement of characters in program text **2.10**

Representation (of a type and its objects) **13.1**
  recommendation by a pragma 13.1

Representation attribute 13.7.2, 13.7.3
  as a forcing occurrence 13.1
  with a prefix that has a null value 4.1

Representation clause 13.1; 13.6, D
[see also: address clause, elaboration of..., enumeration
representation clause, first named subtype, length clause,
record representation clause, type]
  as a basic declarative item 3.9

  as a portion of a declarative region 8.1
  cannot include a forcing occurrence 13.1
  for a derived type 3.4
  for a private type 7.4.1
  implied for a derived type 3.4
  in an overload resolution context 8.7
  in a task specification 9.1

Reserved word 2.9; 2.2, 2.3

RESET (input-output procedure)
  in an instance of direct_io 14.2.1; 14.2.5
  in an instance of sequential_io 14.2.1; 14.2.3
  in text_io 14.2.1; 14.3.1, 14.3.10

Resolution of overloading
[see: overloading]

Result subtype (of a function) **6.1**
  of a return expression 5.8

Result type profile
[see: parameter and...]

Result type and overload resolution 6.6

Result of a function
[see: returned value]

Return
[see: carriage return]

Return statement 5.8
[see also: function, statement]
  as a simple statement 5.1
  causing a loop to be exited 5.5
  causing a transfer of control 5.1
  completing block statement execution 9.4
  completing subprogram execution 9.4
  expression that is an array aggregate 4.3.2
  in a function body 6.5

Returned value
[see: function call]
  of a function call 5.8, 6.5; 8.5
  of an instance of a generic formal function 12.1.3
  of a main program 10.1
  of an operation 3.3.3
  of a predefined operator of an integer type 3.5.4
  of a predefined operator of a real type 3.5.6, 4.5.7

Right label bracket compound delimiter **2.2**

Right parenthesis
  character 2.1
  delimiter 2.2

Rounding
  in a real-to-integer conversion 4.6
  of results of real operations 4.5.7; 13.7.3

Run time check 11.7; 11.1

Safe interval 4.5.7

Safe number (of a real type) **3.5.6**; 4.5.7
[see also: model number, real type representation
attribute, real type]
  limit to the result of a real operation 4.5.7
  of a fixed point type 3.5.9; 3.5.10
  of a floating point type 3.5.7; 3.5.8
  result of universal expression too large 4.10

Static discrete range 4.9
    as a choice of an aggregate 4.3.2
    as a choice of a case statement 5.4
    as a choice of a variant part 3.7.3

Static expression 4.9; 8.7
    as a bound in an integer type definition 3.5.4
    as a choice in a case statement 5.4
    as a choice of a variant part 3.7.3
    for a choice in a record aggregate 4.3.2
    for a discriminant in a record aggregate 4.3.1
    in an attribute designator 4.1.4
    in an enumeration representation clause 13.3
    in a fixed accuracy definition 3.5.9
    in a floating accuracy definition 3.5.7
    in a generic unit 12.1
    in a length clause 13.2
    in a number declaration 3.2, 3.2.2
    in a record representation clause 13.4
    in priority pragma 9.8
    whose type is a universal type 4.10

Static others choice 4.3.2

Static subtype 4.9
    of a discriminant 3.7.3
    of the expression in a case statement 5.4

STATUS_ERROR (input-output exception) **14.4**; 14.2.1, 14.2.2, 14.2.3, 14.2.4, 14.2.5, 14.3.2, 14.3.3, 14.3.4, 14.3.5, 14.3.10, 14.5

Storage address of a component **13.4**
    [see also: address clause]

Storage bits
    allocated to an object or type 13.2; 13.7.2 [see also: size]
    of a record component relative to a storage unit 13.4
    size of a storage unit 13.7

Storage deallocation
    [see: unchecked_deallocation]

Storage minimization
    [see: pack pragma]

Storage reclamation 4.8

Storage representation of a record **13.4**

Storage unit 13.7
    offset to the start of a record component 13.4
    size of a storage unit in bits 13.7

Storage units allocated
    [see: storage_size]
    to a collection 13.2; 4.8, 11.1, 13.7.2
    to a task activation 13.2; 9.9, 11.1, 13.7.2

Storage_check
    [see: program_error exception, suppress]

STORAGE_ERROR (predefined exception) **11.1**
    [see also: suppress pragma]
    raised by an allocator exceeding the allocated storage 4.8; 11.1
    raised by an elaboration of a declarative item 11.1
    raised by a task activation exceeding the allocated storage 11.1
    raised by the execution of a subprogram call 11.1

STORAGE_SIZE (predefined attribute) **13.7.2**; A
    [see also: storage units allocated]
    for an access type 3.8.2
    for a task object or task type 9.9
    specified by a length clause 13.2

STORAGE_UNIT (predefined named number)
    [see: system.storage_unit]

STORAGE_UNIT (predefined pragma) **13.7**; B
    [see also: system.storage_unit]

STRING (predefined type) **3.6.3**; C
    [see also: predefined type]
    as the parameter of value attribute 3.5.5
    as the result of image attribute 3.5.5

String bracket 2.6; 2.10

String literal 2.6, 4.2; 2.2, 3.6.3
    [see also: overloading of..., percent mark character, quotation character]
    as a basic operation 3.3.3, 4.2; 3.6.2
    as an operator symbol 6.1
    as a primary 4.4
    must not be the argument of a conversion 4.6
    replaced by a catenation of basic characters 2.10

Stub
    [see: body stub]

Subaggregate 4.3.2

Subcomponent 3.3; D
    [see also: component, composite type, default expression, discriminant, object]
    depending on a discriminant 3.7.1; 5.2, 6.2 , 8.5
    of a component for which a component clause is given 13.4
    renamed 8.5
    that is a task object 9.2; 9.3
    whose type is a limited type 7.4.4
    whose type is a private type 7.4.1

Subprogram 6; D
    [see also: actual parameter, completed subprogram, derived subprogram, entry, formal parameter, function, library unit, overloading of..., parameter and result type profile, parameter, predefined subprogram, procedure, program unit]
    as a generic instance 12.3; 12
    as a main program 10.1
    as an operation 3.3.3; 7.4.2
    including a raise statement 11.3
    of a derived type 3.4
    overloaded 6.6
    renamed 8.5
    subject to an address clause 13.5
    subject to an inline pragma 6.3.2
    subject to an interface pragma 13.9
    subject to a representation clause 13.1
    subject to a suppress pragma 11.7
    with a separately compiled body 10.2

Subprogram body 6.3; 6, D
    [see also: body stub]
    as a generic body 12.2
    as a library unit 10.1
    as a proper body 3.9
    as a secondary unit 10.1
    as a secondary unit compiled after the corresponding library unit 10.3

Static discrete range ● *Subprogram body*

having dependent tasks 9.4
in a package body 7.1
including an exception handler 11.2; 11
including an exit statement 5.7
including a goto statement 5.9
including an implicit declaration 5.1
including a return statement 5.8
including code statements must be a procedure
body 13.8
inlined in place of each call 6.3.2
must be in the same declarative region as the
declaration 3.9, 7.1
not allowed for a subprogram subject to an interface
pragma 13.9
not yet elaborated at a call 3.9
raising an exception 11.4.1, 11.4.2
recompiled 10.3

Subprogram call 6.4; 6, 6.3, 12.3
[see also: actual parameter, entry call statement, entry call, function call, procedure call statement, procedure call]
before elaboration of the body 3.9 , 11.1
statement replaced by an inlining of the body 6.3.2
statement with a default actual parameter 6.4.2
to a derived subprogram 3.4
to a generic instance 12

Subprogram declaration 6.1; 6, D
and body as a declarative region 8.1
as a basic declaration 3.1
as a later declarative item 3.9
as a library unit 10.1
as an overloaded declaration 8.3
implied by the body 6.3, 10.1
in a package specification 7.1
made directly visible by a use clause 8.4
of an operator 6.7
recompiled 10.3

Subprogram specification 6.1
and forcing occurrences 13.1
conforming to another 6.3.1
for a function 6.5
in a body stub 10.2
in a generic declaration 12.1; 12.1.3
in a renaming declaration 8.5
in a subprogram body 6.3
including the name of a private type 7.4.1
of a derived subprogram 3.4

Subtraction operation 4.5.3
for a real type 4.5.7

Subtype 3.3, 3.3.2; D
[see also: attribute of..., base attribute, constrained subtype, constraint, first named subtype, operation of..., result subtype, satisfy, size attribute, static subtype, type, unconstrained subtype]
declared by a numeric type declaration 3.5.4, 3.5.7,
3.5.9
in a membership test 4.5.2
name [see: name of a subtype, type_mark of a subtype]
not considered in overload resolution 8.7
of an access type 3.8
of an actual parameter 6.4.1
of an array type [see: constrained array type, index constraint]
of a component of an array 3.6
of a component of a record 3.7
of a constant in a static expression 4.9
of a discriminant of a generic formal type 12.3.2
of a formal parameter 6.4.1

of a formal parameter or result of a renamed subprogram or entry 8.5
of a generic formal type 12.1.2
of an index of a generic formal array type 12.3.4
of an object [see: elaboration of...]
of a private type 7.4, 7.4.1
of a real type 3.5.7, 3.5.9; 3.5.6, 4.5.7
of a record type [see: constrained record type, discriminant constraint]
of a scalar type 3.5
of a task type 9.2
of a variable 5.2
subject to a representation clause 13.1

Subtype conversion 4.6
[see also: conversion operation, explicit conversion, implicit conversion, type conversion]
in an array assignment 5.2.1; 5.2
to a real type 4.5.7

Subtype declaration 3.3.2; 3.1
and forcing occurrences 13.1
as a basic declaration 3.1
including the name of a private type 7.4.1

Subtype definition
[see: component subtype definition, dependence on a discriminant, index subtype definition]

Subtype indication 3.3.2
[see also: elaboration of...]
as a component subtype indication 3.7
as a discrete range 3.6
for a subtype of a generic formal type 12.1.2
in an access type definition 3.8
in an allocator 4.8
in an array type definition 3.6
in a component declaration 3.7
in a constrained array definition 3.6
in a derived type definition 3.4
in a generic formal part 12.1
in an object declaration 3.2, 3.2.1
in an unconstrained array definition 3.6
including a fixed point constraint 3.5.9
including a floating point constraint 3.5.7
with a range constraint 3.5

Subunit 10.2; D
[see also: library unit]
as a compilation unit 10.4
as a library unit 10.4
as a secondary unit 10.1
compiled after the corresponding parent unit 10.3
not allowed for a subprogram subject to an interface
pragma 13.9
of a compilation unit subject to a context clause
10.1.1
raising an exception 11.4.1, 11.4.2
recompiled (does not affect other compilation units)
10.3

SUCC (predefined attribute) **3.5.5**; 13.3, A

Successor
[see: succ attribute]

SUPPRESS (predefined pragma) **11.7**; 11.1, B

Symbol
[see: graphical symbol, operator symbol]

Synchronization of tasks
[see: task synchronization]

Index

Task unit 9.1; 9
[see also: program unit]
declaration determining the visibility of another declaration 8.3
including a raise statement 11.3
subject to an address clause 13.5
subject to a representation clause 13.1
subject to a suppress pragma 11.7
with a separately compiled body 10.2

TASKING_ERROR (predefined exception) **11.1**
[see also: suppress pragma]
raised by an entry call to an abnormal task 9.10, 11.5
raised by an entry call to a completed task 9.5, 9.7.2, 9.7.3, 11.5
raised by an exception in the task body 11.4.2
raised by failure of an activation 9.3; 11.4.2

Template
[see: generic unit]

Term 4.4
in a simple expression 4.4

Terminate alternative (of a selective wait) **9.7.1**
[see also: select statement]
causing a transfer of control 5.1
in a select statement causing a loop to be exited 5.5
selection 9.4
selection in the presence of an accept alternative for an interrupt entry 13.5.1

TERMINATED (predefined attribute) for a task object **9.9**; A

Terminated task 9.4; 9.3, 9.9
[see also: completed task]
not becoming abnormal 9.10
object or subcomponent of an object designated by an access value 4.8
termination of a task during its activation 9.3

Terminator
[see: file terminator, line terminator, page terminator]

Text input-output **14.3**; 14.2.1

Text of a program **2.2, 10.1**

TEXT_IO (predefined input-output package) **14.3**; 14, 14.1, 14.3.9, 14.3.10, C
exceptions 14.4; 14.5
specification 14.3.10

TICK
[see: system.tick]

TIME (predefined type) **9.6**
[see also: clock, date, day, make_time, month, system.tick, year]

TIME_ERROR (predefined exception) **9.6**

TIME_OF (predefined function) **9.6**

Timed entry call 9.7.3; 9.7
and renamed entries 8.5
subject to an address clause 13.5.1

Times operator
[see: multiplying operator]

Transfer of control 5.1
[see also: exception, exit statement, goto statement, return statement, terminate alternative]

TRUE boolean enumeration literal **3.5.3**; C

Type 3.3; D
[see also: access type, appropriate for a type, array type, attribute of..., base attribute, base type, boolean type, character type, class of type, composite type, constrained type, derived type, discrete type, discriminant of..., enumeration type, fixed point type, floating point type, forcing occurrence, generic actual type, generic formal type, integer type, limited private type, limited type, numeric type, operation of..., parent type, predefined type, private type, real type, record type, representation clause, scalar type, size attribute, storage allocated, subtype, unconstrained subtype, unconstrained type, universal type]
name 3.3.1
of an actual parameter 6.4.1
of an aggregate 4.3.1, 4.3.2
of an array component of a generic formal array type 12.3.4
of an array index of a generic formal array type 12.3.4
of a case statement expression 5.4
of a condition 5.3
of a declared object 3.2, 3.2.1
of a discriminant of a generic formal private type 12.3.2
of an expression 4.4
of a file 14.1
of a formal parameter of a generic formal subprogram 12.1.3
of a generic actual object 12.3.1
of a generic formal object 12.1.1; 12.3.1
of an index 4.1.1
of a loop parameter 5.5
of a named number 3.2, 3.2.2
of an object designated by a generic formal access type 12.3.5
of a primary in an expression 4.4
of a shared variable 9.11
of a slice 4.1.2
of a string literal 4.2
of a task object 9.2
of a universal expression 4.10
of a value 3.3; 3.2
of discriminants of a generic formal object and the matching actual object 12.3.2
of of the literal null 4.2
of the result of a generic formal function 12.1.3
renamed 8.5
subject to a representation clause 13.1; 13.6
subject to a suppress pragma 11.7
yielded by an attribute 4.1.4

Type conversion 4.6
[see also: conversion operation, conversion, explicit conversion, subtype conversion, unchecked_conversion]
as an actual parameter 6.4, 6.4.1
as a primary 4.4
in a static expression 4.9
to a real type 4.5.7

Type declaration 3.3.1
[see also: elaboration of..., incomplete type declaration, private type declaration]
as a basic declaration 3.1
as a full declaration 7.4.1
implicitly declaring operations 3.3.3
in a package specification 7.1
including the name of a private type 7.4.1

of a fixed point type 3.5.9
of a floating point type 3.5.7
of an integer type 3.5.4
of a subtype 13.1

Type definition 3.3.1; D
[see also: access type definition, array type definition, derived type definition, elaboration of..., enumeration type definition, generic type definition, integer type definition, real type definition, record type definition]

Type mark (denoting a type or subtype) **3.3.2**
as a generic actual parameter 12.3
in an allocator 4.8
in a code statement 13.8
in a conversion 4.6
in a deferred constant declaration 7.4
in a discriminant specification 3.7.1
in a generic formal part 12.1, 12.3
in a generic parameter declaration 12.3.1
in an index subtype definition 3.6
in a parameter specification 6.1; 6.2
in a qualified expression 4.7
in a relation 4.4
in a renaming declaration 8.5
in a subprogram specification 6.1
of a formal parameter of a generic formal subprogram 12.1.3
of a generic formal array type 12.1.2
of a static scalar subtype 4.9
of the result of a generic formal function 12.1.3

Type with discriminants 3.3; 3.3.1, 3.3.2, 3.7, 3.7.1, 7.4, 7.4.1
[see also: private type, record type]
as an actual to a formal private type 12.3.2
as the component type of an array that is the operand of a conversion 4.6

Unary adding operator 4.4, 4.5, C; 4.5.4
[see also: arithmetic operator, overloading of an operator, predefined operator]
as an operation of a discrete type 3.5.5
in a simple expression 4.4
overloaded 6.7

Unary operator 4.5; 3.5.5, 3.5.8, 3.5.10, 3.6.2, 4.5.4, 4.5.6, C
[see also: highest precedence operator, unary adding operator]

UNCHECKED_CONVERSION (predefined generic library function) **13.10.2**; 13.10, C

UNCHECKED_DEALLOCATION (predefined generic library procedure) **13.10.1**; 4.8, 13.10, C

Unconditional termination of a task
[see: abnormal task, abort statement]

Unconstrained array definition 3.6

Unconstrained array type 3.6; 3.2.1
as an actual to a formal private type 12.3.2
formal parameter 6.2
subject to a length clause 13.2

Unconstrained subtype 3.3, 3.3.2
[see also: constrained subtype, constraint, subtype, type]
indication in a generic unit 12.3.2

Unconstrained type 3.3; 3.2.1, 3.6, 3.6.1, 3.7, 3.7.2
formal parameter 6.2
with discriminants 6.4.1, 12.3.2

Unconstrained variable 3.3, 3.6, 3.7; 12.3.1
as a subcomponent [see: subcomponent]

Undefined value
of a scalar parameter 6.2
of a scalar variable 3.2.1

Underline character 2.1
in a based literal 2.4.2
in a decimal literal 2.4.1
in an identifier 2.3

Unhandled exception 11.4.1

Unit
[see: compilation unit, generic unit, library unit, program unit, storage unit, task unit]

Universal expression 4.10
assigned 5.2
in an attribute designator 4.1.4
of a real type implicitly converted 4.5.7
that is static 4.10

Universal type 4.10
[see also: conversion, implicit conversion]
expression [see: expression, numeric literal]
of a named number 3.2.2; 3.2
result of an attribute [see: attribute]

UNIVERSAL_FIXED (predefined type) **3.5.9**
result of fixed point multiplying operators 4.5.5

UNIVERSAL_INTEGER (predefined type) **3.5.4, 4.10**; C
[see also: integer literal]
argument of a conversion 3.3.3, 4.6
attribute 3.5.5, 13.7.1, 13.7.2, 13.7.3; 9.9
bounds of a discrete range 3.6.1
bounds of a loop parameter 5.5
codes representing enumeration type values 13.3
converted to an integer type 3.5.5
of integer literals 2.4, 4.2
result of an operation 4.10; 4.5

UNIVERSAL_REAL (predefined type) **3.5.6, 4.10**
[see also: real literal]
argument of a conversion 3.3.3, 4.6
attribute 13.7.1
converted to a fixed point type 3.5.10
converted to a floating point type 3.5.8
of real literals 2.4, 4.2
result of an operation 4.10; 4.5

Updating the value of an object **6.2**

Upper bound
[see: bound, last attribute]

Upper case letter 2.1
[see also: basic graphic character]
A to F in a based literal 2.4.2
E in a decimal literal 2.4.1
in an identifier 2.3

Urgency of a task
[see: task priority]

Use clause (to achieve direct visibility) **8.4**; 8.3, D
[see also: context clause]

as a basic declarative item 3.9
as a later declarative item 3.9
in a code procedure body 13.8
in a context clause of a compilation unit 10.1.1
in a context clause of a subunit 10.2
inserted by the environment 10.4

USE_ERROR (input-output exception) **14.4**; 14.2.1, 14.2.3, 14.2.5, 14.3.3, 14.3.10, 14.5

VAL (predefined attribute) **3.5.5**; A

Value
[see: assignment, evaluation, expression, initial value, returned value, subtype, task designated..., type]
in a constant 3.2.1; 3.2
in a task object 9.2
in a variable 3.2.1, 5.2; 3.2
of an access type [see: object designated, task object designated]
of an array type 3.6; 3.6.1 [see also: array, slice]
of a based literal 2.4.2
of a boolean type 3.5.3
of a character literal 2.5
of a character type 3.5.2; 2.5, 2.6
of a decimal literal 2.4.1
of a fixed point type 3.5.9, 4.5.7
of a floating point type 3.5.7, 4.5.7
of a record type 3.7
of a record type with discriminants 3.7.1
of a string literal 2.6; 2.10
of a task type [see: task designated]
returned by a function call [see: returned value]

VALUE (predefined attribute) **3.5.5**; A

Variable 3.2.1; D
[see also: object, shared variable]
as an actual parameter 6.2
declared in a package body 7.3
formal parameter 6.2
in an assignment statement 5.2
of an array type as destination of an assignment 5.2.1
of a private type 7.4.1
renamed 8.5
that is a slice 4.1.2

Variable declaration 3.2.1

Variant 3.7.3; 4.1.3
[see also: component clause, record type]
in a variant part 3.7.3

Variant part 3.7.3; D
[see also: dependence on a discriminant]
in a component list 3.7
in a record aggregate 4.3.1

Vertical bar character 2.1
replacement by exclamation character 2.10

Vertical bar delimiter 2.2

Vertical tabulation format effector 2.1

Violation of a constraint
[see: constraint_error exception]

Visibility 8.3; 8.2, D
[see also: direct visibility, hiding, identifier, name, operation, overloading]
and renaming 8.5
determining multiple meanings of an identifier 8.4, 8.7; 8.5
determining order of compilation 10.3
due to a use clause 8.4
of a basic operation 8.3
of a character literal 8.3
of a default for a generic formal subprogram 12.3.6
of a generic formal parameter 12.3
of a library unit due to a with clause 8.6, 10.1.1
of a name of an exception 11.2
of an operation declared in a package 7.4.2
of an operator symbol 8.3
of a renaming declaration 8.5
of a subprogram declared in a package 6.3
of declarations in a package body 7.3
of declarations in a package specification 7.2
of declarations in the package system 13.7
within a subunit 10.2

Visibility by selection 8.3
[see also: basic operation, character literal, operation, operator symbol, selected component]

Visible part (of a package) **7.2**; 3.2.1, 7.4, 7.4.1, 7.4.3, D
[see also: deferred constant declaration, private type declaration]
expanded name denoting a declaration in a visible part 8.2
scope of a declaration in a visible part 4.1.3
use clause naming the package 8.4
visibility of a declaration in a visible part 8.3

Wait
[see: selective wait, task suspension]

While loop
[see: loop statement]

WIDTH (predefined attribute) **3.5.5**; A

With clause 10.1.1; D
[see also: context clause]
determining order of compilation 10.3
determining the implicit order of library units 8.6
in a context clause of a compilation unit 10.1.1
in a context clause of a subunit 10.2
inserted by the environment 10.4
leading to direct visibility 8.3

WRITE (input-output procedure)
in an instance of direct_io 14.2.4; 14.1, 14.2, 14.2.5
in an instance of sequential_io 14.2.2; 14.1, 14.2, 14.2.3

Writing to an output file 14.1, 14.2.2, 14.2.4

Xor operator
[see: logical operator]

YEAR (predefined function) **9.6**

Postscript : Submission of Comments

For submission of comments on this standard Ada reference manual, we would appreciate them being sent by Arpanet to the address

    Ada-Comment at ECLB

If you do not have Arpanet access, please send the comments by mail

    Ada Joint Program Office
    Office of the Under Secretary of Defense Research and Engineering
    Washington, DC 20301
    United States of America.

For mail comments, it will assist us if you are able to send them on 8-inch single-sided single-density IBM format diskette - but even if you can manage this, please also send us a paper copy, in case of problems with reading the diskette.

All comments are sorted and processed mechanically in order to simplify their analysis and to facilitate giving them proper consideration. To aid this process you are kindly requested to precede each comment with a three line header

            !section ...
            !version 1983
            !topic ...

The section line includes the section number, the paragraph number enclosed in parentheses, your name or affiliation (or both), and the date in ISO standard form (year-month-day). The paragraph number is the one given in the margin of the paper form of this document (it is not contained in the ECLB files); paragraph numbers are optional, but very helpful. As an example, here is the section line of comment #1194 on a previous version:

            !section 03.02.01(12) D . Taffs 82-04-26

The version line, for comments on the current standard, should only contain "!version 1983". Its purpose is to distinguish comments that refer to different versions.

The topic line should contain a one line summary of the comment. This line is essential, and you are kindly asked to avoid topics such as "Typo" or "Editorial comment" which will not convey any information when printed in a table of contents. As an example of an informative topic line consider:

            !topic Subcomponents of constants are constants

Note also that nothing prevents the topic line from including all the information of a comment, as in the following topic line:

            !topic Insert: "... are {implicitly} defined by a subtype declaration"

As a final example here is a complete comment received on a prior version of this manual:

            !section 03.02.01(12) D . Taffs 82-04-26
            !version 10
            !topic Subcomponents of constants are constants

            Change "component" to "subcomponent" in the last sentence.

            Otherwise the statement is inconsistent with the defined use of subcomponent in 3.3,
            which says that subcomponents are excluded when the term component is used instead
            of subcomponent.